HANDBOOK OF
Educational
Policy

This is a volume in the Academic Press
EDUCATIONAL PSYCHOLOGY SERIES

Critical comprehensive reviews of research knowledge, theories, principles, and practices

Under the editorship of Gary D. Phye

HANDBOOK OF
Educational
Policy

EDITED BY

Gregory J. Cizek

College of Education and Allied Professions
University of Toledo
Toledo, Ohio

ACADEMIC PRESS

San Diego   London   Boston   New York   Sydney   Tokyo   Toronto

Academic Press
a division of Harcourt Brace & Company
525 B Street, Suite 1900, San Diego, California 92101-4495, USA
http://www.apnet.com

Academic Press
24-28 Oval Road, London NW1 7DX, UK
http://www.hbuk.co.uk/ap/

Library of Congress Catalog Card Number: 98-88526

International Standard Book Number: 0-12-174698-4

PRINTED IN THE UNITED STATES OF AMERICA
99   00   01   02   03   04   EB   9   8   7   6   5   4   3   2   1

Contents

Foundational Issues in American Educational Policy

1. WHOSE SCHOOLS ARE THESE AND WHAT ARE THEY FOR? THE ROLE OF THE RULE OF LAW IN DEFINING EDUCATIONAL OPPORTUNITY IN AMERICAN PUBLIC EDUCATION

Diana Pullin

2. THE FINANCE OF AMERICAN PUBLIC EDUCATION: CHALLENGES OF EQUITY, ADEQUACY, AND EFFICIENCY

Margaret E. Goertz

3. INFUSING EDUCATIONAL DECISION MAKING WITH RESEARCH

Mary Kennedy

4. THE ROLE OF PHILOSOPHY IN EDUCATIONAL REFORMS: NEVER THE TWAIN SHALL MEET?

Andrew T. Lumpe

Local, State, National, and International Perspectives

5. EVOLUTION OF EDUCATIONAL REFORM IN MARYLAND: USING DATA TO DRIVE STATE POLICY AND LOCAL REFORM

Hillary R. Michaels and Steven Ferrara

8. MOVING TOWARD AN ACCOUNTABLE SYSTEM OF K–12 EDUCATION: ALTERNATIVE APPROACHES AND CHALLENGES

James G. Cibulka

9. THE ROLE OF THE NATIONAL ASSESSMENT OF EDUCATIONAL PROGRESS (NAEP) IN SETTING, REFLECTING, AND LINKING NATIONAL EDUCATION POLICY TO STATES' NEEDS

Mary Lyn Bourque

10. EDUCATION POLICY IN THE UNITED STATES AND ABROAD: WHAT WE CAN LEARN FROM EACH OTHER

Harold W. Stevenson and Barbara K. Hofer

III

Intersections of Theory, Policy, Politics, and Practice

11. POLICY AND PRACTICAL IMPLICATIONS OF THEORETICAL INNOVATIONS IN EDUCATION

Thomas G. Dunn

14. THE IMPACT OF THE TEACHERS' UNIONS
ON EDUCATIONAL POLICY AND OUTCOMES

Leo Troy

⇁ 15. THE PENDULUM REVISITED:
FADDISM IN EDUCATION AND ITS ALTERNATIVES

Robert E. Slavin

16. THE ROLE OF TECHNOLOGY IN EDUCATION: REALITY, PITFALLS, AND POTENTIAL

J. Kevin Maney

Methodological Advances for Educational Policy Analysis

17. META-ANALYTIC EFFECTS FOR POLICY

Herbert J. Walberg and Jin-Shei Lai

18. MIXED-METHOD RESEARCH: INTRODUCTION
AND APPLICATION

John W. Creswell

19. BASIC CONCEPTS IN HIERARCHICAL LINEAR
MODELING WITH APPLICATIONS FOR POLICY ANALYSIS

J. Douglas Willms

American Educational Policy Making: Past and Future

20. AMERICAN EDUCATIONAL POLICY: CONSTRUCTING CRISES AND CRAFTING SOLUTIONS

Gregory J. Cizek and Vidya Ramaswamy

21. EDUCATIONAL POLICY ANALYSIS: THE TREADS BEHIND, THE TRENDS AHEAD

Anne C. Lewis

Contributors

Numbers in parentheses indicate the pages on which the authors' contributions begin.

Mary Lyn Bourque (213), National Assessment Governing Board, Washington, DC 20002

James G. Cibulka (183), University of Maryland, College Park, Maryland 20742

Gregory J. Cizek (497), Department of Educational Psychology, Research, and Foundations, University of Toledo, Toledo, Ohio 43606

John W. Creswell (455), Department of Educational Psychology, University of Nebraska, Lincoln, Nebraska 68588

Thomas G. Dunn (273), Department of Educational Psychology, Research, and Social Foundations, University of Toledo, Toledo, Ohio 43606

John Engler (129), Office of the Governor, Lansing, Michigan 48933

Steven Ferrara (101), American Institutes for Research, Center for Educational Assessment, Washington, DC 20007

Margaret E. Goertz (31), Graduate School of Education, University of Pennsylvania, Philadelphia, Pennsylvania 19104

Barbara K. Hofer (251), Middlebury College, Middlebury, Vermont 05753

Mary Kennedy (53), College of Education, Michigan State University, East Lansing, Michigan 48824

Jin-Shei Lai (419), University of Illinois at Chicago, Chicago, Illinois 60611

Anne C. Lewis (521), Glen Echo, Maryland 20812

Andrew T. Lumpe (81), Department of Curriculum and Instruction, Southern Illinois University, Carbondale, Illinois 62901

J. Kevin Maney (387), Educational Technology, Miami University, Oxford, Ohio 45056

Hillary R. Michaels* (101), Mid-continent Regional Educational Laboratory, Aurora, Colorado 80014

Diana Pullin (3), School of Education, Boston College, Chestnut Hill, Massachusetts 02467

Vidya Ramaswamy (497), Department of Educational Psychology, Research, and Foundations, University of Toledo, Toledo, Ohio 43606

Edward D. Roeber (151), Advanced Systems in Measurement & Evaluation, Dover, New Hampshire 03821

Robert E. Slavin (325, 373), Center for Research on the Education of Students Placed at Risk, Johns Hopkins University, Baltimore, Maryland 21218

Harold W. Stevenson (251), University of Michigan, Ann Arbor, Michigan 48109

Leo Troy (351), Department of Economics, Rutgers University, Newark, New Jersey 07102

Herbert J. Walberg (419), University of Illinois at Chicago, Chicago, Illinois 60611

Gleaves Whitney (129), Office of the Governor, Lansing, Michigan 48933

J. Douglas Willms (473), Atlantic Centre for Policy Research, University of New Brunswick, Fredericton, New Brunswick, Canada E3B 6E3

Kenneth K. Wong (297), Department of Education, University of Chicago, Chicago, Illinois 60637

*Current address: CTB/McGraw-Hill, Monterey, California 93940.

Preface

In the colonial period of U.S. history, the most difficult educational decision families made was whether to hire a tutor to teach biblical principles or whether to do the job themselves. Compulsory education laws of the time made no mention of school systems as we currently conceive of those terms. Instead, legislation such as the Massachusetts Act of 1642 and the Connecticut Act of 1650 made education the responsibility of families and caregivers. This emphasis is illustrated in the sanctions that could be imposed when the required religious instruction was not provided; according to Pratte, "parents and masters of apprentices who failed to give the children under their care the required training were first to be warned, and if that did not achieve the desired results, they were to be subject to a fine" (1973, p. 40).

Early policy makers mandated education as a means of promoting cultural homogeneity and the virtues necessary to a civil society. Reading skills were taught only incidentally as the tools that would enable children to access religious teachings independently. Nonetheless, parents shared an understanding of the importance of education to the broader community and actively participated in the formation of local educational policy.

Much has changed over 200 years. More formalized and structured school systems have been established. Federal and state responsibilities for and involvement in schooling are widely recognized. The crafting of educational policy is not strictly a local endeavor, but occurs at many levels—often quite remote from the control of individual families—and affects nearly all aspects of what happens in classrooms. One requirement of the educational system has remained unchanged, though: each citizen must take an active role in ensuring that the nation's children acquire the skills and responsibilities necessary for a free and virtuous social order, however those ephemeral elements are defined in rapidly changing times.

The *Handbook of Educational Policy* reflects the unchanging reality that educational policy making is not limited to specialists, but concerns all those interested in improving education. To that end, each chapter in the *Handbook* discusses educational policy issues and analysis in a way that reaches all of those whose business is educational policy. Authors were charged with writing in a style that would enable any person concerned about education—parents, teachers, legislators, etc.—to gain valuable insight into the key issues of education today. Authors were also charged with maintaining academic rigor and objectivity and were encouraged to speculate about future educational policy.

The perspectives of this handbook are as diverse as its intended audience. Its authors bring expertise and experience from state government and departments of education, national policy making boards and organizations, regional educational research laboratories, universities, and classrooms from elementary to graduate schools. This diversity has resulted in chapters that span the range of current policy perspectives, while sharing homogeneity in terms of the quality of analysis.

The ambitious goals of the *Handbook* have been achieved remarkably well. Technically sophisticated and conceptually abstract topics are presented with accessible style, accuracy, and an innovative approach. For example, perhaps no other issue has dominated national educational policy in the United States for nearly so long as has the call for reform of elementary and secondary school mathematics and science. As learned societies promulgate standards for such reform, the issue of epistemology—the nature of knowledge itself—is sometimes debated in scholarly cliques, but remains largely unarticulated in the public discourse of proposed reforms. Andrew Lumpe's chapter on this topic demonstrates the primacy of epistemological questions in a way that is accessible to the broadest possible audience.

Adances in policy research methods are presented unashamedly in the *Handbook of Educational Policy*. John Creswell's introduction of mixed-method research will appeal to those interested in the intersections of quantitative and qualitative research, as well as to policy makers who must interpret research claims. Herbert Walberg and Jin-Shei Lai's chapter on the magnitude of benefits that can be expected of various teaching and learning practices illustrates the practical applications and policy-influencing power of the method known as meta-analysis. Doug Willms provides the conceptual background and practical context necessary for understanding hierarchical linear modeling (HLM), which has become a prominent means of investigating the effects of context (e.g., classroom, school, district) on educational performance.

A number of other chapters examine current or enduring policy questions. For example, the term "standards" is omnipresent in contemporary policy debates. In his chapter, Ed Roeber sheds light on the origins and varieties of standards currently being discussed. James Cibulka relates standards to accountability. Timely analyses of legal issues and collective bargaining are contributed by Diana Pullin and Leo Troy, respectively. A chapter by Margaret Goertz examines the challenge of funding public education. Kenneth Wong analyzes the multiple levels of political institutions that affect American schools. Mary Kennedy examines the complex interactions among educational research, policy, and practice.

Practical approaches to educational policy making are included in the *Handbook* as well. Michigan Governor John Engler's accomplishments and reform initiatives are described by Engler and Gleaves Whitney, with Michigan's course of educational reform frequently acknowledged to be a portent of national trends. The role of the National Assessment of Educational Progress (NAEP, often referred to as "The Nation's Report Card") in coordinating states' needs with national educational policy and the implications of the proposed Voluntary National Tests are summarized by Mary Lyn Bourque. Harold Stevenson and Barbara Hofer link findings from national and international studies, yielding keen insights for both researchers and policy makers. Hillary Michaels and Steve Ferrara offer advice on how policy makers can use data to inform decision making at the local and state level. Bob Slavin reports on an innovative approach to comprehensive schoolwide reform called "Success for All." Kevin Maney addresses issues that schools face as they confront the technological revolution.

Although much of the *Handbook* focuses on practical issues, it does not shy away from controversial issues. A chapter by Gregory Cizek and Vidya Ramaswamy exposes a crisis orientation in education and suggests an alternative approach to defining and confronting the critical educational issues. In his chapter, Tom Dunn wonders whether adequate attention has been paid to the power and effects of students' expectations, and whether well-intentioned educational reform proposals may have unintended adverse consequences. A second chapter by Bob Slavin presents his appraisal of faddism in education and his suggestions on how to stop it. A closing chapter by Anne Lewis chronicles some of the important policy debates that have marked recent years and anticipates some of the critical issues that policy makers will grapple with into the next millennium.

Despite its breadth, some readers might be disappointed that any of hundreds of specific issues were not included in the *Handbook of Educational Policy*. Such omissions do not imply lesser importance. Rather, the *Handbook*—by design—focuses on some of the key features that dominate educational policy debates today and are likely to continue to do so in the coming years, namely, standards, assessment, finance, accountability, collective bargaining, law, and politics. Finally, a unique feature of the *Handbook* is the inclusion of a special "Resources" section, in which electronic and standard resources are provided so that readers can follow up on the ideas presented in a particular chapter. Overall, the *Handbook* is intended to provide the reader with tools and perspectives that might fruitfully be applied to the educational issues of today and to the unknown challenges that lie ahead.

The *Handbook of Educational Policy* itself would not have been possible without the help of many. Academic Press has a long and successful history of publishing important works in the field of education; their Educational

Psychology series, of which this handbook is a volume, consists of handbook topics such as classroom assessment, academic learning, and transfer of learning, among others. I am indebted to Gary Phye, the series editor, for his keen insights during the conceptualization of this volume and his enthusiastic encouragement at every stage of its production, characteristics that are manifested in the previous volumes under his editorship (e.g., Phye, 1997). I am grateful for the assistance of Nikki Levy, Executive Editor, and Barbara Makinster, Editorial Coordinator, both of Academic Press.

My work as editor of this volume was greatly facilitated by the help of Vidya Ramaswamy, a doctoral candidate in educational psychology at the University of Toledo; Carrie Ann Lewis, a graduate research assistant; and Professor Michael LeBlanc of the State University of New York at Oswego. I also appreciate the continuing support provided by the University of Toledo College of Education and Allied Professions.

Certainly, this volume would not have been possible were it not for the generous contributions of the authors, whose collective willingness to labor in the interest of promoting a more informed academy and body politic is one of the highest forms of public service.

Finally, I acknowledge the support of my wife, Rita, and our children, Caroline, David, and Stephen, with whom I join in thanking God for showering His abundance on the American educational system and in pleading for His continuing favor.

Gregory J. Cizek

References

Phye, G. D. (Ed.) (1997). *Handbook of classroom assessment: Learning, adjustment, and achievement.* San Diego, CA: Academic Press.

Pratte, R. (1973). *The public school movement.* New York: McKay.

Foundational Issues in American Educational Policy

CHAPTER

1

Whose Schools Are These and What Are They for? The Role of the Rule of Law in Defining Educational Opportunity in American Public Education

DIANA PULLIN
Boston College

From the earliest years in what came to be the United States, law has played a major role in defining important public policy issues concerning the nature, content, and extent of public education (Spring, 1997; Tyack, James, & Benavot, 1987). Legislative bodies and courts quickly became the forums for debates on the role of schools in society and the nature of the relationships between school and family. Since the earliest days of American colonial history, government officials, including state legislators, board of education members, members of Congress, and federal, state, and local education officials have used the rule of law to articulate and enforce public policies defining the role of schools in society and the changing norms concerning the meaning and functions of the American "common school" (Spring, 1997).

The history of American education has been marked by an ongoing fundamental ambivalence about whether public education should be considered primarily a public good, providing shared societal benefits, or a private good for individuals (Apple, 1996; Carnoy & Levin, 1985; Cohen, 1984; Green, 1982; Howe, 1997; Spring, 1997). Labaree (1997) noted that this ambivalence has

Handbook of Educational Policy

led to a continuous conflict over the emphasis to be afforded to the demo-cratic egalitarian goals of preparing citizens; the social efficiency, marketplace-driven goal of training for the workplace; and the private and increasingly dominant social-mobility goals of preparing and credentialing individuals to compete for social positions. It has been suggested (Apple, 1996) that many of these contemporary pressures are at least in part efforts to return to traditional, class, gender, and race hierarchical structures. The tension be-tween the public and private goals of the American system of public elemen-tary and secondary education marks the nation's educational history. Even shared public goals for public education have always been the subject of dispute over the appropriate nature and outcomes of our nation's schools.

As the United States moves toward the next millennium, these differences over the role of schools and the intended primary beneficiaries of schooling are becoming increasingly strident. As Labaree asserts:

> More than ever in the past, the publicness of public education is being called into question, so that it is increasingly acceptable, even canonical, to think of education as a commodity whose purpose is to meet the needs of individual educational con-sumers . . . the pursuit of educational advantage has inadvertently threatened to transform the public educational system into a mechanism for personal advance-ment. In the process, the generous public goals that have been so important in defining the larger societal interest in education—to produce politically capable and socially productive citizens—have lost significant ground to the narrow pursuit of private advantage at public expense. (1997, pp. 12-13)

In many respects, the evolving role of the rule of law in education and public policy reflects the history of our tensions over the role of schools in society. The law of education in this nation provides "a map of patterns of power" in conflicts over schools and schooling (Tyack et al., 1987, p. 4). Struggles over the nature and content of schools and schooling reflect an ongoing debate over differing political, social, and economic viewpoints on education (Spring, 1997).

A HISTORICAL INTRODUCTION TO U.S. EDUCATIONAL LAW AND POLICY

Although many of its framers strongly acknowledged the public benefits of education (Silva, 1994), the U.S. Constitution does not make any provisions for education. As such, under the provisions of the Tenth Amendment, mat-ters of education were left to the states. Over the years, beginning most vigorously in the mid 1860s, each state began to address matters concerning elementary and secondary education in statutes and in constitutional provi-sions (Tyack et al., 1987).

In the Massachusetts Bay Colony in the mid 1630s, education was primar-ily limited to young Protestant men not already apprenticed to a master and the purpose of schooling was literacy training to promote Bible study, economic productivity, and good citizenship; children from elite familites attended private schools and poorer, but unapprenticed children attended public schools. Even masters, however, had an obligation to ensure minimal reading and writing skills for their apprentices. A hundred years later, educational efforts were explicitly focused in such places as New York and Pennsylvania on using the schools to ensure the dominance of Anglicization. Even in these early years, part of the education debate was a dispute over allowing multicultural influences—particularly Catholic, German, and Native American—in the public schools (Mayer, 1975; Spring, 1997).

By the middle of the 19th century, when the movement to require compulsory schooling of both boys and girls began, part of the perceived role of schooling was not strictly educational, but also addressed both the protection of children from the harms of child labor and the protection of adult workers from cheap, youthful competition (Cremin, 1951). At this same time, the first widespread efforts to voluntarily educate students with disabilities began, in part because teachers and administrators had difficulty accommodating these students in the classrooms children were mandated to attend (Spring, 1997). In some states, however, there were simply blanket exemptions written into state law that children with disabilities could be excused from attendance or excused if school administrators declared them uneducable (Butts & Cremin, 1953). It was not until the last half of the 20th century that American educational policy really began to address a public commitment to educate all of the nation's children.

In addition to an evolving conception of who should be educated in the nation's public elementary and secondary schools, there has been a continuing debate over the curriculum of these schools. Benjamin Franklin was an early leader in the effort to ensure that the public schools of the 18th century were firmly Anglican in content (Spring, 1997). By the late 19th century, as the immigrant population exploded and industrialization increased, more children of varying backgrounds began to attend public schools and high schools began to offer separate vocational curriculum tracks that would allow practical programs of manual, vocational, trade, and domestic studies to replace academic studies (Nasaw, 1979; Pullin, 1994; Sedlak, Wheeeler, Pullin, & Cusack, 1986). By the late 20th century, the debates over curriculum included such controversies as the effort to limit bilingual education for students whose primary language is not English and the effort to limit the teaching of evolution.

EDUCATION POLICY AND THE ROLE OF LAW

Although the law, both judge-made and legislative, has always played a role in the nation's educational decision making, the role of law has become somewhat more extensive and significantly more visible in American public education during the last half of the 20th century. Where state and local policy makers and education authorities are at odds with federal initiatives, the federal court system, particularly the United States Supreme Court, plays a somewhat unifying function in making declarations on the role schools in our society (Wirt & Kirst, 1989). Even though the judiciary is not, by nature, a particularly innovative public body, in the past 50 years, courts have begun to play more of a role in disputes over contentious social policy issues involving race, religion, gender, ethnicity, and other cultural issues (Tyack et al., 1987; Tyack & Benavot, 1985). In 1954 the United States Supreme Court's landmark decision in *Brown v. Board of Education* firmly recognized the importance of education in our society, noting that the provision of public education was "perhaps the most important function of state and local governments" (347 U.S. 483, 493). Ever since, legal and other public policy makers have been struggling to define just what this means, and whereas the powerless have been unable to influence policy makers, they increasingly have turned to the courts to seek redress of their concerns about issues of educational opportunity. These public policy disputes have been most bitter over issues concerning race discrimination, particularly in school desegregation disputes concerning mandatory busing, financing desegregation, and disputes over affirmative action (Armor, 1995; Kluger, 1975; Orfield, 1996; Spring, 1998).

In recent years, consistent with a general outcry over the litigiousness of American society, there has been a fairly widespread perception of a rising tide, or tidal flood, of litigation against schools (Imber & Gayler, 1988). In fact, although there are frequent—and frequently highly visible—cases pending in many courts, particularly the United States Supreme Court, the nation's schools are far from being overcome by the volume of lawsuits involving public elementary and secondary schools. In fact, a growing number of school-related cases were filed in both state and federal courts in the years after the *Brown* decision, from 1954 to 1977. The total number of reported court decisions concerning education doubled from 1960 to 1977. After 1977, however, the volume of reported education law court decisions declined 20% from 1977 to 1987 (Imber & Gayler, 1988; Imber & Thompson, 1991). These cases raised a wide range of issues about schools and schooling.

The most common claims against schools or educators have involved an assertion that school officials were negligent in maintaining school property or supervising students or employees. By a substantial majority, the most frequent types of cases to be decided by both state and federal courts involved disputes over teacher employment and termination; one study identified more than 4000 reported court decisions from the state and federal courts in the period 1965–1986 over disputes concerning the employment of teachers (Hooker, 1988; Imber & Thompson, 1991). Although there have been about 250 cases of court-supervised school desegregation in the nation

(Heise, 1996), by far the most common type of discrimination claims have been those involving school employees, not students. Similarly, the most common types of complaints about disciplinary action have been brought by employees, not students (Imber & Thompson, 1991).

Litigation over employment disputes and allegations of negligence generally provoke little public controversy. However, the most visible court cases and the most controversial statutes often reflect struggles to agree, or at least reach peace, over the roles of schools in our society. Some have suggested that the perception of a dangerous increase in education litigation is a reflection of anxiety that many of the new legal rights and challenges have been asserted on behalf of groups that were politically, economically, or socially powerless before Brown and the Civil Rights Act of 1964 (Tyack et al., 1987). Current legal trends and new types of litigation theories may indicate that the next wave of legal issues are a reaction by social and religious conservatives, based on a rejection of these liberal political initiatives and the progressive educational theories that accompanied them.

LEGAL ISSUES IN ELEMENTARY AND SECONDARY EDUCATION: CURRENT CONCERNS

The remainder of this chapter will examine only a few of the many categories of education law disputes of the last half of this century to assess the role of law in disputes over the role of elementary and secondary schools in our society. Although many different types of laws and court cases could be assessed, five types of controversies are discussed here, selected because of the opportunities they present to highlight the issues in our ongoing struggle to define who should be educated and what they should learn. Disputes over the right to education, the education of students with disabilities, student discipline and student rights, parent choice, and current efforts to require standards-based education reforms provide an opportunity to review the role of the rule of law in our system of public elementary and secondary education.

Special Education

Federal law has played a significant role in the education of students with disabilities for the past 25 years. These federal policies are mirrored in provisions of state law and regulations. In the second half of this century, both federal laws and laws in all the states have been designed to promote social policy goals of access to educational opportunity for all students with disabilities. The pursuit of access to education for students with disabilities has embraced several key policy goals: every child with a disability is educable and should be educated; students with disabilities should be educated to the maximum extent appropriate in the same settings and classrooms as their nondisabled peers; all students with disabilities should receive an individually appropriate education as defined in an individualized educational program (IEP); and procedural safeguards should be in place to protect the rights of disabled students (Lazerson, 1983; McDonnell, McLaughlin, & Morison, 1997; Minow, 1990; Ordover, Boundy, & Pullin, 1996); Sarason & Doris, 1979; Turnbull, 1993; Tweedie, 1983; Underwood & Mead, 1995).

Federal policy goals concerning the education of students with disabilities have been promoted in two ways. Under the Individuals with Disabilities Education Act (IDEA), students with disabilities in need of special education are the intended beneficiaries of a program providing financial aid to the states, passed through to local school districts. The IDEA funding is contingent on state and local compliance with a series of substantial procedural and substantive protections for students, a requirement that has led each of the 50 states to implement state laws that closely parallel IDEA. In addition to IDEA, two federal civil rights statutes (Section 504 of the Rehabilitation Act of 1973 and the Americans with Disabilities Act) are designed to protect the interests of students with disabilities who need assistance or accommodations but do not need special education.

There is no dispute that there have been dramatic improvements in the access to educational services now afforded to students with disabilities as a result of these laws; few, if any, individuals needing services have not been identified (Aleman, 1995; Gartner & Lipsky, 1987). Some commentators have reported that the overall quality of services to students with disabilities has improved since the federal law was first enacted (Singer & Butler, 1987). However, there has been controversy over how extensively the federal law and the analogous state laws have affected the day-to-day educational opportunities provided to students as well as the relationship between families and educational institutions, and over the consequences of the legalization of special education (Kirp & Neal, 1985; Yudof, 1984). Now there is growing controversy over whether students with disabilities are receiving more educational opportunities than are students without disabilities.

Implementation and Enforcement of Special Education Policy

Under current state and federal special education policy, the burden of implementation falls primarily on local educators. The burden of enforcement largely rests on parents and advocacy groups. Both the state and federal laws include procedural protections for families during the special education evaluation and placement processes to ensure a mechanism for family participation in decision making and for impartial review of disputes that may arise between a family and educators concerning the education of a student with a disability. The use of procedual protections to ensure the access of students with disabilities to appropriate education resulted in what has been called the *legalizing* (Yudof, 1984) or *legalization* of special education (Kirp & Neal, 1985). There has been a high level of compliance with the procedural components of the law requiring parental notification and participation and the right to an impartial review of disputes between family and school (Singer & Butler, 1987; Weatherley, 1979). But these procedural protections have not protected against misdiagnosis and segregation of students with disabilities and disputes over the sufficiency of the educational opportunities to be provided students with disabilities have continued (Gartner & Lipsky, 1987; Handler, 1986; Skrtic, 1991). These consequences are in part due to the fact that has been easier for educators to comply with procedural requirements than the substantive components of IDEA, which require the provision of an appropriate education individually formulated for each student in need of special education (Smith & Brownell, 1995; see also Clune & Van Pelt, 1985, and Kirp & Neal, 1985). The procedures required under the law are at least fairly straightforward. However, the IEP process, where substantive decisions on the nature of the appropriate education required for a student have to be negotiated between school officials and parents, often becomes a political bargaining process more than anything else, with enormous pressures on parents to comply with educators' recommendations. The collective effect of all these pressures results in considerable momentum against the high level of individualization required by state and federal laws (Handler, 1986; Weatherley, 1979).

Beyond participating in the IEP process, parents have generally been reluctant to pursue procedural protections for review of disagreements of disputes with educators over implementation of special education (Engel, 1991; Weatherley, 1979). With a few exceptions when advocacy groups have become involved, most of those who have pursued procedural remedies have been more affluent families (Engel, 1991). Many parents report that they are unsatisfied with the overall experience in terms of the hearings process; school officials, on the other hand, are more often satisfied with the hearings process. However, both parents and school officials seem to share an ultimate belief in the subjective fairness of the current system; both agree that due-process protections in the law are necessary, if not essential, and that the current procedural protections are not sufficient (Goldberg, 1989; Goldberg & Kuriloff, 1991).

Several commentators have decried what they perceived as an alarming increase in litigiousness on special education issues (Melnick, 1994; Zirkel & Richardson, 1989). By 1982 there had been nearly 300 federal and state court cases bearing on the meaning of the federal special education law; most of the cases concerned disputes over IEPs (Yudof, 1984). One study found that during the 1980s a total of 342 federal cases and 99 state cases were reported under IDEA and the earlier versions of that law (Zirkel & Richardson, 1989).

In fact, the total number of administrative hearings and court cases seem quite small given the detailed substantive and procedural protections built into IDEA to ensure equality of educational opportunity and the fact that almost 4 million students annually received special education under IDEA.

More useful than an assessment of the volume of court cases and administrative hearings is an assessment of the role that legalization has had on the daily activities of educators, the relationships between educators and families, and the improvement of eduational opportunities for students with disabilities. Policy analysts began studying the impact of efforts to regulate the provision of special education services as early as the 1970s and have generally concluded that educators, the "street-level bureaucrats" responsible for implementing state policy, make efforts to incorporate the law's provisions but do so in ways most consistent with past practices and procedures (Weatherley, 1979; Weatherley & Lipsky, 1977; see also Wise, 1979).

Under the law, the public policy goals of promoting educational opportunity for individuals with disabilities were to be furthered through the use of an IEP formulated cooperatively by school and familty to define the education appropriate to a student's needs. Research on the development and implementation of the IEP has documented several areas of concern about the effectiveness of the document, particularly as an accountability tool (McDonell et al., 1997). The state and federal courts have played a role in refining state laws and the IDEA statutory and regulatory provisions, spelling out the requirements for appropriate and individualized education for students with disabilities on student-by-student basis. The landmark U.S. Supreme Court decision in *Board of Education v. Rowley* (1982) provided the guiding federal court standard for assessing whether a student had been afforded the appropriate education granted under IDEA. Under the *Rowley* standard, appropriate education for a student with diabilities in need of special education is one that is designed according to the IDEA requirements for an IEP, meets the state's educational standards, and is reasonably calculated to provide the student with educational benefits.

The difficulty of applying an individualized determination of whether a student with disabilities receives an appropriate education has left much room for controversy over the impact of the *Rowley* decision on subsequent disputes over defining IEPs for other individuals. Some commentators have asserted that there has been no uniformity among the lower federal courts in following the *Rowley* standard (Kirp & Neal, 1985; Melnick, 1994; Weber, 1990; Wegner, 1985). Others have argued that the courts have effectively utilized the *Rowley* standard and applied it to the individualized appropriateness disputes before them (Broadwell & Walden, 1988; Gallegos, 1989; Osborne, 1996; Rothstein, 1990; Strope & Broadwell, 1990; Turnbull, 1993). One commentator concluded that few courts ignored the spirit of *Rowley*, and when the issue looks simply like a battle between disagreeing experts, then judges will defer to the school, particularly if the state and local officials do not disagree with each other (Gallegos, 1989). Others have noted that districts have generally been successful in court if they demonstrated that they made an earnest attempt to do all they could for a student (Broadwell & Walden, 1988; Osborne, 1996). Yet another commentator has asserted that many courts misconstrued the *Rowley* admonition to stay out of disputes over educational methodology and, as a result, have failed to determine whether the IEP produces an appropriate education (Huefner, 1991).

As the case law under IDEA began to develop in the years following *Rowley*, the lower courts did clearly begin to expand slightly their interpretations of the educational benefit criteria, as did the U.S. Supreme Court itself. In its decision in *Irving Independent School District v. Tatro*, the Supreme Court gave fairly broad meaning to the "related services" students were also entitled to under IDEA (see Gallegos, 1989; Wegner, 1985). However, even though the related services requirement of IDEA expanded the scope of benefits available to students with disabilities, federal courts were consistent in adherence to the determination made in *Rowley* that the appropriateness standard of IDEA did not require a "maximization of benefit" for a student with disabilities unless this higher standard of service had been adopted by a state legislature, as it was in some states (Osborne, 1996; Rothstein, 1990; Strope & Broadwell, 1990; Turnbull, 1993; Wegner, 1985).

Current Controversies in Special Education Policy

The IDEA appropriate education requirements have begun to provoke criticism from some social conservatives and parents whose children do not have disabilities that IDEA and its state law counterparts are affording unfair educational opportunities for students with disabilities (see, for example, Melnick, 1994). These complaints are being joined by those from fiscal conservatives who decry the high cost of educating many students with disabilities, particularly those who are placed in private schools at public expense to address the IEPs designed for them (Zernicke, 1997). The rhetoric of concern escalates because of expensive private special education placements and also the implementation of the IDEA's least restrictive environment (LRE) requirement in local schools around the country. The LRE requirement has resulted in the placement of many special education students, including students with significant physical or intellectual needs, into regular classrooms to receive education and related services.

In some states, the high costs of some private special education placements have become the focus of controversy when school expenditures in other areas are limited, but the expenses for special education appear to be increasing. The alternative to private school placement to meet the needs of students with disabilities is placement in classrooms in regular public schools. Under the IDEA and state law requirements for LRE, all students with disabilities are entitled to the provision of education, to the extent appropriate, in either the regular classroom or a setting as close an approximation to it as possible (Benveniste, 1986; Minow, 1990). A growing number of high-profile court cases focus on these issues (e.g., *Board of Education v. Holland*, 1994; *Oberti v. Board of Education*, 1993; *Daniel R.R. v. State Board of Education*, 1989). More than 70% of students with disabilities now spend at least 40% of their school day in regular classrooms (U.S. Department of Education, 1996). Most of these students have mild disabilities and blend in easily and without particular notice of their special needs by other students. However, with increasing frequency, students with more significant disabilities are being educated in regular classrooms as the result of medical advances that make this more possible and the mainstreaming or inclusion movements, which seek greater integration of students with disabilities into education and the rest of our social, economic, and political institutions and activities (Wang et al., 1986; Will, 1986).

The increased costs for some forms of special education and related services paid by states and local schools and the increasing visibility of individuals with disabilities in regular school and other settings have given a new face to the differing perceptions of the role of schools in our society (Shanker, 1994). Questions are raised not only about the amount of public monies paid for special education but also about the perceived unfairness of affording students with disabilities a standard of educational services that may be higher than that afforded to students without disabilities. The Commonwealth of Massachusetts, for example, is one of the few states that, by state statute, has for more than 25 years mandated a higher level of service to students with disabilities than the federal law requires. There has been a vigorous debate in the legislature and the press over an effort to rewrite the state law to remove its mandate that students with disabilities receive an education designed to provide them "maximum feasible benefit" on grounds that it is too expensive and is unfair to other students (White, 1998; Zernicke, 1997).

The often unspoken issue in the current debate over special education is whether it is justifiable to expend significant resources on individuals who may not be able to fully participate or substantially contribute to the economic well-being or the civic functioning of the community. Somewhat less oblique are the implications that every dollar spent on special education and related services leads to reduced resources for those who will be full participants in the competition for personal economic and social advancement. These issues have the potential to become a major focus of contention in the beginning of the next century not only over the education of students with disabilities but also over the role of education in furthering either our individual or communal interests. Little attention has been paid to date to any of the human capital or social justice issues about the extent to which short-term investments in special education pay off over the long term in increased human dignity, reduced costs for later social and medical services, and increased economic productivity.

Summary

A legal mechanism has been created that details, for a specific subset of the school-age population, a clear presumption about the type of educational service that should be provided and a particularly detailed set of procedural protections to ensure that disputes arising in the implementation of the laws are resolved. The procedural protections are most certainly more generous than those afforded to students without disabilities. These procedural protections were added into the state and federal laws because of a clear recognition that youngsters with disabilities had been significantly disadvantaged by the nation's educational system and faced the prospect of ongoing discrimination. The substantive guarantees in the special education laws have been more of a struggle to implement, in part because of the uncertain meaning of the entitlement to an appropriate education and the fact that the laws require that the entitlement be given meaning on an individualized basis for each student. There are, in many states, no analogous guarantees to an appropriate education for students without disabilities. However, given the ambiguity over how courts have interpreted and applied the appropriateness standard, it is far from clear that the right to an apppropriate education held by students with disabilities is any better than the level of service to which any other student is entitled. And, as will be discussed later, there are now state court decisions recognizing that many state constitutions guarantee all students the right to an education that is "adequate" or "thorough and efficient." Although these legal protections are not intended to be implemented on an individualized basis, as required in special education, these levels of service may be at least as beneficial to students without disabilities as the appropriateness standards allow for special education students.

The right to private education at public expense for students with disabilities is also asserted by some to be an unfair extra benefit for students needing special education not available in the public schools. However, the current movement to allow public support for private education through school choice, charter school, or voucher systems creates mechanisms quite similar to the system of public support for some special education students. For those private special education placements that are particularly expensive, many of the embedded costs are attributable to expenses that if not assumed by the public educational system would instead be paid by public or private medical insurance, social service, or other systems for expense burden-shifting. In these instances, particularly given the potential communal economic benefit associated with a more self-sufficient population of individuals with disabilities, the assumption of cost burdens by the educational system in lieu of other funding sources may be, simply, inconsequential. However, the willingness of the general population to assume the expenses associated with a full range of special education services depends to a large part on a willingness to recognize the collective communal and individual benefit of paying for these services as educational expenses.

Student Discipline and Student Rights

Another occasion for testing the nation's collective commitment to educating all children arises in the context of student discipline, especially discipline that can result in exclusion from educational services and discipline that may affect rights of free speech and rights to access particular information. Many commentators hailed a new era of student rights in 1969 when the U.S. Supreme Court issued its decision in *Tinker v. Des Moines Independent School District* (1969). The *Tinker* holding that high school students are entitled to constitutional protections at school was hailed by many outside the schools for its recognition of the importance of education to inculcate fundamental values necessary to the maintenance of a democratic political system (see also *Ambach v. Norwick*, 1979). Six years later, in *Goss v. Lopez* (1975), the Court expanded these student rights when it spelled out the right to rudimentary procedural due-process protections (notice and the right to be heard) for students subject to a disciplinary exclusion from school for 10 or fewer days.

Safe Schools

Now student demonstrations have dwindled to a whimper and litigation over the rights of students has not expanded as might have been predicted after *Tinker* but has, instead, diminished (Stefkovich, 1995). Today, public policy makers and the legal system have turned their focus to issues of perceived violence and student drug and alcohol abuse. For example, in 1994 Congress passed the Safe Schools Act seeking to ensure that the nation's schools would be drug and alcohol free by the year 2000. State legislatures have enacted various statutes designed to ensure that students behave themselves both in school and in the community. In Massachusetts, for example, a massive education reform law included a provision (Chapter 380) to allow school principals to permanently expel from school students who were carrying dangerous weapons. Michigan has a similar zero-tolerance law (Michigan Code of Laws Section 380.1311, 1997). In its first case interpreting its state zero-tolerance law, Massachusetts' highest court held that a tiny, half-inch blade inside a lipstick tube given to a girl as a joke by her boyfriend's mother and never used to threaten anyone constituted a weapon sufficient to justify permanent expulsion from school with no provision for alternative education (*Doe v. Worcester Public Schools*, 1995). The expulsion power given to Massachusetts principals resulted in more than 1100 students being expelled—many permanently—from the public schools in the 1996–1997 school year; only about 44% of these students were afforded some form of alternative services, such as home instruction, to ensure that their educational opportunities are not eliminated entirely as a result of the discipline problem (Massachusetts Department of Education, 1997). Now the state's governor is proposing that classroom teachers be given unilateral authority to suspend misbehaving students from their classrooms.

The disciplinary exclusion from school of students with disabilities has presented a particular challenge for legislatures and the courts. The issue also provides a useful illustration of the challenge of reconciling conflicting perceptions of the public good. Based on the right to appropriate education and the procedural protections set forth in IDEA, courts recognized that the use of disciplinary exclusions on students with disabilities could result in the unlawful denial of educational opportunities for these students. In 1988 the U.S. Supreme Court determined that schools could use their ordinary disciplinary proceedings and exclude students for up to ten days of school to address violations of school rules by students with disabilities. But the Court found that unless they were dangerous, students with disabilities were entitled to "stay put" in school until their educational needs could be addressed through the ordinary IDEA and state procedures (Honig v. Doe, 1988). By the reauthorization of the IDEA in 1997, however, many educators and parents of students without disabilities were sufficiently outraged that students with disabilities might be treated differently in school discipline situations that Congress included a new provision in the law to allow educators greater latitude in discipline. At the same time, however, requirements were added to ensure that students with disabilities were not punished for acts that are manifestations of their disabilities.(Public Law 105-17, 1997).

The so-called safe schools proponents argue that stern measures are necessary to ensure proper decorum and a safe learning environment and that students unwilling to meet the expectations of the school community are not entitled to be there. Disciplinary practices, however, that result in a total exclusion from educational services, even services provided in an alternative environment, raise serious issues about our commitment to education as a public good. Long-term or permanent school exclusions may mean increased opportunities for juvenile or criminal misconduct for the youngsters left on the street due to their exclusions from school. Further, the cessation of educational services almost certainly guarantees decreased economic productivity.

Free Speech

At the same time that the potential for severe disciplinary sanctions has increased, the scope of the power of school authorities to regulate student speech and extracurricular activities has also changed. Although *Tinker* and *Goss* created a strong presumption in favor of the constitutional rights of students within the school and during school activities, recent U.S. Supreme Court rulings have demonstrated a clear reluctance on the part of the justices to allow either elementary or secondary students the full range of rights that might be enjoyed by their older student counterparts. For example, in 1967 the Court recognized the importance of preparing college and university students for democratic participation through campus exposure to a wide and robust exchange of ideas (*Keyishian v. Board of Regents*, 385 U.S. 589, 1967). But in 1988, in *Hazelwood School District v. Kuhlmeier*, the Court articulated a strong deference to school officials and teachers to limit student expression, even if it meant censoring the content of a student newspaper. The Court held that a high school student newspaper could, if it was conducted under the supervision of a teacher and part of the curriculum of the school, be subject to prior censorship of its content to avoid exposing students to information about teen pregnancy.

School officials were later allowed to punish the use of sexual innuendo in a student nominating speech at an assembly before student government elections on grounds that the punishment of the student was not aimed at a political expression and a viewpoint but was rather an action that intruded on the work of the schools and the rights of other students. The role of schools, according to this decision, is to prepare students for citizenship and to "inculcate the habits and manners of civility," values that include taking into account the sensibilities of others (*Bethel School District v. Fraser*, 1986, at 681).

While the Supreme Court has never explicitly moved from its consistent articulation of the role of schools in preparing students for participation in a democratic society (Ingber, 1995), the conditions for this preparation have narrowed. The applicability of the *Tinker* decision now appears to have been limited and its protections for student speech are limited in activities that are school-sponsored (Ingber, 1995). At least one commentator has noted that these changes in the law are in direct conflict with recent developments in cognitive psychology that would indicate that student expression is important to the development of individuals' capacity for rational deliberation (Roe, 1991).

The tension between preparation for engaging in free speech and the other activities of democratic citizenship and educators' need for school order and discipline has not been resolved. Many commentators argue that the First Amendment should have little or no role in public elementary and secondary schools and that any judicial limitations on the authority of teachers and administrators inappropriately diminish the quality of the educational process and foster social reconstructionism (Dupre, 1996; Hafen, 1987). Others argue that to be educated for citizenship, students must learn civility and must be exposed to beneficent authority at school, while at the same time being exposed to the experience of liberty (Garvey, 1979; Ingber,

1995). The tension between promoting a commitment to community while fostering individualism means that each act of inculcating official values at the same time diminishes the opportunity to promote individualism (Ingber, 1995; Yudof, 1979; 1984).

Privacy

At the same time that the U.S. Supreme Court has been reinforcing the power of education officials to limit student expression and to exclude students from school for disciplinary reasons, it has also expanded the power of schools to redefine the atmosphere for schooling. In 1985 the Court, while reiterating that students have rights under the federal constitution, drew a clear distinction between the legal rights afforded individuals in the criminal and juvenile justice systems and those available to students; students were not to be afforded the same rights as other citizens. The result was a determination that school officials need establish only a reasonable suspicion to justify an intrusive search into a student's private space, such as a pocketbook or a backpack, rather than having to show evidence that there was probable cause to believe that a rule or law had been violated and that evidence of this will be found in the place to be searched (*New Jersey v. T.L.O.*, 469 U.S. 325). Later the Supreme Court expanded the power of school officials to regulate the conduct of students by upholding a high school's mandatory urine testing of student athletes (*Vernonia School District v. Acton*, 1995).

More than one commentator has noted the increasing restriction of student rights (Edwards, 1989; Stefkovitch, 1995). The courts often articulate some ambivalence about the discpline of students where, as one U.S. Supreme Court justice has commented:

> Schools are places where we inculcate the values essential to the meaningful exercise of rights and responsibilities by a self-governing citizenry. If the Nation's students can be convicted throught the use of arbitrary methods destructive of personal liberty, they cannot help but feel that they have been dealt with unfairly. (Stephens, J., TLO, at 373-74)

Local school officials, left by the federal courts with the discretion to have significant latitude dealing with student discipline, are left with the choice to either enhance or diminish student rights (Stefkovitch, 1995). State statutes may reinforce this latitude for local educators or place even greater constraints on their discretion. However, public outrage over the perceived safety and educational achievement problems in schools may be the most powerful influence of all. The result is an incoherence between articulated democratic goals and the nature of an educational process in which educators are pressed to maintain order at the expense of individual rights (Edwards, 1989; Stefkovich, 1995).

The recent state law changes and U.S. Supreme Court decisions concerning the relationships between school officials and students over privacy rights, freedom of expression, and access to information reflect an ongoing ambiguity over the role of schools, and school officials, in determining the nature and content of public education. If children can be excluded from school, even from access to any alternative educational services, then both the individual benefts of education and the collective social, economic, and civic benefits of an educated society are lost. If student expression and access to information at school can be significantly limited without offending the Constitution, then perhaps we also have changed our commitment to the tenet articulated in *Brown v. Board of Education* that education is a fundamentally important function of government because "it is a principal instrument in awakening the child to cultural values" (1954, at 493; see also *Ambach v. Norwick*, 1979; *Plyler v. Doe*, 1982, at 221). The value of tolerance, critical thinking, and the free flow of ideas is a critical component of a democractic society; if children do not learn these principles in school, where will they learn them?

Curriculum

The curriculum of the public schools is now, and always has been, heavily influenced by the social, cultural, economic, and political forces at work at the time the curriculum is adopted. Curriculum, whether it is the official curriculum of a local school district or the unofficial curriculum embedded in national textbook series, is always a reflection of particular cultural values (Apple, 1996; Spring, 1998). It has been argued that the history of American public elementary and secondary education is in large part a history of the struggle to ensure the domination of Protestant, Anglo-American culture (Spring, 1998). Law has always played a role in defining the official knowledge embedded in the curriculum and in weighing out attempts to challenge curricular norms.

The courts have regularly noted the importance of public schools in educating for citizenship (*Pierce v. Society of Sisters*, 1925; *West Virginia State Board of Education v. Barnette*, 1943). However, the Supreme Court in the early part of this century recognized the liberty rights of parents include the right to determine the type of education a child should receive; states may compel attendance in schools, but parents retain the right to choose to send their children to private schools, including Catholic schools (*Pierce v. Society of Sisters*, 1928). On similar grounds, it struck down a state law forbidding German-language instruction in elementary schools (*Meyer v. Nebraska*, 262 U.S. 390, 1923).

The U.S. Supreme Court has recognized the rights of parents to object, on First Amendment religious grounds, to participation in meeting some educational requirements. In *Wisconsin v. Yoder* (406 U.S. 205, 1972), the Court exempted Amish families from the requirements of a state compulsory attendance law when students reached an age where participation in schooling would expose them to knowledge that contravened family religious values and where the families could show that their community afforded a mechanism for ensuring that their children would be fully prepared for economic self-sufficieny and good citizenship. Justice Douglas offered a provocative ⟵ separate opinion dissenting in part from the decision in the case in which he argued that more consideration should have been paid to the preferences of the children involved, rather than resting a decision solely on the wishes of their parents, but this issue roused none of the other justices.

Allowing parents to pursue private or home school options or the alternative practical education option of the Wisconsin Amish has provided judges with relatively few difficulties. More difficult have been the judicial struggles over what the curriculum at school should contain and how to handle challenges from parents who want to opt out of the official curriculum. Although the Supreme Court recognized that school officials may not "prescribe what shall be orthodox in politics, nationalism, religion, or other matters of opinion" (West Virginia State Board of Education v. Barnette, 1943, at 642), it has subsequently inserted itself several times into disputes over the content of curriculum. The Supreme Court, in reviewing a case challenging a state law forbidding instruction of evolution, noted both the restraint with which courts must look at disputes involving schools but also the importance to which courts must attach the protection of the First Amendment rights of those in schools as "essential to safeguard the fundamental values of freedom of speech and inquiry and of belief. . . . The vigilent protection of constitutional freedoms is nowhere more vital than in the community of American schools" (Epperson v. Arkansas, 1968, at 104). On similar grounds, 20 years later, the Court struck down the Louisiana legislature's popular requirement for teaching creationism as a violation of the separation of church and state (Edwards v. Aguillard, 1987).

In a dispute over a school board's removal from the junior high and high school library of novels it deemed objectionable, the Supreme Court noted the importance of protecting student free expression rights, including the right to receive information. The plurality opinion of the Court states the importance of allowing local school authorities to transmit fundamental community values in the school through curriculum decisions and decisions about what to add to the library, but not in decisions to remove things from school libraries (Board of Education v. Pico, 1982).

Summary

At the end of the 20th century and probably well into the next, stuggles between educators, policy makers, and parents over control of curriculum are again increasing (Fine, 1993). Educators and many policy makers now shy away from any reference to so-called outcomes-based approaches to promote achievement. Similarly, promotion of the use of higher-order thinking skills, independent and collaborative learning, and the capacity for students to understand their personal strengths and weaknesses are now also politically controversial. These reactions are due in no small part to the complaints of social conservatives who have successfully cast such initiatives as efforts to promote particular values, ethics, and cultural norms and an intrusion on parental First Amendment rights to determine the upbringing of their children (Pullin, 1994).

The most powerful strategy for those who oppose current curriculum offerings of the public schools is, of course, the school-choice movement. Educational vouchers and other privitization initiatives allow parents the option to abandon the public school curriculum almost entirely. The free-market approach to elementary and secondary education gives parents the power to engage in total devotion to the individual benefits of education and to avoid altogether the effort to achieve consensus on the role of schools (Apple, 1996; Labaree, 1997).

Right to Education

Perhaps the most vivid reflection of the nation's ambivalence over the role of schools in our society is the ongoing struggle to define access to educational opportunity for all students. The extraordinary and painful inequities in educational opportunity available to some students as a result of the states' various mechanisms for financing public education have been powerfully portrayed (Kozol, 1991). Gross disparities in the resources available for schooling between and within school districts have resulted in variable access to educational programs and services. The problem plays itself out further in not only the provision of adequate physical facilities, but also access to qualified teachers (Darling-Hammond, 1997).

Most of the states have now had state court litigation addressing allegations of inequity in the ways schools are funded from district to district; nearly half of these suits found inequities that violated state constitutional provisions. The disputes in both state and federal courts over the financing of public elementary and secondary education reflect the tensions over the functions of schooling. In a dispute over Texas's system for financing public schools, the Supreme Court determined that the U.S. Constitution does not create a fundamental right to education (*San Antonio Ind. School Dist. v. Rodriguez*, 1973). Later, however, in a circumstance in which the state of Texas contemplated a scheme that would have denied the children of illegal alien parents access to educational opportunities, the U.S. Supreme Court held that once a state undertook to provide a system of public education, it was required to administer that system fairly so that children would not be denied education on the basis of a condition over which they did not have control (*Plyler v. Doe*, 1982).

School Finance

The constitutions of all 50 states contain provisions setting forth each state's responsibilities for educating its citizens. Recently, lawsuits have been brought in at least 27 states alleging that the state's systems for financing and operating public schools violate these state constitutional mandates. Some cases have focused solely on funding inequities, aiming to increase and more equitably distribute resources among local school districts. Others have gone further, challenging the substantive adequacy of the education support provided by the state. These cases require state courts to assess the impact of language in their state constitutions concerning the parameters of a constitutionally adequate education. In 17 states, a constitutionally adequate public education system has been found to be one designed and operated to enable students to meet the broad educational outcomes anticipated by the relevant state constitutional provisions (Goetz, this volume; McCusic, 1991; Underwood, 1995).

In Kentucky, the state Supreme Court held that the Kentucky Constitution, which requires that the legislature "provide for an efficient system of common schools throughout the state" means that *"every child . . .* must be provided with an equal opportunity to have an adequate education." The decision went on to specify a number of outcomes that could be expected for educated persons:

> (i) sufficient oral and written communication skills to enable students to function in a complex and rapidly changing civilization; (ii) sufficient knowledge of economic, social, and political systems to enable the student to make informed choices; (iii) sufficient udnerstanding of governmental processes to enable the student to understand the issues that affect his or her community, state, and nation; (iv) sufficient self-knowledge and knowledge of his or her mental and physical wellness; (v) sufficient grounding in the arts to enable each student to appreciate his or her cultural and historical heritage; (vi) sufficient training or preparation for advanced training in either academic or vocational fields so as to enable each child to choose and pursue life work intelligently; and (vii) sufficient levels of academic or vocational skills to enable public school students to compete favorably with their counterparts in surrounding states, in academics, or in the job market. (*Rose v. Council for Better Education,* 1989, 790 S.W. 2d at 212)

The same approach has been taken in Alabama (*Opinion of the Justices,* 1993), Massachusetts (*McDuffy v. Secretary of the Executive Office of Education,* 1993), and New Hampshire (*Claremont School District v. Governor,* 1993), where each state's highest court has articulated a state constitutional right to adequate education as defined by the seven criteria set forth in the Kentucky case.

At the heart of the school finance disputes is a tension between resource-rich schools and those with insufficient property wealth or other resources to raise sufficient funds to offer the level of educational services available in more affluent communities. The difficulty presented by the proposed remedies for these inequities strikes at the heart of our national ambivalence over public education. The elimination of funding inequities across school districts requires, in essence, a redistribution of wealth. To equalize resources for schools, districts with property wealth must constrain their local spending in order to shift resources to less wealthy districts. This presents one of the most powerful issues over the role of schools in society. If schools do in fact serve the common interests of all citizens, then resource reallocation should not present a significant problem. If, however, the goal is more local or individual in nature, then such efforts to ensure that all children have access to equalized resources must surely be resisted. In several states, efforts to remedy constitutional violations concerning access to education have resulted in interminable debates over new legislation. In Texas, for example, the matter of remedying the school finance violations found by the state's highest court has been presented to the state legislature no fewer than three separate times and still remains unresolved (Augenblick, Myers, & Anderson, 1997).

Summary

Equity in funding is not the only issue in dispute in the state right-to-education cases. Funding sources aside, the more recent state school finance cases have focused less on the funding patterns for schools and more on the adequacy, or sufficiency, of educational opportunities and outcomes. There is every reason to believe that this will be the wave of the future in school finance litigation and, perhaps, state legislation. The focus on asserting a right to an adequate education and on the opportunities required to provide that education may represent a powerful shift in the efforts to define the nature and role of schools. Or the consideration of issues of adequacy may be the point at which the ambigious dialogue over the nature and role of schools may finally break down. If every child is to be the recipient of an adequate education, can we agree on a definition of the nature and content of this education? Is an adequate education for all children the same as the appropriate education we have agreed to provide students with disabilities? And if we can agree on what should be provided, can we agree to provide the resources to make this education available for *all* children?

Standards-Based Education Reform

At about the same time that state courts discovered that many state constitutions required the provision of an adequate system of elementary and secondary education, efforts began in many states and at the national level to undertake a new approach to promoting educational achievement based on the definition of content and performance standards that students would be expected to meet (McDonnell et al., 1997; McLaughlin & Shepherd, 1995). Although the nature of these initiatives varied from place to place, they generally included efforts to define content-based standards of what students should be taught, performance standards to define what students should know and be able to do, and a system of testing or assessment to determine how well individuals or groups of students were progressing toward achieving these goals. All 50 states are now either heavily involved in implementing standards-based reform or on their way to adopting some version of such a system (see Roeber, this volume).

The federal government, although very cautious about federal mandates to the states as a result of the congressional elections in 1994, took a clear stand to promote standards-based education reform in the Goals 2000: Educate America Act (Public Law 103-227, 1994) and in the Improving America's Schools Act of 1994 (Public Law 103-328, 1994). Although states are not required to employ standards-based education reforms, these approaches are strongly supported, in part through federal funding (Ordover et al., 1996). However, once a state undertakes a standards-based reform approach, it is required to ensure that *all* students participate in the program.

Whereas the first version of the federal law encouraged states to meet "opportunity to learn" standards to ensure that the necessary resources were in place to allow all students, including the educationally disadvantaged, to have a fair opportunity to learn the state's content standards. This provision is not now in the federal law on grounds that it would be too much of a federal intrusion on the states, although the federal law does state that "all students can learn and achieve to high standards and must realize their potential if the United States is to prosper" and that "all students are entitled to participate in a broad and challenging curriculum" (Public Law 103-227, Section 301, 1994). In the Improving America's Schools Act (IASA), Congress reconfigured its largest federal education aid program, Title I, to "enable schools to provide opportunities for children served [under Title I] to acquire the knowledge and skills contained in challenging State content standards and to meet the challenging State performance standards developed for all children" (Public Law 103-328, Section 1001, 1994). The provisions of IASA also specified that students with disabilities were to be full participants in these programs. In 1997, when Congress reauthorized the IDEA, it firmly set forth a series of conditions designed to ensure that in every state utilizing standards-based reforms students covered by IDEA were to fully participate in the endeavor under the conditions deemed appropriate by each student's IEP team (Public Law 105-17, 1997).

The current wave of standards-based reform initiatives presents a new and challenging opportunity for testing the nation's commitment to defining and delivering educational opportunity. For the most part, courts have not yet become involved in the inevitable disputes over the implementation of standards-based education reform. But the state legislatures have created the opportunity to bring some resolution to these issues. It has been argued that the standards-based reform initiative is the ultimate attempt by social conservatives to bring about the end to public education and allow total privatization of the elementary and secondary education market (Apple, 1996). Whether this will be the case remains to be resolved in the next century.

Whether the nation is prepared to ensure that the federal requirement for participation by *all* students does, in fact, mean a commitment to *all* students will be one important question for the start of the new millenium. One set of issues will focus on the content of standards for curriculum and instruction, another on the means for assessing achievement, and yet another on the consequences of the new systems. It has been observed that the current standards-based reform proposals have been forged by an unusual new co-alition led by the social conservatives but drawing support among political forces that have not traditionally been coalitions (Apple, 1996; Pullin, 1994). It has also been asserted that the effect of movement will be to legitimize inequality, to create the illusion that all schools have something in common when, in fact, vast disparities still exist in the resources available to individ-ual schools (Apple, 1996). As noted earlier, Apple (1996) has argued that standards-based reform is simply one step in the effort of social conserva-tives to achieve their ultimate goal of privitization of all education. Given the very poor performance on standards-based assessments experienced in many districts, including some quite affluent districts (Harp, 1998), there is good reason to believe that the results of these assessments may be used as the best argument against the continuation of our system of public schools.

The content and assessment of the performance standards will be another important focal point for the ongoing debate over the nature of schooling. Students who complete all other graduation requirements may be denied high school diplomas on the basis of performance assessments. Teachers may lose their jobs if students perform poorly or receive significant financial incentives if students perform successfully. Control of school districts or school buildings may be taken away from localities and given to the state, all based on test performance. The very high stakes for students and educa-tors associated with these programs will ensure that significant portions of each school day will be devoted to the content and performance standards. Indeed, this is exactly what the program proponents wanted. However, how this content is defined and measured will represent a particular vision of schools and schooling, as have all other curriculum initiatives. Recent dis-putes in California and Massachusetts have already highlighted the contro-versial nature of any decision to include or exclude particular content or ways of assessing achievement in the content areas. Yet the implementation of these initiatives is not far enough along for members of the public to have felt the full impact of some of the painful consequences of implementation. What will be the response to large numbers of failures among minority or disability groups or, for that matter, to high failure rates among affluent and otherwise successful schools? Over a few years of implementation of these initiatives, will the nation be any closer to a consensus on the role of schools and the nature and content of schooling? Or will more of our ambiguous feelings be played out in yet another round of education litigation?

THE FUTURE ROLE OF THE RULE OF LAW

There is no particular reason to believe that there will be any growing wave of education litigation to sweep the nation's public elementary and secondary schools over the traditional types of legal issues that have been presented to the courts (Imber & Thompson, 1991; Zirkel & Richardson, 1989). However, there is ample reason to believe that the prognosis for the 21st century is that, so long as Americans are unable to resolve our collective ambivalence about schools and schooling, education legislation and education litigation will continue to be active forums for an ongoing debate.

Many will probably continue to blame the courts for at least some of the ills that arise in schools. However, judges can be no better than we as a society are in resolving the many confrontations and contradictions that ensue from our uncertaintly about what we want from schools for our children. It has been argued that, despite repeated waves of reform, reform remains the steady work of educators, policy makers, and policy analysts (Elmore & McLaughlin, 1988). In many respects, little has changed in the nation's system of public schooling. Public education remains an inherently bureaucratic, reproductionist, class-bound enterprise (Katz, 1971). More than one commentator has opined that we will probably continue to blame schools for all of the social and economic dysfunctions in our society and that "we are doomed to reproduce an endless cycle of high or diminishing hopes, rhetorical reforms, and broken promises" about our system of public education (Apple, 1996, p. 97).

The complexity and difficulty of defining a shared view of the role of schools and the nature and content of schooling cannot be understated. In an era in which there appears to be an increased focus on the private benefits of schooling, the difficulty of this endeavor is increased. Despite the national rhetoric about the importance of high standards for all, the nation is far from achieving a shared view of what schools should do. To some extent, the standards-based reform movement and the definitions imbedded within tests and assessments of what students should know and be able to do is moving faster than the public discussion, or even the consensus of educators, on the appropriate outcomes of schooling.

At the same time, however, an important advance has been made in the states in which courts or legislatures have articulated the rights of all students to receive an adequate education. It is far too early to assess the impact of these recent legal initiatives. There has not been enough time even to assess whether there is a common understanding of the seven standards for assessing educational adequacy articulated by judges in Kentucky, New Hampshire, and other states. Certainly many difficult battles lie ahead to define an adequate education. Many struggles also lie ahead to determine whether there is a shared commitment to shoulder the financial burdens associated with ensuring that *all* children will in fact have access to at least an adequate education. These will be among the most significant legal and educational policy issues at the start of the next millenium and may well be the most monumental debates in the nation's educational history.

References

Aleman, S. R. (1995, March). *Special Education: Issues in the State Grant Program of the Individuals with Disabilities Education Act*. Washington, DC: Congressional Research Service, U.S. Library of Congress.

Ambach v. Norwick, 441 U.S. 68 (1979).

Apple, M. (1996). *Cultural politics and education*. New York: Teachers College Press.

Armor, D. J. (1995). *Forced justice: School desegregation and the law*. New York: Oxford University Press.

Arons, S. (1983). *Compelling belief: The culture of American schooling*. New York: New Press.

Augenblick, J. G., Myers, J. L., & Anderson, A. B. (1997). Equity and adequacy in school funding. *The Future of Children*, 7, 63–78.

Benveniste, G. (1986). Implementation strategies: The case of 94-142. In D. Kirp & Jensen (Eds.), *School days, rule days* (pp. 146–165).

Bethel School District v. Fraser, 478 U.S. 678 (1986).

Board of Education of Hendrick Hudson Central School District v. Rowley, 458 U.S. 176 (1982).

Board of Education Island Trees Union Free School District v. Pico, 457 U.S. 853 (1982).

Board of Education, Sacramento City Unified School District v. Holland, 14 F. 3d. 1398 (9th Cir. 1994).

Broadwell, C. A., & Walden, J. (1988). "Free and Appropriate Public Education" after *Rowley*: An analysis of recent court decisions. *Journal of Law and Education*, 17, 35.

Brown v. Board of Education, 347 U.S. 483 (1954).

Butts, F., & Cremin, L. (1953). *A history of education in american culture*. New York: Henry Holt.

Carnoy, M., & Levin, H. M. (1985). *Schooling and work in the democratic state*. Stanford, CA: Stanford University Press.

Claremont School District v. Governor, 635 A. 2d 1375 (N.H. Sup. Ct. 1993).

Clune, W. H., & Van Pelt, M. H. (1985). A political method of evaluating The Education for All Handicapped Children Act of 1975 and the several gaps of gap analysis. *Law and Contemporary Problems*, 48, 7.

Cohen, D. (1984). The American common school: A divided vision. *Education and Urban Society*, 16, 253–261.

Cremin, L. (1951). *The American common school*. New York: Teachers College Press, Columbia University.

Daniel R. R. v. State Board of Education, 874 F. 2d 1036 (5th Cir. 1989).

Darling-Hammond, L. (1997). *The right to learn: A blueprint for creating schools that work*. San Francisco: Jossey-Bass.

Doe v. Worcester Public Schools, 421 Mass, 117 (Mass. Supr. Jud. Ct., 1995).

Durpe, A. (1996). Should students have constitutional rights? Keeping order in the public schools. *George Washington Law Review*, 65, 49–105.

Edwards, T. B. (1989). Shedding their rights at the schoolhouse gate: Recent Supreme Court cases have severely restricted the constitutional rights available to public schoolchildren. *Oklahoma City University Law Review*, 14, 97–130.

Edwards v. Aguillard, 482 U.S. 578 (1987).

Elmore, R., & McLaughlin, M. (1988). Steady Work: Policy, practice, and the reform of American education. Santa Monica, CA: Rand Corporation.

Engel, D. M. (1991). Law, culture, and children with disabilities: Educational rights and the construction of difference. *Duke Law Journal*, p. 166.

Epperson v. Arkansas, 393 U.S. 97 (1968).

Fine, M. (1993, Summer). [Ap]parent Involvement: Reflections on parents, power, and urban public schools. *Teachers College Record*, 94.

Gallegos, E. (1989). Beyond Board of Education v. Rowley: Educational benefit for the handicapped? *American Journal of Education*, 97, 258.

Gartner, A., & Lipsky, D. K. (1987, November). Beyond special education: Toward a quality system for all students. *Harvard Educational Review*, 57, reprinted in Hehir, T., & Latus, T. (1992). *Special education at the Century's end*. Cambridge, MA: Harvard Education Review.

Garvey, J. H. (1979). Children and the First Amendment. *Texas Law Review*, 57, 321.

Goldberg, S. S. (1989, Summer). The failure of legalization in education: Alternative dispute resolution and the Education for All Handicapped Children Act of 1975. *Journal of Law and Education*, 18, 441.

Goldberg, S. S., & Kuriloff, P. J. (1991, May). Evaluating the Fairness of Special Education Hearings. *Exceptional Children*, p. 546.

Goss v. Lopez, 419 U.S. 565 (1975).

Green T. F. (1982). Excellence, equity, and equality. In L. Shulman, & G. Sykes. (Eds.) *Handbook of teaching and policy*. New York: Longman.

Hafen, B. C. (1987). Developing student expression through institutional authority: Public schools as mediating structures. *Ohio State Law Journal*, 48, 663–731.

Handler, J. F. (1986). The conditions of discretion: Autonomy, community, bureaucracy. New York: Russell Sage Foundation.

Harp, L. (1998). *Education Week*.

Hazelwood School District v. Kuhlmeier, 484 U.S. 260 (1988).

Heise, M. (1996). Assessing the efficacy of school desegregation. *Syracuse Law Review*, 46, 1093–1117.

Honig v. Doe, (484 U.S. 305 1988).

Hooker, C. P. (1988, September). Teachers and the courts. *Education Law Reporter*, 48, 7–18.

Howe, K. R. (1997). *Understanding equal educational opportunity*. New York: Teachers College Press, Columbia University.

Huefner, D. S. (1991). Judicial Review of the Special Education Program Requirements under the Education for All Handicapped Children Act: Where have we been and where should we be going? *Harvard Journal of Law and Public Policy*, 14, 463–516.

Imber, M., & Gayler, D. E. (1988, February). A statistical analysis of trends in education-related litigation since 1960. *Educational Administration Quarterly*, 24, 55.

Imber, M., & Thompson, G. (1991, May). Developing a typology of litigation in education and determining the frequency of each category, *Educational Administration Quarterly*, 27, 225.

Ingber, S. (1995). Liberty and authority: Two facets of the inculcation of virtue, *St. John's law review*, 69, 421–479.

Irving Independent School District v. Tatro, 468 U.S. 883 (1984).

Katz, M. (1975). *Class, bureaucracy, and the schools*. New York: Praeger.

Keyishian v. Board of Regents, 385 U.S. 589 (1967).

Kirp, D., & Neal (1985). The allure of legalization reconsidered: The case of special education. *Law and Contemporary Problems*, 48, 63.

Kluger, R. (1975). *Simple justice: The history of Brown v. Board of Education and Black America's struggle for equality*. New York: Vintage Books.

Kozol, J. (1991). *Savage inequalities: Children in America's schools*. New York: Crown Publishers.

Labaree, D. (1997). *How to succeed in school without really trying: The credentials race in American education*. New Haven: Yale University Press.

Lazerson, M. (1983). The origins of special education. In J. Chambers & W. Hartman (Eds.), *Special education policies: Their history, implementation, and finance*. Philadelphia, PA: Temple University Press.

Massachusetts Department of Education. (1997). *Student expulsions in Massachusetts public schools.* Malden, Massachusetts: Massachusetts Department of Education.

Mayer, M. (1975). *The schools.* New York: Harper & Brothers.

McCusic, M. (1991). The use of education clauses in school finance reform litigation, *Harvard Journal on Legislation, 28.*

McDonnell, L., McLaughlin, M., & Morison, P. (1997). *Educating one and all: Students with disabilities and standards-based reform.* Washington, DC: National Academy Press.

McDuffy v. Secretary of the Executive Office of Education, 615 N.E. 2d 516 (Sup. Jud. Ct. Mass. 1993).

McLaughlin, M., & Shepherd, L. (1995). *Improving education through standards-based reform: A report of the National Academy of Education Panel on Standards-Based Reform.* Stanford, CA: The National Academy of Education.

Melnick, R. S. (1994). *Between the lines: Interpreting welfare rights.* Washington, DC: Brookings Institute.

Meyer v. Nebraska, 262 U.S. 390 (1923).

Michigan Code of Laws Section 380.1311 (1997).

Minow, M. (1990). *Making all the difference: Inclusion, exclusion, and American law.* Ithaca, NY: Cornell University Press.

Nasow, D. (1979). *Schooled to order: A social history of public schooling in the United States.* Oxford: Oxford University Press.

New Jersey v. T.L.O., 469 U.S. 325 (1985).

Oberti v. Board of Education of Borough of Clementon, 995 F. 2d 1204 (3rd Cir. 1993).

Opinion of the Justices No. 338, 624 So. 2d 107 (Ala. 1993).

Ordover, E., Boundy, K., & Pullin, D. (1996). *Students with disabilities and the implementation of standards-based education reform: Legal issues and implications.* Washington, DC: Center for Law and Education.

Orfield, G. (1996). *Dismantling desegregation: The quiet reversal of Brown v. Board of Education.* New York: New Press.

Osborne, A. G., Jr. (1996). *Legal issues in special education.* Boston: Allyn and Bacon.

Pierce v. Society of Sisters, 268 U.S. 510 (1925).

Plyler v. Doe, 457 U.S. 202 (1982).

Public Law 103-227, Goals 2000: Educate America Act (1994).

Public Law 103-328, Improving America's Schools Act (1994).

Public Law 105-17, Individuals with Disabilities Education Act Amendments (1997).

Pullin, D. (1994). Learning to work: The impact of curriculum and assessment standards on educational opportunity. *Harvard Educational Review, 64,* 31–54.

Roe, R. L. (1991). Valuing student speech: The work of the schools as conceptual development. *California Law Review, 79,* 1269.

Rose v. Council for Better Education, 790 S.W. 2d 186 (Ky. 1989).

Rothstein, L. F. (1990). *Special education law.* White Plains, NY: Longman.

Safe Schools Act of 1994 (20 U.S.C. 5961).

San Antonio Ind. School Dist. v. Rodriguez, 411 U.S. 1 (1973).

Sarason, S., & Doris, J. (1979). *Educational handicap, public policy, and social history.* New York: Free Press.

Sedlak, M., Wheeler, C., Pullin, D., & Cusack, P. (1986). *Selling students short: Classroom bargains and academic reform in the American high school.* New York: Teachers College Press, Columbia University.

Shanker, A. (1994). Where we stand: Inclusion and ideology. *New York Times.*

Silva, D. (1994). *Toward lawfulness in schooling: Components in program development.* Lanham, MD: University Press of America.

Singer, J. D., & Butler, J. A. (1987, May). The Education for All Handicapped Children Act: Schools as agents of social reform. *Harvard Educational Review, 57,* 125, reprinted in Hehir, T., and Latus (Eds.), *Special Education at the Century's End* (1992).

Skrtic, T. M. (1991, May). The special education paradox: Equity as a way to excellence. *Harvard Educational Review, 61,* reprinted in Hehir, T., & Latus, *Special Education at the Century's End* (1992).

Smith, S. W., & Brownell, M. T. (1995, September). Individualized education program: Considering the broad context or reform. *Focus on Exceptional Children*, 28, 1.

Spring, J. (1997). *The American School: 1642–1996* (4th ed.). New York: McGraw-Hill.

Spring, J. (1998). *Conflict of interests: The politics of american education* (3rd ed.). Boston: McGraw-Hill.

Stefkovitch, J. (1995). Students' Fourth and Fourteenth Amendment Rights after *Tinker*: A half full glass? *St. John's Law Review*, 69, 481–513.

Strope, J. L., & Broadwell, C. A. (1990). How P.L. 94-142 has fared in the supreme court. *Education Law Reporter*, 58, 13.

Tinker v. Des Moines Independent School District, 393 U.S. 503 (1969).

Turnbull III, H. R. (1993). *Free appropriate public education: The law and children with disabilities* (3rd ed.). Denver, CO: Love Publishing.

Tweedie, J. (1983). The politics of legalization in special education reform, In J. Chambers & Hartman (eds.), *Special education policies: Their history, implementation, and finance.*

Tyack, D., & Benavot, A. (1985). Courts and public schools: Educational litigation in historical perspective. *Law and Society Review*, 19, 339.

Tyack, D., James, T., & Benavot, A. (1987). *Law and the shaping of American public education: 1785–1954.* Madison, WI: University of Wisconsin Press.

Underwood, J. K., & Mead, J. F. (1995). *Legal aspects of special education and pupil services.* Boston: Allyn & Bacon.

U.S. Department of Education. (1996). *Eighteenth annual report to congress on the implementation of the Individuals with Disabilities Education Act.* Washington, DC.

Vernonia School District v. Acton, 115 S Ct. 2386 (1995).

Wang, M., et al. (1986). Rethinking special education. *Educational Leadership* 44, 26.

Weatherley, R. A. (1979). *Reforming special education: Policy implementation from state level to street level.* Cambridge, MA: MIT Press.

Weatherley, R. A., & Lipsky, M. (1977). Street-level bureaucrats and institutional innovation: Implementing special education reform. *Harvard Educational Review*, 47, 171.

Weber, M. C. (1990). The transformation of the Education of the Handicapped Act: A study in the interpretation of radical statutes. *University of California, Davis Law Review*, 24, 349.

Wegner, J. W. (1985). Variations on a theme—The concept of equal educational opportunity and programming decisions under the Education for All Handicapped Children Act of 1975. *Journal of Law and Contemporary Problems*, 48, 169.

West Virginia State Board of Education v. Barnette, 319 U.S. 624 (1943).

White, K. A. (1998, February 13). Effort to revise Massachusetts special education law fails; Study planned. *Education Week*, p. 23.

Will, M. C. (1986). Educating children with learning problems: A shared responsibility. *Exceptional Children* 52, 411.

Wirt, F., & Kirst, M. (1989). *The politics of education: Schools in conflict* (2nd ed.). Berkeley, CA: McCutchan.

Wisconsin v. Yoder, 406 U.S. 205 (1978).

Wise, A. E. (1979). *Legislated learning: The bureaucratization of the American classroom.* Berkeley, CA: University of California Press.

Yudof, M. G. (1979). Law and education research: Past and future. *New York University Education Quarterly.*

Yudof, M. G. (1984). Library book selection and the public schools: The quest for the Archimedean point. *Indiana Law Journal*, **59,** 527.

Zernicke, K. (1997). *Boston Globe.*

Zirkel, P. A., & Richardson, S. N. (1989). The explosion in education litigation. *Education Law Reporter*, 53, 767–791.

CHAPTER 2

The Finance of American Public Education: Challenges of Equity, Adequacy, and Efficiency

MARGARET E. GOERTZ
University of Pennsylvania

In the United States, the authority for public elementary and secondary education resides in the states, a reserved power arising from the Tenth Amendment of the U.S. Constitution. But the state role in education finance dates back to 1647 when the General Court of Massachusetts passed the Old Deluder Satan Act, requiring every town to set up a school or pay a sum of money to a larger town to provide educational services. The act required that these schools be supported by masters, parents, or the inhabitants in general (Odden & Picus, 1992). Initially, local communities established one-room elementary schools, often fully supported by a small local tax. By the mid-19th century, several states had created not only statewide systems of public education, but mechanisms for funding these schools. In New York State, for example, an 1849 statute provided for a state share of school funding of 52%. Yet the fixed appropriation could not keep up with rising school costs, and local real property taxes had to bear an increasing share of the burden (Berke, Goertz, & Coley, 1984).

Today states play a major role in the funding of education. With states providing nearly half of all public school revenues, elementary and secondary education now commands the largest share of state budgets; about one-third of state expenditures are devoted to this function (Raimondo, 1992). But legislators must grapple annually (or biennially) with many of the same

Handbook of Educational Policy

issues as their predecessors: the size of the state education aid budget, the allocation of these funds to local districts, and the consequences of these decisions for the level and adequacy of local educational spending, state and local taxes, and funds available for other public services. The design, enactment, and implementation of state education finance policies are complex tasks that require consensus on such philosophical questions as the meaning of equality of educational opportunity, the appropriate balance between the state's constitutional responsibility for education and local control, how much a good education should cost, and who should pay the bill. Education funding decisions are also intertwined with broader tax policy issues. The public, dissatisfied with rising property taxes, wants the state to play a larger role in the funding of public education. At the same time, state policy makers are being pressured to reduce or stabilize state taxes and spending.

This chapter introduces the reader to four major policy questions in the funding of elementary and secondary education: (1) What is the state's responsibility in funding education? (2) Who should pay for education and how? (3) How can policy makers design funding systems to support education reform? and (4) Who should be responsible for making spending decisions? A discussion of these issues also surfaces tensions among three basic values in education: equity, adequacy, and efficiency. Equity focuses on equalizing or distributing educational resources and opportunities to meet moral or societal goals. Adequacy focuses on the use of these resources to support professional or publicly determined standards of quality or proficiency. Efficiency focuses on holding educators accountable for the performance of their schools and students or rendering schools more productive (Guthrie, 1980). These values come to the forefront when policy makers design education reform policies. How much money should be spent on education to provide quality services to all students? What aspects of the educational program should be equalized? How can the state ensure the most efficient and effective use of public dollars? How much control should states or school districts have over education spending decisions?

THE STATE'S ROLE IN FUNDING EDUCATION

School districts receive revenues from three sources: the federal government (6.8%), state government (46.8%), and local taxes (46.4%). These national averages for the 1994–1995 school year mask major variation in sources of revenues across the states. In that year, state support for elementary and secondary education ranged from a low of 7.3% in New Hampshire to a high of 90.2% in Hawaii. Similarly, the local share of education funding varied from 89.6% to 2.4% in these states, respectively (NCES, 1998).

The level of local education revenues is driven by the interaction of the wealth and tax effort of a community. This close relationship between wealth and revenues makes it possible for a rich district to raise more revenue for education than a poor district, even though are both applying the same education tax rate. For example, a community with property wealth of $100,000 per student can raise only $1000 per student in local tax revenues with a ten-mill tax rate, whereas a wealthier neighboring community with a tax base of $500,000 per student can raise five times as much, or $5000 per student, with that same tax effort. Although most state aid systems are designed to compensate for these wealth-based disparities in educational spending, state aid is generally insufficient to offset these differences in community wealth. The result of these school finance systems is that poor school districts cannot generate sufficient revenue for an adequate education program or one that matches the programs provided by their more fortunate neighbors.

What is the responsibility of the state to address these funding inequities? To what extent must states equalize spending across their school districts? What is the state role in ensuring that all of its students have access to an adequate education? How does a state define adequacy and design a funding system that supports an adequate education? The answers to these questions are emerging from 30 years of school finance litigation, legislation, and political debate.

School Finance Litigation

Education is explicitly designated a state responsibility in state constitutions, although the wording of these guarantees varies across states. For example, the constitution of Kentucky requires its legislature to establish an efficient system of common schools, whereas the New York constitution calls only for the creation of a statewide system of free public schools. Other constitutions mandate the provision of basic, adequate, thorough and efficient or liberal systems of free public schools. State courts have used their authority to interpret these state education clauses to define the scope and substance of states' responsibilities for education and the degree and type of equity required of school funding systems. The policy directions set by state courts, however, reflect not only the language of constitutional provisions but the states' constitutional and legal history and the activism of the state justices (Hershkoff, Cohen, & Morgan, 1995; Underwood, 1994).

Wealth-based disparities in educational spending evident in the 1960s sparked the first legal challenges to state education finance systems. This first wave of litigation, which spanned the 1970s and early 1980s, was characterized by equity cases that focused primarily on the relationship between school district wealth and spending. Seventeen state high court decisions were handed down in this period: seven overturned existing school finance plans, and ten upheld them. This new judicial activism spurred states to restructure and expand their education funding systems. Twenty-eight states enacted school finance reform measures between 1971 and 1981, state education revenues rose by one-third, and the state share of funding rose from 40 to 49% (Brown & Elmore, 1982; NCES, 1998).

School finance activity lessened in the 1980s as state policy makers turned their attention to issues of excellence in education. The equity issue laid dormant until four new school finance decisions were handed down in 1989 and 1990 in Kentucky, Texas, Montana, and New Jersey. These decisions breathed new life into traditional equity cases and focused the courts' attention on issues of educational *adequacy* as well. State courts rendered 21 decisions between 1989 and 1997, 12 of which declared their state's school funding systems unconstitutional (Hickrod, McNeal, Lenz, Minorini, & Grady, 1997). Cases are pending in another dozen or so states.

Three issues appeared to have triggered this new round of litigation. First, in a few states, like New Jersey, reform laws that were enacted after the first round of litigation failed to close spending gaps. Second, reformers were concerned that the educational excellence movement of the 1980s would leave educationally disadvantaged students further behind because their communities could not provide the level of education resources necessary to meet new and rigorous state academic standards. Third, the educational adequacy theory reopened the legal door for states that had been unsuccessful in litigating an equity claim.

A Focus on Fiscal Equity

Most of the school finance cases argued over the past 30 years emphasized traditional fiscal equity arguments— that in spite of similar or often higher tax effort, low-wealth communities are unable to raise the same level of education revenues, and therefore provide comparable educational opportunities, as their wealthier neighbors. When state courts determined that these wealth-based disparities in educational spending violated state constitutional guarantees of equal educational opportunity, they usually ordered their legislatures to design state school finance systems that ensure that all children have substantially equal access to similar educational revenues. Although most of these courts gave their legislatures a fairly general charge, some were more prescriptive. In California, for example, the state court ordered that wealth-related per pupil spending not vary by more than $100 per pupil (*Serrano v. Priest*, 1976). The Texas Supreme Court called for a funding structure that more specifically ties equality of spending to similar levels of tax effort (*Edgewood v. Kirby*, 1989). In its *Abbott v. Burke* (1990) decision (hereafter *Abbott* II), the New Jersey Supreme Court focused on spending disparities between the state's poorest urban and wealthiest suburban districts, calling for expenditure parity between these two groups of districts (which together educate about 40% of the state's students).

The most common state policy for reducing the disparity in spending levels across a state is the foundation program. In place in 40 states in 1993–1994 (Gold, Smith, & Lawton, 1995), this approach focuses on expenditure equity, by guaranteeing that every student's education is supported by an equal amount of money, or foundation, regardless of the wealth of the individual school district. Local school districts must contribute to this state-prescribed amount, typically by applying a state-established tax rate to the local property tax base. Low-wealth districts will have a smaller required contribution and thus receive more state aid than those districts with greater taxable wealth. States use different criteria for setting the foundation amount; some link it to the state average per pupil educational expenditure. The foundation formula, however, leaves a district free to spend above the foundation level, if it chooses to tax itself at a higher rate. Known as *local leeway*, this choice can lead to wealth-based expenditure disparities above the foundation amount, especially if the foundation level is set at or below the state average expenditure.

Some of the newer school finance reform laws, such as those in Kentucky and Texas, address the issue of local leeway by creating a second tier in their funding formulas. This additional tier equalizes some of the local leeway by providing additional state aid when districts choose to tax and spend above the state-prescribed foundation amount. This approach equalizes districts' capacity to raise money for education, but it leaves them free to determine how much of that capacity they choose to tap. Although these state aid structures guarantee equal dollars for equal effort, they too can result in expenditure disparities if districts choose differing tax rates.

In most states, school finance reform legislation has been designed to equalize spending among school districts by providing additional state aid to low-wealth communities. These increases in state aid are often accompanied by increases in state taxes. For example, the New Jersey legislature increased that state's income tax by $1.1 billion to fund its 1990 school finance reform law (Goertz & Goertz, 1990). Kentucky raised state taxes by more than $600 million a year to support its new funding law (Koch & Willis, 1993). Recently, however, legislatures have turned to other ways of equalizing educational revenues—through tax-base sharing or the redistribution of local tax revenues. The Texas legislature, for example, established county education districts (CED) to levy local school taxes, which had the effect of substantially equalizing the range of property tax bases in the county. When CEDs were declared unconstitutional in 1992 because they violated a constitutional prohibition against statewide property taxes, the legislature required Texas's wealthiest districts to reduce their per-pupil property wealth by transferring the taxing authority for nonresidential property to another school district or by sending funds to the state or other school districts (Picus & Toenjes, 1994). Vermont's Act 60, passed in response to that state's

1997 school finance decision, established a statewide property tax to tap the wealth of the state's so-called gold towns, primarily ski and tourist areas (Goldberg, 1997).

Addressing the Special Needs of Students, Schools, and School Districts

States began to address a second kind of educational equity issue during the 1970s: meeting the needs of students with physical, mental, and environmental disadvantages. Led by the urban states of California, Massachusetts, and New York, by 1980, 23 states had enacted special funding programs to support services to educationally disadvantaged students; an equal number funded the instruction of limited-English-proficient students. All 50 states had enacted programs for students with disabilities that conformed to federal law, although they varied in how they were financed (Winslow & Peterson, 1982).

Legislation, litigation, changing demographics, and the rising cost of programs for special needs students continue to pose fiscal, as well as programmatic, challenges for schools, school districts, and states. For example, the percentage of students in poverty rose from 16% in 1979 to 20% in 1996. As states implemented the landmark federal legislation, the Education for All Handicapped Children Act of 1975 (P.L. 94-142) and subsequent amendments to the law, the number of students receiving special education services increased from 4.1 to 5.6 million children between 1980 and 1995. The number of children living in immigrant households rose by 24% in the 1980s, and the number of limited English proficient (LEP) students grew by almost 26% (GAO, 1994). In this section, we focus on the particular policy issues related to the financing of programs for students with disabilities and economically-disadvantaged students.

Special Education

In 1993–1994, about 12.4% of the school-aged population received special educational services at an estimated expenditure of $32 billion. States and localities pay most of the cost of these programs. Although the formula for federal support provides that states may receive up to 40% of the national average per-pupil expenditure for each child with a disability, the federal government picks up less than 10% of the bill (Parrish, 1996). As the number of students eligible for, and receiving, special education services grew during the 1980s, special education spending accounted for a large part of rising school budgets. In New York State, for example, school districts spent about one-third of their new dollars on special education between 1980 and 1992. Special education's share of school district budgets rose from 6 to 15% during this period. At the same time, the percentage of the budget allocated directly to regular education teaching dropped from 53.6 to 49.2% (Lankford & Wyckoff, 1995b). It is not surprising, then, that the cost and financing of special education services have come under heightened public scrutiny, with charges that special educational spending is encroaching on the regular education program.

These fiscal pressures will continue as rising special education enrollments intersect with slow growing school district budgets. Between 1988 and 1992, for example, participation in special education programs grew at approximately 3½ times the rate of the general education population growth. This increase reflected the extension of special education programming to infant and preschool children and other disability categories (e.g., autism and traumatic brain injury) and increasing numbers of students with characteristics that are related to learning problems and developmental disabilities, such as poverty, low birth rate, and substance abuse (Parrish & Chambers, 1996). At the same time, per-pupil education expenditures were flat during the first half of the 1990s, reflecting the interaction of enrollment growth, stagnant tax bases, and taxpayer resistance. This budget situation intensified the competition for funds within the education sector, leading some states to freeze or limit increases in state aid for special education or to cap the percentage of students eligible for state special education funds.

Policy makers in nearly two-thirds of the states have been prompted to pursue new ways of funding special education by fiscal pressures and three other special education finance issues: (1) the desire to remove fiscal incentives for restrictive special education placements, (2) demands by local administrators for increased flexibility in the use of special education dollars, and (3) a movement to include students with disabilities in standards-based general education reforms. These new approaches include *census funding,* which allocates some or all special education aid based on district enrollments rather than special education child counts. Census funding raises a number of issues, however. First, if the prevalence of disabling conditions varies across districts, the allocation of funds using total enrollments will be inequitable. Second, as special education funding formulas become more flexible, states must develop other mechanisms to ensure that the rights and needs of students with disabilities are recognized and that funds intended to support special education services are used appropriately. Third, in addition to changing the structure of formulas, states must address the incentive structure embedded in federal, state, and local special education regulations and in current school and teacher practice.

Programs for At-Risk Students

The rise in youth poverty, a growing concern with the large academic performance gap between poor and nonpoor and between minority and majority students, and a call for all students to meet more rigorous academic standards have also focused policy makers' attention on the educational needs of students who are most at risk of school failure. As the justices of the New Jersey Supreme Court wrote in their 1990 decision:

> [T]he children of poorer urban districts are as capable as all others; . . . their deficiencies stem from their socioeconomic status; and . . . through effective education and changes in that socioeconomic status, they can perform as well as others. Our constitutional mandate does not allow us to consign poorer children permanently to an inferior education on the theory that they cannot afford a better one or that they would not benefit from it (*Abbott* II at 340).

The New Jersey court identified those social and economic needs that they felt would hinder the academic performance of poor children: inadequate food, clothing, and shelter; the lack of close family and community ties and support; the lack of helpful role models; and "the needs that arise from a life led in an environment of violence, poverty and despair" (*Abbott* II at 369). The court then directed the state to identify, fund, and implement special supplemental programs and services to address these disadvantages. A report prepared for the New Jersey Supreme Court recently put the price tag for needed early childhood, summer school, and social services at about $600 million— approximately $2200 per pupil above the cost of the regular education program (King, 1998).

Whereas the *Abbott* decision appears to go the furthest in defining a state's responsibility for meeting the needs of disadvantaged students, a few other states have adopted similar kinds of programs, although on a smaller scale. For example, as part of its comprehensive reform law, the Kentucky Education Reform Act (KERA), the Kentucky legislature created new categorical aid programs that support preschool, extended school services, and social services for students and their families. These programs accounted for about 20% of Kentucky's new state aid dollars.

Clune (1994) characterized the kinds of policies implemented in KERA and mandated by the New Jersey court as *equity plus*. Equity is achieved by guaranteeing an equal expenditure base. The *plus* is represented by compensatory aid and services targeted on poor school districts. Clune viewed equity plus as a transition from school finance formulas that address traditional equity issues to ones that focus primarily on adequacy—that is, ensuring that school districts have sufficient resources to bring low-achieving students and schools up to state outcome standards. In his view, funding formulas that emphasize equality of spending reflect adequacy by focusing on what students actually achieve rather than on equal access to tax bases or tax revenues. Compensatory programs reflect adequacy by recognizing the special problems of poor students in meeting educational standards. But while equity plus responds to the emerging goal of higher standards for all students by targeting additional resources on low-outcome schools and districts, it lacks the policy, implementation, and governance structures necessary to ensure that resources are spent in an instructionally effective way.

Educational Adequacy

School finance equity cases and policies have focused primarily on whether school districts of different wealth and tax effort receive similar levels of funding. In contrast, educational adequacy cases are concerned about whether this level of funding is sufficient to prepare all students for higher education, skilled employment, and other experiences of adult life (Hershkoff et al., 1995). Although issues of educational adequacy are often raised in equity cases to illustrate the negative effects of inadequate funding on educational opportunities, educational adequacy claims relate the level of educational resources provided to students to some measure of an adequate education as defined by the state in its constitution, in a court's interpretation of that constitution, or in state statute.

The first state to confront the adequacy issue was West Virginia, where the court concluded that the state's constitutionally mandated thorough and efficient education system required equal programs and services so that students could develop their capacities in eight areas, including literacy, mathematical operations, knowledge of government, and interests in the creative arts (*Pauley v. Kelley*, 1979; *Pauley v. Bailey*, 1982). In the *Abbott* II decision, the New Jersey Supreme Court defined its state's constitutional obligation as assuring that students in poor urban communities have the opportunity to compete in, and contribute to, the society entered by their relatively advantaged peers. Subsequent decisions by courts in Alabama, Kentucky, and Massachusetts defined their states' obligations in terms of more specific educational outcomes, such as

> sufficient mathematical and scientific skills to function in [their state] and at national and international levels, ... sufficient understanding of the arts to enable each student to appreciate his or her cultural heritage and the cultural heritage of others, ... [and] sufficient support and guidance so that every student feels a sense of self-worth and ability to achieve. (*Harper v. Hunt*, 1993, at 166)

State policy makers face several new challenges in responding to the new adequacy decisions by the courts.[1] The first challenge is defining and measuring an adequate education. Should states use input standards—such as minimum class size, number of computers in a school or minimum facilities standards—or should they determine what kinds of programs are necessary to help students achieve the outcome standards being established by state boards of education, legislatures, and courts?

States have begun to define the parameters of an adequate education as they develop content and student performance standards in academic disciplines. In 1997, 49 states were developing common academic standards for their students, and 46 states either had or were in the process of developing

[1]A complete discussion of these adequacy challenges is beyond the scope of this chapter. The interested reader can find additional information, however, in Goertz (1994) and related articles in a special issue of *Educational Policy* (1994).

assessments aligned with these standards (Gandal, 1997). (See also Cibulka, this volume; Roeber, this volume.) State content standards vary, however, in terms of how broad or generic versus specific they are, whether they are primarily academic or comprehensive (that is, including affective domains and career standards, as well as traditional academic disciplines), and in the number of academic fields they cover. In a few states, such as California, consensus on the content of the standards has broken down, particularly in the areas of mathematics and language arts, resulting in fragmented and contradictory messages about what outcomes are expected of students. State policy makers must also establish performance goals. What level of student outcomes is a state seeking? Has the state ensured an adequate education when 70% of its students meet state standards? 50%? All students? Is the goal to have students meet a basic proficiency standard or achieve a more advanced level? These are the same questions that policy makers face when designing new performance-based accountability systems for their schools and school districts.

If and when a state has defined the substance of an adequate education, it must then determine what a school finance system based on adequacy will look like. By definition, school funding formulas allocate inputs, so to speak of an outcomes-based finance system is a non sequitur. Therefore, the second challenge is determining the level and mix of educational services and resources required to enable all students to meet these new standards. Linking inputs to outcomes depends on a production model, however, and until one is articulated well (see, for example, Monk, 1992), all attempts to build a funding formula on notions of adequacy will be intuitive at best.

Policy makers and researchers have responded to this lack of a scientific model with three other ways of defining appropriate resource levels. Policy makers in New Jersey and Wyoming have used *expert judgment* to identify the level and mix of resources that they felt schools will need to provide an adequate education (NJDE, 1996; Guthrie et al., 1997). One limitation of this approach, however, is a failure to link these resource decisions to any measures of student achievement. A second approach, used most recently in the states of Illinois and Ohio, addresses this limitation by identifying the *actual expenditure levels* of districts with satisfactory levels of student performance (Augenblick, 1997; Hinrichs & Laine, 1996). Third, economists are using *econometric models* to predict the level of funding needed to produce a certain level of output, such as average student achievement on a state assessment, given different characteristics of schools and their students (see, for example, Duncombe, Ruggiero, & Yinger, 1996).

Regardless of the approach, additional research is needed to address the following questions: What programs are successful for what kinds of students in meeting what types of outcomes? Are fundamentally different programs needed for low-risk and high-risk students? What are the necessary preconditions for successful academic programs, such as preschool and full-day kindergarten programs? What is the necessary infrastructure for these programs? For example, poor, high-need school districts have two kinds of infrastructure needs. The first is a lack of infrastructure for any kind of program and includes replacing dilapidated facilities, addressing a shortage of instructional materials and equipment, and adding the kinds of staff found in less needy school systems (e.g., more teachers and support staff). Once this basic infrastructure is in place, districts must provide additional resources to offset the educational, social, and economic disadvantages poor children bring to school. These services are truly compensatory—that is, they go beyond what is needed in more affluent school systems.

Once a state determines the basis of an adequate education, it must then determine the cost of this education for students with differing needs and design a state school finance system that supports an adequate education. Most states establish an entitlement in their education funding formulas— a funding guarantee that is related to some standard, such as the average expenditure or the number and mix of staff per 100 students. The issue in educational adequacy is where and how to set that standard. Is the standard the cost of meeting state outcomes for regular students, with an add-on for special needs districts that reflects their additional programmatic needs? Short of developing individualized allocations for each school district, there must be a base cost on which to build a formula.

New Jersey is the first state to tackle these issues head on, and the ongoing litigation over the state's current formula points out the major policy issues in such a design. In 1996 the New Jersey legislature enacted a new funding law, the Comprehensive Educational Improvement and Financing Act (CEIFA), that purported to link state support of elementary and secondary education with what it will cost for students to meet specified state educational goals: 56 core curriculum content standards in seven academic content areas and five cross-content workplace readiness standards. The cost of this education is driven by a set of input standards, such as class size, administrators/teachers per student, schools per district, and types and amount of classroom supplies, services, and materials that the state department of education considered to be sufficient to achieve the state content standards (even though the state currently lacks any way of measuring how well students perform on these standards). Any other district expenditures are deemed nonessential and must be funded only from local revenue sources.

In a 1997 review of the constitutionality of CEIFA, the New Jersey Supreme Court was the first court to accept a state's academic content standards as a reasonable definition of the educational opportunity required by a state constitution (Abbott v. Burke IV, 1997). The court determined, however, that these standards alone do not ensure substantive academic achievement. Because the funding provisions are derived from a model district that has few characteristics of any of the state's successful districts, and because

CEIFA does not link the content standards in any concrete way to the actual funding needed to deliver that content, the court declared CEIFA unconstitutional as applied to New Jersey's special needs districts. As in past decisions, the court used the expenditure levels of wealthy (and usually high-performing) school districts as its measure of a constitutionally adequate education for poor urban districts.

Summary

State court decisions have expanded states' constitutional responsibility for education from one of ensuring equal access to educational revenues to one of ensuring that most, if not all, students have access to an adequate education. At the same time, the standards-based reform movement is defining the scope and content of that education by specifying what every student should know and be able to do to function in the 21st century. State policy makers are thus confronted with the challenge of designing school funding systems that ensure equal access to those programs and services that help all students meet high academic standards. Yet no one is sure what programs work for which kinds of students, how much they cost, or how states and local communities will pay for them.

WHO PAYS FOR EDUCATION?

At the same time that states are confronted with the cost of equalizing educational opportunities for all students, legislators face opposition to raising taxes for education, especially the local property tax. Voter concerns about high and rising property taxes are justifiable. For example, per capita property taxes increased by over 120% in New York between 1981 and 1992; adjusted for inflation the growth exceeded 40% (Lankford & Wyckoff, 1995a). Nationally, school property taxes rose from $1.36 to $1.50 per $100 of personal income during about the same time period (Gold, 1995). Before Michigan restructured its tax system in 1994, per capita property taxes in that state were 33% higher than the national average (Kearney, 1995).

Taxpayer resistance to increasing property taxes has manifest itself in four kinds of policies designed to limit local property taxes and to encourage a more efficient use of education dollars: limiting the growth of education expenditures or revenues; capping or rolling back property tax rates; limiting growth in assessed valuations; and replacing local property taxes with state taxes, including a statewide property tax.

In 1976, New Jersey enacted the first statutory limitation on expenditures or tax revenues at both state and local levels. Initially, increases in local school budgets were limited by growth in local property valuations—the major source of local school district revenue. In later years, the growth in both state education aid and local school district expenditures were restricted primarily to changes in state per capita income, reflecting a philosophy that both state and local property taxes are paid out of personal income. The tax limitation movement gained momentum in the late 1970s when several states limited the combined property taxes of all local government units (municipalities, counties, school districts, etc.) to a certain percent of the property's full value. For example, the combined limit is 1% in California (Proposition 13) and 2½% in Massachusetts (Proposition 2½) (Kearney, 1995). In both states, these voter-initiated referenda had the effect of not only capping but substantially reducing property tax rates. More recently, voters enacted property tax rollbacks in Oregon and Colorado. In Oregon, for example, property tax rates for education were reduced by two-thirds over a 4-year period.

Some states also enacted limitations on growth in the assessed value of property. In California, for example, the assessed valuation of property does not change until the property is sold, when it is revalued at full market value. Other states limit increases in the value of taxable property to a small percentage each year or the rate of inflation, whichever is lower.

A fourth response to the call for property tax relief has been to specifically replace local property taxes with state tax revenues. In a dramatic vote in 1993, the Michigan legislature eliminated the local property tax as a source of funding for elementary and secondary education, leaving a $6.5 billion gap in education budgets. (See also Engler & Whitney, this volume.) The legislature and voters subsequently replaced most of these lost dollars—which represented two-thirds of school districts' revenues—with a state property tax, a 2-cent increase in the state sales tax, and a limited local property tax levied primarily on nonresidential property. As a result, the state share of educational funding jumped from 33% to nearly 80%, and the use of property taxes to fund education was cut in half—from two-thirds to only one-third of total education revenues (Kearney, 1995).

The Michigan experience generated national interest in abolishing local property taxes. Similar legislation was considered in other states, but to date only Vermont and Kansas have replaced the local property tax with a state-wide property tax. Vermont's Act 60, which was enacted in response to that state's school finance ruling, replaced most local funding for education with a statewide property tax. Unlike the Michigan legislation, which reduced property taxes across the state, Vermont's new tax plan redistributes property tax revenues from the state's wealthiest communities, primarily resort towns, to a large number of poorer districts. A much smaller portion of the burden is shifted to nonproperty-tax sources, such as increased sales taxes on gasoline and hotel rooms.

The continuing pressure to reduce reliance on local property taxes to fund elementary and secondary education thus raises three policy issues. First, as states limit the role of *local* property taxes, to what extent and how should states replace lost dollars? Second, what is the appropriate balance between the property tax and other broad-based taxes? Third, who should pay for education? What are the equity implications of state tax reform policies?

Not all states that cut property taxes made provision for replacement revenues. For example, neither California, Massachusetts, nor Oregon enacted new taxes or raised rates on existing taxes to offset the loss of local property tax revenues (Kearney, 1995). A large state surplus generated by California's booming economy initially replaced local dollars lost under Proposition 13, but subsequent downturns in the state's economy and constitutional limitations on state spending restricted growth in local school budgets (Picus, 1991). Average per-pupil spending dropped from the national average in 1979–1980 to 85% of the national average in 1990–1991 (NCES, 1998). Local school budgets were slashed in Massachusetts in the wake of Proposition 2½ (Ladd & Wilson, 1985), but high rates of economic growth in the 1980s and fewer limits on state revenues dramatically boosted average per-pupil spending. Oregon provided replacement revenues for only 4 years after its property tax reduction legislation.

As discussed earlier, other states such as Kansas, Michigan, and Vermont explicitly replaced local property tax revenues with a statewide property tax and increases in other state revenue sources. The Michigan and Kansas reforms addressed a long-standing imbalance among their major sources of tax revenues: property, sales, and income tax. But all three states chose to keep the property tax as a major revenue source. What are the advantages of retaining the property tax? First, the property tax raises a lot of money for education (as well as for other local government functions). Property taxes accounted for three-quarters of local tax revenues in 1991 (ACIR, 1993) and one-third of all state and local tax revenue in 1992 (Gold, 1995). Second, the property tax is a more stable source of revenue than either income or sales taxes. The stability of the property tax results from the relative insensitivity of property valuations to economic cycles, particularly downturns in the economy. Third, the burden of the property tax is shared among renters, homeowners, and businesses. In fact, one intended consequence of recent tax changes in Michigan and Vermont has been to shift some of the property tax burden from resident homeowners to nonresidential and vacation property owners.

Thus, depending on how it is structured, a move from the local property tax to statewide tax sources can have implications for who pays for education and therefore the equity of the school funding system. The statewide property tax in Vermont will both equalize property tax rates and shift some of the tax burden from local property owners in poor communities to property owners in wealthy "gold" towns, many of whom live out of state. Tax relief for Vermont's residents is augmented by a cap on the amount of property taxes that households earning less than $75,000 a year must pay. The increase in gasoline and hotel taxes shifts even more of the burden onto non-Vermonters.

The reassessment-on-sale ("Welcome Stranger") provisions in the California and Michigan laws create inequities between new and long-term property owners in the same town. Whereas both are subject to the same tax rate and own homes of similar market value, their tax bills are significantly different, reflecting variations in their assessed values. By taxing different classes of property at different rates, Michigan policy makers have also created inequities between types of property owners in the same community. A shift from local property taxes to state sales or income taxes also has the potential to redistribute tax burdens from lower to moderate or higher income families and from business owners to individual taxpayers.

LINKING EDUCATION FINANCE AND EDUCATION REFORM

An increased emphasis on educational adequacy and the public's concern over the high cost of education is focusing policy makers' attention on the efficiency and effectiveness of educational spending, as well as on the equity and adequacy of state aid allocations. Policy makers argue that added funding for education will lead only to increased benefits for teachers or will be consumed by an "administrative blob," rather than being directed to the instruction of children. Although studies have shown that new dollars generated by school finance reform are used to hire more teachers, provide additional support services, purchase more instructional materials and equipment, and replace aging facilities (Adams, 1994; Firestone, Goertz & Natriello, 1997; Picus, 1994), other researchers argue that spending more dollars in these traditional ways will not produce significant gains in student performance (Hanushek, 1989; Odden & Picus, 1992).

Researchers and policy makers have identified three fiscal strategies with a potential for increasing the efficiency and effectiveness of schools: school-based incentive programs, competency-based pay, and whole-school program designs. *School-based incentive programs* are intended to change the behavior of educators in ways that promote student learning by providing financial rewards for improvements in student achievement and other outcomes, such as attendance and dropout rates. For example, Kentucky gives cash rewards to educators in schools that move beyond a performance threshold established biennially by the state. In 1995 the state distributed more than $25 million directly to 14,100 teachers and administrators across 480, or 35%, of the state's schools (Elmore, Abelmann, & Fuhrman, 1996). Maryland's incentive program is more modest and rewards schools, not teachers. In 1996 the state allocated nearly $3 million to 100 elementary and middle schools (about 10% of the total) for having shown a statistically significant change in student performance over a 2-year period. Schools and teachers must use the rewards for instructional improvement, not for monetary payments to individual staff.

School-based incentive programs are relatively new, and little is known about how these incentives work. In designing these kinds of programs, policy makers must consider how they will measure the performance to be rewarded, who should be rewarded (teachers, schools, school districts), how much state aid will be allocated through an incentive program, and how incentive funds can be used by recipients. They must also ensure that these programs are fair, comprehensible to educators and the public, and do not produce perverse consequences, such as narrowing the curriculum to tested subjects or excusing low-achieving students from the test. For example, should teachers be held accountable for students who are new to a school? Should states make some adjustment for socio-economic differences among students, or will these kinds of adjustments institutionalize low expectations for poor or low-achieving students? Finally, incentive programs assume that educators have the knowledge but not the will to improve student performance. Teachers, however, are being asked to teach not only to higher standards, but in significantly different ways. Therefore, state policy makers must be willing to develop or fund technical assistance in assessment, evaluation, instruction, and curriculum (Clotfelter & Ladd, 1996; Elmore, Abelmann, & Fuhrman, 1996). Rewards may be necessary, but they are not sufficient to dramatically change educational practice.

School-based incentive systems emerged, in part, in response to the limited success of teacher-based incentive programs such as merit pay or career ladders. It has been argued that these latter programs were ineffective at motivating teachers because they were based on a flawed understanding of teacher motivation and of school organizational context. *Competency-based pay programs* are designed to overcome these problems by addressing both the intrinsic motivation of teachers—to help students achieve, to work collaboratively with other teachers, and to expand their professional skills to assist students—and extrinsic rewards, such as higher salaries (Odden & Kelley, 1997). Under a competency-based compensation system, indirect measures of teacher skills, such as years of experience and course credits, are replaced with more direct measures of teacher knowledge and skills. Teacher pay increases are tied to increased expertise in three broad areas: depth of knowledge in content, curriculum, and instruction; breadth of skills in nonteaching functions, such as curriculum development and counseling; and management skills necessary to work in site-based managed schools (Odden & Kelley, 1997). Competency-based pay plans are just now being implemented on a small scale in two school districts: Robbinsdale, Minnesota, and Douglas County, Colorado (Bradley, 1998).

Whole-school reforms seek to improve student achievement by reallocating school resources in support of research-based educational programs. These reform programs provide models for change, are designed for replication, and support networks of professional development. Some reforms, such as James Comer's School Development Program, Henry Levin's Accelerated Schools, Ted Sizer's Coalition of Essential Schools, Robert Slavin's Success for All/Roots and Wings and additional models supported by the New American Schools Design Corporation (NAS), are comprehensive designs that address to varying degrees curriculum, instruction, school operation, assessment, and parent and community involvement. Whereas all focus on improving student outcomes of at-risk students, they differ in the substance of their curricula (from E. D. Hirsch's Core Curriculum to Outward Bound's learning expeditions) and reliance on technology (from a little to a great deal). Other programs focus more narrowly on curriculum and instruction in language arts or mathematics (e.g., Reading Recovery, Direct Instruction, Comprehensive School Mathematics Program, and Cognitively Guided Instruction) (Fashola & Slavin, 1997; Slavin & Fashola, 1998; Stringfield, Ross, & Smith, 1996).

Odden and Busch (1998) described the staffing and other resource configurations required of the seven NAS designs and estimated the start-up and annual operating costs of each model for an elementary school of 500 students. After comparing these costs with the resources available in a national average school, they concluded that the average school in America has sufficient resources to finance a NAS design. What is required, however, is a reallocation of resources away from regular education specialists (e.g., art and music teachers), categorical program specialists (particularly federally funded Title I staff), and pupil support specialists to the core NAS program, which is staffed, organized, and run differently from the traditional school design. Bodily (1998) has argued, however, that it is difficult for schools to implement the type of restructuring called for in the NAS designs without giving schools greater control over their budgets.

WHERE SHOULD SPENDING AUTHORITY RESIDE?

School finance policy in the United States focuses primarily on raising revenues and allocating resources to local school districts. Districts then determine how they will allocate resources to schools. In most cases, districts allocate staff positions; schools control only a small amount of money for instructional supplies and equipment. In the past decade, however, many researchers, educators, and policy makers have advocated the use of school-based management (SBM) and school-based budgeting (SBB) as ways of improving educational quality and student performance (Malen, Ogawa, & Kranz, 1990).

Five arguments have been put forth in support of SBM and SBB. First, school-based management and budgeting structures bring the perspectives of those closest to students to the decision-making process, leading to better decisions and decisions more focused on the interests of children (Hess,

1995; Wohlstetter, Mohrman, & Robertson, 1997). Second, increasing school-level control over budgeting, hiring, and curriculum will enable schools to tailor their programs to the unique needs of their students and their communities and provide the flexibility needed to target resources to appropriate programs and services (Clune & White, 1988; Hess, 1995). Third, shared decision-making empowers administrators, teachers, parents, and other school constituents, increasing their willingness to make and support change (Clune & White, 1988; Ladd, 1996; Wohlstetter, et al., 1997). Fourth, the cost structure and use of site resources differs across innovative school designs, such as the New American Schools models. Thus, schools need the budget authority to reallocate their resources to the requirements of their chosen designs or programs (Odden, in press). Fifth, in making the current intradistrict allocation of resources more transparent to the public, school-based budgeting and school-based financing will spark a debate regarding equity—among schools within districts and among elementary, middle, and high schools (Odden & Busch, 1998).

Thousands of school districts across the United States have implemented SBM in at least some of their schools and many models of high-performance schools, such as the New American Schools, incorporate some measures of local school control (Wohlstetter et al., 1997). Yet few of these districts have devolved significant portions of their operating budgets to school sites and there is little research on the design, implementation, and impact of school-based budgeting in the United States (Wohlstetter & Buffett, 1992).

One recent study of site-based budgeting in four cities in the United States—Chicago, Fort Worth, New York, and Rochester—found that as currently structured, school-based budgeting in these districts takes place at the margins. True discretionary funds were limited to less than 20% of their resources, and schools were constrained in their use of these funds by collective bargaining agreements or district policy. Second, while one rationale for SBB is to promote more innovative educational programming, school-based budgeting in these four sites did not appear to provide an impetus for schools to do business differently. They used their budgetary flexibility to make traditional resource allocation decisions, such as reducing class size or providing enrichment programs. These decisions may reflect external constraints, a lack of knowledge of more comprehensive reform approaches, the organizational culture of the district or school, or educators' views of what kinds of programs are effective in improving student achievement. Third, although successful implementation of school-based management and budgeting requires the dissemination and use of financial and strategic planning information, teachers and parents in these districts reported they had limited access to information on or knowledge about school budgeting (Goertz & Hess, 1998).

Implementation of school-based budgeting structures raise issues of equity as well. Analysis of the allocation of resources across schools in Chicago, Fort Worth, New York, and Rochester showed that the allocation of general education expenditures was relatively equal across schools (reflecting, perhaps, the impact of federal Title I comparability requirements). Although high poverty schools received more state and federal compensatory education aid, there were few instances of these schools receiving a larger allocation of general education funds. Average teacher salaries were lower in schools with larger concentrations of poor and, in some cases, minority students, however. This relationship was compensated for at times by placing relatively more teachers in higher poverty schools (Berne & Stiefel, 1994; Berne, Stiefel, & Rubenstein, 1998; Rubenstein, 1998).

In 1997–1998, four different school districts—Broward County (Florida), Cincinnati, Pittsburgh, and Seattle—developed school-based financing systems to support the implementation of New American School (NAS) designs. The experiences of these and other districts highlight a set of policy issues around the design and evaluation of school-based finance and budgeting structures (Goertz & Stiefel, 1998; Odden, in press). First, districts must determine which functions should remain at the central office and which should be devolved to the schools and, correspondingly, how much money to retain centrally and how much to allocate to the school sites. Second, districts must identify which student and school factors (e.g., school size, students' educational needs, grade level, curriculum enhancement) should be considered when allocating funds to the school sites and establish equity criteria against which to evaluate the resulting allocations. Equity analyses also require integrated databases containing information on staff positions and student demographics and outcomes, as well as dollars. Third, districts must develop site-based accounting systems that generate detailed and timely budget and expenditure data, and they must train school staff, parents, and community representatives in how to use budget, personnel, program, and performance data. Fourth, as policy makers devolve more dollars and budgetary powers to the school site, they must consider who is ultimately responsible and how for the fiscal and academic performance of schools. What happens if schools fail to improve?

SUMMARY

State and local policy makers face many challenges as they design school funding systems that provide equitable and adequate educational opportunities to all students and foster an efficient use of educational resources. Changing student demographics and more challenging educational expectations require new approaches to preparing students to be effective citizens and to compete in a global economy. At the same time, a tax-weary public demands that educators find more efficient and effective ways of spending their education dollars. Unfortunately, there are no easy answers or cheap solutions to these problems. The public and policy makers must come to a legally, morally, and politically defensible consensus about their state's responsibility in education, and then they must develop a fair way of funding that responsibility. Policy makers and educators must also look to the growing body of educational research to inform the design of effective and efficient educational programs and funding structures. The bottom line, however, is that the education of every child in a state is ultimately the responsibility of every citizen of that state. This is the message of school finance court decisions, and perhaps the most difficult lesson for policy makers and the public to learn and accept.

References

Abbott v. Burke, 119 N.J. 287 (1990). (Abbott II)

Abbott v. Burke, 149 N.J. 145 (1997). (Abbott IV)

Adams, J. E., Jr. (1994). Spending reform dollars in Kentucky: Familiar patterns and new programs, but is this reform? *Educational Evaluation and Policy Analysis*, 16, 375–390.

Advisory Commission on Intergovernmental Relations (ACIR) (1993). *Significant features of fiscal federalism*: 1993, Vol. 2 (Report No. M-185-11.) Washington, DC: Author.

Augenblick, J. (1997). *Recommendations for a base figure and pupil-weighted adjustments to the base figure for use in a new school finance system in Ohio*. Columbus, OH: Ohio Department of Education.

Berke, J. S., Goertz, M. E., & Coley, R. J. (1984). *Politicians, judges and city schools: Reforming school finance in New York*. Russell Sage Foundation.

Berne, R., & Stiefel, L. (1994). Measuring equity at the school level: The finance perspective. *Educational Evaluation and Policy Analysis*, 16, 405–421.

Berne, R., Stiefel, L., & Rubenstein, R. (1998). Intra-district equity in four large cities: Methods, data and results. *Journal of Education Finance*, 23, 447–467.

Bodilly, S. (1998). *Lessons from New American Schools' scale-up phase: Prospects for bringing designs to multiple sites*. Santa Monica, CA: RAND Corporation.

Bradley, A. (1998, February 25). A better way to pay. *Education Week*, p. 29.

Brown, P. R., & Elmore, R. F. (1982). Analyzing the impact of school finance reform. In N. H. Cambron-McCabe & A. R. Odden (Eds.), *The changing politics of school finance* (pp. 107–138). Cambridge, MA: Ballinger.

Clune, W. H. (1994). The shift from equity to adequacy in school finance. *Educational Policy*, 8, 376–394.

Clune, W. H., & White, P.A. (1988). *School-based management: Institutional variation, implementation and issues for further research* (Rep. No. RR–008). New Brunswick, NJ: Rutgers University, Consortium for Policy Research in Education.

Clotfelter, C. T., & Ladd, H. F. (1996). Recognizing and rewarding success in public schools. In H. F. Ladd (Ed.), *Holding schools accountable: Performance-based reform in education* (pp. 23–63). Washington, DC: Brookings Institution.

Duncombe, W., Ruggiero, J., & Yinger, J. (1996). Alternative approaches to measuring the cost of education. In H. F. Ladd (Ed.), *Holding schools accountable: Performance-based reform in education* (pp. 327–356). Washington, DC: Brookings Institution.

Edgewood Indep. School Dist. v. Kirby, 777 S.W. 2d 391 (Tex. 1989).

Educational Policy. (1994). W. H. Clune (Ed.), Vol. 8, No. 4. [Special Issue].

Elmore, R. F., Abelmann, C. H., & Fuhrman, S. H. (1996). The new accountability in state education reform: From process to performance. In H. F. Ladd (Ed.), *Holding schools accountable: Performance-based reform in education* (pp. 65–98). Washington, DC: Brookings Institution.

Fashola, O. S., & Slavin, R. E. (1997). Promising programs for elementary and middle schools: Evidence of effectiveness and replicability. *Journal of Education for Students Placed at Risk*, 2, 251–307.

Firestone, W. A., Goertz, M. E., & Natriello, G. (1997). *From cashbox to classroom: The struggle for fiscal reform and educational change in New Jersey*. New York: Teachers College Press.

Gandal, M. (1997). *Making standards matter 1997*. Washington, DC: American Federation of Teachers.

General Accounting Office (GAO). (1994). *School-aged children: Poverty and diversity challenge schools nationwide*. GAO/HEHS–94–132. Washington, DC: U. S. General Accounting Office.

Goertz, M. E. (1994). Program equity and adequacy: Issues from the field. *Educational Policy*, 8, 608–615.

Goertz, M. E., & Hess, G. A., Jr. (1998). Processes and power in school budgeting across four large urban school districts. *Journal of Education Finance*, 23, 490–506.

Goertz, M. E., & Stiefel, L. (1998). Introduction: School-level resource allocation in urban public schools. *Journal of Education Finance*, 23, 435–446.

Goertz, R. K., & Goertz, M. E. (1990). The Quality Education Act of 1990: New Jersey responds to *Abbott v. Burke*. *Journal of Education Finance*, 16, 104–114.

Gold, S. D. (1995). *The outlook for school revenue in the next five years* (CPRE Research Report Series RR–034). New Brunswick, NJ: Rutgers University, Consortium for Policy Research in Education.

Gold, S. D., Smith, D. M., & Lawton, S. B. (1995). *Public school finance programs of the United States and Canada, 1993–94*. Albany, NY: American Education Finance Association and State University of New York, Center for the Study of the States, The Nelson A. Rockefeller Institute of Government.

Goldberg, C. (1997, December 19). School tax law splits 'haves' and 'have nots.' *The New York Times*, p. A34.

Guthrie, J. W. (1980). United States school finance policy 1955–1980. In J. W. Guthrie (Ed.), *School finance policies and practices: The 1980s: A decade of conflict* (pp. 3–46). Cambridge, MA: Ballinger.

Guthrie, J. W., Hayward, G. , Smith, J., Rothstein, R., Bennett, R., Koppich, J., Bowman, E., DeLap, L., Brandes, B., & Clark, S. (1997). *A proposed cost-based block grant model for Wyoming school finance*. Sacramento, CA: Management Analyst & Planning Associates.

Hanushek, E. A. (1989). The impact of differential expenditures on school performance. *Educational Researcher*, 18(4), 45–51.

Harper v. Hunt, Opinion of the Justices, 624 So.2d 107 (Ala. 1993).

Hershkoff, H., Cohen, A. S., & Morgan, M. I. (1995). Establishing education program inadequacy: The Alabama example. *University of Michigan Journal of Law Reform*, 28, 559–598.

Hess, G. A., Jr., (1995). *Restructuring urban schools: A Chicago perspective*. New York: Teachers College Press.

Hickrod, G. A., McNeal, L., Lenz, R., Minorini, P., & Grady, L. (1997). Status of school finance constitutional litigation. Web site: http://coe.ilstu.edu/boxscore.htm.

Hinrichs, W. L., & Laine, R. D. (1996). *Adequacy: Building quality and efficiency into the cost of education*. Springfield, IL: Illinois Board of Education.

Kearney, C. P. (1995). Reducing local school property taxes: Recent experiences in Michigan. *Journal of Education Finance*, 21, 165–185.

King, M. P. (1998, January 22). Report and decision of remand court. The Superior Court of New Jersey, Chancery Division in the civil action, *Abbott v. Burke*, Supreme Court of New Jersey, Docket No. M–622–96.

Koch, K., & Willis, T. (1993, March). *The Kentucky Education Reform Act of 1990: A review of the first biennium*. Paper presented at the annual meeting of the American Education Finance Association, Albuquerque, NM.

Ladd, H. F. (1996). Introduction. In H. F. Ladd (Ed.), *Holding schools accountable: Performance-based reform in education* (pp. 1–22). Washington, DC: Brookings Institution.

Ladd, H. F., & Wilson, J. B. (1985). Education and tax limitations: Evidence from Massachusetts. *Journal of Education Finance*, 10, 281–296.

Lankford, H., & Wyckoff, J. (1995a). Property taxation, taxpayer burden, and local educational finance in New York. *Journal of Education Finance*, 21, 57–86.

Lankford, H., & Wyckoff, J. (1995b). Where has the money gone? An analysis of school district spending in New York. *Educational Evaluation and Policy Analysis*, 17, 195–218.

Malen, B., Ogawa, R. T., & Kranz, J. (1990). What do we know about school-based management? A case study of the literature—a call for research. In W. H. Clune & J. F. Witte (Eds.), *Choice and control in American education, Vol. 2, The practice of choice, decentralization and school restructuring* (pp. 289–342). New York: Falmer.

Monk, D. H. (1992). Education productivity research: An update and assessment of its role in education finance reform. *Educational Evaluation and Policy Analysis*, 14, 307–331.

National Center for Education Statistics (NCES). (1998). *Digest of education statistics, 1997* (NCES 98–015). Washington, DC: U.S. Department of Education, Office of Educational Research and Improvement.

NJDE (New Jersey Department of Education). (1996, May). *Comprehensive plan for educational improvement and financing*. Trenton, NJ: Author.

Odden, A. R. (in press). School-based financing in North America. In Ross, K., & Levacic, R. (Eds.), *Needs-based resource allocation in schools via formula-based funding*. Paris: UNESCO, International Institute for Educational Planning.

Odden, A., & Busch, C. (1998). *Financing schools for high performance: Strategies for improving the use of educational resources*. San Francisco: Jossey-Bass.

Odden, A. R., & Kelley, C. (1997). *Paying teachers for what they know and do*. Thousand Oaks, CA: Corwin.

Odden, A. R., & Picus, L. O. (1992). *School finance: A policy perspective*. New York: McGraw-Hill.

Parrish, T. B. (1996). Special education finance: Past, present and future. *Journal of Education Finance*, 21, 451–476.

Parrish, T. B., & Chambers, J. G. (1996). Financing special education. *The Future of Children: Special Education for Students with Disabilities*, 6(1), 121–138.

Pauley v. Bailey, No. 75–1268 (Cir. Ct. Of Kanawha Co., W. Va., 1982).

Pauley v. Kelley, 162 W. Va. 672, 255 S.E.2d 859 (1979).

Picus, L. O. (1991). Cadillacs or Chevrolets? The evolution of state control over school finance in California. *Journal of Education Finance*, 17, 33–59.

Picus, L. O. (1994). The local impact of school finance reform in four Texas school districts. *Educational Evaluation and Policy Analysis*, 16, 391–404.

Picus, L. O., & Toenjes, L. (1994, March). *Texas school finance: Assessing the equity impact of multiple reforms*. Paper presented at the annual meeting of the American Education Finance Association, Nashville, TN.

Raimondo, H. J. (1992). *Economics of state and local government*. New York: Praeger.

Rubenstein, R. (1998). Resource equity in the Chicago public schools: A school-level approach. *Journal of Education Finance*, 23, 468–489.

Serrano v. Priest, 18 Cal. 3d 728 (1976).

Slavin, R., & Fashola, O. (1998). *Show me the evidence! Proven and promising programs for America's schools*. Thousand Oaks, CA: Corwin.

Stringfield, S., Ross, S., & Smith, L. (Eds.) (1996). *Bold plans for school restructuring: The new American schools*. Mahwah, NJ: Lawrence Erlbaum.

Underwood, J. (1994). School finance litigation: Legal theories, judicial activism, and social neglect. *Journal of Education Finance*, 20, 143–162.

Winslow, H. R., & Peterson, S. M. (1982). State initiatives for special needs students. In Sherman, J. D., Kutner, M. A., & Small, K. J. (Eds.), *New dimensions of the federal-state partnership in education* (pp. 46–62). Washington, DC: Institute for Educational Leadership.

Wohlstetter, P., & Buffett, T. (1992). Promoting school-based management: Are dollars decentralized too? In A. R. Odden (Ed.), *Rethinking school finance: An agenda for the 1990's* (pp. 128–165). San Francisco: Jossey-Bass.

Wohlstetter, P., Mohrman, S. A., & Robertson, P. J. (1997). Successful school-based management: A lesson for restructuring urban schools. In D. Ravitch & J. P. Viteritti (Eds.), *New schools for a new century* (pp. 201–225). New Haven, CT: Yale University Press.

CHAPTER 3

Infusing Educational Decision Making with Research

MARY KENNEDY
Michigan State University

You would think it would be relatively noncontroversial to say that educators should attend to research when making educational decisions. But this simple proposition has been the subject of a great deal of debate and hand-wringing. One reason for this is that it has been difficult to find evidence of anyone actually using research, despite the apple-pie merits of the idea. Another is that some critics of research have suggested that research should not, in fact, be a major contributor in educational decisions, either because of flaws in the research itself or because of the greater salience of community values. These arguments have been underway for several decades, though each has taken a slightly different cast as each debate reflects the actual educational decisions being made in each period.

This discussion organizes the literature on the relationship between research and educational practice into three broad categories: (1) the influence of research on policy, (2) the influence of research on teaching practice, and (3) the influence of policy on research. Each of these topics is pertinent to educational administrators and policy makers—the first because these groups have a professional responsibility to formulate policies as carefully and productively as they can, the second because they have an ethical obligation to promote research use as a way to enhance teaching and learning, and the third because many of them also are in positions to influence research itself by establishing policies for the funding of educational research.

Handbook of Educational Policy

THE INFLUENCE OF RESEARCH ON POLICY

The notion that social science might be able to contribute to public policy is a uniquely 20th-century idea. Mitchell (1985) has traced its origin to the 1951 publication of Lerner and Lasswell's (1951) *The Policy Sciences*, which both proposed and developed the idea of using social science research to help settle policy debates. But research designed explicitly to contribute to public policy did not become commonplace until the late 1960s, when President Johnson began waging his war on poverty. Education was a central part of President Johnson's war on poverty and during this period Congress launched the Head Start Program, the Follow Through Program, the Elementary and Secondary Education Act, the Community Services Act, and a variety of other related, though smaller, programs.

This proliferation of programs, often based on untested premises, stimulated an interest in program evaluation and in the systematic testing of public policy. Alice Rivlin's (1971) *Systematic Thinking for Social Action* presented an optimistic view of how research could, and should, contribute to social policy. Rivlin's book laid out an approach to rational policy decisions in which program evaluation research played a central role. At the same time that government officials became interested in marrying research and policy, so did researchers. Donald Campbell (1969; 1973), for instance, tirelessly promoted the idea that policy variations should be studied experimentally before being adopted on a nationwide scale. Others, such as Boruch (1975) and Cook et al. (1980) argued for strong experimental designs, even when research was being conducted in natural settings.

The Rise of Program Evaluation

In the context of this optimism, the federal government began commissioning studies of a wide range of education and other social service programs. Large-scale national evaluations were conducted of federal programs, and carefully-controlled studies were also tried, as a way of experimentally testing alternative policy initiatives. Findings from many of these studies were disappointing, in part because they were fraught with methodological compromises and in part because they did not yield the positive findings that program advocates had expected. Because of design problems, it was easy to attribute the apparent negative outcomes to poor evaluation designs. Disadvantaged students, for instance, were frequently inappropriately compared to more advantaged students. These initial disappointments increased the calls for stronger experimental designs, and the use of appropriate comparison groups, so that policy research could provide more definitive statements about the effects of these policies.

Advocates for experimental testing of public policy were not, as many people accused them, trying to usurp a political process and govern as Plato's philosopher-kings through their social science expertise. But they did believe that policy making could be improved through systematic experimentation and evaluation. Campbell (1973), for instance, argued that policies should be made through a largely *unscientific* process—a political process. He argued that the job of the social scientist was not to say what *should* be done but rather what *has been* done and what effect it had. He chastised his colleagues for veering into advocacy by trying to advise policy makers on what they should do next, rather than confining their remarks to the evidence at hand.

At the same time these large national studies were underway in the 1960s, virtually all of the legislation of that period also began requiring local program evaluations to be conducted by local grantees. As a result, thousands of school districts and all 50 states developed or expanded their evaluation offices and conducted evaluations aimed at contributing to local program decisions (McLaughlin, 1975). This expansion created a new profession and ultimately led to a new Evaluation Research Society, a new division within the American Educational Research Association on School Evaluation and Policy Analysis, several new evaluation and policy analysis journals, a host of textbooks on evaluation methods, and new courses on program evaluation and policy analysis in graduate programs in government, public administration, and education throughout the country.

Education Evaluation and Research Utilization

Even as this huge evaluation enterprise developed and expanded, though, it quickly became apparent that systematic research and evaluation evidence were not contributing to policies in the ways that advocates had been hoping for. Evaluation reports proliferated, but so did questions and doubts about their value. Some of these doubts had to do with the extent to which policy makers actually attended to evidence when they made policy decisions. Some had to do with the quality of the studies themselves, and whether they were sound enough to influence policy. Still others had to do with indications that findings were being distorted to fit into political agendas.

What was going wrong? Several hypotheses were put forward, ranging from methodological problems in the research to cultural differences between researchers and policy makers (Snow, 1959). The two-community theory suggested that scientists and policy makers belong to different communities, with different norms for communicating, different decision-making practices, different rules of evidence, and so forth. The differences create a lack of understanding and a distrust of one another. Policy researchers and program evaluators responded to this possibility by reducing the amount of report space devoted to methods and by adding executive summaries in front of their reports.

They also, being social scientists, began to study their problem systematically. Policy researchers created a completely new topic for research: *research utilization.* Some researchers did case studies of evaluations to determine how these studies influenced policies. Others asked policy makers to read samples of research and comment on their potential benefit. Still others examined the policy making process to see whether or how research was pulled into the deliberations along the way. Researchers examined the connections between research and policy at the federal, state, and local levels in a number of substantive areas to learn how relevant research and evaluation contributed to policy formulations. Interest in this issue was nearly as widespread as interest in applied research and evaluation itself, and it ultimately led to the development of still more new research journals, this time focusing on the diffusion, dissemination, and use of research. Two relatively thorough reviews of this work are Cousins and Leithwood (1986) and Love (1985). Among the more influential of these many studies were Mitchell's (1981) study of state legislative decision making, Caplan, Morrison, and Stambaugh's (1975) study of federal executive office decision making, Weiss's study of executive decision making (1977), and Knorr-Cetina's (1981) and Kennedy's (1983; 1984) studies of local decision making.

Competing Models of Research Use

These studies, when taken together, significantly altered our understanding of the relationship between research and policy. The first, and perhaps still most important, message emanating from this body of work was the difference between *instrumental* and *conceptual* uses of research. The advocates for social science were envisioning an instrumental role for research. They assumed that the kind of decisions policy makers made were analogous to the kind of decisions researchers were trying to make when they tested alternative treatments. For instance, in a medical experiment, a researcher might compare dosages of 5 mg, 10 mg, and 20 mg of a drug to see which dosage is most beneficial. If 5 mg turns out to be the best dosage, then that becomes standard medical practice. The experiment is an instrument for determining which alternative will be most effective and which, therefore, should be used. But policy decisions rarely involve selecting among clearly defined alternatives, all of which are aimed at solving a clearly defined problem. Instead, policy makers often must struggle to determine what the problem actually is, must negotiate among multiple and conflicting goals, and must devise compromise actions that adjust existing policies at the margins rather than making radical changes.

As researchers studied the phenomenon of research utilization they discovered that research rarely provided direct, instrumental guidance in the way that, say, findings from a medical study might, for two important reasons. First, research rarely yielded definitive findings, telling policy makers that method A was clearly superior to method B in solving a specific problem. But second, and perhaps more important, was that policy decisions rarely involved such clear choices. Given the kinds of decisions that policy makers made there was no instrumental role to be played. Consequently, most of the rhetoric about enhancing the policy-making process by infusing it with systematic research was based on an erroneous conception of the kinds of decisions that policy makers routinely made.

As researchers began to debunk their own naive *instrumental* model of how social science should influence the policy-making process, they also created an alternative, *conceptual* model of research use. This new conceptual model was much more grounded in the realities of the policy world. Research on research use not only revealed the complex and often subtle ways in which policies were formulated; it also revealed the complex and subtle ways in which research findings found their way from the pages of arcane reports into public consciousness. For instance, Cohen and Garet (1975) pointed out that even though social science could not possibly make a strong, instrumental contribution to policy, it could nonetheless contribute to the *climate of opinion* in such a way that future discussions, actions, and decisions would be altered to reflect a different way of conceptualizing the problem. Similarly, Weiss (1977; 1980) stressed the enlightenment function of research, noting that policy makers did gain new insights from research and that these insights enabled them to reformulate their problems and to make a wide range of small adjustments in their decision making rather than making big visible decisions differently. Weiss summarized the subtle interaction between research and policy making in a 1980 article titled "Knowledge Creep and Decision Accretion." Policies develop incrementally, she argued, through a continuous process of tinkering, rather than through a rational process of selecting from among radically different alternatives. At the same time, knowledge from research accumulates, seeps into conversations, and eventually influences the thoughts and actions of policy makers. She also pointed out that just as decisions tend to be made incrementally, knowledge tends to accumulate gradually, and the two do adjust to one another over time so that knowledge contributes in a more subtle way to the thinking and actions of policy makers.

Another important finding from research on research utilization was that policies must necessarily be built from a variety of other kinds of knowledge: personal experiences, financial audit information, public attitudes, and, especially, social values. All of these contribute to the policy making process, and all of them have a legitimate role in that process. The nature of public decision making is such that we should never expect social science to provide definitive knowledge. Lindblom and Cohen (1979) emphasized that social science must necessarily be one of many inputs into a policy-making process and that there is no particular reason to believe that it is inherently better or more persuasive than any of the others. They also pointed out that it is entirely possible to solve problems without such understanding, and, conversely, it is entirely possible that such understanding will not help with the solution. This point was more recently brought home by Cooper (1996), a social scientist who served on a school board. He pointed out that much of policy making consists of competitions among interest groups to define the issues. The terms used by competing factions are designed to be emotion-laden. In the abortion issue, for instance, neither side is *against* anything: One side is prolife, the other is prochoice. The terms each side uses to define the issue are designed to appeal to wide audiences. The definitions that eventually are adopted frequently imply the policy positions that need to be taken.

The third important finding from this research was that in order for social science knowledge to be used it had to be incorporated into the composite of ideas and knowledge that comprise each decision makers' knowledge and the knowledge of the community as a whole. That is, knowledge from research must be blended with experiential knowledge, personal values, common beliefs, and so forth. As it is blended, the knowledge is interpreted in light of these other sources of knowledge (Kennedy, 1983) and eventually becomes part of a coherent body of working knowledge, which provides the basis for actions at given moments. Working knowledge is a continually evolving body of ideas that shapes decisions and is shaped by them as well The process of integrating research evidence into working knowledge is also a continual process, for each participant in the community continues to revise his or her ideas in conversations with others as well as when confronting new research evidence and, of course, having new experiences. Knorr-Cetina (1981) suggested that we think of research as analogous to legal precedents or rules. Both research and legal rules have an aura of authority and invariability about them, but in fact each requires *situated interpretation*. Knorr-Cetina suggested that a certain opportunistic logic governs practical actions, such as policy decisions, and in these practical contexts the value of any given idea depends on the context. All ideas must be interpreted and reinterpreted in light of the specific situations. Even goals are continually modified and altered to respond to changing contingencies.

Contemporary Thinking about Research and Policy

Our current understanding of the relationship between research and policy making, then, derives in part from a reconceptualization of the policy-making process itself and in part from a reconceptualization of the nature of social science knowledge and how it fits with other kinds of knowledge. Rather than envisioning policy making as a process of evaluating alternative courses of action and then selecting the most effective alternative, policy making is now viewed as a much more complicated and messy process, one that involved continual negotiation, redefinition, and tinkering rather than one that involves selecting from among clearly defined alternatives the one that best matches a clearly defined goal. Rather than envisioning social science as providing definitive or authoritative conclusions, we now see that it can only be understood when it is reconciled with all the other sources of ideas and knowledge that people use to interpret their surroundings. Donmoyer (1995) called policy making a process of practical deliberation and suggested that research provides a heuristic function—a stimulus for conversation.

But this view of the policy-making process outlines a much more ambiguous role for research, one that offers terrific potential for failure. Kennedy (1983) noted that misunderstandings and distortions of research were frequent, as various audiences tried to reconcile discrepancies between research findings, on one hand, and their goals, their values, or their experiences, on the other. Weiss (1995) has also noted that this model of research use is somewhat chancy, as findings can easily be lost of misused. Moreover, because the field of education research itself is large and diverse, it sends multiple and inconsistent messages to policy makers, thus further threatening the potential for social science to make a coherent contribution to social problem solving and further increasing the opportunities for distortions.

If using systematic research to inform policy was the dominant idea of the 1960s, then the question of whether and how systematic research can actually influence policy dominated the 1970s. Questions about the appropriate relationship between research and policy continue to be discussed, as both researchers and policy makers strive to improve the mutual complementarity of these two enterprises. But it is safe to say that by the early 1980s most researchers and policy makers felt they had come to understand better both the real and the ideal relationships between these two enterprises. In the 1980s a new question came to the forefront, and that had to do with the relationship between research and educational *practice*.

THE INFLUENCE OF RESEARCH ON TEACHING PRACTICE

Educational research consists of much more than the body of program evaluations and policy analyses designed to serve the policy-making community. In addition to all of that work is a body of research aimed at helping us understand the nature of education more broadly and the nature of teaching and learning more particularly and ultimately aimed at improving the quality of teaching and learning in schools. There are many parallels between research on teaching and its relationship to teaching practice, on one hand, and policy research and its relationship to policy, on the other. One parallel is that both fields of scholarship became prominent in the 1960s. Berliner (1984) placed the origin of research on teaching at the publication of Gage's (1963) *Handbook of Research on Teaching*. Another parallel between the two is that early advocates for research on teaching expected it to make a strong contribution to teaching practice and to make an instrumental contribution as well, whereas more recent observers have become more skeptical about the likelihood of such an outcome from research (Kennedy, 1997). Questions about how research on teaching should find its way into the classroom parallel questions about how evaluation research and policy analysis should find their way into new policies.

One important difference between these two issues, however, is that most evaluation research can be transmitted directly from the researcher to the policy maker, whereas most research on teaching requires some intermediaries to carry the message. The sheer size of the education industry in the United States prohibits almost any imaginable method of direct communication between researchers and teachers. This fact means that policy makers are implicated in the relationship between research and classroom practice, for they can, and often do, either become intermediaries themselves or try to support other intermediaries. Policy makers may try to tighten the connection between research and practice by (1) developing regulations or.incentives for practice that reflect research findings, (2) sponsoring the dissemination of research findings, or (3) sponsoring professional development.

Regulating Practice

If the 1960s and 1970s can be characterized by undue optimism about the potential of research to inform policy, the 1980s can be characterized by undue optimism about the potential of research to inform classroom teaching practices. A particular genre of research, called *process-product* research, was widely used and was expected to make substantial contributions to practice. The label "process-product research" came about because researchers were interested in discerning the relationship between classroom *processes*, on one side, and student achievement (the *product*), on the other. Most of this work was correlational: Researchers observed and tallied up numerous specific teaching practices and then correlated their use with gains in student achievement gains. The logic was relatively straightforward: We should learn the difference between the practices of teachers whose students gain a lot during the school year and the practice of teachers whose students do not make such gains. We should then describe the practices of the relatively more effective teachers and try to teach these to the relatively less effective teachers. Process-product research often required complex observation schemes to define the specifics of teaching practices and complex statistical procedures to correlate those practices with students' gains in achievement.

Advocates for this line of work were as optimistic about its potential as early advocates for policy research were for its potential. Gage (1985), for instance, effused about the volume of knowledge we were acquiring and about its significance for teaching practice. Like advocates of policy research,

Gage did not expect social science to *replace* the practitioner's decision making, but instead to *inform* it. He referred to this body of research as providing a *scientific basis for the art of teaching*.

Findings from this research were extensive and were, indeed, informative. For comprehensive syntheses of this work, see Walberg (1986) and Brophy and Good (1986). Some of the ideas from this research, such as *time on task* and *student engagement*, gained substantial momentum as they became the focus of more and more research. Researchers learned, for instance, that teachers differed dramatically in the amount of time they allocated to each school subject. For instance, one fifth-grade teacher might spend 68 minutes a day on reading, whereas another spends 137 minutes—double the time of the first teacher! Similarly, one second-grade teacher might spend 16 minutes a day on mathematics, whereas another spends 51 minutes (Berliner, 1984). Even apart from the time allocated to different subjects, some teachers managed to cover a lot more material during the course of a semester than other teachers did.

Whereas the time allocated to each school subject may seem like an obvious contributor to student outcomes, other variables identified by process-product researchers were less obvious. *Wait time* is an example of a less-obvious practice. The phrase *wait time* refers to the amount of time teachers wait, once they have posed a question, for some student to volunteer an answer. Teachers with short wait times tended to interject an answer of their own before students had a chance to formulate their answers. Researchers have found that longer wait times increase student achievement, presumably because the additional time gave students a chance to think about the question, and perhaps formulate an answer to it, before someone else answered it for them.

Optimism about the potential value of such findings spread from researchers to policy makers and they became grist for the policy mill. Ironically, although policy makers took interpretive liberties when drawing on research in their own decision making, they did not mind creating policies that imposed research findings on teachers. Several states devised teacher assessment instruments that evaluated teachers according to their use of the effective teaching practices identified by researchers. The idea that such practices should be imposed on teachers, without regard for local teaching context or for teachers' professional judgement, was challenged by many researchers. Critics identified several problems.

One set of criticisms was based on the merits of the research itself. For even as this body of research began to accumulate and to create some relatively consistent findings, its validity came to be hotly debated. One problem was that the work was frequently based on lower-elementary grade levels, on volunteer teachers, and on students from low socioeconomic classes, so that it was not clear that these findings should be generalized to teachers working in different grade levels, in different settings, and with different types of students. Another problem was that these studies used standardized achievement tests almost exclusively as their outcome measure, and many critics felt these outcomes were far too narrow to represent the full range of outcomes we want from our schools (Cruickshank, 1990).

Another set of concerns had to do with the meaning of discrete teaching behaviors when they were described outside of their original context. Teaching does not consist of discrete behaviors, this argument goes, but rather of meaningful *patterns of behaviors*. Policies that focus on discrete behaviors, without regard to their meaning and conceptual basis, reduce teaching to an unworkable list of rules devoid of rationale (Anderson & Burns, 1990; Doyle, 1990; Fenstermacher, 1982). It is not clear that the behaviors themselves will produce the desired outcomes if they are not employed in the same meaningful patterns as the original teachers employed them.

Yet another set of criticisms focused on the nature of the teaching practice and teacher decision making. Researchers noted that teaching is inherently a reflexive practice. It requires moment-to-moment judgments that respond to the particulars of the situation. It cannot be governed by rules (Fenstermacher, 1982; Myers, 1987; Richardson-Koehler, 1987). In many respects, these critics were making an argument similar to that made by Knorr-Cetina (1981) and Kennedy (1983) about the role of research in policy: For research to be used, it must be interpreted, and in order to be interpreted, it must be blended with other sources of knowledge—beliefs, values, and experiences— and it must be situationally interpreted. Instead of trying to enforce a list of seemingly unrelated and inexplicable behaviors on teachers, therefore, we might be more likely to improve teaching practice if we could help teachers understand the *rationale* for these practices, so that they could interpret the findings in light of their own situations and draw on them as they saw fit.

That research on teaching would find such direct, instrumental translation into policy may seem ironic: We have seen that policy makers' own use of research is largely strategic and conceptual, rather than systematic and instrumental; yet despite their own experiences with decision making, they seemed to be as naïve about how others—in this case, teachers—could or should use research as researchers had been naïve about how policy makers could and should use research. Eventually, though, many policy makers turned to other avenues to try to infuse research into teaching practices. One idea that has been popular for several decades is dissemination.

Sponsoring Dissemination Systems

Rather than trying to force teachers to comply with research findings, many policy makers have taken an interest in dissemination programs—networks, newsletters, or other devices that increase the likelihood that teachers will at least be informed about relevant research findings. One important staple in the education landscape today is the large storage and distribution systems known as the Educational Resources Information Clearinghouse (ERIC), a system sponsored by the federal government. The ERIC system abstracts some 30,000 new pieces of literature each year (Mitchell, 1985) and makes these abstracts available on CD-ROM and over the Internet. Another staple in education is the network of educational research centers and regional educational laboratories, also sponsored by the federal government. Centers conduct research on topics deemed to be of national significance, whereas labs conduct research that meets local needs and disseminate research findings throughout their respective regions. In addition to these apparently enduring institutions, a variety of other federal systems have come and gone: technical assistance centers, national diffusion networks, and others. Many states sponsor intermediate school districts whose job is, in part, to provide information and workshops to administrators and teachers in local education agencies. Many professional associations sponsor professional networks, which help motivate practitioners and keep them informed about new developments in their fields. School districts, too, frequently sponsor in-service workshops for teachers to keep them abreast of the latest developments. The Internet has also made research more accessible to teachers and several sites have been established to provide ideas and techniques to teachers.

There are therefore many potential routes for research knowledge to take on its way from dusty journals to living classrooms. Research is made available through national, state, intermediate, and local education agencies, through professional associations, and through private vendors. Despite this tremendous volume of activity and the tremendous variety of routes research can take on its way to practice, most observers are not satisfied with the results. Critics of education believe that teachers are not performing as well as they should be, given what we know about teaching and learning, but at the same time, teachers believe that research has not been particularly useful to them.

One thing that seems increasingly clear is that making research knowledge *available* does not necessarily make it *acceptable*. When the National Education Association (NEA) surveyed teachers several years ago and asked them to rate the relative value of several sources of knowledge, teachers rated local in-service programs dead last (Smylie, 1989) and ranked other kinds of formal education programs near the bottom as well. Sources of knowledge that were ranked at the top included their own experience and interactions with colleagues. Similarly, when Carl Kaestle (1993) interviewed educational leaders and legislators to learn their views of research, he summarized his findings in the title of his article: "The Awful Reputation of Educational Research." One reason for the problem, Kaestle noted, is that everyone has been to fourth grade. This simple fact is true of teachers as well as local education administrators, parents, businesspeople and policy makers. Each of us has his or her own store of experiences in school, and because of the potency of that firsthand experience, each of us believes we know what is needed to fix the system. Cooper (1996) quoted local school board members as saying, essentially, "I don't know anything about research, but I know what is good for children." Even when we are aware that others disagree with us, we still believe that our solutions are self-evidently correct. When we read research findings, we often view them as either so obvious as to be trivial or as obviously wrong.

Although part of the problem is that we all believe we already have a strong knowledge base of our own, an added complication is that research findings are frequently communicated without enough detail for audiences to thoroughly understand their meaning—to make the kind of situational interpretations that are needed to render the research useful. Just as policy makers need to blend research findings with the rest of their continually evolving working knowledge, and need to make situated interpretations of research findings, so do local education administrators and teachers. Dissemination programs that strip research of its conceptual underpinnings and convey to teachers simple bottom-line admonitions do not give teachers a chance to interpret the findings. Without enough detail to thoroughly understand the research, teachers have only two options: accept the findings or reject them. If these are the only possible responses, rejection is the more likely one to occur.

A third part of the problem is that a great deal of intellectual effort is required to merge research findings with firsthand experiences, especially when such a merger requires one to change one's thinking or one's habits. In fact, Kennedy (1989) has argued that people rarely change their behavior simply because research suggests that they should, but instead because they interpret *their own situations* as requiring behavior changes. Even people who quit smoking rarely claim that this difficult and important change in behavior was stimulated by research. Instead, they are likely to say it was stimulated by their own experiences—they became aware of shortness of breath or nagging coughs, for instance. Yet they would not have noticed these experiences, nor interpreted them as danger signals, had it not been for the research. How long it takes each individual to reinterpret his experiences and behaviors in light of new research findings depends on many factors, including the strength of one's commitment to the old habits, the extensiveness of one's familiarity with the research findings, and the extent to which one participates in a community whose climate of opinion is changing in response to new research findings.

A fourth important part of the dissemination problem in education is that there is little incentive to engage the hard work of translating research findings into personal experiences in order to improve one's practice. In this sense, education practice differs from practice in other professions. McGuire (1984) listed several features of the medical dissemination system that make it successful, and nearly every feature listed is missing in educational dissemination: (1) The general public has a strong interest in seeing that physicians use the latest knowledge. (2) The press gives a lot of coverage to medical breakthroughs. (3) Patients pressure physicians to use new knowledge that they have read about. (4) Physicians' reputation and income depend on their willingness to respond positively to these pressures. (5) Because medicine is highly specialized, professional communities are small and tightly linked and enable more functional communication networks. (6) Pharmaceutical companies also disseminate research findings: after spending millions on research, they engage extensive and expensive marketing programs.

These features are nearly all missing in the education infrastructure. The press gives little attention to education research; parents and students are more interested in teachers who satisfy their personal needs or respond to popular fads than in teachers who draw on research findings; teachers work in isolation and few other adults actually know whether they are using or not using research findings, and their salaries and prestige do not depend on such improvements; and textbook publishers, though they invest in marketing, are more likely to use opinion polls than research on learning to develop their products.

The incentive problem is a serious one in education and has been noted by several researchers (Cohen, 1988; Fullan, 1994; Kaestle, 1993; Kennedy, 1997; Price, 1996). Indeed, the high volume of new ideas that are continually foisted on teachers, whether from research, policy, or popular fads, may actually reduce teachers' interest in responding and motivate them instead to concentrate on their own narrow agenda and to resist all incoming signals. Throne (1994) described the effect of these numerous messages on teachers, saying that policies frequently impose a certainty that is missing in real teaching, and that the only way teachers can cope with "bureaucratic certainty" is to quietly shut their doors and teach. She also suggests that, if the door is to remain open, communications have to be two-way.

This is not to say, of course, that no local administrators or teachers are interested in improving their own practices, but rather that such improvements are both intellectually and emotionally difficult to make, that there are few official incentives to do so, and that rapidly changing and frequently fad-driven changes in admonitions can in fact create a disincentive to seriously reconsider one's practices. Practitioners differ, and some researchers have tried to learn more about why some practitioners are more receptive to research than others are. There is little evidence that taking courses in research better enables teachers or principals to read and draw on research findings (Green & Kvidahl, 1993–1994; Walker & Cousins, 1984), but there is evidence that career commitments and self-confidence matter. Walker and Cousins (1984) found that teachers and principals who were receptive to research tended to be more experienced and tended to have a stronger sense of their own self-efficacy. It is likely that confidence in their own ability made them more willing to entertain new ideas. Similarly, Saha, Biddle, and

Anderson (1995) determined that principals who perceived more value in research were those who intended to remain in this line of work. Interestingly, these relatively more-interested principals also were people who did not work extensive hours, which Saha and Biddle speculated might contribute to burnout and fatigue.

The bottom line is that the most a dissemination program can do is lead the horses to water; it cannot make them drink. Dissemination programs can make research available to teachers, but most are not designed to help teachers take the intellectually and emotionally difficult step of situationally interpreting—of personalizing—the findings. Nor are they designed to alter the incentives to use research. Weaknesses in dissemination programs and recognition of the substantial intellectual and emotional requirements involved in personalizing research findings have led many observers to propose that policy makers support long-term, sustained professional development programs. This idea is clearly the idea of the 1990s.

Sponsoring Professional Development

As investigators have examined teaching in more detail and have examined the nature of knowledge that contributes to teaching, a new set of ideas about the relationship between research and teaching is beginning to emerge. Under this view, research can only contribute to practice when teachers have ample time to think about and digest the implications of research, and this kind of deep understanding is most likely to occur in extended professional development programs. The aim for professional development in the 1990s has not been to encourage teachers to obediently implement lists of specific practices, without regard for how well these practices fit their situations, but instead to promote a new type of teacher, one who is able to *create* a practice that was grounded in research. Fenstermacher (1986) has proposed a model of practical decisions that illustrates how such a teacher's practice might look. In this model, teaching decisions are based on *practical arguments*. Like formal arguments in logic, practical arguments consist of both premises and conclusions. But practical arguments include a wider range of premises. They include value judgements about goals, empirical evidence about how to get there from here, and estimates about the salient features of particular situation. These premises, taken together, lead the teacher to take a particular practical action.

In fact, though, few teachers have a sufficiently detailed or deep understanding of research to enable them to develop practical arguments in this way, for a variety of reasons. Moreover, there are features of practice that may discourage such rational decision making. Just as researchers have developed a more sophisticated understanding of the nature of policy making, and of how research can contribute to policy making, so they have devised more sophisticated understandings of the nature of teaching. Most of these findings point to inherent tensions within teaching that prevent teachers from attending more to research or to policy imperatives. We have seen that policy making has its own inherent tensions, but teaching also has some inherent tensions, and these are worth outlining, for the nature of teaching has a great deal to do with whether or how research might be able to influence teaching.

One of the earliest in-depth studies of teaching is Lortie's (1975). Lortie noted that teaching has a number of inherent contradictions. First, our society holds multiple, conflicting, and controversial goals for education. We want children to learn to be able to think for themselves, yet we also want them to respect authority, for instance. Second, the organization of the work is unclear, and there are multiple lines of influence into the classroom. Teachers must respond to district, state, and federal policies, but also to the wishes of parents and the local community. These multiple sources will not likely agree on many points, so teachers must find ways to negotiate among these conflicting ideas. Third, because no adults witness their work, there is no external approval or disapproval for it. Finally, the work itself if highly ambiguous. It is very difficult to know whether or what students have learned, it is difficult to even say what counts as evidence of learning, and it is difficult to see a clear relationship between teaching and learning. The ambiguity of the situation, combined with the ambiguity of goals, motivates teachers to try to narrow their range of concerns and to stabilize their intellectual work as much as possible. Teachers perceive other adults as interfering with their work and complicating matters, so they strive for autonomy and independence from outside influences. But they also simplify the work by focusing on immediate results and narrow, achievable goals rather than longer-term, more ambiguous or ambitious goals.

Meyer (1983) has added to these observations by noting that education in the United States, because it is decentralized, is more susceptible to fads than education in most other countries. Because fads come and go quickly, evidence usually does not appear until well after the idea has lost favor (Kennedy, 1997; Slavin, 1989). Because solid evidence is rarely available when new ideas are being espoused, these new educational ideas are promoted by exaggerated claims or moral imperatives rather than by evidence of their merits. These arguments rarely can be sustained once the ideas are translated into real practices, and they nearly always counteracted at that time. Ironically, these fads further motivate teachers to privatize their practice and to protect themselves from the so-called help of outsiders.

Fullan (1994) has also contributed to our understanding of the nature of teaching and the potential for research to contribute to it. The two most critical problems noted by Fullan are as follows:

1. *Overload.* Teachers spend a higher fraction of their time actually performing (as opposed to planning, studying, rehearsing, etc.) than do pro-

fessionals in almost any other area. As a result, they have little time to think seriously about what they are trying to accomplish or to seriously evaluate their efforts. Fullan also suggested that the numerous prescriptions and fads that come to teachers through dissemination channels, in-service programs, and changing state and district policies may actually exacerbate this problem by further cluttering and fragmenting teachers' harried intellectual lives.

2. *Isolation.* Teachers work in isolation from one another and from other adults. As a result, "privatism" becomes a habit. Because they are physically separated from others and have no time to talk to others or to engage in systematic analysis of their own practice, they tend to turn inward and to create private sets of standards for their work. That is, they shield themselves from outside influences, including influences from well-intentioned re-searchers, disseminators, and policy makers.

Cohen (1988) has pointed out yet a further problem with teaching. The academically ambitious reforms that many policy makers are currently striv-ing for place even greater demands on teachers. Reformers today want more rigorous academic content, they want students to work on more complex types of problems, and they want a broader spectrum of students to partici-pate in this curriculum. These ambitious goals, if adopted by teachers, would add even more uncertainty and ambiguity to their work. Moreover, it would increase their dependency on students' motivation and students' coopera-tion. To the extent that teachers try to accomplish these more ambitious educational goals, they become even more vulnerable than they already are. If teachers stick to their traditional, more limited educational goals, they can be assured of at least a modicum of success.

These observations are pertinent to any reform, dissemination, or profes-sional development plans. For if all these things are true—if (1) the work of teaching is inherently complicated and difficult to understand; (2) it is dif-ficult to know when students have learned or what caused them to learn; (3) teachers are regularly bombarded by new innovations and moral impera-tives from parents, researchers, disseminators, and policy makers; (4) teachers have no time to think through and interpret all their experiences, much less to reason about the relative merits of all these new proposals, in light of their experiences; *and* (5) teachers must develop and sustain their practice in virtual isolation—then it should not be surprising that their practices tend to become rigid, that they reject outside ideas, that their thinking is not very systematic, or that their practices are not very responsive to new research findings.

It should not be surprising, in fact, to learn that teachers use a *craft orien-tation*, rather than a research orientation, to formulate their practice (Huber-man, 1983). Huberman characterized a craft orientation as one in which the practitioner focuses on short-term outcomes, prefers intuitive judgements to empirically justified practices, and tends to believe there is no real underlying order to the process of teaching and learning. Even more disturbing are the findings from Schwille and others that teachers' decisions about what to teach are based on such factors as their personal enjoyment of the subject more than on a sense for its relative importance to student learning (Schwille et al., 1981).

For all of these reasons then, contemporary reformers tend to advocate a different approach to the improvement of teaching. Policies that aim to regulate practice, and those that send research bulletins to schools, tend to increase teachers' defensiveness and decrease their receptiveness to new ideas. The alternative approach currently being tried is to alter teachers' working conditions and to alter the professional climate of schools. One such change might be to modify the ratio of time spent directly with children relative to time spent in planning and evaluation. Such a change would be consistent with the scheduling of teachers' time in Asian countries, where Stigler and Stevenson (1991) found that greater time available for planning and evaluation of teaching practices stimulated a much more self-critical attitude among teachers and a greater willingness to consider alternative approaches to their practice.

Another such change would be to encourage more collegiality among teachers, so that teachers learn to draw on one another as resources and so that teachers might develop the kind of professional community that fosters continual professional development through its climate of opinion and its peer pressure. The idea behind such proposals is not merely to change the structure of teachers' work—altering the teachers' work schedule and increasing the amount of time spent in collegial interactions—but also to alter the professional climate of teaching so that teachers would be more able and perhaps, therefore, more willing to read research, to reflect on its meaning, and to consider its implications for their teaching practices.

But these are merely ideas. So far, no state or local agencies have found ways to create such structural changes, nor to create or fund the kind of long-term, intellectually coherent schoolwide professional development that might foster these changes in private attitudes or in broader climates of opinion. It is too early, therefore, to say whether such changes might foster the kind of relationship between research and teaching that many strive for.

THE INFLUENCE OF POLICY ON RESEARCH

The first two sections of this chapter have examined the ways in which research influences policy decisions and the ways in which research might be able to influence local practice, with the help of policy. One further relationship between research and policy needs to be considered. This third aspect of the relationship reverses the direction of influence and examines the ways in which policies can or should influence research. Policies may influence research in a number of ways: First, since educational research is sponsored by local, state, or federal education agencies, funding policies can substantially influence the volume of educational research that is conducted as well as influence its content and form. Sponsored educational research is a relatively small business compared to medical research or technological research, for instance, but it is large enough to necessitate that policy makers examine the appropriateness of their investments. Second, policies frequently stimulate new research by putting forward new ideas that in turn raise new questions. New policy initiatives ranging from preschools, to career ladders, to charter schools have motivated significant new bodies of research as researchers examine the implementation and consequences of these new initiatives. Finally, policy makers may influence research symbolically, for virtually all public pronouncements carry with them nuances and attitudes toward evidence, or toward researchers, that may ultimately and indirectly influence research activities. The latter two influences of policy on research are likely to be side effects, however, of policies whose primary intention lies elsewhere. The main avenue policy makers use to intentionally influence research is through funding; this section therefore concentrates on proposals for funding research.

Recall that policy research in education originated roughly in the 1960s and that research on teaching also originated around that time. It should not be surprising to learn that funding for educational research also originated around that time. The U.S. Congress legislated the national network of education research centers and regional educational laboratories in 1963 and formed National Institute for Education (NIE) in 1972. Between these two dates, federal funding for educational research rose some 2000% (Bloom, 1966). But this euphoric period of optimism did not last long. The NIE was mired in political battles over its usefulness almost as soon as it came into existence and has steadily lost appropriations almost ever since.

One early debate over research funding had to do with the fraction of funding that should go to basic research versus applied research, an argument that eventually received serious scholarly attention (Atkinson & Jackson, 1992; Cronbach & Suppes, 1969; Shulman, 1970). Policy makers clearly wanted research that would have direct and immediate payoff in classrooms, whereas researchers tended to think that fundamental understanding would have a greater long-term benefit. One reason for the disagreement, however, was that at that time, most research on learning was conducted in laboratory settings, where researchers could carefully control the effects of all potential influences. Since then, researchers have moved out of the laboratory and into the classroom, where they routinely collaborate with practicing teachers, so the difference between basic and applied research has virtually disappeared.

Two things have happened. First, researchers have discovered that they cannot develop coherent and plausible theories without testing them in practical settings (Brown, 1992) Second, researchers have discovered that practitioners need theory to understand research findings and to generate situated interpretations. As a result, theories turn out necessarily to be intensely practical. Research findings that can be reduced to bumper sticker slogans have little impact on practice for they do not convey the details and conceptual underpinnings that enable teachers to generate situational interpretations of the findings. Since the 1960s, research has become much more applied, and its applications have become much more theoretical. The distinction, then, between theoretical research and applied research has virtually disappeared.

There continues to be, however, a variety of arguments about the types of research that are most likely to be useful to teachers, and these arguments are important to any policy makers who hope to sponsor research that might contribute to practice. One of the earliest of these arguments was offered by Bolster (1983), who suggested that traditional empirical research yielded a form of knowledge that was incompatible with the kind of knowledge teachers held. Bolster argued that researchers aim for universal generalizations—nomothetic knowledge—whereas teachers are interested in ideographic knowledge—knowledge of the particulars of their situation. Research knowledge is also verified differently, as researchers rely on rigorous formal procedures whereas teachers rely on the trial and error of experience. Finally, knowledge from research is codified into static propositions such as "if X, then Y," whereas teacher knowledge has a holistic, narrative form that recognizes multiple and reciprocal causes and influences.

Bolster suggested that these differences in forms of knowledge might account for teachers' lack of interest in research. He thought that if researchers were to engage in ethnographic, or anthropological research, which yields the kind of holistic, multifaceted, and situational understanding that teachers bring to their own practice, perhaps teachers would find research to be more compelling. The idea was for research knowledge to simulate the knowledge teachers tended to hold, so that teachers would be more able to understand it and connect it to their practice.

Bolster's argument has been revised, refined, and recycled a number of times in the past several years, and it anticipated a great deal of research into the nature of teachers' knowledge. Much of this literature takes on a laudatory tone as researchers marvel at the number of decisions teachers make in a given hour (30-45—Clark & Peterson, 1986), or the number of questions they ask students within an hour (up to 150—Gall, 1970). Tacit, if not explicit, in much of this literature is the notion that teaching must necessarily depend far more on *craft* knowledge, which develops from personal experience, than it possibly can on research produced by faraway experts.

The idea that research should emulate the natural thinking of teachers has been challenged, however, on two important grounds. First, even though the knowledge drawn on *in situ* is dynamic and holistic, we should still expect teachers to be able to justify their actions with reference to generally agreed on principles of pedagogy, just as physicians or other professional practitioners do. These generally accepted principles will likely take on the static "if X, then Y" form of propositions. The two kinds of knowledge, then, need not be incompatible, but should in fact complement one another. Second, findings from ethnographic studies are necessarily limited to descriptions and interpretations of existing conditions—the status quo—and therefore may not be able to guide teachers toward better practices or toward solutions to the widely recognized problems in the current situation (Cazden, 1983). Tom and Valli (1990) have suggested a possible rapproachment on this argument, proposing that perhaps such studies can help if they provide "generative potential"—the potential to stimulate teachers to generate new practices of their own.

Another proposal for improving the potential utility of research has been that researchers should engage in more collaborative research efforts with teachers or other local educators. The U.S. Office of Educational Research and Improvement (OERI) has been attracted to this idea and has, at varying times, required its funded researchers to show evidence of collaboration with practicing teachers. One prominent promoter of this idea is Michael Huberman (1989), who has studied the effects of research when researchers engage in what he calls *sustained interactivity* with their clients. In sustained interactivity, researchers interact with teachers prior to conducting the study, to be sure that they understand the teachers' problems and point of view; they interact during data collection, to be sure that the data they are collecting are relevant and valid; they interact during data analysis; and, of course, they interact when reporting their findings. When researchers and teachers interact continuously, Huberman has argued, teachers are far more likely to use the findings once the study is completed. Huberman argued that one reason this sustained interactivity makes a difference is that it increases the likelihood that teachers will have a deep understanding of the meaning of the research by the time the study is finished.

Huberman's idea is an attractive one, and it has been suggested by other researchers as well (see, e.g., Bennett & Desforges, 1985; Donmoyer, 1989). But several criticisms can be made of this proposal. First, good research is frequently critical of the status quo, and it is hard to imagine that a researcher working closely with teachers would feel free to report findings that were heavily negative, or even that disagreed sharply with the teachers' perspective, unless these findings were on relatively innocuous topics. Second, collaborative research is not a large-scale solution to the problem of knowledge use, because its direct benefits accrue only for those teachers who actually participate in the study. The size of the education community in the United States prohibits genuine participation in education research by all practitioners. The third criticism of this line of reasoning is that, to the extent that teachers each hold a unique body of knowledge built from their own private experiences, it is not clear that the participation of one group of teachers will necessarily assure that the findings will be meaningful to other groups of teachers. So although many researchers are discovering the benefits of collaborating with teachers, many go to great lengths to find compatible teachers with whom to work. Enforcing such collaboration as a condition of funding may not yield the intended benefit.

Another proposal for research funding policies is to focus research on important *topics*, rather than worrying about the forms or processes of the research. This line of reasoning suggests that policy makers should not think about the *form* of the research (ethnographic versus correlational studies, for instance) nor should they think about the *process* of the research (research done in collaboration with teachers versus not); instead they should think about the *topics* that researchers address. Shulman has made this argument more than once (Shulman, 1970, 1986) and on both occasions argued that we need more research on the teaching and learning of specific school subjects. When Shulman first made this argument, in 1970, he was concerned about the volume of research on learning that was being conducted in laboratories, most of which studied learning by asking adults to memorize lists of random syllables. He suggested that researchers move out of the laboratory and into the classroom, and focus on learning of real children learning real school subjects. When he made the argument the second time, researchers had moved almost entirely into real classrooms to conduct their research, but much of their attention was focused on issues of classroom management and discipline rather than on the character and intellectual integrity of the content being taught. If policy makers believe that teaching and learning particular subjects is important, and that researchers are not giving sufficient attention to the teaching and learning of specific subjects, they should organize their funding to support research in those areas.

Policy makers who aim to sponsor research face difficult decisions when it comes to establishing funding priorities that will be most likely to benefit practitioners, for researchers themselves are of mixed minds about how to proceed. Moreover, these different ideas are not necessarily complementary. It would not necessarily make sense to sponsor research that was (1) ethnographic, so that it matched the holistic character of teachers' thinking, (2) done in collaboration with teachers, and (3) focused on the subject matter being taught and learned. Using highly interpretive ethnographic methods in studies involving collaboration with teachers, for instance, might invite research that is essentially self-congratulatory for teachers. Requiring that research be done on a predefined topic and also collaboratively may also backfire, for funding agencies may not be able to find strong combinations of teachers and researchers who share an interest in the funding agency's favored topics.

Though there are still many unknowns regarding the optimal forms or topics to encourage through funded research, some things do seem clear. One important conclusion is that funding agencies need to think of research as yielding *knowledge about* teaching rather than *techniques for* teaching. Research on the nature of teaching and teacher thinking, the nature of teacher learning, and the relationship between research and practice all agree that teachers gain more from understanding general ideas that they can situationally interpret than they gain from lists of techniques that lack conceptual underpinnings. One reason for this, I suspect, is that no technique exists that can be used repeatedly over the day or over many days. Both teachers and students need variety. If teachers understand the principles underlying research findings, they can build a variety of teaching episodes that are consistent with those principles but that also adapt to their particular daily situations and needs.

Another important conclusion is that funding agencies need to think of this knowledge as something that will *necessarily* be situationally interpreted rather than blindly implemented and that the hoped-for improvements in student learning are more likely to come about if teachers can create their own research-based practices than if teachers are simply given admonitions that they must accept or reject without question. This means that the most likely methods for influencing practice will not be written communications or brief workshops, but instead will probably be longer-term and conceptually oriented programs.

SUMMARY AND CONCLUSION

If we view research in the context of the entire history of education, we can see that it is a relatively new innovation. Much of the United States' educational history, especially at the beginning of this century, has been taken up with expansion—expanding the number of grade levels that comprise the compulsory years, expanding the number of students who attend schools, expanding the curricular offerings available within the comprehensive secondary school, and expanding the number and variety of offerings available to students once they have completed their high school education. Associated with this great expansion was a continuing concern with finding enough teachers to meet new and expanding demands (Lucas, 1997). Throughout most of this period, our most salient educational problem consisted of finding enough warm bodies to fill the classrooms, so we did not worry much about finding ways to improve the quality of their teaching.

Consequently, teachers have historically received few incentives to improve their practices and even fewer guidelines as to how they might improve their practices. Left to their own devices, teachers have devised their practices largely by emulating the practices of the people who taught them a generation earlier (Cuban, 1984; Lortie, 1975). Not surprisingly, teaching came to be thought of as a conservative profession, one on which traditional content and pedagogy were sustained over time and in which innovations were shunned.

It was not until the 1960s, as our school population finally stabilized, that we began to think seriously about the quality of teaching and learning in our classrooms. This was also the period when most of our research endeavors began in earnest. It has really been only in the past 30 years or so that research has been considered as a potentially important contributor to education—to teaching or to educational policy making. Viewed in this way, perhaps it is too soon to determine whether research has had a suitable impact, either on policy making or on teaching practices. Viewed from the vantage point of history, we can see that the idea that research could or should contribute to educational practices and policies is a relatively new idea.

The literature referred to in this chapter has yielded three important findings regarding the relationship between research and educational policy and practice. First, it has shown that the naïve model of research use, called the instrumental model, does not fit. Instead, both teachers and policy makers use research conceptually. They weigh its findings in light of their own personal values, their own particular situations, their own experiences, and the values and beliefs of those with whom they are in daily contact. Second, research use entails situational interpretation and adaptation. People cannot take research findings as they arrive, but instead must translate the findings into their own contexts, bending and adjusting the ideas to make them fit. Finally, and closely related to the first two points, is the finding that *knowledge* from research has a greater impact than *prescriptions*. This third point makes sense if we recognize that research will be used conceptually rather than instrumentally, and if we recognize that people must translate and adapt research findings to their particular situations. It is hard to make such adjustments with prescriptions, but knowledge provides us with greater flexibility.

One could argue that, given the relatively recent entry of research into the education landscape, it has had a remarkable impact. Many of the ideas that motivate contemporary policies, and many of the ideas that motivate contemporary teaching, have come from research. Moreover, much of the perceived lack of research use really derives from faulty expectations for what research use *should* look like. In the area of policy, optimistic government planners and researchers hoped to forge a new, empirical and rational kind of policy making. When they did not see policy makers making rational choices among alternative policies, they thought that research had had no impact. In fact, research had had a great deal of influence on the thinking of individual policy makers and on the climate of opinion. These influences, in turn, affected the continual negotiations and tinkering that policy makers engaged in. The problem was not in the value of research, but rather in the naïve expectations for how research should contribute.

Similarly, when policy makers tried to use research to regulate teaching behaviors, they were disappointed when they discovered that teachers did not obediently implement whatever procedures were required of them. But this disappointment, too, derived from a naïve notion of what research use should look like in the classroom. For just as policy makers need to negotiate with others in their environments and need to adjust research findings to accommodate their values, experiences, and the beliefs and values of their colleagues, so too do teachers need to adapt research findings to their particular circumstances. Both groups must engage in situational interpretations of research findings. If we put aside our naïve expectations for research use among teachers, we can see that even though teachers have been unable or unwilling to implement techniques prescribed by others, they have nevertheless altered their practices in numerous subtle ways to reflect new ideas they have encountered, and many of these ideas originated in research.

These new insights into the potential for research to influence practice also have implications for how policy makers might influence research through their funding practices. We now see, for instance, that there is virtually no distinction anymore between applied research and theoretical research, and we see that the applications that follow from research can only occur when the findings are accompanied by a principled rationale. Thus research-sponsoring agencies may want to focus their efforts on identifying important topics rather than on identifying the best methods or structural relationships for research.

Associated with these three important findings regarding research use are findings about the nature of educational decision making. Whether the educator in question is a policy maker, a teacher, or an administrator, he or she is engaged in a practical enterprise that must be continuously adjusted to accommodate changing environmental pressures. Educational decisions are not choices among clear alternatives, but rather inventions designed to accommodate as many constraints and as many ideals as possible. No decision ever satisfies all the goals and constraints one faces, so there is a continual need to adjust. The fact that educators must regularly adjust their practices to accommodate continuing constraints, continuing unmet goals, and continually changing circumstances means that research knowledge must compete for attention with all of these other pressures. But such a situation does not necessarily mean that research is not valuable, nor that it has no place in educational thought. Rather it simply means that research faces tough competition for educators' attention.

References

Anderson, L. W., & Burns, R. B. (1990). The role of conceptual frameworks in understanding and using classroom research. *South Pacific Journal of Teacher Education*, 18(1), 5–18.
Atkinson, R. C., & Jackson, G. B. (1992). *Research and educational reform: Roles for the Office of Educational Research and Improvement*. Washington, DC: National Academy of Science.
Bennett, N., & Desforges, C. (1985). Ensuring practical outcomes from educational research. In M. Shipman (Ed.), *Educational research: Principles, policies and practices* (pp. 81–96). Philadelphia, PA: Falmer.

Berliner, D. C. (1984). The half-full glass: A review of research on teaching. In P. L. Hosford (Ed.), *Using what we know about teaching* (pp. 51–77). Alexandria VA: Association for Supervision and Curriculum Development.

Bloom, B. (1966). Twenty-Five years of educational research. *American Educational Research Journal*, 3(3), 211–221.

Bolster, A. S. J. (1983). Toward a more effective model of research on teaching. *Harvard Educational Review*, 53(3), 294–308.

Boruch, R. F. (1975). On common contentions about randomized field experiments. In R. F. Boruch & H. W. Reichen (Eds.), *Experimental testing of public policy*. Boulder, CO: Westview.

Brophy, J., & Good, T. L. (1986). Teacher behavior and student achievement. In M. C. Wittrock (Ed.), *Handbook of research on teaching*. (3rd ed., pp. 328–375). New York: Macmillan.

Brown, A. (1992). Design experiments: Theoretical and methodological challenges in creating complex interventions in classroom settings. *The Journal of the Learning Sciences*, 2(2), 141–178.

Campbell, D. T. (1969). Reforms as Experiments. *American Psychologist*, 24(4), 409–429.

Campbell, D. T. (1973). The social scientist as methodological servant of the experimenting society. *Policy Studies Journal*, 2, 72–75.

Caplan, N., Morrison, A., & Stambaugh, R. (1975). *The use of social science knowledge in policy decisions at the national level*. Ann Arbor, MI: University of Michigan.

Cazden, C. B. (1983). Can ethnographic research go beyond the status quo? *Anthropology and Education Quarterly*, 14, 33–41.

Clark, C. M., & Peterson, P. L. (1986). Teachers' thought processes. In M. C. Wittrock (Ed.), *Handbook of research on teaching* (3rd ed., pp. 255–296). New York: Macmillan.

Cohen, D. K. (1988). Plus ça change. In P. Jackson (Ed.), *Contribution to educational change: Perspectives on research in practice issues*. National Society for the Study of Education Series on Contemporary issues. (pp. 27–84). Berkeley, CA: McCutchan.

Cohen, D. K., & Garet, M. S. (1975). Reforming educational policy with applied research. *Harvard Educational Review*, 45, 17–43.

Cook, T. D., Levinson-Rose, J., et al. (1980). The misutilization of evaluation research: Some pitfalls of definition. *Knowledge: Creation, Diffusion, Utilization*, 1(4), 477–498.

Cooper, H. (1996). Speaking power to truth: Reflections of an educational researcher after 4 years of school board service. *Educational Researcher*, 25(1), 29–34.

Cousins, J. B. & Leithwood, K. A. (1986). Current empirical research on evaluation utilization. *Review of Educational Research*, 56(3), 331–364.

Cronbach, L. J., & Suppes, P. (Eds.). (1969). *Research for tomorrow's schools: Disciplined inquiry for education*. New York: National Academy of Education and Macmilan.

Cruickshank, D. R. (1990). *Research that informs teachers and teacher educators*. Bloomington, IN: Phi Delta Kappan.

Cuban, L. (1984). *How teachers taught: Constancy and change in American classrooms, 1890–1980*. White Plains, NY: Longmans.

Donmoyer, R. (1989). A research agenda: Theory, practice, and the double-edged problem of idiosyncrasy. *Journal of Curriculum and Supervision*, 4(3), 257–270.

Donmoyer, R. (1995). Empirical research as solution and problem: Two narratives of knowledge use. In T. Barone (Ed.), The uses of educational research. *International Journal of Educational Research*, 23, 151–168.

Doyle, W. (1990, April). *Teachers' curriculum knowledge*. Paper presented at the AERA, Boston.

Fenstermacher, G. D. (1982). On learning to teach effectively from research on teacher effectiveness. *Journal of Classroom Interaction*, 17(2), 7–12.

Fenstermacher, G. D. (1986). Philosophy of research on teaching: Three aspects. In M. C. Wittrock (Ed.), *Handbook of Research on Teaching* (3rd ed.. pp 37–49). New York: Macmillan.

Fullan, M. G. (1994). Teachers as critical consumers of research. In Tomlinson, T., & A. C. Tuijnman (Eds.), *Educational research and reform: An international perspective*. Washington, DC: OERI/OECD.

Gage, N. L. (Ed.). (1963). *Handbook of research on teaching*. New York: Macmillan.

Gage, N. L. (1985). *The scientific basis of the art of teaching*. New York: Teachers College Press.

Gall, M. D. (1970). The use of questioning in teaching. *Review of Educational Research*, 40, 707–721.

Green, K. E., & Kvidahl, R. E. (1993–1994, Fall/Winter). Teachers' opinions and practices regarding research: Effects of a research methods course. *Teacher Education and Practice*, 29–35.

Huberman, M. (1983). Recipes for busy kitchens. *Knowledge: Creation, Diffusion, Utilization*, 4(4), 478–510.

Huberman, M. (1989). Predicting conceptual effects in research utilization: Looking with both eyes. *Knowledge in Society: The International Journal of Knowledge Transfer*, 2(3), 6–24.

Kaestle, C. F. (1993). The awful reputation of educational research. *Educational Researcher*, 22(1), 23–31.

Kennedy, M. M. (1983). Working Knowledge. *Knowledge: Creation, Diffusion, Utilization*, 5, 193–211.

Kennedy, M. M. (1984). How evidence alters understanding and decisions. *Educational Evaluation and Policy Analysis*, 6(3), 207–226.

Kennedy, M. M. (1989). Studying smoking behavior to learn about dissemination. *Knowledge: Creation, Diffusion, Utilization*, 11, 107–115.

Kennedy, M. M. (1997). The connection between research and practice. *Educational Researcher*, 26(7), 4–12.

Knorr-Cetina, K. D. (1981). Time and context in practical action. *Knowledge: Creation, Diffusion, Utilization*, 3(2), 143–165.

Lerner, D., and Lasswell, H. D. (Eds.). (1951). *The policy sciences*. Stanford, CA: Stanford University Press.

Lindblom, C. E., & Cohen, D. K. (1979). *Usable knowledge*. New Haven, CT: Yale University Press.

Lortie, D. C. (1975). *Schoolteacher: A sociological study*. Chicago: University of Chicago Press.

Love, J. M. (1985). Knowledge transfer and utilization in education. In E. W. Gordon (Ed.), *Review of research in education* (pp. 337–386). Washington, D.C.: American Educational Research Association.

Lucas, C. J. (1997). *Teacher education in America: Reform agendas for the twenty-first century*. New York: St. Martin's Press.

McGuire, C. H. (1984). Diffusion and application of new knowledge in medicine. In P. Hosford (Ed.), *Using what we know about teaching* (pp. 13–17). Alexandria, VA: Association for Supervision and Curriculum Development.

McLaughlin, M. W. (1975). *Evaluation and reform: The elementary and secondary education act of 1965/Title I*. Cambridge, MA: Ballinger.

Meyer, J. W. (1983). Innovation and knowledge use in American Public Education. In J. W. Meyer, W. R. Scott, B. Rowan, & T. E. Deal (Eds.), *Organizational environments: Ritual and rationality*. Beverly Hills, CA: Sage.

Mitchell, D. E. (1981). *Shaping legislative decisions: Education policy and the social sciences*. Lexington, MA: D. C. Heath.

Mitchell, D. E. (1985). Research impact on educational policy and practice in the USA. In J. Nisbet, J. Megarry, & S. Nisbet (Eds.), *World Yearbook 1985: Research, policy and practice* (pp. 19–41). New York: Kogan Page.

Myers, M. (1987, January). When research does not help teachers. *The Educational Digest* 14–17.

Price, W. J. (1996). Educational research and the practitioner: The great divide. *AASA Professor*, 19(2), 1–4.

Richardson-Koehler, V. (1987). What happens to research on the way to practice? *Theory into Practice*, 26(1), 38–43.

Rivlin, A. (1971). *Systematic thinking for social action*. Washington, D.C.: Brookings Institution.

Saha, L. J., Biddle, B. J., & Anderson, D. S. (1995). Attitudes towards education research knowledge and policymaking among American and Australian school principals. In T. Barone (Ed.), The Uses of Educational Research. *International Journal of Educational Research*, 23, 113–124.

Schwille, J., Porter, A., Belli, G., Floden, R., Freeman, D., Knappen, L., Kuhs, T., & Schmidt, W. (1981). *Teachers as policy brokers in the content of elementary school mathematics* (NIE Contract No. P-80-0127): Michigan State University Institute for Research on Teaching.

Shulman, L. S. (1970). Reconstruction of educational research. *Review of Educational Research*, 40(3), 371–396.

Shulman, L. S. (1986). Paradigms and research programs in the study of teaching: A contemporary perspective. In M. C. Wittrock (Ed.), *Handbook of research on teaching* (3rd ed., pp 3–36). New York: Macmillan.

Slavin, R. (1989). PET and the pendulum: Faddism in education and how to stop it. *Phi Delta Kappan*, 70, 752–758.

Snow, C. P. (1959). *The two cultures and a second look: Expanded version of the two cultures and the scientific revolution.* London: Cambridge University Press.

Smylie, M. A. (1989) Teachers' views of the effectiveness of sources of learning to teach. *Elementary School Journal*, 89(5), 543–558.

Stigler, J. W., & Stevenson, H. W. (1991, Spring). Polishing the stone: How Asian teachers perfect their lessons. *American Educator*, pp. 12–48.

Throne, J. (1994). Living with the pendulum: The complex world of teaching. *Harvard Educational Review* 64(2), 195–208.

Tom, A. R., & Valli, L. (1990). Professional knowledge for teachers. In W. R. Houston, M. Haberman, & J. Sikula (Eds.), *Handbook of research on teacher education* (pp. 373–392). New York: Macmillan.

Walberg, H. J. (1986). Synthesis of research on teaching. In M. C. Wittrock (Ed.), *Handbook of Research on Teaching* (3rd ed., pp. 214–229). New York: Macmillan.

Walker, C. A., & Cousins, J. B. (1984, November). *Influences on teachers' attitudes toward applied educational research.* Paper presented at the American Evaluation Association, Boston.

Weiss, C. H. (1977). Research for policy's sake: The enlightenment function of social research. *Policy Analysis*, 3(4), 531–545.

Weiss, C. H. (1980). Knowledge creep and decision accretion. *Knowledge: Creation, Diffusion, Utilization*, 1(3), 381–404.

Weiss, C. H. (1995). The haphazard connection: Social science and public policy. In T. Barone (Ed.), The uses of educational research. *International Journal of Educational Research*, 23(2), 113–124).

CHAPTER 4

The Role of Philosophy in Educational Reforms: Never the Twain Shall Meet?

ANDREW T. LUMPE
Southern Illinois University

When I was in graduate school, I frequently engaged in long discussions with colleagues about philosophy and its role in education. Whenever my wife, a high school mathematics teacher, overhead our conversations, she would get a contorted look on her face and question why we spent so much time talking about esoteric issues that have nothing to do with the everyday world of the classroom teacher. In a more recent example, I was involved in a curriculum restructuring meeting. The purpose of this meeting was to re-design the scope and sequence of a university's undergraduate elementary education program. All prospective elementary and middle school teachers articulate through this program and most school districts in the region hire graduates of the program. A professor who teaches a course designed to provide a background on the social and historical foundations of schools made the following comment: "The first thing I tell my students is that there is no such thing as truth." She went on to insist that this is a primary goal of her course and that schools should be based on this premise. At first, this comment may be easily brushed aside. However, it is rife with philosophical implications may that eventually work their way into school curricula and instruction.

WHY PHILOSOPHY?

As a former middle and high school science teacher, teacher educator at the college level, parent of four children, and a school board member, I have come to realize that philosophical issues serve as the foundation for everything done in education. All changes in schools are predicated on some philosophical cornerstone. Hence, the primary thesis of this chapter is that philosophy and educational reform are inextricably linked—a quick answer to the question in the title. In defense of this thesis, I offer Butler's (1968) statement regarding this link:

> It is difficult to define education without implying an educational philosophy. Philosophy is theoretical and speculative; education is practical. Philosophy asks questions, examining factors of reality and experience many of which are involved in the educative process; whereas the actual process of educating is a matter of actively dealing with these factors, i.e., teaching, organizing programs, administering organizations, building curricula. (pp. 10–11)

Recent policy shifts in education contain certain philosophical assumptions with which one may or may not agree. It behooves everyone who is directly or indirectly involved with education to clearly understand the philosophical issues that underlie educational reforms and policy initiatives. Because this chapter appears early in this handbook, the reader is encouraged to use it as a basis to ponder the current educational policy issues outlined in the rest of this book.

This chapter provides a historical background of philosophical issues related to teaching and learning. This background includes some unavoidable definitions—many of which end with the suffix *ism*. Next is an examination of the current prominent philosophical viewpoint in education—constructivism. The implications of constructivism for curriculum and classroom instruction is delineated, and the of role of philosophy in the recent wave of academic standards is examined. Finally, the chapter offers suggestions on how educators can approach this critical subject. Numerous scientific examples are presented in this chapter, most of which are applicable to all the core disciplines.

A HISTORICAL PRIMER

Before discussing how philosophy impacts today's schools and educational policies, we must first understand some history. Butler (1968) outlined two great problems in philosophy: *epistemology* and *ontology*. Epistemology deals with the issue of knowledge generation. It seeks to answer the question, "How do we come to know something?" Ontology deals with issues of reality. It attempts to explain "What is real?" Butler emphasized the importance of philosophical theories in education stating, "no theory is fully expressed until it is expressed in practice" (p. 12). Education is the ideal place to examine the connections between ontology, epistemology, and educational practice. To set the stage for identifying the role of philosophy in educational reform, we first outline epistemological issues.

Objectivism

Objectivist epistemology was the dominant philosophical perspective for many centuries. The basic tenets of this view are that reality is objective and external to the mind. The conviction is that human knowledge conforms to the object. Several branches of objectivist philosophy exist, including rationalism, empiricism, and logical positivism.

Rationalist trains of thought essentially began with René Descartes in the late 16th and early 17th centuries (Gardner, 1985). Descartes declared that the mind is capable of establishing valid knowledge if rational, logical thought processes were used to make sense of the world. These powers of reasoning are imposed on the sensory experience. Rationalists believe that knowledge is formed as people test ideas about the world through deductive reasoning. Mathematical models are a part of this school.

The empiricist school of thought, exemplified by John Locke, maintained that mental processes reflect the sensory perceptions (Gardner, 1985). Locke contended that the only reliable source of knowledge is the senses. He stated that ideas do not prove the existence of anything. The powers of observation were stressed as a way of accurately knowing the world. Empiricists believe that knowledge comes from conclusions inductively drawn from observations.

In the 17th and 18th centuries, philosophers such as Hume and Berkeley attacked these two schools of thought, arguing that neither one alone could account for the way people learn about the world (Fabricus, 1983; Gardner, 1985). These philosophers argued for an integration of rationalist and empiricist ideas; the result was logical positivism. Philosophers following this vein of thought believe that the mind inductively gathers ideas from the senses and then tests these ideas using deductive reasoning. This epistemology pervaded scientific thought for centuries and still shows up in school textbooks as what is called the scientific method.

Because it is obvious that humans' senses are fallible, empiricism and positivism began to be questioned. Thus, philosophical discussions of learning began to swing in the opposite, subjectivist direction with a focus on human cognitive structures.

Subjectivism

In the 1700s, Vico argued that knowledge does not conform to the object but is built of conceptual structures that people consider usable. He stated that people can know nothing but the cognitive structures they themselves have put together (Glasersfeld, 1989). Building on Vico's ideas, Kant, a German philosopher of the late 1700s, explained the processes of thought by stating that the person depends on and is stimulated by the outside world but can only understand the external world through experience with that world (Gardner, 1985). Thus, Kant tried to synthesize rationalist and empiricist ideas. He developed the idea of schemata, which he viewed as a combination of raw sensory data and abstract categories. These schemata provide the basis for our interpretation of the world. They can be thought of as part sensory and part intellectual.

Modern epistemologists, psychologists, and learning theorists began to use the ideas of Kant and Vico to explain learning. Piaget, a well-known epistemologist, used a lifetime of investigations with children to posit that knowledge is not a representation of the real world but is a set of conceptual structures used by humans to adapt and function in the world (Fabricus, 1983; Favell, 1963; Glasersfeld, 1989). To Piaget, the learner is engaged in an active process of trying to understand the external world.

Thus, objective epistemology was eventually replaced with subjective epistemology as the dominant philosophy. Subjectivists believe that there exists a connection between the learner and the world, but the object has not imposed its version of reality on the learner, and the learner has not imposed reasoning on the object. Knowledge is what turns out to be feasible; it is the product of self-organization and is not passive. The learner actively constructs knowledge over a lifetime. This characterization of knowledge has come to be called *constructivism*. The learner actively constructs knowledge based on personal experiences, beliefs, and previous knowledge. Knowledge can be constructed by individuals as they interact with the environment or knowledge can be constructed by groups of people as they collectively interact and agree on the knowledge base. The agreed on knowledge of a collective group is called public or social knowledge. In summarizing constructivism, Wheatley (1991) noted that learners actively build knowledge via their experiences and that through the processes of learning, people do not achieve truth but simply construct viable explanations of experiences.

Matthews (1994) outlined two basic forms of constructivism: psychological and sociological. The former is reflected in Glasersfeld's (1984, 1989) detailed accounts of individual learning based on Piagetian theory and Vygotsky's (1962) theory of the role of language in learning. Social constructivists (e.g., Berger & Luckman, 1966; O'Loughlin, 1992) criticize Piagetian-based theories as being too focused on individuals. Social constructivists argue that culture, power, and social discourse must be considered when describing learning.

Constructivism has rapidly become the prominent epistemology in education (Matthews, 1994; Phye, 1997). In fact, in teacher preparation, it is often the only epistemology discussed. Many education conferences devote large numbers of sessions to constructivism. It is a prominent feature of curriculum standards (see, e.g., NCTM, 1989) and professional literature. In fact, a handbook similar to this one was devoted solely to constructivism (Phye, 1997).

Constructivism can take on a variety of forms. Phillips (1995) outlined several competing forms or sects of constructivism. Regardless, most constructivists would agree that traditional instructional practices such as lecture and rote memory are not effective in helping all children learn. Many constructivists propose classrooms where students choose the curriculum and learn via discovery-inquiry methods.

Many educators treat constructivism simply as a learning theory. However, Matthews (1992, 1994) asserted that constructivism cannot simply serve as a psychological theory of learning; it contains major philosophical implications. In a book describing constructivist teaching practices, Henderson (1996) reminded us that constructivism contains complex ideological issues. These ideological-philosophical issues are the topic of the next section.

Realism versus Idealism

A discussion of ontology—the nature of reality—naturally arises from any discussion of constructivism. Giere's (1988) description of two opposing ontologies, *realism* and *idealism*, is helpful in a continued discussion of constructivism. Giere maintained that people can be categorized into one of these two camps. (The definitions for realism and idealism presented below will allow the reader to contemplate his or her own ontological view.) For the remainder of this chapter, these two ontologies and the implications they have for education will serve as the basis for further discussion. Furthermore, it will soon be evident that constructivism is firmly grounded in one of these two ontologies.

Idealists holds that reality is a matter of the mind and matter does not exist except as ideas in the mind. Idealists imply that people rely heavily on the senses to produce ideas, but ideas cannot inform us about the material world. Truth would not be a goal of the idealist other than to say that truth is in the mind of the thinker. Truth is replaced by the notion of viability or utility; good ideas are useful (Osborne, 1996). Poole (1995) provided a succinct definition of idealism:

> Idealism, in its various forms, shares the common belief that the so-called "external world" is somehow created by the mind. Physical objects are viewed as existing only in relation to an experiencing subject, so that reality is conceived of in terms of mind or experience. (p. 45)

Bronowski (1973) clarified the idealist position:

> There is no absolute knowledge. And those who claim it, whether they are scientists or dogmatists, open the door to tragedy. All information is imperfect. We have to treat it with humility. That is the human condition. (p. 353)

Conversely, *realists* accept the existence of a real, external world. For realists, a forest of trees exists whether or not humans are present to think about it. Many varieties of realism exist, and most modern writers would adhere to a *critical realist* position that takes into account the role of the learner but acknowledges a real, external world. In other words, there is a real world but humans' prior knowledge and senses mediate their perceptions of that world. This position concedes the "human condition" posited by Bronowski (1973). Realists set forth to learn the truth about the world around them. Barbour (1974) summarized this view:

> The critical realist thus tries to acknowledge both the creativity of man's mind and the existence of patterns in events not created by man's mind. Descriptions of nature are human constructions but nature is such as to bear descriptions in some ways and not others. No theory is an exact account of the world, but some theories agree with observations better than others because the world has an objective form of its own. (p. 37)

At this point, the reader may be asking, "What do these philosophies have to do with schools, teaching, curriculum, and policy?" The answer lies in the fact that much of the literature on constructivism clearly identifies it with idealistic philosophy. Almost 30 years ago, Perry (1970) noted the shift in worldview toward idealism. It is clear that this shift is becoming evident in education through the emphasis placed on idealistic constructivism. Poole (1995) stated, "One of the challenges to objectivity, which has achieved great prominence in science education, uses some of the language of idealism and goes under the umbrella term of constructivism" (p. 45). This link is reiterated in a book on pedagogy written for classroom teachers.

> One cannot have an interest in the notions of constructivism without grappling with questions of perception and reality. Is there one, fixed, objective world that we all struggle to come to know, or are there many different worlds, dependent for their definition upon individual perception? (Brooks & Brooks, 1993, p. 24)

Problems with Realism and Idealism

Both ontologies possess inescapable problems. Realism has been criticized because it does not take into account the role of the human mind in learning. Some would say that it is a throwback to the views of objectivist epistemologies: empiricism, rationalism, and positivism. On this front, realism is susceptible to attack. It is obvious that humans cannot perceive reality with 100% accuracy. A brief look at the history of any discipline quickly reveals that our views of the world have changed over time. Our observations are theory laden and theories are routinely replaced by new ones. For example, Issac Newton's theories of gravity and forces have been replaced by Einstein's theories of relativity for explaining space, time, and motion. To address these criticisms of realism, some have offered a moderate form of realism called critical realism (Harre, 1986; Osborne, 1996). This position was described earlier.

The problems of idealism appear to be more problematic without feasible solutions. Trigg (1980) noted, "Idealists have assumed that men are everywhere the same and that therefore a single reality will be constructed" (p. ix). Yet a simple observation of cultures reveals that this idea quickly degenerates into Berger and Luckman's (1966) social construction of reality in which scientific knowledge becomes merely the mental construction of societies of academicians. Carrying this logic forward would lead one to conclude that the only goal of schools is to develop mental constructions that are *viable* and not to impart knowledge or discover truth. Fields of study become relegated to social constructions and not noble disciplines. Perhaps this explains the general mistrust of science in today's generation (Gross & Levitt, 1994). Giere (1988) stated that under the banner of idealism, "the science of the paranormal could, in different social circumstances, be normal science" (p. 4). This very problem, in fact, was recently noted by Loving (1997). She described a research presentation where Australian Aborigine and Alaskan Native American myths were presented by an educational researcher "as equally valid as a kind of scientific explanation in terms of having an equal place in science class" (p. 436). This equality was stressed in spite of the fact that the myths led to potentially dangerous medical and scientific consequences. As Poole (1995) concluded, idealism leads down the slippery slopes of relativism; truth becomes whatever an individual or social groups believe it to be.

In an idealistic world, history is free to be rewritten. Political and governmental systems become social constructions of the powerful. Science and medicine are questioned. All ideas are equal in value no matter the source. At this point the reader must consider, "Could our current knowledge base have been developed in an idealist world?"

It is clear that constructivism is firmly based on idealistic ontology. Poole (1995) presented his objections to the idealistic foundations of constructivism:

> From a stance of realism, some of the language of constructivism . . . is linguistically odd. As matters stand at present, it needs to be said that although you can construct a theory or a model, or a view of reality or an interpretation of the world, you cannot construct reality and you cannot construct the world. Furthermore, the aim of pupils constructing their own meaning of the world will have little to commend it unless it has as its touchstone the world itself. (p. 47)

Theses are also Matthew's (1992) and Suchting's (1992) objections to the idealistic foundation of constructivism. Matthews noted, "Constructivist epistemology is fraught with grave educational and cultural implications that are seldom thought through. Constructivism leads directly to relativisms of all kinds" (1994, p. 158). Given these implications, Matthews asks serious questions: "Can children construct knowledge as sophisticated as experts?" "Who selects school curriculum if knowledge is based solely upon our experiences?" "Is knowledge relegated to a personal belief?" "Are cultural traditions up for negotiation?" "Are real-world problems dismissed because there are no objective facts?"

At its practical conclusion, schools based on idealism are necessarily doomed to produce illiterate children as literacy is currently conceptualized. In contemplating perceived problems in his own childrens' education, Morrison (1997), a Nobel laureate scientist, recently reviewed a book by Cromer (1997) and summarized these problems in science education:

> Cromer gradually compares science and its methodology with the ideas of the "post-modernists," who question the objectivity of science and even the existence of objective reality. What I found particularly worrying . . . was the author's description of how postmodernists have applied their ideas to education. In that arena, the movement is called constructivism. . . . I often hear American scientists lament the low standard of education in their public schools. After reading . . . of how constructivists have worked their ideas into science teaching programs and introduced their non-scientific ideas, I can well understand how these actions have exacerbated the problems.

An additional problem with constructivism is that many of the constructivist writers and philosophers tend to be radically idealistic in their beliefs (Phillips, 1995), which leads to confusing and quixotic philosophies. Perhaps educators should adopt a new terminology or simply clarify their positions to avoid this confusion. Poole (1995) commended certain aspects of constructivism, but he stringently objected to the strange idealistic overtones of some constructivist writings. He objected to constructivism on the grounds that it mixes realism with idealism. His view seems to be that constructivism would be more palatable if the idealistic aspects were abandoned.

What Do Educators Believe?

Talk of idealistic ontology begs the question, "What are educators' beliefs about such philosophies?" Some researchers have begun to seek an answer to this question. A study conducted by Alters (1997) demonstrated that philosophers do not agree with the basic philosophical tenants of educators. He demonstrated that most philosophers are realists. Haney, Czerniak, and Lumpe (1998) analyzed the constructivist beliefs of school personnel, students, and parents. They found that constructivist ideas do not dominate the belief systems of these groups, all of whom held relatively negative beliefs toward constructivist practices. The findings from these studies indicate a clear conflict: The personal philosophical positions of educators stand in direct conflict with the constructivist thoughts of educational theorists and most of the professional literature.

Phillips (1995) has gone so far as to question the intentions of some constructivist educators. He has argued that Glasersfeld desires to see education undergo a massive shift toward a student-centered approach where there is no commonly accepted set of ideas or standard curriculum. Progressive education proponents with roots in the philosophy of John Dewey intend to redesign schools in order to change society. Feminist and other political constructivists desire to use their constructivism to redistribute power and wealth. Cromer (1997) concurred with Phillips when he noted:

> Contemporary progressivism is, in fact, reactionary, since it reaches back to ideas and practices that failed over a century ago. It would be of little interest to us, except that it's very strong today among educators and academics, being the common denominator of constructivism, postmodernism, multiculturalism, radical feminism, ecoradicalism, and political correctness. (p. 114)

Phillips clarified his exposé by indicating that people can be sympathetic to these causes without agreeing with their use of constructivism to achieve the goals.

In spite of his comment that "in a very broad and loose sense . . . all of us these days are constructivists" (p. 5), Phillips (1995) expressed concerns about this prevailing educational philosophy. His view is that educators can be classified along a continuum he has called "humans the creators versus nature the instructor" (p. 7) (see Figure 1). Those who believe that knowledge is imposed from the outside are placed at one end of the continuum. To borrow a term from earlier in this chapter, such people would be called objectivists, empiricists, or positivists. Philosophers such as Locke, Descartes, Hume, and Berkeley would be classified at this end of the continuum. The other end of the continuum would represent those who believe in idealistic constructivism. Vico, Piaget, Vygotsky, Glasersfeld, and Berger and Luckman would be placed here. People who believe that the best philosophy of learning is somewhere in the middle on this continuum would probably agree with Phillips' (1995) summary of Karl Popper's philosophy of learning

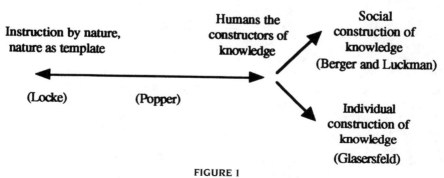

FIGURE 1

Humans the creator versus nature the instructor. Adapted from Phillips, 1995, p. 8. Copyright 1995 by the American Educational Research Association. Adapted by permission of the publisher.

"man proposes, nature disposes" (p. 9). In other words, nature is real and as such has a certain structure; however, people interpret nature using their own experiences and senses. This view, critical realism, represents a more palatable philosophy than either naïve empiricism or idealistic constructivism.

CONSTRUCTIVISM AND EDUCATION

Earlier in this chapter, it was noted that the modern philosophical movement of constructivism is ingrained in today's educational culture, and the idealistic foundations of constructivism were demonstrated. We must now turn our attention to the practical applications of constructivism in the classroom.

The Link between Philosophy and Classroom Practice

Cobern (1990) outlined a linear connection between ontology (i.e., the nature of reality), epistemology (i.e., the nature of learning), and *pedagogy* (i.e., the nature of instruction). The question we must ask at this point is, "What is the connection, if any, between idealist ontology, constructivist epistemology, and classroom practice?"

In a book designed to provide practical advice for classroom teachers, Brooks and Brooks (1993) outlined 12 principles the book's authors believe characterize constructivist teaching practice. They assert that teachers who practice constructivist principles should do the following:

1. Encourage student autonomy.
2. Use primary data sources.
3. Use cognitive terminology.
4. Allow students to drive lessons, shift strategies, and alter content.
5. Inquire about students' understandings of concepts.
6. Encourage students to engage in dialogue.
7. Encourage student inquiry.
8. Seek elaboration of student's initial responses.
9. Engage students in experiences that might engender contradictions to their initial hypotheses and then encourage discussion.
10. Allow wait time after posing questions.
11. Provide time for students to construct relationships.
12. Nurture students' natural curiosity. (pp. 103-116)

Notice that discipline-based content—the product of a discipline—is curiously missing from this list. As noted earlier, the Brooks' are clearly idealists, and therefore the emphasis on content is minimized. But, for the sake of argument, let us assume that Brooks and Brooks built their 12 principles with the purpose of only characterizing effective instructional strategies. At first glance, many educators would agree with most, if not all, of the 12 principles. Many current educational reform efforts and policy initiatives incorporate these principles as well.

But can such principles serve as a pedagogical foundation for schooling? Matthews (1994) criticized such constructivist practices as those mentioned by Brooks and Brooks. He argued that in a constructivist classroom, students will oftentimes construct knowledge that is different than the accepted view of experts. Should educators tell a child that he or she is wrong? This has grave implications for the explication of curriculum. Both Matthews (1994) and Hodson (1988) have maintained that children cannot discover scientific truths and may not possess the sophisticated skills to conduct investigations leading to concept development. Hodson stated:

> The suggestion that initial, unprejudiced observations lead infallibly to conceptual explanations is both philosophically and psychologically absurd. For children to "discover" anything at all they need a prior conceptual framework. (1988, p. 23)

Education based on idealism is necessarily experienced based. In other words, the process of a discipline, not its product or content, is the primary educative goal. A constructivist would embrace student experimentation, student-centered projects, informality, and discussion. A constructivist may also include certain content from a discipline. But that content is simply a means to an end, the end being the construction of the student's own view of the world.

Do idealists have the market on student-oriented teaching strategies? Realists propose that educators should use a variety of teaching methods to educate students, to help them understand the real world around them. Does realism lead to rote memorization and destructive lecture models as many constructivists argue? Not necessarily. In citing a critical realist perspective on the educative process, Butler (1968) noted that realism does not lead to a mechanical process where knowledge is transmitted directly from teacher to pupil. Indeed, mastery of subject matter becomes much more than memorization of facts. It includes the skillful use of this information to address real issues and problems through research, experimentation, critical thinking, and evaluation. In fact, rote memorization may be necessary for some curriculum objectives such as multiplication tables, spelling, rules of proper language usage and writing, and definitions of terms used in a discipline. Without these key foundations, students cannot begin to venture into problem-oriented learning. The classroom of a realist would be a place where a variety of instructional strategies are employed in an effort to reach all students. Indeed, Broudy (cited in Butler) has pointed out that even in a realist classroom, "the mind is active — reaching out to its object" (p. 316).

Does all this mean that effective teaching practices are the sole property of constructivists? Matthews (1994) and Osborne (1996) have made a case for the nonconstructivist foundation of many effective teaching practices. It is Osborne's (1996) belief that learning style research goes farther to support effective teaching practice than does constructivist epistemology. Contrary to constructivist writers, his contention is that at the exclusion of other viable pedagogical strategies, constructivism has only "offered a singular pedagogy where meaning is negotiated through a process of cultural apprenticeship" (p. 77).

Current pedagogical policy promoting active learning strategies are commonly based on cognitive learning theories and constructivist epistemologies. However, as noted earlier, there is much disagreement about the ultimate ontological foundation of such practice. If the foundation of inquiry-based classroom practice is idealism, then its foundation is a weak one.

If one was to make a logical extension from idealist ontology, to constructivist epistemology, to science classroom pedagogy, then the classroom would look rather unguided and chaotic. Some constructivists even reject the notion of curriculum as a body of knowledge and instead stress the development of skills. There would be no standards for learning and no way to indicate whether students really achieve. In fact, achievement becomes negotiated instead of based on an external standard.

All of these philosophical issues are salient at this junction in American education. We are currently enmeshed in an unprecedented era of educational policy; national standards for learning are being developed and published at a rapid clip. Educators are being bombarded with curricular innovations. States and local school districts adopt curriculum frameworks based on these new standards and innovations. The next section examines the role constructivism plays in school curriculum.

The Link between Philosophy and Curriculum

If schools are based on constructivism, then a systematic curriculum becomes contradictory and knowledge is simply idiosyncratic, ephemeral, and socially negotiated. Learning involves activities with no defined objectives. In a constructivist dominated classroom, will the accepted theories in a discipline take a backseat—or at least a side seat—to students' own constructed views? Herein lies the danger of constructivism. In certain forms of constructivism, "the scientific enterprise is reduced to a study of what socially conditioned believers believe" (Poole 1995, p. 47). There is no longer any agreed on curriculum. A standard curriculum become a moot point. Learner outcomes are what the learner decides to construct. Or as Dewey (1916) proposed, an understanding of the processes of a discipline are more important for children to learn than are the products or content of a discipline.

As recent developments in educational policy have demonstrated, this practice is far from reality. On the heels of national mathematics standards developed by the National Council of Teachers of Mathematics (1989), other professional societies organized to develop content, teaching, and assessment standards for their disciplines. Typically, these professional societies have developed standards through a consensus process involving all stakeholders in the discipline (i.e., teachers, experts, business executives, government agencies). These societies have published and disseminated standards to broad audiences; others continue to do so.

These standards have become extremely important policy statements. At the national level, they have been used to by the White House for suggesting education policy and are emphasized in federally funded programs administered by the United States Department of Education and the National Science Foundation. States have also used these standards to develop statewide curriculum, high-stakes tests, and block grants to local schools. Many federal and state grant programs require recipients to use the new standards. Local school districts have begun to use the new standards to redesign educational programs.

In spite of their emphasis on content standards for learning, there is abundant evidence that constructivist philosophy is prevalent throughout the standards. The National Social Studies Standards (National Council for the Social Studies, 1997) makes this very clear when asking the question, "How can the social studies curriculum help students construct an accurate and positive view?" (p. 3). The English Language Arts Standards (International Reading Association & National Council of Teachers of English, 1996) state, "language development starts at birth as they begin to hear language, process it, and construct meaning with it" (p. 18) and "the processes of language are active, not passive" (p. 19). The National Science Education Standards (National Academy Press, 1996) define learning as an occurrence in which "students describe objects and events, ask questions, acquire knowledge, construct explanations of natural phenomena, test those explanations in many different ways and communicate their ideas to others" (p. 20). All of the standards documents refer to learning as an active process where students' prior knowledge interacts with desired knowledge. The standards use terms that are commonly used in constructivist literature to describe teaching and learning, such as construct, use, interpret, explore, speculate, propose, investigate, inquiry, discourse, engage, and collaborate.

Here is an essential conflict. The standards documents represent a strange blend of constructivism, with all its idealistic problems, and realistic goals for learning. This is evident in the fact that most of the standards devote considerable length to outlining detailed content standards for student learning. In fact, the science standards (National Academy Press, 1996) devote more than 100 pages to specific concepts, principles, theories, and laws that students should learn within the life, earth/space, and physical sciences. On the other hand, the science standards stress a "shifting emphasis away from teachers presenting information and covering science topics" (p. 20) and toward "enabling students to have a significant voice in decisions about the content . . . of their work" (p. 46). Why was so much energy spent on defining content standards? On this point, the idealist must ask, whose standards are these? In light of the schizophrenic personality of the standards, it is reasonable to assert that the developers of the standards desire to promulgate effective pedagogy but do not believe in a curriculum built on the foundations of idealistic constructivism.

The Link between Philosophy and the Role of Schools

We have looked at philosophy in curriculum and instruction; now we must examine the role of schools in society. Idealists and realists have differing positions regarding the role of schools. As Cromer (1997) has observed:

> There is an inevitable contradiction between the progressive doctrines of educators—with their emphases on naturalism and individualism—and the practical needs of schools, businesses, and society as a whole for discipline and order. (p. 118)

Many educational policy makers believe that the role of schools is to maintain society and culture and prepare children for the workforce. Much of the standards movement is based on the view that there are certain skills, knowledge, and dispositions that students need in order to be functional citizens. Such is the case with Goodlad's (1987) core curriculum. Pleas for more scientists and engineers coupled with increasing threats of global competition have led policy makers to delineate and stiffen the requirements for school children.

Others see schools as a vehicle to change society. Children, young minds to be molded, become the avenue for bringing about societal change. Dewey (1938/1974) advocated individual expression, free activity, learning through experience, and preparing students for a changing world. Some progressives see the primary role of education as bringing about social justice. Extremist groups, such as People for the Ethical Treatment of Animals (PETA), develop and distribute educational materials advocating social and cultural change. As was noted earlier, Phillips (1995) has laid bare the underlying intentions of some constructivists. Some of these intentions include reforming schools so they become the driving force for a change toward their own political and sociological views.

Cromer (1997) posited that a middle-of-the-road educational system, one based on moderate constructivist strategies, would be wiser than its more ideological foundations. Whichever philosophical position a person espouses individually, it is clear that in a democratic society schools must maintain the desires of its citizens while at the same time preparing students for the rapid changes occurring in today's technological society. Cromer's proposed balance would be a wise choice for policy makers.

EDUCATORS, PHILOSOPHY, AND
EDUCATIONAL POLICY

It should be clear to the reader that idealistic-based constructivism is an unsuitable match for education. Johnson (1995) warned educators against using idealist philosophies for the foundation of societal systems such as science, law, and education. In fact, Johnson would argue that these philosophies provide no foundation at all and will eventually lead to chaos and an eventual breakdown of society. Cromer (1997) concurred,

> But if there can be no objective knowledge about human behavior, how can there be any rational basis for making public policy? On what basis do we decide how and what to teach our children? (p. viii)

No matter how esoteric philosophical issues may appear, educational policy makers, curriculum developers, school board members, school administrators, and classroom teachers should be aware of these important issues. All should clarify their own philosophical beliefs before making decisions that will impact schools, children, and ultimately society.

Constructivism, as a philosophical referent or foundation, should be seriously questioned. Its blind acceptance could spell doom for our educational systems. Of course, many constructivists see constructivism as a way to change a system supposedly in need of major reform (Berliner & Biddle, 1995). The educational community should carefully consider the constructivism bandwagon and all of its philosophical implications before jumping on board. Many teachers, parents, and policy makers neither know about, nor agree with, the philosophical roots of constructivism.

On the other hand, certain pedagogical strategies arising from constructivist literature appear to be extremely useful and effective in teaching and are documented to be reasonably efficacious in the research literature. The following dilemma arises from this state of affairs: "Can one be a constructivist without being an idealist?" Based on the rhetorical force with which some constructivist writers push its idealistic foundations, the answer is emphatically no. Does this mean that teachers should throw out the effective teaching strategies presumably linked with constructivism? Obviously not. As Osborne (1996), among others, made clear, constructivists cannot claim all effective strategies as their own. Critical realism and learning style research provide excellent foundations for inquiry, project-based, and group learning activities.

From a policy maker's viewpoint, philosophy and education have met. From a teacher's viewpoint, perhaps the two are not even related. Academicians—professors and policy makers—tend to overtheorize in lieu of practicality. Teachers, the daily practitioners, often do not believe that theory applies to their everyday lives. Perhaps both groups need to realize the important role philosophy plays in both policy and classroom practice. University-based teacher-educators are in an ideal position to facilitate such discussions. This may be difficult given our pluralistic society where philosophical differences, primarily between idealists and realists, are so prevalent. However, it is clear that many policy makers have assumed—perhaps unwittingly—an idealistic viewpoint without consulting all the major stakeholders.

So where does this leave us? Perhaps local control of education allows communities to decide their own policies and programs. The United States is one of few countries that maintains local control of education. In spite of local control, states continue to promulgate standards, high-stakes tests, and funding policies to ensure that prescribed policies are followed. State government school personnel need to be aware of the variety of philosophical viewpoints before suggesting policy recommendations to local schools and legislatures. Idealistic constructivism is rife with philosophical implications with which the majority of the populace does not agree.

School administrators and board members should be aware of the philosophical views of their constituents before determining school policy. Philosophy may appear in a school's mission statement, goals, adopted curriculum materials, and instructional models. Those involved in making decisions at the local level need to be cognizant of the philosophical beliefs of the school community before making decisions. School personnel should clarify their curricula and adopt a variety of instructional strategies that allow all students to learn.

At least for the near future, policy makers would do well to avoid extremism in terms of epistemology; balance in most matters has its benefits. Extremism in education must be prevented for a multicultural democracy to be sustained. Hodson (1982) proposed a compromise philosophy in education, which he called *critical realism*. Critical realism provides a sound philosophical alternative to idealistic constructivism. If educators accept a critical realist position—that is, a belief in an objective reality but with the possibility for human interaction—then some pedagogical strategies supposedly linked to constructivism and a standard curriculum become palatable, even wise choices. As Cromer so eloquently stated, "I share the liberal's desire to improve the human condition and I share the conservative's belief that human nature, and the laws of physics, limit what's possible" (p. x).

References

Alters, B. J. (1997). Whose nature of science? *Journal of Research in Science Teaching*, 34, 39–55.

Barbour, I. G. (1974). *Myths, models, and paradigms*. London: SCM Press.

Berger, P., & Luckman, T. (1966). *The social construction of reality: A treatise in the sociology of knowledge*. Garden City, NJ: Doubleday.

Berliner, D. C., & Biddle, B. J. (1995). *The manufactured crisis: Myths, frauds, and the attack on America's public schools*. New York: Longman.

Brooks, J. G., & Brooks, M. G. (1993). *In search for understanding: The case for constructivist classrooms*. Alexandria, VA: Association for Supervision and Curriculum Development.

Bronowski, J. (1973). *The ascent of man*. Boston: Little, Brown and Co.

Butler, J. D. (1968). *Four philosophies and their practice in education and religion.* New York: Harper Row.

Cobern, W. W. (1990, November). *Education research will not profit from radical constructivism.* A paper presented at the annual meeting of the Arizona Education Research Organization, Tempe, AZ.

Cromer, A. (1997). *Connected knowledge: Science, philosophy, and education.* New York: Oxford University Press.

Dewey, J. (1916). *Democracy and education.* New York: Free Press.

Dewey, J. (1938/1974). *Experience and education.* New York: Collier Books.

Fabricus, W. V. (1983). Piaget's theory of knowledge: It's philosophical content. *Human Development, 26,* 325–334.

Favell, J.H. (1963). *The developmental psychology of Jean Piaget.* New York: Van Nostrand.

Gardner, H. (1985). *The minds new science.* New York: Basic Books.

Giere, R. N. (1988). *Explaining science.* Chicago: University of Chicago Press.

Glasersfeld, E. von (1984). An introduction to radical constructivism. In P. Watzlawick (Ed.), *The invented reality: How do we know what we believe we know? Contributions to constructivism* (pp. 17–40). New York: Norton.

Glasersfeld, E. von (1989). Cognition, construction of knowledge, and teaching. *Synthese, 80,* 121–140.

Goodlad, J. I. (1987). A new look at an old idea: Core curriculum. *Educational Leadership, 44(4),* 8–16.

Gross, P. R., & Levitt, N. (1994). *Higher superstition: The academic left and its quarrels with science.* Baltimore, MD: Johns Hopkins University Press.

Haney, J. J., Czerniak, C. M., & Lumpe, A. T. (1998, January). *Constructivist beliefs about science teaching: Perspectives from teachers, administrators, parents, community members, and students.* A paper presented at the annual meeting of the Association for the Education of Teachers of Science, Minneapolis, MN.

Harre, R. (1986). *Varieties of realism: A rationale for the natural sciences.* Oxford: Basil Blackwell.

Henderson, J. G. (1996). *Reflective teaching: A study of your constructivist practices.* Englewood Cliffs, NJ: Merrill.

Hodson, D. (1982). Science—the pursuit of truth? Part II. *The School Science Review, 64,* 23–30.

Hodson, D. (1988). Toward a philosophically more valid science curriculum. *Science Education, 72,* 19–40.

International Reading Association & National Council of Teachers of English (1996). *Standards for the English language arts.* Newark, DE: Author.

Johnson, P. E. (1995). *Reason in the balance.* Downers Grove, IL: Intervarsity Press.

Loving, C. C. (1997). From the summit of truth to its slippery slopes: Science education's journey through positivistic-postmodern territory. *American Educational Research Journal, 34,* 421–452.

Matthews, M. R. (1992). Constructivism and empiricism: An incomplete divorce. *Research in Science Education, 13,* 106.

Matthews, M. R. (1994). *Science Teaching: The role of history and philosophy of science.* New York: Routledge.

Morrison, D. R. O. (1997, November). Bad science, bad education. In *Scientific American* [Online], Available: http://www.sciam.com/1197issue/1197review1.html [1998, January 25].

National Academy Press. (1996). *National Science Education Standards.* Washington, DC: Author.

National Council for the Social Studies (1997). *A sampler of curriculum standards for social studies: Expectations of excellence.* Upper Saddle, NJ: Prentice-Hall.

National Council for Teachers of Mathematics (1989). *Curriculum and evaluation standards for school mathematics.* Reston, VA: Author.

O'Loughlin, M. (1992). Rethinking science education: Beyond Piagetian constructivism toward a sociocultural model of teaching and learning. *Journal of Research in Science Teaching, 29,* 791–820.

Osborne, J. F. (1996). Beyond constructivism. *Science Education, 80,* 52–82.

Perry, W. G. (1970). *Forms of intellectual and ethical development in the college years: A scheme.* New York: Holt, Rinehart & Winston.

Phillips, D. C. (1995). The good, the bad, and the ugly: The many faces of constructivism. *Educational Researcher, 24(7),* 5–12.

Phye, G. D. (Ed.). (1997). *Handbook of academic learning: Construction of knowledge*. San Diego: Academic Press.

Poole, M. (1995). *Beliefs and values in science education*. Buckingham, England: Open University Press.

Suchting, W. A. (1992). Constructivism deconstructed. *Science & Education*, 1, 223–254.

Trigg, R. (1980). *Reality at risk: A defense of realism in philosophy and the sciences*. Sussex, England: Harvester Press.

Vygotsky, L. S. (1962). *Thought and language*. Cambridge, MA: MIT Press.

Wheatley, G. H. (1991). Constructivist perspectives on science and mathematics learning. *Science Education*, 75, 9–22.

Local, State, National, and International Perspectives

CHAPTER

5

Evolution of Educational Reform in Maryland: Using Data to Drive State Policy and Local Reform

HILLARY R. MICHAELS
Mid-continent Regional Educational Laboratory

STEVEN FERRARA
American Institutes for Research

It is a common assertion that the standards-based educational reform movement grew out of A *Nation at Risk*, the 1983 report by the National Commission on Excellence in Education that decried the state of public education (cf. Ravitch, 1995; Shepard, 1993). The report also raised the public's level of awareness of American public education. Since 1983, public concern has continued and was addressed in the education summit report, *The National Education Goals Panel* (NEGP) *Report: Building a Nation of Learners* (1991). The six goals listed in the NEGP report include references to competencies that all students should master so that they can be productive learners, citizens, and employees (National Education Goals Panel, 1991).

Many states responded to these reports by reflecting on their current education policies and changing them. After A *Nation at Risk* was released, one of the first to respond was Bill Honig, then state superintendent of California's public schools. He led an effort to revise California's content standards and curricular frameworks beginning in 1983 (Marzano & Kendall,

1996). Other states that responded by reforming their educational policy include Arizona, Maryland, and Vermont.

In this chapter we use Maryland as an example of a state using data to inform policy decisions. Maryland has used data in this way for three policy iterations since the mid-1970s: the Accountability Testing Program, Project Basic and the Maryland School Performance Program. Maryland uses national reports and trends, state and local data, and public needs and requirements to inform educational policy. To inform the Maryland School Performance Program, Maryland used information from A *Nation at Risk*, the National Education Goals Panel report, and state trends from the National Assessment of Educational Progress (NAEP). This information, along with the *Report of the Governor's Commission on School Performance* and Project Basic results helped to create an innovative, data-driven assessment system. The centerpiece of this program is the criterion-referenced performance assessment, the Maryland School Performance Assessment Program (MSPAP).

Maryland is only one of several states using data to inform policy. Therefore, it is useful to examine the state's achievements and deficiencies to inform others. In addition, the process used by local school districts in Maryland has elements similar to the processes advocated in the *Profiling Handbook* (Northwest Regional Educational Laboratory, 1995) and *Data-Driven School Improvement* (Johnson, 1996). All of these methods recycle information into the local system to inform the district's educational improvement plans.

This chapter is divided into four sections. Each section refers to the use or implications of data use at different levels of policy construction. The first section highlights assessment policy focusing on the history of Maryland's assessments. The second section focuses on the experiences of a specific school that has used data to inform school improvement policy and practice. The next section discusses how data can be used and misused to create policy, and the final section speculates about the future use of data to inform decision making.

HISTORY OF MARYLAND'S SCHOOL REFORM EFFORTS

Maryland's standards-based educational reform effort includes regular public reporting of school performance, explicit standards-focused school improvement efforts, and high expectations for the learning and performance of all students in all schools. Called the Maryland School Performance Program, it is actually the third evolutionary phase of efforts in Maryland to improve the quality of public education. The first phase, the Maryland Accountability Testing Program, began in the mid-1970s and operated through the 1980s. It required school systems to report school performance using nationally normed tests and to base instructional improvements on these test results. The Accountability Testing Program was supplemented in 1977 by a second evolutionary phase, Project Basic. Project Basic requires schools to teach basic skills in a state framework and for students to pass four minimum-competency tests in order to receive a high school diploma. In the early 1990s, the Maryland School Performance Program became the policy for reporting data, evaluating school performance, and guiding school improvement. Today, the Maryland School Performance Program reports school performance and monitors improvement in relationship to standards for school quality (i.e., student achievement in basic and applied skills and knowledge, attendance, dropout rates) and provides sanctions and rewards for schools based on their performance.[1]

The following sections briefly trace the evolution of educational reform efforts in Maryland. They focus specifically on ways that policy makers have used (1) data to formulate and compel reform policies and (2) data and conclusions produced in each phase to set the stage for subsequent phases.

Phase 1: Public Accountability for Student Achievement

In the mid-1970s the Maryland state legislature began to focus its attention on the quality of public education in light of spending. Expenditure of local, state, and federal funds on public schools had been expanding rapidly, and legislators and their constituents were calling for an accounting of the uses and impacts of these dollars. The combined weight of several factors probably motivated the Accountability Testing Program. These included rapid increases in spending on education throughout the late 1960s and into the 1970s, media attention on declining SAT scores, other indicators taken as signs of the decline of American public education, and, perhaps, increasing concerns about public education that resulted from public information campaigns (e.g., widely publicized dropout prevention and literacy campaigns).

In response, the Maryland state legislature passed an educational accountability law in 1972 that mandated statewide goal setting and testing. Each year the Maryland State Department of Education published the Maryland Accountability Testing Program report, which included average grade equivalent scores from the California Achievement Tests, Form C (CAT-C) in reading comprehension, language skills, and mathematics at Grades 3, 5, and 8 for every school and all 24 school systems in the state. Although school report cards are fairly common today, in the 1970s it was innovative and even revolutionary to provide a public accounting for the performance of individual schools. However, these accountability reports suffered from several shortcomings compared to today's school report cards:

[1]Education policy includes many elements. However, for the purpose of this chapter, we will focus on assessment systems as they are often powerful tools that states use to implement educational policy.

1. The reports contained only norm-referenced test information and no information about attendance, performance of student subgroups, or other indicators of school performance.
2. The reports contained no information on the percentage of students enrolled in each school and school system whose CAT-C scores were included in the report, and they actually obscured the fact that considerable percentages of students—as many as 5 to 10%—were not tested or included in the report.
3. The CAT-C, like all nationally normed and commercially published tests, matched state and local curriculum in broad ways (e.g., it tested English conventions skills like capitalization and punctuation) but was not tightly linked to state and local curricula (e.g., it did not reflect Maryland's increasing emphasis on writing as a composing process in which adherence to conventions is only one component).
4. The norms for CAT-C, established in the late 1970s, were soon outdated, and CAT-C results suffered from the Lake Woebegone effect (Cannell, 1987) in which virtually all schools and school systems performed at or above the national average.

Phase 2: Basic Skills Curriculum and Minimum-Competency Testing

These and other shortcomings of the accountability reporting system became apparent to the public, as did the need to focus attention on the large numbers of high school graduates who entered higher education and the job market with inadequate skills in basic reading, writing, and mathematics. The well-known report, A *Nation at Risk* (National Commission on Excellence in Education, 1983) provided a compelling metaphor that resonated with the public, "the educational foundations of our society are presently being eroded by a rising tide of mediocrity" (p. 5). The Maryland Accountability Testing Program report did not account for this problem. In fact, the report contributed to a dissonance about public education. On average, Maryland students were at or near grade level even though test students appeared to the public to lack adequate skills in reading and arithmetic. The evidence for this belief came from regular reports in the media about the decline in average SAT scores, popular books like *Why Johnny Can't Read and What You Can Do About It* (Flesch, 1955), and concerns expressed by business and industry about the inadequate basic skills of recent high school graduates. The policy response in Maryland was called Project Basic, which was initiated by Maryland's state superintendent, David Hornbeck, and the state board of education.[2]

[2]Hornbeck was an architect of Kentucky's standards-based reform effort that began in the early 1990s and currently is leading reform efforts of the Philadelphia public schools as its superintendent.

Project Basic had two components: (1) a basic skills framework of 165 competencies that all schools were required to cover in their local curricula by the end of Grade 8 and (2) minimum-competency tests in reading, writing, mathematics, and citizenship skills that all students were required to pass in order to receive a high school diploma. Project Basic was Maryland's version of two converging national movements: a focus on basic literacy skills and minimum-competency testing. A concurrent national movement—teaching writing as a composing process as well as teaching Engligh conventions— also led to the rise of large-scale essay testing. The Maryland Functional Tests in reading, writing, mathematics, and citizenship skills, developed in the early 1980s, were phased in as high school graduation requirements between 1986 and 1989. As state and system level results were reported in the media and as educators examined school level results, the limits of Project Basic and the Maryland Functional Tests became evident. Educators and policy makers around the United States came to acknowledge that requiring explicit instruction and mastery of basic skills by the end of middle school is important but not enough, for several reasons:

1. The required skills and standards for passing minimum-competency tests were not rigorous or challenging for most students.
2. Typical basic skills objectives came to be viewed as overly narrow, and passing some of the tests (e.g., the Maryland Test of Citizenship Skills) was likened to a game of "trivial pursuit" (Henry, 1987).
3. The combination of a required basic skills curriculum and high-stakes minimum competency tests seemed to encourage some curriculum narrowing (e.g., Wilson & Corbett, 1991), at least for some students.
4. Preparing students to pass the tests often meant teaching to the test; this approach involved frequent administration of practice tests that were developed by local school systems to parallel the state tests (Ferrara, Willhoft, Seburn, Slaughter, & Stevenson, 1991) in place of teaching the skills and knowledge intended in the basic skills curriculum.

Despite these shortcomings, policy makers saw the power of high-stakes testing and measurement-driven instruction (Popham, 1987). The prevailing, though not unanimous, view among policy makers was that the observable positive impacts of driving instruction and learning with high-stakes tests outweighed the risks of negative impacts like curriculum narrowing. Policy makers may or may not have been aware that they could influence day-to-day classroom activities from as far away as the state house and state department of education. But they were aware that they could shape public education this way at relatively little cost. Further, they seemed to be aware that public reporting of results from these high-stakes testing programs acted as lightning rods. Test results and public debates about the tests themselves attracted public concerns about the quality of public education and the welfare of children. These concerns could be used as launching pads for political careers and provocative issues for re-election campaigns.

Phase 3: Standards-Based Reform
and Standards-Based Assessments

Other ideas about what students should know and be able to do became widespread in the national educational movements of the mid-1980s. Perhaps most prominent was the notion that students should master higher-order or critical thinking skills in addition to basic skills. In the late 1980s, various calls for more authentic performance-based assessments that could assess broader and higher-order skills converged with the higher-order thinking skills movement. These movements coincided with large and well-publicized analyses of the quality of graduates coming to business and industry (e.g., Secretary's Commission on Achieving Necessary Skills, 1991). The policy response in Maryland was to commission a 2-year study by a specially appointed staff and panel of national consultants and publication of the "Report of the Governor's Commission on School Performance" (Commission on School Performance, 1989).[3]

The governor's commission report pointed out that (1) the accountability program reported performance in relation to national norms but not in terms of curriculum and did not require schools to take action to improve achievement and (2) the Maryland Functional Testing Program reported performance in relation to standards for students but not schools. The report also provided a blueprint for reforms to the state board of education. The blueprint called for a state framework for school improvement with school accountability as the focus for reporting school performance and monitoring school improvement. It made explicit that the responsibility for improving schools and providing a rigorous education for all children is the responsibility of each school, school system, and the state as a whole. It also explicitly directed focus toward educational outputs (i.e., student achievement) in addition to educational inputs (e.g., per pupil expenditures).

Maryland School Performance Program

In response to these challenges, the state board of education implemented the Maryland School Performance Program (MSPP) within months of receiving the commission's report. The four major elements of MSPP are as follows:

1. Indicators of student participation and achievement in school, called *data-based areas*, and standards for satisfactory and excellent school performance in each data-based area

[3]The report is commonly referred to as the "Sondheim report," named for Walter Sondheim, the chair of the governor's commission. Sondheim is a well-known and respected civic leader in Maryland. He has been a member of the Baltimore school board, he was an architect of Baltimore's fiscal and infrastructure revitalization in the 1970s, and he is a current member of the Maryland State Board of Education.

2. Public accounting of school performance through annual publication of school report cards
3. Development of school improvement plans in schools whose performance is low or declining, with reconstitution as a potential option for schools that do not begin to improve[4]
4. Sanctions for schools that are performing poorly or declining in the data-based areas and rewards for schools that improve in the data-based areas for 2 or more years

The data-based areas and standards in the Maryland School Performance Report (see Figure 1) are intended to provide a reasonably comprehensive view of school quality for the school system, local school districts, and schools. Not all of the data-based areas have standards applied to them. The data-based areas are as follows:

1. Performance data as indicated by student mastery of basic skills on the Maryland Functional Testing Program (MFTP) and school performance on highly challenging content area learning outcomes, as indicated by the Maryland School Performance Assessment Program (MSPAP)
2. Student participation data as indicated by student attendance and dropout rates
3. Supporting information not compared to a standard, such as total student enrollment, student mobility, and students receiving special services such as free and reduced lunch or Title I
4. Other factors that may influence student performance, such as staffing per 1000 students, financial information, first graders with kindergarten experience, documented postgraduation plans for high school seniors, and school improvement notes

An example of the 1996–1997 performance report card is shown in Figure 1. It shows that school performance is reported in terms of the percentages of students performing at the satisfactory and excellent levels in each of the data-based areas for which standards are set. In addition to this report, school performance is evaluated using a school performance index and a change index. These indexes combine the data elements in a manner similar to other well-known composites such as the Consumer Price Index and Dow

[4]School reconstitution—the takeover of a school by another authority—is a process rather than an event in Maryland. Takeover of a school by the local school system or the state is the last and most drastic option. It has not occurred in Maryland since the inception of MSPP in 1990. The typical process in the more than 50 reconstituted schools has involved school improvement goals and a highly visible and active role for the school improvement team, which guides strategic planning and implementation of school improvement efforts. The most drastic school reconstitutions to date have included actions like assignment of a new principal who is freed to release or retain current teachers and staff and given additional resources to hire outside consultants or additional staff (e.g., master teachers, reading specialists) and to buy equipment (e.g., computers) and materials for the school.

MARYLAND

Maryland, with a population of 4,983,900, ranks forty-second in size and nineteenth in population among the fifty states. The State Department of Education is housed in Baltimore. There are twenty-four local school systems and 1,309 public schools and centers.

STUDENT PERFORMANCE
School Year 1996-1997

ASSESSED STUDENT KNOWLEDGE

MARYLAND FUNCTIONAL TESTS — Grade 9 Status

Grade 9 Status	Standard Percent Ex	Sat	1993** Percent Passing	1996 Percent Passing	1997 Number Taking	Number Absent	Number Exempt	Percent Passing	Ex	Sat	Not Met
Reading	97	95	97.4	97.2	61,361	935	1,117	97.3	✓		
Mathematics	90	80	79.2	83.0	61,464	829	1,119	84.9		✓	✓
Writing	96	90	93.5	82.5	59,330	2,279	1,564	89.0		✓	✓
Citizenship	92	85	83.8	83.1	56,102	2,213	981	84.5		✓	✓

MARYLAND FUNCTIONAL TESTS — Grade 11 Status

Grade 11 Status	Standard Percent Ex	Sat	1991** Percent Passing	1996 Percent Passing	1997 Number Refused	Number Exempt	Percent Passing	Ex	Sat	Not Met
Reading	99	99	99.4	99.6	•	760	99.6	✓		
Mathematics	99	97	96.5	95.9	0	763	95.9		✓	✓
Writing	99	98	97.7	97.7	0	1,016	98.0		✓	✓
Citizenship	99	96	96.4	95.5	•	747	95.5		✓	
Passed All Tests	96	90	93.1	91.8	0	699	91.8		✓	✓

MARYLAND SCHOOL PERFORMANCE ASSESSMENT PROGRAM

Assessment Program	Standard Percent Ex	Sat	1993** Percent at Ex	Sat	1996 Percent at Ex	Sat	Tested	Absent/ Excused
3 Reading	25	25	—	—	4.3	35.3	56,666	2,370
3 Writing	25	25	9.2	35.1	11.8	40.9	61,025	1,695
3 Language Usage	25	25	9.0	29.4	13.4	45.2	58,193	1,577
3 Mathematics	25	25	2.1	28.6	6.0	38.7	59,707	1,907
3 Science	25	25	2.3	31.1	5.3	36.0	60,691	2,029
3 Social Studies	25	25	1.1	31.9	2.0	29.1	61,516	1,204
5 Reading	25	25	2.3	24.7	3.7	33.7	55,281	1,798
5 Writing	25	25	11.7	36.8	19.1	42.3	59,684	1,470
5 Language Usage	25	25	10.4	26.8	22.4	45.3	56,961	971
5 Mathematics	25	25	5.8	39.5	9.6	47.8	59,355	1,799
5 Science	25	25	4.0	33.3	8.1	44.8	59,134	2,020
5 Social Studies	25	25	3.0	31.3	10.0	42.8	60,201	953
8 Reading	25	25	1.2	24.6	1.6	28.6	52,608	3,848
8 Writing	25	25	9.0	36.3	15.2	43.0	—	—
8 Language Usage	25	25	8.6	36.9	16.5	52.9	53,738	3,222
8 Mathematics	25	25	4.1	35.8	8.1	43.3	55,927	2,015
8 Science	25	25	—	—	12.2	46.8	53,974	3,968
8 Social Studies	25	25	2.8	25.9	4.5	36.2	55,260	2,682

*Fewer Than 5 Students   **Indicates Baseline Year Data   KEY: Ex = Excellent,   Sat = Satisfactory

STUDENT PARTICIPATION

ATTENDANCE RATE (Yearly)

	Standard Percent Ex	Sat	1990** Percent	1996 Percent	1997 Percent	Ex	Sat	Not Met
Grades 1 - 6	96	94	94.2	95.1	95.1		✓	
Grades 7 - 12	96	94	90.1	91.4	91.4		✓	

Students Absent

	1996 Percent	1997 Percent
Fewer than 5 days	33.5	32.2
More than 20 days	13.6	13.8

DROPOUT RATE (Yearly)

	Standard Percent Ex	Sat	1990** Percent	1996 Percent	1997 Percent	Ex	Sat	Not Met
Grades 9 - 12	1.25	3.00	6.5	4.58	4.66			✓

MARYLAND SCHOOL PERFORMANCE ASSESSMENT PROGRAM — Participation

Assessment Program	1997 Number ESL Exemptions	Special Education Exemptions	Second Semester Transfers	1997 Percent at Ex	Sat	Not Met
3 Reading	1,239	4,194	500	5.0	36.8	✓✓
3 Writing	970	765	514	13.2	40.0	✓
3 Language Usage	1,261	3,434	504	20.8	49.5	✓
3 Mathematics	1,058	1,786	511	6.6	41.4	✓✓
3 Science	970	765	514	6.7	38.2	✓✓
3 Social Studies	970	765	514	3.6	35.8	✓✓
5 Reading	598	4,680	407	6.0	35.6	✓✓
5 Writing	414	773	423	18.4	39.3	✓✓
5 Language Usage	617	3,808	407	24.1	46.8	✓✓
5 Mathematics	414	773	423	11.9	48.2	✓✓
5 Science	414	773	423	9.3	46.3	✓✓
5 Social Studies	414	773	423	11.6	43.7	✓✓
8 Reading	465	2,109	426	2.9	26.3	✓
8 Writing	—	—	431	18.1	49.2	—
8 Language Usage	424	1,641	431			✓
8 Mathematics	383	694	437	9.1	45.9	✓✓
8 Science	383	694	437	13.4	45.9	✓✓
8 Social Studies	383	694	437	7.8	41.0	✓✓

8

MARYLAND SUPPORTING INFORMATION
School Year 1996-97

ENROLLMENT	1995-96	1996-97
Pre-Kindergarten	19,092	19,639
Kindergarten	63,232	61,856
Grades 1 - 6	381,463	387,851
Grades 7 - 12	328,655	335,999
Ungraded Special Education	13,102	13,238
TOTAL ENROLLMENT	805,544	818,583

STUDENT MOBILITY	1996 Number	Percent	1997 Number	Percent
Entrants	92,980	11.9	97,357	12.2
Withdrawals	97,255	12.4	101,715	12.8

STUDENTS RECEIVING SPECIAL SERVICES	1996 Number	Percent	1997 Number	Percent
Limited English Proficient	15,104	1.9	16,035	2.0
Title 1	62,125	7.7	107,457	13.1
Free/Reduced Price Meals	249,611	31.0	253,010	30.9
Special Education	96,543	12.0	99,928	12.2

OTHER FACTORS	1996	1997
Wealth per pupil	$232,924	$235,664
Per pupil expenditure	$6,337	$6,446
Instructional staff per 1,000 pupils	57.7	58.6
Professional support staff per 1,000 pupils	8.6	8.9
Instructional assistants per 1,000 pupils	9.9	10.0
Average length of school day for pupils	6.4	6.5
Length of school year for pupils	180	180

GIFTED AND TALENTED EDUCATION INFORMATION

FIRST GRADERS WITH KINDERGARTEN EXPERIENCE	1996 Number	Percent	1997 Number	Percent
	66,753	97.6	67,689	97.0

Maryland defines a gifted and talented student as an elementary or secondary student who is identified by professionally qualified individuals as having outstanding abilities in the areas of: general intellectual capabilities; specific academic aptitudes; or the creative, visual, or performing arts. Gifted and talented students need services in addition to those normally provided by the regular school program in order to develop their potential. Gifted and talented information for each local school system is listed on the following pages of this report.

HIGH SCHOOL PROGRAM COMPLETION	1997 Number	Percent
Maryland High School Certificate	509	1.2
Maryland High School Diploma	42,856	98.8
Students with Maryland High School Diploma who met:		
a. University System of Maryland Course Requirements	23,695	53.1
b. Career and Technology Education Program Requirements	6,384	14.3
c. Both University and Career/Technology Requirements	2,417	5.4
d. Rigorous High School Program Indicators	8,677	19.5
e. One or more of Categories a, b, c, or d	32,904	73.8

GRADE 12 DOCUMENTED DECISIONS TO:	1996 Percent	1997 Number	Percent
Attend a four year college	42.9	17,266	43.8
Attend a two year college	17.1	6,870	17.4
Attend a specialized school or specialized training	2.5	1,067	2.7
Enter employment (related to high school program)	4.0	1,636	4.2
Enter employment (unrelated to high school program)	8.5	3,089	7.8
Enter the military	3.8	1,504	3.8
Enter full-time employment and school	3.7	1,297	3.3
Enter part-time employment and/or school	11.9	4,599	11.7
Other and no response	5.7	2,092	5.3

School Improvement Notes

Maryland's Student Performance results are aggregates of the twenty-four local school systems' results. Overall, satisfactory standards were met for: Maryland Functional Tests—grade 9 in mathematics and grade 11 in writing and passed all tests; and student attendance in grades 1-6. Excellent standards were met for: Maryland Functional Tests—grades 9 and 11 in reading. We did not meet the satisfactory standards for: writing and citizenship in grade 9, mathematics and citizenship in grade 11, student attendance in grades 7-12, dropouts, and all grades and subject areas in the Maryland School Performance Assessment Program (MSPAP). In the MSPAP, our scores decreased in grades 3 and 5 in writing, and in grade 8 in reading, language usage, and science; however, our scores increased in twelve of the eighteen areas assessed. We will continue to work with local school systems to improve the quality of instruction to move us to our goal of achieving all standards.

FIGURE 1

The 1996–1997 Maryland school performance report card pages. Source: Maryland State Department of Education, (1997). (*Maryland school performance report, 1997.*) Baltimore, MD: Author.

Jones Industrial Average. The school performance index includes all elements for which the state has determined standards. Therefore, the school performance index includes the following areas (which differ depending on the grade levels included in a school):

1. Student mastery of basic skills, as indicated by the Maryland Functional Testing Program
2. School performance on highly challenging content area learning outcomes, as indicated by the Maryland School Performance Assessment Program
3. student attendance
4. student retention, as indicated by dropout rates (high schools only)

School awards and sanctions are based on changes in the school-change index over 3 years.

Maryland School Performance Assessment Program

The Maryland School Performance Assessment Program (MSPAP) results are reported as percentages of students in each school who have performed at or above the satisfactory and excellent levels in reading, writing, language usage, mathematics, science, and social studies (see Figure 1). MSPAP results are perhaps the most salient of the elements in the Maryland School Performance report and are featured prominently each year when the report is released in a large press conference. Certainly they are a primary focus of the elementary and middle school administrators and faculty who are actively striving to meet state standards for satisfactory school performance.[5] Improvement at the state level in school performance on MSPAP and the composite performance index has been incremental. This incremental growth has helped the state board of education withstand criticisms of the fairness of the standards and challenges in the legislature. Although desired by many reformers, rapid increases in MSPAP scores would likely raise suspicions about the rigor of the standards. Lack of incremental growth would likely raise cries about their fairness and appropriateness. Incremental, and sometimes rapid, growth in MSPAP scores in schools that have focused a great deal of energy on improving performance has also lent some credibility to the MSPAP standards.

Maryland High School Assessment Program

During the 1990s, observers and critics of educational reform began to express concerns about the content standards that formed the basis for reform.

[5]Schools in which 70% or more of students achieve the satisfactory level in an MSPAP content area meet the satisfactory school performance standard for that content area. School performance standards are the same in all six MSPAP content areas.

For example, the Maryland Learning Outcomes have been criticized as merely process goals (i.e., reflecting only procedural knowledge) without content (i.e., declarative knowledge) specified. Critics borrowed from a popular TV commercial for a fast-food hamburger chain to complain, "Where's the beef?" Though often tacitly acknowledged as rigorous learning goals, the Maryland Learning Outcomes were explicitly criticized as too fuzzy and too vague to guide teachers on what to teach (e.g., American Federation of Teachers, 1995; "Quality Counts," 1997). These first reviews of the standards for what should be taught seemed consonant with Hirsch's notion of cultural literacy (1987). Related criticisms of performance-based assessments pointed to scoring and other technical problems, complicated logistics and operational problems, and relatively high dollar and administration costs in relation to traditional norm-referenced testing programs. Critics cited the demise of the California Learning Assessment System (CLAS) and of new standards-based performance assessments in Arizona, Colorado, Indiana, and elsewhere. They cited some early and well-publicized problems with Vermont's writing and mathematics portfolio assessment system. The policy response around the United States was to feature declarative knowledge in content standards and to include multiple-choice items along with constructed response items in new assessments. Examples include recent editions of norm-referenced tests from the commercial test publishers, the National Assessment of Educational Progress (NAEP), and the proposed Voluntary National Tests in Grade 4 reading and Grade 8 mathematics. In response to these criticisms the Maryland State Department of Education moved in 1998 to refine the Maryland Learning Outcomes by making content knowledge more explicit; in 1996 it decided to include both multiple-choice and constructed response items in the new high school assessment system, which will be implemented as a high school graduation requirement for the class of 2004.

LOCAL USE OF DATA FROM THE MARYLAND SCHOOL PERFORMANCE PROGRAM

Maryland School Performance Program (MSPP) data shape but do not fully define school improvement plans and activities. As noted earlier, the Maryland report card lists the percentages of students in a school who have met the state standards for satisfactory or excellent performance. Schools are expected to reach these standards by the year 2000. This section examines a Maryland elementary school's use of data in its efforts to improve its performance and reach the MSPP satisfactory goals. The section begins, though, with some details on the Maryland School Performance Assessment Program (MSPAP) to aid understanding of Maryland's school improvement technology.

Background on MSPP and MSPAP

The Maryland School Performance Program (MSPP) was created as a school accountability and school improvement program. As part of the accountability system, the performance of schools, local school systems, and the state are compared to the state standards for satisfactory and excellent performance in assessed student knowledge and participation. The results for the accountability portion of the program are used to produce the school performance index and change index. The Maryland State Department of Education provides schools with specific information on student outcome performance from MSPAP. Maryland outcomes are defined subsets of a larger content area—such as geometry, which is an outcome within mathematics. This information, along with other local information (e.g., local assessment information or teacher comments or logs), is intended to help guide school improvement planning. The reports do not provide solutions for school improvement but highlight areas of strengths and needs.

MSPAP is a criterion-referenced performance assessment based on the Maryland Learning Outcomes in reading, writing, language usage, mathematics, science, and social studies. The tests are administered in May for approximately 9 hours in 5 days to all third-, fifth-, and eighth-grade students. Students are not tested in their classrooms, but they are randomly assigned to testing groups that take different test forms. There are three new test forms per grade per year and one equating form that had been used the previous year administered. These nonparallel test forms assess different portions of each content area through matrix sampling. In other words, the content areas are distributed throughout the different test forms.

MSPAP results include scale scores for each content area. These scale scores range from 350 to 700 with a mean of 500 and a standard deviation of about 50. Scale scores from the same grade level and content area have the same meaning and can be compared from year to year. However, scale scores across grade levels are not comparable. The scale score ranges for each content area are divided into proficiency levels. There are usually five proficiency levels, 1–5. For students, satisfactory performance is defined as performance at Level 3; and excellent performance is defined as Levels 1 or 2. Schools and systems with 70% or more of their students at Level 3 are considered satisfactory. Schools and local systems with 70% or more of their students at Level 3 and 25% or more of their students at or above Level 2 are considered excellent.

Each content area includes learning outcomes. For example reading includes three measured outcomes: reading for literacy experience, reading for information, and reading to perform a task. The Maryland State Department of Education (MSDE) also reports outcome scores, which are estimated scores. Using the subset of items a student took in an outcome, the outcome score indicates how they would have scored had they taken the entire domain of items within a given outcome. Because outcome scores are not comparable from year to year, outcome scale scores are also calculated. They are expressed on the same scale as the content scale scores.

Information Yielded by MSPAP

MSDE provides several reports to schools and school districts: the Standards Report, which is for school accountability; the Proficiency Level and Participation Report, for accountability and improvement; the Outcome Score Report, for school improvement; and the Outcome Scale Score Reports, for school improvement. According to Beverly Pish, test development specialist for Prince George's county public schools, schools that use their data to inform school improvement activities achieve growth, although slow, in their MSPAP scores and confidence in their ability to improve student learning (personal communication, January 18, 1998). Prince George's County, in conjunction with MSDE, has created worksheets for school improvement teams to highlight instructional targets, refine instruction, and enhance professional development activities. These worksheets, specific for MSPAP data, are included in Figures 2 and 3.

Figure 2 is the worksheet for the Standards Report and the Proficiency Level and Participation Report. This worksheet helps school improvement teams know in which content areas their students are performing well or poorly. Because the content areas are broad, another worksheet, Figure 3, was created to aid in the determination of specific outcomes within a content area on which a school can focus its school improvement efforts. This worksheet focuses on the Outcome Score and Outcome Scale Score reports. It also prompts school improvement teams to rank each outcome as a short-term or long-term goal for the school. These worksheets include only MSPAP score report information. To create targets for the school, the improvement team should incorporate the data from the worksheets with other information, such as other test results, participation information, and teacher comments.

MSDE describes a process for school improvement in the *Score Interpretation Guide* (MSDE, 1996). First the school improvement team needs to gather available information on school performance and student learning, including student grades, school or student assessment information, and what teachers know about their students. If information exists about the implementation of new instructional programs, that should be used as well. School administrators and faculties need to review the learning outcomes or standards in the grade level(s) and content(s) of interest, such as reading. It is not uncommon that educators know the names of the outcomes but do not define the outcomes as MSDE does. Once everyone has a shared understanding of what the learning outcomes include, teachers need to verify that the outcomes or standards are included in everyday curriculum materials and instructional programs throughout the school. Outcomes and standards

**WORKSHEET FOR THE MSPAP STANDARDS REPORT
AND THE PROFICIENCY LEVEL AND PARTICIPATION REPORT**

This worksheet should aid you in understanding the information located on the Standards Report and the Proficiency Level and Participation Report. Additionally, this information can be used to set short-term and long-term goals for your school which should relate to your students' achievement and participation.

Standards Report

Content Area:	Percent at/above Satisfactory [1]	Percent at/above Excellent [2]

Note 1:   To meet the Satisfactory standard, 70% of the students in a grade must score at proficiency levels 1, 2, or 3.

Note 2:   To meet the Excellent standard, 70% of the students in a grade must score at proficiency levels 1, 2, or 3 and 25% of these students must score in proficiency levels 1 or 2.

The satisfactory percentages in the Standards Report are calculated by dividing the total number of students scoring at or above level 3 by the total number of students tested added to the number of student absent/excused.

$$\frac{\text{number of students scoring at or above level 3}}{\text{number of students tested + number of students absent/excused}}$$

The excellent percentages in the Standards Report are calculated by dividing the total number of students scoring at or above level 2 by the total number of students tested added to the number of student absent/excused.

$$\frac{\text{number of students scoring at or above level 2}}{\text{number of students tested + number of students absent/excused}}$$

Proficiency Level and Participation Report

	Number	Percent
Level 1		
Level 2		
Level 3		
Total at/above Satisfactory		
Level 4		
Level 5		
Total at Levels 4 and 5		

FIGURE 2

Worksheet for the MSPAP standards report and the proficiency level and participation report. Source: Maryland State Department of Education. (1996). (*Score interpretation guide.*) Baltimore, MD: Author.

Eligible Takers

Using the information from both the Standards Report and the Proficiency Level and Participation Report, you can determine how many more students must achieve level 3 for your school to reach the satisfactory standard. Fill in your data below.

Note: This worksheet assumes that the results from the previous year will be the starting point for next year. It also assumes linear growth within an area.

Step 1: Number of students tested   _____

Step 2: Number of students absent/excused   _____

Step 3: Total of Steps 1 and 2   _____

Step 4: Number of students needed to meet the
satisfactory standard   _____
        To calculate take Step 3 and multiply by 0.70 *

Step 5: Number of students at/above the satisfactory standard   _____

Step 6: Number of eligible students needed to meet the
satisfactory standard   _____
        To calculate subtract Step 5 from Step 4

Step 7: Number of remaining MSPAP administrations before the   _____
year 2000

Step 8: Divide the number of students in Step 6 by the number   _____
of years in Step 7
        This number represents the number of students
        you need to move into proficiency level 3 to reach
        the satisfactory standard by the year 2000.

*: 0.70 is the proportion of students needed to be at proficiency levels 1, 2, or 3 to meet the satisfactory requirement.

Issues for Consideration

Using the Standards Report, what are your strongest and weakest areas in terms of the percentages of students are satisfactory?

What is the distribution of students on the Proficiency Level and Participation Report for each content area?

Review the number of additional students your school needs to meet the satisfactory requirement? How many students are in Proficiency Level 4? Were there many students who were absent or excused? (Remember that not all of the absent students will be in Level 3.)

FIGURE 2 (*Continued*)

that are not adequately covered can become targets for instruction and learning.

To determine additional targets using the worksheets or another process, the data from the MSPAP reports can be used to identify the learning outcomes in which students are more or less successful. These reports identify where students are in terms of proficiency levels. Another strategy for determining learning targets includes reviewing the descriptions of what stu-

1996 Worksheet for the Outcome Score and Outcome Scale Score Reports Grade 3

The information below should help you understand the information on the Outcome Score (OS) and the Outcome Scale Score (OSS) Reports. Additionally, it can highlight the relationships between these reports.

School: Elementary   Grade: 03

CONTENT AREA DOMAIN	I Within 10 points of next lower level			Proficiency Level 3 Cut-Off Score*	I Within 10 points of next higher level		Rank: short-term or long-term goal?
	From the OS: % in 0-25	From the OS: % in 26-50	From the OSS: MDN (Median Score)		Distance from Proficiency level (+or-)	Proficiency Level of Median score*	
Reading							
For Literary Experience				530			
To Be Informed				530			
To Perform A Task				530			
Writing							
To Inform				528			
To Persuade				528			
To Express Personal Ideas				528			
Language Usage							
Language In Use				521			
Mathematics							
Problem Solving				531			
Communication				531			
Reasoning				531			
Connections				531			
Number Concepts and Relationships				531			
Measurement / Geometry				531			
Statistics				531			
Probability				531			
Patterns and Relationships				531			
Science							
Concepts of Science				527			
Nature of Science				527			
Habits of Mind				527			
Processes of Science				527			
Applications of Science				527			
Social Studies							
Political Systems				525			
Peoples of the Nation & World				525			
Geography				525			
Economics				525			
Skills and Processes				525			
Valuing Self and Others				525			
Understandings and Attitudes				525			

*Score Interpretation Guide   1996 MSPAP and Beyond   Table 1

This form developed in conjunction with Dr. Hillary Michaels, MSDE and Prince George's County public schools.

FIGURE 3

Worksheet for the 1996 outcome score and outcome scale score reports for Grade 3. Source: Maryland State Department of Education. (1996). (*Score interpretation guide.*) Baltimore, MD: Author.

dents at each of the proficiency level know and can do. Using these descriptions, teachers can focus on what skills and knowledge are needed to move students from lower proficiency levels to higher ones.

Once learning targets have been established, they need to be prioritized. Some schools have prioritized their targets by the areas of greatest need as determined by data reports and teacher input. After establishing priorities and determining resources that may be needed to help meet them, these instructional materials and activities need to be incorporated as part of daily classroom activities. Schools need to monitor student progress on the outcomes and standards that have been targeted. This monitoring will help school administrators and teachers refine classroom activities as the school year progresses.

Discrepancies between the State's Plan and School Plan

The plan that MSDE produces works well up to the point of defining what schools should examine or set as instructional targets. However, these steps fail to acknowledge the cyclical nature of school improvement. Steps dealing with implementation plans and evaluation should be included (Johnson, 1996), not just monitoring student progress. Ideally a school would determine a school plan, implement the plan, and then evaluate it. By doing this, the staff could then take ownership of the data and plan. In other words, all staff members would understand the data and agree with the plan goals. However, the data that schools and local districts collect or receive are often perceived to be for someone else's purposes or do not match with local educational goals (Levesque, Bradby, & Rossi, 1996).

Previous sections have identified steps that schools use or modify when creating an informed decision based on their data. What follows is an example of how one school uses the data forms and steps outlined earlier to inform its school improvement process.

Kenilworth Elementary School: An Example of a School's Use of Data

Kenilworth School, a comprehensive elementary school in Maryland, has been using data to inform its instructional decisions for several years. Key features of the process that Kenilworth uses include timely use of data, sustained staff development, and multi-grade-level school improvement teams.

Beginning each December with the release of MSPAP data, school staff prioritize educational indicators, such as learning outcomes or student participation. Many other schools in the district create plans during the summer because Prince George's County public school district requires schools to submit their plans by July. However, the Kenilworth staff members prefer to adjust teaching according to their most recent data; therefore, the Kenilworth school improvement plan is completed by February. Multi-grade-level teams review the data reports produced by the state and incorporate what they know about their students from their experience and from that of the supplemental services team (T. Scherr, assistant principal Kenilworth Elementary School, personal communication, March 5, 1998). By using multi-grade-level teams and culminating in a vote, the staff decides whether to accept the school improvement plan. Thus, the entire school staff recognizes its responsibility to and ownership of the plan.

Table 1 presents part of the Kenilworth school improvement plan for the 1997–1998 school year. Objectives, strategies, milestones, and evaluation are identified in the plan for each targeted area. This global plan guides the more specific actions that are determined by content area groups in their planning meetings.

In these planning meetings, teams identify and define targets, such as the science outcome concepts of science, using the overall school improvement plans (see Table 1) and data worksheets (see Table 2). In planning meetings, the teams identify and define targets. Working through the School Based Management Worksheet, the staff members discuss ways to meet targets by generating sample scenarios and ways to apply the learning targets in their classes. In doing so, the team reflects on resources and materials that may be needed to enhance staff or student knowledge. The last step includes creating a sequential plan for kindergarten through sixth grades. For example, the 1998 science plan includes the following:

> To correct the big gap in understanding of science, each teacher of science (K–6) will keep an ongoing Science Fair backboard or bulletin board with the appropriate headings to use for completed investigations. These headings are Question, Hypothesis, Materials, Procedure (independent, dependent, and controlled variables), Results (with graphs), and Conclusion.

To aid in meeting a targeted goal, the school improvement plan includes staff development. The staff development calendar typically includes seven events per month. Teachers are encouraged to attend the activities ranging from literacy workshops and portfolio classes to health workshops. By obtaining additional funding from the county and other sources, Kenilworth purchases resources and provides in-service opportunities for teachers. Teachers are given release time or are reimbursed for working outside of the school day to accommodate this ongoing staff development.

Attention to data has helped Kenilworth meet its school improvement goals. The school now has the highest composite score of all the elementary schools in Prince George's County. Since 1994 the Kenilworth Elementary School composite has risen from 39.7 to 70.8. In a newspaper account of Prince George's County's MSPAP results, Kenilworth principal, Richard Melzer, commented that the three best things Kenilworth has going for it are "excellent students, supportive parents, and a wonderful staff" (Frazier, 1997, p. Md. 9). In addition, Melzer noted that the school analyzes its data to develop school improvement plans and to determine areas of focus. Kenilworth Elementary School was used as an example of how one school has made informed decisions using data and has therefore sustained consistent growth.

TABLE 1

Excerpt from the Kenilworth Elementary School's Improvement Plan for Science

Objective	Strategies/activities	Person(s) responsible	Milestones	Evaluation
By June 1998, the percent of students achieving satisfactory or higher on the MSPAP science test for grade 3 will meet or exceed 50% and for grade 5 will meet or exceed 66.7%.	1. Improve *Habits of Mind* by providing students with the opportunity to • recognize and design a fair test in order to collect valid data during scientific experiments. • develop a set of procedures to test hypotheses. • use quantitative measurement to gather data (rulers, clocks, scales, etc.) • utilize supporting evidence in order to justify a conclusion. • recognize that a conclusion must answer the question. • demonstrate an awareness that the results collected from a scientific investigation may change prior ideas.	Principal, EIA, science chairperson, instructional staff	1. At the end of the second quarter, 40% of grade 3 and grade 5 students will score at the satisfactory level or higher on a school selected science performance assessment (Science Plus), which measures outcomes taught to date.	1. The 1998 MSPAP Report will document the percent of students who scored at or above proficiency level 3 on the MSPAP assessment as follows: Grade 3 Science: 47.4% Grade 5 Science: 66.7%

TABLE 2

Excerpt from the Kenilworth Elementary School's 1997 Worksheet for the Outcome Score and Outcome Scale Score Reports for Grade 5 Science

Content area/ domain	From the OS: % in 0–25	From the OS: % in 26–50	From the OSS: Median score	Proficiency level 3 cutoff score	Distance from PL 3 (+ or −)	PL of median score	Rank: Short-term or long-term goal?
Concepts of Science	2.3	46.5	541	525	+16	3	1
Nature of Science	19.8	34.9	553	525	+28	3	3
Habits of Mind	18.6	27.9	562	525	+37	3	5
Processes of Science	8.1	36.0	553	525	+28	3	4
Applications of Science	14.0	23.3	554	525	+24	3	2

Notes: OS: Outcome Score Report; OSS: Outcome Scale Score Report; PL: Proficiency Level.
Proficiency Level 3 cutoff scores begin the range for the satisfactory proficiency level.

ISSUES IN DATA USE AND INTERPRETATION

Data obtained from the Maryland Functional Testing Program and the Maryland School Performance Assessment Program serve as influential factors in shaping Maryland's educational policy. When using assessments to modify classroom practice, Cuban (1991) and others have warned of restricting the curriculum, in particular neglecting untested curriculum such as the arts. The result of the Functional Testing Program was a narrowing of the curriculum (Wilson & Corbett, 1991). One of the purposes of MSPAP was to broaden the curriculum by including authentic, integrated assessment items and focusing on application of knowledge and skills. MSDE would like teachers to focus instruction on the Maryland Learning Outcomes and performance-based activities like those in MSPAP. By teaching to MSPAP, teachers equip students with knowledge and skills that can be applied in everyday situations.

Even though the state collects data on participation, student characteristics, and supporting information, student achievement is most heavily weighted when determining school performance on the standards. Therefore, it is relevant that the public believes that student achievement is paramount to judging a school. More important, the assessments must be seen as valid indicators of student and school achievement. If the indicators are not trusted, then the data will no longer have meaning in the process of information school reform. However, because the tests are so important, the possibility of test score pollution always exists (Cuban, 1991).

Test score pollution causes test scores to lose their meaning. This can occur with standardized norm-referenced tests when teachers instruct students on test items or analogies. For example, teachers may reinforce or teach the capitalization of proper nouns, such as New Year's Day, just before the standardized norm-referenced test is given. Test score pollution can occur with assessments such as MSPAP as well. Instead of explaining to students why it is important to label all parts of a graph, teachers may just require this when doing MSPAP type items. Another type of test score pollution is cheating. Policies have been implemented by which MSDE determines which schools may be investigated for cheating and how the investigation will proceed (e.g., Ferrara, 1997).

MSPP has enjoyed the support of the Maryland State Teacher's Association. According to a recent survey, 60% of the responding teachers supported MSPAP and 83% believed that it is moving schools in the direction that they should be going (R. A. Peiffer, assistant state superintendent, School and Community Outreach Office, Maryland State Department of Education, personal communication, February 26, 1998). Moreover interviews of principals about accountability in their states revealed that they believe "performance assessments are beneficial to reform; they model good instruction, draw attention to standards and outcomes, and provide data for school improvement" (Mitchell, 1997, p. 264).

Other researchers provide cautions about data misinterpretation or manipulation (e.g., Jaeger & Hattie, 1996; Mehrens & Kaminski, 1989). Jaeger and Hattie described different ways in which data can be manipulated. In one example, they examine levels of per-pupil expenditure compared to the performance of nations on international assessments, state ranks on an eighth-grade NAEP mathematics assessment, and the average eighth-grade student's NAEP mathematics scores within a state. They found that even if a relationship existed at one level of analysis (e.g., state NAEP rankings and per-pupil expenditures), one should not assume that this relationship generalizes to other levels of analyses (e.g., students and per-pupil expenditures). To make sound decisions using data, the nature of the data must be understood. Otherwise, policy makers and others can misinterpret data or incorrectly manipulate the numbers.

When using assessment to inform policy decisions or school improvement plans, careful attention to what the assessment domain includes is helpful in making inferences from the data. As Mehrens and Kaminski (1989) have pointed out, once a test score has been created, there is a tendency to over interpret what the score means. Therefore, policy makers need to be careful when they use data to support their decisions, or the data may be interpreted to support erroneously a point of view. An erroneous decision may negatively influence what students are learning and the manner in which they are presented information. Policy makers and local school personnel also need to be careful to not create policies out of anecdotal evidence, but rather to use credible data in a systematic manner.

SOME SPECULATIONS ABOUT THE FUTURE OF DATA-BASED DECISION MAKING

Conventional wisdom in the social sciences suggests that the best predictor of future performance is past performance. We have already made a similar assertion by suggesting that each subsequent phase of educational reform in Maryland evolved from earlier phases. The first three evolutionary phases of educational reform in Maryland suggest the outline of future phases. This prediction assumes that no unanticipated events (e.g., sharp economic downturns, political shifts, operational errors) will cause rapid evolution or even sudden, catastrophic change in the evolutionary process.

Scenario 1: Sustained School Improvement Efforts and Stable Reform Policy

Perhaps the most likely scenario for the next 5 to 10 years of educational reform policy in Maryland involves continuing incremental growth in MSPAP scores and school composite indexes and sustained efforts to meet the current standards for satisfactory and excellent school performance. Political opponents of the current reform policy would find little ammunition for mounting successful attacks in this scenario. However, continuing refinements to current policy to account for emerging issues are expected. For example, in 1996 Maryland's governor, Parris Glendening, allocated several million dollars to provide awards for improving schools. Other possible adjustments might include adding other school performance indicators to the school report card and composite index (e.g., as is planned for the new high school assessments) and shifting or increasing funding for schools that are not improving despite reasonable efforts. In addition, refinements to MSPAP and the report card should be expected if a perception develops that growth in MSPAP scores represents test score inflation rather than real growth in student learning and real school improvement. Finally, year-to-year changes in test and composite index scores tend to be somewhat chaotic. Even when the general trend is upward over several years, results tend to fluctuate up and down by several percentage points each year and may exhibit upward or downward spikes (i.e., an occasional sharp rise or decline of 5 to 10 or more percentage points). Erratic changes within a general trend are especially prevalent for individual schools and small school systems because of percentages calculated using small numbers of students.

We might also anticipate initial pass rates in the new high school assessment program to be similar to those of the Maryland Accountability Testing Program, Functional Testing Program, and School Performance Assessment Program. It is reasonable to expect initial pass rates on these new, rigorous end-of-course examinations to be fairly low (e.g., around 50%) in the first years of implementation. Subsequently, we might expect incremental growth in percentages of students who pass the tests the first time they take them. However, because these exams will be used to make decisions about conferring and denying diplomas, it is also likely that passing standards set in the first years of the program will be low enough for larger percentages of students to pass the exams on first try (i.e., perhaps 80 to 90%) and that passing standards would be ratcheted up in subsequent years. Also, based on history in Maryland and elsewhere, we might expect pass rates of disadvantaged subgroups (e.g., students in low socioeconomic status neighborhoods) to be considerably lower than pass rates of other students.[6] Adjustments can be expected to the high school examinations, the content objectives they assess,

[6]It is likely that policy makers and advocacy groups will continue to focus on substantial test performance differences between white and minority students. In fact, it is often the case that performance differences can be demonstrated for low versus high socioeconomic status students, independent of race/ethnicity. For example, we have shown that subgroup performance differences are as high when comparing high and low SES subgroups that include white, African American, and Hispanic students as when comparing white and minority student subgroups (see Ferrara & Michaels, 1994; Michaels & Ferrara, 1995).

or passing standards as such results emerge and debate begins. In the end, incremental improvement is likely to be accompanied by incremental changes in reform policy. Of course, unexpected events could result in accelerated evolution or even radical revisions to Maryland's educational reform efforts.

Scenario 2: Catastrophe and Policy Changes

Of course, an unanticipated "catastrophe" (see Brown, 1995) could cause a sudden shift in the evolution of Maryland's educational reform policy. For example, the successful launch of the *Sputnik* satellite on October 4, 1957, by the Soviet Union has been identified as a force that launched the U.S. space program and as an influence to increase federal aid to education and development of new mathematics and science curricula. Likewise, years of increases in federal, state, and local spending on education along with economic inflation, set the stage for state and local tax caps in the later 1970s. These caps limited local education spending (e.g., Proposition 2½ in California, Proposition 13 in Massachusetts). It seems plausible that changes in political priorities could pave the way for passage of federal and state legislation to reduce education spending and government influence on state education reform policy.

Operational errors in state assessment programs or in implementing educational reform policies could lead to "catastrophic" changes in education reform policy. Operational errors in complex assessment programs like MSPAP and implementation errors in high-stakes accountability and reform programs like MSPP are always a possibility. The 1986 NAEP reading anomaly (Beaton & Zwick, 1990) illustrates the considerable disruption caused by contained errors. This anomaly did not cause permanent damage to NAEP. In fact, the forthright and competent manner in which it was discovered, disclosed, researched, and adjusted for may have actually strengthened NAEP quality control and credibility. Likewise, small equating anomalies in the 1993 MSPAP results required suppressing results for Grade 3 reading and Grade 8 science. These anomalies did not permanently damage MSPAP; however, small anomalies or errors in more volatile political environments have been more damaging. For example, an equating error in the Kentucky assessment program in 1997 was damaging enough to lead to cancellation of a multiyear contract for operating the testing program.

Multiple or particularly egregious errors in a politically volatile environment could have a catastrophic effect on educational reform policy. The evolution of California's reform efforts is a case in point. The California Learning Assessment System (CLAS) of the early 1990s included high-stakes assessments that were designed to guide and goad educational reform. A combination of errors in the first statewide field test of CLAS led to its demise. Some of these errors included problems with accurate scoring of open-ended items, cost overruns for scoring tests of all students in all schools, errors in reporting school scores when these reports were based on random samples of enrolled students, inclusion of controversial and questionable reading selections, and advocacy of whole language approaches to teaching and assessing reading to the exclusion of phonics and other word-analysis skills. CLAS and the accompanying reform policy were replaced by a more conservative state-testing program. Although one might not anticipate any of these "catastrophic" policy changes or errors in Maryland, the fact that they have occurred elsewhere in the past suggests that they could occur in Maryland as well.

CONCLUSION

This chapter demonstrated how high-quality data can be useful to many audiences. With assessments being legislated to determine what occurs in schools, policy makers need valid information to determine what is resulting from their policies. Additionally, valid data should be used to appraise what changes are taking place as a result of the assessment policy. Used judiciously, data can also be used to help guide what should be happening in classrooms, local school districts, and states.

Caution needs to be taken when interpreting data because, as Mehrens and Kaminski (1989) and Jaeger and Hattie (1996) have pointed out, erroneous data interpretation may lead to incorrect conclusions. Some educational policy makers, reformers, and observers are anxious to see immediate improvements in student achievement as a results of reform efforts. They may seek out and publicize analyses and data that can accelerate and expand the rate and extent of change in educational practice and performance. So long as the interpretations that are made accurately reflect any data constraints, publicizing results is not necessarily wrong.

What is probably not clear to policy makers and the general public is that discrepancies among various assessment results may be logical, even though they may seem anomalous. However, explanations of differences in Maryland's performance on MSPAP, state NAEP, and commercial norm-referenced tests due to differences in test items and specifications, motivational conditions, and test performance standards will not be persuasive. If the U.S. Congress approves continuation beyond 1998 of the Voluntary National Tests in Grade 4 reading and Grade 8 mathematics, this dilemma may be further exacerbated.

However, interpreted appropriately, data can be a powerful tool in informing policy and change. Just as data were used in the creation of the Maryland's current assessment system, data are being used in schools to bring instructional practices and curriculum more in line with school assessments and philosophies. Used in this manner, data aid to inform practices that can increase student learning and preparation for future participation in an informed and productive society.

References

American Federation of Teachers. (1995). *Making standards matter: A fifty state progress report on efforts to raise academic standards.* Washington, DC: Author.

Beaton, A. E., & Zwick, R. (1990). *Disentangling the NAEP 1985–86 reading anomaly.* (No. 15-TR-21) Princeton, NJ: Educational Testing Service.

Brown, C. (1995). *Chaos and catastrophe theories.* Thousand Oaks, CA: Sage.

Cannell, J. J. (1987). *Nationally normed elementary achievement testing in America's public schools: How all fifty states are above the national average.* Daniels, WV: Friends for Education.

Commission on School Performance. (1989). *Report of the Governor's Commission on School Performance.* Available from the Maryland State Department of Education, Baltimore, MD.

Cuban, L. (1991). *The misuse of tests in education.* Washington, DC: Office of Technology Assessment. (ERIC Document Reproduction Services No. ED 340 780).

Ferrara, S. (1997). *Test security issues for high stakes performance assessments: Consideration of ethics, validity, and data integrity.* Invited symposium presentation at the annual meeting of the National Council on Measurement in Education, Chicago. IL.

Ferrara, S., & Michaels, H. R. (1994, June). *A preliminary study of black–white performance differences in the Maryland School Performance Assessment Program.* Presentation at the National Conference on Large Scale Assessment, Albuquerque, NM.

Ferrara, S., Willhoft, J., Seburn, C., Slaughter, F., & Stevenson, J. (1991). Local assessments designed to parallel statewide minimum competency tests: Benefits and drawbacks. In R. Stake & R. O'Sullivan (Eds.), *Advances in program evaluation: Vol. 1. Effects of mandated assessment on teaching.* Greenwich, CT: JAI Press.

Flesch, R. F. (1955). *Why Johnny can't read and what you can do about it.* New York: Harper.

Frazier, L. (1997, December 18). County's schools are near bottom on state tests. *The Washington Post*, Md. 1, 9.

Henry, M. (1987, June 22). A true test or a trivia game? *Newsweek*, pp. 10, 11.

Hirsche, E. D., Jr. (1987). *Cultural literacy: What every American needs to know.* Boston: Houghton Mifflin.

Jaeger, R. M., & Hattie, J. A. (1996). Artifact and artifice in education policy analysis: It's not all in the data. *The School Administrator, 53*, 24–29.

Johnson, J. H. (1996, May). *Data-driven school improvement.* Eugene, OR: Oregon School Study Council.

Levesque, K., Bradby, D., & Rossi, K. (1996). *Using data for program improvement: How do we encourage schools to do it?* Washington, DC: Office of Vocational and Adult Education. (ERIC Document Reproduction Services No. ED 392 983).

Maryland State Department of Education. (1996). *Score interpretation guide.* Baltimore, MD: Author.

Maryland State Department of Education. (1997). *Maryland school performance report, 1997.* Baltimore, MD: Author.

Marzano, R. J., & Kendall, J. S. (1996). *A comprehensive guide to designing standards-based districts, schools, and classrooms.* Alexandria, VA: Assocaition for Supervision and Curriculum Development.

Mehrens, W. A., & Kaminski, J. (1989). Methods for improving standardized test scores: Fruitful, fruitless, or fraudulent. *Educational Measurement: Issues and Practices*, pp. 14–22.

Michaels, H., & Ferrara, S. (1995, April). *Minority/majority performance differences on Maryland's performance assessment.* Invited symposium presentation at the annual meeting of the American Educational Research Association, San Francisco.

Mitchell, K. (1997). What happens when school reform and accountability testing meet? *Theory into Practice*, 36, 262–265.

National Commission on Excellence in Education. (1983). *A nation at risk: The imperative for educational reform*. Washington, DC: U.S. Government Printing Office.

National Education Goals Panel. (1991). *The national education goals report: Building a nation of learners*. Washington, DC, Author.

Northwest Regional Educational Laboratory. (1995, May). *Profiling handbook*. Portland, OR: Author.

Popham, W. J. (1987). The merits of measurement-driven instruction. *Phi Delta Kappan*, 68, 679–682.

Quality Counts. (1997, January 22). *Education Week*.

Ravitch, D. (1995). *National standards in American education: A citizen's guide*. Washington, DC: Brookings Institution.

Secretary's Commission on Achieving Necessary Skills (SCANS). (1991). *What work requires of schools: A SCANS report for America 2000*. Washington, DC: U.S. Government Printing Office.

Shepard, L. (1993). *Setting performance standards for student achievement*. Stanford, CA: National Academy of Education, Stanford University.

Wilson, B. L., & Corbett, H. D. (1991). *Two state minimum competency testing programs and their effects on curriculum and instruction*. Washington, DC: Office of Educational Research and Improvement. (ERIC Document Reproduction Services No. ED 377 251).

CHAPTER

6

Michigan: The State of Education Reform

JOHN ENGLER AND GLEAVES WHITNEY
Office of the Governor

It has been quipped that the United States has an established church—it is called public education. Certainly the quip applies to Michigan, as much in the 1990s as at the state's origin 2 centuries ago. The most famous provision of the Northwest Ordinance of 1787, which provided the legal framework for the territory that would become Michigan, underscored the importance of education in building up the new nation: "Religion, morality, and knowledge being necessary to good government and the happiness of mankind, schools and the means of education shall forever be encouraged."

This statement was reaffirmed, word for word, at the constitutional convention that crafted the state's current constitution of 1963. Article VIII, Section 1 of the constitution of the state of Michigan lifts verbatim the language of the Northwest Ordinance. Further, Section 2 states: "The legislature shall maintain and support a system of free public elementary and secondary schools as defined by law. Every school district shall provide for the education of its pupils without discrimination as to religion, creed, race, color, or national origin."

During the 1990s, Michigan has amply met its constitutional obligation to education. Public schools have not just been encouraged; they have been robustly supported. Funding is at an all-time high—more than $11.8 billion—which represents a 50% increase since 1991. Inflation during the same period has been 28%. Average per-pupil spending for the 1998–1999 school year was projected at $5462. Truly this represents a world-class level of commitment and funding.

Just how world class? Recent numbers are hard to come by, but comparison of the G-7 nations shows that in 1992 the United States ranked first in public expenditure per K–12 student, and that Michigan's per-student expenditure has historically been higher than the U.S. average (U. S. Department of Education, 1996, pp. 208–219).

But to have a world-class education system, it is necessary to have more than world-class funding. It is necessary to have world-class performance. Michigan students are not just competing against each other. They are competing against students in the other 49 states and the rest of the world. And the competition is fierce. For example, as of February 1998 the Third International Mathematics and Science Study (TIMSS) found that U.S. high school seniors performed worse than those of 20 other nations. In addition, U. S. seniors scored near the bottom in the calculus test. As William Schmidt of Michigan State University put it, these results destroy the myth that America's best students are world-class (Foreign Students Beat Even Our Best, 1998, p. 1A).

The future of the 1.6 million school-aged children in Michigan public schools is of paramount importance to the state's success in the 21st century. To put it bluntly, the state with the best schools wins. Michigan can cut taxes, trim red tape, downsize government, and restructure welfare and health care. But if the state does not benchmark its students to the best in the world or prepare them to be the best in their class, Michigan will never be first in the 21st century. We cannot have the kind of state that we want, with incomes rising and job opportunities multiplying, without workers who are highly knowledgeable and skilled.

The aims of this chapter are to review Michigan's success with recent education reforms and to point in the direction of future reforms. Michigan is an ideal state to study because in many ways it reflects the diversity and contrasts that define America. Many of the education successes in our "laboratory of democracy" arguably apply to other states.

THE CRISES LEADING TO THE 1993 REFORM

It has been said that every crisis is an opportunity in disguise. To understand how and why far-reaching education reforms have taken place in Michigan in the 1990s, it is necessary to review the events that unfolded during the summer and fall of 1993—the *annus mirabilis*—when a funding crisis touched off heated debate over public education.

Wait a minute: A *funding* crisis triggering *education* reform? Although at first it may seem that there is little necessary connection between the two, recall that the French Revolution also began as a funding crisis. In Michigan in

1993, no sooner had the funding crisis appeared than the debate swelled like a torrent, overflowing its original banks and sweeping up everything concerning education in its path. Not just the topic of school finance, but parental choice, higher standards, safer classrooms, and greater accountability were all taken up.

It is interesting to note that Governor William Milliken had identified most of the major issues that would come to the surface in 1993, but a quarter-century earlier. On October 9, 1969, in an address to the Michigan Legislature, Governor Milliken warned:

> In my special message to the Legislature on education . . . I outlined the major problems facing Michigan because of the inadequate, inequitable, and antiquated structure we have for operating and financing our schools. I said that collectively these problems add up to an educational crisis in Michigan, and that if we failed to move toward educational reform intelligently in the very near future, the crisis would become an educational disaster.
>
> Evidence of this mounting crisis is upon us. It is evident in the loss of public confidence in the State Board of Education. It is evident in strike-torn school districts. It is evident in the collective bargaining whipsaw effects that are forcing too many districts into deficit financing. It is evident in the large number of unresolved contract disputes. It is evident in student disorders. It is evident, above all, in the growing public dissatisfaction with our educational processes. We must move now, and we must move with boldness. (Milliken, 1969, p. 12)

The terms of the debate, it turned out, had not changed appreciably for a quarter century.

The School-Finance Quagmire

How did the funding crisis originate?[1] It was noted earlier that the Michigan Constitution of 1963 commits the legislature to "maintain a system of free public elementary and secondary schools." But Article VIII nowhere spells out how to fund those schools. Education funding historically evolved out of a combination of state appropriations and local property taxes. The state portion was voted on by the legislature each year. The local portion was collected through a millage approved by local voters.

Michigan's traditional system for funding public schools evolved in a 19th-century agrarian economy. In such an economy, wealth was usually measured in terms of property. As a general rule, the more land one had, the more wealth. The land yielded its riches through farming or ranching, logging or mining. Thus, it was reasonable to fund public education out of property taxes, because it was property that generated the lion's share of wealth.

---

[1]For the technical information in this section, we are indebted to State Treasurer Douglas B. Roberts and his staff, Bobbie McKennon, Robbie Jameson, and Mark Haas. Especially helpful were two documents: Engler (1993a) and McKennon (1996).

For most property owners in the 20th century, however, the reality is quite different. Real estate is simply where their home is, and it does not yield additional wealth. Few property owners are farmers, ranchers, loggers, or miners.

In short, Michigan's 19th-century system of financing schools failed to adapt to 20th-century realities. As Michigan was transforming the Arsenal of Democracy into the Automotive Capital of the World, funding for public schools remained stuck in the patterns of the past and relied heavily on an archaic system of property taxes. By 1993 the average millage rate used to fund local schools had climbed to 36 mills. In terms of average property tax burden, this put Michigan 30% higher than the national average (Mark Haas, personal communication, Michigan Department of Treasury, Office of Revenue and Tax Analysis, September 1993).

Powerful teachers' unions, led by the Michigan Education Association, exacerbated the problem of rising millage rates. The unions were frequently able to negotiate new contracts with raises higher than the rate of inflation, to the point that Michigan educators became among the best paid in the nation. Indeed, when retirement and health benefits were added to salaries—and the cost of living was factored in—Michigan educators were the highest paid in the United States. This fact looms even larger when one realizes that teacher and administration costs amounted, on average, to 80 to 85% of a school district's budget in 1993 (Robbie Jameson, Michigan Department of Education, personal communication, September 1993).

Many local school boards became, in effect, millage committees. They were pressured to acquiesce to union demands because of illegal strikes. These strikes held families hostage; working mothers and fathers suddenly had to make day-care arrangements or stay home from work, as their children could not attend school. Although Michigan law had long prohibited strikes by public employees, teachers—who are public employees—continued to strike with impunity.

Thus in school districts across the state, there was upward pressure to raise taxes. It was not unusual for state assessment of property values to rise at more than twice the rate of inflation. This laid the groundwork for property taxes to increase significantly. Skyrocketing property taxes became especially burdensome for homeowners on fixed incomes. It was not unusual for senior citizens who had been paying a fixed monthly mortgage to find themselves face to face with an even higher monthly property tax bill. The Engler administration regularly received letters from distressed senior citizens who urged prompt action so that they would not have to move to a state with lower property taxes.

Not only was this archaic system imposing a burden on individual property owners; it was also creating a growing equity gap among Michigan's 558 school districts. Districts with a large percentage of wealthy residents living in tony neighborhoods were able to rake in large returns for each mill levied.

But districts with a large percentage of residents with below-average income and living in modestly priced houses were able to squeeze out only a small return for each mill levied: obviously 36 mills collects more school funding against a $250,000 house than against a $50,000 house.

As the years rolled by, this system of funding that relied on local property taxes resulted in intolerable inequities. Depending on the districts being compared, the difference in revenues per pupil could exceed $7000. For example, during the 1993–1994 school year, the Sigel Township No. 3 School District had per-pupil revenues of only $2759. By contrast, the Bloomfield Hills School District that same year had per-pupil revenues of $10,290.

Another way to visualize the problem is to compare the spending ratio between the highest and lowest spending districts. By 1980 the ratio between the highest and lowest spending districts was 2.75. The problem was not addressed the entire decade. The gap kept growing: the rich were getting richer; the poor, (relatively) poorer. By 1990 the ratio was 3.33 and clearly getting out of hand. The Engler administration and the legislature began to address the problem in the early 1990s, and the ratio came down from a peak of 3.33 in 1990 to 3.07 prior to major reform in 1993—but it was still much too high (Robbie Jamison, financial analyst, Michigan Department of Education, personal communication, September 1997).

These two problems—the inequity in per-pupil funding and the local property-tax burden—fueled a 20-year debate in Michigan on what was wrong with the existing system and how it could be modified to provide equity to both students and taxpayers. Over that same 2 decades, no fewer than 12 unsuccessful statewide school funding referenda were held and countless legislative proposals were defeated, leaving a broken system in utter disrepair. The public was truly concerned. A Michigan State University poll released in late September 1993 revealed that two of every three Michigan citizens believed the huge spending gap between rich and poor school districts was a serious problem, and an overwhelming majority favored letting the state collect and redistribute taxes to ease the disparity. "We were shocked at the depth of how seriously people view the disparity problem," said Jack Knott, director of MSU's Institute for Public Policy and Social Research ("School Funding Gap," Bell 1993b, p.1B). Michigan was headed for a court-imposed solution if something were not done, and quickly.

The Public School Assignment System

Besides the worsening school-finance quagmire, another historic problem came to a boil in 1993. It had to do with school choice. Traditionally, not just in Michigan but across the United States, school districts have assigned children to attend the public school of the district's choosing. Critics of the assignment system have argued that the needs and desires of families are often left out of the equation. The assignment system seems inherently unfair. After all, is it not families that are paying the taxes to support public schools? Do not families deserve to be involved when it comes to decisions about their children's education?

In the months leading up to the fall of 1993, there were a number of highly publicized reports of the assignment system's inflexibility, which could reach ridiculous extremes. One of the more prominent stories concerned Kay and Roger Pettipas and their 8-year-old son, Rory. Rory took a battery of tests that showed he was gifted in math and reading. But his mother did not think he was challenged enough academically. She asked the school and Rory's teachers if they could do more to challenge her son. Remarkably, the administration got upset with *Rory's mother* for making waves. They said they did not have the extra resources Rory required. So Rory's parents tried to transfer him. But the local school board refused permission to transfer. One board member frankly admitted that the issue was money, that the board was more interested in receiving state aid because of Rory than in doing what was best for him (Kay Pettipas, personal communication, September 1993).

Rory's mother tried to be understanding. In a telephone conversation with the authors she said, "I realize the money issue is important to them. But our child and his academics are important to us. We are responsible parents and we must send him to [a better school]" (Kay Pettipas, personal communication, September 1993). Rory's mom and dad eventually made their decision—the only choice they had, and the only legal choice open to Michigan parents in the early 1990s. To do the right thing for Rory, they had to sell their house and move to another school district.

Other high-profile stories also illustrated just how oppressive the governmental assignment system had become. One concerned an Eaton Rapids kindergartner who had to ride a bus 2 hours a day because his school district would not release him to attend a school 10 minutes down the road but which happened to be in another district. Another story was about a mother who went to court and gave up custody of her son so that he could live with relatives in order to attend a higher-quality school. Still another story was about school districts hiring "family police" at taxpayer expense to investigate where children lived and fining parents who did not send their kids to the assigned school (cited in Engler, 1993a, p. 6).

Critics of the assignment system raised questions of fundamental importance in the freest nation on earth. Who was really being served by the public education establishment? The system or the children? To what extent should parents be allowed to exercise their natural right as the first and foremost teachers of their children? Had the nation's commendable dedication to a system of common schools become coopted by special interests?

Proponents for more choice argued that the freedom to choose is why this nation was founded. America's political and economic system is built on this fundamental right. This right encompasses, to this day, many phases in a child's education. Parents have complete freedom to choose where to send their children to preschool, and when their kids grow up, parents have complete freedom to choose where to send them to college. So why the educational gulag between kindergarten and the 12th grade? Why were families denied this fundamental American right? It was especially unjust, critics contended, that the people denied this freedom were the very people paying for the schools—middle-class families like Rory's.

1970 Constitutional Amendment

These questions involved not just parents' right to choose the schools most appropriate for their children but whether they could do so, at least in part, at public expense. These issues also relate to questions involving school funding, but this time the issue was whether nonpublic schools could be funded by taxes.

Critics of the notion of a rigid separation of church and state have pointed out that schools are rarely given over entirely to sectarian interests. After all, when a religious or private school is teaching algebra or English grammar to its students, it is performing a public service that yields public benefits. There is not a Catholic way of teaching the quadratic equation, nor a Jewish way of understanding Newtonian physics, nor a Protestant way of correcting run-on sentences and dangling participles. Yet parents who send their children to a private or religious school have to pay twice—once in property taxes for the neighborhood public school and a second time in tuition at the private school of their choice.

These concerns came to the fore in 1970 when Michigan citizens were given the opportunity to vote on a constitutional amendment that would prohibit virtually all public funding from going to sectarian or private schools. Once again, a little history will be useful for understanding how the 1970 election came about.[2]

At the beginning of the chapter, it was noted that Article VIII, Section 1, of the Michigan Constitution of 1963 borrowed a famous passage from the Northwest Ordinance of 1787. In adopting this language, Michigan citizens were asserting not only that education is fundamental to our democratic way of life, but that knowledge is vitally connected to morality and religion. Historically, this understanding had been confirmed in practice. Until the middle of the 19th century, a number of states appropriated some public funds in support of sectarian schools. To the extent that they taught subjects considered to be basic—such as reading, writing, and arithmetic—these nonpublic schools were rewarded for contributing to the commonwealth (see Whitney, 1995).

---

[2]Much of this information in this section is drawn form Anderson, Overton, McLellan, and Wolfram (1997) and Citizens Research Council of Michigan (1970). We are indebted to these authors for their work.

This arrangement was largely abolished for reasons that are too complex to detail here. Suffice it that in Michigan in the early decades of the 20th century, there was still some blurring between sectarian and public schooling. For example, so-called *shared time* classes were held involving both private and public school students, a practice that continued until 1970. Shared time applied to children who spent most of their time in nonpublic schools, but who received some secular instruction in a public school.

Further complicating the picture was a law passed in 1929 that prohibited the state from giving direct support to sectarian schools. Yet since at least 1939, indirect support for private schools was being provided for such activities as transportation, testing, health, and special services for disabled children.

As is well known, interpretations of the First Amendment to the United States Constitution since the 1940s have strictly limited the extent to which government can support religious institutions, including schools. Some of the prominent U.S. Supreme Court cases that relate to education funding and reform include *Everson v. Board of Education* (1947), *Lemon v. Kurtzman* (1971), *Committee on Public Education v. Nyquist* (1973), *Mueller v. Allen* (1982), and *Rosenberger v. Rector and Visitors of University of Virginia* (1995). The debate over the meaning of the First Amendment not only gave rise to competing visions of what the separation of church and state means, it also shaped Michigan's current constitution. The story of how and why the constitution was amended comprises one of the most contentious chapters in the state's postwar history.

In the 1960s, many parents who were paying both property taxes to support public schools and tuition to send their children to nonpublic schools championed taxpayer funding for religious and private schools. As a result, the legislature passed, and then-Governor Milliken signed, Public Act 100 of 1970. This act (PA 100) was the school aid bill for that year. It provided direct support to eligible private schools and restricted public funding to instruction in nonreligious subjects. Michigan's law was similar in content and inspiration to those passed in a handful of other states, such as Pennsylvania and Rhode Island.

When the Michigan law was challenged, the state Supreme Court upheld it, ruling in an advisory opinion that "the Constitution of the State of Michigan did not prohibit the purchase with public funds of secular educational services from a nonpublic school" (Advisory Opinion, 1970). The law, in other words, did not appear to involve excessive entanglement, which had become a chief criterion in both state and U. S. Supreme Court decisions.

Since PA 100 passed constitutional muster, it may have seemed that the question was settled. On the contrary, passage of the law sparked a rancorous campaign against taxpayer funding of nonpublic schools. The Council against Parochiaid was established to direct a petition drive whose purpose was to place the constitutional amendment on the ballot. The amendment would prohibit any public funding going to religious or private schools.

The campaign was acrimonious and hard-fought on both sides. Proponents of the amendment argued that state dollars would not just be used for private education but for proselytizing on behalf of specific denominations. An antiCatholic tone crept into the debate, as the Parochiaid slogan was used to arouse ancient Protestant prejudices against Catholic citizens. Besides the use of unsavory tactics, a number of confusing statements surfaced in the proponents' campaign. In fact, the state supreme court later opined that the "voter was barraged by contradictory statements," including those made by prominent supporters and public officials (*Traverse City v. Attorney General*, 1971, note 2).

As if the campaign were not confusing enough, the petitions were thrown out after the attorney general, and later the board of canvassers, found that the petitions did not let signers know whether the proposed amendment would abrogate the existing education section of the constitution. A split panel of the court of appeals, and then a five-to-two majority on the state supreme court, nevertheless ordered the proposal onto the November 1970 ballot. It was known as Proposal C.

When citizens went to the polls on November 3, 1970, they approved Proposal C by a margin of 338,098 votes: 1,416,838 to 1,078,740. The new language added to Article VIII, Section II, consisted of two sentences that were quite restrictive. Passage of Proposal C scotched any chance that parents would receive tuition help when their children were receiving nonsectarian instruction in religious or private schools. The amendment read:

> No public monies or property shall be appropriated or paid or any public credit utilized, by the legislature or any other political subdivision or agency of the state directly or indirectly to aid or maintain any private, denominational or other non-public, pre-elementary, elementary, or secondary school. No payment, credit, tax benefit, exemption or deductions, tuition voucher, subsidy, grant or loan of public monies or property shall be provided, directly or indirectly, *to support the attendance of any student or the employment of any person at any such nonpublic school or at any location or institution where instruction is offered in whole or in part to such nonpublic school students* [emphasis added]. The legislature may provide for the transportation of students to and from any school."[3]

The amendment went into effect December 19, 1970. However, it was still causing resentment more than 2 decades later. As Anderson et al. put it:

> With the 1970 amendment, Michigan's Constitution became one of the most repressive in the nation with respect to parental choice involving nonpublic schools. . . . The passing of more than two decades has brought about change in Michigan. Nonpublic schools are attracting more students, support for parental choice in education is growing rapidly, and it is not clear that 1970's Proposal C would pass in our present day. It is time to reevaluate the language that is openly hostile and punitive to parents

[3]Significantly, the italicized portion of the second sentence was ruled unconstitutional, void, and unenforceable because it contravened free exercise of religion guaranteed by the United States Constitution and violated the equal protection provisions of the U. S. Constitution (*Traverse City v. Attorney General*, 1971).

who would like to send their children to a nonpublic school without having to pay twice. (1997, p. 26)

Lagging Performance

In addition to inequitable funding, debates over school choice, and a rancorous campaign to pass the 1970 amendment, there was yet another concern that helped make education reform in Michigan come to a head by 1993. That year the National Education Goals Panel issued its 1993 goals report to the nation. The report was a wake-up call to Americans from coast to coast:

> At no stage in a learner's life—before formal schooling, during the school years, or as adults—are we doing as well as we should be or as well as we can. The nation has fallen behind its own expectations and behind the progress of our global competitors (Engler, 1993a, p. 3).

Harold Stevenson at the University of Michigan reported that "On tests given to students from 20 countries, American eighth graders ranked tenth in arithmetic, twelfth in algebra, and sixteenth in geometry. Twelfth grade students fared just as badly" (cited in Engler, 1993a, p. 3).

The 1993 goals report, along with related research, exposed a number of specific weaknesses in Michigan's system of public education, especially regarding student performance. Data showed that high school graduation rates had been barely above 70%; only one in five 10th graders was passing the statewide mathematics test; only two in five were passing the statewide reading and science tests. Moreover, in 1992 there were 15 school districts where more than 75% of incoming seniors could not pass a 10th-grade test and earn a state-endorsed diploma. In 253 districts, more than half of incoming seniors could not pass the 10th-grade test and earn a state-endorsed diploma. Despite investing billions of dollars on K–12 education over the previous decade—despite countless reform efforts—SAT scores had remained virtually flat and at about the national average (cited in Engler, 1993a, pp. 3–4).

If it is true that "the state with the best schools wins"—and we believe that it is—then it would be imperative to break 2 decades of gridlock in Michigan's capital and shake up the status quo. Another generation of children could not be consigned to a monopoly of mediocrity.

THE PIVOTAL YEAR: 1993

For all these reasons, by the summer of 1993 the stage was set for far-reaching education reform. But something was needed to spark the engine of change. That opportunity came in the form of a dicey game of political chicken, when a Democratic aspirant to the governor's office tried to outflank Republicans on the issue of taxes. On July 20, 1993, State Senator Debbie

Stabenow, who was a candidate for the Democratic nomination for governor, introduced an amendment to a bill in the Michigan Senate that would eliminate all school-operating property taxes.[4] If passed, it meant that no local property taxes would be used to fund public schools. This proposal was perhaps the most dramatic change of course ever attempted in Michigan school-funding history.

Politics, not school reform, was the motivation behind Senator Stabenow's proposal. In proposing to eliminate property taxes for schools, the Democratic senator assumed a Republican governor would never sign it. The Engler administration, she thought, would be forced to reject the very property tax relief that had been promised in the 1990 gubernatorial campaign. This rejection would supposedly expose Republicans as hypocrites and hurt GOP candidates in the 1994 election cycle.

The senator and her Democratic colleagues were surprised when the governor, immediately seizing this unparalleled opportunity to break 2 decades of gridlock, urged leaders in both houses of the legislature to rise to the challenge. The amendment and the bill passed the senate the same day it was introduced—July 20, 1993—and passed the house in the early afternoon of the following day. The action was historically unparalleled, cutting almost $6 billion in funding for public schools and giving property owners the largest tax cut in Michigan history (Bell et al., Engler Took Dems' Dare, 1993a, p. 1A).

The legislation was then sent to the governor's desk, and Senate Bill One was signed on August 19, 1993, in Dearborn, in front of the Scotch Settlement School where Henry Ford had learned to read and write. At the bill-signing ceremony, the governor's office revealed the scope of its intentions:

> Senate Bill One is about much more than cutting property taxes. Ultimately, Senate Bill One is about a promise we are making to the people of Michigan. It is a promise to improve education, find a fair way to finance our schools, and do what's best for our children. . . .
>
> How do you bring about an education revolution in Michigan, and make our schools the best in the world? You begin by focusing on the education of our children rather than on the needs of "the system." You empower our families with choice. You expand our charter schools. You set up rigorous academic standards. You make schools accountable for meeting those standards. You free up our teachers and reward the best ones with merit pay. You inform parents with a Report Card that grades school performance, building by building. You accept nothing less than quality and excellence. These are some of the ways to build a high-performance education system and make Michigan schools the best in the world. (Engler 1993b, p. 2)

The practical effect of signing Senate Bill One into law was a huge property tax cut made possible by abolishing 65% of public school funding. Now Michigan public schools had only the state's portion of their funding, or 35%.

[4]The original property tax-cut legislation, Senate Bill One, was introduced by Republican Senator Gil DiNello. Senator Stabenow's amendment to Senate Bill One was to exempt all property from millage levied for local school operating purposes. This proposal cost Stabenow the Democratic nomination for governor. She became instead the Democratic candidate for lieutenant governor in 1994, after losing the August primary to Howard Wolpe.

The question of funding, not just for the 1994–1995 school year but for the next generation of students, was looming large. The challenge was how to replace those revenues.

In early August of 1993, the governor appointed a task force under the leadership of State Treasurer Douglas B. Roberts. His charge was to come up with a plan by late September that not only would put school funding back on track but simultaneously would propose much-needed education reforms. The task force held its initial meeting on August 16. Over the next 6 weeks, a team of 12 men and women in state government tackled numerous issues, worked round the clock, and met its deadline. On October 5, 1993, the governor addressed a special joint session of the Michigan legislature and unveiled a comprehensive, far-reaching education and school finance reform plan.

The plan plumbed many aspects of reform—including school finance, parental choice, and the lagging performance of students — but for purposes of the present discussion it boiled down to two major components.

More Public School Choice through Charter Schools

The keystone of education reform was to give families more choice—and that meant giving them the freedom to send their children to the public school they thought best. It should be noted that no attempt was made at this time to repeal Article VIII, Section 2, of the constitution of 1963. Polling indicated that Michigan was not yet ready for that debate. Nor did any groundswell of support for such a change arise. The governor, sworn to uphold the constitution, therefore championed reforms that fit within the framework provided by Article VIII, Section 2, as amended by the 1970 vote against so-called Parochiaid.

To assure an array of public school choices for families, particular emphasis was placed on charter public schools. Charter schools are publicly sponsored autonomous schools, substantially deregulated and free of direct administrative control by the government.

Innovative, autonomous, flexible, accountable—these words begin to describe how charter schools differ from mainstream public schools. They are free to try new ideas, free of geographic boundaries and can accept students on a nondiscriminatory basis from anywhere in the state, free to help children reach the highest standards of excellence the way teachers deem best, and free to unleash all the talent in the education community on behalf of our children.

Charter schools were seen as a driving force in the effort to improve education quality and performance. That is because charter schools would infuse public schools with a dynamic that for too long has been missing—competition. Charter schools would offer choices in an otherwise monopolistic system. They would give creative teachers, concerned parents, and far-sighted employers the opportunity to break free from overregulated mainstream schools. Because of their autonomy and flexibility, charter schools could show Michigan— and the United States—what education reform really looked like.

Even before charter schools became law, public school superintendents responded to the governor's October 5 address by conceding that the mere existence of charter schools would leverage change throughout their district. Psychologically, a powerful impetus for ongoing improvement had been provided.

School Finance Reform

How would such far-reaching reforms be financed, and could they be funded in a way that restored accountability to Michigan families and taxpayers? The key was to funnel funding not into the system directly but to students and their families—letting them choose the public school that best fit their needs and expectations, then applying a foundation grant to their school of choice.

Under the plan, each Michigan child who attended a public school was guaranteed a minimum foundation grant of $4500. That would ensure greater fairness in the system. Indeed, all children would be ahead of where they had been. Students in the 234 districts that spent less than $4500 per pupil would be brought up to that amount, students from average spending districts, which spent between $4500 and $6500 per pupil, would be protected; and students from the highest spending districts, which spent more than $6500 per pupil, would have the opportunity to maintain funding at high levels.

The plan provided school replacement revenue, yet also guaranteed a net property tax cut of some $4 billion to Michigan's families. The average home owner would save $356 a year. To ensure that families saw permanent property tax relief, the plan called on Michigan voters to approve a 2-cent hike in the state sales tax, capped in the constitution, so that Michigan students could receive world-class funding. The sales tax had the advantage of putting part of the tax burden on out-of-state tourists. In addition to the sales tax, further revenues were to be raised by the following:

- Increasing the Single Business Tax a half percent
- Implementing a real estate transfer tax
- Hiking the tax on a pack of cigarettes by 50 cents; and
- Levying a 16-mill property tax on businesses, second homes, and non-resident property, also to be capped in the constitution.

It was also proposed that the package of replacement revenues be backed up by long overdue cost-containment measures. The administration proposed to rein in skyrocketing spending in ways ways that would not sacrifice quality learning in the classroom. Competitively bidding out health care, food service, custodial work, landscaping, and transportation would save millions of dollars annually. Under the plan, 100% of the savings could be put back into children's education, where the money belonged.

Over the next 77 days, the debate over the governor's plan and the future of public education in Michigan was fully joined. In all, 26 bills were drawn up to implement the administration's proposals. Negotiations were intense; the most famous marathon session went into the wee hours of Christmas Eve. The *Detroit Free Press* reported: "For many of the participants, the Legislature's frantic December rush to retool Michigan's public schools was the work of a lifetime. Gov. John Engler called it the most important challenge he has faced in his 23 years in Lansing" (Some Legislators Skipped Votes, 1993b, p. 1A).

The Engler administration, while it did not win every battle with the house of representatives, which was evenly split between Republicans and Democrats, got much of what it fought for. The administration's school-finance plan won out over competing schemes. Families would have greater choices. Years of lagging student performance were going to be seriously addressed.

The proposed constitutional amendment to restructure school funding went on the ballot as Proposal A. Michigan voters passed it overwhelmingly on March 15, 1994, thereby changing forever the way Michigan schools would be financed. A *New York Times* editorial fittingly summed up the 1993 Michigan school-finance reforms, calling them "a revolution in the way [to] finance public schools" ("Rich Are Wary of Michigan's Revolt," 1994, p. 19A).

1994–1997

In the 4 years after 1993, Michigan implemented many of the proposals that were championed in the governor's October 5, 1993, address. Since that time, the train of successes has been significant. Without hyperbole it can be said that Michigan is leading the states in education reform—indeed, in the opinion of many it has become the state of education reform.[5]

Gone are the days when millage elections were failing and property taxes were skyrocketing. The Engler administration fixed that problem with Proposal A, which slashed property taxes and constitutionally guaranteed funding for every student.

Gone is an archaic funding system, whereby the rich got further ahead, the poor fell further behind, and the kids got trapped in the middle. Again, that problem was fixed with Proposal A. By 1998 the equity gap had been cut in half and was continuing to close, and every student in every school was receiving at least $5100.

[5]The accomplishments and data presented in the following paragraphs are drawn from Engler (1998).

Executive order (EO) cuts to education have been eliminated. The previous two governors had signed EOs cutting education by $400 million. In the 1990s, with stabilized funding, there were no more executive order cuts. In fact, between 1990 and 1998, education spending rose 50% and topped $11.8 billion. During that period Michigan was the only state in the nation to balance its budget 6 years in a row, cut taxes 24 times, and *increase* education spending every single year.

No longer can students bring guns and knives to school with impunity or just a slap on the wrist. So far some 600 arms-bearing students have learned that lesson by being expelled from school.

Illegal teacher strikes have ceased. Now, teachers are teaching and children are learning from Day 1.

Families no longer have to change houses to change schools thanks to choice, charter schools, and competition. With Public Act 362 of 1994, Michigan could boast one of the most far-reaching public charter school laws in the United States. In the Great Lakes State, more than 20,000 children are enrolled in more than 100 charter public schools, giving Michigan the third largest number of charter public schools in the nation.[6] These are not elitist institutions, as some critics claim. On the contrary, Michigan leads the nation in the number of minority students enrolled in charter schools—53%; in fact, 47% of the children in these schools are African American. And school after school has long waiting lists. The creation of new charter schools cannot be accomplished quickly enough, especially in cities like Detroit, where the school board has been reluctant to issue charters—despite tremendous unmet demand.

In addition to charter schools, nearly 8000 families took advantage of the schools-of-choice initiative in the first year alone—proving that this was an idea whose time had come. Because of charter schools and schools of choice, the system was finally responding to children's needs, reflecting Michigan's perspective that education is the Number 1 indicator of success in life.

At one time newspapers carried sports scores but not test scores. Now, through the Internet, the data from the Michigan School Report on school performance is accessible to every parent.

[6]According to the Center for Education Reform (CER), the leading charter school states are Arizona (241 schools), California (128), Michigan (108), and Colorado (50). CER shows that the four leading states have about two-thirds of all charters. Michigan has 14% and almost exactly the same percentage of students. The variety of Michigan charter schools must also be emphasized. Examples of charter schools include (1) Excel Academy, emphasizing outstanding academics; students in the program for 2 years on average progress 3.4 years on the Metropolitan Achievement Test; (2) Henry Ford Academy of Manufacturing Arts and Sciences, which demonstrates the potential of partnerships among business, cultural institutions, and public education; (3) Washtenaw Technical Middle College, which is developing the role of community colleges in high-school-level programs; (4) Marvin L. Winans Academy of Performing Arts, where every child takes violin lessons; and (5) Detroit Community High School, with many at-risk students, including several on electronic tethers.

Complaints about teacher tenure have also been addressed. Tenure reform means that bad teachers are moving out, and good teachers are moving up.

The use of technology and computers in classrooms has increased. State resources, combined with local and federal funds, have given Michigan schools unprecedented access to the Internet and to the world. The state is devoting hundreds of millions of dollars to infuse more classrooms with state-of-the-art technology and to put trained teachers in those classrooms. Interactive technology—and teachers trained to use it—are becoming more available in Michigan classrooms, enabling all students to enrich their lives and maximize their potential.

To battle unfunded mandates, red tape, and threats to local control, the state has overhauled the school code and dumped some 200 obsolete sections. The state's intention is to empower school boards and, more important, trust parents.

To reduce class sizes, Michigan's $4 billion increase in school funding has, in the 1990s, improved the ratio of teachers to students. In fact, since 1991, Michigan public schools have hired an additional 6700 teachers, and in 1998 launched a $20 million initiative for even smaller classes.

Whereas school boards members spent all their time talking about the problems just catalogued, they are now free to tend to their real mission—delivering a quality education to every child.

Michigan's reforms, combined with the efforts of dedicated teachers and concerned parents, are getting results. Rising test scores are one proof. In a national science test, the level of improvement among Michigan students was best among the ten largest states in the United States. Over the period from 1990 to 1996, Michigan's eighth-grade math scores showed the greatest improvement in the nation. No matter which test one looks at—ACT, SAT, MEAP, the High School Proficiency Test—Michigan students are performing better.

DIRECTIONS OF FUTURE REFORM

In seven short years of intense education reform, Michigan has come far and is a different state in the late 1990s compared to the late 1980s. But much remains to be done. First, despite the waiting lists for charter schools, the Michigan legislature has imposed an unreasonable cap on the number of such schools that can be opened. The cap on university-authorized schools is 125 in 1998 and will rise to 150 in 1999. It should be lifted.

Second, voluntary performance standards should be adopted by the states, especially in mathematics, science, reading, and writing. Some critics seem to get all caught up in the content and method of the testing. While well intentioned, such discussions are unnecessarily distracting. Plant managers and CEOs know what skills are needed in the workplace. The sum of 2 plus 2 is the same in Michigan as it is in Texas. In this highly integrated global economy, we should be able to compare student peformance across state lines.

Third, some proponents of school choice believe that the public nowadays is more receptive to repealing much of the restrictive language of Article VIII, Section 2, of the Michigan Constitution. Their aim is to give middle-class and poorer families even greater choices, so that all children will have the chance to attend the best schools. The next year or two may see an effort to launch a petition drive on behalf of a universal tuition tax credit in Michigan (see Anderson et al., 1997). There is also a growing movement, headed by Paul DeWeese, president of the Teach Michigan Education Fund, for limited experimentation with vouchers; it has garnered its strongest support among African Americans in Detroit.

In time, constitutional change may occur. But in the meantime, there is a more basic challenge to tackle. The federal and state budgets may be balanced, but there is a terrible deficit all across America—a *reading* deficit. This introduces the fourth major proposal (see Engler, 1998). Data compiled by the U. S. Department of Education show that the average reading proficiency of 12th-graders declined significantly in the early and mid-1990s. Almost one in three high school seniors, despite having spent more than a decade in school, could not read at the basic level as defined by the National Assessment of Educational Progress (NEAP).

Younger children are also not reading as well as they should. In Michigan results from a recent administration of the Michigan Educational Assessment Program (MEAP) tests, while showing improved reading scores, indicate that 51% of fourth graders still cannot perform at grade level. That means not even half of the state's fourth graders are good readers.

This is tragic. Nothing is more basic than the ability to read. Reading changes lives. The inability to read also changes lives. It means falling behind classmates, dropping out of school, and spending a life in an unfulfilling job or, worse, in prison. If our children are not reading, Michigan will never be first in the 21st century.

Yet the best research, conducted by the National Institutes of Health, shows that it is realistic to teach almost 100% of our kids to read at grade level *if* they are screened early for learning difficulties and are taught using effective methods (Dr. Reid Lyon, Bethesda, MD, personal communication, March 30, 1998).

The governor's state of the state message of January 1998 set before the legislature this challenge: Children who start kindergarten in the fall of that year must be able to read by the time they reach the fourth grade. No exceptions. No excuses.

Now, making every child a reader will take commitment—the commitment of parents, teachers, school boards, and state government. In January 1998, the Engler administration sent a directive to the Department of Education to launch an ambitious Reading Plan for Michigan (RPM). This RPM strategy will help children even before they enter school. The Early Childhood Office in the Department of Education will develop reading readiness kits and get them into parents' hands as early as possible. The Department of Education will also do the following:

- Assure that every child is assessed from the first day of school with the best diagnostic tools to determine reading readiness
- See that every child is monitored on an ongoing basis to ensure reading progress
- Design a model summer reading program to reinforce reading year round

In the future, if a child is not reading by the end of the third grade, he or she will be required to attend a summer school program designed to ensure the ability to read at grade level. The goal is to end the practice of social promotions in the state.

Michigan has many wonderful and dedicated teachers. Dedicated as they are, they cannot do the job alone. Nor can government ever be a substitute for Mom and Dad. It is imperative that parents become more involved in their children's education. To assist parents, a statewide resource guide will be made available so they will know who to call to get the help their youngsters need.

Fortunately, in addition to teachers and parents, many individuals and organizations already volunteer. The administration strongly supports the expansion of its highly successful Alliance for Children's Education (ACE). Michigan's ACE initiative has already developed mentoring programs for reading in more than 150 schools.

Many other groups are involved: Help One Student to Succeed (HOSTS), Success to All Readers (STAR), literacy councils such as Kent County's Project One to One, the SUCCEED Program, Reading Is Fundamental (RIF), Read Indeed, the National Center for Family Literacy, local libraries, and the Michigan Reading Association. These and others are important allies. Michigan is blessed with a wealth of reading organizations who are working together to guarantee that Michigan children will be readers.

ON WASHINGTON'S ROLE IN K–12 EDUCATION

This discussion of the future of education reform in Michigan has a caveat. Nothing could derail state-based reforms like the heavy hand of the national government. Washington's role in education should be minimal.

William Bennett and Lamar Alexander put it best when they said, "Education in America is the constitutional responsibility of the states, the social responsibility of communities, and the moral responsibility of families." In other words, there need not be, and should not be, the heavy hand of the national government on the states when it comes to education (Alexander & Bennett, 1995, p. 2).

By most estimates, Americans collectively spend more than $290 billion every year on primary and secondary public education. That is about $1.5 billion spent every school day (Consortium on Productivity in the Schools, 1995). Much of that money, however, is diverted through Washington. Recently a congressional committee, chaired by Michigan Representative Peter Hoekstra, identified 760 federal education programs throughout 39 agencies spending more than $120 billion annually—staggering numbers all. Further, 50% of the paperwork that the states must deal with comes from Washington. In fact, one of the most amazing figures to come to light is that there are 487 steps to go through to complete the average U. S. Department of Education grant (cited in Engler, 1997).

This raises questions: For all the billions that Washington spends on public education each year, is there proof that it is helping public schools achieve their fundamental mission, which is to improve the mind and character of American children?

Many federal dollars end up going to bureaucrats—but no bureaucrat ever taught children a thing. Furthermore, bureaucracies do not respond well to market pressures and commonsense reforms. The intrusiveness and sluggishness of bureaucracies should give us pause. It has gotten to the point where, in Michigan, less than half of every education dollar spent—48 cents, to be exact— actually makes it into the classroom. Much of the rest is going to administration and to the bureaucracies. Michigan's fear is that more federal involvement will not only reduce the amount actually going to the classroom but may come with so many strings attached that the state will never be able to cut through the thicket of rules and regulations. There is no way to reform a monopoly that has become gummed up with red tape.

As a favor to Michigan's children the governor's office would like to cut the red tape being manufactured inside the Beltway that is streaming out and strangling the states. More of the money could bypass Washington altogether and go directly to children in the classrooms.

One step in the right direction would be to simplify federal involvement through congressional utilization of block grants. Block grants have enabled the states to enact far-reaching welfare reforms and would likely give similar flexibility with regard to education. This remedy will allow the state to cut through the existing thicket of rules and regulations and stop much of the current paper chase, which is wasting so much of its public resources.

If what has been said about Washington sounds harsh, it should be quickly added that the Engler administration practices what it preaches. Neither Lansing nor any other state capital should have a heavy-handed education bureaucracy. That is why, in 1994, the governor signed two executive orders that trimmed the size of the Michigan Department of Education

(MDOE) from 2000 to fewer than 1000 staff members. Now, due to its retirement program, the MDOE has fewer than 500 staff members.

Reels of red tape have been cut at the state level. The number of state forms for reporting has dropped from 217 to 149. Of the 149 forms, 67 are required, and 82 are voluntary.

In addition, in the past 2 years, the administration has rescinded one-third of all MDOE regulations. In 1995, the MDOE had 771 rules; today it has only 507. Of all the rule reductions among the Michigan state departments in the 1990s, the MDOE reductions represent the greatest percentage. Moreover, in 1996, the Michigan legislature eliminated more than 200 sections of the school code.

CONCLUSION

Most parents, educators, and policy makers want the same goals for children. We want our children to attend schools that equip them with the knowledge and skills they need to earn a living, to become responsible citizens, and to fulfill their potential as individuals and as members of families and society.

Yet for years public education has been under attack. The widespread belief is that, despite the billions being spent annually on K–12 education, the majority of children are simply not receiving adequate preparation to take their place in the world of the future. There is much truth in this perception. By the 1980s, if the United States was a nation at risk, then Michigan was certainly a state at risk.

But the Michigan experience of the 1990s proves that a state facing historically daunting challenges can in fact meet those challenges—and surmount them. Michigan modernized its school-finance system by dragging it out of the 19th century and designing it for the 21st century. The state encouraged competition and opened up the public school system so that it offers more choices to families. It got tough on weapon-wielding students who made it difficult for everyone else to learn, and it focused on the basics and set the bar high. Like its children, education in the state of Michigan is a work in progress. But rising test scores in math, science, reading, and writing indicate that the reforms are producing results.

Without diminishing the need for further action, Michigan can nevertheless affirm that it has realized a significant number of education reforms in a few short years. That is because all groups have worked together—Republicans and Democrats, cities and townships, local and state government. After all, the well-being of our children transcends ethnic divides, party lines, racial tensions, gender wars, and geographic barriers. Kids may be only 25% of Michigan's population, but they are 100% of the state's future. If the Michigan experience teaches anything, it is that by working together and putting children first, a state can have a lasting impact on the world and the future.

References

Advisory Opinion re: Constitutionality of PA 100, 384 Mich. 82 (1970).

Alexander, L., & Bennett, W. (1995, January 26). *Abolishing the Department of Education in order to Liberate Parents and Schools.* Testimony presented to the House Economic and Educational Opportunities Committee, Subcommittee on Oversight and Investigation, Washington, DC.

Anderson, P. L., McLellan, R., Overton, J. P., & Wolfram, G. (1997). *The universal tax credit: A proposal to address parental choice in education.* Midland, MI: Mackinac Center for Public Policy.

Bell, D., et al. (1993a, July 23). Engler took Dem's dare: He doubted they'd try tax cut; when they did, he pounced. *The Detroit Free Press*, p. 1A.

Bell, D., et al. (1993b, September 28). School funding gap bothers many Michiganders. *The Detroit Free Press*, p. 1B.

Citizen Research Council of Michigan (1970). State ballot Issue C: Prohibit the use of public money for support of non-public schools. *Council Comment*, 833, p. 1–4.

Committee on Public Education v. Nyquist. 93 S. Ct. 2955 (1973).

Consortium on Productivity in the Schools. (October, 1995). *Using what we have to get the schools we need: A productivity focus for American education.* New York: Institute on Education and the Economy, Teachers College, Columbia University.

Engler, J. (1993a, October 5). *Our Kids Deserve Better.* Remarks presented to a special session of the Michigan legislature, Lansing, MI.

Engler, J. (1993b, August 19). Remarks presented at the signing of Senate Bill 1, Dearborn, MI.

Engler, J. (1997, October 2). Testimony presented to the U.S. House of Representatives Committee on Education and the Workforce, Subcommittee on Oversight and Investigations, Muskegon, MI.

Engler, J. (1998, January 29). *Taxpayers' Agenda VIII: Taking the Next Steps to Make Michigan First in the Twenty-first Century.* Governor's 1998 State of the State address, Lansing, MI.

Everson v. Board of Education, 67 S. Ct. 504 (1947).

Lemon v. Kurtzman, 91 S. Ct. 2105 (1971).

Lyon, R. (March 30, 1998). Chief of Child Development and Behavior Branch, National Institute of Child Health and Human Development, National Institute of Health, Bethesda, MD.

McKennon, B. (1996). Proposal A: Michigan's experience with school reform. Unpublished manuscript.

Milliken, W. (1969, October 9). Special message to the Fall Session of the Legislature on Education Reform. Library of Michigan Archives, Lansing.

Mueller v. Allen, 103 S. Ct. 3062 (1982).

Rich are Wary of Michigan's Revolt. (1994, March 23). *The New York Times*, p. 19A.

Rosenberger et al. v. Rector & Visitors of the University of Virginia et al. 115 S. Ct. 2510 (1995). Thomas, C. concurring.

Schulz, T. (1998, February 25). Foreign students beat even our best. *Lansing State Journal*, p. 1A.

Some legislators skipped votes on school plan: 'Nutcracker' frustrations are among reasons (1993, December 30). *The Detroit Free Press*, p. 1A.

Traverse City Public School District v. Attorney General of Michigan, 384 Mich. 390 (1971).

U.S. Department of Education. (1996). *Education indicators: An international perspective.* Washington, DC: National Center for Education Statistics.

Us against them (1997, December 22). *The Lansing State Journal*, p. 1A.

Whitney, G. (1995). Wither American education? *University Bookman*, 35, 3–7.

CHAPTER

7

Standards Initiatives and American Educational Reform

EDWARD D. ROEBER
Advanced Systems in Measurement & Evaluation

The citizens of the United States have long been concerned about the educational attainments of its students, particularly how well the American educational system is preparing the youth of the country for the future. In the post–World War II environment, the United States became increasingly concerned about the achievement of its students, particularly in relationship to students in other countries. In the 1950s, the United States began a competition to beat the Soviet Union and other communist countries to the moon, and to the classroom. A heated debate began as well about how (or if) the country should try to correct differences in funding and achievement across the states.

In 1965 the Elementary and Secondary Education Act (ESEA) was adopted, a landmark piece of educational legislation at the national level designed to correct differences in educational achievement presumably due to economic imbalances in the United States. Although proponents of federal aid to education at that time had wanted to pass legislation to provide general aid throughout the educational system, a more limited compensatory education bill was adopted, in part because of a political environment of concern about federal intrusion into education. In the ensuing years, billions of dollars have been spent attempting to correct the impact of poverty on the educational attainments of poor students.

In the late 1960s, a federal initiative called the National Assessment of Educational Progress (NAEP) began collecting data on the achievement of students across the country. It revealed deep differences among students by region, by community type, by gender, and by race. During the 1980s, the NAEP added state-by-state testing and demonstrated the substantial differences between states, particularly those with many students in poverty. Although some students performed quite well, others did poorly on assessments such as these. When the NAEP set standards for student performance during the 1980s, the relatively poor performance of many students became even more apparent.

During the 1970s and 1980s, a number of states began assessing student performance as well. Quite a few of these states, mainly in the southeast, used off-the-shelf norm-referenced tests such as the *Stanford Achievement Test*, the *Iowa Test of Basic Skills*, the *California Achievement Test*, and others to test all students at certain grade levels. In a few other states, starting with California and Michigan in the early 1970s, educators defined what knowledge and skills students needed to know and be able to do, and these became the basis of state-developed, criterion-referenced tests that were administered to students in one or more grades. In still other states, such as Florida, students were required to take and pass tests in order to receive a high school diploma. Although these programs began in the 1970s, each can still be found today.

It was the publication of A *Nation at Risk: The Imperative for Educational Reform* (National Commission on Excellence in Education, 1983), however, that stirred the country to action in recent years. The "rising tide of mediocrity" (p. 5), which this report documented, awakened the country once again to the issue of whether the country's students were learning enough to be economically competitive in the global marketplace in which the United States was increasingly finding itself. Business leaders and politicians began again to discuss whether students were leaving high school sufficiently educated to go to college, to go to work, and to succeed as adults in American society.

A *Nation at Risk* also spurred state-level discussions and reports, stirring many states to action. Among the actions that states took were the adoption of plans to define and assess what students should know. The impact of A *Nation at Risk* has been an ongoing struggle to define in educationally and politically acceptable terms what students will need to know and be able to do, to assess students on these knowledge and skill factors, and to use the assessment information to help schools change and improve so that students acquire the needed skills.

THE PROMISE OF STANDARDS-BASED REFORM

The phrase *standards-based reform* refers to the reform of education at the school, school district, or state levels that is based on student standards set at these levels. Standards-based reform uses the student knowledge and skill standards as the basis of organizing the teaching activities of educators and others to help students achieve the standards. Reform based on these standards means changing the educators' actions to improve the achievement of the content standards by students.

The standards movement's basic assumption is that students are not learning the types of knowledge and skills that they need to be successful later in school or at work. A *Nation at Risk* began a debate about what students should be learning. This debate focused both on the nature of the skills (which often became debates about factual knowledge versus applied knowledge) and the depth of skills or rigor of what schools should be teaching. The basis of this debate has been the knowledge and skill levels needed to succeed in college and the workplace.

Standards-based reform also helped to shift the attention of policy makers and the public from concern about inputs, or the resources provided to the educational system, to a concern about outputs, or what the educational system and the students it serves have accomplished. Chester Finn, former U.S. assistant secretary of education, described this shift in education:

> Under the *old* conception . . . education was thought of as process and system, effort and intention, investment and hope. To improve education meant to try harder, to engage in more activity, to magnify one's plans, to give people more services, and to become more efficient in delivering them.
>
> Under the *new* definition, now struggling to be born, education is the result achieved, the learning that takes root when the process has been effective. *Only* if the process succeeds and learning occurs will we say *education* happened. Absent evidence of such a result, there is no education—however many attempts have been made, resources deployed, or energies expended. (1990, p. 586, emphasis in original)

Policy makers came to believe that past reform efforts—such as higher graduation requirements that required additional Carnegie units for graduation or the passage of tests in order to receive a high school diploma—would not work, and that other steps would be needed to help reform schools. Ramsay Selden, former director of the State Education Assessment Center at the Council of Chief State School Officers, noted the following:

> [T]here was a feeling of urgency that the educational system needed to be stronger, and that in addition to what states and districts and individual schools were doing— we needed a stronger presence at the national level. . . . We recognized that we didn't need a national curriculum, so national goals and voluntary national standards came to be seen as a good mechanism for providing a focus. (quoted in O'Neil, 1995, p. 12)

A basic premise of this discussion was that students were not sufficiently challenged by the instruction that they received, resulting in lower levels of achievement by many students. By setting more rigorous standards for students, it was hoped that the general level of student achievement would rise, thus better preparing students for post-secondary educational opportunities and employment. By changing the nature of the instruction students received, the assumption was that students would not only learn more, but they would be more actively engaged in this learning and thus retain a higher proportion of what they had learned.

A concomitant goal was that current inequities in student performance—well-documented by a variety of state and national student assessment programs—would narrow or actually disappear. Equity in educational achievement has been an important goal for the American educational system for more than 3 decades. Past reforms of education in the United States have not resulted in closing the gaps in student achievement between white students and other groups of students, because these often focused on providing *equal* resources, not the resources needed to close the gap in achievement.

The hope was that by setting higher standards for all students and by attending to what all students were actually achieving, the students who have traditionally done poorly in schools would achieve at much higher levels. It was hoped that a focus on *standards*, using these as a basis for reform, would help educators focus on what students are achieving rather than the resources expended, which is the basis of the assumption that gaps in student achievement can be closed while raising standards for the entire educational system.

Another basic premise of standards-based reform was that if educational agencies can define what knowledge students need to know and skills they need to be able to do, schools will rise to the challenge and help students accomplish these knowledge and skill goals. This is more likely to occur in schools where the knowledge and skills needed by students form the basis of the schools' curricula and instruction, are used as the basis of the assessments that students take, and are supported by the professional development in which the educators are engaged.

This means, of course, that reform of educational systems would not occur simply by setting standards, assessing these standards, and reporting the accomplishments of students. Instead, attention will need to be paid to how well educators are prepared and motivated to provide instruction that will help students achieve the standards set by the system. This fact has implications for state education agencies and the resources they can provide, as well as for local education systems and how they address the standards set at the state and local levels.

RECENT STANDARDS-BASED REFORMS
AT THE STATE AND NATIONAL LEVELS

In the early 1990s the terms *content standards* and *performance standards* were first used at the national levels. Although these terms were first applied in recent years, the concept of setting standards or goals for schools is not at all new at the state or local levels. The status of standards-based reform at the national and state levels is described in the following sections.

Standards-Based Reform at the National Level

Although reform based on standards and assessments is not new in many states, such reform efforts have begun in some states in earnest only since the late 1980s. In 1989 President Bush and the nation's governors met in Charlottesville, Virginia, in the first educational summit involving all fifty states in the nation's history. This educational summit yielded six national educational goals (National Educational Goals Panel, 1991) that were to be accomplished by the year 2000 and led to the formation of the National Education Goals Panel to monitor the states' progress in accomplishing each of the goals. Two of the goals focused on student achievement in subject areas such as English, mathematics, science, geography, and history. The list of subjects was subsequently expanded to include the arts, civics and government, economics, and foreign languages.

One major activity that followed the educational summit was a commitment to develop content standards at the national level for each subject area, similar to those that the National Council of Teachers of Mathematics (1989) had established for the area of mathematics. Federal support was provided to permit content standards to be developed in several subject areas. In a few other subjects where federal support was not forthcoming (such as social studies, physical education, and health education), content standards were developed using private support. Standards were set by national professional groups or groups composed explicitly for the standards-development effort; these standards focused on higher-order skills, with a particular emphasis on problem-solving and conceptual understanding skills. The intent was to set high-level, rigorous standards that would nonetheless be appropriate for all students.

In all cases, however, support for the development of the standards was relatively thin, perhaps due to the fact that the impetus for developing national standards came from a relatively small number of politicians, bureaucrats, business leaders, and educational leaders and did not represent a groundswell of popular support. Neither the policy approval nor the financial support for the various efforts to set standards proceeded through the normal channels involving approval by Congress. Because Congress was not included in the original planning of the National Education Goals Panel and the follow-up content standards development activities (and in fact, congressional representatives did not participate in the panels that approved the standards development activities), it was necessary to revisit the panel's original recommendations for standards and assessments.

An interim group, called the National Council on Education Standards and Testing (NCEST), was formed on an ad hoc basis. NCEST took almost a year to review the recommendations on the development of content standards and assessments, adding recommendations regarding the use of assessments in high-stakes situations. The group developed criteria for *opportunity-to-learn* standards, or standards relating to the learning opportunities that students have, for the equitable use of the assessments to make important decisions about students or the schools that they attend.

The result of the NCEST activities was the introduction of federal legislation, America 2000, during the final years of the Bush administration, based on bipartisan support. However, partisan debate and differences over the funding of charter schools led to the narrow defeat of America 2000 in the waning days of the Bush administration.

President Clinton, who had attended the educational summit as the governor of Arkansas, shared the commitment to federal activity to help the country set standards for its students. In March 1994, the Goals 2000 legislation was narrowly adopted by Congress and approved by President Clinton. Goals 2000 became the focal point of other federal legislation such as Improving America's Schools Act (IASA), the reauthorized version of the original ESEA. Goals 2000 called for the establishment of a National Education Standards and Improvement Council (NESIC) that would review and certify state content standards and assessments as well as federal support for the development of states' standards and assessments.

A year later, when Republican majorities were elected in both the House and the Senate, an effort was made to overturn Goals 2000, led primarily by conservative members of Congress who believed that Goals 2000 represented a major unneeded and harmful intrusion of the federal government into state and local education systems. The debate was heated, but in a narrow vote, the development of a federally supported group (NESIC) to review and certify states' standards and assessments was dropped, although the basic premises of Goals 2000 were affirmed. Federal financial support for the development of state standards and assessments was maintained, however. Most states voted to accept the federal funds available under Goals 2000, although a few (e.g., New Hampshire and Virginia) decided not to accept the funds, at least initially.

This debate about the appropriate level of federal support for states (and the extent to which the federal government should lead or push state educational support), plus controversies in the development of content standards in the areas of history (Stearns, 1996) and English language arts, led a number of observers by 1995 to ponder whether the standards-based reforms were dead in the water. Although states continued to develop content standards—whether or not states called them by this name—the impetus for national action slowed substantially. Ron Brandt (1995), former editor for the ASCD publication *Educational Leadership*, noted:

> Now that some of the original sponsors are disappointed in the new standards because they are not what was expected, what does this mean for educators? Apparently, these standards will not soon become a national curriculum or the basis for a set of high-stakes tests. Under the circumstances, educators can breathe a sigh of relief and, with discretion, put them to use in the endless task of improving curriculum and instruction. (p. 5)

To jump-start the momentum for the development of content standards, President Clinton and most of the nation's governors (as well as key business leaders selected by the governors) met in a second national education summit in 1997. At the summit, the nation's education policy makers and business leaders renewed their commitments to developing standards. They also vowed to establish a privately funded group to review states' standards to determine whether they are world-class and rigorous and to review the assessments being used and their alignment to those standards.

In 1997 the National Governors' Association formed Achieve with private support to review states' standards and assessments. Achieve began work on the development of criteria for what constitutes "rigorous" or "world-class." Achieve has implemented plans to review states' standards and provide commentary and assistance to states as they develop standards. Additional plans have been made for comparable work in reviewing and commenting on student assessments, and in early 1998 state officials met to discuss interest in working together to develop standards and assessments collaboratively.

Standards-Based Reform at the State Level

For decades, several states have had student expectations, academic goals, student outcomes, or other definitions of the skills that students need to know and be able to do. Similar efforts have taken place nationally since the late 1980s; however, at the state and local levels, the definition of student expectations is not nearly as new. This does not mean that state (or local) definitions of student expectations are necessarily rigorous nor uniform across states. In some states, this has been a relatively recent phenomenon, started since the national impetus to develop content standards began in the mid-1990s.

Both in terms of format and content, the standards that states have set vary in both depth and quality. Historically, these differences are partially due to the purposes or reasons for states' work in defining student expectations. In some states, particularly those with well-defined, mandated state curricula, the statements of student expectations were necessary to provide concrete definitions of what schools were expected to teach. In other states, particularly those without explicit state curricula or high school graduation requirements, the statements of student expectations defined a minimum recommended program. In these states, statements of student expectations guided or suggested what schools should be teaching without actually requiring schools to do so. States that have used testing as a requirement for grade promotion or high school graduation have also tended to focus on the minimum levels of accomplishment needed for promotion or graduation, thereby focusing schools' attention on these minimum skills.

However, as schools have focused on these minimum-level skills, and textbooks and tests have been prepared to reinforce these expectations, the perceived result has been so-called dumbed-down instruction. Critics believe that the emphasis on minimum basic skills has denied most students the opportunity to learn the challenging skills they need to go beyond the basics and to acquire the skills needed to succeed in post-secondary educational environments, the workplace, and as citizens. The textbooks, the tests, and the drill sheets have focused the nation's attention on low-level mathematics and reading skills, to the exclusion of higher level skills needed in these areas, much less the skills needed in areas beyond these subjects.

These critics have seen that even the curricula for college-bound students are filled with facts to be memorized and multiple-choice tests on which students can rely on guesswork. Students languish in classes where they go unchallenged and unmotivated, striving to achieve the minimum level needed to pass the tests and get into a good college. The largest worry for students in these classes is what is on the test. Past attempts at reform have simply added more to the curriculum to be completed before students graduate. Lacking are the expectations needed to help students learn and be able to do more.

A recent report on standards-based reforms by the National Academy of Education (McLaughlin & Shepard, 1995) has captured the spirit of the changes that critics of this minimum skills approach believe are needed at the state level:

> Much of current instructional practice is based on behavioral-learning theory from the early part of this century. According to this theory, learning occurs by reinforcement of low-level skills that become the building blocks for more complex understandings. An unfortunate practical consequence of this approach is that thinking and reasoning about core concepts are postponed, for some students indefinitely. In more recent decades, learning researchers have demonstrated that memorizing facts does not lead automatically to an ability to analyze and apply what has been learned. Learning requires thinking. Even reading the simplest texts requires that students actively comprehend what the text is saying or decide to reread if they don't. According to current theories, learning requires the active construction of mental models or representations by the learner. Each person has an organized set of ideas in his or her head about how concepts are related in math, science, or history; for learning to occur, when new information or ideas are encountered, the individual must think about and figure out how they fit within the existing structure or must reorganize their mental schema to accommodate the new knowledge. (p. 9)

These changes are not simply in the type and level of student expectations. To successfully accomplish the underlying transformations needed in student learning, the manner in which students are taught also needs to change. Teachers need to emphasize meaningful content and learning that is set in contexts understandable to students and based on experimenting, solving realistic problems, and applying knowledge and skills to real-life settings. As conceptualized, such instruction does not eliminate the need to know facts or key concepts from memory. However, knowing, particularly in the abstract, is not sufficient. It is important that teachers provide the opportunities for students to learn knowledge and to apply their understand-ings in contexts filled with meaning for the student, not simply for students to memorize information in isolated contexts devoid of meaning. By assem-bling knowledge, the assumption is that students will learn more, will retain this learning, and will be able to use and apply this learning more broadly and hence more effectively.

A major impact of the recent national efforts to develop content standards at the national level has been a flurry of state-led work to create or to revise student expectations at the state level that are much more rigorous and far more challenging. Efforts are under way to reform schools and the instruc-tion they provide by changing the nature of the standards that are set by states in order to move schools and students from the minima to much higher levels of achievement.

Recent state efforts have not been simply to make the curriculum more difficult nor simply to add more to it. Instead, there has been a conscious effort to add depth and rigor to the curriculum, with a distinct flavor of "less is more." Recent state reforms have differed substantially from current prac-tice by emphasizing the teaching and learning of fewer concepts (particularly unconnected factual information) and the use of the information learned in meaningful ways so that the information is retained and can be used by students to understand and solve unique and challenging problems.

Beginning in the mid-1980s, some states asserted a definition of skills that went beyond the minimum levels of expected performance and set a new course for influencing curriculum and instruction. These states adopted a policy strategy known as *standards-based systemic reform*. In these states, sys-temic efforts were made to set high standards for schools and students and to use these as the basis for instructional development, professional devel-opment, school improvement, and student assessment.

More states joined the effort following the establishment of the national educational goals, with support and encouragement coming from Washing-ton, DC (through funding provided by Goals 2000, the National Science Foundation, the Office of Educational Research and Improvement, and other federal sources) and state legislation. By 1998 every state except Iowa had developed state-level content standards in one or more content areas, many having established standards in a number of content areas.

Measuring Progress in State Reforms

It is often difficult to gauge the degree of change in the 50 states (and the myriad number of local school systems), much less to characterize the nature of these changes. Have states substantively increased what they expect of students? Are these changed expectations communicated well to local school districts? Are they being used as the basis for changed instruction with students? These are not easy questions to answer. Even the issue of what constitutes a rigorous or world-class content standard is not an easy one to settle.

There have been several attempts to measure the status and progress of states' standards reform efforts. One of these has been a series of studies conducted by researchers at the Consortium for Policy Research in Education (CPRE), as they have studied educational reform efforts in a number of states. A recent CPRE study (Massell, Kirst, & Hoppe, 1997) examined the persistence of standards-based reform efforts in nine states and 25 school districts within those states. A summary of excerpts from the study follow:

> In the nine states studied by CPRE, 1994–95 was characterized by a disjuncture between change-orientated political rhetoric and steady, incremental progress implementing the kinds of standards-based instructional guidance policies that have evolved over the past five to ten years. Policy rhetoric calling for greater free-market choices in education, smaller government, deregulation and the removal of categorical programs characterized both the state and federal level. . . .
>
> Standards-based, systemic reform has made impressive gains in recent years, despite the many difficulties inherent in such a sustained and complex effort. Indeed, policymakers on both sides of the political aisle and across all levels of government—federal, state, and local—have broadly agreed on the merits and worth of this approach to school change. As a consequence, states have persisted with the strategy despite substantial turnovers in leadership, criticisms about the content of particular standards and assessment policies, and real cuts in educational spending. (p. 9)

Another, much more widely known series of studies of states' efforts to set standards has been the annual critiques of state standards and assessments conducted by the American Federation of Teachers (AFT). Each state's standards and assessments have been critiqued and rated on dimensions using criteria established by AFT. These critiques and criteria will be among those used by Achieve, the privately funded effort established by the nation's governors and business leaders at the second education summit held in 1996. At the time of this writing, however, Achieve was just beginning its work and had not prepared any report on states' standards-reform efforts. The 1997 AFT report contained several key findings. Among them were the following:

- *The commitment to standards-based reform remains very strong in the states.* Every state except Iowa is setting common academic standards for its students and most consider standards a work in progress. Forty-nine states are developing common academic standards for their students. Thirty-nine states have developed new or revised standards since the 1996 report.
- *Over the course of the year since the American Federation of Teachers 1996 report on states' standards and assessments, the quality of state standards has improved.* Fourteen states produced new standards that are stronger than the versions reviewed in 1996. Only three states produced standards that are weaker than their previous versions. Most states (29) have standards in at least three of four core subjects that are clear, specific, and well grounded in content (up from 21 in 1996).

- *Most states still need to improve some of their standards to provide the basis for a common core of learning.* Only 17 states have standards in *all four* core subjects that are clear and comprehensive enough to lead to a common core of learning across the state (up from 15 last year). The other 32 states have standards that need improvement in one or more subjects.
- *States continue to have more difficulty setting strong standards in English and social studies than in math or science.*
- *Some state standards are exemplary and should be considered models for other states to emulate.*
- *More states recognize the need for internationally competitive standards but lack the resources to determine whether their standards are world-class* (American Federation of Teachers, 1997, pp. v, 11–12).

It appears from these studies that some states have successfully tackled the issue of developing rigorous content standards, whereas other states' efforts can be characterized as works in progress. It is highly likely that states' efforts will continue in the foreseeable future, and that such development efforts will improve both the rigor and utility of the content standards.

PERILS AND PITFALLS OF STANDARDS-BASED REFORM

Much progress appears to have occurred in states and local districts as they have created content standards for their schools and students. However, this progress has not taken place without controversy and concerns being expressed. In fact, the creation of content standards at the national and state levels has raised a number of issues. The success of standards-based reform hinges on the successful resolution of issues such as these, since broad-based support for standards-based reform rests on popular support for such definitions of what schools should teach and students should learn.

Some of the major concerns that have been raised with standards at the national level were summarized in the National Academy of Education (McLaughlin & Shepard, 1995) report on standards and assessment. These concerns include the following:

- *Diverting attention from more fundamental educational needs.* Serious questions have been raised about whether the standards movement is what is needed most to improve schools. Excellence in academic achievement requires more than setting goals and expecting students to meet them. What if reformers focused instead on the necessary conditions of a highly literate and well-educated nation? . . . An exclusive focus on outcomes may prevent debate about how instruction should be delivered or how learning could be supported by the community, and it could avoid attention to adequacy of resources which would be more costly than developing standards. . . . (pp. 12–13)

- *Undermining professional and local responsibility for student learning.* In the Panel's judgment, curriculum standards developed by national professional associations would be helpful as tools for informing and guiding state and local curriculum building, teaching practice, and assessment development. Where they are well conceived and well constructed, they may help local educators reflect on and evaluate their own efforts at reshaping classroom and school-level practices, particularly when concepts of knowledge are changing. . . . Critics of the standards movement are less sanguine, however, about the public education system's ability to use standards as tools rather than as mandates or prescriptions for instruction. They fear that national standards may be a step down the road to a highly specified national curriculum and argue that, given the diversity of human experiences and the need to build on prior knowledge in the learning process, it is neither wise nor reasonable to make centralized decisions about what, when, and how ideas should be taught or how student understanding should be tested. . . . (pp. 13–14)

- *Heightening educational inequities.* Arguments that standards could worsen inequities have two key components. First, it is likely that traditionally disadvantaged groups will have the least access to the kind of instruction needed to reach high standards. The vision of new standards, exemplified by the NCTM math standards, requires that most teachers make substantial shifts in their teaching practices. Teachers in urban and poor school systems, where instruction is currently often characterized by drill and practice, will have the biggest changes to make but are least likely to be provided with needed staff development resources. Second, negative consequences of failing to meet the standards will further impede already disadvantaged students. The intention in having students repeat a grade or be placed in a remedial class to prepare for retesting is to help them academically. Past research has consistently shown, however, that students are very often worse off not only academically but also socially, following these placements. (p. 14)

- *Threatening basic-skills instruction.* The intended changes in curriculum and instruction described in the section on challenging standards . . . are opposed by a number of groups each with slightly different reasons for their objections. Some fear that the deemphasis of skills instruction, especially in mathematics, will leave students ill prepared to take important tests such as the SAT. Some groups worry that advanced students will be slowed down by a common set of standards for all students. Others oppose the emphasis on a "thinking" curriculum because critical thinking and questioning threaten strongly held beliefs and introduce value issues into the school curriculum. In some local applications involving integrated curricula, people see goals aimed at effective communication and cooperative learning as a watering down of rigorous academic content. Specific objections differ from community to community, depending upon the particular features of proposed standards and curriculum and the beliefs and values of parents and community members. Occasionally, groups with philosophically incompatible perspectives form coalitions against the common enemy—standards-based reform. (pp. 14–15)

Another study of the standards-based reform movement (National Association of State Boards of Education, 1996) also listed a series of criticisms that have been raised about the standards movement:

- *Resources.* Some saw the standards movement as a major drain on resources that should be used for more pressing needs such as basic educational materials. . . .
- *Educational apartheid.* Other critics saw the standards movement as another burden that would be placed on the shoulders of those who traditionally do not do well in schools. . . .
- *Standards as new attempts at previous failed reforms.* Still others saw the standards movement as a thinly veiled attempt at a type of educational reform that had been tried a number of times before . . . the efficiency movement of the early 1900s . . . and the behavioral objectives movement of the 1960s. . . .
- *Content.* In addition to its association with the flawed efficiency and behavioral objective movements of the past, the standards movement received a fair amount of criticism for the very content it promoted. . . .
- *Volume of material.* Perhaps the ultimate criticism of the national efforts to establish standards was the charge that, once developed, they were simply too cumbersome to use. (pp. 5–6)

It is clear that regardless of the logic used to promote standards-based reform in a state or a local school district, some groups might still oppose such efforts based on real or imagined threats to their belief systems or on the grounds that the problems or issues that standards-based reforms are designed to address will only worsen if such reforms are implemented.

Often, the debates that have raged during the past decade surrounding standards-based reform have at their heart fundamental disagreements about what will help all students achieve academic and life success. The advocates for reform urge such reforms based on the idea that rote learning (in their view, often followed by immediate forgetting) hinders students later in school and at work when they are presented with novel problems to solve or those requiring creative solutions. Hence, they advocate instruction that relies on hands-on problem solving and stresses the application of knowledge in more or less unique, real-world settings.

The advocates for basic skills, however, see such reforms as intending to provide all students with a false sense of accomplishment. They assert that it is nearly impossible to solve problems and be truly creative without a strong background in fundamental knowledge and skills that can be learned in no better way than rote memorization. They argue that collaborative learning, promoted by many standards advocates, might encourage weak students to feel good about themselves, but supplants real learning.

Debates have also focused on the nature of the standards needed to guide reform in several subject areas. In English language arts, debate has centered on whether general or specific statements of intended student accomplishment are needed. The controversy surrounding the creation of the national standards in English (federal funds were used to create an initial draft, then were withdrawn over the nature of that draft, and the standards were completed by professional groups in the areas) have caused some educators and other citizens to reject the resulting standards as inappropriate and misguided. States such as Virginia have rejected these standards, as has organizations such Family Research Council, a major Washington, DC-based Christian citizen organization that monitors and reports on federal legislation and programs.

In the area of mathematics, debates have focused on whether and how basic computational skills should be emphasized, as well as whether or how calculators should be used in instruction and assessment.

In history, the viewpoint of instruction was often debated. That is, should history be taught from the perspective of European discovery of America or from the perspective of a native American whose land is invaded and conquered. Are the historical "dead white male" accomplishments of the past to be set aside or diminished in favor of stressing the accomplishments of women and minorities?

Such disagreements, often heatedly debated in public or in policy circles, cite studies of student learning from state and national testing programs or surveys to back up their claims. For example, one study might reveal that few employers are able to find and hire the potential employees that they need, whereas another study might reveal that few students can find their country on a world map, can identify when Columbus discovered America, or can name the president of the United States. As a result, strongly held, extreme positions are often staked out and the various groups argue vociferously from these extremely held vantage points. The result is that, depending on who wins the argument, the standards on which reforms rest can vary from one extreme to another between the states. It also means that content standards may change substantially from one year to another at either the state or local levels as one group or the other gains power or political office. More effective strategies are needed if content standards are to serve as the basis for curricular and instructional planning, much less systemic school reform.

WORK NEEDED ON CONTENT STANDARDS

The AFT report cited earlier (American Federation of Teachers, 1997) lists several general recommendations for states as they continue to develop and refine their content standards. These include the following:

1. States need to be encouraged to revise and improve their academic standards.
2. States need help to make sure their standards are rigorous and internationally competitive.
3. States should draw on the best work of other states.
4. States should supplement their standards with curriculum guides or frameworks that provide clearer guidance to districts and schools without sacrificing local control.
5. States need to make sure their assessments are based on strong standards.
6. States need help determining whether their standards and assessments are aligned.
7. States should establish plans for phasing in incentives or consequences, otherwise students will not take the standards seriously.
8. States must provide extra help to students who are not meeting the standards. (pp. 27–31)

The AFT report also indicates why these recommendations are so important:

> Building an education system based on standards is analogous to building a house. The standards serve as the foundation, and everything else gets built upon them. The curriculum is based on the standards, assessments are based on the standards, textbooks are based on the standards, teacher training is based on the standards, and all accountability measures are based on the standards as well. With so much resting on the standards, states need standards that are very clear and very strong. (p. 27)

Clearly, the content standards developed by states are important. One of the ways in which this importance is demonstrated and emphasized is the use of the content standards as a basis for the student assessments used at the national, state, and local levels.

ROLE OF ASSESSMENT IN STANDARDS-BASED REFORM

Student assessment often plays a critical role in standards-based reform efforts, particularly at the state and national level. It is often the creation of the assessment program that triggers the development of the content standards that will guide not only the assessment program but the broader efforts at curricular and instructional reform. In addition, assessment programs are often perceived to be the single best mechanism for communicating changing standards of student expectations and the levels of student performance.

The assessment program may concurrently communicate to educators and the public the goals and specific levels of instruction that should take place, the levels of performance that are needed at each level of the educational system, and the types of teaching and learning that must take place to reach these levels of desired performance on the standards set for students and the educational system.

Thus, the role of student assessment in standards-based reform is a pivotal one. The nature of what is tested is important in establishing the rigor of the system, because rigorous-appearing standards can be assessed in a simplistic manner and serve to reinforce a mediocre status quo in the educational system. This means that care needs to be taken in what is selected to measure at each level of the assessment program, and the quality of the assessment measures themselves needs to be carefully examined.

In addition, because the nature of assessment may influence how the results are used, some attention needs to be paid to the manner in which the content standards are assessed. There is some evidence that the nature of the assessment—whether multiple-choice or extended constructed response—can influence the manner in which students receive instruction on the standard (Roeber, 1997). This was one of the major forces behind the development of criterion-referenced assessments during the 1970s, because they were thought to attend more to the nature of the skills being assessed and how these would be taught. With this in mind, some states have introduced extended constructed response exercises as some or all of the formats used to assess students.

Indeed, standards-based assessments differ from traditional assessments used in the past in several important ways. First, because the intent of assessing the content standards is to improve student learning on the content standards, there is a stronger tie between assessment and instruction built into the system. This helps to assure the linkages between student expectations, student performance, and instruction. More traditional forms of assessment were linked less directly to one set of standards.

Second, because standards-based assessments are built on content standards expected of all students, it is more logical to compare a student's performance to the set of standards being measured rather than to the performance of other students. This is a more criterion-referenced approach to reporting student performance. From the perspective of standards-based assessment, what matters is not necessarily whether one student has achieved more than another, but whether they have each achieved a satisfactory (or higher) performance on the standards. In traditional norm-referenced, commercially available tests, student performance (at the individual or group levels) is compared to a norm group and performance is expressed in comparative terms. Of course, using a standards-based approach, it is still feasible to compare the number of students achieving a satisfactory performance across schools, districts, states, or even nations when scores are reported relative to the content standards.

Third, because the content standards may incorporate a broader range of student expectations, it is logical that assessment formats other than multiple-choice exercises may be required. If students are to provide a unique solution to a complex problem, they must be permitted to solve the problem in an extended constructed-response exercise, as opposed to selecting one of several possible solutions provided in a multiple-choice exercise. Traditional, norm-referenced tests tend not to assess such skills and typically contain, exclusively or primarily, multiple-choice items.

Fourth, because the assessments themselves can exemplify the content standards and illustrate how well students can perform, they serve as a motivator for professional development in two areas: standards-based instruction and the assessment of student performance. One significant difference between standards-based assessments and more traditional forms of assessment is the belief that both classroom instruction and the assessments that teachers use in their classrooms should be aligned with both the content standards and large-scale assessments of the standards. Professional development is needed to help educators see the alignments and to implement the instruction (and assessments) that will permit students to achieve the standards.

To carry out the intent of standards-based reform, assessments must possess certain qualities. These include not only the traditional measures of quality (e.g., reliability and validity) but additional concerns as well (e.g., alignment and utility). As standards-based assessments have been implemented, even the traditional measures of assessment quality need to be examined.

Reliability of the measures used has been and remains a primary concern. As new student outcomes and ways of measuring student performance have been adopted, the traditional concern about the internal consistency of measures, as well as their replicability, are prime concerns, regardless of whether a student is assessed using multiple-choice or constructed-response exercises. Even hands-on, individually administered exercises must be reliable. In such cases, reliability would address questions such as "If students are asked to sing a song, would their performance be the same each time they sang the same song? Would different songs yield different student performance?"

The concerns about the *validity* of the measures used to assess the content standards is not much different than more traditional concerns about the match of tests to the assessment framework used to guide assessment development. In each case, content validity is judged by content experts against the standards, the curriculum, or the set of expectations being measured. The concept of alignment between the standards and the assessments is now being emphasized so that the assessment measures what is judged to be important (the content standards) in a manner that will encourage schools to provide the instruction students need.

More recently, some assessment developers have begun to stress a new conception of *consequential validity* (Messick, 1989). Consequential validity refers to whether the assessment, when results are reported to local educators, leads to uses of the results that are viewed as useful or positive improvements.

In the view of these developers, the ultimate validity of the measure is whether it leads to positive consequences for the educational system and students. Examples of such positive consequences might include changes in the manner in which instruction takes place (e.g., a shift from drill and practice to more hands-on, constructed learning) or changes in student performance (e.g., the improvements in student learning shown on the assessment in question or on other assessments). Critics of this conception of validity rightfully point out the many mediating factors that determine whether test results are used at all, much less successfully used.

STATUS OF ASSESSMENT EFFORTS AT THE STATE AND NATIONAL LEVELS

Although the use of content standards as the basis of assessment is relatively new, attention to assessment at the national and state levels is not. This section provides an overview of the status and trends in state and national testing. In some states, statewide testing has been going on for decades, whereas in others, little or no statewide testing has occurred. However, because standards-based assessment is relatively new, the manner in which states are implementing such programs is changing, in some cases rather dramatically.

The Association of State Assessment Programs (ASAP) was formed by several states with an interest in statewide student assessment as a vehicle by which states could help one another to develop quality assessment programs with a minimum of wasted effort and controversy. Early ASAP meetings consisted of discussions about the procedures for developing criterion-referenced tests and surviving the inevitable legal challenges to the minimum competency tests, as the landmark legal case *Debra P. v. Turlington* (1979) was then taking place. To provide the maximum time for discussion of issues, annual surveys of states' assessment efforts were begun and continue to the present, conducted under the auspices of the Council of Chief State School Officers (CCSSO) (1996). The most recent CCSSO report on the status and trends in statewide student assessments programs (Council of Chief State School Officers, 1997) is the basis for the information presented in this section.

In the mid-1970s, two strong innovations occurred in state-level, large-scale assessment that were spreading throughout the states. First, states such as Michigan adopted the then-new form of measurement called *criterion-referenced testing*. Scores were reported as the proportion of the objectives passed, rather than comparing student (or school or district) scores to national norms. Second, states began to use tests to determine whether students had learned enough to receive a high school diploma. This use of minimum competency testing for high school graduation was exemplified by the landmark program in Florida.

The predominant form of large-scale assessment at that time was norm-referenced testing (NRT). Interest in criterion-referenced tests (CRTs) was stimulated not only by the states that had adopted CRTs as a form of assessment but also by the National Assessment of Educational Progress (NAEP), due to the fact that several states (such as California, Connecticut, Minnesota, and Wyoming) gave the early NAEP assessments in conjunction with their own state tests in order to obtain state and national data on their students. Not only did this practice introduce these states to CRTs, it also introduced the concept of the state NAEP assessment program.

Advent of Writing Assessment

In the 1970s, assessment was limited usually to mathematics and reading. NAEP, however, added assessments in a number of additional subject areas, including science, social studies, citizenship, music, visual arts, career and occupational development, literature, and writing. Assessments included both conventional approaches such as multiple-choice items and less conventional approaches such as constructed-response and individually administered, hands-on performance measures. Many of these innovative approaches to assessment (and even the subject areas) were dropped as a result of budget cuts in the 1970s, but performance measures in the area of writing survived.

The NAEP assessments of writing in the early 1970s encouraged the belief that having all students at one or more grade levels actually write essays would be feasible. Although more expensive than the much more prevalent multiple-choice tests of writing, actual writing demonstrations (e.g., essay tests) were thought to be more content valid, and many believed that this format would lead to better teaching of writing. Substantial debate about the costs versus benefits of this type of assessment occurred in the 1970s. However, belief in the use of performance testing to assess writing skills was so strong that it remains the prevalent form of assessment used by states today. The use of similar, open-ended performance exercises has also spread to other subject areas.

Expansion of Student Assessment Programs

During the 1980s, additional states adopted large-scale assessment programs as a tool for school reform and improvement. Each year, one or two states would add some form of large-scale assessment. In addition, states began to develop assessments in other subject areas, such as science, social studies (or one or more of its components, such as history or geography), health education, physical education, the arts, and vocational education.

Educators in many states also began to show interest in sharing assessment items or tasks among the states, since so many new states were now interested in large-scale assessment. Attempts were made to create item banks among the states, but these generally proved to be unsuccessful as states tended to cling to their own sets of student expectations, making sharing of corresponding items challenging at best.

Performance Assessment

The latter part of the 1980s also brought more attention to the form of assessment. Multiple-choice tests were (and still are) the primary assessment format used by most states, with the exception of states that assessed writing using a writing sample. In the late 1980s, a couple of trends began. First, a small group of states (Maryland, Kentucky, California, Arizona, and Maine) began to use performance assessments (constructed-response formats) as the primary form of assessment. (Other states considering developing such programs included Massachusetts and Delaware.) These states demonstrated that it is feasible to administer alternative forms of assessment in a relatively cost-effective manner.

However, concerns about test content caused the innovative assessment programs in Arizona and California to be shelved and caused Kentucky to add a norm-referenced test to its assessment program. In Arizona and California, it was the content of particular constructed-response items as well as the technical adequacy of each program that raised concerns, whereas in Kentucky, the concern was whether gains on the state test were artifacts of that assessment and would not show up on other tests.

Second, a number of states were working on other alternatives. This innovative work included performance assessments that could be administered to individuals or small groups of students, that were based on curriculum-imbedded tasks in which assessment is intricately interwoven within teaching and assessment information is collected over several weeks or months, portfolios of student work that were collected and later scored, and other innovative forms of assessment. The annual survey of states' student assessment programs indicated that few states have actually implemented these innovative alternative forms of assessment, but given the number of states reporting such work, these numbers might increase in the future.

It is likely that, given the costs of alternative assessment in terms of money and time, most states will move toward the concept of an *assessment system* using different forms of assessment at different levels. For example, large-scale, standardized assessments with some alternative approaches might be used for state-level reporting, whereas more extensive programs of performance and portfolio assessment might be used to meet school or classroom assessment needs. Such a program has been illustrated in

Oregon. Several states report that such innovative performance assessments are being developed for use by local educators.

A real challenge for states considering innovative approaches to assessment are the costs (both financial and instructional time) involved in using such measurement strategies, as well as the technical concerns about these new approaches to assessment. Although they have a strong advantage of illustrating better approaches to teaching and learning, alternative assessments may be less reliable for reporting individual student or school results, and they are certainly more expensive. Therefore, in recent years, several states have considered the use of a *mixed* assessment model in which students are assessed using a combination of multiple-choice and open-ended exercises. This approach has the advantage of allowing states to assess more content, but at lower cost than an entirely open-ended assessment. Kentucky has and will be using this approach and Massachusetts will be implementing it.

Another approach to broader content coverage is the use of every-pupil matrix sampling designs. In matrix sampling, the entire assessment is broken up into subtests and each student takes only a portion (e.g., one or more subtests) of the entire assessment. This approach is useful when school and district information are more important than individual student results. One drawback to matrix sampling is that it makes individual student-level reporting difficult, particularly if any one student takes so few items that reliable results for that student cannot be prepared. Kentucky and Maryland have used this approach for several years.

Professional Development on Assessment

Attention to the forms of assessment, as well as thinking about assessment systems used at both the state and local levels, has encouraged another trend at the state level. As state-level policy makers and educators have debated the form(s) of assessment appropriate for the state to use, increasing attention has been paid to the training of classroom teachers to collect and use information that might be gathered from innovative approaches to assessment used within their classrooms. This trend is actually the convergence of several trends, including changes in student standards to emphasize thinking and problem-solving skills (while de-emphasizing memorization of content knowledge), and increased support for alternative approaches to assessment (such as projects, exhibitions, demonstrations, and the use of portfolios).

The result is that many local districts and some state agencies are now providing classroom teachers with assessment learning experiences that teachers can apply in their classrooms. The state of Washington uses this approach, and other states (e.g., Wisconsin) are considering how to provide such training to all teachers. This attention to professional development on assessment for classroom teachers is particularly appropriate given that few, if any, teachers receive much in the way of preservice training on assessment (Stiggins, 1991).

Norm-Referenced Tests

When the ASAP group began meeting in the mid-1970s, the most commonly used assessments were commercially available, norm-referenced tests. Despite the attention that has been paid to other forms of measurement such as criterion-referenced assessments, over the past two decades, norm-referenced tests are still a significant feature of large-scale assessment in the United States. The trend in recent years, however, has been a slight decrease in the number of states requiring the use of norm-referenced tests at one or more grade levels. In 1993, 31 states used norm-referenced tests, 30 reported using them in 1994, 31 states reported using norm-referenced tests in 1995, and 29 states reported using them in 1996.

This number was expected to fall even further, given the de-emphasis on norm-referenced assessments in the Improving America's Schools Act (IASA), the reauthorization of the Elementary and Secondary Education Act (ESEA). As a result of this legislation, states no longer were required to use norm-referenced assessments for the evaluation of Title I compensatory education programs or for monitoring individual Title I student improvement. This was a major change in the legislation, which opponents of norm-referenced tests fought for and won. Instead, states are required to develop and operate comprehensive assessment systems capable of reporting whether individual students and school programs are making adequate yearly progress.

Two events conspired to confound the prediction of declining reliance on norm-referenced tests. First, the November 1994 election brought to power chief state school officers, state board of education members, legislators and governors with strongly held ideas about student standards and assessments. These ideas often included deeply held concerns about the new forms of assessment and the standards on which they are based. These individuals felt more comfortable with tests sold by major test publishers than home-grown assessments developed by educators in their states. They believed that the tests sold by publishers were more objective and did not require that large sums of money be spent to develop them.

In addition, many policy makers and members of the public wanted to be able to make national comparisons at the student, school, and school district levels. Given problems in some of the innovative assessment efforts first implemented in Arizona, California, and Georgia, to name a few, policy makers pushed to set aside newer approaches to assessment and to return to commercially available, norm-referenced tests. States such as Alabama re-implemented norm-referenced tests in addition to their criterion-referenced testing programs, as many policy makers preferred to rely on comparative data using test instruments developed outside of their individual states.

Second, the changes implemented in the IASA legislation have proved to be less far-reaching than originally thought. As the result of political pressures, states will be required to change their statewide assessments substantially less than originally thought. For example, states have until the 2000–2001 school year to develop and implement a final comprehensive assessment system—and only in mathematics and reading, not in all of the national goal areas (unless the states assess students in other subject areas).

In the interim, states can use transitional assessments of virtually any type (norm-referenced, criterion-referenced, or performance assessments), so long as they are deemed by the states to "measure challenging state content standards," which is left poorly defined in the federal legislation. Some states have even proposed using norm-referenced tests as their final assessments for IASA Title I; apparently the use of such assessments in this manner will meet with federal approval.

For these reasons, it is likely that norm-referenced tests will continue to be a major type of assessment used in states. To satisfy the desire for normative information, but using measures of higher-level standards, some states (such as Kentucky and North Carolina) have administered the National Assessment of Educational Progress (NAEP) assessments to samples of students taking their statewide assessments in order to provide NAEP-like scores to buildings and districts, as well as for their own state.

The use of the NAEP in providing normative information promises to allow states to pursue new forms of assessment while providing external referents for scores on the statewide assessments. It is even possible that some form of individual student NAEP test might be made available as well. It will be interesting to monitor the success of these efforts and to determine if this becomes a trend for the future.

In the state of the union address in early 1997, President Clinton proposed voluntary national tests (VNTs) of fourth-grade reading and eighth-grade mathematics. His proposal was similar to one proposed in 1996 by Governor Engler of Michigan, then cochair of the National Education Goals Panel. The president's proposal calls for the development (at federal expense) of a mixed assessment based on (but different than) the NAEP frameworks in these subjects to yield individual student scores and to be given at federal expense beginning in 1999. States' participation would be voluntary. Several states have proposed methods of linking the VNTs to their current assessments, not unlike how Kentucky and North Carolina linked the NAEP assessments to their state assessments in the past.

The VNTs have been warmly received by some who view them as a means of gauging state performance on national content standards, while avoiding some of the pitfalls seen by critics in the use of commercial norm-referenced tests. However, several states have expressed concerns about the viability of both the NAEP assessments and their own statewide assessments if the VNTs are implemented.

During 1997 the specifications for the mathematics and reading tests were created by national panels under the direction of the Council of Chief State School Officers and the U.S. Department of Education. The U.S. Department of Education originally stated that it did not need congressional approval to develop or administer the tests, but it later sought congressional approval of the testing plans, as well as the necessary appropriations to develop them. In the heated debate that ensued, a compromise proposal was adopted.

Policy direction for the new VNTs was assigned to the National Assessment Governing Board (NAGB), the policy board responsible for NAEP. Second, the U.S. Department of Education was requested to carry out at least two studies: one study would examine whether the same information that a national test would provide could be obtained from nationally available, norm-referenced tests, and the other study would examine the same question relative to the assessments that states are using. The National Academy of Sciences' Board on Testing and Assessment has begun each of these studies.

In addition, NAGB was given responsibility for determining whether the government's contract for developing the VNTs—which involved many of the national testing companies—should be continued. Each of these determinations is scheduled to be completed in 1998, and reports to Congress and the subsequent approval of Congress are necessary before progress beyond pilot testing occurs. This has pushed back the possible implementation of the VNTs from 1999 to no sooner than 2001.

It is too soon to tell what the long-term impact of the VNTs will be on states or the testing industry. At the current time, most states and districts that planned to administer VNTs had planned to add them to their assessment programs and, at least initially, do not plan to drop any of their current assessment components.

NATIONAL EFFORTS AT JOINT DEVELOPMENT

Another trend is worth noting. Until 1990 most assessment development was carried out by individual states working alone or with the assistance of a testing contractor. Since then, two innovations in collaboration among the states have taken place. The first is the New Standards project, codirected by the University of Pittsburgh Learning Research and Development Center and the National Center for Education and the Economy, which has been working with a number of states and local districts to design and develop innovative assessment systems in areas such as mathematics, language arts, and science. The second is the Council of Chief State School Officers' State Collaborative on Assessment and Student Standards (SCASS), which is currently involved in nine projects in which states work together to develop innovative assessment designs or innovative student assessment program components.

Both of these activities mark a first for collaboration among the states. States are actively working together to develop assessments that they will share and use, rather than simply exchanging information about innovative assessment approaches, as has been the case in the past. This collaborative work has demonstrated the feasibility of states working together to develop shared assessment program strategies and components, including common instruments. This work is based on the demonstrated similarity among states' standards in areas such as science and social studies, as well as the emerging realization that states can share assessment developmental work to increase quality and reduce costs. This effort is beginning to give rise to the belief that common instruments across states are both feasible and desirable.

Along these lines, in 1998 Achieve proposed extending this collaborative work to include the establishment of mathematics and reading tests that are jointly developed by several states. Mathematics and reading tests are frequently the most well-funded programs among the states, so the incentives for collaborative development work are the lowest. Thus, it is uncertain how successful this effort will be. However, this approach does offer an interesting alternative to the development of the VNTs by NAGB, because a common test that is shared between several participating states would allow direct state-to-state comparisons and, with an appropriate national sample, state-to-nation comparisons as well. This is another trend that bears watching.

Accommodating Students with Disabilities

One issue that states are now facing is how to provide accommodations on many of the statewide assessment components for students with disabilities. Much work is taking place to encourage local school districts to use various accommodations to increase the participation of these students, for several reasons. First, advocacy groups for students with disabilities have brought concerns regarding participation in large-scale assessment programs to the forefront. Second, federal agencies (e.g., the Offices of Special Education Programs and of Educational Research and Improvement of the U.S. Department of Education) have provided substantial funding to states to investigate methods and procedures for accommodating students with disabilities. States have used funds to develop new assessments, to develop new accommodations policies, to research the impact of these accommodations policies, and to develop materials explaining appropriate accommodations.

Third, national organizations such as the National Center for Educational Outcomes at the University of Minnesota have been tireless in their efforts to assist states in providing accommodations to all students and have collaborated with organizations such as CCSSO in working with state assessment and special education staffs to design appropriate accommodations.

Finally, the reauthorized *Individuals with Disabilities Education Act* (IDEA) requires states to provide accommodations to students needing them, alternate assessments for individuals for whom the accommodations still do not permit full participation in state or district assessments, and reports of results of accommodated and alternate assessments in a disaggregated manner. The IDEA also sets deadlines and schedules for these milestones to be accomplished.

All of this work has resulted in a wide variety of accommodations being provided by states for many of the assessment components run by states. The categories of accommodations being provided include accommodations regarding presentation format, test setting, response setting, and timing/scheduling. The variety has resulted, at least for the time being, in some unusual practices. For example, accommodations permitted in one state may be specifically prohibited in another state.

Although many states offer a broad number of accommodations, relatively few provide alternate assessments for students still unable to participate in the large-scale assessment program. In the CCSSO survey, only six states reported providing alternate assessments (such as an alternate portfolio assessments) that collect and report information on students. Of course, such alternate assessments raise various policy and technical issues. Accommodations and alternate assessments are not typically provided in the cases in which states use commercially available, norm-referenced tests. Accommodations on norm-referenced tests and the development of alternate assessment procedures are among the major areas of assistance needed by states and school districts as they address the requirements of the IDEA.

Assessing English-Language Learning Students

As much work as appears to be occurring in providing accommodations for students with disabilities, substantially less work appears to be occurring in assessing students with limited-English proficiency. The CCSSO survey found that more states permitted the automatic exclusions of students from large-scale assessment requirements and that fewer accommodations are provided for these students. In addition, fewer alternate assessments are provided. A few states with large numbers of non-English-speaking students require English proficiency measures to be used annually with students who do not participate in the state's large-scale assessment programs. These policies are intended to encourage local school districts to help students acquire English proficiency as soon as possible. Clearly, assessment of students with disabilities and students with limited English proficiency are two areas in need of both policy and technical development among the states. Much work is needed to help states in developing appropriate assessments and accommodations for these students.

Future Issues and Their Impact on State Assessment

An examination of the changes in large-scale assessment programs during the past 20 years shows a substantial change in the number of states with such programs, the subject areas assessed, and the types of assessment measures being used, as well as the types of assessment measures being developed and the manner in which this development is proceeding. The pace of these changes has increased substantially in the past few years as public attention to the quality of schools has increased. There is no sign of this interest abating.

Not surprisingly, these changes have led a number of states to reexamine assessment program designs that were adopted in years past. Several states are examining whether their current assessment designs are still adequate and are looking at how such programs as NAEP, the New Standards project, SCASS, IASA Title I, IDEA, and a possible VNT fit within their overall assessment purposes and design. Given the number of states that are conducting such reviews, further changes in state's large-scale assessment programs are likely.

Several trends occurring at the state and local levels may have a long-term impact on the shape of large-scale assessment programs at the state level. Certainly, the current emphasis on performance assessment and other alternative assessment formats is likely to continue. Along with the successes (such as in Maryland and Kentucky), there have been setbacks in California, Arizona, Indiana, and elsewhere, which indicates that widespread acceptance of performance assessment is not automatic.

Technical issues related to alternative assessments need to be addressed in a sound manner, and policy makers and the public need to understand the reasons for such measures, the student standards that they measure, and why both innovative standards and assessments are needed. Educator support is also vital; teachers and administrators must see that the additional time and costs associated with the use of such measures are appropriate. States and others interested in innovative forms of assessment will need to make sure important parties such as parents, legislators, and other members of the public are on board before engaging in this new developmental work. More than rhetoric is needed.

Certainly, there will be some impact of the drive now under way in some states to deregulate public education and return control of it to local school districts. Because this drive is taking several forms, it would not be unexpected for these pressures to affect the extent and types of state-level student assessment in the future. In some cases, this phenomenon may mean less attention to statewide student expectations and measures; in other places, it may mean just the opposite.

The need for appropriate assessment training and experiences for classroom teachers is also not likely to abate. Both IASA Title I and IDEA require educators who understand and can use large-scale and classroom assessment information. Several states have undertaken assessment literacy projects for educators, policy makers, and others.

The collaborative work between states is likely to spread innovative approaches to assessment more quickly than has occurred in the past. In addition, the outside political pressures to use assessment as a tool for school reform is not likely to lessen. Changes brought about by federal legislation such as Goals 2000 and IASA will occur as well, but perhaps at a slower pace than once thought.

Finally, recent congressional reauthorizations of the NAEP program have brought several changes that also may affect states. In recent years, NAEP has offered the trial state-NAEP programs, but unfortunately recent appropriations for the program have not permitted a full-scale state-NAEP program to be offered. A number of changes to NAEP have been proposed, and with the voluntary national test being assigned to NAGB, additional changes may take place. It is uncertain at this point how many of these changes will be implemented for NAEP, what the shape of the program will be in the future, nor how the NAEP of the future will affect states. In addition, it is uncertain how the drive to develop a voluntary national test will affect NAEP, the use of norm-referenced tests, or states' large-scale student assessment programs. One thing is sure, however: many swirling, cross-cutting trends at the state level are affecting large-scale assessment programs, and it is likely that these trends will affect the nature of statewide assessments in the future.

PROGNOSIS FOR STANDARDS-BASED REFORM FOR EFFECTIVE SCHOOL IMPROVEMENT

There are strategies that states and local school districts can use to effectively implement standards-based efforts to reform curriculum and instruction at the state and local levels. The challenge is not only to create a set of standards to guide the system that can survive politically, but also to implement wide-scale reforms based on these standards for all students. These strategies were described in a recent publication by the Education Commission of the States (ECS) on standards-based assessment systems. The ECS recommendations for policy makers can be summarized as follows:

- *Build state and local consensus.* If public opinion polls are any indication, the concept that students should be held to high academic standards enjoys broad support.... The diversity of opinion on what students should learn and schools should teach makes it imperative to involve the public in the development of standards *and* assessments.
- *Provide strong standards.* Achieving consensus on standards that are broad and vague is no challenge.... Available evidence suggests that many states' current standards are not strong enough to support rigorous content-based assessment.
- *Align standards with assessment and instruction.* Some states patch together assessment systems using whatever assessments are available, sacrificing the custom fit they would gain by developing assessments from scratch.... Ultimately, classroom curriculum and instruction should also be aligned with standards and assessments. Yet this alignment depends in turn on teachers' ability to understand—and obtain the resources and expertise to help their students meet—the expectations embodied by new assessments.

- *Assure accurate measures.* To furnish a stable estimate of student capability, most assessments now being developed incorporate a broad range of tasks, reflecting the full scope of the standards.
- *Define progress.* The progress of schools, districts, and states is typically defined by the performance of successive cohorts of students: Are more fourth-graders, for example, demonstrating proficiency in math standards this year than last?
- *Set the stakes.* What schools do with assessment results—whether simply reporting them, at one end of the spectrum, or making graduation contingent on them, at the other—can have a profound effects on students.
- *Include all students.* Standards are designed to raise expectations for *all* students. Including limited English speaking students and students with disabilities in an assessment may require a variety of different accommodation strategies. . . .
- *Build local capacity.* . . . [T]eachers need time to become familiar with new standards, assessments and administration requirements; to understand how new forms of assessment are developed and scored; to apply criteria for assessing students' work; and to acquire enough information and pedagogical knowledge to change their practices. Providing appropriate resources and sufficient opportunities for professional development is equally important.
- *Distinguish assessments.* An assessment that attempts to perform too many functions—student diagnosis, curriculum planning, program evaluation, instructional improvement, accountability, certification, public communication—will inevitably do none well. It is important, therefore, to distinguish appropriate roles for different assessments, at the district, school and classroom level. (Linn & Herman, 1997, pp. iv–vi)

It is clear that the vision for standards-based reform of America's schools includes the development of rigorous, well-thought-out content standards, the development and implementation of challenging assessments that are aligned with the content standards, and setting challenging levels of performance expected of students and schools, with consequences for both. What is equally clear is that relatively few states and school districts can say that they have successfully done all of these. Although the record is checkered, their lack of success cannot be attributed to a lack of effort. Every state has developed some form of content standards (whether called this or not), almost all have implemented some form of assessment, and slightly more than half of the states have developed assessments specifically aligned with their state's content standards.

What is equally apparent is that efforts to improve the quality of both the content standards and assessments are continuing in many states. States are not satisfied with simply developing and assessing a set of standards; they have been engaged in a repetitive process of refinement and improvement of their standards and assessments, leading even critics to see progress toward the development of high-quality, useful, and aligned systems.

Even more important than the ongoing nature of the development and refinement of standards, and the use in statewide assessment programs, has been the use of the content standards as the basis for education reform efforts at the state and local levels. In many states, the content standards have served as the basis for the provision of professional development opportunities for educators (on curriculum, instruction, and assessment), the development of instructional resource materials, school improvement activities, accountability programs (including rewards and sanctions often included with such efforts), and even specially funded state improvement programs. In other words, within a decade or less, content standards have become the heart of efforts to bring about change and reform at the state and local levels.

Of course, simply defining what students need to know and be able to do, and measuring and reporting how many students perform at desired levels, will not in itself improve education. Additional, innovative policy initiatives are needed to promote the translation and implementation of state reform efforts at the local level. Both the policy initiatives and the implementation efforts must be monitored for effectiveness and refined before state standards-based reform efforts will bear great success in improving student achievement. At the state level, legislators, educational administrators, and policy makers need to keep in mind the concerns and criticisms raised so that they can avoid the pitfalls and perils and instead demonstrate success in helping all students to achieve high standards.

The struggles will be ongoing, and undoubtedly there will be setbacks that cause some jurisdictions to choose to retreat from standards-based efforts aimed at educational reform. However, for at least the foreseeable future, schools in many states across the country are likely to continue using content standards and assessments based on them to guide standards-based efforts at the national, state, and local levels.

References

American Federation of Teachers. (1997). *Making standards matter 1997: An annual fifty-state report on efforts to raise academic standards.* Washington, DC: Author.

Brandt, R. (1995). Overview: What to do with those new standards. *Educational Leadership,* 52(6), 5.

Council of Chief State School Officers. (1996). *Key state education policies on K-12 education: A fifty-state report.* Washington, DC: Author.

Council of Chief State School Officers & North Central Regional Educational Laboratory. (1997). *The status of state student assessment programs.* Washington, DC and Oak Brook, IL: Authors.

Debra P. v. Turlington, 474 F. Supp. 244 (M.D. Fla. 1979), 644 F.2d 397 (5th Cir. 1981); 564 F. Supp. 177 (M.D. Fla. 1983), 730 f.2d 1405 (11th Cir. 1984).

Elmore, R. F. (1996). Getting to scale with good educational practice. *Harvard Educational Review,* 66(1), 1–26.

Finn, C. E. (1990). The biggest reform of all. *Phi Delta Kappan,* 71(8), 584–592.

Linn, R. L. & Herman, J. L. (1997). *A policymaker's guide to standards-led assessment.* Denver, CO: Education Commission of the States.

McLaughlin, M. W., & Shepard, L. A. (1995). *Improving education through standards-based reform.* Stanford, CA: National Academy of Education.

Massell, D., Kirst, M., & Hoppe, M. (1997). *Persistence and change: Standards-based systemic reform in nine states* (Research Brief 21, April, 1997). Philadelphia, PA: University of Pennsylvania.

Messick, S. (1989). Validity. In R. L. Linn (Ed.), *Educational measurement* (3rd ed., pp. 13–103). New York: Macmillan.

National Association of State Boards of Education. (1996). Issues in brief: The fall and rise of standards-based education. Alexandria, VA: Author.

National Commission on Excellence in Education. (1983). *A nation at risk: The imperative for educational reform.* Washington, DC: U.S. Government Printing Office.

National Council of Teachers of Mathematics. (1989). *Curriculum and evaluation standards for school mathematics.* Reston, VA: Author.

National Educational Goals Panel. (1991). *The national education goals report: Building a nation of learners.* Washington, DC: Author.

O'Neil, J. (1995). On using standards: A conversation with Ramsay Selden. *Educational Leadership, 52*(6), 12–14.

Roeber, E. D. (1997). Coordinated assessment systems. Washington, DC: Council of Chief State School Officers.

Shields, P. M., & Knapp, M. S. (1997). The promise of school-based reform. *Phi Delta Kappan, 79*(4), 288–294.

Stearns, P. N. (1996). A cease-fire for history? *The History Teacher, 30*(1), 65–82.

Stiggins, R.J. (1991). Relevant classroom assessment training for teachers. *Educational Measurement: Issues and Practices, 10*(1), 7–12.

Tanner, D. (1998). The social consequences of bad research. *Phi Delta Kappan, 79* (5), 344–349.

CHAPTER

8

Moving toward an Accountable System of K–12 Education: Alternative Approaches and Challenges

JAMES G. CIBULKA
University of Maryland, College Park

Accountability policy is the most recent thread in the educational reform movement. It has emerged in response to two intersecting political forces. First, continuing evidence that American schoolchildren are not scoring well on standardized tests when compared with their peers in other nations has fed the perception that additional reform is needed. Within the political mainstream, these amplified reform nostrums take several paths. At the national level, performance standards for students and the creation of charter schools are popular initiatives. Mayors in major cities are advocating local reforms intended to make the public schools of their cities more accountable.

A second converging development has both propelled the initiatives endorsed within the political mainstream and created another impetus for reform. The political right has seized on the failure of public schools as a major political issue, prompting some members of Congress to fight for school vouchers and educational savings accounts.

One justification that advocates of all these reform approaches use is the need for more accountability in running schools. For example, standards are said to make students and teachers more accountable. Likewise, charters are defended as a way to improve performance because they improve accountability for results. In other words, although there is no consensus on what approach to take in reforming schools, accountability has emerged as a legitimate goal framing education policy debates. Because there are such wide differences in proposals for reforming American schools, it follows that the approaches to accountability take different forms and have different theories of action embodied within them.

This chapter examines various approaches to accountability, some of the assumptions embedded in these approaches as a theory of change, and the difficulties these approaches entail. First, however, it is important to address how accountability can be understood as a governance value existing alongside of, and to a degree in competition with, other values. The larger significance of accountability policies cannot be understood without taking this larger perspective.

ACCOUNTABILITY AS A GOVERNANCE VALUE

It is generally understood that the American political system embraces a number of legitimating values or principles. Indeed, these values are so fundamental that they are part of modern democratic systems in widely different nations. Without attempting to be complete, we can identify these values as liberty or choice, equality, tradition, progress, fairness, efficiency, effectiveness, popular control, representativeness, expertise, responsiveness, and accountability.

These values are to some degree in competition with one another. They cannot all be achieved simultaneously because many of them push in opposite directions. Equality and choice, for example, are not easily reconciled. For example, the American system of relying heavily on the local property tax has been defended as consistent with local control of schools, yet it has led to widespread inequalities in spending and educational opportunities among communities with different property wealth and different levels of willingness to fund education. Nor are popular control, representativeness, and expertise necessarily consistent with one another. In the United States, a federal system has allowed many different approaches to coexist, depending on the branch of government or governmental institution in question or the state or local jurisdiction in question. Moreover, different governance approaches have come into play at different stages in the nation's history. Kaufman (1956) presented one of the classic formulations of these value frameworks. Americans value neutral competence—that is, strong professional control of institutions—but they also embrace the ideals of executive leadership and representativeness. Institutions rarely are pure embodiments of a singular approach, but we are inclined to lean in one or another direction depending on ideas that are in vogue at a particular historical moment and problems that are paramount.

The recent public interest in accountability represents a challenge to the concept of professional control of school. *Professional governance* models lean heavily on an internal approach to accountability. Professional standards and norms determine who makes key decisions about policy and shape the criteria employed in those policies. The assumption is that policy ought to be guided by the expertise of these professionals. The model, while not ignoring entirely the role of values in shaping policy, tends to frame policy choices in largely value-neutral terms.

This professional governance approach heavily influenced the development of educational administration in elementary and secondary schooling. Scientific management was a wing of the Progressive reform movement (Callahan, 1962; Tyack, 1974). School professionals sought to establish autonomy from outside political pressures. In many U.S. cities political machines had controlled jobs and resources and been a mechanism for responding to parent and neighborhood concerns. The new profession of educational administration sought to replace this politicized and loosely managed approach with a system of education based on standardization, efficiency, and other values influenced heavily by corporate America. Large educational bureaucracies were built in cities, school districts were consolidated, and school boards were made smaller and restructured to encourage membership by civic elites who would set policy while leaving administration to the new school professionals. At the state level, reformers also sought to professionalize state departments of education, to give state superintendents more authority and autonomy, and to create state boards of education with policy making authority.

This professional governance strategy reduced emphasis on representativeness as a legitimating principle. Professional governance required decision making based on technical criteria and merit rather than decision making growing out of one's likeness with a particular group or based on an obligation to be responsive to preferences expressed by particular constituencies. At the local level reformers were successful in reducing the size of school boards so that they no longer represented concerns and needs of individual schools and neighborhoods. Efforts were made, with greater success in some places than others, to have board members represent a citywide perspective rather than wards or sectional interests. This view of representation emphasizes trusteeship, which requires the exercise of independent judgment concerning what is in the best public interest. Although board members are not expected bring the same professional knowledge to their role as school experts possess, they are assumed to have complementary specialized expertise or at least a broad perspective that qualifies them to make good policy decisions.

The legitimating value of *executive leadership*, like professional governance, differs somewhat from representativeness. At the federal level presidential initiative rather than congressional power is emphasized. It also is different from professionalism in its focus on restoring accountability through external means, such as placing "outsiders" in charge of an institution, who are presumed to bring new skills and perspectives.

In short, although accountability is itself a legitimating value, it draws in different ways on certain complementary principles such as executive leadership, while downplaying others such as representativeness and professionalism.

ACCOUNTABILITY AS A REFORM IMPULSE

Accountability deals with the relation between an authority and some external authority to whom the official answers. To be specific, if we do not trust that school officials will use their own professional judgment wisely, then someone else must hold them to account. But who is this external agent of accountability? It is not clear. Accountability's agents can be the public, the family, bureaucrats, politicians, executive leaders, or consumers. Efforts to reform schools in recent years have relied on each of these agents to one degree or another. For example, the idea that the public should hold officials accountable is rooted in populism. California's initiative system permits voters to express their views on a variety of issues such as taxes, funding levels for schools, and affirmative action. In reforms that emphasize greater opportunities for choice of schools, the parents or caregivers of children make decisions on behalf of the child's interests, presumably holding school officials accountable. Alternatively, state bureaucrats can intervene by expanding their regulatory authority if they find local schools are not performing adequately, even closing failing schools. Elected politicians such as governors and mayors, on the other hand, argue that they should be accountability's agents. In still another approach, superintendents may be replaced by other kinds of executives, such as business leaders or military officials, on the premise that they will bring greater accountability to the educational system. Each of these approaches to accountability carries a potentially different theory of action concerning how school officials will be answerable to the external agent, even though the theory in use may not be stated. Six types of current approaches to accountability are discussed in the following sections.

Publication of Performance Information

The publication of performance information about schools by state departments of education is a relatively new development, having gained momentum since the 1980s. All but a few states now produce some kind of report. These reports go under a variety of names (report card, performance report, accountability report, etc.) and have been evolving in format and importance. Many states now produce multiple reports. Data included in the reports vary widely. State assessments of student achievement, dropout/graduation rates, and other student performance indicators are most common. Descriptive data on students, families, and communities may be included. Expenditure data, staffing characteristics, and other ostensible indicators of quality are provided in some cases. The data are aggregated in different ways. The unit of analysis can be the school, the district, or the state. Data may or may not permit comparisons against a norm or standard. In a few cases, student assessment results are adjusted statistically to even the playing field when comparisons are made among schools or districts, although this approach remains controversial. Some school districts, large ones and urban districts in particular, publish reports. Figure 1 shows selected portions of a prototype, district-level report proposed for use in Ohio. Ohio's report illustrates many of the features noted. An example of a report used in Maryland is shown in Michaels and Ferrara (this volume, Figure 1).

The federal government produced a state-by-state wall chart until the early 1990s but discontinued it in response to criticism from some states. The National Educational Goals Panel produces an annual report with a variety of educational and social indicators related to the eight national goals for educational progress. The U.S. Department of Education will require publication of school performance indicators regarding the major federally supported education program for the educationally disadvantaged, Title 1 of Improving America's Schools Act, beginning in 2002. Overall, performance reporting has become a common feature at all levels of government.

Beyond a generally accepted impulse to disclose these performance data, however, there is little clarity about how the reports are expected to improve government performance. As a general premise about what is wrong with government, the presumption is tied to a lack of information about performance, but beyond that highly imprecise characterization of the problem's source are many points of possible confusion. First is the issue of who the targets of the information are. One possible audience is the public, writ large. This approach has populist undercurrents. Disclosure of information is assumed to lead the public to demand that school officials take corrective action, insofar as it is warranted. This is, of course, a variant of direct democracy, because it implies direct action by a concerned public. In this case, information is assumed to provide the public with a source of power ordinarily denied to it. The ability to obtain information about how government is performing supposedly was a strong feature of small-town democracy. The size and complexity of modern government makes this direct relationship between citizen and government officials less plausible. Performance reporting is a kind of functional equivalent to the annual town meeting. Accountability consists, in other words, of raising public awareness. As a theory of change, as well as a theory of democratic accountability, this informational strategy is incomplete.

A second approach to performance reporting views the target of the information as school officials themselves, either school board members who represent the public by setting educational policy or professionals who

State of Ohio
1998 School District Report Card

PROTOTYPE #7

ABC School District

- How well did **your school district** perform last year?

- Are **children in your community** receiving a quality education?

- How can **your community** help improve local schools?

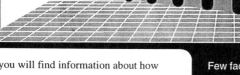

Inside you will find information about how well your local schools are doing — where they are succeeding and where there is room for improvement. While this report card cannot tell you everything about your school district's performance, it is a good starting point for discussions with teachers, administrators and school board members in your community.

Few factors have greater impact on student performance than parent and community involvement. The State Board of Education and Ohio Department of Education encourage you to contact local district officials to find out how you can become more involved in efforts to improve your local schools.

NOTE: The information presented in this report card is for an imaginary school district.

FIGURE I
Sample state school performance report (Ohio).

implement policy. The theory of change here bypasses the public, thereby shortening the chain of influence required between the publication of the information and its employment for systemic improvement. Depending on

HOW WELL DID YOUR DISTRICT PERFORM LAST YEAR?

In August 1997, the Ohio General Assembly passed Senate Bill 55, which requires the Ohio Department of Education to issue report cards to every school district in Ohio beginning in 1999. This report card is a "prototype" of the first official report cards that will be distributed in 1999.

Senate Bill 55 calls for each Ohio school district to receive a performance accountability rating based on *18 performance standards* established by the Ohio General Assembly. These 18 standards are *minimum* performance goals for public education in our state.

The State Board of Education and Ohio Department of Education are working to define appropriate levels of assistance and intervention for school districts, depending on the rating they receive.

YOUR DISTRICT'S RATING:

(No Ratings Will be Given Until 1999.)

How Your Rating Is Determined

Effective districts meet 17 or more standards.
(XX districts statewide received this rating.)

Continuous Improvement districts meet 10 - 16 standards.
(XX districts statewide received this rating.)

Academic Watch districts meet 6 - 9 standards.
(XX districts statewide received this rating.)

Academic Emergency districts meet 5 or fewer standards.
(XX districts statewide received this rating.)

Your District's Results At a Glance

18 Performance Standards	Minimum State Performance Standard	Your District's 3-Year Average	Did Your District Meet the Standard?
	Percentage of Students Who Passed Tests		
Grade 4 Proficiency Tests			
1. Citizenship	75%	96.3%	Yes
2. Mathematics	75%	85.9%	Yes
3. Reading	75%	92.4%	Yes
4. Writing	75%	91.2%	Yes
Science	*	76.1%	*
Grade 6 Proficiency Tests			
Citizenship	*	57.0%	*
Mathematics	*	52.5%	*
Reading	*	71.5%	*
Writing	*	71.4%	*
Science	*	43.9%	*
Grade 9 Proficiency Tests — 9th Grade Students			
5. Citizenship	75%	76.2%	Yes
6. Mathematics	75%	62.9%	No
7. Reading	75%	83.9%	Yes
8. Writing	75%	81.3%	Yes
Science	*	NA	*
Grade 9 Proficiency Tests — 10th Grade Students			
9. Citizenship	85%	91.6%	Yes
10. Mathematics	85%	82.1%	No
11. Reading	85%	94.1%	Yes
12. Writing	85%	93.6%	Yes
Science	*	NA	*
Grade 12 Proficiency Tests			
13. Citizenship	60%	88.9%	Yes
14. Mathematics	60%	76.1%	Yes
15. Reading	60%	94.3%	Yes
16. Writing	60%	88.1%	Yes
Science	*	57.9%	*
17. *Student Attendance Rate*	93%	93.6%	Yes
18. *Dropout Rate*	3%	24.9%	No

Your District Met 15 of the 18 State Standards.

* No minimum state standards have yet been established for the tests marked with an asterisk (*). However, state law calls for these tests to be used in determining your district's rating at a future date.

FIGURE 1 (*Continued*)

which unit of analysis is reported, the implied theory of change differs to some degree. If information is only provided at the state level, then the primary (although not exclusive) audience presumably is state officials. They

NINTH-GRADE PROFICIENCY TEST RESULTS

One important measure of a district's performance is how well students perform on Ohio's Ninth-Grade Proficiency Tests, *which students must pass in order to receive a high school diploma*. The bar charts below show the percentage of ninth-grade students in your district who passed each test, as well as those who passed all required tests.

Your district's passing rate is compared to "similar districts" and to the overall state average. Similar districts were identified based on (1) size; (2) poverty level; (3) family income, education levels and professions; (4) factors related to urban or rural location; and (5) district property tax wealth.

Percentage of Students Who Passed the Tests

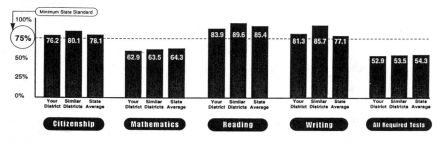

All test scores are 3-year averages for 1994-1997. Science tests are not included because they are not required for graduation until after September 15, 2000.

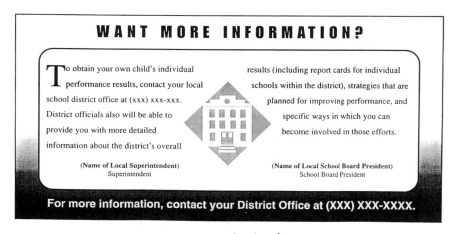

FIGURE 1 (*Continued*)

must set policies that effectively elicit change at appropriate lower levels of the system (districts, schools, or teachers). Providing district information makes it possible for officials at that level to take corrective action without

8. Moving toward an Accountable System of K–12 Education

Targets	Comparisons	Trend
Minimum state *Performance Standards* have been established by the Ohio General Assembly. For districts that do not meet these minimum standards, beginning in 1999 the State Board of Education will identify annual *Improvement Goals* that represent satisfactory levels of progress.	These columns show how well your district performed in comparison to "similar districts" and to the overall state average. For similar districts, the average passing rate and the highest passing rate in the group are provided. Similar districts were identified based on size; poverty level; income, education levels and professions; factors related to urban or rural location; and property tax wealth.	These columns show your district's results for each of the last three years. This information can help you see whether performance in these areas is improving, declining or staying about the same.

PERCENTAGE OF STUDENTS WHO PASSED THE TESTS

State Performance Standard %	Your District's Improvement Goal %	Your District's Average %	SIMILAR DISTRICTS Average % of Group	Best % in Group	Overall State Average %	1994-95 Results %	1995-96 Results %	1996-97 Results %
75%	NA	96.3	90.1	95.6	84.1	NA	96.1	96.4
75%	NA	85.9	87.2	92.4	73.2	NA	83.7	88.1
75%	NA	92.4	95.4	98.0	82.4	NA	94.2	90.5
75%	NA	91.2	87.8	93.2	79.3	NA	92.4	89.9
NS	NA	76.1	76.7	84.1	59.6	NA	73.5	78.6
NS	NA	57.0	58.6	65.3	61.2	NA	56.4	57.5
NS	NA	52.5	49.5	54.7	45.4	NA	53.6	51.3
NS	NA	71.5	75.8	81.9	73.8	NA	71.0	71.9
NS	NA	71.4	73.9	78.7	63.6	NA	72.7	70.0
NS	NA	43.9	49.3	53.0	42.9	NA	42.8	45.0
75%	NA	76.2	80.1	85.6	78.1	70.2	79.1	79.4
75%	NA	62.9	63.5	69.2	64.3	59.6	62.3	66.7
75%	NA	83.9	89.6	93.1	85.4	81.7	82.4	87.7
75%	NA	81.3	85.7	91.0	77.1	78.3	79.1	86.4
NS	NA	NA	NA	NA	NA	NA	NA	NA
85%	NA	91.6	94.4	99.2	82.1	89.4	92.4	93.1
85%	NA	82.1	85.5	91.8	70.3	81.6	80.5	84.1
85%	NA	94.1	93.2	97.6	89.8	92.5	95.8	94.0
85%	NA	93.6	90.3	96.7	80.7	93.7	93.2	94.0
NS	NA	NA	NA	NA	NA	NA	NA	NA
60%	NA	88.9	80.2	85.2	69.4	NA	94.7	82.3
60%	NA	76.1	75.4	81.3	61.3	NA	79.5	70.1
60%	NA	94.3	88.3	94.6	80.5	NA	97.6	90.0
60%	NA	88.1	76.5	83.1	67.6	NA	94.1	77.8
NS	NA	57.9	60.7	68.5	54.8	NA	56.8	58.9

NOTE: The percentage of students who take and pass all five sections of the state proficiency tests at each grade level will be provided in the year 2000 report card.

Targets	Comparisons	Trend

State Performance Standard %	Your District's Improvement Goal %	Your District's Average %	SIMILAR DISTRICTS Average % of Group	Best % in Group	Overall State Average %	1994-95 Results %	1995-96 Results %	1996-97 Results %
93%	NA	93.6	94.7	99.7	93.4	93.6	93.9	93.4
NS	NA	NA	NA	NA	NA	NA	NA	NA
NS	NA	3.4	2.9	—	2.7	4.1	3.3	3.2
NS	NA	97.0	99.4	—	97.8	98.6	99.7	95.7
NS	NA	98.0	98.2	—	95.5	97.7	96.1	99.8
NS	NA	75.1	74.6	82.0	74.3	NA	75.0	75.2
NS	NA	6.5	15.0	19.2	13.5	NA	7.4	5.0
3%	NA	24.9	26.2	21.3	25.7	NA	25.0	24.8

FIGURE 1 (*Continued*)

requiring a regulatory response at the next higher level of the system, and so on.

Despite the fact that performance reporting is so widely used, until recently it has not been seen as a pivotal strategy for reforming schools. There have been a number of impediments to its effectiveness. When the public is the target of the published information about the educational system, more

Performance Results For Student Groups Within Your District

B reaking down your
district's overall
performance record to show
how different groups of
students have performed gives
a more complete picture of how
well your district is doing.

It also helps to ensure that no
group of students is overlooked
because the district as a whole
is doing well.

**Questions to Discuss
In Your Community:**

✔ Are there big differences in
the passing rates of
different groups of students?

✔ If yes, what factors (such as
economic factors) might be
contributing to those
differences?

✔ What is your district doing
to address the differences
and to raise all students'
performance to satisfactory
levels?

State Proficiency Tests:

			Female		Male	
			Your District's %	State Average %	Your District's %	State Average %
4th Grade Tests		Citizenship	90.8	76.7	94.6	75.4
		Mathematics	78.7	51.6	80.3	52.3
		Reading	84.2	68.6	76.4	61.7
		Writing	74.3	74.8	68.7	59.5
		Science	85.1	58.1	84.6	60.0
6th Grade Tests		Citizenship	71.3	67.6	70.7	63.6
		Mathematics	58.3	50.9	53.2	51.8
		Reading	82.4	79.6	76.8	76.1
		Writing	90.7	82.3	76.4	65.8
		Science	44.5	40.8	51.5	45.5
9th Grade Tests		Citizenship	82.3	78.1	81.5	78.4
		Mathematics	69.3	64.0	64.0	69.9
		Reading	86.1	90.8	87.9	85.1
		Writing	87.7	89.8	82.3	76.3
		Science	NA	NA	NA	NA
9th Grade Tests (10th Grade Students)		Citizenship	96.7	88.3	92.1	88.4
		Mathematics	81.7	76.5	84.4	81.9
		Reading	95.9	95.4	93.2	92.1
		Writing	100	95.2	85.7	86.8
		Science	NA	NA	NA	NA
12th Grade Tests		Citizenship	65.1	70.5	81.5	70.8
		Mathematics	47.3	55.1	63.8	60.4
		Reading	90.4	82.6	79.6	74.7
		Writing	73.1	76.9	64.7	59.2
		Science	53.6	54.3	66.7	57.2

NOTE: All results are 3-year averages, unless not available.

Attendance, Discipline, Promotion and Graduation

	Female		Male	
	Your District's %	State Average %	Your District's %	State Average %
Student Attendance Rate	92.7	93.3	93.8	93.4
Percentage of Students Suspended	NA	NA	NA	NA
Average Length of Suspensions (Number of Days)	2.8	2.6	15.9	2.7
Percentage of 4th Grade Students Promoted to 5th Grade	97.7	98.0	95.9	97.6
Percentage of 6th Grade Students Promoted to 7th Grade	96.3	96.4	96.4	94.7
High School Graduation Rate	81.4	81.3	73.6	73.5
Percentage of Graduates With State Honors Diploma	3.5	16.0	8.7	10.6
High School Dropout Rate	18.6	18.7	26.4	21.5

Graduation and dropout data are 2-year averages for 1995-97.

NA = Not available.
NR = Not reported by the district.
NC = Not calculated for fewer than 10 students.

FIGURE 1 (Continued)

often than not the approach has not led to widespread demands for reform.
Access to the reports, except as reported by the media, often is difficult. In
many cases the reports are not user-friendly; they are too voluminous or do
not arrange the data in ways that make interpretation easy for a layperson.
As a result, after a brief flurry of interest (if that) the reports tend to be
forgotten. Perhaps the biggest users of the reports have been realtors, who

Percentage of Students Who Passed the Tests

Students with Disabilities		African American		Hispanic		White		Other	
Your District's %	State Average %	Your District's %	State Average %	Your District's %	State Average %	Your District's %	State Average %	Your District's %	State Average %
NA	NA	55.6	50.3	NC	62.9	92.0	79.4	68.1	70.0
NA	NA	28.7	21.2	NC	32.2	79.3	55.8	42.4	40.3
NA	NA	42.4	39.5	NC	50.4	81.3	68.3	62.6	59.1
NA	NA	46.8	45.1	NC	59.2	78.0	69.4	68.3	63.4
NA	NA	29.4	26.2	NC	41.2	78.7	63.5	53.2	49.0
NA	NA	NR	38.1	NC	53.6	71.0	68.7	63.4	60.4
NA	NA	NR	20.0	NC	36.8	56.9	54.9	58.6	44.2
NA	NA	NR	53.8	NC	64.7	80.5	77.6	73.4	73.6
NA	NA	NR	58.9	NC	70.3	84.7	75.3	72.1	70.9
NA	NA	NR	12.2	NC	25.7	48.7	47.0	42.3	36.4
69.2	68.5	63.4	55.6	61.2	60.0	82.1	82.4	78.1	75.7
54.7	53.6	39.2	33.0	44.3	46.6	67.7	72.7	61.6	59.3
83.6	82.4	76.5	74.2	78.9	77.7	86.7	90.5	86.4	87.4
77.4	76.3	72.3	69.6	73.6	71.4	84.2	85.3	87.3	84.1
NA	NA	NA	NA	NA	NA	NA	NA	NA	NA
75.6	74.2	76.4	72.8	79.1	76.6	93.4	90.7	85.4	83.2
68.4	67.3	52.3	49.7	68.2	63.9	83.1	83.2	68.3	69.6
82.6	81.5	89.1	87.1	86.1	87.0	94.6	94.9	91.4	90.2
84.1	83.2	86.3	84.1	87.4	85.9	92.7	92.0	88.9	86.4
NA	NA	NA	NA	NA	NA	NA	NA	NA	NA
NA	NA	NR	57.2	69.2	60.6	74.9	72.5	67.3	66.7
NA	NA	NR	36.3	48.3	46.1	55.1	59.9	53.5	49.7
NA	NA	NR	69.4	76.1	74.4	84.5	80.3	84.6	83.0
NA	NA	NR	60.9	63.2	60.9	69.9	69.5	68.4	67.7
NA	NA	NR	33.0	46.4	43.6	60.2	58.1	48.8	45.8

All test scores have been adjusted to reflect higher proficiency test standards that will take effect in the year 2000.

Students with Disabilities		African American		Hispanic		White		Other	
Your District's %	State Average %	Your District's %	State Average %	Your District's %	State Average %	Your District's %	State Average %	Your District's %	State Average %
92.4	92.0	92.9	89.4	91.2	90.1	93.5	94.1	91.3	93.1
NA	NA	NA	NA	NA	NA	NA	NA	NA	NA
2.7	2.5	3.6	2.8	2.8	2.9	3.3	2.6	3.8	2.6
96.3	97.2	49.1	92.7	100	91.6	98.3	98.8	98.2	97.3
93.2	95.2	100	87.2	94.2	86.4	97.0	97.1	96.7	94.2
62.8	55.9	51.4	60.2	100	59.1	77.7	80.0	73.2	69.6
0	0.9	0	3.5	3.1	5.4	6.4	14.3	9.2	8.5
37.2	44.1	48.6	44.1	0	40.9	22.3	20.0	26.8	30.4

FIGURE 1 (Continued)

provide the data to prospective residents of a neighborhood or school district.

Adoption of Performance Standards

An exception to this generalization is where a state or local jurisdiction aligns the performance information to other elements of its educational policy system. Nearly every state is in the process of adopting content or per-

DISTRICT PROFILE (1996-97 DATA)

Questions to Discuss In Your Community:

✔ What economic factors may impact your district's performance results?

✔ What effect do teacher qualifications and attendance have on student learning?

✔ How is your district spending its money compared to other districts and the state as a whole?

✔ Does the district's overall performance represent a good return on the community's investment?

	Your District	Similar Districts	State Average
GENERAL			
Enrollment	2,140	2,784	2,793
Students with Disabilities	8.7%	12.0%	12.2%
Students in the District Less Than Half the Year	5.1%	5.0%	5.6%
Students in the Same School Less Than Half the Year	4.3%	4.6%	4.8%
Economically Disadvantaged Students*	1.3%	1.8%	2.0%
Median Household Income	$28,461	$26,774	$24,588
*Students from families receiving Temporary Assistance to Needy Families.			
TEACHERS			
Average Number of Students Per Teacher	22.5	19.6	20.7
Teachers Not Certified in Their Teaching Area	NA	NA	NA
Teacher Attendance Rate	97.6%	96.2%	95.7%
REVENUE SOURCES PER PUPIL			
Local Funds	$4,654	$3,878	$3,064
State Funds	$740	$1,502	$2,385
Federal Funds	$254	$289	$354
ANNUAL SPENDING PER PUPIL			
Administration (such as office salaries, supplies, postage)	$684	$704	$708
Building Operations (such as utilities and maintenance)	$1,119	$1,220	$1,163
Staff Support (such as teacher training)	$14	$85	$97
Pupil Support (such as guidance counselor salaries/services)	$511	$665	$634
Instruction (such as teacher salaries and classroom materials)	$3,010	$3,515	$3,434
Total Annual Spending Per Pupil (operating costs only)	$5,338	$6,189	$6,036

NA = Not available. • NR = Not reported by the district. • NC = Not calculated for fewer than 10 students.

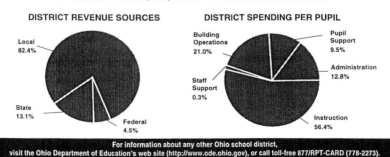

DISTRICT REVENUE SOURCES

Local 82.4%
State 13.1%
Federal 4.5%

DISTRICT SPENDING PER PUPIL

Building Operations 21.0%
Staff Support 0.3%
Pupil Support 9.5%
Administration 12.8%
Instruction 56.4%

For information about any other Ohio school district, visit the Ohio Department of Education's web site (http://www.ode.ohio.gov), or call toll-free 877/RPT-CARD (778-2273).

FIGURE 1 (*Continued*)

formance standards for student performance (see Roeber, this volume). In turn, these standards may be tied to curricula and student assessments and in some cases to policies for intervening in low-performing schools. Performance accountability has now emerged as a central feature of many state educational accountability systems in which standards, student assessments, and rewards and sanctions for performance are coordinated components (Elmore, Adelman, & Fuhrman, 1996). Although not all states have adopted this approach, it has become perhaps the dominant model, and it is flexible enough to permit many variations when it is applied in different states.

Relation beween Performance Standards and Reports

When publication of a state report card is linked to a larger reform agenda, then the performance information tends to receive more attention by the public, policy makers, and education professionals. The creation of standards, in other words, creates pressure to publish information about progress on the standards. In Maryland, for example, the results of the annual School Performance Report are announced with great fanfare by state officials, and the report is the object of widespread attention by the media, the public, and school officials (see Michaels & Ferrara, this volume). Part of the reason is that the state has set a long-term goal for student performance on the Maryland School Performance Assessment Program (MSPAP), and each year's performance can be measured against that benchmark. Financial rewards are given to high-performing and high-improving schools, and the state has a policy for monitoring and assisting low-performing schools that it deems eligible for reconstitution. The responsibility for turning around a school's performance is considered to be a local one, not that of the state.

This kind of approach to reform has come to be known as *high-stakes* because serious consequences are attached to the performance results. Yet there are many ways of constructing an accountability policy so that consequences flow from a level of performance. In Maryland, there have been no consequences for students, although the state is embarking on a high school assessment initiative in which graduation from high school may be tied to satisfactory performance on a series of rigorous standards-based, end-of-course assessments. A number of states already have these high stakes for high school students. An earlier generation of these assessments emphasized performance in basic skills as a requirement for graduation, but they differ from the new assessments in the level of rigor.

Some states have predicated their performance reporting on the premise that the information should be locally controlled rather than imposed by the state. In Colorado, for instance, the approach has been to allow local districts wide leeway in implementing performance assessment and reporting, reflecting the state's strong tradition of local control (Cibulka & Derlin, 1998). A Standards and Assessment Development and Implementation council, known as SADI, was established and made responsible for preparing specific content standards and assessments for twelve educational/discipline areas. However, local school districts may adopt or revise the state-level standards or develop unique local standards as long as they meet or exceed the state standards. Nor are local districts required to adopt the state assessment system as long as they develop performance levels and student assessments that are reported to the state Department of Education. Although annual education reports must be broadly communicated to local constituents, the means by which local districts achieve this is widely varied, and authority for the development of school improvement plans and the assessment of progress toward educational goals is broadly diffused through a previously established hierarchy of school and district accountability committees.

Florida is even more wedded to a local control model in the development and reporting of performance data. The Florida School Public Accountability Report is specific to each of the schools in the state. In 1993–1994 the responsibility for producing a school report shifted from the state department of education to the individual school, although much of the data are provided to the school by the state. Florida has developed one of the most comprehensive databases on educational indicators, which are organized by the state's educational goals. The rationale for this shift was primarily to enlist the commitment of school officials in the use of data for developing an annual school improvement plan, which is approved by each school district.

In sum, a wide variety of approaches to performance reporting has evolved. These various approaches speak to different levels of the policy system and address a host of different performance indicators. Some performance systems are centralized, others locally controlled or developed. Some are high stakes, others low stakes. Some are directed at the public, others at school officials. Some are isolated policies; others are part of a coordinated, systemic reform strategy. Despite these difficulties in generalizing, what can be said of all these policies is that information alone is at best an incomplete strategy for creating an accountable educational system.

Despite the attempt to enhance accountability by providing substantive data, the release of information can be an empty formality or it can empower citizens and professionals to be more effective change agents. To accomplish the latter, usually there must be some strategy for assuring that the information will be used in transforming the school or district about which information is provided. The requirements for making this happen are complex, and there is a growing recognition (if still simplistic in its assumptions) that other strategies are needed to complement performance information alone. Like performance reporting, these fall in the category of governance reforms. Two strategies that are sometimes employed in concert with the former are new institutional models emphasizing executive leadership and heightened bureaucratic oversight. Here accountability means giving over influence or ultimate control to another set of factors. If information answers the question "Accountable for what?" then the following strategies provide an answer to an entirely different question: "Accountable to whom?" It is, in other words, an *authoritative* rather than substantive approach to the problem of accountable government.

Institutional Reform: Executive Leadership

Whenever public dissatisfaction with an institution runs high, there is the tendency to look for alternative ways of governing it. Schools are not unique in this regard. In the mid-1970s New York City's financial crisis led to special financial oversight arrangements (Peterson, 1981). Urban school systems have witnessed external interventions, such as the School Finance Authority in the case of the Chicago Public Schools (Cibulka, 1987). Recently, a number of urban school systems such as Baltimore, Boston, Chicago, Milwaukee, Newark, and Washington, DC, to name some of the most prominent, have undergone restructuring, and similar reforms are being debated in other cities. A common element in these plans is the emphasis on strong executive leadership. In some cases this has meant bringing in a nontraditional educator to act as superintendent, such as Howard Fuller (a former community activist and state executive) in Milwaukee and Julius Beckton, Jr. (a retired general), in Washington, DC. Stronger mayoral oversight is part of this focus on executive leadership, as in Chicago and New York City, although in Baltimore and Washington, DC, the mayor's powers were actually curbed on the logic that political interference in the schools had been detrimental. The underlying reform impulse, therefore, is a variation on an old story in electoral politics: Throw the rascals out, whoever the rascals today are!

Despite variation on the mayoral dimension, often executive leadership is taken to mean a shift to private-sector management skills and models. Under this model school heads are not longer superintendents. They become chief executive officers (CEOs) instead. Chief financial officers often are invested with special powers and qualifications, sometimes independent of the CEO. Many variations exist, but the common underlying assumption is that strong executive leadership can ameliorate the maladies besetting urban school systems. A concomitant assumption has been that representativeness should be curbed. School boards should be restructured to emphasize expertise and neutral competence as against affiliation with and allegiance to one or another constituency.

The 1997 restructuring of the Baltimore City Public Schools (BCPS) provides a good example of this reform logic. In this case the party exercising more bureaucratic (and legislative) oversight is the state. The school system had operated as a department of city government with no independent fiscal or personnel authority. School board members were appointees of the mayor. The administration of the school system was, as a consequence, highly politicized, reflecting mayoral preferences, elements of patronage, and a central administrative bureaucracy that had weak professional norms. As a result of multiple lawsuits involving special education and school finance, an

out-of-court settlement was reached in 1996 involving the state superintendent of schools, state board of education, and the governor, which was in
turn ratified in early 1997 by the Maryland legislature. The legislation provided $230 million over 5 years to assist in the implementation of the man-
agement and education accountability reforms in BCPS.

A new nine-member board of commissioners has been appointed jointly
by the mayor and governor, based on a nominating slate provided by the
state board of education. The kinds of affiliations and expertise required for
these members were made explicit in the legislation: at least four must
possess a high level of expertise concerning a large business, nonprofit, or
governmental entity; at least three must have a high level of knowledge and
expertise in education; at least one member must be a parent of a BCPS
student; and at least one member must possess knowledge or experience in
the education of children with disabilities. Unlike the previous board, which
had been appointed and was controlled by the mayor, the new board is
vested with full authority and responsibility for running the school system.
The reform law does require that a 14-member parent and community advisory board be convened to solicit parental input and involvement.

The Baltimore reforms also require a CEO who reports directly to the
board and whose contract must specify demonstrable and continuous improvement in the academic performance of students and sound management
of BCPS. The CEO, subject to board approval, appoints a chief academic
officer, responsible for systemwide curriculum and instruction, and a chief
financial officer. Both these officers also have contracts that are contingent
on the effective performance of their duties.

The board operates under considerable state oversight. A transition plan
and annual master plans must be provided by specified dates. These plans
must meet detailed requirements such as the use of the new state dollars in
the first year, implementation of reforms in the areas of curriculum, instruction, and assessment, and so on. The master plan must include, among other
things, a comprehensive plan for improvement of school management and
accountability. Also, the additional state aid must be targeted on specific
things: improved educational performance for schools with high concentration of children in poverty, reconstitution-eligible schools and marginal
schools, teachers salaries to close the gap between BCPS salaries and those
in nearby Baltimore County, and so on. The law also requires that an independent consultant be retained by the state board of education to prepare
an interim review and evaluation of the progress of reform in BCPS, a comprehensive review and evaluation, and an annual report.

Given the great focus on master plans, reviews, and evaluations, the Baltimore reform clearly includes performance information in its reform strategy. This information is to be used both by BCPS officials and by the state to
determine if sufficient progress is occurring. The law is silent on what the
consequence will be if the school system's educational performance does

not improve. The new reform was labeled a "partnership" by state officials, even though it was viewed by many in Baltimore as capitulation to the state by ceding too much authority from the mayor. The state's response has been that BCPS should operate much the same as any of the other 23 school districts in the state, although the new law clearly imposes more restrictions on BCPS than any of its counterparts.

A partnership, however vaguely structured, provides significant risks for state officials because they may share in the responsibility if BCPS fails to improve. On the other hand, it holds promise of developing a new working relationship that bridges the differences in hierarchical authority between the two entities. It is hard to predict whether the partnership can thrive despite being inevitably buffeted by the often conflicting political agendas of Baltimore's mayor, the governor, the state superintendent, and legislative leaders, not to speak of the separate institutional interests of the city, the school system, the state board, and the state legislature. The attempt to restructure BCPS to make it more accountable, in the end, fails to clarify who will be accountable to whom for the success or failure of Baltimore school-children. What emerged was a compromise, as most institutional arrangements are, crafted under political, legal, and time constraints. Whether that compromise will prove better than the old largely discredited system remains to be seen. The appearance of accountability resides in creating a new regime with somewhat different ground rules. But whether that restructuring will be symbolic or effective remains murky.

Heightened Bureaucratic Oversight of Poorly Performing Schools

Another governance reform has been closer bureaucratic oversight of poorly performing schools. Most states have had educational "bankruptcy" statutes on the books for years, directed at school districts, but except for cases of clear financial mismangement or illegal activity, states rarely invoked them. More recently enacted statutes focus more on breaches of academic accountability. A growing number of states and local school districts have developed policies to deal with failing school districts or failing schools (Fraga, Anhalt, & Lee, 1998; O'Day, 1997). Some jurisdictions have developed gradations of intervention, first giving schools or districts an opportunity to improve before more drastic measures are taken. In Maryland, for example, schools that fall below a certain threshold of performance and have been declining in performance over several years are identified by the state as reconstitution eligible. They must file a transition plan to avoid actual reconstitution by the state, which if approved qualifies the school for financial assistance. State monitoring and some initial additional funds are provided until the school has improved sufficiently to warrant being taken off the list (none have been thus far). If a school fails to improve, the state reserves the right to reconstitute the school, including instituting management by an alternative provider. Chicago and San Francisco have taken this next step by actually closing schools and reorganizing them (see Wong in this volume).

Interest in this reform strategy has been widespread among policy makers, but the approach is so new that little firm evidence can be found that regulatory oversight of failing schools will work. The potential effectiveness of the policies may depend on many details of the way the policies themselves are constructed. If we assume that there are a variety of reasons why schools perform poorly, it follows that policies that are sensitive to this multifaceted etiology of failure are likely to enjoy a greater likelihood of success. What are some of the choices available to policy makers in designing the policy? First, there is the issue of whether to send an advance signal to the school that it needs to improve or merely to reorganize the school *ispo facto*. The first approach places faith in the willingness and capacity of school officials to reverse a prior pattern of failure, temporarily setting aside the interests of children who may be the victims if this strategy of buying time does not prove to be a fruitful gamble. The second approach, which moves immediately to reconstitute the school, implicitly rejects the assumption that sufficient progress can occur without dramatic changes in leadership and staffing, among other things. It assumes that school leaders have been doing everything possible—within their control—to address the failure, and that additional time would not matter. It also assumes that the latter approach has a greater likelihood of success. This seems plausible enough until one considers that certain boundary conditions may prove to be unsurmountable constraints, such as a shortage of qualified teachers to staff the reconstituted schools.

If the first path of early warning is chosen, what might be an effective strategy on the part of the regulator/interveners? At one end of the continuum we might find an approach that relies entirely on monitoring with virtually no consequences attached, and at the other extreme is an approach that is grounded entirely in support—that is, capacity building. If support is chosen, who is in the best position to offer it—state officials, local district officials, a third party partner such as a university, or some other option?

Closely related to these choices, but independent of them, is whether to attach consequences, such as rewards or sanctions, to the monitoring or support. The choice of strategy is not inconsequential, because these polarities are grounded in different sets of assumptions about what motivates individuals and social systems to improve. To what motivational theory do we subscribe? At a rhetorical level, accountability policy often seems grounded in a view of human nature that focuses on responsiveness to external stimuli, particularly to threat of punishment or prospect of reward. The policies themselves may include rewards (positive external inducements), and they may focus on providing opportunities for people to improve. Under what circumstances do individuals improve in response to threats (here, of having their school closed) or offers of help? This is a problem of motivating an entire group and not merely individuals, as individual decisions about how to respond will be influenced by the other individuals in the group. Few of these subtleties are well incorporated in the thinking that occurs when policies are crafted, but they become relevant when policy implementation occurs.

Almost all policies that intervene in failing schools require school officials to develop a plan to improve. This requirement is itself imbued with a questionable set of assumptions: that school officials have the capacity, using data about their performance, to identify clearly the problems of their school and to design appropriate solutions, that they will be honest in stating these problems to a regulatory agency rather than merely presenting a good image in a plan, and finally, that they are capable of working together over a sustained period to implement a plan. If any one of these assumptions is incorrect, then the rational planning requirement may fall down as a methodology for reversing decline. It is not unreasonable to question the capacity of local school officials to engage in continuous improvement given the fact that schools traditionally have not built their organizational cultures around collaboration or problem solving.

The reason that a theory of change is so blurry in these policies is, to return to an earlier point, that they focus on accountability as a problem of "accountability to whom?" External authorities are the embodiment of accountability. When attention shifts to what the authorities must do to elicit improvement from school officials, another set of problems comes into focus.

Rewards for Good Performance

Whereas executive leadership and bureaucratic oversight approaches to accountability attempt to address failures, rewards for performance deal with success. A small number of states (e.g., Kentucky and Maryland) and local jurisdictions (e.g., Dallas, Texas, and Harford County, Maryland) provide financial rewards to schools. The underlying assumption about the problem that must be fixed is that resources have not been allocated in public education according to performance. In fact, low-performing schools often qualify for additional federal or state revenue on the basis of need. Critics charge that this system of resource allocation sometimes has created a disincentive for school officials to improve achievement.

There are various different approaches to financial reward systems. All rely on performance reporting systems to allocate the rewards, but some systems focus on absolute levels of high student performance, whereas others emphasize improvement above a baseline. The approaches that stress improvement tend to qualify a wider range of schools, including the historically low-performing ones, while at the same time attempting to push the high performers to do even better. Most plans give money to a school to spend rather than individual teachers, although some approaches permit local discretion in deciding which approach to take.

Financial reward systems have not been popular in public education because of the widespread perception among teachers and much of the public that it is an unfair way to allocate resources. Some jurisdictions have eliminated their programs. For example, in California the Cash for CAP (California Achievement Program) was plagued with reporting irregularities by local districts and complaints that students were blackmailing teachers by threatening not to try hard on the CAP. Kentucky experienced other problems in implementing its financial reward program. Therefore, while giving rewards theoretically is an attractive alternative to the use of sanctions for poor performance because it relies on positive rather than negative inducements to modify individual and system behavior, the policy approach has not really caught on.

Contractual Approaches to Accountability

Still another approach to accountability is to establish a contractual relationship to bind the parties. The authorizing agent is a school board, the state board of education, or some other public authority such as a university. This authorizing agent in turn contracts with an organization to run a school or group of schools. Accountability resides in the binding relationship between the parties, contained in the details of the contract itself. To the degree that the contract specifies concrete expectations for performance, the relationship between the parties focuses on accountability for results. Here the question shifts from accountability to whom to accountability for what.

The few experiments with contracting between school boards and external parties to run schools have proved to be problematic. This is partly because the development has been interpreted by some stakeholders as an effort to introduce privatization to public schooling. Privatization has been defended (Savas, 1987). as centering on four types of pressure: pragmatic, ideological, commercial, and populist. Pragmatic arguments are built on the assumption that privatization can lead to more cost-effective approaches to funding services. Ideological arguments rest on the idea that government is too large and unresponsive when compared with private provision. Closely related to this is the commercial economic argument that private firms will better use public tax dollars than government monopolies will. Finally, populist defenses of privatization emanate from the idea that citizens *qua* consumers should have a greater choice in public services. Operating in concert, these rationales have led to more efforts toward privatization of public services.

Although privatization of public services has been increasingly common in other local governments such as municipalities and counties, as well as in some state and federal services, it has met with more resistance in public education. Those who oppose its use in the provision of education at K–12 level assert that education is different from other services such as sanitation or the supervision of welfare clients. Public education is regarded as sacrosanct because it is part of the nation's civil morality—equality of opportunity, the melting pot, and so on. According to this view, this secular religious quality of public education means that it is an activity in which people should not profit. The complexity of schooling also is cited as a reason why private provision would be inappropriate.

One of the main opponents of contracting has been teacher unions, who potentially stand to lose salary and benefits, favorable working conditions, and job security in collective bargaining agreements. Working with existing educational bureaucracies and with school boards also has proven complicated. Educational Alternatives, Inc., had experiments in Baltimore to run nine elementary schools, and in Hartford, Connecticut, to manage an entire district, both of which ended in failure (White, in press; Williams & Leak, 1996). Other corporations such as Sylvan Learning Systems proved to be more successful in developing working relationships (White, in press). It is also the case, however, that despite K–12 education being a potentially large market, Wall Street investors have not jumped in with large infusions of capital. The Edison Project had to scale back its ambitious plans to establish 1000 private schools due to a lack of investors, despite a considerable infusion of funds from the Whittle Corporation to jump-start the effort. Potential investors remain skeptical as to whether such ventures can be profitable (Harrington-Luecker, 1996).

The rapid growth of charter schools in the United States represents another form of contracting. The theory behind charter schools is that they can be more successful than existing public schools because the schools are freed of many of the typical regulatory burdens of other public schools (see Nathan, 1996 and Engler & Whitney, this volume). In exchange for this freedom they enter into a contractual agreement with the sponsoring agent (the local school board, the state department of education, etc.) on performance goals. Charter schools potentially have some of the ostensible advantages of private schools (clear focus, strong commitment by parents, a shared culture among teachers, etc.) but remain under public oversight and carry some restrictions, such as no overt selectivity in admissions. In practice, state charter school laws differ widely in the degree to which they loosen state and local regulatory oversight and in the contractual requirements under which the charter school must operate (Bierlin, 1996).

Contract theory also does not answer the key question of how to evaluate charter school success. The issue of how to assess student achievement has long been debated in public education. Both norm-referenced and criterion-referenced tests have limitations, and performance assessments are still at a developmental stage. Because charter schools are efforts to innovate on a variety of dimensions (content, pedagogy, governance, etc.), this traditional problem assessment is even more vexing for them. This is one of the major questions in the fledgling charter school movement (Nathan, 1998).

The contractual process also must answer what to do when a charter school is not meeting the goals set out in the contract. To date, only a small number of charter schools have been closed by their sponsors, which may reflect the newness of this reform movement. Over the longer term, however, the issues of what enforcement mechanisms charter school contracts will carry to deal with performance failures has yet to be clarified. There will be a delicate balance to strike between the rights of children already enrolled in those schools (as well as potential applicants) and the legitimate goal giving the charter school sponsors a reasonable period to make their experimental school successful. Some of the same issues that arise when state and local school officials seek to intervene in failing public schools arise in this context. Obviously, then, a contractual approach to accountability does not eliminate, much less resolve, fundamental issues of how to measure success and failure. Charter schools open up a process for creating schools that may have a greater likelihood of success, leaving to the performance contract the nettlesome question of how to specify and measure success at the student and school levels.

Markets as Accountability Devices

A final approach to accountability seeks to define its essence through market mechanisms. In a sense, elements of a market logic can be found in contracting, particularly in the charter school movement. When school boards contract with a private firm to offer a service, they are seeking choice in the provider, but the consumer may or may not have access to choice among providers. Charter schools do operate with some element of choice for consumers, although in many states a ceiling on the number of charters that can operate effectively constrains a competitive market from operating. This limits access to market alternatives for a wide range of consumers. It also has implications for the consumers who have selected the charter school, because if they are dissatisfied they may have few alternatives besides returning to the local public school serving their neighborhood. From an economic standpoint, this would deny a key principle in the theory of markets—namely, that the supply of schools will represent allocative efficiency. That is, the supply of schools should accommodate the full range of consumer preferences. Charter schools are as much rooted in theories of direct democracy as they are markets.

Market theory, by contrast, introduces the idea that schools will compete for clients and thereby be more responsive than institutions such as public schools, which often operate in monopolistic or quasi-monopolistic conditions and therefore have little incentive to be responsive to parents and students. Rather, critics charge that they are responsive to bureaucratic and political imperatives, which allegedly interfere with their responsiveness (Chubb & Moe, 1990).

Market accountability, therefore, resides in the essence of the economic exchange relationship between school officials (the producers) and parents and their children (the consumers or consumers and clients). This exchange relationship consists of a number of critical elements. The school offers a service and provides information to prospective consumers. Parents make a choice based on certain preferences and information. The school and parents/students enter into a working relationship in which the obligations and expectations of each party need to be articulated. The school attempts to be responsive to these expectations. If the consumer is dissatisfied, then parents/students must articulate those concerns, and the school has an opportunity to be responsive. Finally, parents/students decide whether to remain at the school.

In the case of schools, there are a number of complications in operationalizing the market exchange relationship. This fact does not worry many economists, because the pure market is rarely if ever found in the real world. Nonetheless, these complexities are seized on by critics of educational choice to point to the fallacious logic inherent in attempting to operate schools as markets and hope that accountability will result in improved learning outcomes for most pupils when compared with the present public education system.

We shall not try to summarize here the debate on school choice. (For two critiques see Fuller & Elmore, 1996, and Smith & Meier, 1995). Some of the major complications in the exchange relationship do bear mention. First, there is the nature of the information available to and utilized by parents and students in selecting a school. Is the information provided accurate? Do parents make the choice based on educational considerations or convenience factors? These factors influence the expectations parents have for a school and how accountable they will hold the school for meeting their child's needs. Second, do the consumers choose the school, or does the school choose the consumer it is willing to enroll? The range of choices available to consumers may be limited, allowing school officials to be highly selective in whom they decide to admit and whether they will keep a student who is having problems in the school. To the degree that schools are free to choose from an oversupply of applicants, this potentially acts as a sharp constraint on accountability from the school to the consumer. Third, education is a complicated process, and it is delivered in many steps over an extended period. The problems for the parent in gaining accurate information on which to make judgments, of understanding accurately what is being delivered, and finally in communicating expectations are therefore considerable. These are compounded by the time constraints under which both teachers and parents operate. These barriers to information, understanding, and communication may be greater for less well-educated parents. In other words, there are complications on both the demand and supply side of the market exchange. Fourth, with these complications, would parental satisfaction with schooling and student achievement actually improve, or might it grow worse? Finally, the nature of the provider and the regulatory environment within which the provider operates are certainly relevant to how well the school will be accountable. Nonprofit schools such as those run by religious organizations certainly have a different approach to defining their mission than do for-profit schools. The degree to which the school is free to define its mission, its curriculum, and its staff free of external state (or school district) regulation is also a significant factor, particularly for public schools of choice.

Quite apart from these theoretical issues, there has been little widespread experimentation with educational choice involving private schools. Only Milwaukee and Cleveland have such programs. Legal challenges have been made to both programs, and the Milwaukee program has been barred from involving religious schools, pending further court appeals. There have been major debates over the effectiveness of the Milwaukee program. (Cleveland's program is still a fledgling, but similar arguments over results already have begun.) Although Greene and Peterson (1996) and Rouse (1996) have provided strong evidence concerning the effectiveness of the Milwaukee program, challenging earlier evaluations by Witte (1996), their findings have been disputed as well. This echoes a larger debate about the effectiveness of Catholic schools first launched by Coleman, Hoffer, and Kilgore (1982), which remains unresolved. However, recent reanalyses of the data point to the effectiveness of Catholic schools (Hoffer, in press; Schiller, in press).

Choice within the public school sector provides another approach, such as public magnet schools (Smrekar and Goldring, in press) and interdistrict open-enrollment plans. (Magnet schools, for example, rarely are freed from regulations of the school district, although magnet school officials may have freedom to select their students. Consequently, it is difficult to generalize about markets as accountability systems. In practice, most market systems operate within regulatory constraints and therefore must be evaluated with that in mind. It is unlikely that expansion of public school choice, charter schools (to the extent that they can be viewed as choice arrangements at all), or voucher plans would proceed without significant governmental oversight. Thus, the idea that markets substitute accountability for performance for traditional accountability for process is only a matter of degree. Despite its hybrid character, the inclusion of market processes in the definition of accountability is an important development that departs in quite important, if not fundamental, ways from other approaches to defining accountability.

CONCLUSION

This chapter examined six approaches to improving accountability in American public K–12 education. Key aspects of these approaches are summarized in Table 1. Each of these approaches addresses a part of the accountability puzzle, but each is, not surprisingly, an incomplete specification of the requirements for effective accountability to occur. Information alone will not cause accountability to occur, although it seems to be a precondition. Moreover, who the targets of the performance accountability are, both as objects of change and its agents, remains fuzzy.

Performance reporting portrays the accountability problem as lack of information on which to act. Yet, depending on how the performance reporting is structured, the strategy has many alternative targets: the public, government regulators, school officials, and others. The strategy does nothing to address how this information will be employed by the agents of change or its targets. Unless one assumes that information is empowering in and of itself, which is highly questionable, performance reporting is an incomplete strategy.

Executive leadership as a strategy for reform invests all its logic in an authoritative view of the accountability problem: putting new officials in charge and giving new authority will cure the problem. Part of the logic of this approach is to imbue schools with more of the trappings of private-sector approaches to management. As an institutional renewal strategy, however, the theory is incomplete. It does not speak to what these authorities will do to restore

TABLE 1
Six Approaches to Accountability in Education

Accountability type	Key premise concerning problem needing to be addressed	Target(s)
Information	Performance data are needed to create greater accountability.	Public, government, school officials
Executive leadership	New leaders are needed.	Public
Bureaucratic oversight	Regulatory intervention is needed where schools fail.	Schools, districts
Rewards for performance	Resources need to be allocated according to performance to create positive incentives to improve student achievement.	Schools
Contracting	New providers need to be empowered with less regulation and held accountable for results.	Schools, districts
Markets	Consumers need more choices.	Consumers, schools

confidence or to whom they will be accountable for improving results. The strategy has a symbolic dimension in that its target is the general public, whose confidence may be restored for a time when new authorities are appointed.

A *bureaucratic oversight* strategy captures the essence of the accountability problem as an insufficient regulatory authority. It is directed at schools and districts. This approach has its limitations as well. It is not directed at making all schools more accountable, only those that are targeted as performing poorly using criteria employed by the regulators. Also, heightened regulation may not result in improvements. It must increase both incentives to change and capacity to do so, and the requirements for making this happen depend on many factors, all of which may not be addressed by the accountability policy or even under the jurisdiction of those who are the agents of the increased bureaucratic oversight.

Rewards for performance emphasize positive incentives for school officials to maintain high performance or improve against a previous record or benchmark. Like bureaucratic oversight, it assumes that teachers and administrators are motivated by extrinsic factors. The approach also assumes that those not receiving a reward will have increased motivation to succeed. However, if the perception is that there is not an even playing field and that opportunity to succeed is unfairly distributed, the program could have the opposite effect. The differences in motivation and commitment to succeed could widen rather than narrow. Like the implicit theory behind reconstitution for failing schools, these assumptions have not been tested by research.

Contractual approaches to accountability use the opposite strategy. They *decrease* regulation rather than increase it, and they focus on the creation of new schools, not fixing failing ones. Accountability is defined legalistically, through the essence of a performance contract that obligates the school to meet certain standards of performance in student achievement and other measures. Yet this approach, whose targets are schools and districts, has difficulties. What the performance standards should be is open to dispute, particularly in schools whose *raison d'etre* is to break the mold and provide new models of successful schooling. This strategy does not address how to maintain accountability when the school fails to meet its agreed-upon goals, much less how to scale up the successful cases.

Market approaches target the consumer of educational services as the agent of accountability and school officials as its objects. Accountability exists in the incentives created for school officials to be responsive when they depend on consumers, who have the power to make choices for their children. This approach to reform addresses an element missing in the other models: incentives for both the provider and the consumer to act in ways that makes accountability possible. Here again, however, establishing an accountability relationship is formalistic unless it actually results in educational improvements. Satisfied customers may be one measure of improvement, but other information is needed to establish whether the market exchange actually has served students will. Critics of choice worry about the negative externalities associated with markets, particularly effects on those children who are denied a choice because of a lack of a supply of good schools among which to choose. They claim that choice will reduce general financial support for public education among the middle class if they are allowed to flee public schools for private ones with vouchers. Among those who do exercise the opportunity to choose a school, the reasons for selecting a particular school and the responsiveness of school officials may depend on many factors, such as availability of accurate information about the school, the balance of demand and supply, and so on.

From these examples it should be clear that accountability is a broad legitimating principle of governance, which can lead to many specific approaches to reform. Each approach defines the essence of accountability differently. From one view, each approach has a theory in use that is incomplete and needs greater specification in the policy itself. The assumption is that creating a more accountable educational system involves getting each particular policy strategy right. Even if they are not entirely compatible, well-crafted policies that compete with one another can lead to a more accountable educational system. From another perspective, the tensions and incompatibilities among these policies are a problem. If fragmentation in the policy system also is problematic, these multiple paths to accountability may contribute to greater incoherence in the policy system. Indeed, as pressure to move along one policy path (such as markets) increases, arguably it will only accelerate inclinations to introduce alternative approaches to accountability in hopes of restoring public confidence.

The focus on making the educational system more accountable is a welcome development if it leads to improvements in the performance of American students. Few would argue with that goal at the level of generality it is stated here. Whether any one of the approaches discussed is the necessary, much less sufficient, route to achieving that goal is entirely unclear. Moreover, it is an empirical question whether the overall menu of approaches, taken together, will move the educational system in this direction of improved results. As indicated earlier, accountability is only one of the legitimating principles of the American political system, many of which operate in tension with one another. Will accountability policies make the educational system more efficient in use of resources? Will they address the inequities inherent in the current system, such as wide disparities in educational opportunity available to pupils depending on family background, race, and place of residence? Those who see policy as ideologically loaded and reflecting the deep structures of society, rooted in inequalities among the nation's social classes, will be skeptical about accountability. Those who view policy as a rational process striving toward optimization of outcomes and making a difference depending on the design of the policy in question will hold out more hope that accountability policies can be salutary if they are improved. These are legitimate differences of perspective for which there are no clear answers.

References

Bierlin, L. A. (1996, February). *Charter schools: Initial findings.* Denver, CO: Education Commission of the States.

Callahan, R. E. (1962). *Education and the cult of efficiency.* Chicago: University of Chicago Press.

Chubb, J. E., & Moe, T. M. (1990). *Politics, markets, and America's schools.* Washington, DC: Brookings Institution.

Cibulka, J. G. (1987). Theories of education budgeting: Lessons from the management of decline. *Educational Administration Quarterly,* 23(1), 7.40.

Cibulka, J. G., & Derlin, R. L. (1998). Authentic education accountability policies: Implementation of state initiatives in Colorado and Maryland. *Education Policy,* 12(1–2), 84–97.

Coleman, J. S., Hoffer, T. B., & Kilgore, S. (1982). *High school achievement: Public, Catholic, and other private schools compared.* New York: Basic Books.

Elmore, R. F., Abelman, C. H., & Fuhrman, S. H. (1996). The new accountability in state education reform: From process to performance. In H. F. Ladd (Ed.), *Holding schools accountable: Performance-based reform in education* (pp. 65–98). Washington, DC: Brookings Institution.

Fraga, L. R., Erlichson, B. A., & Lee, S. (1998). Consensus building and school reform: The role of the courts in San Francisco. In C. Stone (ed.), *Changing urban education* (pp. 66–92). Lawrence, KS: University of Kansas Press.

Fuller, B., & Elmore, R. F. (1996). *Who chooses? Who loses? Culture, institutions, and the unequal effects of school choice.* New York: Teachers College Press.

Greene, J. P., & Peterson, P. E. (1996). Methodological issues in evaluation research: The Milwaukee school choice plan. Unpublished manuscript, Department of Government and Kennedy School of Government, Harvard University.

Hoffer, T. B. (in press). Social background and achievement in public and Catholic high schools. In J. G. Cibulka (Ed.), *Educational choice: Lessons from private and public schools.* Greenwood, CT: Greenwood Press.

Kaufman, H. (1956, December). Emerging conflicts in the doctrines of public administration. *American Political Science Review,* pp. 1057–1073.

Harrington-Luecker, D. (1996, April). The high-flyer falls. *The American School Board Journal,* pp. 26–33.

Nathan, J. (1996). *Charter schools: Creating hope and opportunity for American schools.* San Francisco: Jossey-Bass.

Nathan, J. (1998). Heat and light in the charter school movement. *Phi Delta Kappan,* 79(7), 499–505.

O'Day, J. (1997, April). *Reconstitution in San Francisco: A new model of accountability.* Paper presented at the meeting of the American Educational Research Association, Chicago, IL.

Peterson, P. E. (1981). *City limits.* Chicago: University of Chicago Press.

Rouse, C. E. (1996). Private school vouchers and student achievement: An evaluation of the Milwaukee parental school choice program. Princeton, NJ: Firestone Library, Princeton University.

Savas, E. S. (1987). *Privatization: The key to better government.* Chatham, NJ: Chatham House.

Schiller, K. A. (in press). The Catholic school advantage: A continuing debate. In J. G. Cibulka (Ed.), *Educational choice: Lessons from private and public schools.* Greenwood, CT: Greenwood Press.

Smith, K. B., & Meier, K. J. (1995). *The case against school choice: Politics, markets, and fools.* London: M. E. Sharpe.

Smrekar, C., & Goldring, E. (in press). *Magnet schools in urban districts: What's our choice.* New York: Teachers College Press.

Tyack, D. (1974). *The one best system: A history of American urban education.* Cambridge, MA: Harvard University Press.

White, S. B. (in press). Privatization in education. In J. G. Cibulka (Ed.), *Educational choice: Lessons from private and public schools*. Greenwood, CT: Greenwood Press.

Williams, L. C., & Leak, L. E. (1996, October). The UMBC review of the Tesseract program in Baltimore City. Unpublished manuscript, Center for Education Research, University of Maryland, Baltimore County, MD.

Witte, J. F. (1996). Reply to Greene, Peterson, and Du: "The effectiveness of school choice in Milwaukee: A secondary analysis of data from the program's evaluation. Unpublished manuscript, Robert LaFollette Institute of Public Affairs, University of Wisconsin-Madison, WI.

CHAPTER 9

The Role of the National Assessment of Educational Progress (NAEP) in Setting, Reflecting, and Linking National Education Policy to States' Needs

MARY LYN BOURQUE
National Assessment Governing Board[1]

The nation's report card, the National Assessment of Educational Progress (NAEP), is the only nationally representative and continuing assessment of academic achievement in the United States. Since 1969, surveys of what American students know and can do have been conducted periodically in various school subjects. Although relatively unknown to practitioners in the early years, NAEP has gained in currency over the past decade. Currently, NAEP data have informed many national policy debates and are an integral part of the nation's evaluation of educational progress at the national, state, and local levels.

As the next millennium grows near, NAEP is quickly approaching its 30th anniversary as the premier survey of academic achievement in the United States. Though its original architects, Francis Keppel and Ralph W. Tyler,

[1]The views expressed in this chapter do not necessarily reflect the policy or positions of the National Assessment Governing Board.

Handbook of Educational Policy

could not have known, NAEP has achieved a stature as a national program unlike many other federally funded initiatives of recent memory. Over the past 30 years NAEP has changed, in some ways significantly, from the program intentionally created by its early planners. However, in large measure such changes have been the result of the sociopolitical milieu in which a program like NAEP operates.

This chapter examines briefly the development of NAEP through the first three decades, with a particular emphasis on policy shifts in the program during the 1990s. It also develops the themes and ideas that are part of the redesign of NAEP that will take it into the next century. Finally, the chapter examines the latest developments in the individualized version of NAEP, the voluntary national test, focusing on the policy ramifications of a federally sponsored national test.

BACKGROUND

From the beginnings of the United States until 1865, the federal government had virtually no interest or involvement in education. Education of the nation's youth was solely the responsibility of the colonies and states. It was not until 1865, when the U.S. Office of Education (USOE) was established, that the federal government developed an interest, and national data collections in education became more systematic. The primary mission of the USOE was to collect and report on various characteristics of education across the nation. Such data collection included the number of schools and teachers, the number of school-age children, the number and type of private schools, and other similar observations. For almost 100 years these simple descriptive statistics were the only data the federal government collected. It was not until 1957 and the launch of the USSR's *Sputnik*, that the federal government began to take a more active role in shaping national educational policy with the passage of the National Defense Education Act (NDEA). The NDEA poured federal dollars into science and mathematics education and foreign language training, all three areas being viewed as necessary prerequisites for our national defense and successful competition in a global market.

EARLY NAEP, 1969–1982

In 1961 when Francis Keppel was first appointed U.S. commissioner of education, USOE took a policy position that it should collect and report data on student academic performance, and thus the National Assessment of Educational Progress was born. The sociopolitical climate at this time was one of a postwar expanding economy and growing school enrollments. Under the Johnson administration, the federal role in education expanded (e.g., Congress passed the first Title I legislation), even in the face of strong state and local autonomy. The time seemed to be right for changing the way a nation reported to its people on how well its youth were achieving academic success in school subjects. As Keppel stated "Americans know more about steel production, garment prices, and the raising of cattle than the proficiency of students . . . we have no reliable means to judge the vast output of some 33,000 heterogeneous school districts." However, political pressures dictated that the design of NAEP had to be such that it posed no real threat to the constitutionally protected authority of state and local agencies for educating the nation's youth.

The first National Assessment was defined more in terms of what it would *not* do than what it *would* do; it would *not* collect or report data on individual students, on classrooms or grades, on schools or districts, on states or jurisdictions. NAEP's primary purpose was to focus on what students in the nation *know and can do* and to report on changes in academic performance at the national level. Consequently, many of the design features of the original NAEP were intended to support these goals (Jones, 1996), as well as to preclude inappropriate uses of the data and provide political assurances that a national curriculum was not lurking behind the next proverbial assessment bush. So, for example, item-examinee sampling (also known as *matrix sampling*) was viewed as an efficient means to achieve broad coverage of the content. Matrix sampling is a method for sampling both test items and students such that a subset of the exercises in the item pool are administered to a subset of the examinee sample. Matrix sampling allows more comprehensive coverage of the content domain while minimizing the testing burden on any individual examinee. This approach yielded results for nationally representative samples of students and, at the same time, since no students answered all the survey questions, precluded individual student scores. Age-defined samples (as opposed to grade-level samples) provided a uniformly defined sampling criterion while precluding grade-level accountability. Nationally representative samples provided results for the nation as a whole and broad regions of the country, while precluding state or jurisdictional reporting, or for that matter policy shifts at the state or jurisdictional level. NAEP's original design was both clever and wise given the tenor of the times: a national program without federal intrusion; national and regional results while maintaining individual and jurisdictional anonymity. Data collection under the original design continued more or less unchanged from 1969 through 1982.

The early NAEP assessments were both varied in scope and innovative in approach. Subject areas tested included art, music, the social sciences, and the core academic areas of reading, writing, mathematics, and science. These latter four have become institutionalized over the years as the Long-Term Trend assessment and continue to be administered on a regular, but somewhat less frequent, basis today.

NAEP's REDESIGN FOR THE 1980s

During the first dozen years of NAEP, the limitations of the original design became apparent. Age-defined samples, for example, generally included students from three grade levels: the modal grade, one grade higher, and one grader lower. Consequently, linking the age-based results to grade-level practices was not possible. Policy decisions regarding program effectiveness are frequently grade-level focused because schools are organized generally around a grade structure, not age. Therefore, using achievement results for 13-year-olds to help guide and inform program decisions at the appropriate instructional level was difficult at best.

One of the primary initial purposes of NAEP was to track educational progress and to report on trends in academic subjects. However, NAEP could not do this very well either. In the early years, reporting was done at the exercise level (Phillips et al., 1993). That is, NAEP results were reported using the percentages of students responding correctly to individual survey questions. Trends initially were reported by using those same questions year after year and reporting changes in the percentages correct from year to year. However, this method of tracking trends in NAEP was cumbersome and failed to give readers of NAEP reports the gestalt of student achievement as measured by the NAEP assessments. To understand the results, readers needed more summary measures—ways of aggregating the data into a meaningful whole—using a reporting metric that could communicate to a general audience of policy makers, educators, and the citizenry. Some improvements were realized in this area by summarizing percentages correct for item clusters and reporting these for the population of students and for selected subgroups as well. However, this methodology is dependent on the particular items being used, and, as the items in the cluster changed from assessment to assessment, the possibility of mistaking changes in item difficulty with changes in trends was apparent.

A New Design for a New Era

Because of these limitations, in the early 1980s, under the guidance of the National Institute of Education, NAEP was redesigned to address some of the weaknesses noted (Messick, Beaton, & Lord, 1983). The implementation of the program was moved from the Education Commission of the States in Colorado to the Princeton, New Jersey-based Educational Testing Service (ETS). Matrix sampling was retained as an efficient approach to covering the very broad content domains that were NAEP's hallmark, while minimizing student burden in terms of individual testing time required. In addition, age-defined samples were supplemented with grade-defined samples to make NAEP more useful in the policy and instructional arenas. Because there was considerable interest in reporting by demographic subpopulations, over-sampling of underrepresented subpopulations became part of the redesign.

Analytical techniques were approved allowing for reporting of domain (and subdomain) scores. Most important, perhaps, trend reporting was achieved through a new item Response Theory (IRT) scaling procedure.[1]

Under the guidance of the newly established cabinet Department of Education, the National Assessment flourished in the 1980s. New subject areas were added to NAEP's repertoire, including computer literacy and geography. (Some other subjects, such as music and art, were dropped and not returned to NAEP until the late 1990s.) New and innovative assessment exercises were used to measure what students know and can do. New item sampling techniques were instituted to gain maximum coverage of content domains and at the same time to minimize the student and school burden. The Balanced Incomplete Block (BIB) design became standard fare in NAEP administrations. The BIB design refers to the manner in which NAEP allocates the grade-level item pools to smaller testing units called *blocks*. Because each block contains a subset of the item pool, it is *incomplete*. However, in the assembly of examinee test booklets, each block is included in different positions in the booklet and in combination with alternative blocks in a balanced way. Thus, the term BIB has been coined to describe this procedure.

Table 1 shows a BIB design for the 1998 writing assessment, which has 20 prompts/blocks for Grade 4. Because the writing assessment consists of prompts measuring the three types of writing, narrative (N), informative (I), and persuasive (P), blocks (one prompt per block) are arranged in the BIB designs such that pairs of prompts appear together in a single examinee test booklet. Because not all possible pairs are selected, the result is 40 Grade 4 test booklets, 9 of which are the NN and NI types, 7 are II, and 5 are PP, NP, and IP. The order of NI, I, and P, is varied in their position in the booklet.

Similarly, state-of-the-art analytical methods were developed to make NAEP estimates of proficiency more accurate and stable from year to year. NAEP trends were established not only for the 1980s and into the future but also for the past, back to 1970 in some cases. Under the ETS grant, data from the early years of NAEP were reexamined using the new IRT approaches so that long-term trend lines could provide policy makers and others with a longitudinal picture of American student achievement.

A Nation at Risk

In 1983 the *Nation at Risk* (National Commission on Excellence in Education, 1983) was released, which cited numerous concerns about American public education and its relation to the expanding global economy. The National

---

[1]Item Response Theory is a statistical procedure for estimating unobservable traits (achievement) from observable student performance (correct or incorrect answers) that does not depend on the pool of test questions used or on the particular sample of students used to estimate the performance. In NAEP these characteristics are quite desirable because only a sample of students in a grade level are assessed and because each student in the sample takes only a portion of the full item pool.

TABLE I
1998 NAEP Writing Assessment: Balanced Incomplete Block Design for 20 Prompts in 40
Booklets Comprising Two Exercises Each

Booklet no.	Block order	Booklet no.	Block order
1	$N_4 I_{16}$	21	$N_8 P_{22}$
2	$I_{16} I_{11}$	22	$P_{22} I_{13}$
3	$I_{11} N_3$	23	$I_{13} N_9$
4	$N_3 P_{18}$	24	$N_9 N_4$
5	$P_{18} P_{19}$	25	$N_4 N_3$
6	$P_{19} P_{20}$	26	$N_3 N_5$
7	$P_{20} I_{12}$	27	$N_5 N_6$
8	$I_{12} N_7$	28	$N_6 N_7$
9	$N_7 P_{21}$	29	$N_7 N_8$
10	$P_{21} P_{22}$	30	$N_8 N_9$
11	$P_{22} P_{18}$	31	$N_9 N_{10}$
12	$P_{18} I_{14}$	32	$N_{10} I_{11}$
13	$I_{14} N_5$	33	$I_{11} I_{14}$
14	$N_5 P_{19}$	34	$I_{14} I_{17}$
15	$P_{19} I_{17}$	35	$I_{17} I_{12}$
16	$I_{17} N_6$	36	$I_{12} I_{15}$
17	$N_6 P_{20}$	37	$I_{15} I_{13}$
18	$P_{20} P_{21}$	38	$I_{13} I_{16}$
19	$P_{21} I_{15}$	39	$I_{16} N_{10}$
20	$I_{15} N_8$	40	$N_{10} N_4$

Commission's report claimed the United States was a nation at risk, citing increasing dropout rates, lack of school readiness for young children, and high school graduates' lack of preparation for the postsecondary school environment (including the workplace, military service, and higher education), as indicators of such deficiencies. According to the report, the American educational system was not producing highly qualified graduates, and consequently the potential for being competitive in a global economy was very much at risk. At the same time, the U.S. Department of Education was releasing the *Wall Chart*, which compared the performance of students in one state against those in another. However, the indices being used for these comparisons were far from ideal. For example, the Scholastic Aptitude Test (SAT) results for self-selected samples of students in states were one of the major indices used in the chart. Similarly, the student scores from the American College Testing (ACT) program were also major entries. This, and other indices with fundamental comparability problems and policy flaws, caused the Council of Chief State School Officers (CCSSO) along with the National Governors Association (NGA), to call for better state comparability data.

The Nation's Report Card

The CCSSO and the NGA turned their attention to the nation's report card, the National Assessment of Educational Progress. However, a fundamental limitation of the NAEP design was that it provided only national and some regional data, but no data on a state-by-state basis. In response to the CCSSO and NGA needs, then-Secretary of Education William Bennett appointed a blue ribbon panel in May of 1986 to examine the National Assessment carefully and to determine whether NAEP could answer some of the fundamental questions on the educational policy table:

1. How well are American students performing school?
2. What are they learning?
3. Are schools doing a good job?
4. Are learning and teaching better than they used to be?
5. Will students in our state be able to compete successfully in the future?

In the process of answering such questions, the whole structure of NAEP was reexamined: what was being assessed, how NAEP policy decisions were being made, whether standards of performance were integral to the Nation's Report Card, and how best to achieve these new goals of the nation's only continuing measure of American achievement.

1988 NAEP Reauthorization and the Birth of NAGB

The results of the blue ribbon panel were formulated in the Alexander-James Report (1987) and ultimately became the basis for Congress' reauthorization of NAEP (Public Law 100-297) signed into law on April 28, 1988. The main thrust of the 1988 reauthorization was to make NAEP more responsive to national and state policy needs. If NAEP could provide achievement results for states and jursidictions that were fair and comparable, then unacceptable entries in the Wall Chart could be replaced with NAEP statewide results. The 1988 legislation was responsive to such needs and the Trial State Assessments (TSA) were inaugurated for the first time in 1990.

Similarly, if the policy decisions affecting the National Assessment could be formulated by a broadly representative, bipartisan panel, this would ensure that such decisions reflect states' as well as national needs, would provide continuity and stability to NAEP policies, and could limit future policy decisions from being unduly influenced by political pressures. Thus, the 1988 legislation also created such a panel, called the National Assessment Governing Board (NAGB). Congress described in the legislation the categories of membership for the NAGB that would cover a broad spectrum of constituencies including governors, state legislators, chief state school officers, local and state school board members, teachers, curriculum specialists, testing experts, members of the business community, and members of the general public. This broad representation has survived a subsequent reauthorization in 1994 and an anticipated reauthorization in 1999, leaving the NAGB with its current 26 members of geographical, racial/ethnic, and gender diversity.

The Trial State Assessment

The single most significant change in NAEP in 2 decades has been the authorization for the Trial State Assessment (TSA) program, which continues to be a highly successful state-level component of the National Assessment. In 1990, 40 U.S. states and territories (often referred to jointly as jurisdictions) participated in the first ever TSA in Grade 8 mathematics. The NAGB anticipated participation by about 25 jurisdictions and was somewhat surprised by such an overwhelming response. This was followed 2 years later by 44 jurisdictions signing on for Grades 4 and 8 mathematics and Grade 4 reading. As of 1998, 43 jurisdictions participated in the reading and writing assessments in Grades 4 and 8. This degree of participation is surprising and speaks to the broad sense of need and acceptability of NAEP in an era when most states have their own statewide assessments in various subject areas, when there is much discussion about the amount of time American students spend taking tests, and in an environment in which NAEP is still considered to be a low-stakes assessment.

In the 1994 reauthorization, Congress removed the "trial" designation from the TSA, but required that the state assessments be considered *developmental* until evaluated and judged to be both reliable and valid. Currently, the program is under evaluation by the National Academy of Sciences, whose report was released in the fall of 1998. The Academy recommended removal of the designation *developmental* to give the TSA full stature in NAEP.

The Role of the National Assessment Governing Board

The second major change under the 1988 reauthorization was the creation of the NAGB to oversee NAEP activities. The NAGB is required under the current law (Public Law 103-382, 1994) to carry out a number of policy functions including selecting subjects to be assessed; developing student performance standards; developing assessment frameworks and test/item specifications; designing the methodology of the assessments; developing guidelines for reporting and disseminating NAEP results; developing standards for state, regional, and national comparisons; and improving the form and use of NAEP. In addition, the NAGB judges the appropriateness of all cognitive items and takes steps to ensure that all items selected for use are free from racial, cultural, gender, and regional biases.

The National Education Goals

At about the same time that NAEP was beginning to address some of the residual issues stemming from the *Nation at Risk* report, the nation's governors, in conjunction with the Bush administration, gathered in Charlottesville, Virginia, to rethink the states' responsibilities for education through a decentralized educational system. Could the governors agree on national goals that would adequately address the diverse needs of 50 heterogeneous jursidictions? And if they could agree, could they begin to measure how well the nation's youth were achieving such goals? Participants at the Charlottesville summit believed a common set of goals would serve this nation well and articulated six priority areas: (1) school readiness, (2) school graduation rates at 90%, (3) competency over challenging subject matter in nine school subjects, (4) the challenge to be first in the world in math and science by the year 2000, (5) adult literacy, and (6) drug-free and violence-free schools (National Governors Association, 1991). These six goals became codified in the 1994 Goals 2000 legislation (Public Law 103-227), along with two additional goals: parent involvement and teacher preparation.

Because there was much discussion at the time on the distinctions to be made between *content standards* and *performance standards*, the National Education Goals Panel (NEGP) issued a study report that articulated the differences between the two (NEGP, 1993). NAEP is well positioned to provide indices of performance regarding the third and fourth original goals. Since 1990, the NEGP has been employing the NAEP results to report to the American public on school achievement.

POLICY SHIFTS IN NAEP UNDER THE GOVERNING BOARD

The 1990s saw a number of new initiatives for NAEP under the direction of the National Assessment Governing Board. NAEP was now considered to be not only the national barometer of American student achievement but also the standard by which the states could measure their successes and failures against themselves and each other. The NAGB adopted a position of listening and attending to states' needs as it went about the business of adopting policies for NAEP. Involving state and local education agencies in the decision-making processes was necessary to make NAEP responsive and sensitive to what states wanted in an external criterion measure. State administrators and curriculum personnel participated in nearly every advisory group, which provided recommendations to the NAGB on a specific topic.

The National Consensus Process in NAEP

One area where states' involvement was most important was in developing the assessment frameworks and test and item specifications for NAEP. Although there is no formal NAGB policy on consensus, two major principles are the driving forces behind the NAGB's work: (1) The national consensus process shall produce assessment frameworks for the NAEP subject area that are grounded in research and best practice and that reflect state-of-the-art assessments (the so-called *balance principle*), and (2) the national consensus process shall be carried out by a broadly representative body of teachers, curriculum specialists, local school administrators, parents, and concerned members of the general public in a working atmosphere that is open, free of constraints and partisan political influence (called the *participation principle*).

The *balance principle* requires that assessment frameworks must maintain a balance between present instructional efforts, curriculum reform in the particular field, research results about cognitive development and ways of learning, and the nation's future needs and desirable levels of achievement. This delicate balance between *what is* and what *should be or will be* is the essence of the NAEP frameworks.

The consensus process begins by thoroughly identifying all the current instructional and measurement issues in the content area. This summary is designed to serve as a springboard for committee discussions and framework development. The consensus panels consider a wide variety of resources as the deliberations proceed, including curriculum guides produced by the states as well as those produced by curriculum organizations (e.g., National Council of Teachers of Mathematics, 1989), key reports having significant national and international importance, and, of course, the frameworks of earlier NAEP assessments.

The *participation principle* speaks to the issue of representation in the consensus process. The guiding statute requires the active participation of various publics in the endeavor. In addition, the deliberations must be governed by the principles of equity and fairness throughout the process. The NAGB has always required the consensus panels to be as representative as possible in terms of gender, race/ethnicity, geographic region, and pedagogical point of view. The representativeness in pedagogy extends as well to the broadly inclusive review process of draft materials and public input into the overall process. The process attempts to obtain continued reviews of materials from a wide audience of stakeholders, including content experts, state and local education agencies, users of assessment data, policy makers, and those who ply their trade in the content area under discussion (e.g., scientists, geographers, historians, writers, and political scientists). Consensus panels are encouraged to explore the question, "What is the best asessment?" in an environment that is free, open, and evenhanded. To the greatest extent possible, the consensus environment is protected from the inappropriate influences of various interest groups in part due to the fact that these groups are afforded equal access to the process.

The current NAEP reading assessment framework, developed by the NAGB in 1990, was the first of many using a *national consensus* approach. The steering and planning committees who guided that work for the NAGB included diverse points of view regarding reading instruction and assessment. Then, as now, there were opposing views on the importance of teaching reading using methods such as phonics or whole language. Rather than inviting particular points of view to the national consensus table at the exclusion of others, all were invited to participate and to work through the differences. The NAGB has always viewed the national consensus process as an opportunity to define and measure *outcomes* rather than the *instructional means* for achieving such outcomes. The NAGB ultimately adopted a view of reading for the 1992 NAEP assessment framework (National Assessment Governing Board, 1991) that was not necessarily shared and embraced by all or even most reading professionals. However, it has stood the test of time. The National Academy of Education (1994) in its evaluation of the NAEP program has stated, "In general, the 1994 studies, like those conducted for 1992, confirmed the validity of the NAEP reading assessment and framework on which it was based, finding them reasonably well aligned with current research as well as with common classroom practices" (p. 15). Many states have adopted the structure of the NAEP reading assessment in their own assessment programs, using longer passages drawn from published literary or information sources that the student might encounter, employing constructed response exercises in their item pools, and asking questions that go beyond the literal interpretation of texts, probe the reader/text connections, and encourage critical thinking skills in students.

Of more recent origins are the consensus efforts in science, mathematics, U.S. history, world geography, writing, and civics. Each of these curriculum areas has its own set of dissonances, which were brought to the NAEP consensus table. In each case, the NAGB tried to achieve a balance among competing views in these subject areas. In U.S. history for example, there is a tension between the Eurocentric and multicultural views of American history. Whether a particular classroom, school, district, or state espouses one view over the other is somewhat immaterial. The NAEP assessment framework (National Assessment Governing Board, 1992) attempts to measure the fundamentals of American history, the common ground that all students should reach at the end of their instructional sequence irrespective of which view may have been more or less heavily weighted in students' instructional exposure.

Similarly, the 1998 NAEP writing assessment framework (National Assessment Governing Board, 1997) makes no assumptions about *how* students are taught to write. Those who may have been exposed to process writing skills are encouraged to use the approaches they have been taught, although other approaches to writing are neither excluded nor penalized. Scoring rubrics are built on commonly accepted elements of good writing, such as organization, sequencing, sentence structure, word choices, audience awareness, voice, and other linguistic features.

The national consensus process in NAEP works to produce an assessment framework that is recognizable as measuring quality outcomes, not divergent inputs. The process has always sought the active involvement of teachers and curriculum experts, state and local administrators, members of the general public who are knowledgeable in the subject area under consideration, and, most important, parents of school-age children. The litmus test is that these frameworks have been widely acknowledged as models of sound assessment frameworks that advance the state-of-the-art in the field of large-scale assessments.

Setting Student Performance Standards on NAEP

If ever there was a controversial feature of the NAEP design it has been the development of the student performance standards also known as *achievement levels*. The inaugural effort in 1990 to set achievement levels in mathematics was fraught with difficulties. The National Academy of Education's evaluation of the process was unfavorable (NAE, 1993a, 1993b), the NAGB's own evaluation team was critical of the approach (Stufflebeam, Jaeger, & Scriven, 1991), and Congress initiated a General Accounting Office probe (U.S. GAO, 1992). In spite of the lack of political consensus on the issue, the NAGB was committed to moving ahead on its statutory mandate, "to set goals for each grade and subject tested under the National Assessment" (Public Law 100-297, Sec. 3403). The effort to set student performance standards enjoyed the support of the Bush administration. In a letter, Secretary of Education Lauro F. Cavazos urged the NAGB to go forward with its plan to set such standards saying that "[it] is not only in keeping with the charge of the law, but is a constructive and complementary addition . . . to the work of the President and the Governors as they establish goals for performance of the Nation's education system" (L. F. Cavazos, Letter to National Assessment Governing Board, January 24, 1990). By the time of the 1994 NAEP legislation, NAEP assessments were clearly tied to the governor's national goals, as were the NAGB's achievement levels.

Contrasting Anchor Points and Achievement Levels

An initial effort to make NAEP more relevant was reporting results using the 0-to-500 scale developed by ETS in the early 1980s. For reporting purposes the interpretability of the scale was improved by selecting arbitrary points (150, 200, 250, 300, and 350) and describing what students know and can do at or around these points. These were known as *anchor points* and were the primary means for describing student performance on NAEP for more than a decade. The history and development of the scale and the anchoring procedure used to interpret specific points are well described in other sources (e.g., Phillips et al., 1993).

However, because these scale points were arbitrary they did not answer the question, "How good is good enough?" Figure 1 displays the descriptions of the anchor points for the 1990 science assessment. Because scale level 250 represents the mean, the interpretation is that this point represents average (grade-level) performance—that is, what students know and can do. However, it says little about desired performance or about what students *should* know and be able to do. In contrast to the arbitrary nature of the anchor points, the purpose of the achievement levels is to describe this intended performance. The levels set the standard for what it means to demonstrate *basic*, *proficient*, and *advanced* achievement in a subject area.

There are other important differences between the anchor points and the achievement levels. For example, the anchor points initially establish a fixed

Level 200   ***Understands Simple Scientific Principles***

Students at this level are developing some understanding of simple scientific principles, particularly in the life sciences. For example, they exhibit some rudimentary knowledge of the structure and function of plants and animals.

Level 250   ***Applies General Scientific Information***

Students at this level can interpret data from simple tables and make inferences about the outcomes of experimental procedures. They exhibit knowledge and understanding of the life sciences, including a familiarity with some aspects of animal behavior and of ecological relationships. These students also demonstrate some knowledge of basic information from the physical sciences.

Level 300   ***Analyzes Scientific Procedures and Data***

Students at this level can evaluate the appropriateness of the design of an experiment. They have more detailed scientific knowledge and the skill to apply their knowledge in interpreting information from text and graphs. These students also exhibit a growing understanding of principles from the physical sciences.

Level 350   ***Integrates Specialized Scientific Information***

Students at this level can infer relationships and draw conclusions using detailed scientific knowledge from the physical sciences, particularly chemistry. They also can apply basic principles of genetics and interpret the societal implications of research in this field.

FIGURE 1

1990 science anchor level descriptions. From NCES, 1990 Nation's Report Card in Science.

percentage of students at or above each level because, by definition, the points delimit the area under a normal curve. These percentages are the same for all subject areas. Over time, the percentages may change according to growth or decline in performance. This is in contrast to the achievement-level standards, which, because they are judgments, can initially vary across subject areas. The change to achievement levels reflects the concern that it did not make sense to report that the percentage of students achieving a particular level is the same whether or not there had been any curricular attention paid to the subject. Also, the change recognized that the expectations for reading and math should not be the same as, for example, the expectations for civics or art.

Another salient difference is the interpretation of the scale points: The levels are judgmentally derived, whereas the anchor points were empirically derived. The achievement levels reflect student performance in relation to the content of the assessment, whereas the anchor points described proficiency in terms of national norms.

In terms of the measurement characteristics of the two, neither the system of anchor points nor the system of achievement levels has yielded completely satisfactory evidence of reliability or validity (Lissitz & Bourque, 1995). According to the National Academy of Education (NAE, 1993a), "[T]here has been no theoretical or developmental model underlying the NAEP scales. Rather the scales have been created statistically, without evaluating the implied developmental model that underlies them" (p. xxx). The NAEP achievement levels probably have been the most critiqued standard-setting effort in the history of the country (ACT, 1993; NAE, 1993a, 1993b, 1994; U.S. GAO, 1993; NAGB & NCES, 1995). It is fair to conclude that, to date, the evidence of reliability or validity of the achievement levels has not been completely satisfactory to any evaluating agency or group.

Setting Student Performance Standards on the NAEP

The initial policy framework developed by NAGB (1990) viewed standard setting as an opportunity to make a transition in NAEP from a normative assessment to a standards-based assessment. The ability to craft descriptions of the specific content students *ought* to be expected to know at each grade level would, in the NAGB's view, make NAEP much more useful as a *national barometer* of educational achievement. The NAGB judged this standards-based approach to be NAEP's central mission.

The first effort at standard setting was in mathematics in 1990. The unfavorable evaluations of this initial work influenced the NAGB to set the mathematics levels again during the 1992 NAEP cycle and to not use the 1990 results as benchmarks for progress toward the national goals. Among the significant procedural improvements made between 1990 and 1992 were

(1) an external contractor with considerable experience in the area of standard setting was selected to conduct the work, (2) internal and external advisory teams were established to monitor all technical decisions throughout the process, and (3) state assessment directors were assigned to provide expertise at key stages in the project. Although there were no significant differences between the 1990 and 1992 mathematics levels, the latter have been adopted as the benchmark for the NAEP short-term trend line in mathematics and as the starting point for marking progress toward the national goals.

Salient Features of the NAEP Achievement Levels

The NAEP achievement levels have some special characteristics unlike other educational standards. First, there are three levels for each grade. The issue of whether to have a single standard or multiple standards is hardly ever addressed, except by assumption. For example, few school districts sometimes use a Pass/Fail decision rule to evaluate student performance in course work like algebra. The more typical grading frameworks employ an A-to-F scheme or a numerical equivalent of this, for example, 95-to-60 or less percent correct. It is assumed that multiple points are necessary to adequately distinguish student performances in the course. Likewise, the move to alternative assessments during the 1990s has generated the need for scoring protocols that employ a multiple-grading schema that captures the range of performance in the content area. This approach stands in contrast to the single standard that was employed by most minimum competency programs in the 1960s and 1970s and by many states and school districts as part of the back-to-basics movement.

There were several policy reasons why the NAGB chose to develop more than one standard for each grade. In the initial planning phases of the work, public hearings were held in various parts of the United States. One of the common outcomes of the hearings was an interest in being able to hold out standards that would be reachable and reasonable for all ranges of the performance distribution. The argument proposed was that if only a single standard was adopted by NAEP, then there would be large proportions of the population who would be unable to reach it—ever. So, in the interest of inclusion, and with a sensitivity to groups of students who may be underachieving as well as those whose performance is at or above grade level, the three levels were proposed. Moreover, the NAGB is committed to preserving trend results in NAEP, and having three levels accommodates reporting on growth (and possible declines) in all ranges of the performance distribution. Paul Barton (1997) commented on the need for multiple national performance standards in a recent report on the inequality in higher education when he said, "The idea of a single performance standard strains credulity when one confronts the dispersion in achievement. . . . Standards that are too low will encourage mediocrity at the high-achieving end, while standards that are too high will leave many students behind" (p. 21).

The achievement levels were labeled *basic, proficient, and advanced,* and the policy definitions articulating the expectations for each level are displayed in Figure 2. Although there are three levels, the central level—the level to which all students should aspire—is the proficient level. The NAGB has always adopted the position that basic is not good enough—even though the largest percentage of population falls in this level, it is still not the desired level. Basic has been conceptualized in early NAGB documents as somewhat higher than minimum competency and a necessary prerequisite for being proficient.

Although the specific language of the policy definitions evolved over time, they are still statements of what students should know and be able to do. Initially these statements included references to "students [at the proficient level] being well prepared for the next level of schooling, . . . democratic citizenship, responsible adulthood, and productive work," and at the advanced level "[students showing] readiness for rigorous college courses, advanced technical training, or employment requiring advanced academic achievement" (NAGB, 1990, p. i). The current definitions are less far-reaching and neither state nor imply criterion goals that cannot be validated.

A second characteristic of the NAEP achievement levels that sets them apart from most other standard-setting activities is the legislated national

---

Basic   **Partial Mastery**

This level denotes partial mastery of the prerequisite knowledge and skills that are fundamental for proficient work at each grade.

Proficient   **Solid Academic Performance**

This level represents solid academic performance for each grade assessed. Students reaching this level have demonstrated competency over challenging subject matter, including subject matter knowledge, application of such knowledge to real-world situations, and analytical skills appropriate to the subject matter.

Advanced   **Superior Performance**

This level signifies superior performance beyond proficient.

FIGURE 2
NAEP achievement levels policy definitions.

consensus process through which they are developed. The current statute requires almost an identical process for developing the levels as for developing the assessment frameworks. Who should be involved in the standard-setting process is as much a political question as it is a policy question. NAEP standard setting has been a widely inclusive activity, carried out by a broadly representative body of teachers, nonteacher educators including curriculum specialists and local and state administrators, and noneducators including parents, concerned members of the general public, employers, scholars, and specialists in the particular content area. Long before the current legislation and continuing today, the standard-setting panels were constituted to be about 70% educators and 30% noneducators (NAGB, 1990). The latter category is composed of individuals who never had a career in education, though they need to have expertise in the subject area under consideration. For example, in 1998 the writing standard-setting panels could include noneducators who are authors of children's literature, editors in the news media, technical authors, and others whose employment requires formal writing skills.

As in the assessment development consensus work, the NAGB has implicitly adopted the *balance* and *participation* principles. The *balance* principle addresses the issue of ensuring that the expectations of the levels are not too far ahead of reality. There will always be a tension between what students know and what students should know. However, the magnitude of the difference must be reasonable, otherwise the standards will simply be ignored. The *participation* principle ensures that the major players in the development of the standards include not only educators, but also those who have a vested interest in the high achievement of students in the American educational system. Such groups include parents of school-age children; the business and industry communities, which will ultimately employ graduates of the system; employees in the content area who have an understanding of the necessary entry-level skills; policy makers; and members of the general public whose tax dollars are providing the fiscal resources for the ongoing support of the system. In NAEP, the NAGB contends that the magnitude of the decisions regarding what students should know and be able to do is simply too important a decision to seek involvement from a narrow slice of those concerned about American education, such as professional educators alone. That decision must have the benefit of the collective wisdom of a broadly representative body, educators and noneducators alike.

The position of the NAGB on this issue is certainly the prevailing wisdom among agencies responsible for setting standards for academic achievement. Today, many state agencies typically seek to involve the constituencies that could be most affected by the results. There are a number of ways in which an agency can assemble panels of participants for the standard-setting process. The type of participants desired may dictate how this task is accomplished. For example, if an agency wants a panel of expert participants, then obviously random sampling of knowledgeable individuals will not work. If an agency wants to represent a constituency—for example, the population of teachers in the state—the agency might want to sample from a list of all eligible teachers. One might also be interested in ensuring that both large and small districts are represented or that teachers who primarily serve both regular and special education are included. A recent study of the standard-setting process for the national Teachers Examinations (NTE) investigated the effect of using different types of participants to set certification standards (Busch & Jaeger, 1990) and found that there were some initial differences between teacher-practitioners and university faculty. However, these differences were reduced (though not eliminated) during the second stage of the standard-setting process due to discussion and the use of normative data in the process.

Similarly, the size of the panels should be responsive to what the research is demonstrating—namely, that the size of the panels is dependent on the variance of the test standards of individual panelists, how many items each panelist is rating, the type of participant on the panel, and perhaps even the kind and amount of training panelists are given.

Setting educational standards is both an art and a science. As an art, it requires judgment. This precisely why Glass (1978) took such a strong position against standard setting. He claimed that all extant methodologies were arbitrary and thus flawed. On the other hand, there is the more generally accepted view as articulated by Cizek (1993), who recognized the judgment involved in standard setting but who suggested it can be accomplished in a defensible way through the established, replicable, systematic application of judgment. In the case of NAEP, the policy board exercises this judgment. State and local boards and others charged with the responsibility of setting standards for their assessment programs often make that judgment as well. As a *science*, standard setting requires solid technical advice based on a sound technical process. Good judgment, no matter how well-intentioned, is not a sufficient condition for setting standards that are reasonable and dependable and that invoke the balance and participation principles. On the other hand, a sound technical process, without some judgment about the consequences and the vision of policy planning, is merely measurement for the sake of measurement. Both judgment and technology have a beneficial moderating effect on each other in the standard-setting process.

Sociopolitical Climate of the 1990s

The 1990s has been an interesting and challenging period for NAEP. Already the NAEP appropriation had increased from $4 million in the early 1980s to about $17 million in 1990 with the first state NAEP. The NAEP appropriation for 1998 is about $36 million. Concurrent with these substantial increases in the NAEP funding was the congressional call to smaller government and with that, less domestic spending on those programs that have their epicenter in Washington, DC. During the past several years, NAEP and NAGB have been able to elude the budget cuts that other programs have suffered. On the other hand, the handwriting was on the proverbial wall: NAEP needed to rethink its program and its spending. Could NAEP be more efficient in the future, accomplishing more with less? Could NAEP be redesigned to meet the needs of the nation and the states—and do this with level funding? By the mid-1990s, NAEP was asking these questions, but did not yet have answers. The needs of policy makers were clear: They wanted more data in more subject areas on a more regular basis. For example, in the last decade of this century, NAEP has provided assessment results only in mathematics and reading on more than one occasion: 1990, 1992, and 1996. On the other hand, science assessment data were first available in 1996 and would be again in 2000—only two data points to measure whether or not American students were achieving world-class standards in science (one of the national goals). U.S. history and world geography would be assessed only once (1994) during this decade; world history, economics, foreign language, literature, and the arts would not be assessed at all. How could NAEP continue to measure all nine subjects in the national goals at this pace? If NAEP were to be responsive to the national goals, to the needs of the states, and to the needs of the American public, something in the program had to change radically. The NAGB's redesign effort described next offers some broad policy directions for probing possible solutions to such questions.

NAEP's REDESIGN FOR THE FUTURE

The redesign of NAEP for the next century has been developed through a thoughtful process that began in late 1994 and culminated in mid-1996 when the National Assessment Governing Board adopted the *Policy Statement on Redesigning the National Assessment of Education Progress* (NAGB, 1996). That document articulates the goals of the redesign in broad brush strokes included under each of the three objectives shown in Figure 3. A broad policy approach was necessary because the specific details of the future NAEP program would only be articulated in planning for the operational grants awarded by the National Center for Education Statistics, the agency responsible for implementing the National Assessment program in accordance with NAGB policies.

Objective 1: Timely, Fair, and Accurate
Comparative Data

The NAEP redesign focused almost exclusively on how to improve reporting NAEP data to the American public. The redesign examined reporting *to whom,*

Objective 1

-- To measure national and state progress toward the third National Education Goal and provide timely, fair, and accurate data about student achievement at the national level, among the states, and in comparison with other nations.

Objective 2

-- To develop, through a national consensus, sound assessments to measure what students know and can do as well as what students should know and be able to do.

Objective 3

-- To help states and others link their assessments with the National Assessment and use National Assessment data to improve educational performance.

FIGURE 3

NAEP redesign objectives.

in *how many* subjects, *how frequently*, and what design changes would have to be made to reach these new goals. The section examines the issues, the rationale for the policy positions, and the trade-offs between goals and design elements.

Reporting to the American Public

The primary audience for reporting NAEP results under the redesign is the American public. Although this may not sound so new and innovative, it represents a significant change in the way NAEP reports assessment information. Even though the NAEP program is supported by public funds, it has not for the past several years been widely accessible to the public. The NAEP reports are highly respected in the psychometric and research communities. However, they are written, primarily, by measurement specialists for measurement specialists. Typically, the NAEP reports are products of the National Center for Education Statistics, and as such they display extensive amounts of statistical detail, are very much text bound with few tabular or graphical displays, and cover every possible aspect of the assessment. A good example is the 1992 NAEP mathematics report, which contained more than 1800 pages of text and numbers in its report to the American people on the performance of students in Grades 4, 8, and 12 in school mathematics. The number of different reports in a single subject area has proliferated over the years as well, including *First Look* reports, the *Nation's Report Card*, *State Report Cards*, *Technical Reports* for the nation and for the states, curriculum-oriented reports, data compendia, data almanacs, and shorter type focus reports, not to mention Web page summaries and the like.

Although one cannot argue that such full and complete disclosure is note-worthy, it does not serve the broader American public well. The redesign calls for NAEP reports to be written to and for the American public saying that they should be "understandable, jargon free, easy to use, and widely disseminated" (NAGB, 1996, p. 3). There is a commitment to maintain tech-nical accuracy in the more public reports, but simplicity is the sine qua non for the utility of such reports. The redesign policy statement indicates that the intent of the NAEP reports is to "support [national and state policy makers' and educators'] efforts to interpret reults to the public, to improve education performance, and to perform secondary analysis" (NAGB, 1996, p. 4).

Measuring All Subjects in the National Goals

To provide clarity and stability to the direction in which NAEP was moving, NAGB adopted a schedule of assessments covering the NAEP cycles over the next 10 years. Table 2 shows that statewide assessment will be offered bien-nally in Grades 4 and 8 only starting in 2000, and the assessment will al-ternate between mathematics and science (2000) and reading and writing (2002). The national assessment component will be offered on an annual basis in Grades 4, 8, and 12: In the even-numbered years the four subjects will be assessed in the same way as the state assessments, whereas the remaining five subjects and the long-term trend will be covered in the odd-numbered years. For example, the 2001 assessment will cover U.S. history and world geography, and the 2003 assessment will cover civics, foreign language, the long-term trend, and so forth. The primary purpose of this regularized schedule was to serve as a response to states that want to be able to count on NAEP as a part of their state system of assessments. This represents a significant coordination of state and national educational pol-icy, assessment, and priorities.

Currently, there are some minimal state NAEP costs, which could increase in the next several years. If that is the case, states need to be able to build this into their budget planning operations, which frequently run 24 months ahead. The regularized schedule supports long-range fiscal planning among other things. States also may conduct additional assessments in alternate subjects and grades at their own cost. For example, states interested in pur-suing a Grade 12 world history or economics assessment could do so when those subjects are tested on the NAEP in 2005, even though it is not part of the regularly scheduled state assessment program.

Providing National Assessment Results for the States

As discussed earlier, the number of states and jurisdictions participating in the state NAEP program has grown substantially since its beginnings in 1990. However, as the number of subjects being assessed increases so does

TABLE 2
NAEP Schedule for 1996 through 2010

Year	National	State
1996	Mathematics Science Long-term trend* (reading, writing, mathematics, science)	Mathematics (4, 8) Science (8)
1997	Arts (8)	
1998	Reading Writing Civics	Reading (4, 8) Writing (8)
1999	Long-term trend*	
2000	Mathematics Science	Mathematics (4, 8) Science (4, 8)
2001	U.S. History Geography	
2002	Reading Writing	Reading (4, 8) Writing (4, 8)
2003	Civics **Foreign Language** (12) Long-term trend*	
2004	**Mathematics** Science	**Mathematics** (4, 8) Science (4, 8)
2005	**World History** (12) **Economics** (12)	
2006	**Reading** Writing	**Reading** (4, 8) Writing
2007	**Arts** Long-term trend*	
2008	Mathematics **Science**	Mathematics (4, 8) **Science** (4, 8)
2009	**U.S. History** **Geography**	
2010	Reading **Writing**	Reading (4, 8) **Writing** (4, 8)

Note: Grades 4, 8, and 12 will be tested unless otherwise indicated. Comprehensive assessments are indicated in **bold**. All other listings are standard assessments.

the number of schools and students. The assessment burden has grown, partly due to the fact that the samples for each component (i.e., national, state, and long-term trend) are drawn separately and are kept partitioned in the administration of the assessment. The redesign tries to address this issue by requiring a more creative approach to NAEP sampling. At the time of this writing a few ideas have surfaced that appear to have merit. A sampling design that would augment the schools selected for the national component in order to derive state estimates of performance is a possibility. This option would relieve the burden on some of the larger jurisdictions such as California, New York, and Texas. However, this is only a partial solution and does not address those states whose grade-level population is small, such as Rhode Island or Delaware with fewer than 10,000 students per grade, or those states whose individual school enrollments are very small, such as Montana or Alaska with fewer than 25 students per grade per school. Policy waivers have tried to address the needs of these states, but they have done so more or less unsatisfactorily. However, research is now underway by the NAEP Validity Panel (a congressionally mandated study group that conducts ongoing validity studies about NAEP), which would suggest that the required number of schools (approximately 100) and students per state (approximately 2500) may be excessive and that substantially smaller and more efficient samples could be used along with appropriate statistical corrections to ensure comparability from state to state (Chromy, 1998).

Reducing Time Lag between Data Collection and Reporting

One of the less desirable characteristics of NAEP has been the unusually long time lag between data collection and the public reporting of the data—as much as two years in some cases. This is a serious deficiency and one which is particularly unresponsive to states' needs. Why would states be interested in participating in the state NAEP component if the fourth-grade results are returned when the sampled students are in the sixth grade? This seemingly intractable problem was carefully examined during the planning phases for the NAEP redesign. The *Design Feasibility Report* (Forsyth, Hambleton, Linn, Mislevy, & Yen, 1996) laid out some of the causes of the problem and how these could be eliminated, or at the very least ameliorated, in the NAEP redesign. In their report, Forsyth et al. defined something called the *critical path*—the series of tasks that are interdependent and must be completed to produce a NAEP report. Tasks include test scoring, preliminary sample weighting, differential item functioning (DIF) analysis, scaling and conditioning on background data, and, finally, report writing, revision, and review. The report states that "No task should appear on the critical path between data collection and reporting if it can be done before or if it is not essential to the report," (p. 3–2). Some of these tasks may seem fairly straightforward, but in NAEP they present severe challenges. For example, conditioning on background data—a statistical procedure used for obtaining more accurate estimates of student achievement—currently requires that all background data from student, teacher, and school questionnaires be entered into the data files, that teacher questionnaire data be matched and merged with specific student files, and that every data element be analyzed before any reports are developed. Currently all this lies on the critical path. Moreover, there are test-scoring issues such as the extraordinarily large number of constructed response items that are scored by human raters (rather than machine scored). There is also a very lengthy process of reviewing and revising NAEP reports after they have been written. On this latter issue, an evaluation conducted by KPMG Peat-Marwick & Mathtech, Inc. (1996) of the NAEP program indicated that one of the major causes of delays in reporting is the typical 12-month review and revision of final NAEP reports.

Timely reporting is an area where NAEP could learn a lesson from the states. Commercial testing companies typically report information back to clients in 2 to 4 weeks. Similarly, states that have their own testing programs can return scores to districts and schools in less than six weeks generally, even if the state does in-state scoring of constructed response items (e.g., the scoring of writing samples).

So what is the solution under the redesign? Forsyth et al. (1996) suggest a few options that could be explored in future NAEP cycles. One solution is to move many of the tasks listed into a *norming year* for NAEP—that is, by adding one additional planning year to the NAEP cycle before going operational with a particular assessment. This would require a pilot testing of items much the way they are piloted currently, whereas the field testing would need to be completed using nationally representative samples of students (not intact groups as is currently the case). The data from the field testing would then be of sufficient quality to conduct bias analyses, scale the assessment, set the achievement levels, and complete other technical analyses which are now on the critical path and currently completed after the operational data are collected.

This approach could be implemented at the time of adopting of new assessment frameworks—about every 10 years—and would produce what is termed a *comprehensive* assessment report, much like the current version. Subsequent uses of a particular assessment framework after this initial use would result in a *standard* assessment—a more limited version of NAEP that would be parsimonious with respect to the number of background variables collected, the number of conditioning variables used, the number of subscales reported, and the total number of reports. Accepting these constraints, and keeping the cognitive item pools identical (or nearly so) from cycle to cycle, will result in an assessment that is very much like the long-term trend assessment and can be reported on in 6 months or less—the goal of the redesign.

Both of these suggestions (i.e., the additional norming year and varying the intensity of data collection and reporting) could be implemented either independently or in tandem. Both would reduce the time lapse from data collection to reporting by many months. If the 6-month reporting goal was achieved, states would receive feedback on fourth and eighth grade performance in the fall of the year of testing—a laudable goal for a large-scale national assessment program like NAEP.

Simplifying NAEP Trends

It is useful to think of NAEP not as a single assessment program but as three entirely independent assessment programs: (1) the cross-sectional national assessments, (2) the national assessment state component, and (3) the long-term trend national assessment, which dates back to 1970 in some cases. At some time in the near future, NAEP will be operating four entirely independent assessments: the current three plus the national assessments reflecting the new assessment frameworks scheduled to begin in 2004 with mathematics. At that point the burden on states will be enormous and might cause many, if not all, states to decline participation. This leaves the National Assessment Governing Board asking the question: How can we move to *new* assessment in the next century and transition the current cross-sectional assessments into the *new* long term? *The Design Feasibility Report* (Forsyth et al., 1996) offered some models for *managed change*. Quite simply, the concept of managed change means moving one assessment off-line after two overlapping cycles and allowing the new assessment to replace the old, as shown in Figure 4. While the concept sounds very simple, there is great reluctance to retiring the long-term trend assessment permanently. The Forsyth et al. report (1996) suggests keeping the long-term trend assessment on the shelf for occasional use, perhaps every 10 years, "just to see how today's students are faring with tasks that were deemed important to students of the past" (p. 6–15). This suggestion, coupled with the more efficient sampling measures suggested in earlier sections of this chapter, may indeed reduce the sampling burdens on the states and maintain interest and motivation to participate fully in the NAEP program.

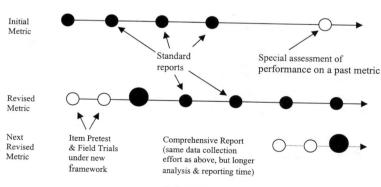

FIGURE 4
Managed change in NAEP. From Forsythe et al., 1996.

Using International Comparisons

International comparisons of student performance represent an area where NAEP is still a novice and learning many lessons. The Third International Mathematics and Science Study (TIMSS) was administered in 1995 to 43 participating countries including the United States. Although TIMSS was primarily a curriculum study, there was an assessment component that measured student performance in the two curricular areas in Grades 3 and 4, 7 and 8, and 11 and 12. There were a number of distinguishing features between NAEP and TIMSS including the proportion of item formats (e.g., multiple choice and constructed response), the content of the assessments, the scaling model used, and so forth, not to mention the cross-country translations, sampling, curriculum policy features such as the degree of calculator usage, and other salient assessment differences.

An attempt was made to link NAEP to TIMSS at Grades 4 and 8, those grades in which there appeared to be the greatest similarity and overlap in content between the two assessments. *Linking* (in this context) refers to the process of statistically connecting the performance distributions of two assessments, NAEP and TIMSS, such that one can predict the performance of students on the TIMSS assessment knowing only the students' NAEP scores. That linking has been only partially successful. Validity studies have not supported the linking functions derived from Grade 4 (National Center for Education Statistics (NCES), 1998). The Grade 8 linking was reviewed by an independent statistical review panel to examine possible explanations for the anomalies in the data, and the panel recommended that NCES not release the data since it could lead to misinterpretations of both assessments.

International comparative data is an area in which states are interested. However, according to a report by the American Federation of Teachers (AFT), interest has not necessarily resulted in action. Only a dozen states have tried to compare their state results to those in other countries (AFT, 1995). Recently, the state of Maryland, for example, administered its statewide assessments in several countries for the purposes of being able to judge its own students against some international measure of performance. Similarly, two states, Colorado and Illinois, participated in the TIMSS assessment and received state reports on how their students compared to the United States and the other 42 participating countries. The NAEP redesign supports these kind of international comparisons and will provide such comparisons as feasible.

Moving NAEP into the Technology Age

The current NAEP has employed technological innovations in several key areas. Technology has been introduced in the scoring of constructed response items through an image scoring system and in the sophisticated statistical analysis techniques that are part of the NAEP methodology (including conditioning, multiple imputations, and plausible values).[2] In reporting state results, an artificial intelligence system has been used to generate customized state reports. However, in terms of development and administration, NAEP has lagged behind other large-scale assessment programs. In the last academic year, for example, the Graduate Record Examinations offered a computer version, as did some of the College Board's entrance examinations, and ACT's COMPASS, which is a placement assessment for college freshmen in the areas of mathematics, reading, and writing.

Incorporation of computer administration of assessments is an unchartered area for NAEP but one where the NAEP program could exert leadership among the states. Bennett (1997) argued that the future of large-scale assessment is about to change in radical ways, saying that

> [L]arge-scale assessment will reinvent itself to serve both summative and formative purposes, become curriculum-embedded and performance-based, occur at a distance, and incorporate constructs newly valued by society. This reinvention will be enabled chiefly by new technology and by advances in cognitive and measurement science. (p. 2)

Some of what Bennett describes as first-generation computer-based tests is envisioned for the NAEP administrations beginning in the year 2000. The NAEP assessments of the immediate future will resemble paper-and-pencil tests except they will be administered via computer. At this point in time, there is no requirement to make these tests adaptive. However, future assessment frameworks (starting in 2004 with mathematics) may require not only adaptive testing but also new item formats such as dynamic stimuli, three-dimensional graphics and art that are integral to the presentation of the test item, and they may have audio/visual characteristics not permissable with static two-dimensional (paper-and-pencil) presentations. Future NAEP frameworks may move in the direction of measuring new cognitive dimensions, a recommendation of the National Academy of Education (1997) in its most recent evaluation report of the National Assessment.

Objective 2: Balanced Measurement

Stability of Frameworks

It is a stated goal of the redesign to keep NAEP frameworks and test specifications stable for about 10 years. The redesign policy states, however, that "in rare circumstances, such as where significant changes in curricula have

---

[2]Discussion of the technical procedures used in NAEP is well beyond the scope of this chapter. However, readers interested in more specific details are referred to the most recent NAEP Technical Report, Allen, N. L., Swinton, S. S., Isham, S. P., & Zelenak, C. A. (1997). *Technical report of the NAEP 1996 state assessment program in science*. Washington, DC: National Center for Education Statistics.

occurred, the . . . Board may consider making changes to test frameworks and specifications before ten years have elapsed (NAGB, 1996, p. 15). This may not seem like such a realistic goal when one considers the history of the National Assessment and realizes that it is rare indeed that the same framework and specifications were ever used in the same subject for two consecutive cycles. However, this goal does not mean that the item pools cannot be refreshed for each cycle, since IRT scaling allows replacement exercises at a modest level. Generally, in NAEP about 40% of the grade level items are replaced each time. The remainder are held for cross-cycle linking and measuring trends. Long-term stability in frameworks means that states can link to NAEP assessments without having to worry that their investment may be lost due to fluctuations in the NAEP content. It opens the door to NAEP's becoming a part of the states' system of assessments wherein states can plan on receiving regularized information in certain subject areas on their own students' performance and have the assurance that such data demonstrate credibility, reliability, validity, and are free from the "Lake Wobegon" effect, claimed to be indigenous to other assessments (Cannell, 1987).

Appropriate Mix of Item Formats

A second aspect of redesigning balanced measurement in NAEP is the mix of multiple choice (MC) and constructed response (CR) items. Over the past decade, NAEP has gradually increased the percentage of CR items from a low of about 20% of the grade-level item pool in the 1990 mathematics assessment to a high of about 80% in the 1996 science assessment and 100% of the items in the 1998 writing assessment. Some academic subjects such as writing are best measured using writing samples, and NAEP will continue to do this into the future. However, for other subject areas, the appropriate mix is determined by the kinds of knowledge and skills about to be measured. Large numbers of CR items have made their way into both commercial tests and statewide assessments. Nonetheless, constructed response items continue to have unresolved technical problems including lack of generalizability across tasks and lower reliability due to the reduced numbers of items that can be included in the assessment because of time constraints. Moreover, CR items are costly because they are hand scored rather than machine scored. All in all, CR items are generally less efficient than MC items.

It is the policy position of the NAGB that the proportion of CR items used in the future will be a serious consideration as the assessment frameworks are developed, and cost will be part of the cost-benefit equation. In fact, a study is underway to determine how to reduce the costs associated with the 2000 NAEP science assessment by reducing the sample size for the hands-on tasks that were part of each examinee's booklet in 1996. The study is looking into whether or not a sample size reduction can be made without losing the trend line started in 1996. If the answer is yes, then NAEP could realize substantial savings of approximately $2 million through reducing the number of science kits purchased and in the professional scoring of the exercises in these blocks.

Objective 3: Linking NAEP to Other Assessments

There has been some initial work done in a few states to link their statewide assessments to NAGB. North Carolina and Kentucky are good examples. This is an area in which several states have expressed an interest and which NAEP has taken seriously. However, to do so NAEP needs to be designed in such a way as to permit, and even encourage, linking. Currently, the NAEP design is so complex that linking is done only by states that can arrange for this feature with a contractor or a research agency who has highly qualified technical staff. Simplifying the NAEP design would make NAEP more accessible and user-friendly and allow states to use NAEP as an external criterion—a so-called gold standard—so that individual states could compare their own tests with NAEP and give them the benchmarks needed to do cross-state comparisons as well. It is the stated goal of the redesign policy that NAEP "shall be designed so that others may access and use . . . frameworks, specifications, scoring guides, results, questions, achievement levels, and background data" (NAGB, 1996, p. 17).

It is the hope of the NAGB that the redesign of NAEP will lead to greater use of the wealth of data afforded by this large-scale assessment and that, through the mining of the data, states and other agencies will have access to the best possible technical information to help inform policy decisions of the future.

THE VOLUNTARY NATIONAL TEST

The voluntary national test (VNT) has a history not unlike NAEP in many respects. The evolution of the VNT has taken many twists and turns since the first announcement in President Clinton's February 1997 state of the union address. This is not the place to document the very short but complicated history of the VNT, except to say that 9 months after that historic announcement by the president, Congress gave exclusive authority for VNT development to the National Assessment Governing Board (Public Law 105-78, 1997). It is appropriate, however, to provide a brief synopsis, and to compare and contrast the policy ramifications for an individual student testing program in the United States with a program such as NAEP.

Currently, the fate of the VNT is unknown. As of this writing, without further authorization and an appropriation from Congress, the VNT could come to an abrupt halt on October 1, 1998.[1] The current authorization (1) limits the use of FY 1998 appropriations to test development planning activities only (stopping short of pilot testing item pools or field testing student booklets); (2) gives NAGB exclusive control over developing the VNT; and (3) incorporates three national Academy of Sciences (NAS) studies on fairness, linking the VNT to commercial assessments and the accuracy of the information resulting from the VNT. The results of the NAS studies will play a large role in the congressional deliberations to determine future authorizations of the VNT.

Notwithstanding, NAGB is currently proceeding with care and thoughtfulness to craft a VNT that could eventually win the political and social support it will need if it is to be successful. The overall schedule has been realigned to allow a sound development process and to ensure that the test will meet all the technical standards in the field. The first annual VNT in fourth grade reading and eighth grade mathematics is currently being planned for spring 2002, with pilot testing of the item pool as early as spring 2000 and field testing of parallel forms and subsequent linking to NAEP and TIMSS in spring 2001.

From its original inception, the VNTs in Grade 4 reading and Grade 8 mathematics have been proposed as tests to help teachers and parents know how students are progressing by comparing individual student performances to state, national, and international assessment results. This comparison is achieved by linking the VNT to NAEP (Grade 4 reading and Grade 8 mathematics) and to TIMSS (grade 8 mathematics). There are some obvious differences between the VNT and NAEP/TIMSS. Table 3 highlights some of the salient differences in the design and implementation of the VNT in contrast to NAEP/TIMSS. Although NAGB is trying to make decisions that will support linking the VNT to NAEP/TIMSS, there are some nontrivial differences among the assessments, which could reduce the strength of the links. Some of these will be discussed in a later section of this chapter.

There are many serious issues to be dealt with concurrent with the test development process. What is the purpose of the VNT? How is that purpose different from NAEP's purpose, after which it is modeled? What are the policy implications for state and local jurisdictions that might use the VNT? What technical problems will need to be overcome to make the VNT a sound measurement instrument? There are also a host of questions that may not be answered until well into the future of the VNT, such as how will jurisdictions use the VNT to make decisions about individual students? Or what does it mean to be a *voluntary* national test? Or what will be the impact of the

---

[1]In fact, the legislation passed in October 1998 requires explicit congressional authorization for the administration of the VNT; limits all current VNT activities to planning and test development only; and requires several new studies from the National Academy of Sciences and a report from the NAGB on the purposes and use of the VNT, as well as on the issue of the flawed nature of the achievement levels.

TABLE 3
Comparison of Design Elements of NAEP, TIMSS, and VNT

Design/implementation element	NAEP	TIMSS	VNT
Student sampling	Random sample produces group results	Random sample produces group results	Individuals—produces individual scores
Item sampling	Each student takes about 25% of total item pool	Each student takes about ___% of total item pool	All students take all items
Item types	Mix: 40% multiple choice, 60% constructed response	Mix: 75% multiple choice, 25% constructed response	Mix: 80% multiple choice, 20% constructed response
Test length	Approximately 3.5 hours	Approximately 3.25 hours	90 minutes
Scaling	IRT 3-parameter model	IRT one-parameter model	IRT 3-parameter model
Content subscales	5, multidimensional	6	None, unidimensional
Process subscales	3	4	None, unidimensional
Accommodations for special needs students	Yes	Exclusions up to 10% for special needs students allowed	TBD
Adaptations for limited English proficient students	Math—bilingual Reading—none	30 Languages + English 11 cultural adaptations for English	TBD
Achievement levels	Yes: Basic, proficient, advanced	No	Yes: Predicted B, P, A

VNT on state assessment programs and on commercial testing programs? The next sections of this chapter will explore some of the more immediate questions as their solutions are currently unfolding through the work of the National Assessment Governing Board.

Measurement Objectives of the VNT

The purposes of the VNT, like a chameleon, take on different colors depending on which lens is being used. As one might expect, the U.S. Department of Education, which spearheaded the initiative at the beginning, has always ascribed great potential to the VNT. It was viewed by the department as a means of leveraging change or leveling the playing field for underserved students. Some public statements from the administration spoke of educational reform, raising standards, or informing parents and teachers of how well their students fare in comparison to national and international standards. It is hard to disagree with such lofty and worthwhile measurement goals for the VNT. However, it is equally difficult to believe that a 90-minute NAEP-like student test is going to measure up to such expectations.

NAGB has not yet tried to articulate a purpose for the VNT. To do so, no doubt, would require taking at least a philosophical position regarding its merits. In an effort to remain a neutral participant in the ongoing conversation about a national test, NAGB has refrained from any discussion of purposes. At this early juncture in the test development process, NAGB may still enjoy the luxury of neutrality. However, as issues and other questions need to be resolved, the question of purposes *will* be answered, if not explicitly, at least tacitly by a series of policy decisions affecting test development. In one sense this may be good for the VNT. If NAGB as an independent and broadly representative body can listen to the national commentary and incorporate a broad national consensus on why the VNT should exist in the first place, then there is greater assurance that the NAGB policy decisions will be informed by state and local needs. Consequently, the VNT could be a more effective measurement instrument in meeting these needs. What is currently missing is the political and social will for a national test. To secure this requires a national debate that will encourage a full examination of all sides of the issue in an open and public conversation with those most apt to be affected by the final outcomes. NAGB needs to be positioned to broker that historic exchange in the very near future.

What are some potential uses of the VNT? By itself, the VNT may be nothing more than the measurement twin of the color patch placed on a child's forehead to find out if the child is running a temperature. The VNT may be the "quick and dirty" estimate of academic health in primary school reading and middle school mathematics. Reported in conjunction with the NAEP achievement levels, parents and teachers would know if the student was below the basic level, or at or above one of the levels, basic, proficient, or advanced. If VNT reporting is developed well, parents and teachers may also know some of the skills and knowledge that an individual student has mastered, as well as those areas that may still need remediation. Taken in conjunction with teachers' grades and local and state individual student test results, it may be an early warning sign that something is amiss. It is quite clear, however, that if diagnostic information is needed, further testing will be required with longer content batteries and administered on an individual basis.

Will the VNT be able to serve the program evaluation function? Probably no more than it can serve as a diagnostic instrument. No assessment instrument with 60 or so items can adequately measure the breadth and depth of a content area sufficiently, particularly when this is a one-size-fits-all test and not tailored to the ability level of the individual examinee.

Will the VNT be able to serve a placement function, assigning students to various levels of reading or math instruction? Again, this is best done by multiple measures, including teachers' grades, classroom evaluations, and local tests; the VNT could effectively be part of this mix. Can the VNT be used for grade retention and promotion? Or for teachers' evaluation? Such uses, which have serious consequences for individuals, are probably not going to be legitimate given test length and other technical aspects of the VNT.

Policy Implications for Users of the VNT

There will be tremendous pressures at the user level to make the VNT serve more functions than can reasonably be assured. Notwithstanding, there are policy decisions that could come about as a result of a poor showing on the VNT. At the classroom level, teachers might be inclined to study the scores of examinees for areas of the delivered curriculum where all or most students are doing poorly. This might signal either poor instruction—or no instruction—or a lack of curriculum alignment with the VNT content frameworks. It could point to a lack of classroom resources, to pedagogical differences between teaching and testing, or perhaps to beyond-school structures that are nonsupportive of a healthy learning environment. In most of these instances, the classroom can make a difference by taking a course of corrective action.

At the school level, similar kinds of observations apply. Poor results for individuals on the VNT might be a sign that there is a discrepancy between the intended curriculum and the delivered curriculum. Poor instruction and lack of resources is a correctable problem. Schools need to ensure that all students have the opportunity to learn whatever is being tested. Parents have the right to expect that their children are reaping the maximum benefits from their time in school. Compulsory schooling is meaningless without the assurance of equity.

Local and state control, which often has been used in this debate as the reason for not having a national test, could be augmented by the VNT. Local and state control is not just about control, it is also about local and state responsibilities. The VNT could alert local and state educators to the needs of their students in a way that other testing programs cannot. Because the VNT is an individualized version of the NAEP, at least initially, it will not be victim of the "Lake Wobegon" effect. It will be secure, and it will be linked to the NAEP student performance standards—which have a reputation for being high, world-class standards. Local and state educators should seize the opportunity to have access to an individualized version of the NAEP gold standard.

How do parents score on this one? Parents are winners, for sure. This is the first time that the federal government has acknowledged that parents are the real partners in education. It is a first that the government is about to spend money to tell parents how well John or Susan are doing with respect to their classmates in their state and their counterparts in the United States and in other nations as well. For most parents it is altogether too late to find this out when the student's hopes for post-secondary education are dashed or when the military rejects the student's application. Parents are winners if they are positioned to provide early guidance and parental support that is informed by an understanding of their children's potential.

Selected Technical Hurdles for the VNT

The major technical issues for the VNT are just beginning to be discussed in a variety of forums (Skaggs & Bourque, 1998). The major technical hurdle for the VNT is probably linking to NAEP and TIMSS. Linking NAEP to other assessments is very problematic as evidenced by a number of recent studies (Beaton & Gonzalez, 1993; Ercikan, 1993; Linn & Kiplinger, 1995; Pashley & Phillips, 1993; Williams, Billeaud, Davis, Thissen, & Sanford, 1995; and NCES, 1998). Although each of these studies had its own particular challenges and used different linking procedures, there were some common issues which impacted all of them: (1) the content of the linked assessments was dissimilar, (2) test lengths were different, (3) the reliability of the assessments was different, and (4) in at least in one case language translations were required because both assessments were not in a common language. The VNT may not need to solve this latter problem, but the remaining problems will be difficult at best given the VNT design. There will be differences in test content even though the NAEP frameworks are the basis for the test (e.g., shorter reading passages in the VNT than in NAEP). There will be other differences in the administration of the VNT, which could impact the linking (e.g., the use of calculators and formula sheets in the VNT mathematics). Similarly, the test will have substantially fewer items (e.g., 60 items as compared to approximately 200 in NAEP mathematics).

A second area of concern is the IRT model used in the assessment designs. NAEP employs a multidimensional 3-paremter logistic (3PL) model, whereas the VNT uses a unidimensional model to fit the data. For example, in the NAEP mathematics, each of the five content strands are scaled independently, and a weighted composite of the five subscales is used to estimate overall proficiency. Similarly in Grade 4 reading, there are two subscales. The VNT will estimate individual student proficiency directly without employing subscales.

NAEP has always used blocks of items, which are administered at more than one grade level. About two-thirds of the Grade 8 assessment in mathematics uses those same items in Grades 4 and 12. Although this approach makes for parsimony in constructing NAEP, it is not an appropriate design for the VNT and is expected to cause problems in linking the two assessments.

Finally, the NAEP achievement levels take on a new meaning in the context of the VNT. The purpose of the standards now is more than simply describing the performance of the population. The VNT achievement levels need to reliably classify individual students and to report accurately on that performance to students, parents, and teachers. On the basis of the report, serious decisions could be made about individual students, about teachers and classes, about schools and districts.

The brief description of the myriad technical issues surrounding the VNT is not exhaustive. Other aspects that will have to be addressed in the long term include issues of data aggregation, appropriate accommodations for students with disabilities and how to properly report their nonstandard scores against the NAEP standard norms, and appropriate adaptations for English-language learners and how to norm their scores.

The NAGB will be engaging a number of individuals, groups, and local, state, and federal agencies to initiate this long-term conversation on the future of the VNT. Much of what happens will be determined by the social and political milieu of the next 5 years. As in the past, the outcomes will be shaped by the players involved, by the tenor of the times, and by the wisdom of those entrusted with the power and responsibility for moving American education forward into the next millennium.

SUMMARY

This chapter has discussed the role of NAEP in setting, reflecting, and linking national education policy to states' needs. The National Assessment has been termed a *national treasure* by some precisely because it has the potential to illuminate and guide development of both national education policy and states' policy decisions as well. The redesign of NAEP is likely to make this large-scale assessment program even more valuable in the future. The future of America lies in the potential of its youth. Policy makers, educators, and the American public are urged to continue to engage in a conversation about the role of society in providing a supportive learning environment, one in which all children can reach their potential, meet high standards, and find personal and intellectual fulfillment. It is hoped that NAEP will play a pivotal role in that exchange and will influence the outcomes as a catalyst, such that education will see substantive—even revolutionary—change in the next century.

References

Alexander, L., & James, H. T. (1987). *The nation's report card: Improving the assessment of student achievement.* Washington, DC: U.S. Department of Education.

Allen, N. L., Swinton, S. S., Isham, S. P., & Zelenak, C. A. (1997). *Technical report of the NAEP 1996 state assessment program in science.* Washington, DC: National Center for Education Statistics.

ACT. (1993). *Setting achievement levels on the* 1992 *National Assessment of Educational Progress in mathematics, reading, and writing: A technical report on reliability and validity.* Iowa City, IA: Author.

American Federation of Teachers. (1995). *Making standards matter: A fifty-state progress report on efforts to raise academic standards.* Washington, DC: Author.

Barton, P. E. (1997). *Toward inequality.* Princeton, NJ: Educational Testing Service.

Beaton, A. E., & Gonzalez, E. J. (1993). *Comparing the* NAEP *trial state assessment results with the* IAEP *international results.* Paper prepared for the Panel on the Evaluation of the NAEP Trial State Assessment of the National Academy of Education, Stanford, CA.

Bennett, R. E. (1997). Speculations on the future of large-scale educational assessment. (Research Report 97-14). Princeton, NJ: Educational Testing Service.

Busch, J. C., & Jaeger, R. M. (1990). Influence of type of judge, normative information, and discussion on standards recommended for the National Teacher Examinations. *Journal of Educational Measurement*, 27, 145–163.

Cannell, J. J. (1987). *Nationally normed elementary achievement testing in America's public schools: How all 50 states are above the national average.* (2nd ed.), Daniels, WV: Friends for Education.

Chromy, J. R. (1998). *The effects of finite sampling corrections on state assessment sample requirements.* Paper (Draft No. 3) prepared for the NAEP Validity Studies Panel. Palo Alto, CA: American Institutes for Research.

Cizek, G. J. (1993). Reconsidering standards and criteria. *Journal of Educational Measurement*, 30, 93–106.

Erickan, K. (1993). Predicting NAEP. Unpublished manuscript. Monterey, CA: CTB Macmillan/ McGraw-Hill.

Forsyth, R., Hambleton, R. W., Linn, R., Mislevy, R., & Yen, W. (1996). *Design/Feasibility Team: Report to the National Assessment Governing Board.* Washington, DC: National Assessment Governing Board.

Glass, G. V. (1978). Standards and criteria. *Journal of Educational Measurement*, 15(3), 237–261.

Jones, L. V. (1996). A history of the National Assessment of Educational Progress and some questions about its future. *Educational Researchers*, 25(7), 15–22.

Jones, L. R., Mullis, I. V. S., Raizen, S. A., Weiss, I. R., & Weston, E. A. (1992). *The* 1990 *science report card: NAEP's assessment of fourth, eighth, and twelfth graders.* Washington, DC: National Center for Education Statistics.

KMPG Peat-Marwick LLP & Mathtech, Inc. (1996). A review of the National Assessment of Educational Progress: Management and methodological procedures. Study conducted for the U.S. Department of Education, National Center for Education Statistics. Washington, DC: Author.

Linn, R. L., & Kiplinger, V. L. (1995). Linking statewide tests to the National Assessment of Educational Progress: Stability of Results. Unpublished manuscript. Center for Research on Evaluation, Standards, and Student Testing: University of Colorado at Boulder, CO.

Lissitz, R. W., & Bourque, M. L. (1995). Reporting NAEP results using standards. *Educational Measurement: Issues and Practice*, 14(2), 14–23.

Messick, S., Beaton, A. E., & Lord, F. (1983). *National Assessment of Educational Progress reconsidered: A new design for a new era.* Princeton, NJ: Educational Testing Service.

National Academy of Education. (1993a). *Setting performance standards for student achievement.* Stanford, CA: Author.

National Academy of Education. (1993b). *Setting performance standards for student achievement: Background studies.* Stanford, CA: Author.

National Academy of Education. (1994). *Quality and utility: The* 1994 *trial state assessment in reading.* Stanford, CA: Author.

National Academy of Education. (1997). *Assessment in transition: Monitoring the nation's educational progress.* Stanford, CA: Author.

National Assessment Governing Board. (1990). *Setting appropriate achievement levels for the national Assessment of Educational Progress: policy framework and technical procedures.* Washington, DC: Author.

National Assessment Governing Board. (1991). *Reading framework for the national Assessment of Educational Progress:* 1992. Washington, DC: Author.

National Assessment Governing Board. (1992). U.S. *history framework for the National Assessment of Educational Progress*: 1994. Washington, DC: Author.

National Assessment Governing Board and National Center for Education Statistics. (1995). *Proceedings of the joint conference on standard setting for large-scale assessment* (Vols. I and II). Washington, DC: Author.

National Assessment Governing Board. (1996). *Policy statement on redesigning the National Assessment of Educational Progress*. Washington, DC: Author.

National Assessment Governing Board. (1997). *Writing framework for the National Assessment of Educational Progress*: 1998. Washington, DC: Author.

National Center for Education Statistics. (1998). *Linking NAEP and TIMMS*. Washington, DC: Author.

National Commission on Excellence in Education. (1983). *A nation at risk: The imperative for educational reform*. Washington, DC: U.S. Department of Education.

National Council for Teachers of Mathematics. (1989). Curriculum and evaluation standards for school mathematics. Reston, VA: NCTM.

National Education Goals Panel. (1993). *Promises to keep: creating high standards for American students*. Washington, DC: Goals 3 and 4 Technical Planning Group on the Review of Education Standards, National Education Goals Panel.

National Governors Association. (1991). *Educating America: State strategies for achieving the national education goals*. Washington, DC: Author.

Pashley, P. J., & Phillips, G. W. (1993). *Toward world-class standards: A research study linking international and national assessments*. Princeton, NJ: Educational Testing Service.

Phillips, G. W., Mullis, I. V. S., Bourque, M. L., Williams, P. L., Hambleton, R. K., Owen, E. H., & Barton, P. E. (1993). *Interpreting NAEP scales*. Washington, DC: U.S. Department of Education, Office of Educational Research and Improvement.

Public Law 100-297. (1988). National assessment of educational progress improvement act (Article No. USC 1221). Washington, DC.

Public Law 103-227. (1994). Goals 2000: Educate America act. Washington, DC.

Public Law 103-382. (1994). Improving America's schools act. Washington, DC.

Public Law 105-78. (1997). Labor, health, and Human Services and Education Appropriations Act, 1998. Washington, DC.

Skaggs, G., & Bourgue, M. L. (1998). *Overview of the most difficult technical issues on the VNT*. Paper presented at the National Council for Education Measurement Annual Meeting, San Diego, CA.

Stufflebeam, D., Jaeger, R., & Scriven, M. (1991). Summative evaluation of the National Assessment Governing Board's inaugural effort to set achievement levels on the National Assessment of Educational Progress. Unpublished manuscript, The Evaluation Center Western Michigan University, Michigan.

U.S. General Accounting Office. (1993). *Educational achievement standards: NAGB's approach yields misleading interpretations*. Washington, DC: Author.

Williams, E. A., Billeaud, K., Davis, L. A., Thissen, D., & Sanford, E. (1995). *Projecting to the NAEP scale: Results from the North Carolina end-of-grade testing program*. Technical Report #34. Chapel Hill, NC: National Institute of Statistical Sciences, University of North Carolina, Chapel Hill.

CHAPTER

10

Education Policy in the United States and Abroad: What We Can Learn from Each Other

HAROLD W. STEVENSON AND BARBARA K. HOFER
University of Michigan

Discussions of educational policy, especially when they concern other countries, often devolve into heated arguments. Some persons disregard comparative studies with the indictment that cultures differ so greatly from each other that attempts to transfer educational policies and practices from one culture to another are bound to fail. Other persons are more positive, proposing that information about the policies and practices of other countries can serve us well by helping us to understand our own culture; policy makers and educators are better able to reconsider and reevaluate what exists in our own society when provided with information from other cultures.

Cross-cultural study, according to the anthropologist, Melford Spiro (1990), is that which makes the familiar strange and the strange familiar. This phrase summarizes the goals of this chapter. By comparing practices related to the education of children and adolescents in several different cultures, this chapter will illustrate how the most interesting revelations are not what we discover about other societies, but come from what we learn about the United States. Everyday events seen in this new context suddenly demand our attention and concern; events once considered to be novel or unique become commonplace when consistently encountered elsewhere.

Most of the comparisons in this chapter involve Germany, Japan, and the United States, all of which were examined in the Case Study Project of the

Handbook of Educational Policy
Copyright © 1999 by Academic Press. All rights of reproduction in any form reserved.

Third International Mathematics and Science Study (TIMSS), a project that involved interviewing hundreds of students, parents, teachers, and educational administrators and observing scores of classrooms in several locations within each of the three countries.

LEARNING FROM EACH OTHER

Several examples may help illuminate what we can learn from comparative studies of educational policies and practices. One example of radically different policies held by the three countries concerns the grade level at which students are first separated into different tracks. All countries face the problem of aligning students' widely different levels of academic achievement with the level of difficulty of the academic curriculum. In Germany, all levels of ability are accommodated in the same all-purpose school during the first 4 years of elementary school. Beginning in fifth grade, however, children are tracked and are assigned to one of several different types of secondary school. Some are admitted to elite *gymnasien*, which serve students whose performance in the earlier grades reflects a high degree of academic ability and strong motivation to succeed in school. Curricula in the gymnasien emphasize academic courses that are considered to be necessary for entrance to a university. Other students are assigned to secondary schools where the curriculum is less demanding and is likely to involve vocational training.

In Japan, on the other hand, the decision to separate university-bound students from their peers does not occur until the tenth grade. This late separation is based on the assumption that appropriate placement in academic or vocational high schools depends strongly on the students' scores on a high school entrance examination. Scores on this examination are considered to reflect the suitability of the student for admission to the demanding academic high school curriculum. Any form of tracking is prohibited until the student enters high school. In marked contrast to the egalitarian practices governing enrollment in elementary schools, high schools in Japan are organized hierarchically, ranging from the most prestigious academic high schools to the most occupationally oriented vocational schools. Entrance to an academic high school is a critical step for Japanese students who hope to attend a university. Moreover, it is through study at a highly ranked academic high school that the student is likely to attain a score high enough on the college entrance examination to ensure admission to a prestigious university.

The Japanese and German cultures subscribe to different beliefs about when a student's likelihood of succeeding in high school can be reliably evaluated. German policy makers, reflecting German culture, subscribe to the belief that natural ability and the likelihood of future academic success can be discerned by the time the child is 10 years old. Japanese policy makers express the belief that academic success is strongly dependent on the child's motivation and diligence, qualities that are hard to evaluate reliably until the student has experienced the more demanding years of junior high school.

The fact that these cultures prohibit tracking of any type, at least until after the fourth grade, contrasts with the fact that children in U.S. classrooms may be tracked into learning groups according to their skill in reading or mathematics as early as the first grade. Having all-purpose elementary, junior high, and high schools seems natural to Americans. The justification for this form of tracking is that children enter school with different levels of preparation. Proponents of early tracking argue that the early separation of children according to their level of academic achievement is necessary to give all children the necessary backgrounds for later success in school. But one must ask several questions: What are the consequences of such early tracking? What are the effects on students of attending high schools where tracks exist and students are aware of each other's track? Is motivation increased or decreased when all students attending a high school have common goals in mind?

Another example of cultural differences that force one to reconsider U.S. practices concerns the length of the school day and of the school year. Some U.S. policy makers have proposed that students from top-performing countries do well because they spend more time in school than do American students. They conclude that improving academic achievement can be accomplished by increasing the number of hours in the school day or lengthening the school year. Although such a conclusion might seem logical, this recommendation is counter to the modifications of practices that are occurring in several East Asian countries. The Japanese Ministry of Education, for example, has taken steps to shorten the number of days each year that students spend in school. The ministry has concluded that the 6-day week places too strong an emphasis on study and provides too few opportunities for students to enjoy other activities. As a result, Saturday classes have been eliminated for 2 weeks each month and soon all Saturday classes will be canceled. Similarly, in Taiwan, where students also have attended school for a half day on Saturdays, many teachers now tell their pupils not to bring their books to school on Saturdays because the days will be spent on extracurricular activities rather than on further academic study.

Western observers have also noted that East Asian students, compared to American students, spend a greater number of hours each day in school. Seeing elementary school students returning home from school in late afternoon and high school students returning home during the evening, observers assume that the students have been spending long hours at school attending classes and studying. Although the school day in East Asia may be an hour longer at the upper grades than in the United States and students may spend some time after their last classes studying together, the main reason students remain at school longer is that they are engaged in extracurricular activities. In Japan, for example, participation in extracurricular activities in the form of school clubs is required after the fourth grade. Elementary school students must participate in the activities of at least one club; secondary school students may choose to belong to as many as five or six clubs. What appeared to be an unusual dedication to academic activities proves on closer observation to be an involvement in enjoyable social activities. Clubs and other extracurricular activities are a source of heightened enthusiasm about attending school, for the longer school day provides additional opportunities for students to interact with their friends, play games and sports, and enjoy other aspects of group life. If the United States were to increase the length of the school day, would provision be made for a richer program of extracurricular activities? Would a longer school year mean more academic classes or greater opportunities for activities such as excursions, field trips, sports and cultural events, and school carnivals?

Studies of other cultures reveal natural experiments in progress, but to obtain reliable and valid information we must have more than curiosity and goodwill. To be useful, the studies must yield reliable data and present valid descriptions of the practices and beliefs characterizing different cultures. Thus, before discussing any of the studies in detail, it is important to describe what must be taken into account when efforts are made to conduct research on educational practices and policies in other countries.

CONDUCTING CROSS-CULTURAL STUDIES

Reading about other cultures or even visiting other countries and observing educational practices firsthand may add an exotic aspect to research in education. Unfortunately, many of the descriptions of educational practices in other countries are based on short-term visits to a small number of schools by an individual or a few individuals who know little of the culture and must rely on an interpreter to gain any understanding of what is going on in the classrooms. Reputable newspapers and magazines appear to find no problem in sending reporters to characterize policies in other countries on the basis of a 2- or 3-day visit. More than any other source these reports shape America's perceptions of educational practices in other countries. Even when delegations actually visit other countries for several weeks they are often ill prepared and spend much of their time gaining familiarity with another culture rather than acquiring sound information about that country's educational practices.

Because so many of the comparative studies of educational practices are subject to criticisms such as these, it is useful to discuss some of the factors necessary for sound comparative research in education. These include such factors as sampling of respondents, language facility, familiarity with the cultures, and construction of research instruments.

Sampling

To generalize about the characteristics of a culture it is necessary to involve a broad sample of individuals from that culture. This is usually a difficult task, with the result that few comparative studies of educational practices are based on representative samples of locations or of respondents. The visitor typically relies on friends or government officials to make arrangements for visits to schools and for conversations with teachers, parents, members of boards of education, or school administrators. It is unlikely, given this task, that arrangements will be made to visit other than the most effective, best equipped, or most unusual schools in the city. To do otherwise requires experience in the country or well-developed relations with school officials. As a result, many Americans are stunned when they find that the descriptions they have read are as uncharacteristic of the schools in the country being discussed as a report of visits to private schools in mid-Manhattan would be of American schools.

Journalists have been especially errant in including anything approximating representative samples of respondents. As a result, the descriptions they offer about other cultures are often stereotyped pictures of some of the culture's most dramatic or unusual aspects. Although their efforts do not constitute formal studies, logic dictates that they should attempt to interview more than a few exceptional persons if they are to write responsibly about the other cultures.

Language

Dependence on a translator poses special problems in investigating other cultures. Translators may be facile with everyday terms or have special areas of expertise, but few have the dual qualifications of language facility and competence in the field of education. As a result, mistakes are often made in obtaining accurate explanations and descriptions of educational practices and policies. An especially vivid example of the lack of equivalence of terms is evident in the translation of *ochikobore*, a Japanese word that is translated as "school dropout." The translation seems straightforward until a teacher describes a child who is present as being *ochikobore*. When asked about this apparent discrepancy, the teacher explains, "Oh no, it refers to an inattentive child, not just to one who fails to attend school." Thus while *dropping out* in the United States refers to leaving school, the term in Japan can indicate physical presence but mental disengagement. Slippages such as this can occur with alarming frequency and sometimes unpleasant consequences. Translations convey incomplete or inaccurate understanding unless the translator is familiar with differences in the nuances of meaning or takes the time to probe more thoroughly about the implications of the words in the two languages. Translation and back-translation, common practices in cross-cultural research, are unlikely to reveal such differences.

Culture

Reliance in comparative studies is sometimes placed on informants, members of a culture who attempt to instruct the foreign visitor about the characteristics of the culture. More than a single informant is necessary to ensure that the description is reliable and accurate, and observation by the visitor to substantiate the description is essential.

Cultural differences are expressed in many ways. For example, making arrangements for conducting a study may follow a very different path in China from that followed in the United States. An American, eager to make the arrangements necessary for beginning a research project, may pause briefly to enjoy a cup of tea but then quickly wants to begin discussing the details of the research. The potential Chinese collaborator may often appear to be less goal directed, discussing the weather, asking about the American's family, and engaging the visitor in general conversation. It becomes apparent that the goals of the two persons are different: the American has been concerned about the details of the research; the Chinese has sought assurance that cooperation will be fruitful. Unless this phase of the interaction is reconciled to the satisfaction of each party, the possibility of gaining a clear understanding of the procedures for the study is reduced.

Similarly, an American may become impatient with Japanese collaborators when faced with the frequent situation wherein only one member of the Japanese team does all the talking. The Japanese participants, rather than run the risk of having disagreements emerge during the course of a group meeting, may already have spent hours discussing all aspects of the arrangements and have reached a consensus that can be represented by a single member of the group. The same procedures are followed in discussions about education. Consensus is reached by the Japanese about acceptable answers before a meeting is held with the foreign visitor, and only rarely will dissenting opinions appear during the course of the discussions. This difference in style of group interaction makes meaningful discussion between the two groups difficult to achieve.

Instruments

Behavioral science is much more popular in the United States than in many other countries and a great deal of time and money has been invested in developing surveys, questionnaires, tests, and interview protocols for use in research. As a result, these instruments are often translated into other languages and used in comparative studies, at times with dubious results. Perhaps the most egregious examples of misuse of research instruments occur in cross-cultural studies of intellectual functioning. A high percentage of the intelligence tests used comparatively are constructed in English by U.S. psychologists; translated versions of the tests are then used to gauge the intellectual levels of children and adolescents in other countries. It is doubtful that these translated tests are useful clinically or possess the predictive validity that the tests have in their U.S. versions.

Attempts to adapt personality tests for use in other cultures are also laden with problems. For example, several years ago an American psychologist attempted to adapt the well-known Minnesota Multiphasic Personality Inventory for use in China. The Chinese collaborator confronted the American with the problem that one of the items dealt with the respondent's desire to attend wild parties, insisting that "we have no wild parties in Beijing." The American's response was that the item had to be retained to preserve the scale's integrity, regardless of the usefulness of the inventory for the Chinese population.

The problems associated with developing instruments in one language and in one culture and translating them for use in other cultures become evident in studies involving interviews and questionnaires. Items tapping information that may be relevant and acceptable in one culture may be considered to be intrusive in another. Americans and members of some other industrialized societies are familiar with rating scales, where they are asked to indicate their evaluations or reactions to statements or situations by selecting what they consider to be the most appropriate answers. Members of many other cultures have not had these kinds of experience and find psychometric scales difficult to understand and hard to evaluate.

Equally problematic are questionnaires provided to teachers to assess their responsibilities and requirements. For example, teachers in most countries, especially at the elementary grades, are expected to remain at school throughout the school day. This is not the case in Germany, where teachers' schedules vary from day to day, and when there is a free hour in their teaching schedule teachers are permitted to leave school, go shopping, or engage in other activities. Without a German representative in the group that constructed the questionnaire, this possible difference between the daily lives of German teachers and teachers in other countries might not emerge. In a similar fashion, German teachers leave school at noon or at the latest at 1:30 in the afternoon. The assumption that the day's work is completed by this time is wrong. German teachers prefer to do their preparation and grading at home. Japanese teachers, who work in a more collaborative fashion, prefer to remain at school throughout the day so that they can interact and cooperate with their colleagues. U.S. teachers are in between; they do much of their work at home but seldom leave school immediately after their pupils have departed. In view of these variations, it would be inappropriate to ask only about the time teachers spend at school or at home in their preparation of lessons.

Alternatives are not difficult to suggest. Materials should be simultaneously constructed by members of all of the societies involved. Most importantly, the words used in the various versions of the test should be equally familiar to children in all of the languages involved. This can be accomplished through reference to the textbooks used by the children and to word frequency counts that are available in various languages. Unless these minimal requirements are met it is not immediately evident that the test will be a fair assessment of the reading abilities of the children in the different cultures.

A related set of problems concern the use of instruments consisting of open-ended questions such as, "Which have you enjoyed more, high school or junior high school? Why is one more enjoyable than the other?" Answers to the second question by members of various cultures differ markedly in their completeness. Japanese and Chinese respondents are likely to be terse, providing only the essential elements of an explanation. German and American respondents tend to be more voluble and proceed to discuss various reasons and implications of their choice. Unless the interviewer is skilled in probing for more complete answers the assumption might be that Japanese and Chinese respondents are less capable of self-analysis than are Westerners. Alternatively, the explanation may be that the cultural differences lie in the person's willingness to engage in speculation and psychological analysis rather than in an inability to do so.

A second problem encountered in answers to open-ended questions lies in the development of a coding scheme. Categories of response developed for coding answers obtained in one culture do not necessarily constitute an exhaustive sample of responses elicited by the question. It is critical in comparative studies that the coding scheme for open-ended questions include responses that may be idiosyncratic to a particular culture as well as those that are common across all cultures involved.

APPLYING RESULTS

Meeting the requirements for sound comparative research is difficult and few studies reported in the research literature have been conducted with the care and attention called for in the preceding discussion. Difficulties in conducting research in education are no excuse, however, for failing to impose rigorous standards in evaluating research. More than in most areas of social science, implementing innovative programs can have profound consequences for everyday practices. Indeed, many critics of the field of education express dismay at the ease with which changes in practice are instituted on the basis of incomplete or inadequate research evidence. Change may result in positive effects, of course, but it can also have unexpected, unfortunate consequences. Adopting a new but ineffective approach to teaching reading may result in a precipitous decline in reading scores. Introducing a totally new curriculum in mathematics may lead to a rapid drop in morale of teachers who feel they are inadequately prepared to teach this new approach.

One of the most ill-informed arguments concerns the relation of high academic standards to students' mental health. A common misperception in the West is that students in high-performing countries of East Asia are subject to psychological maladjustment due to pressure for performance and a high incidence of suicide. This assumption has been used as an argument against raising education standards in the United States. It is argued that if more demanding standards were adopted, American students would be more likely to develop the kinds of problems evidenced by East Asian students. There is little evidence to support this position. Self-reports of students in Japan, China, and Taiwan do not reveal a greater incidence of maladjustment than do the reports from their American counterparts. For example, when asked to indicate the frequency with which they feel stress, depressed mood, anxiety, aggression, or various psychosomatic disorders, East Asian students are no more likely than American students to describe difficulties in adjustment (e.g., Crystal et al., 1994). Rates of suicide among secondary school students in Japan (the only East Asian country for which data are available) are, if anything, lower than those in the United States.

What is the basis of the belief that efforts to cope with high standards may result in maladjustment? It is not from formal research, for there is no evidence for this view in the research literature. Part of the explanation lies in the tendency of the Japanese public to pay great attention to any evidence of misbehavior on the part of Japanese students. Stories of teasing or physical abuse by students appear as front-page news in Japan. A student's suicide becomes an item of national concern. In an effort to explain these events, blame is often placed on the demanding curriculum and the difficult high school and college entrance examinations, whether or not these are actually the major causes.

Another common misinterpretation of what exists in other countries is the failure to distinguish between guidelines and a national curriculum. There is little support in the United States for adopting a national curriculum that specifies the content of lessons, the time they will be studied, and the manner in which they will be taught throughout the country. However, such stringently defined curricula do not characterize the national guidelines that exist in many other countries. The 16 independent states in Germany, for example, attempt to coordinate their curricula through meetings of the Conference of Ministers of Education. These meetings result in commonly agreed upon guidelines for what will be taught in school, the organization and basic goals of education, course requirements, periods of instruction, and requirements for school completion. But whether these guidelines are adopted depends on the states. Moreover, whether schools adhere to the guidelines depends on the teachers and school authorities. Teachers who disagree with the recommended content and sequence of lessons feel free to substitute their own ideas and materials. Thus, guidelines are much less restrictive than might be the case when a curriculum is defined by national law.

Japanese guidelines, like those in Germany, follow a similar general approach. For example, the English version of the guidelines describes what students should be able to accomplish in Japanese language classes in high school:

> To comprehend accurately the subject and points of a speech or passage in accordance with the description. To comprehend the writer's way of developing an idea and his points of emphasis, paying attention to the structure and development of the passage. To summarize or explain in full detail the content of a speech or passage according to the need. To read and appreciate the characters, scenes, and sentiments described in accordance with its expression. . . . To read, paying attention to the features of expression and the characteristics of styles suitable for the content and form of a passage. To deepen the comprehension and appreciation of a passage by declamation. (Ministry of Education, Science, and Culture, 1983, p. 16)

There is no demand for rigid adherence to a predetermined content or schedule, but the guidelines offer a general picture of the purpose and approach recommended by the Ministry of Education. These guidelines, along with textbooks approved by the ministry but chosen by the teachers, provide a degree of comparability in lessons offered throughout the country.

A final example of misperception concerns *juku* and *buxiban*, the afterschool classes offered by private companies to Japanese and Chinese students. In an effort to explain the consistently high level of performance of Japanese and Chinese students in comparative studies of academic achievement, some Westerners have attributed the students' success to attendance at these classes. What weakens this explanation are statistics indicating that attendance at these classes is not universal, but depends on the grade level of the student, the family income, and the region of the country and size of the city in which the student resides. *Juku* attendance is much higher, for example, on the corridor of large cities stretching from Tokyo to Nagoya and Osaka than in other regions of the country. Attendance is also higher during the later years of junior high school than at other times. Further weakening this explanation of higher achievement is the fact that the afterschool classes do not function solely for preparing students for tests. There are *juku* classes for slow learners, for students who seek to go beyond the content of their lessons at school, and for students who want to become better calligraphers, practitioners of martial arts, flower arrangers, or abacus operators. In addition, many students explain their attendance at the afterschool classes as providing opportunities for socializing with their friends.

Information about the operation of these classes comes primarily from students and their parents because, as competitive operations, owners of *juku* and *buxiban* are reluctant to reveal data that might influence their enrollments. What we do know is that although attendance at extra classes may be helpful to some students, the relatively limited number of students actually attending *juku* for academic acceleration cannot explain the high standing of the East Asian students in comparative studies of academic achievement.

As is evident from these examples, errors of interpretation or attribution are easy to make and hard to correct in the absence of reliable information. Although much can be learned from what is done in other countries, the wisest course for the present seems to be that of remaining cautious about promoting changes in U.S. policy and practices on the basis of what is occurring in other countries.

CONTRIBUTIONS FROM THE UNITED STATES

Thus far we have emphasized ways in which practices and policies of other countries differ from those of the United States. It is also appropriate to describe ways in which educators and policy makers from other countries look to the United States for new ideas about policies and practices.

Creativity

It is inevitable in discussions of education that East Asians will mention the high degree of creativity of American students, the high incidence of Nobel prize winners from the United States, and the remarkable scientific advances made by American researchers. East Asians are not so self-effacing that they de-emphasize the high levels of academic achievement of their primary and secondary school students, but they express dismay at what they consider to be the weakness of their schools in producing creative children and adults. How much this perception is due to a deficiency in fostering creativity in students and how much it is a result of the governments' modest investments in research through construction of laboratories, support of research teams, and provision of up-to-date materials and equipment is a matter of debate. Nor does a look at contemporary Japanese architects, fashion designers, novelists, dramatists, and composers support the charge of a lack of creativity in Japan. Resolution of this dilemma will depend on further research, but thus far cross-cultural research on creativity has been minimal because researchers in both East Asia and the West have lacked the creativity to devise useful tests of creative thinking.

Flexibility

Americans at nearly any age have the opportunity to enroll in some type of institution of higher education, whether it is a junior college, community college, or a four-year college or university. This is not the case in other countries, where entrance is limited to persons who have completed the school-leaving examination (the *Abitur* in Germany) or a college entrance examination in Japan. The flexibility of training as reflected in the wide range of schools and their accessibility is an envied aspect of U.S. education.

Higher Education

Not only is some form of post–high school education available throughout the United States, the quality of a high percentage of colleges and universities is also high. This is evident in the large number of foreign students who seek admission to undergraduate and graduate programs in American universities each year. Enrollments in some colleges and departments, such as engineering, the physical sciences, statistics, and computer science, have shown increasing percentages of foreign students. The high level of training in the social sciences and the arts offered by American universities also has begun to attract more and more students from other countries. Which policy of investment is more productive for a country: well-supported and highly developed primary and secondary schools or outstanding universities? This will be one of the most strongly debated policy questions in the coming decades, when scientific and technological superiority will play an important role in each country's economic future.

Special Education

The United States has led the way in developing programs for exceptional children, including programs for learning disabled, emotionally disturbed, and dyslexic students, as well as for students who are unusually talented academically. American schools have had several decades of experience in designing special programs and courses for these students, and educators from other countries have been especially interested in visiting and learning about these innovations.

RECENT RESEARCH

We can convey our recommendations about how comparative studies of education can provide useful information to policy makers by describing in detail the design and implementation of one recent large-scale study in educational policy. This description enables us to look in greater depth at both the process of conducting cross-national educational research and at current findings that can help shape policy. The example with which we are most familiar is the Third International Mathematics and Science Study (TIMSS). A comprehensive study of math and science achievement in 41 nations, TIMSS is one of the most rigorous and extensive studies of its kind, covering selected topics of special importance to policy makers. The TIMSS project, conducted in 1995, involved the testing of more than 500,000 students at three stages of schooling. Results from this large-scale multimethod research endeavor provide the opportunity for U.S. educators to evaluate educational policies and practices in an international context. In addition to math and science tests, the study included questionnaires for students and teachers, curriculum analyses, videotaped observations of mathematics lessons, and an analysis of key policy issues in Germany, Japan, and the United States. It is this case study, which our research team at the University of Michigan designed and coordinated, which we will describe in the context of the broader TIMSS project.

Results of the TIMSS testing at the fourth, eighth, and twelfth grades indicate that students in the United States performed poorly in comparison to their counterparts in other countries, falling progressively further behind with each grade level of testing. The most positive results appear at the fourth grade, where American students' scores were just above the average for all countries in mathematics and were higher in science, with scores surpassed only by Korean students and comparable to those in Japan. American fourth graders outperformed their peers in nine countries in both math and science. Among eighth graders, students in the United States scored slightly below the international average in math and slightly above it in science. The only countries that American students outperformed in both subjects were Cyprus, Iran, Lithuania, and Portugal. By twelfth grade, student achievement in the United States was near the bottom, with only two countries scoring significantly lower, Cyprus and South Africa. The results, for the most part, are not surprising, for in the first and second international math tests students in the United States also received scores below the international average. (For a review of these and other comparative studies, see Stevenson & Lee [1998]).

The results of this achievement testing provide important indicators about the comparative performance of students in the United States, but we need other types of research to interpret these findings and to inform decisions concerning educational policy. Because it is difficult to introduce reforms in education solely on the basis of test scores, the TIMSS study included additional research questions and approaches. The questionnaire component of the TIMSS study provided indices of student attitudes and practices; the curriculum analyses permitted an examination of differences in the content and organization of math and science curricula; and the videotape study enabled researchers to examine differences in actual classroom teaching practices in eighth-grade math classes in three countries (the United States, Germany, and Japan). The TIMSS Case Study Project offers an in-depth, qualitative analysis of selected policy issues.

The Case Study Project has served as a complement to the other components of TIMSS, providing the possibility of rich interpretation of data collected by the other methods. For example, whereas results of the eighth-grade questionnaires suggested that Japanese teachers assign less homework than U.S. teachers (Peak, 1996), this seemed puzzling in the light of the achievement differences between the two countries. Results from the case study give us a fuller portrait. Interviews with students revealed that Japanese students did spend less time doing out-of-class work directly assigned by teachers but that they put considerable effort into studying each night. Unlike many of their peers in the United States, Japanese adolescents described reviewing the day's lesson and actively preparing for the next lesson, whereas American students typically reported doing assigned homework on a daily basis and were much less likely than the Japanese students to pursue independent study—unless a test was imminent. Furthermore, American students reported that they often did their homework during schooltime, either during study hall or at the end of a class period during time set aside by the teacher, a practice seldom found in Japan. One of the suggested implications is that teachers might do well to help students develop practices leading to more frequent self-motivated study.

The Case Study Project has also served as a means for gathering information not easily accessible through quantitative methodologies. For example, understanding the role that school plays in adolescents' lives in Germany, Japan, and the United States involved observations of students both during classes and in extracurricular activities, and interviews and conversations with students, their teachers, families, and school administrators. We were able to make comparisons both between and within countries about a series of complex contextual issues that could not have been addressed through questionnaires.

Conducting the TIMSS Case Study Project

The Case Study Project was designed to address four key topics of interest to U.S. policy makers, which were selected by the Department of Education: educational standards, how schools deal with differences in academic ability, the role of school in adolescents' lives, and the training and daily lives of teachers. Exploration of these topics was undertaken in the United States and two key economic competitors whose students in the past have performed well in math and science: Japan and Germany. The U.S. Department of Education and the National Science Foundation provided funding for this component of the study. The development of this study and how it was conducted provide an example of the application of the research practices outlined earlier.

Sampling issues in conducting case studies are critically important. One primary site and two secondary sites in other regions were selected as representative within each country. We selected sites that were as similar as possible both geographically and demographically across the three countries. Primary sites were large metropolitan areas and their surrounding towns; secondary sites were smaller. With assistance from local authorities, we chose schools within these sites that represented the range of educational environments typical in these countries. We included both academic and vocational high schools, for example, as well as schools that represented a wide range of student achievement.

One of the early steps in the research process was to review the literature on the four topics. This was accomplished through a thorough analysis of materials from each country, read and summarized by native speakers trained as social scientists and with a professional interest in education. These reviews provided the foundation for developing general lines of inquiry for the study.

The development of interview instruments followed the guidelines described earlier. Native speakers from each of the countries studied worked as an interdisciplinary social science research team to develop semistructured interviews for each topic. The topics were based on the literature reviews and our knowledge from previous studies and were developed in consultation with policy boards composed of professional experts on the educational system of each country. Where relevant, researchers were to interview students, parents, teachers, and administrators at each of the three levels of schooling addressed by TIMSS. For example, for the topic of how schools deal with differences in academic ability, all of these populations at each level served as relevant informants; by contrast, when the role of school in adolescents' lives was discussed, there was no need for the researchers to visit elementary schools. For the topic of educational standards, it was also necessary to meet with a variety of educational and government officials. This mapping of questions, subjects, and educational levels formed a complex design that guided the work of the researchers.

Semistructured guidelines for the interview provided uniformity of data collected by different interviewers but gave the interviewers flexibility in pursuing the overall purposes of the research. These guidelines were open to modification in other ways. A draft was presented to the researchers during a week-long training and subsequently revised, and interviewers communicated through computers with each other on-line while in the field and were able to suggest additional avenues of inquiry to the central staff and to one another.

Given the importance of linguistic and cultural skills in conducting cross-cultural research, it was critical in this study that the researchers be fluent in the country's language, familiar with the culture, and knowledgeable about and comfortable in school settings. The research team was primarily composed of native speakers of English whose fluency had been gained either in bilingual homes or through extended residency in Germany or Japan, but the team also included a native speaker of Japanese and one of German, both of whom had been educated in the United States. The core researchers were nearly all recent Ph.D. recipients who had done their dissertation field research in the countries to which they were assigned. Because of this familiarity, it was not necessary for them to spend long periods of time acquainting themselves with the communities they visited, a practice common to most ethnographic work. Because of their prior work in schools, they also were able to understand the social practices and customs necessary for gaining entrée and the confidences of those interviewed.

The researchers typically spent 2 to 3 months at the primary site and 2 to 3 weeks at the secondary site. The research team in each country consisted of at least three primary researchers and several supplementary researchers. For example, the U.S. team included an African American and a Hispanic researcher, each of whom primarily interviewed students and parents from their own ethnic backgrounds. All interviews were conducted in the language of the country where the interview took place (with the exception of some interviews with Hispanic parents in the United States conducted in Spanish), were tape-recorded, and were translated into English so that cross-cultural analyses could be conducted more easily.

Even with well-trained researchers and a carefully developed interview protocol, the study was not without its cultural problems. The topics selected by U.S. policy makers were those of interest in the United States but not necessarily of primary relevance in the other two countries. In the case of how schools deal with individual differences in ability, the topic was not only of little interest in Japan, but discussions of such a concept were often deemed impolite, inappropriate, or simply puzzling. In a culture that emphasizes Confucian values of malleability and effort, focused inquiry about innate ability carries embedded assumptions about our own American cultural values. Although we were aware of these issues in advance and had attempted to develop questions that were as sensitive as possible under these circumstances, this topic still provided difficulties for researchers.

The analyses of the large amount of ethnographic data collected on each topic for each country were facilitated by the use of computer software designated for qualitative research. Researchers working on each of the four topics began with a common set of key words, which they subsequently expanded during the coding process. Finally, one researcher for each topic analyzed the data for that topic, including interviews, observations, and artifacts, and wrote a final report.

The results of the Case Study Project are reported in five volumes (Stevenson & Nerison-Low, in press). Three of the volumes are organized by country, with a chapter on each of the key topics. A fourth volume contains the review of the literature and the fifth volume compares and summarizes the overall results. Most important for future researchers interested in additional analyses, the entire computer database of interviews, conversations, and observations will be made available through the Department of Education.

CONCLUSIONS

It is immediately obvious to anyone reading reports of comparative studies that there are both remarkable commonalities and striking differences among countries in nearly all aspects of education. On the basis of our work on the TIMSS Case Study Project and from other comparative studies conducted by our research group at the University of Michigan and by others, we have compiled a list of factors that appear to be the most salient in improving academic achievement. We list these factors not as established facts but as hypotheses that merit further study. Table 1 shows some of the findings from the comparative studies that we believe are relevant for educational policy and that have emerged as viable possibilities for improving students' academic achievement.

We conclude from our comparative studies that the Japanese, whose students' test scores exceed those of German and U.S. students in mathematics and science tests of TIMSS, also demonstrate more of the positive attributes described in Table 1 than do members of the other two countries. Japan is characterized by the high standards and great importance it places on education and by its highly involved parents, versatile and excellent teachers, and highly motivated students. Such conditions exist in some sections of the United States, especially in advantaged neighborhoods, and in Germany, notably in many of the *gymnasien*, but for the most part they share fewer of the positive attributes described than does Japan.

Further investigation of the relevance of the policies reached in our explorations will clarify the conditions that appear to result in successful achievement. Study of Singapore, Korea, Hong Kong, and the Czech Republic, whose students were high scorers on the TIMSS mathematics and science tests, would be especially informative, as would studies of countries whose students did not do well on the TIMSS tests. What differentiated Cyprus, Kuwait, Colombia, and South Africa, all among the lowest-scoring countries, from countries whose students were more successful? Studies of the education policies of low- and high-achieving countries, combined with studies of U.S. schools that receive the highest and the lowest scores on achievement tests, would add further depth to our understanding of effective schooling and would alert us to conditions that may be relevant to discussions about improving education in the United States.

TABLE I
Case Study Findings Relevant to Educational Policies

- All students, including those in vocational as well as academic programs, can be exposed to mathematics and science throughout their schooling if there are appropriate adaptations to the students' levels of ability.
- Providing national guidelines that describe the expectations for accomplishment at each grade level leads to greater comparability across school systems and assists teachers and parents in knowing what to expect from students at successively higher levels of education.
- Active participation by teachers in decisions concerning the standards, content, and implementation of the school curriculum establishes a sense of teamwork throughout the school.
- Approval of textbooks by state or national ministries of education results in more uniform implementation of guidelines and of the curriculum throughout the state or nation.
- Funding schools through local property taxes results in inequities both within and between school districts in the opportunities provided to students for obtaining an effective education.
- Keeping groups of students together with the same teacher over a period of several years aids students' socialization and teachers' understanding of the strengths and weaknesses of individual students.
- Extracurricular activities transform the school from a place where there is concentration on academic matters to one that fosters students' social development and provides greater engagement in schooling.
- A de-emphasis on the limitations imposed by differences in innate ability and a greater emphasis on the contributions of diligence and study to successful achievement promotes the belief by teachers and students that students are capable of meeting the demands of the curriculum.
- Conversely, although effective instruction and hard work are likely to improve overall academic performance, individual differences among students in their rate of learning will persist.
- Belief in the efficacy of self-initiated study makes it unnecessary for students to rely solely on assignments by the teachers for clarifying and reinforcing the goals of classroom instruction.
- Late channeling of students into different tracks allows students to have a longer period to demonstrate their potential for further academic training and may result in more appropriate placement than that resulting from early assignment of students to different curricula.
- Vocational programs that include both academic and applied experiences increase students' motivation to continue in school and improve their chances of obtaining productive employment after graduation.
- Emphasis on learning in group settings rather than in isolation improves students' motivation and level of academic achievement.
- College entrance examinations are a source of anxiety but they also motivate teachers and students to strive to cover the curriculum more fully.
- The esteem of teaching as a profession is enhanced when teachers' salaries are competitive with those of other professions requiring comparable degrees of education.
- Assistance from a mentor, observation of effective teaching, and a high degree of interaction and sharing of information among teachers improves the quality of teaching.
- Teachers are likely to be kept up to date if opportunities exist for learning from appropriate in-service training and visits to resource centers and successful programs.
- Teachers benefit from opportunities for guided practice in effective techniques of teaching.
- Placing emphasis in instruction on interaction among and between students and teacher results in helpful support, counsel, and models for appropriate response.

References

Crystal, D. S., Chen, C., Fuligni, A. J., Stevenson, H. W., Hsu, C.-C., Ko, H.-J., Kitamura, S., & Kimura, S. (1994). Psychological maladjustment and academic achievement: A cross-cultural study of Japanese, Chinese, and American high school students. *Child Development*, 65, 738–753.

Ministry of Education, Science, and Culture. (1983). *Course of study for upper secondary schools in Japan*. Tokyo: Monbusho.

Peak, L. (1996). Pursuing excellence: A study of U.S. eighth-grade mathematics and science teaching, learning, curriculum, and achievement in international context. Washington, DC: Department of Education, National Center for Educational Statistics.

Spiro, M. E. (1990). On the strange and the familiar in recent anthropological thought. In J. W. Stigler, R. A. Schweder, & G. Herdt (Eds.), *Cultural psychology: Essays on comparative human development* (pp. 47–61). New York: Cambridge University Press.

Stevenson, H. W., & Lee, S. (1998). An examination of American student achievement from an international perspective. In D. Ravitch (Ed.), *The state of student performance in American schools* (pp. 1–52). Washington, DC: The Brookings Institution.

Stevenson, H. W., & Nerison-Low, R. (in press). *To sum it up: Case studies of education in Germany, Japan, and the United States*. Washington, DC: U.S. Government Printing Office.

Intersections of Theory, Policy, Politics, and Practice

CHAPTER

11

Policy and Practical Implications of Theoretical Innovations in Education

THOMAS G. DUNN
University of Toledo

Educational policy and educational theory frequently intersect in interesting and unpredictable ways. Ideas proposed by theorists are often popularized and woven into practice long before they have been refined, tested, or evaluated. Slavin (1989) has deftly illustrated this process in his article "PET and the Pendulum: Faddism in Education and How to Stop It." This phenomenon represents what might be called a more formal or structural version of how theorizing affects educational policy and practice.

Educational theorists also influence policies and practices in less formal ways. For example, many parents may not be able to label certain practices as behaviorist or name educational theorists associated with behaviorism. Many practicing teachers may not be familiar with books or articles devoted to particular theoretical perspectives in education, tending instead to professional development that directly improves their daily activities in practical ways. Nonetheless, nearly all parents and teachers would probably regard the use of compliments, encouragement, and so on (*praise*, to use behaviorist terms) as effective—indeed, necessary—for improving behavior and increasing a student's self-esteem. This phenomenon represents what might be called the less formal version of how educational theorizing affects policy and practice.

The primary purpose of this chapter is to examine the formal and informal pathways by which educational theorizing affects what happens in classrooms,

Handbook of Educational Policy
Copyright © 1999 by Academic Press. All rights of reproduction in any form reserved.

in families, and in contemporary American society. Because what occurs in classrooms is, to a great extent, influenced by what happens in a student's home and family life, the effects of educational theorizing on home environment and parenting practices are also examined.

This chapter also attempts to investigate the intersections between education and psychology in ways not often contemplated by researchers or policy analysts. For example, particular attention is given to potential undesirable effects on psychological characteristics such as a student's personal happiness brought about by otherwise desirable educational innovations and societal changes.

One caution is in order, however. In the course of examining these intersections, a number of popular educational reforms, practices, and policies are used to illustrate key points. These innovations usually have a strong foundation in the literature commending their use. Because these innovations are used to illustrate the potential for unanticipated undesirable consequences, the context is ripe for the misinterpretation that these innovations should be abandoned. The reader is cautioned against making this unwarranted inference. Instead, the purpose is to stimulate all those concerned about American education—parents, teachers, administrators, researchers, and policy makers—to begin consideration and systematic research on the potential undesirable effects of both current practices and proposed educational reforms *prior* to their implementation.

In the following section, a brief vignette is first presented to illustrate the phenomena of interest. Subsequent sections focus on (1) how expectations impact emotions; (2) general patterns of rising expectations; (3) specific societal shifts and changes in students' lived experiences—both at home and in school—that may influence the development of these rising expectations; and (4) how these rising expectations are inevitably violated, with the near certain results of unhappiness, disillusionment, and disengagement in both familial and scholastic settings. The chapter closes with recommendations for how to break the cycle, including suggestions that are applicable and relevant to educational practitioners, theorists, students, and their families.

AN EDUCATIONAL DILEMMA

Mark's parents, Pauline and Rob, read much on child-rearing practices. They were both college educated and had taken several psychology courses. They were guided in their child rearing by the ideas developed by several writers and theorists, including Benjamin Spock, Jean Piaget, and John Dewey. For example, Pauline and Rob believed that it is important for children to learn to make choices and that this process should begin early, so beginning when Mark was about two years old they would often ask him what he wanted to eat at mealtimes. Although this resulted in extra meal preparation time,

Pauline and Rob felt it was an excellent opportunity to develop choice-making skills. They followed through fairly consistently in other types of situations as well, such as allowing Mark to select a book for reading before going to bed and choosing which parent would read the book and put him to bed.

As is the case in so many families, Pauline and Rob's lifestyles placed Mark in situations where he could make other choices. For example, owing in part to their busy schedules, they ate out at least once a week. In these instances Mark made choices regarding what to eat, but certainly from a wider selection. As another example, both Pauline and Rob wanted Mark to get involved in music. Periodically they asked him if he wanted to learn to play a musical instrument and if he did, what he wanted to play. He never did choose to learn how to play a musical instrument.

Mark's early school experiences were somewhat rocky. Teachers noted two types of situations that were particularly troublesome for Mark. One was a general problem with sharing. If Mark wanted something that another child also wanted, he would get frustrated. It was not that he fought, pushed, or shoved to get his way. He would just get exasperated, cry, and go off to a corner. Another common situation that caused difficulty for Mark was when he was assigned a project or task that had specific guidelines. He would get frustrated when the teacher wanted him to do something in a particular way. Mark did not like school.

Tension developed between the teacher and Mark's parents. Pauline and Rob wanted the teacher to be more responsive to Mark's need to make creative choices, whereas the teacher thought it important that Mark learn to share and follow directions. A counselor recommended that they find outlets for Mark where he could still make choices. In doing so his creativity would not be stifled and he would not be so anxious and exasperated. Pauline and Rob bought Mark a computer for his room and encouraged him to choose computer games that he liked. To do this they went to a software store once a month where Mark could chose a game that he liked from the many available. They also bought a VCR for his room and he could choose tapes he wanted to see (except for R-rated ones). Overall the situation did not improve. Mark's problems in school persisted, and after awhile the novelty of the computer and VCR seemed to wear off.

Problems such as those faced by Pauline, Rob, and Mark are not unusual. One could argue about possible solutions, take the parents' position or that of the teacher, or perhaps even take Mark's position. However, it is not the intent of this chapter to present problems and propose practical solutions. Instead, it is more important to understand how many of the difficulties that parents and teachers experience in their everyday activities with children are at least in part due to changes in society. Further, some of these changes are rooted in the recommendations of philosophers, psychologists, counselors, teachers, and others who are professionally involved in education. These changes have in turn influenced children's expectations regarding many aspects of their lives. Educational and social problems arise when these expectations are violated. The case for these points will be made in the following sections: (1) a brief presentation on the general impact of expectations, particularly, violated expectations; (2) an information-processing explanation of how mediated cognitions affect our emotions; (3) a discussion of two patterns of rising expectations with examples dealing with marriage and schools; (4) a portrayal of how changes in the home and in school have affected children, especially with regard to rising expectations; (5) a specific illustration of how the quest for relevance may have been harmful by leading to rising expectations; and (6) some final comments and recommendations.

THE IMPACT OF EXPECTATIONS

Research indicates that expectations have a strong influence on inclinations, attitudes, actions, and motivation (Bandura, 1986; Covington, 1992; Schunk & Meece, 1992; Weiner, 1985). The effect of expectations is particularly influential regarding personal emotions. As Seligman (1988a) has suggested, expectations may help explain why there is more depression today compared to earlier decades in this century. Seligman has argued that since World War II there has been an increase in individualism and a decrease in involvement with the larger, supporting social institutions such as family, religion, and country. The increase in individualism has been accompanied by rising expectations about what individuals should be able to have, to do, and to be. When these rising expectations cannot be met, and people do not or cannot turn to larger institutions for support, feelings of helplessness ensue. The risks for, and incidences of, depression increase.

Consider, for example, that many people expect to experience personal fulfillment in their vocations. As Seligman stated: "Work now needs to be ecologically innocent, comforting to our dignity, a call to growth and excitement, a meaningful contribution to society—and deliver a large paycheck" (1988b, p. 52). But can this expectation really be possible for the majority of workers? Surely there are millions of jobs in any complex society that cannot be described as life fulfilling. Thus, as Seligman predicted, if people expect such fulfillment, they are at increased risk for depression. Finally, Seligman observed that previous generations had no such expectations about the relationship between personal fulfillment and work. For them, work was work. The effect of this change on expectations is clear: "[It was] as if some idiot raised the ante on what it takes to be a normal human being" (1988b, p. 52).

The notion of increasing—and possibly unrealistic—expectations may also explain why so many American students, like Mark, feel unhappy, frustrated—both at home and in school—and in general suspect that they are being treated unfairly. As probable behavioral indicators of these feelings it is germane to consider the increasing levels of depression, suicide, illegitimacy, school violence and criminal behavior since the 1950s (see Damon, 1995, chap. 1).

A particularly important corollary to the idea of increasing and unrealistic expectations is that some events elicit distressful reactions in individuals today that would not necessarily have done so in the recent past. Specifically, is it possible that some current responses to problematic educational conditions and social changes have engendered rising expectations and, ironically, led many students to feel less free as they negotiate the inevitable and unavoidable hassles in life? It is a central thesis of this chapter that well-intentioned responses to yesterday's societal ills in general and educational ills in particular (e.g., injustice, regimentation, lack of communication, restriction of students' personal freedoms, and irrelevant content) have actually contributed to an increase in distressful and dysfunctional behaviors on the part of today's students.

To pursue that thesis, the following sections examine the relationships among children's expectations, violations of those expectations, and their perceptions of and reactions to home and school.

COGNITIVE MEDIATION AND OUR EMOTIONS

What causes us to be depressed, anxious, or angry? Or, in the specific vignette presented earlier, what causes Mark to get upset? Generally, most people point to rather obvious external stimuli as likely culprits. The road rager views the cause of his rage to be the motorist who just cut him off. The test-anxious student points to the actual test as the source of her anxiety. Perhaps Mark blames the teacher because he cannot do an assignment the way he wants to do it. However, research in cognitive psychology over several decades suggests that it is cognitive representations of events, and not the events themselves, that induce states of unhappiness. Psychologists and counselors are certainly well aware of this, as indicated by the proliferation of cognitively based therapies that were introduced in the 1970s (e.g., Beck, 1976; D'Zurilla & Goldfried, 1971; Ellis & Harper, 1975; Mahoney, 1974; Meichenbaum, 1977). The theoretical perspective supporting cognitive approaches revolves around the central position of *mediation*, as described by Stone:

> [T]he mediational model...suggests that there is quite a lot of action going on between input and output. The person does not have direct access to a real world of tables, chairs, and people. The only knowledge available about reality is mediated information. That is, individuals respond to the world in terms of their symbolization of it. Thus the stimulus world is more or less transformed in its contact with sense organs and the more complex systems of information processing. Such transformations occur through the person actively contributing to the production of his or her

experiential world by "actively" seeing, hearing, imaging, thinking, and remembering. And it is information, the basic unit of learning in a cognitive-behavioral perspective, that is attended to, transformed, stored, and retrieved. (1980, p. 5)

An essential aspect of mediation is that an individual's cognitive representations of events are based on *schemas*—that is, existing knowledge structures in long-term memory—which are relevant in some ways to the external event. These schemas can be very elaborate and all encompassing, affecting the individual's overall view. But the content of schemas can also be quite situation specific, giving rise to beliefs and expectations about the way things are or *should be* with respect to specific events and experiences. Individuals classify situations based on these schemas and then follow scripts (i.e., rule-governed behavior or productions) associated with these schemas (see Lazarus, 1982; Meichenbaum, 1977, chap. 1.) The development, organization, integration, and activation of these schemas has been represented in information-processing models of human cognition and memory (see, for example, Gagné, 1985, p. 71; Mayer, 1987, p. 10).

From an information-processing perspective, integrated cognitive structures in long-term memory encompass related values, idiosyncratic interpretations, productions (possible actions to take), and—notably—expectations. The expectations can be quite specific; for example, prior experiences with proofs influence a student's expectation for success on a geometry assignment. Additionally, more general and deeper-level expectations of a global nature, similar to what has been called *tacit knowledge* (Emery & Tracy, 1987; Polanyi, 1966), can affect how a student reacts to a variety of situations. For example, a student's beliefs about his or her inadequacy can affect how the student feels about participating on school sports teams, in social gatherings (e.g., the Homecoming dance) and—importantly—in academic endeavors. Attribution theory (Weiner, 1985) provides explanations regarding how, depending on attributions, individual's expectations can be both specific and more general and how they affect subsequent emotions and behavior.

In the situations described, both specific expectations and more global beliefs regarding self-worth are present. The more global beliefs often remain nonverbalized; indeed, they usually escape conscious awareness (Ellis & Bernard, 1985). Nevertheless, such beliefs (e.g., "I'm just not as smart as most people") also affect expectations. It is these latter expectations that are potentially the most troublesome because they are so pervasive, tacit, and difficult to identify.

According to basic information-processing models, information activated in long-term memory is then available in short-term memory (or its functional equivalent, working memory) where more conscious deliberations are carried out (Gagné, 1985; Mayer, 1987). At this point, a person's thoughts about an interpreted event can range from a shortcut recognition (e.g., "Oh no! It's going to be a multiple-choice test!"), to self-instructions regarding likely responses, some of which may be quite maladaptive (e.g., "I'll probably freak when I see the first question and after that I won't recognize anything"). Affective, behavioral, even physiological responses then follow, which complete a cycle. The key is that these responses are based not on an unarguably objective reality but on an interpreted and constructed reality in which the cognitive structures in long-term memory play a significant role. Individuals are generally aware of their behavioral and emotional responses but are often unaware of the cognitive interpretation processes preceding them (Meichenbaum & Cameron, 1983). This phenomenon is particularly important because the individual's interpretative processes set up expectations that can—cruelly—be violated by reality.

RISING EXPECTATIONS—HOW AND WHY

If it is the case that external events have less to do with causing emotional distress than our interpretation of these events, then it would be helpful to have some insight as to how and why these interpretations have come about. More specifically, if our interpretation/construction of events is a function of preexisting schemas, how might we characterize the content of these cognitive structures so as to better understand how they may induce different expectations today than would have been the case years ago? In this regard I will discuss two clusters or patterns of rising expectations.

Rising Expectations I—Some Degree of Change and Improvement or the Possibility of Escape from Perceived Difficulties

> We used to think that revolutions are the cause of change. Actually it is the other way around: change prepares the ground for revolution (Eric Hoffer, *The Temper of Our Times*, 1967, p. 8)

It is ironic but apparently true that we get more upset and frustrated after events start going in our direction and not before. Several authors have expressed this phenomenon very well. For example, in commenting about the decade of the 1960s, Glazer (1988, p. 4) saw, among other things, a revolution of rising expectations. An unfortunate consequence was that "rising expectations continually enlarge the sea of felt and perceived misery, whatever happens to it in actuality" (1988, p. 4). Sykes (1992), in describing the relationship between unfulfilled expectations and social policy, offered a possible explanation:

> Before the twentieth century, people had more or less accepted the vagaries of fate. Sudden reverses could ruin farmers or businessmen; death, disease, and accident were familiar presences. Faith cushioned many of the shocks, but it could do nothing to eliminate them. But with the decline of religion and the rise of technology and

science, society began to lose its belief in both the inevitability of suffering and the need for stoicism in the face of adversity. (p. 125)

Almost 30 years ago, Silberman, in commenting about the American social turmoil of the 1960s, found historical support for this tendency of rising expectations in the writings of de Tocqueville. He quoted de Tocqueville from *Democracy in America*, written in 1837:

The evil which was suffered patiently as inevitable seems unendurable as soon as the idea of escaping from it crosses men's minds. . . . All the abuses then removed call attention to those that remain, and they now appear more galling. The evil, it is true, has become less, but sensibility to it has become more acute. (Quoted in Silberman, 1970, p. 20)

Certainly we see evidence of anxiety, frustration, and even depression in the lives of many women today, who, even though they certainly have more choices than perhaps their mothers had, are probably not discernibly happier. The freedom to choose to work, go to school, be a wife, and be a mother certainly does not feel like freedom.

The idea that the possibility of escaping an unpleasant situation may make it more difficult to cope with that situation can be countered with another view—that believing you cannot do anything to escape an unpleasant situation may lead to learned helplessness (Seligman, 1975). Which position is correct? The latter may be easier to understand and less subtle than the former. The latter is also more acceptable as an explanation because of society's popularized notions of anxiety and depression. That is, if a particular situation or relationship causes a person anxiety then he or she should get out of that situation or relationship. Consider the following discussion of divorce where these two points of view are presented.

Divorce rates are higher today than they were 40 years ago. If divorce is not out of the question then other alternatives look more attractive or at least feasible: Others, including friends, have done it and they ended up okay (modeling); their religious community did not condemn them and still welcomes them in church; their parents, although certainly unhappy about the divorce, did not disown them. There is more freedom to explore other alternatives and relationships. Under these conditions individuals are likely to consider as at least possible that a divorce could solve the problem. This might include imagining what life would be like in the future when the stress of the present relationship is no longer. It is at least reasonable to conjecture that some individuals in this situation experience more frustration, discomfort, anxiety, or depression in what is presently an unhappy marriage precisely because they can consider other options—with less sanction than previously—and begin wondering if their lives would be better if they chose separation or divorce.

What would be the case if divorce were not an option and, for example, there were strict religious sanctions against divorce and strong societal disapproval? It could be argued that without divorce as an alternative people would not be as unhappy. This may take some convincing, because so many people can think of men or women, perhaps themselves, who are in unpleasant marriages and feel trapped. They would view the situation from their perspective and conclude that in such strict religious environments people would have lived lives of quiet desperation. It is tempting to believe this view. However, it is apparently not the case that 40 or 50 years ago millions of men and women were depressed because they saw no alternative but to stay in unhappy marriages. If this were the case, rates of depression would have been relatively higher in those decades; however, to the contrary, rates of depression are much higher today than they were 40 or 50 years ago (see, e.g., Goleman, 1995, chap. 15; Seligman, 1988a).

If divorce is not an option it is possible that some people can cut their losses, so to speak, and get on with their lives. If so they might not be dwelling as much on their perceived plight. The present-day caricature of a married couple in the 1940s quietly going about their lives being unhappy most of the time and surrendering their wants and desires and the very essence of their individual selves to keep a marriage together may not have been that common at all.

Instead of feeling trapped and incapable of doing anything that will make a difference in life, a couple's commitment to the marriage may have enabled them to proceed in other directions of relatively better mental health. First of all, adhering to what they considered to be important religious beliefs may have helped them to deal with more earthly difficulties. Religious beliefs apparently can serve as a buffer against suffering and setbacks (Seligman, 1988a). For example, in Catholic theology, "offering it up to the poor souls in purgatory" was a way to find value in personal suffering. Second, they may have felt a degree of fulfillment in raising their children and a degree of contentment in adhering to what was believed to be a primary responsibility of married life. Third, if not overwhelmed with negative thoughts about the desperate state of their existence, they may have been more open to experience whatever pleasant aspects of life may have come their way, and some of these may have involved each other.

The major points in this example are (1) it is consistent with mediation theory in cognitive therapies, which asserts that it is primarily our thoughts that make us unhappy; (2) it indicates how the possibility of escape from perceived unpleasantness, even if somewhat remote, may incidentally increase unhappiness in the present situation; and (3) if escape from a perceived difficult situation is not an option and instead the individual commits to the present situation, the frequency of thoughts contributing to unhappiness may decrease.

Can this first pattern of rising expectations, introduced previously in the context of marriage, be extended to school environments? That is, are there situations where students believe that they may, or should, be able to escape a perceived unpleasant situation and that subsequent lack of commitment on their part to the present situation will result in increasing frequency of troublesome thoughts leading to anger, frustration, impatience, and so on?

As an example consider Pam, a student in a sixth-grade gifted education program. It is a matter of choice—Pam did not have to be in this program—but both she and her parents were pleased that she qualified. In class, the teacher challenged students with comprehensive projects that involved considerable reading and writing. This was more work than Pam's friends did in their "regular" classes. Pam complained to her parents and they told her to see how it goes for awhile, with the implication that if things did not go well she would be permitted to leave the gifted program. The teacher encouraged the parents to have Pam commit to the program for the entire school year. The parents were reluctant to do this because they recgonized that the program was voluntary and that their daughter was demonstrating what appeared to be bona fide signs of unhappiness and distress. Pam remained in the program for three more weeks. During that time she complained every day and grudgingly did some work of rather low quality. The content of her complaints was familiar, with comments such as "I wish I wasn't in this program" and "It's not fair that I have to do all this extra work when my friends don't have to."

But how might Pam have reacted if there had been no option of leaving the program or that she would have to be in the program for at least a year? Would she have felt trapped? Would it have been a miserable experience? Or would the commitment for a specified period of time have freed her of these stress-engendering cognitions and at least provided her opportunities for developing more adaptive responses? In Pam's case we will never know the answers—nor will her parents and teachers. However, it is important that parents, educators, and educational policy makers at least be aware of this phenomenon. Why? Because numerous educational innovations share the same characteristic of offering the possibility of escaping a perceived uncomfortable situation when previously this was not the case. Consequently, it is reasonable to be concerned that these changes in educational policy and practice might also share the same consequence of engendering self-defeating cognitions.

Rising Expectations II—Proliferation of Short-Term Reinforcers and the Promotion of Individualism: The TV Remote—Bane or Boon?

What do the following have in common? VCRs, the Internet, cable TV, fast-food restaurants, ATMs, and the TV remote? With apologies for stating the obvious, these items (1) are relatively recent innovations, (2) are ubiquitous in our society, (3) depend on advances in technology to a considerable extent, (4) are widely enjoyed by people, and (5) provide high-powered short-term reinforcement. And, with the possible exception of fast-food restaurants, what's not to like about these innovations? Well, one characteristic of these innovations is that they carry with them the risk of promoting individualism and retarding the development of delayed gratification.

To illustrate this principle, I will refer to an undergraduate educational psychology course that I teach in which I have used the TV remote in discussions of reinforcement. The discussion was always meant to be lighthearted and it involved a behavior with which all students could identify. Although my discussions have remained lighthearted, I have become convinced that there are serious issues both with the specific use of the TV remote and what it symbolically represents.

First of all, the use of the remote is highly reinforcing to the one who uses it, and the reinforcement is quite immediate. To be more accurate, this would qualify as negative reinforcement as the purpose of pressing the button on the remote is usually to get rid of a commercial or a TV show, which at that moment is less than desirable. The immediacy of the reinforcement is very powerful and the use of the remote, over time, resembles an addiction. Just as smokers need to smoke, otherwise they do not feel well, expert TV remote users need to use it or else they are often frustrated and, indeed, unhappy.

If you settle in for an evening of "must see TV" and the remote does not work, what do you do? Many of my students report being miserable if their remote does not work. Some do not know how to change the channel without it. They also listen in fascination when I tell them about the old days when I had to get out of my chair, walk across the room, and change the channel. It sounds downright primitive. The unhappiness that people experience when the TV remote does not work or is lost is an interesting example, even somewhat humorous, of a situation that causes distress today that would not have been the case years ago.

Other possible problems with the use of the remote are that it may (1) contribute to short attention span, (2) promote selfish behavior, and (3) prevent the development of delayed gratification attributes. This may seem to be quite a condemnation, or the cranky ramblings of an anachronistic Luddite. Rest assured: I am not advocating banning the remote, closing down Blockbuster videotape stores, or returning to the "better days" of vacuum tubes and transistor radios. However, it is important to realize the downside to innovations: As much as we may like them, in the long run, they seldom make us happier. Instead, rising expectations following the introduction and wide availability of innovations may actually set us up to be more unhappy.

The possibility that innovations can affect schools, families, and society in negative ways is not remote; the phenomenon is beginning to attract increased attention on the part of educational and psychological researchers. For example, Seligman (1988a) has discussed similar, recent cultural developments that have had a dramatic influence on what he refers to as

individualism. These developments include the increasing benefits of technological advances and the increasing isolationism resulting from waning at-
tachment to traditional social institutions.

First, technological advances have enabled large scale cutomization to
suit individual tastes and increased individual purchasing power. Second, a
decline in the importance of, and our reliance on, "communities" such as
religion, the family, and the nation have produced increased alienation. As a
result, individuals can get more and have more, but they are at the same
time forced to rely more and more on themselves for reconciling doubt,
failure, misfortune, or unhappiness.

In rather strong arguments, Damon (1995) discussed similar dual themes
of self-centeredness and loss of spirituality:

> The elevation of self and the loss of spirituality are not in themselves responsible for
> all the misconceptions about childhood that prevail in contemporary society, but they
> have created a cultural context where the misconceptions have flourished. They have
> established a receptivity to ideas that once would have been ridiculed or dismissed
> out of hand. They have desensitized us to the inane nature of some currently fashion-
> able childrearing practices. Moreover, these misconceptions about children have con-
> tributed to their own perpetuation; for the consequences of the misconceptions have
> been precisely to promote self-centeredness and a spiritual void in the generations
> of youth who have been raised in their wake. (p. 68)

In his popular book, *Emotional Intelligence*, Goleman (1995) is clear about
his concern for individualism and the inability to tolerate *delayed gratification*.
He has equated the ability to delay gratification with impulse control—"the
eternal battle between impulse and restraint, id and ego, desire and self-
control, gratification and delay" (p. 81). With a combination of compelling
argument and scholarly research, Goleman credited delayed gratification as
enabling people to be effective in relationships, in school, and on the job
and to go beyond competence to expertise. According to Goleman, "There
is perhaps no psychological skill more fundamental than resisting impulse"
(p. 81).

Mischel and colleagues' research on delayed gratification is particularly
noteworthy. It is their contention that delayed gratification may be a crucial
ingredient of "intelligent social behavior" that includes social and intellectual knowledge and problem-solving competencies (Mischel, Shoda, &
Peake, 1988; Shoda, Mischel, & Peake, 1990). In a series of studies covering
more than 10 years, they compared the delayed gratification ability of 4-year-
olds with aspects of their cognitive and self-regulation competence years
later when they were adolescents. For the delayed gratification task, the
children were given a choice. They could have one marshmallow now or two
marshmallows later if they could wait till the experimenter got back. The
primary dependent variable was delay time—that is, how long could they
wait until signaling for the experimenter to come back. The signal essentially
meant that they would opt for the one marshmallow now. Children who

waited until the experimenter got back without signaling (15 minutes) could have the two marshmallows.

Over a decade later, delay time was compared to SAT scores and the results of questionnaires in which parents assessed their child's self-regulation and coping competencies. Children who were able to delay gratification at the age of 4 were judged to be more socially competent, assertive, reliable, and dependable as adolescents. Those who were not able to delay were judged to be relatively shy, stubborn, and easily upset by frustrations. In addition, those who were able to delay had significantly higher SAT scores than those who were more impulsive (the reader is encouraged to read these studies, as there were several different conditions in the initial studies and follow-up data covered as much as 5 years). Goleman's discussion of these studies, within the context of his views on emotional intelligence (1995, chap. 6), lends dramatic support for the importance of the ability to delay gratification. The implications of these studies are striking. As early as 4 years of age, a child's ability to defer gratification predicts a wide variety of self-regulation and cognitive abilities at adolescence. It would appear that families and primary-grade educators should be extra sensitive to those factors in the environment that contribute to the development of what Goleman has referred to as the "master aptitude" (1995, chap. 6) and also those factors that would retard or prevent its development.

INNOVATION AND CHANGE: IMPACT ON CHILDREN

With the apparent importance of delayed gratification, some changes affecting children deserve closer inspection. In that regard, several examples of changes in the home and school are presented in the following paragraphs. Although further research is required before suggesting broad policy shifts, it is likely that policies designed to address these changes would be beneficial across economic, racial, and gender lines. Indeed, as Damon (1995) has argued, these changes may have even greater impact on the most disadvantaged communities.

As noted earlier, many of the changes affecting school-aged children have resulted in greater freedoms than children experienced in previous generations. It is probably the case that children in the 1990s have more input and make more decisions than children did 30 or 40 years ago regarding such things as what to eat, where to live, what to wear, what to watch on TV, what to listen to, when to do homework, how to do homework, what time to go to bed, where to go on vacation, and so on. Children today are also more likely to have their own bedroom and to choose what it will look like. Children are more likely to have discretionary money and to have more of it.

Many children have their own TVs, telephones, CD players, and computers. In general, it is more likely that children growing up today can see what they want on TV when they want to see it and hear what they want to hear when they want to hear it. The buying power of children and adolescents has certainly increased, as evidenced by the increases in advertising budgets and campaigns targeting children. Possessions that children believe to be essential today in the past were considered to be luxuries.

Again there is nothing inherently wrong with these changes and innovations. However, their potential power to retard the development of delayed gratification is quite evident. Notice also that getting used to these often short-term reinforcers develops expectations that would make dealing with their absence very difficult. This further exacerbates the developmental tendency for children's expectations to be quite egocentric, a tendency that persists at all stages of cognitive development, even through early formal operations (Elkind, 1970).

Cognitively oriented practitioners also find this to be the case. For example, Ellis and Bernard (1985) reported on a multitude of irrational beliefs and expectations that influence the development of depression and anxiety. However, they reduced these to three basic beliefs: (1) I must do extremely well and win approval, or else I am a rotten person; (2) others must treat me considerately, kindly, and in precisely the way I want them to treat me; if they don't, society and the universe should blame, condemn, and punish them for their inconsiderateness; and (3) the conditions under which I live must be arranged so that I get practically all that I want comfortably, quickly, and easily and get virtually nothing that I don't want. The dramatic, egocentric nature of these beliefs is obvious.

Although psychologists have recognized these changes and documented their effects on, for example, personality and adjustment, parents, educators, and educational policy makers have been comparatively slower to recognize their meaning and ramifications for schooling. Whereas the impact of these changes in the lives of children is easily understood, the impact of changes on schools may be more subtle. Despite a wealth of literature supporting many educational innovations, there has been comparatively little examination of the potential they have to bring about unanticipated negative consequences. To be fair, because we are dealing with the ill-structured knowledge domain of human behavior, we cannot expect these innovations to be immediately successful. However, given the conditions in society as a whole that may contribute to expectations of immediate gratification and retard the development of delayed gratification, we ought to be particularly sensitive to educational conditions and innovations that do the same. Table I presents a necessarily partial list of innovations that come to mind as potentially yielding negative consequences along with the good. The list is presented with some trepidation because of the passion it may elicit. It is important to clarify that there is nothing inherently wrong with these innovations; the essential objective is merely to recognize that beneficial changes can have unforeseen consequences.

TABLE I
Innovations and Changes in Schools That May Have
Unforeseen Negative Consequences for Children

Changes in Educational Theory and Practice
More comfortable school environments
Mastery learning
Group projects
Relaxed dress codes
Increasing student choices
Student-centered teaching
Developmentally appropriate practice
Constructivist teaching
Culturally sensitive practices
Emphasis on students' self-esteem
Incorporation of handheld calculators
Parents who question what teachers do

Student and Parent Awareness of a Variety of Controversies
Anxiety
Relevance
New teaching methods
Disciplinary methods
Multiple intelligences
Learning styles
Promotion/retention
School reform efforts

Although this is quite a list, only a few of the items will be highlighted here. The philosophy, theory, and research forming the foundation for these innovations, such as student-centered teaching, developmentally appropriate practice, and constructivist teaching, go back some time. The authors are formidable indeed, including John Dewey, Jean Piaget, and Lev Vygotsky. Putting their ideas into practice—or putting any theoretical ideas into practice—has never been straightforward.

Damon made a strong case that some applications of child-centered ideas have led to promoting self-centeredness in children (1995, chap. 5). Part of this is due to the needless, but all too common, polarity between child-centered and adult-centered practices. In schools these poles are student-centered and teacher-centered teaching practices. Damon's concern is not with the original authors whose work ostensibly supports these innovations (e.g., Piaget)," but of the ways in which they [notions] have been misapplied by our media, by many institutions, by some professional experts, and by most of our childrearing gurus" (p. 21).

Such polarization of viewpoints is not new. The debates between behaviorism and humanism (see e.g., Rogers & Skinner, 1956) dealt with similar views. On the one hand is the belief that the lives of children should be structured and consequences should be provided to increase the likelihood that particular behaviors will occur more often and other behaviors less often. The opposing view is that we provide a nurturing climate in which children proceed at their own pace, pursue their own intersts, and learn from their own actions. It is the latter view that, in Damon's view, has led to children being more self-centered.

It may be worthwhile to return for a moment to the young student, Mark, who found it difficult to do assignments the way his teacher wanted him to do them. He would rather do them his own way. At the risk of polarization, I would add that Mark's parents were following what they believed to be child-centered advice—that is, they would refrain whenever possible from imposing their view on what Mark should do and how he should do it. The teacher, who may have implemented various student-centered ideas in other contexts, nonetheless wanted students to obediently follow directions for other assignments. Hence the conflict. If the teacher had been completely consistent, the assignments in question would also have been more student centered and Mark may have had more choices in carrying them out. He may not have been upset and, at least for the present, there would not have been a confrontation.

However, sooner or later, Mark will not be able to have things his own way, whether it be in school, at play, or at home. The real world does not bend to our wishes. If educators do not provide an environment where children can learn this, their expectations will surely be violated and they will be unhappy.

Ironically, school environments based originally on sound ideas may be contributing to expectation violations as surely as the more obvious influences of rampant consumerism. It is these conditions that may contribute to a substantial increase in potential for personal agency in the child's environment—so much so that children are more likely to believe that they should have control over these issues. This is a key issue, of course. Just how much control should children have over what courses they will take, what projects they will complete, the format for these assignments, when they should be done, and so forth? Educational researchers have not yet provided good answers to these questions. But if early in their school careers children are led to believe that they should have control over these and related factors, it is reasonable to hypothesize that when events do not conform to these new expectations, anger, frustration, anxiety, depression, and other varieties of inappropriate behavior are more likely to occur.

The psychological theories supporting many of the innovations shown in Table 1 are well established. In the long run, they may lead to positive results. However, at least in the immediate future, these changes may instead (1) create expectations of self-agency that cannot be met, (2) lead to frustration at a level that was only reached in the past as a result of comparatively more serious events, and (3) delay or prevent the development of a more decentered (i.e., less egocentric) outlook toward one's environment and others in the environment.

THE QUEST FOR RELEVANCE AND RISING EXPECTATIONS

Expectation violations can also result from what most educational researchers would consider to be important characteristics for educators to possess. Consider, for example, the well-intentioned advice of encouraging relevance in textbooks, assignments, activities, and classroom instruction.

The plea for relevance in schools has been invoked over the centuries as critical to the reform of education (Dewey, 1920, 1938; Rogers, 1969; Rousseau, 1762/1979). The plea is very strong today and can be found, for example, in virtually every educational psychology textbook used in teacher-preparation courses at colleges around the country. Not surprisingly, relevance issues are found in these texts in discussions of student-centered instruction and constructivism (see e.g., Eggen & Kauchak, 1997, chap. 11; Woolfolk, 1998, chap. 13). Generally speaking, learning materials and experiences are considered relevant if students (1) like them, (2) feel that they contribute in some fashion to their present life, or (3) feel that they will contribute in some fashion to their future life. Although there is a certain degree of relevance if students realize that they need to know material for a test, this is not considered to be appropriate relevance because it may lead to a performance (only for the test) orientation as opposed to a mastery (to learn it) orientation (Ames & Archer, 1988).

Among educators, questioning the essential role of relevance is like objecting to motherhood or the flag. However, cavalier application of the goal of relevance may cause more harm than good. One critical problem is that adults have consistently viewed the issue from a contemporary perspective. Such a view involves reflecting on the knowledge hypothesized to be appropriate and needed in the current everyday life of adulthood in comparison with what had to be learned in school. When we, as adults, do not see a match, it is easy to conclude that "because I do not use this knowledge now, I did not need to learn it." Such conclusions have often been reached regarding foreign languages (e.g., "Everyone speaks English, so why should I take Spanish"), history ("Why do I need to know who discovered the St. Lawrence river?"), and geography ("Who cares about the average rainfall in Paducah, Kentucky?"), for example. This has been an enduring concern of all educators. How can knowledge be taught that will be relevant tomorrow in ways that are compelling today?

Unfortunately, the very quest for relevance can be problematic. First of all, it is possible that adults are often mistaken regarding the usefulness of what they have learned. Research in cognitive psychology (e.g., Bransford, 1979; Glaser, 1984; Chi & Bassok, 1989; Alexander, 1996) has pointed out the value of a rich, highly developed, knowledge base and how that knowledge base enables individuals to make sense of their experiences. Because we do not find a need to talk explicitly about the Spanish explorers today does not mean that those related cognitive structures have forever remained dormant and unused. At the very least, this knowledge has provided a perspective within which we have viewed history and current events of all kinds over many years.

There may be an even more insidious problem regarding this quest for relevance. That is, we may be giving students the unintended message that what they perceive to be irrelevant may not be worth putting in the effort required to learn. It is unrealistic to suppose that students do not pick up on the educational—indeed, societal—affinity for relevance. They hear it from their parents. They hear it from their peers. Most importantly for educators, they almost certainly perceive pervasive emphasis on relevance in their classrooms.

Just how far is the cognitive distance for students from a societal plea for relevance to students' expectations that they should be able to see relevance in everything they study in school? It may be very short indeed. Critically, the real issue here is not that students fail to see relevance in what they are supposed to learn; it is the possibility that this realization constitutes a violated expectation that they *should* see relevance.

Of consequence for educators and policy makers is the fact that these violated expectations influence educational achievement. Along these lines, it is useful to consider some of the possible choices of action for students who believe that what is being taught has no relevance for them. First, it is possible that some students may strive to attain meaning on their own. They may ask the teacher, ask parents, or perhaps engage in personal quests to find some meaning. Unfortunately, many students will simply feel justified in not putting in the effort required to do well. "Blowing it off" is how this is often expressed.

Under conditions not involving expectancy violations, it is a difficult enough task for teachers to encourage students to put in the required effort. With the student-held perspective of expected relevance, the teacher's task is even more daunting and students will likely feel entirely justified in avoiding difficult tasks. De facto "blowing it off" precludes *ever* finding future relevance, thereby reinforcing the students' point of view. Still another possibility is that some students persist and do put in some effort to learn, but resent the need to do so for something deemed irrelevant. This resentment may take other forms; for example, less patience, less persistence, more frustration, and increased resistance to education. Again, unhappiness from a violated expectation.

It is essential to note that providing relevant instruction and helping students see relevance in what they are learning is critical. Teachers at all levels should be so motivated. But the question is, how do educators help students see this relevance? In some content areas the answer may come fairly easy. For example, the relevance of requiring skill in using a calculator to do the basic arithmetic involved in balancing a checkbook seems straightforward. The practical usefulness of imaginary numbers is another story.

To their credit, some teachers are highly skilled at showing relevance for even the most abstruse content. However, not all teachers are able to do this to the same degree. More important, in our quest to ensure relevance we may fail to take into consideration that students' failure to see relevance is related to their ability to understand instruction. Ironically, the very inability to understand instruction can be interpreted by students as bad or irrelevant instruction, especially if social environments exist in which these ideas are reinforced. Have we inadvertently created circumstances that make it easy—and more likely—for students (and perhaps parents) to blame academic difficulties on any number of innocents? If so, this circumstance may be one of the most damaging conditions extant in schools today, far outweighing the negative effects of putatively irrelevant content.

DISCUSSION AND RECOMMENDATIONS

As this chapter has indicated, and consistent with information processing and recent cognitive therapies, it is our thoughts about events rather than the events themselves that make us unhappy. This chapter presented two clusters or patterns of rising expectations: those resulting from some degree of improvement or escape from perceived difficulties and those resulting from the proliferation of short-term reinforcers. This chapter also examined specific changes and innovations in society that in particular retard the development of delayed gratification. Finally, this chapter elaborated on the specific case of relevance.

With regard to the latter, should educators try to help students see relevance in what they teach? Absolutely! Much of the current educational literature focuses on ideas associated with relevance. Relevance is certainly a major focus of situated cognition (Brown, Collins, & Duguid, 1989), constructivism (Cobb, 1994), authentic assessment (Ferrara & McTighe, 1992), and what Damon (1995) referred to as project learning. Also relevant here is Schön's work on the reflective practitioner (1987). Although Schön's work deals primarily with adult learners in professional practice environments, his emphasis on learning in actual practice situations, as opposed to the technical rationality of school learning, speaks directly to relevance. I find the work of these authors to be both challenging and compelling, and look forward to a time when educators will be much more effective in providing learning situations that are both relevant *and* intellectually demanding, while also economically and logistically feasible.

In the meantime, should teacher educators encourage future teachers to make their instruction relevant? I think so. Should experienced teachers encourage novice teachers to include activities that will add to the relevance of their teaching? Of course. Should teaching be deemed inadequate if students do not see relevance in what is being taught? I say no. Should failure to see relevance in what is being taught be sufficient justification for an insufficient effort to learn? Absolutely not!

Because pervasive societal changes are at the heart of many of these educational dilemmas, what can parents, teachers, theoreticians, and educational policy makers do to reduce the impact of expectation violations? Many strategies have been recommended for addressing academic and behavioral problems. For example, going back a few decades, the reinforcement of acceptable behaviors (Madsen & Madsen, 1974), the practice of empathy and unconditional positive regard (Rogers, 1969), and reference to logical consequences of behavior (Dreikurs, 1968) are familiar and viable options. More recent theoretical and empirical work, such as promoting developmentally appropriate practice (Bowman, 1993), targeting students' zones of proximal development (Brown & Palinscar, 1989), and developing authentic, integrated assessments (Ferrara & McTighe, 1992), seem promising.

I mention only a few of the well-known possibilities for intervention to promote learning and adjustment; all of the models and theories from which they derive have exhibited varying degrees of practical promise. Unfortunately, the incidence of educational problems resulting from strategies intended to ameliorate educational problems such as those described in this chapter persist despite—indeed, often as a result of—application of those strategies.

Psychologists, educational researchers, and other social scientists have a special responsibility for addressing the problem of expectation violations; it is often the implementation of their theories and principles that contributes to educational problems. Whether one's educational philosophy is aligned with the tenets of behaviorism, humanism, developmentalism, multiculturalism, constructivism, or postmodernism (to name a few) is—to some extent—irrelevant. A critical point for those interested in crafting beneficial educational policies derived from any of these perspectives is this: The translation of these theoretical and philosophical views into educational practice will always be fraught with unforeseen difficulties and results. As with regard to the press for relevance, the difficulties that result may contribute to conditions that, at least temporarily, are potentially more troublesome than those that motivated the "solutions."

The general problem may go beyond expectancy violations to all research/theory-based policies and practices. For example, in the past some educators carried out activities that would be considered by present standards to be developmentally appropriate, although these educators lacked a theory to guide their efforts. Now—with theory—when educators deliberately set out to design instruction that is developmentally appropriate, we face the coincident possibility of unintentionally lowering standards and achievement expectations for some students as well (see Damon, 1995, chap. 5).

As another example, previous generations of educators may have worked to establish environments in which students received reinforcement for behaviors that would presently be termed "on task," although they may not have been engaging in a conscious, explicit attempt to do so. Now, however, armed with psychological principles, empirical research, and a theoretical perspective to view behavior, we do not find it easier to manage classroom learning and indeed we find that rewards can under certain circumstances diminish intrinsic motivation for achievement and self-regulation (e.g., see Lepper, Keavney & Drake, 1996).

Educational policy makers specifically and social scientists generally must begin to approach theoretical innovations with this fact in mind: Even admirable, well-grounded, consensually benevolent programs have unforeseen, erratic, often negative consequences when applied in classrooms. Any innovations will affect the expectations of those involved, not just teachers and parents but also students. In our quest for a better world in which individuals will not be oppressed, and in which they will be free to develop their potential, might it not be beneficial for us to assume a more modest posture—one that avoids ephemeral, ethereal postulates that promise more than they can deliver?

Beyond this, when we see troublesome conditions in the home or in schools, we should not affix blame on an anonymous "them," on an ostensibly outdated paradigm, or on some other "ism." Rather, it may be fruitful to begin looking at how we may have contributed to the very conditions we view as in need of correction.

As Slavin (1989) has demonstrated, the practical applications of our research seldom, if ever, match the convictions and expectations of the researchers and theorists who formulate them. Whatever successes can be documented are often equaled by unforeseen consequences of the innovations we suggest. Certainly the successes are not rivaled by the impact of rather substantial sociological and cultural changes that take place regardless of the quality of a well-supported reason for the innovation. All those concerned about education in American can profit from these observations.

Parents are in particularly difficult situations today. They hear about psychological and educational issues on a daily basis. Years ago parents knew relatively little of these issues. Now there are innumerable TV talk shows, magazines, and pop psychology books wherein important topics are scrutinized ranging from intelligent presentation and discussion to shameful hucksterism. However, parents should remember some basic ideas. First, human behavior is unpredictable and any psychologically based innovations will necessarily be imperfect. Second, however good some innovations may sound, they should not prevent the development of delayed gratification. Third, angry, anxious, and frustrating reactions to schoolwork do not necessarily indicate that there is anything wrong with the schoolwork.

Similar recommendations would be helpful for *teachers* also. However, teachers are professionals. Knowledge of development, learning, and teaching is the sine qua non of their profession. They cannot settle for pop psychology. They should not settle for an exciting workshop. They need to check the research literature for themselves. What innovations are supported by research? What can they do to determine the impact of innovations in their own classrooms? Teachers should not wait until innovations are thrust on them. Instead, they should actively enlist the aide of educational researchers and professional teacher educators and take advantage of the recent encouragement of collaborative and action research (e.g., see Noffke, 1997).

Educational researchers and teachers need to be more knowledgeable about prior movements, writings, and research that underlie innovations. Apparently, lack of knowledge contributes to superficial implementation of potentially important innovations (Alexander, Murphy, and Woods, 1996). In addition, educational researchers should ask, "What might be the unintended consequences of our ideas for children, classroom teachers, and parents? What unintended meaning might students, teachers, and parents construe from our research and development efforts?" In essence these become research questions worthy of investigation.

Finally, *educational policy makers* would do well to adapt a cautious stance. For example, in constructing homes, bridges, commercial buildings, and other structures, it is common for an environmental impact study to be conducted to ascertain the likely unforeseen results that will accrue from the ostensibly noble goals of providing for improved transportation, commerce, or housing. Prior to reconstructing or reforming educational systems, it might be wise to precede innovations with an educational environment impact study that examines the intended, unintended, and ecological effects of our proposals.

References

Alexander, P. A. (1996). The past, present, and future of knowledge research: A reexamination of the role of knowledge in learning and instruction. *Educational Psychologist* 31, 89–92.

Alexander, P. A., Murphy, P. K., & Woods, B. S. (1996). Of squalls and fathoms: Navigating the seas of educational innovation. *Educational Researcher*, 25(3), 31–39.

Ames, C., & Archer, J. (1988). Achievement goals in the classroom: Students' learning strategies and motivation processes. *Journal of Educational Psychology*, 80, 260–267.

Bandura, A. (1986). *Social foundations of thought and action: A social cognitive theory.* Englewood Cliffs, NJ: Prentice-Hall.

Beck, A. T. (1976). *Cognitive therapy and the emotional disorders.* New York: International Universities Press.

Bowman, B. (1993). Early childhood education. In L. Darling-Hammond (Ed.), *Review of research in education* (pp. 101–134). Washington, DC: American Educational Research Association.

Bransford, J. D. (1979). *Human cognition: Learning, understanding and remembering.* Belmont, CA: Wadsworth.

Brown, A. L., & Palinscar, A. S. (1989). Guided, cooperative learning and individual knowledge acquisition. In L. B. Resnick (Ed.), *Knowing, learning, and instruction* (pp. 393–451). Hillsdale, NJ: Erlbaum.

Brown, J. S., Collins, A., & Duguid, P. (1989). Situated cognition and the culture of learning. *Educational Researcher, 18*(1), 32–42.

Chi M. T. H., & Bassok, M. (1989). Learning from examples via self-explanations. In L. B. Resnick (Ed.), *Knowing, learning, and instruction* (pp. 251–282). Hillsdale, NJ: Erlbaum.

Cobb, P. (1994). Where is the mind? Constructivist and sociocultural perspectives on mathematical development. *Educational Researcher, 23*(7), 13–20.

Covington, M. V. (1992). *Making the grade: A self-worth perspective on motivation and school reform.* New York: Cambridge University Press.

Damon, W. (1995). *Greater expectations: Overcoming the culture of indulgence in America's homes and schools.* New York: The Free Press.

Dewey, J. (1920). *The child and the curriculum.* Chicago, IL: University of Chicago Press.

Dewey, J. (1938). *Logic: The theory of inquiry.* New York: Henry Holt.

Dreikurs, R. (1968). *Psychology in the classroom: A manual for teachers* (2nd ed.). New York: Harper & Row.

D'Zurilla, T. J., & Goldfried, M. R. (1971). *Journal of Abnormal Psychology, 78,* 107–126.

Eggen, P., & Kauchak, D. (1997). *Educational psychology: Windows on classrooms* (3rd ed.). Columbus, OH: Merrill.

Elkind, D. (1970). *Children and adolescents.* New York: Oxford.

Ellis, A., & Bernard, M. E. (1985). What is rational-emotive therapy? In A. Ellis & M. E. Bernard (Eds.), *Clinical applications of rational-emotive therapy* (pp. 1–30). New York: Plenum.

Ellis, A., & Harper, R. A. (1975). *A new guide to rational living.* Englewood Cliffs, NJ: Prentice-Hall.

Emery, G., & Tracy, N. L. (1987). Theoretical issues in the cognitive-behavioral treatment of anxiety disorders. In L. Michelson & L. M. Ascher (Eds.), *Anxiety and stress disorders: Cognitive-behavioral assessment and treatment* (pp. 3–38). New York: Guilford.

Ferrara, S., & McTighe, J. (1992). Assessment: A thoughtful process. In A. Costa, J. Bellanca, & R. Fogarty (Eds.), *If minds matter: A foreword to the future* (Vol. 2, pp. 337–347). Palatine, IL: Skylight.

Gagné, R. M. (1985). *The conditions of learning* (4th ed.). New York: Holt, Rinehart, & Winston.

Glaser, R. (1984). Education and thinking: The role of knowledge. *American Psychologist, 39,* 93–104.

Glazer, N. (1988). *The limits of social policy.* Cambridge, MA: Harvard University Press.

Goleman, D. (1995). *Emotional intelligence.* New York: Bantam.

Hoffer, E. (1967). *The temper of our times.* New York: Harper & Row.

Lazarus, R. S. (1982). Thoughts on the relations between emotion and cognition. *American Psychologist, 37,* 1019–1024.

Lepper, M. R., Keavney, M., & Drake, M. (1996). Intrinsic motivation and extrinsic rewards: A commentary on Cameron and Pierce's meta-analysis. *Review of Educational Research, 66,* 5–32.

Madsen, C. H., & Madsen, C. K. (1974). *Teaching/discipline: A positive approach for educational development* (2nd ed.). Boston: Allyn & Bacon.

Mahoney, M. J. (1974). *Cognition and behavior modification.* Cambridge, MA: Ballinger.

Mayer, R. E. (1987). *Educational psychology: A cognitive approach.* Boston: Little, Brown.

Meichenbaum, D. (1977). *Cognitive-behavior modification: An integrative approach.* New York: Plenum.

Meichenbaum, D., & Cameron, R. (1983). Stress inoculation training: Towards a general paradigm for coping skills. In D. Meichenbaum & M. E. Jareko (Eds.), *Stress reduction and prevention* (pp. 115–154). New York: Plenum.

Mischel, W., Shoda, Y., & Peake, P. K. (1988). The nature of adolescent competencies predicted by preschool delay of gratification. *Journal of Personality and Social Psychology, 54,* 687–696.

Noffke, S. E. (1997). Professional, personal, and political dimensions of action research. In M. W. Apple (Ed.), *Review of research in education* (Vol. 22, pp. 305–343), Washington, DC: American Educational Research Association.

Polanyi, M. (1966). *The tacit dimension*. Garden City, NY: Doubleday.

Rogers, C. R. (1969). *Freedom to learn*. Columbus, OH: Merrill.

Rogers, C. R., & Skinner, B. F. (1956). Some issues concerning the control of human behavior. *Science*, 124, 1057–1066.

Rousseau, J. J. (1979). *Emile* (A. Bloom, Trans.). New York: Basic Books. (Original work published 1762).

Schön, D. (1987). *Educating the reflective practitioner*. San Francisco, Jossey-Bass.

Schunk, D. H., & Meece, J. L. (Eds.) (1992). *Student perspectives in the classroom*. Hillsdale, NJ: Erlbaum.

Seligman, M. E. P. (1975). *Helplessness: On depression, development, and death*. San Francisco: Freeman.

Seligman, M. E. P. (1988a). Research in clinical psychology: Why is there so much depression today? In I. S. Cohen (Ed.), *The G. Stanley Hall Lecture Series*, (Vol. 9, pp. 75–96). Washington, DC: American Psychological Association.

Seligman, M. E. P. (1988b). Boomer blues. *Psychology Today*, 22(10), 50–55.

Shoda, Y., Mischel, W., & Peake, P. K. (1990). Predicting adolescent cognitive and self-regulatory competencies from preschool delay of gratification: Identifying diagnostic conditions. *Developmental Psychology*, 26, 978–986.

Silberman, C. E. (1970). *Crisis in the classroom*. New York: Random House.

Slavin, R. (1989, June). PET and the pendulum: Faddism in education and how to stop it. *Phi Delta Kappan*, 70, 752–758.

Stone, G. L. (1980). *A cognitive-behavioral approach to counseling psychology*. New York: Praeger.

Sykes, C. J. (1992). *A nation of victims: The decay of the American character*. New York: St. Martin's.

Weiner, B. (1985). An attributional theory of achievement motivation and emotion. *Psychological Review*, 92, 548–573.

Woolfolk, A. E. (1998). *Educational Psychology* (7th ed.). Boston: Allyn & Bacon.

CHAPTER

12

Political Institutions
and Educational Policy

KENNETH K. WONG

University of Chicago

Public education in the United States is shaped by two distinct structural features of the American political system. First, federalism creates a highly decentralized form of educational governance. It facilitates a division of control among the three levels of government—namely, federal, state, and local. Although the federal government has expanded its involvement in educational policy since the 1960s, public education remains the primary responsibility of state and local government. Second, pluralist democracy enables competing interests to gain access to the decision-making process. Not infrequently, conflicts over educational issues occur. Educational policies are formulated as efforts to mediate contending perspectives. In other words, political institutions—the presidency, the Congress, state legislatures, the judicial branch, state and local boards of education, and others—play a major role in shaping the overall policy environment within which schools and classrooms are situated. The development of educational policy is closely connected to the political structures through which policy development travels.

This chapter aims to specify how political institutions shape public elementary and secondary education. Specifically, it examines the roles of the three levels of government. These roles include the somewhat restrained federal involvement in education, the states' constitutional authority, and the tradition of local control. Further, the American democratic form of government establishes a system of checks and balances. These arrangements

Handbook of Educational Policy

include the separation of power between the executive, legislative, and judicial branches. The following sections explore the relationships between
structural arrangements and major issues in educational policy. Particular
attention is paid to the federal role in promoting equal educational opportunities and school funding reform at the state level. To illustrate policy
changes at the local level, research findings from a study of Chicago's efforts
to restructure school governance are presented.

EDUCATION AS A MAJOR
GOVERNMENTAL FUNCTION

Why do educators need to understand politics and government? For too
long, educators have seen their tasks as largely detached from the broader
political process. Such a misperception needs to be dispelled. Several factors suggest a close connection between public schools and the political
process. First, elementary and secondary education is a major item in the
government's budget, a product of intense political deliberation. In the
1990s, spending on public education accounted for one-third of all state and
local government expenditures. School districts employed 2.5 million teachers and provided instruction to more than 45 million students, or 89% of the
nation's school population. Public schools spent more than $240 billion, or
more than 4 percent of the gross national product (GNP).

Second, education draws from the same fiscal pie that is available to all
public policy domains. Clearly, public education as a policy focus has to
compete with other priorities in the governmental agenda, including post-
secondary education, health care reform, welfare restructuring, and correctional facilities. In many states, spending for correctional facilities and health
care grew much faster than spending for K–12 education in the past decade.
Within public education, contending values include equity issues, political
accountability that respects the tradition of local control, constitutional
guarantees of individual rights, commitment to efficiency in service provision, and maintenance of democratic representation. Governmental institutions and their leaders are expected to manage competing values and
reconcile contending interests in a changing society.

Third, education is a shared governmental responsibility. All three levels
make decisions that affect schools. For example, educational funding comes
from all three levels of government. In 1995, $5907 in current dollars was
spent on the average public school student; 45.3% derived from state funds,
48.1% from local funds, and 6.6% from federal funds. Control over educational policy is distributed among the three levels of government. The constitutional framework enables the states to exercise primary authority over
public education. The state government defines the powers of the local
school board, establishes standards in delivering services, sets teacher cer-

tification requirements, and restricts the taxing and spending practices of districts. Meanwhile, the federal government has been the primary promoter of equal educational opportunities since the Great Society era of the 1960s (as discussed later). And whereas districts are bound by a state-defined school code in providing services to children, local school boards develop the curriculum, negotiate union contracts, and draw up school attendance zones.

Fourth, decisions made by governmental institutions at different levels have an impact in educational quality for all children. Schools and classrooms are nested in a complex, multilayered policy system (Barr & Dreeben, 1983). Clearly, the U.S. Congress and the state legislatures define the purpose of governmental actions, formulate programmatic strategies to pursue the goals, and allocate resources to eligible segments of the student population. In administering programs, educational agencies can create opportunities and impose constraints on curricular and instructional activities in the school building. In some circumstances, federal and state programs provide supplemental resources to students who come from at-risk environments. In other cases, governmental regulations isolate disadvantaged students from the regular classroom setting. Clearly, designers and administrators of educational policy need to develop a proper understanding of the connection between governmental actions and classroom practices.

DEVELOPMENT OF EDUCATIONAL POLICY IN U.S. FEDERALISM

Education is a shared responsibility in American federalism. The ways in which power and functions are distributed within the American federalist system have undergone several phases in the nation's history. Each phase has redefined the role of the government, particularly that of the federal government, in addressing the changing societal needs. Educational policy can be understood in this broader context of shifting authority between the federal and the subnational governments. For analytical purposes, I shall call attention to the early *dual federalism* when social redistribution was a nonissue, *collaborative federalism* when the federal government expanded its power to support the social welfare state beginning in the New Deal era, and the *Great Society* phase when the federal government institutionalized its redistributive policy arrangements. Since the 1980s, the federal government has directed increasing attention to the development of national standards.

Early Phases of Federalism

The nation's founding generation created a system of *dual federalism*, in which powers were divided between the federal government and the states to guard against the danger of having a national government with excessive authority. Article I, Section 8 of the U.S. Constitution specified the "enumerated powers" that Congress enjoyed and the Tenth Amendment granted state autonomy in virtually all domestic affairs, including education. Sovereignty for the states was not dependent on the federal government but instead came from the state's citizenry. Consistent with this view, in *The Federalist Papers*, which were first published during 1787 and 1788, James Madison suggested a line of demarcation between the federal and the states (Hamilton, Madison, & Jay, 1961). He wrote, "The federal and state governments are in fact but different agents and trustees for the people, constituted with different powers, and designed for different purposes." (No. 46, p. 296, 1961) The dual structure was further maintained by the strongly held belief in local control. It came as no surprise that in his description of the American democracy in the mid-nineteenth century, Alexis Tocqueville opened his seminal treatise by referring to local customs in the New England townships. Public education was primarily a local affair. The division of power within the federal system was so strong that it continued to preserve state control over its internal affairs, including de jure segregation of schools, many decades following the Civil War.

Dual federalism was designed to preserve liberty by not turning the national government into a Hobbesian Leviathan with absolute and indivisible power (Hobbes, 1985). However, it became less suitable for social and economic needs in a modern, industrialized society. By the 1930s, intergovernmental collaboration was clearly needed to address social inequity and to promote economic growth. The federal role was redefined to formulate a social welfare state and to integrate the market economy across state lines. Within three decades, between Roosevelt's New Deal in the 1930s and Johnson's War on Poverty in the 1960s, "marble cake" federalism replaced dual sovereignty.

Several changes in the distribution of power between the federal and state governments tended to promote shared responsibilities in domestic affairs. Numerous decisions by the U.S. Supreme Court broadened federal power to regulate interstate commerce and to provide financial assistance to subnational governments and their people. As early as 1819, in *McCulloch v. Maryland*, the Supreme Court rejected the notion that the state of Maryland had the power to levy taxes on the Bank of the United States. As Chief Justice John Marshall pointed out, "[t]hat the power to tax involves the power to destroy; [and] that the power to destroy may defeat and render useless the power to create" (quoted in Lieberman, 1992, p. 200). Equally important, the U.S. Supreme Court viewed the general welfare clause in Article I, Section 8, of the Constitution as an independent power beyond the list of enumerated powers in the article.

The last clause in Article I, Section 8, of the Constitution allowed the U.S. Congress to "make all Laws which shall be necessary and proper for carrying into Execution the foregoing Powers." This "elastic clause" came to provide the constitutional basis for a more activist federal government. In a 1936 case, the Court affirmed Congress's power to allocate tax revenues "for public purposes . . . not limited by the direct grants of legislative power found in the Constitution" (quoted in Lieberman, 1992, p. 501). This decision provided a key basis of the judicial framework that supported the expansion of the federal grants in aid.

Clearly, fiscal mismatch between the federal and subnational levels was demonstrated during the depression of the 1930s when the federal government decided to fund 70% of the relief programs after the states had failed to provide the services on their own. The post–World War II decades saw further expansion in the way the federal government financed nationally formulated policy but not in the way that the state and local governments delivered the services. By the 1950s, the federal government began to assume a significant role in the development of local affairs, including housing, education, health care, and community development.

An Era of Federal Activism

Federal involvement in local affairs sharply increased during the Great Society era of the 1960s and the 1970s. Federal activism in social issues followed the 1954 landmark Supreme Court decision on *Brown v. Board of Education* and the congressional enactment of the 1964 Civil Rights Act. Hundreds of federal categorical (or single-purpose) programs were formulated to provide supplemental resources for local agencies to combat social and economic problems in poor communities. A major example of the federal antipoverty legislation is compensatory education, enacted as Title I of the 1965 Elementary and Secondary Education Act (ESEA). For years, there was political deadlock on ESEA in the Congress. The nonsouthern states were opposed to allocating federal funds to segregated school systems. Whereas some lawmakers refused to aid parochial schools, others wanted to preserve local autonomy from federal interference. These policy disagreements were reinforced by the authority structure of the Congress—a committee system allowed a powerful few bargaining behind closed doors to kill a bill and the seniority privilege granted exclusive powers to the committee chairs (Sundquist, 1968).

The eventual passage of ESEA and other federal programs contributed to a significant increase in intergovernmental transfers. Consequently, total federal grants increased from approximately $8 billion in 1950 to $76 billion in 1975 in constant dollars, or in other words, from less than 1.0% of the GNP in 1950 to 3.3% in 1975. The number of categorical programs was more than doubled, from 160 to 380 during the Lyndon Johnson presidency. By 1980, there were approximately 500 federal categorical programs, including such major antipoverty programs as Aid to Families with Dependent Children (AFDC), medicaid, food stamps, low-income housing, and compensatory education.

The expansion of federal redistributive policy provided the basis for reconceptualizing federalism. According to some analysts, organizational complexity and bureaucratic isolation in the grants-in-aid system can be characterized as "picket fence federalism" (Wright, 1982). Indeed, efforts were made since the Nixon administration to move toward a more decentralized grant system with fewer regulations. Block grants were created to replace categorical programs, including Chapter 2 of the Education Consolidation and Improvement Act under the Reagan administration.

Other research has clarified how the complex implementation process serves the redistributive purpose of many federal programs. Based on a comparative analysis of federal policy in education, health, and housing, Peterson, Rabe, and Wong (1986) presented a differentiated theory of federalism. Their study distinguished two patterns of intergovernmental relations that are closely related to the purpose of federal policy. Although conflict occurs in redistributive policy, intergovernmental cooperation remains strong in developmental programs. They also found that, with the passage of time, even redistributive programs become more manageable. With a few exceptions, local administrative agencies were found to be in compliance with the federal targeting intent. The differentiated perspective not only considers program administration but also draws on the rich literature in fiscal federalism, in which the federal government is seen as encountering fewer structural economic constraints. Whereas the federal government raises its revenues on the ability-to-pay principle, local taxation is primarily based on the benefits-received principle (Oates, 1972; Tiebout, 1956). Consequently, local governments are most likely to adopt developmental programs that promote economic growth in response to economic demands and provide allocational services that correspond to a certain level of efficiency that is acceptable to the taxpayers (Wong, 1990).

With the arrival of the Clinton administration, policy coherence rose to the top of the agenda. In an effort to improve systemic restructuring, Martin Orland (1994) proposed to replace "picket fence federalism" with "chain link federalism." Whereas the former sustains organizational fragmentation with many categorical programs, the latter is designed to foster interdependence among various policy components. In education, Orland sees the importance of placing disadvantaged students within the context of broader systemic reform, where policy is designed to facilitate problem-solving skills for all students and to emphasize outcome-based accountability. A major effort to enhance accountability is the development of standards-based reform, an issue to which we now turn.

Debate over National Standards

In recent years, national debate has centered on developing standards in core subject areas for all students, without excluding students who come from at-risk environments. Since the publication of the national report, A *Nation at Risk* (National Commission on Excellence in Education, 1983), the public has tightened its scrutiny of public school performance. Both presidents Bush and Clinton have focused a great deal of attention on educational standards. In September 1989, President Bush convened an unprecedented summit meeting with the nation's governors—including then-governor Clinton—to develop educational goals for schools and students to attain by the year 2000. Building on the sentiments expressed by the governors, the Bush administration began promoting America 2000, a program that included provisions for school choice and elimination of federal and state education regulations. Amid record federal budget deficits, however, growing skepticism emerged about putting additional resources into public schools.

The political momentum for establishing national standards in education increased when Clinton assumed the presidency in 1993. With Clinton's strong endorsement, the Democratic-led Congress in March 1994 passed the National Goals 2000: Educate America Act, which set eight goals including student readiness to learn, high school completion rates, demonstrated learning in various subject areas, teacher education and professional development, math and science achievement, adult literacy and skills needed in a global economy, a safe and drug-free school environment, and parental participation in children's education. A critical component of the legislation was the establishment of the National Education Standards and Improvement Council (NESIC), which would certify national standards in key academic subject areas. The focus on performance and assessment was not coupled with any legislative efforts to increase funding for needy schools.

Another legislative example of standards-based reform is the 1994 reauthorization of the Elementary and Secondary Education Act (ESEA). It is designed to provide more coherent educational services to schools with a high concentration of students living in poverty and to apply vigorous national standards to all students, including Title I and bilingual students. According to the Clinton administration, "Title I, bilingual education, and dozens of other federal programs will become integral to, not separate from, state and community education reforms that center on high standards" (U.S. Department of Education, 1993). However, standards-based reform encountered political difficulty as the nation's capital entered a new period of divided partisan control following the 1994 midterm election.

Checks and Balances Turn into Partisan Rivalry

What otherwise would have been a history of steady bipartisan support for federal educational programs was punctuated by a year of highly visible institutional conflict in the nation's capital. It was 1995, an unusual year of political change in the nation's political scene. The 1994 midterm election produced a Republican majority in the U.S. Congress for the first time in 40 years. The new congressional leadership attempted to shrink the federal role in social programs and to shift programmatic authority to state and local governments. Policy conflict in 1995 was heightened by two sets of political processes. First, the reorganization of the U.S. House under the Republican leadership weakened the bipartisan support for educational programs in the short run. Second, the adversarial relationship between the White House and the "new" Congress was particularly salient. These two political changes produced what can be described as the politics of deinstitutionalization in the short term.

Deinstitutionalization in U.S. Congress

The process of deinstitutionalization is seen in a comparison of the membership in two crucial education-related committees in the House and the Senate in 1993, the first year of the Clinton administration, and 1995, the first year of the Republican era in Congress. It is important to focus on congressional committees because they are the key decision-making units in the division of legislative labor. Committees comprise lawmakers who share common interests in particular policy areas. Committee members are the ones who set the legislative agenda, write the bills, mobilize political support behind a legislative proposal, debate over the merits of the initiatives, and have the power to block proposals by not reporting them to the full legislative membership for further action.

A study conducted for this chapter based on information found in the *Congressional Quarterly Weekly* revealed that institutional memory and legislative knowledge significantly declined between 1993 and 1995. In the House, the average number of years of legislative experience for committee members of the majority party in the Education and Labor Committee was 7.2 years in 1993. This dropped to 5.0 years in 1995—a decline of 31.3% from the previous session. In the House Appropriations Subcommittee on Labor, Health, and Human Services, there was a decline of 64.5%—that is, from an average of 16.6 years to an average of 5.9 years. Similar patterns were seen in the Senate committees. In 1993 Democratic members of the Senate Labor and Human Resources Committee had an average of 12.9 years of legislative experience. In 1995 the Republican average dropped to only 4.1 years, a decline of 68.2%. Between the 1993 and the 1995 sessions, legislative experience of members of the majority party in the Senate Appropriations Subcommittee in Labor, Health, and Human Services declined by 31.5%, or from 15.9 years to 10.9 years on the average.

These significant changes in membership experience are likely to reduce the importance of seniority, weaken the contribution of policy expertise, and enhance the currency of party loyalty in the legislative process. To be sure, these kinds of fundamental shifts are likely to occur in an institution where one party, regardless of whether it is Democratic or Republican, dominated for 40 years. As one report observes, the Republican takeover in the House has "brought in a large class of junior Republicans who are hungry for action on their agenda and are skeptical of giving power to chairmen [in the committees]" (Cloud, 1995 p. 9). Among the first reforms that restructured the internal operation of the House was a 6-year term limit for committee chairmanship.

Conservative control over the educational agenda is in sharp contrast to the long time liberal dominance of the House Education and Labor Committee. According to Sroufe, this committee under Democratic control was "easily the most liberal in Congress. It include[d] strong representation from radical minorities and women, and ha[d] close ties with both the Black Caucus and the Hispanic Caucus. Issues of equity . . . have seldom been absent from the committee" (Sroufe, 1995 p. 83). Soon after the Republican takeover, the House moved to weaken the institutional practices that gave special attention to various target populations. For example, the new leadership eliminated three standing committees that had long served the Democratic constituencies. These were the committees on the District of Columbia, Merchant Marine and Fisheries, and Post Office and Civil Service. The fiscal 1996 spending bill for the District of Columbia failed to pass in the House because of partisan conflict over the Republic voucher proposal that would authorize $5 million for a program to allow 1500 poor children to enroll in private schools (Nitschke, 1996 p. 549).

Further, the leadership style of the new House speaker, Newt Gingrich, tended to undermine long-term institutional practices in making decisions. Gingrich had gained power under the most unusual political circumstances. His predecessor, Democratic speaker Tom Foley, was the first House speaker who had been defeated since 1860. For one thing, the new speaker conceptualized social and governmental issues in polarizing terms. The naming of his core political caucus, the Conservative Opportunity Society, was a "semantic counterpoise to the three words Gingrich strove to discredit: Liberal Welfare State" (New York Times Magazine, 1996, p. 54). He depicted the government as the major cause of poverty, the bureaucracy as the major source of waste in taxpayer dollars, and the private sector as the only real solution to social inequality. Further, he circumscribed the seniority practice to make sure that his first-term allies gained greater representation in crucial committees. For example, freshmen lawmakers got 9 of 10 open seats on the Commerce Committee, 7 of 11 on Appropriations Committee and 3 of 10 on the powerful Ways and Means Committee (New York Times Magazine, 1996, p. 40). At the same time, Speaker Gingrich handpicked three activist conservativists, side-stepping seniority consideration, to lead three major committees. His direct involvement in drafting the federal budget also placed enormous constraints on the programmatic jurisdiction of committees. To make sure that his legislative agenda was followed, the speaker created task forces to come up with legislative proposals instead of relying on committee support. Consequently, he was able to secure House approval on 9 of the 10 items on his Contract with America.

Rivalry between Two Branches

The heightened political confrontation was highly visible between the Congress and the president during 1995. The 1994 election was the only midterm election for first-term elected presidents in the United States history when the president's party lost the majority in both houses of Congress (Jones, 1995). While the first two years of the Clinton administration brought about major legislative accomplishments (such as the Goals 2000 legislation), the second half of Clinton's first term was marked by a significant loss of political capital. The acrimonious relationship between the two branches was seen in the long impasse on the federal FY 1996 budget that shut down the federal government for weeks.

The gap in educational policy between the Clinton administration and the new Republican majority is evidenced in the congressional response to the administration's budgetary requests between 1993 (Democratic control) and 1995 (Republican control). Republican lawmakers in 1995 wanted to reduce the level of federal funding in education in all major programs as well as reduce the overall budget for the Department of Education. It should be noted that the House Republican proposals would result in actual decrease from the 1995 funding level and not simply a slowing down in the rate of funding growth. Significant disagreements arose over major redistributive programs. For example, the House proposed a 19% cut in compensatory education, a 66% reduction in bilingual programs, and a 7% cut in special education. Overall, the House Republican leadership called for cutting $1.7 billion in federal education spending in fiscal 1996. The proposal included reductions of $73 million from compensatory education, $100 million from safe and drug-free schools, $42 million from Head Start, and $40 million from School-to-Work Opportunities Act. The House GOP also targeted Goals 2000 for elimination. Furthermore, in H.R. 1214, House Republicans proposed legislation that would replace the school lunch program with a block grant, eliminating the federal guarantee of a free or reduced-price meal for every eligible child and slowing down the annual rate of growth in educational funding overall. The cuts proposed by the Senate were less drastic and would have cut only $436 million in education spending. In contrast, the 1993 Democratic Congress was generally supportive of the administration's budgetary requests on such redistributive programs as compensatory education, bilingual programs, and special education.

From a broader perspective, the highly visible partisan conflict in 1995 seems more of an exception than the rule. With Clinton's reelection in 1996, the Republican congressional leadership suspended its quest to eliminate federal involvement in education. In 1997, for example, there was bipartisan support behind several new education initiatives, including a major expansion in public school choice programs. In the course of 3 decades, federal support for educational equity remains unchanged despite partisan shifts in the executive and the legislative branches. Whether there will be another major effort to dismantle federal programs in the future remains to be seen.

POLITICAL AND POLICY DIFFERENCES AMONG STATES

Our constitutional framework enables each of the 50 states to maintain its own educational system. Compared to other industrialized democracies, we have a distinctly decentralized structure of school governance. This decentralized character is cherished by both the public and the poltical leaders. In the official Republican party response to President Clinton's 1997 state of the union message, Congressman J. C. Watts stated that "the state of this union really isn't determined in Washington, D.C. It never has been, and it never will be" (*Congressional Quarterly Weekly Report* 1997). He proclaimed that the Republican party's mission is "to limit the claims and demands of Washington; to limit its call for more power, more authority and more taxes." Similarly, in response to President Clinton's call for national educational standards, Republican governor Tommy Thompson of Wisconsin argued that "Education is a local issue. This is the way our parents and communities want it, and that is how it should be. Afterall, the states and local taxpayers are the ones who pay for schools" (*New York Times* 1997).

At the same time, even when President Clinton endorses a more activist federal role in education, his top aides take a more cautious view on local control. In his 1997 state of American education address, Secretary of Education Richard Riley tried to dispel local concerns about excessive federal control. He argued that, "Reading is reading. Math is math. For these basics, let's not cloud our children's future with silly arguments about federal intrusion" (*New York Times* 1997). The current movement toward goals and standards, according to Riley, is a national challenge and must not be seen as a federal requirement.

State control in education is established by its own constitutional framework. In general, states handle a wide range of important educational policies, including teacher certification, curriculum standards, operation of districts, graduation requirements, and school funding. Across the 50 state educational systems, there are undoubtedly significant variations in fiscal capacity and governance arrangement. First, governance structure varies among states. The selection of state school boards and the state chief school officers is far from uniform. In the 1990s, governors in 32 states appointed the state school board. Eight popularly elected boards appointed a chief school officer (*Education Week* 1997, p. 21). In Georgia, the state board lost substantial power in part due to a 1996 legislation that shifted power from the board to the superintendent and in part due to gubernatorial decisions to replace 9 of its current 11 members. In Illinois, the governor gained new power to appoint a chair of the state board, of which membership had been cut from 17 to 9. According to one analysis of the 13 western states, a greater number of state boards are popularly elected and fewer states allow the governor to appoint the board. At the same time, a greater number of chief school officers are appointed by the state school board, fewer directly elected by the people, and none appointed by the governor (Wong 1991).

Further, there are differences in the state portion of school spending. In 1995–1996, the national average is that the states provided 47.9% of the total school revenues. Although 21 states allocated over 50%, 12 states contributed less than 40% to the total school spending. The level and the scope of state financial support is shaped by a number of political factors, including litigation, the taxpayers' movement, and the structure of the legislature.

School Finance Litigation

School finance litigation has directed the attention of the public and of state policy makers almost exclusively to funding inequalization between rich and poor districts. It should be noted that several failed attempts were made to call for a greater federal role in addressing funding equalization. The most publicized effort was the 1973 ruling on a case in Texas, *San Antonio v. Rodriguez* (1973), in which the U.S. Supreme Court reversed a federal district court ruling. The Supreme Court concluded that since education does not constitute a fundamental interest under the U.S. Constitution, states can choose to preserve local control by not interfering in interdistrict fiscal inequities. Since *Rodriguez*, the pressure for funding equalization has shifted to the states. Plaintiffs from poor districts have grounded their arguments for more state funding on issues of adequacy, sufficiency, and efficiency. Their grievance points to the close connection between disparity in local taxable wealth and inferior educational quality. In virtually all judicial challenges since *Serrano v. Priest* (1971) in California, taxpayers in districts with low property values have been found to carry a heavy tax burden. Students in these high-tax, low-wealth districts do not seem to benefit from the fiscal well-being of the state as a whole. Consequently, states have been asked to restructure their allocative systems to address these disparities (Wong, 1994). As of 1998, the high courts in 18 states have overturned their state school finance system. In 18 states, the courts upheld the funding system. Reform in funding, however, has not been confined to the 18 states.

Taxpayers Movement

Increases in state allocations to resource-poor districts is also a response to the local taxpayer movements. In California, discontent with property taxes became widespread during the much publicized campaign for Proposition 13, which called for a statewide limit on property tax levies. According to a 1978

Gallup poll, 52% of respondents mentioned local property taxes when asked to identify their dissatisfaction with various taxing sources for public schools; only 21% and 20%, respectively, cited federal and state taxes (Phi Delta Kappa 1984). Not surprisingly, between 1978 and 1983, 39 of the 64 tax or spending limitation measures on state ballots were approved (Citrin, 1984). These taxpayer campaigns, in turn, have put pressure on state legislatures to distribute aid so as to ease the local tax burden of virtually all districts.

State Legislative Structure

Finally, school finance packages are substantially shaped by state legislatures, which are structured by geographic representation. To attain the legislative coalition needed to pass a school finance bill, lawmakers are likely to adopt strategies in which no district suffers a reduction in state support. This *leveling up* strategy is consistent with the pragmatic concerns of lawmakers, who are keenly aware of the political effects of spending decisions. Thus, the legislature has the political interests to make sure that school aid would be provided to the greatest possible number of constituents. In New York, for example, the state senate, which has traditionally played a stronger role in education than the assembly, has successfully disbursed state aid to all but 9 of the state's 708 districts (Berke, Goertz, & Coley, 1984).

As state funding becomes more important to schools, state elections often involve partisan contentions over ways to generate revenues. For example, Illinois governor Jim Edgar, touting his record of fiscal responsibility, won reelection in 1994 against a challenger who proposed a major increase in the state income tax both to equalize school spending across districts and to relieve local property tax burdens. Concerned about heavy local property taxes, Michigan governor John Engler and state lawmakers in 1993 developed a plan to make school funding dependent on state revenues; the shift in funding sources did little to resolve funding inequities across the state. In South Carolina, the Republicans, as a result of the 1994 election, gained control of the house for the first time in 118 years. The House GOP and the Republican governor, David Beasley, proposed relieving the property tax burden by eliminating 22 educational programs that were enacted during the term of Democratic governor Richard W. Riley, who now serves as U.S. secretary of education in the Clinton administration. In Kansas, the state senate in 1995 killed a House bill that would have eliminated property taxes as a revenue source for schools. In short, politics also plays a major role in state-level educational policy.

LOCAL CONTROL AND GOVERNANCE REFORM

In public education, local control is predominant. From a constitutional-legalistic point of view, localities are merely political subdivisions of the state and local powers can only be granted with the consent of the state legislature. In reality, once their legal status has been established, local governments enjoy control over critical resources that can be used to sustain their existence. Localities can select their own political representatives, decide on fiscal policies, and choose the scope of their services.

Historically, states moved toward district consolidation to provide more uniform educational services in a more economical manner. Smaller districts were said to have difficulties in retaining high-quality teachers, upgrading school facilities and maintaining an enriched curriculum. Smaller districts often required a much higher per-pupil cost, thereby imposing a heavier burden on the local property taxpayers (Fuller & Pearson, 1969). In part due to these factors, the number of school districts was reduced from about 128,000 in 1930 to about 71,000 in 1951, while the average enrollment in districts increased. The states' efforts to contain school costs by consolidating smaller districts continued in the postwar decades, cutting the number of districts by two-thirds between 1951 and 1967. During this period, the sharpest reductions occurred in Nevada, Colorado, Alaska, and Oregon. For example, following the passage of the School District Organization Act of 1959, Colorado consolidated 950 districts into 180 districts in an 8-year period. Since the 1960s, the pace of district consolidation in the United States has slowed. The number of school districts decreased from more than 23,000 in 1967 to fewer than 14,500 in 1992, representing a drop from 38% to 17% of all local governmental units. States that have a large number of districts include Texas (1,100), California (1,078), Illinois (985), and Nebraska (797). In contrast, far fewer districts exist in Rhode Island (3), Tennessee (14), Nevada (17), Connecticut (17), and Delaware (19).

Differences across Districts

Significant variation exists in fiscal and governance arrangements across the 14,400 school districts in the United States. Clearly, fiscal capacity differs among districts, as indicated by the wide variation in tax rates levied on property values. On the governance side, 95% of the school boards are popularly elected, whereas appointed boards are mostly found in urban systems. Among big-city districts, mayoral control varies. Cities where the mayor appoints members of the board included Chicago, Baltimore, Cleveland, and Boston. Equally diverse are the local political cultures that shape school politics and governance (Clark, 1994).

District Control as Democratic Practices

The existence of thousands of autonomous districts can be justified by three widely held views in the literature. First, district autonomy is embedded in strongly held public beliefs in democratic control over schools. The fact that there are thousands of local school systems operating their own budgets and electing their own boards testifies to the pervasive influence of the tradition of local control. Thomas Shannon (1992), former executive director of the National School Boards Association, has argued that school boards serve several indispensable functions. They develop strategic plans, manage the operation of the system, implement federal and state laws, evaluate educational programs, arbitrate complaints from citizens and employees, and represent the entire population of the district. The boards also negotiate contracts with teachers unions. Boards serve as the middle management buffers between schools and powerful state and federal bureaucracies.

Taking a critical view of local control, Robert Wagner, Jr. (1992), a former president of the New York City Board of Education, warned that "local control of education is out of control." Wagner argued that school boards should avoid micromanagement and focus more on setting policy. Going even farther, Chester Finn (1992), a former Reagan administration official in charge of educational research, has called for the abolition of local school boards. He sees local control as "a legacy of our agrarian past" (p. 22) and no longer an appropriate governing tool for the high-tech future. Finn has characterized this middle management as superfluous and dysfunctional because it is largely detached from the interests of the clients and the taxpaying public. Instead, the board is seen as dominated by various service-provider interest groups, particularly the teachers unions.

Cost Efficiency in District Control

Another strand of the literature on local services argues that the presence of multiple school systems can be cost-efficient. The economic argument for local control is grounded in the notion that the public sector can be treated as a quasi-market arrangement. An educational system with multiple suppliers of services promises a better fit between consumer-taxpayers' preferences and the level and quality of local services. As Tiebout (1956) suggested, taxpayers make residential decisions that would maximize the benefits they expect to obtain from public services and minimize the level of taxes that they have to pay for those services. In particular, middle-class taxpayers who can afford to spend more on goods and services are keenly concerned about the quality of basic services, such as schools. As Hirschman (1970) argued, they are more ready to exit when they perceive a decline in those municipal services that they value. Studies of district-level performance in metropolitan areas suggest that interdistrict competition can improve service quality (Hoxby, 1997).

Roles of Urban Districts

Finally, in the challenging context of large urban districts, the school board and its administration perform important functions. The centralized, bureaucratic model has been the predominant mode of public school governance in urban districts for generations. Between the turn of the century and the 1920s, urban school governance shifted from neighborhood-based councils to citywide school boards. The central office bureaucracy emerged as the locus of power in developing rules to allocate personnel and other resources, in recruiting teachers and administrators, and in insulating the conduct of curricular and instructional affairs from external influences (Callahan, 1962; Cuban, 1990; Danzberger, Kirst, & Usdan 1992; Tyack, 1974). Over time, local school governance came to be characterized by a *strong executive-weak board* arrangement. At the top of the central bureaucracy is the school superintendent, who assumes the educational, managerial, and fiscal responsibilities of the entire district. Board policy and state mandates are implemented through an internal division of labor, which is characterized by specialized bureaus in which program administrators are insulated from one another. When allocating resources, the lay school board becomes merely "an agent of legitimation" (Kerr, 1964), following the recommendations made by professional administrators. To be sure, the centralized, bureaucratic power has served important functions in the public school system: It manages competing interests, routinizes service delivery, distributes comparable resources to schools, enforces federal and state mandates, and above all provides organizational stability to a complex operation that serves a diverse clientele (Boyd, 1983; Wong, 1992).

Bureaucratic Inefficiency?

Despite its many accomplishments, an insulated bureaucracy is increasingly being viewed as ineffective in meeting the current concerns on accountability and performance. First, an oversized central bureaucracy may result in diseconomies of scale. In their study of New York City schools, Ravitch and Viteritti (1997) observed that "most of the necessary functions are overadministered and undersupervised (p. 22)." A large amount of resources are used to support central services instead of allotting to the schools. The New York City board's own analysis showed that only 42% of the budget was spent on classroom instruction during 1995–1996. There were audit inconsistencies in the Division of School Safety, which hired 3000 security officers, and in the Bureau of Supplies, which controlled a $160 million budget for purchases. Although New York's problems may be unique, virtually all urban districts have to face the question of whether some of the centralized functions can be better performed (and at a lower cost) by schools and by private vendors.

A second concern is accountability. Centralized authority has been criticized for its lack of responsiveness to community needs. Beginning in the 1960s, various mechanisms have been instituted to improve district-school communication and collaboration. By the 1990s, virtually all urban districts had implemented some form of shared governance in which parents and community representatives participate in the decision-making structure at the school sites. Examples of these governance arrangements include the New York-style community board; site-based management in Dade County, Florida, Rochester, New York, and Salt Lake City, Utah; and the Chicago experience in establishing a locally elected parent council in each school.

A third concern with the centralized bureaucracy is its mixed results in terms of student performance. In an increasingly technologically oriented, global economy, policy makers, business leaders, and parents often blame bureaucratization for the decline in student performance in the United States. Will high school graduates acquire adequate skills to compete with their peers in other countries in the global economy? Does the projected labor force shortage mean that employers have to hire the less skilled in the future? Can the new workforce perform well in a technologically complex world? The public seems uncertain whether bureaucratized school organizations are effective in meeting these challenges. To be sure, the causes of performance decline are complex, as socioeconomic factors and other cultural barriers continue to influence teaching and learning. Nevertheless, the public's perception of bureaucratic ineffectiveness is often reinforced by accounts on low student performance in standardized tests in urban areas. For example, the 1997 New York state report card showed that 89% of New York City's elementary schools failed to reach the state's expectations on reading performance. These and other kinds of indicators on student achievement are particularly frustrating when the United States is spending a great deal more on education than other western countries (Hanushek, 1994).

Decentralized "Voice" Reform

Giving more powers to parents and professionals in school operation and budget allocation represents one major reform effort to reduce centralized control. Decentralized reforms are directed at reallocating power between the central authority and the schools within the public school system. Though by no means typical, Chicago's experience in parent empowerment since 1988 provides useful information on both the potentials and the limitations of this particular reform effort.

Local School Councils in Chicago

In the United States, a systemwide effort to make sure that parents are indeed the key decision makers is seen in the establishment of the Local School Councils in Chicago. The 1988 Chicago School Reform Act was guided by the belief that parent and citizen empowerment through local school councils (LSCs) would improve educational performance. The legislation was designed to restore public confidence by granting parents substantial ownership over schools.

The 1988 act has changed the structure of Chicago school governance. For example, to enhance accountability, the central office has decentralized policy making to locally elected councils at each school site. The 11-member councils consist of a majority (6) of parents, 2 community representatives, 2 teachers, and the principal. There is also one student member at the high school level. Members of the local council are given substantial authority— they can hire and fire principals (who lost tenure as a result of the 1988 act), allocate lump sums that come from state compensatory fund (Chapter 1), and develop school improvement plans. With training and support from business and public interest groups, local councils have written their bylaws, approved school budgets, and reviewed and ratified the principals' contracts. According to some assessments, about one-third of all the elementary schools have a local school council that is in good operational standing after several years of existence (Consortium of Chicago School Research, 1993).

Not surprisingly, the LSCs have a direct impact on the principal selection. During the 7 years when the LSC model dominated Chicago school governance, selection of principals was often reflective of the racial and ethnic makeup of the LSCs and their neighborhood constituencies (Wong & Moulton, 1996). In Latino neighborhoods, for example, new principals were more likely to reflect the ethnic majority of the community residents. In the first round of contract evaluations, affecting 286 schools in 1990, 38% of the principals were replaced. In 1991, when evaluation was conducted in the remaining 207 schools, 37% of the principals were replaced. Consequently, the percentage of black principals has increased from 37% to 50% and the percentage of Latino principals increased from 7% to 11% between 1989 and 1994. The number of white principals has decreased from 56% to 39% during the 5-year period.

While the LSCs seem to exercise their appointive power fairly visibly throughout the school system, voter involvement in LSCs has been shrinking during the period of decentralization. Voter turnout for LSC elections has declined significantly since the first election in 1989 when 294,213 people turned out to vote in the LSC races throughout the system. In 1991, turnout dropped to 161,089. Even lower voter participation occurred in the 1993 election (the last one before the mayor took over the system), when only 131,798 voters were involved. Overall, voter turnout has declined by 55% over the three LSC elections (Wong & Moulton, 1996). The decline is even more dramatic when measured in terms of just parents and community residents (without including teachers, staff, and students). For this particular electoral subgroup, there was a 59% drop in turnout between 1989 and 1991. Between 1991 and 1993, another 25% decline was seen. Overall, turnout among parents and community residents plunged by 68% in a 5-year period.

As voter turnout has declined, fewer candidates have run for LSC offices. Between 1989 and 1993, the number of candidates running for offices in the LSCs declined from 3.18 to 1.36 per seat (Wong & Moulton, 1996). To be sure, the electoral contest was unevenly distributed among schools. Schools that lacked enough candidates for all the LSC offices have increased from 3% in 1989 to 25% in 1991. By 1993, one out of every three schools in Chicago lacked a full slate of candidates.

Turning to the issue of school effectiveness, the experience in Chicago's decentralized council has been mixed at best. Polsby (cited in Walberg & Niemiec, 1996) found no systematic patterns of improvement in any of the major outcome indicators in Chicago schools, including attendance, graduation rates, and achievement. When he found that high schools were further behind national standards than were elementary schools, Polsby suggested that the longer students enroll in Chicago schools, the less satisfactory their performance. Even the strongest supporters of LSC reform concluded that achievement trends have been inconclusive. Although the school-by-school trends in reading on standardized tests showed fairly sharp declines, math and writing performance was stable between 1989 and 1995 (Bryk, Kerbow, & Rollow, 1997). These trend-line analyses, however, did not include baseline data in the pre-1989 reform era. Only one-fourth of the elementary teachers perceived a positive impact of the decentralized reform on the quality of student academic performance (Sebring, Bryk, & Easton, 1995). From an institutional perspective, one might argue that the unsatisfactory student outcomes are due to the uneven capacity of the LSCs. However, if the LSCs failed to build up their governing capacity in a 7-year period—a fairly reasonable time frame to expect organizational improvement—one has to call into question whether the LSC is an effective model to improve schools system-wide. In light of these concerns, a bipartisan legislative coalition adopted a comprehensive reform proposal that created *integrated governance* in Chicago in July 1995.

Integrated Governance Reform

In response to the ineffectiveness of local school councils and an insulated bureaucracy, a new framework of educational governance is gaining prominence in urban districts across the nation. Integrated governance, as the model has been labeled (Wong, Dreeben, Lynn, & Sunderman, 1997), entails three central components: (1) state legislation that focuses on student achievement at the school site level as a crucial measure of school performance, (2) state legislation that grants districts or the state educational agency new authority to intervene in failing schools, and (3) district or state willingness to use this authority to improve failing schools. This new governance model tends to reverse the decades-long trend toward shared decision making by integrating power and authority at the district level. In short, integrated governance reform is driven by a focus on student performance and is characterized by district-level capacity and willingness to intervene in failing schools.

Mayoral control of urban school systems constitute one prominent form of integrated governance. Several mayors have taken control over urban schools or have begun seeking power from state legislatures to do so. Examples include Cleveland, Baltimore, and Boston, among others. The best example of integrated governance is Chicago, where mayoral control in the last 2 years provides the most detailed information on this new model. The following section assesses the impacts of integrated governance in Chicago.

What Is Integrated Governance?

Decentralization is no longer the dominant reform strategy in the Chicago Public Schools, a system that enrolls 410,000 students in 550 schools. The Chicago School Reform Amendatory Act, which took effect in July 1995, reverses a 7-year trend toward decentralization of authority over school operations and redesigns the governance arrangement so that power and authority are now integrated. Integrated governance reduces competing authorities and coordinates activities in support of systemwide policy goals. Integrated governance in Chicago is characterized by the following:

- Mayoral appointment of board members and top administrators
- Elimination of competing sources of authority, such as the School Board Nominating Commission and the School Finance Authority
- Powers granted to the board of trustees to hold local school councils (LSC) accountable to systemwide standards, elected parents constitute the majority of the LSC
- Creation of the position of a chief executive officer (CEO) that oversees the top administrative team, including the chief education officer

With integrated governance, fewer policy actors compete for decision-making authority. The 1995 law suspended the power of the School Finance Authority, eliminated the School Board Nominating Commission, and diminished the ability of the local school councils to operate independently of board authority. Further, integrated governance is designed to facilitate policy coherence and improve organizational collaboration among major actors. As a result of the 1995 reform, the board, top administration, and the mayor's office are closely linked by appointment decisions emanating from the mayor's office. Finally, integrated governance relies on an administration that enjoys strong managerial authority. The 1995 law expanded the financial powers of the board and enhanced the powers of the chief executive officer to manage the system.

Reducing Institutional and Policy Fragmentation

Although the 1995 legislation left intact some features of the previous arrangements, it reduced competing institutional authority and recentralized administrative authority (Wong, 1996). The law decreased the size of the 15-member board to 5 and put the mayor in charge of appointing board members, the board president, and the chief executive officer in charge of the schools. Because the board appoints the top administrative officers, these changes facilitate an effective link between the mayor's office and the central office. Under this arrangement, education becomes a part of the mayor's policy agenda and gives the mayor the option to decide the amount of political capital he is willing to invest in improving the schools.

Following its appointments, the new school administration acted swiftly to demonstrate a commitment to efficient management by adopting a business management model. The management and maintenance of school buildings, for example, was reorganized to stress customer service and outside contracting for services. The board eliminated the Bureau of Facilities Planning in the central office (resulting in the elimination of 10 jobs), reduced the number of positions in the Department of Facilities Central Service Center by half (26 out of 50 positions were eliminated), and reduced the citywide administration of facilities from 441 positions to 34. Contracts for these services are now with private firms. To oversee the management and maintenance of school property, the board negotiated contracts with five firms to provide property advisory services for each region. Under this arrangement, the firms advise principals and the Department of Operations on property management and provide custodial, engineering, and construction-related services to the schools. In addition, the board prequalified a number of general construction contractors from which the schools can select.

By strengthening the centralized authority of the school system, the 1995 legislation shifted the balance of power between the central office and local school councils. Prior to 1995, the central office competed with the local school councils for authority over the educational agenda. LSCs had broad authority, but there was little direct accountability or oversight. For example, state Chapter 1 funds went directly to the schools, but the board remained accountable if the money was misused. Selection of principals by the LSC was often influenced by the constituencies of the particular neighborhood.

The new administration has signaled the LSCs that they can no longer operate with complete independence and have incorporated the LSCs into the overall system by defining standards and responsibilities to which they must adhere. This policy establishes 15 criteria covering the actions of the principal, staff, local school council, and local school council members. Under the new board policy, the board declared that an educational crisis existed at Prosser Preparatory Center and Nathan Hale School. At each school, the LSC was disbanded. The LSC at Prosser was declared nonfunctional in part because of its failure to approve the school improvement plan or evaluate the principal. At Hale, the LSC was suspended after LSC members were found to have intruded in the day-to-day operations of the school, entered classrooms unannounced and uninvited, and failed to follow the law regarding their powers and responsibilities, among other violations.

Taken together, these actions have improved public confidence in the ability of the board and central administration to govern the schools, giving the top administration the legitimacy it needs to carry out its educational initiatives.

Improving Financial Management

The 1995 governance redesign enhanced the ability of the central administration to perform financial and management functions efficiently. The 1995 law suspended the budget oversight authority of the School Finance Authority, removed the balanced budget requirement, and placed the inspector general under the authority of the board. In addition, the Chicago school board was granted new authorities that expanded its financial powers. A number of funded programs (for example, K–6 reading improvement, substance abuse prevention, Hispanic programs, gifted education, and others) and categorical funds were collapsed into a general education block grant and an educational services block grant, respectively. Although total revenues available to the board declined by 8% in fiscal year 1996 from the previous year, revenues going into the general funds increased by about 2% (or $28.5 million). Additionally, the board acquired greater flexibility over the use of pension fund monies and Chapter 1 funds not allocated to the schools. Finally, there were no longer separate tax levies earmarked for specific purposes.

These changes increased board discretion over school revenues, allowing the board to prepare a 4-year balanced budget and negotiate a 4-year contract, including a raise, with the Chicago Teachers Union. These actions brought both financial and labor stability to the system. Indeed, by March 1996, Standard and Poor's raised the Chicago public schools bond ratings from a BBB– to BBB and Moody's from a Ba to Baa, allowing the board to issue bonds for the construction of new buildings under lower interest rates than before. By the summer of 1997 the Chicago public schools' bond ratings were A– from Standard and Poor's and Baa1 from Moody's. The 4-year teacher's contract meant the board could focus on developing and implementing its education agenda.

Intervening in Low-Performing Schools

The 1995 law incorporated a focus on accountability and academic achievement that compelled the administration to target the lowest performing schools within the system for intervention. Declaring that an educational crisis existed in Chicago, the 1995 legislation directed the board of trustees and the CEO to increase the quality of educational services within the system. It enhanced the powers of the CEO to identify poorly performing schools and place these schools on remediation, probation, intervention, or reconstitution. Prior to 1995, the subdistrict superintendent, not the school board, had the primary responsibility to monitor the performance of the schools and identify nonperforming schools. In the past, to place a school on remediation or probation required the approval of the subdistrict council, which was made up of parent or community members from each LSC within the subdistrict.

With the new legislation, the board and central office responded by focusing on the lowest performing schools within the system. Four kinds of intervention efforts have been made since the beginning of integrated governance in July 1995:

Remediation. In January 1996, the CEO placed 21 schools on remediation for failing to meet state standards on the Illinois Goal Assessment Program (IGAP) for three consecutive years. Only six schools were placed on remediation by the previous administration. At the same time, the board removed two elementary school principals because the schools failed to improve after a year on remediation.

Probation. In September 1996, the CEO placed 109 schools (or 20% of all Chicago schools) under probation because 15% or less of their students scored at grade level on nationally normed tests (Wong and Anagnostopoulos 1998). These schools are being held accountable to their school improvement plans as well as to improvements in their students' scores. Since this initiative began, 9 schools have been removed from the list, and 15 have been added.

Reconstitution. Beginning in the fall of 1997, seven high schools have been reconstituted based on continual low performance of students' test scores (none of the reconstituted schools had more than 7% of their students reading at or above grade level according to test scores). The principals were replaced in five of the seven schools, and 188 of 675 teachers, or 29%, were not rehired. These schools will have to improve their test scores or risk being shut down.

The end of social promotion. In an expanded program from last summer, third-, sixth-, eighth-, and ninth-grade students who did not meet set levels on one of two nationally normed tests (the Iowa Test of Basic Skills [ITBS] or the Test of Academic Proficiency [TAP]) were required to participate in a system-sponsored summer school called the Summer Bridge Program. For example, 61% of eighth graders who participated in the program met the cutoff scores after the 7 weeks. By the end of the summer, 92% of all eighth graders had met the school system's new promotion standards. Teachers in this program were provided with day-by-day lesson plans. Students were promoted to their next grade if they brought their scores to the cutoff point set for their grade. If they did not, they were required to repeat their grade. Repeating students returned to their original schools, unless they were older eighth graders. Half of the repeating eighth graders, who will be 15 by December 1, now attend one of 13 transition centers, which feature a curriculum emphasizing basic skills.

The board and top administration reorganized the central office to reflect the focus on accountability and established the improvement of IGAP scores as the primary objective of the system. While other departments within the central office were eliminated or significantly downsized, the administration created the Office of Accountability, which has grown from a staff of 50 in September 1995 to 90 in July 1996. This office monitors the performance of the schools, identifies low-performing schools, and intervenes in schools that are not performing well.

The Office of Accountability has several departments that are in the process of launching various programs to level up schools where test scores are low. The Department of School Quality Review is working with the Illinois State Board of Education to develop a review process to evaluate all schools once every 4 years. The Department of School Intervention works with schools on the state's Academic Watch List or in remediation. These schools receive a one day visit from the staff in School Intervention, which recommends corrective actions and pairs them with consultants to provide technical support. In December 1995, the board approved $1,335,500 in contracts to universities and colleges to work with 30 schools on the watch list.

Broadening the Political Base of Support

The link between the mayor's office and the board can facilitate political support for the school system. With the redesign of the governance system, Chicago mayor Richard Daley has been more willing to invest his political capital in the Chicago schools. To restore public confidence, the new administration has projected an image of efficient, responsive, and ethical government. The administration has also taken a number of steps to strengthen the support of the business community for the public schools. This support becomes crucial when appealing to the Illinois legislature because the business community can lobby in favor of the board's legislative agenda, thereby lending the board credibility.

The mayor's appointments to the board of trustees reflect a concern with consolidating business support for the schools. Three of the five board members have extensive experience in the private sector. Moreover, the distribution of appointments within the central office reflect the mayor's commitment to improving the fiscal conditions and management of the system. The top appointments in the central office made between July 1995 and December 1996 reflect a diversity of expertise: 11% are from the private sector, 12% from nonprofit organizations, 23% from city agencies, and 54% from within the ranks of the Chicago Public Schools.

To further enhance business support for the schools and the perception of efficient management, the new district administration reorganized the central office according to business principles that stress downsizing and privatization. Within 1 year of implementing the new system, the number of staff positions in the central administration declined almost 21%. The majority of these cuts came from citywide administration and services. The reduction was achieved through awarding contracts to private providers for food services, distribution, and facilities. Other reductions were obtained by consolidating the 11 district offices into six regional offices.

The administration's strategy of focusing on management and budget issues early on can be viewed as a serious effort to establish political credibility. Over the course of the last 3 years, the administration balanced the budget, developed a 5-year capital development plan, and negotiated a 4-year teachers' contract. This strategy paid off with improved public confidence in the ability of the administration to manage the schools and to stabilize relations with the union. Believing that raising test scores is the basis for long-term political support, the mayor, board, and CEO have now adopted this as their primary strategy. Better test scores, it is hoped, will form the basis for increased state funding and the continuation of the current centralized governance with the mayor in control of the schools. This arrangement is likely to shift additional power back to the central office, including the establishment of qualifications for the appointment of principals by the central office, and to further diminish the local school councils' role. Indeed, in August 1996, the legislature adopted legislation that allows the board of trustees to develop additional standards and requirements for school principals.

An Ambitious Agenda in Systemwide Restructuring

As integrated governance moves into its third year, the CEO and the board initiates a broad reform agenda that includes the following components:

- The system has designed and disseminated its own standards (Chicago Academic Standards) in the areas of English language arts, mathematics, biological and physical sciences, and social sciences. Benchmark exams for selected cutoff grades are being developed with the intention of eventually replacing the ITBS and the TAP.
- All high schools have students divided into a junior academy, consisting of 9th and 10th graders, and a senior academy, serving 11th and 12th graders.
- Teachers are expected to participate in professional development that is supportive and consistent with their school's action plan.
- Local school council elections were held on report-card-pickup day to improve parental participation.

What Challenges Lie Ahead?

In the longer run, the success of the integrated governance model in Chicago depends on the extent to which the district is able to address several of the key educational challenges. These challenges can be summarized in terms of several policy questions:

- How will the system serve repeating students? How will high schools address failure rates at the ninth grade?
- How will the system implement curriculum standards in 550 schools? How will teachers make use of assessment to improve curriculum and instruction?
- What incentives will the system provide to expand the supply of well-qualified teachers?
- How will the system monitor progress in the reconstituted schools? What kinds of interim benchmarks are helpful to schools under probation and reconstitution?

These concerns notwithstanding, integrated governance is a promising strategy. Currently, Chicago is the only district where mayoral commitment is highly visible and where political capital is used to improve the system. Further research is needed to better understand how this can work in other urban districts and to identify the crucial components of the redesigned system that are transferable.

CONCLUSION

Given the pervasiveness of federalism and pluralist democratic practices, public education will continue to be shaped by federal, state, and local decisions. At issue is the extent to which governance and policy address our changing social and educational challenges as we enter the 21st century. How will educational policy improve student performance for all? Can public schools become centers of excellence? Do districts and schools have the capacity to promote equal educational opportunities when the broader political climate has shifted toward fiscal retrenchment? These are critical policy issues that have implications for policy makers and researchers. As lawmakers look for ways to improve educational performance, they are likely to call for systemic reform at all levels of our government. New accountability frameworks may emerge and more vigorous content standards may be adopted. In this climate of accountability, teachers and professors are likely to give greater attention to instructional strategies that would raise student performance. The challenge, then, is to ensure a proper balance between excellence and equity.

To be sure, the most extensive efforts to reform school governance are currently underway at the local level. Urban districts and their schools have become a laboratory of innovative ideas. Clearly, since the early 1980s, school districts have gradually moved away from the traditional, centralized model. Increasingly, school systems have adopted a variety of power-sharing arrangements, such as parental empowerment in Chicago. In the past few years, a different kind of centralized model is in vogue that can be called *integrated governance*. Unlike the traditional bureaucratic model, integrated governance, as exemplified in Chicago since 1995, focuses on student outcomes, policy coherence, and greater accountability. Diversity in governing structures is likely to flourish for some time and will continue to deepen our understanding of the most effective ways to improve both quality and equity in schools.

References

Barr, R., & Dreeben, R. (1983). *How schools work*. Chicago: University of Chicago Press.
Berke, J., Goertz, M., & Coley, R. (1984). *Politicians, judges, and city schools: Reforming school finance in New York*. New York: Russell Sage Foundation.
Boyd, W. (1983). Rethinking educational policy and management. *American Journal of Education*, 91(1), 1–29.
Bryk, A., Kerbow, D., & Rollow, S. (1997). Chicago school reform. In D. Ravitch & J. Viteritti (Eds.), *New schools for a new century* (pp. 164–200). New Haven, CT: Yale University Press.
Brown v. Board of Education 347 U.S. 483 (1954).
Callahan, R. (1962). *Education and the cult of efficiency*. Chicago: University of Chicago Press.
Citrin, J. (1984). "Introduction: The Legacy of Proposition 13." In T. Schwadron (Ed.), *California and the American tax revolt* (pp. 1–69). Berkeley: Univ. of California Press.
Clark, T. N. (Ed.). (1994). *Urban innovation: Creating strategies for turbulent times*. Thousand Oaks, CA: Sage.
Cloud, D. S. (1995). Shakeup time. *Congressional Quarterly: Committee Guide*. Washington, DC: Congressional Quarterly Inc.
Consortium on Chicago School Research. (1993). *A view from the elementary schools: The state of reform in Chicago*. Chicago, IL: Author.
Cuban, L. (1990). Reforming again, again, and again. *Educational Researcher*, 19(1), 3–13.
Danzberger, J., Kirst, M., & Usdan, M. (1992). *Governing public schools: New times, new requirements*. Washington, DC: Institute for Educational Leadership.
Finn, C. (1992). Reinventing local control. In P. First & H. Walberg (Eds.), *School boards: Changing local control* (pp. 21–25). Berkeley, CA: McCutchan.
Fuller, E., & Pearson, J. (Eds.). (1969). *Education in the states*. Washington, DC: National Education Association.
Hamilton, A., Madison, J., & Jay, J. (1961). *The Federalist Papers*. New York: Mentor.
Hanushek, E. (1994). *Making schools work*. Washington, DC: Brookings Institution.
Hirschman, A. (1970). *Exit, voice, and loyalty*. Cambridge: Harvard Univ. Press.
Hobbes, T. (1985). *Leviathan*. London: Penguin.
Hoxby, C. (1997). "What do America's "traditional" forms of school choice teach us about school choice reforms?" Paper presented at the National Conference of the Association of Public Policy Analysis and Management, Washington, DC, 1997.
Jones, C. O. (1995, Spring). Bill Clinton and the GOP Congress. *The Brookings Review*, pp. 30–33.
Kerr, N. (1964). "The school board as an agency of legitimation," *Sociology of Education* 38 (1964), 34–59.
Lieberman, J. K. (1992). *The evolving constitution*. New York: Random House.
National Commission on Excellence in Education. (1983). *A nation at risk*. Washington, DC: U.S. Government Printing Office.
Nitschke, L. (1996, March 2). Alternate routes considered for D.C. spending bill. *Congressional Quarterly Weekly Report*, p. 549.

Oates, W. (1972). *Fiscal Federalism*. New York: Harcourt Brace Jovanovich.

Orland, M. (1994). "From the picket to the chain link fence: National goals and federal aid to the disadvantaged." In K. Wong and M. Wang (Eds.) *Rethinking policy for at-risk students* (pp. 179–196). Berkeley: McCutchan Publishing Co.

Peterson, P. E., Rabe, B., & Wong, K. (1986). *When federalism works*. Washington, DC: Brookings Institution.

Phi Delta Kappan. (1984). *Gallup polls of attitudes toward education 1969–1984: A topical summary*. Bloomington, IN: Phi Delta Kappan.

Ravitch, D., & Viteritti, J. (1997). New York: The obsolete factory. In D. Ravitch & J. Viteritti (Eds.), *New schools for a new century* (pp. 17–36). New Haven, CT: Yale University Press.

Sebring, P., Bryk, A., & Easton, J. (1995). *Charting reform: Chicago teachers take stock*. Chicago: Consortium on Chicago School Research.

Shannon, T. (1992). Local control and 'organizacrats.' In P. First & H. Walberg (Eds.), *School boards: Changing local control* (pp. 27–33). Berkeley, CA: McCutchan.

Stroufe, G. (1995). Politics of education at the federal level. In J. Scribner & D. Layton (Eds.), *The study of educational politics* (pp. 75–88). London: Falmer.

Sundquist, J. (1968). *Politics and policy*. Washington, DC: Brookings Institution.

Tiebout, C. (1956). A pure theory of local expenditures. *Journal of Political Economy*, 64, 416–424.

Tyack, D. (1974). *The one best system*. Cambridge, MA: Harvard University Press.

U.S. Department of Education. (1993). *Reinventing Chapter 1: The current Chapter 1 program and new directions*. Washington, DC: Author.

Wagner, R., Jr. (1992, April 30). Can school board be saved? *New York Times*, p. A23.

Walberg, H., & Niemiec, R. (1996, May 22). Can the Chicago reforms work? *Education Week*, p. 39.

Wong, K. K. (1990). *City choices: Education and housing*. Albany, NY: State University of New York Press.

Wong, K. K. (1991). State and local government institutions and education policy. In C. Thomas (Ed.), *Politics and public policy in the contemporary American west* (pp. 355–388). Albuquerque, NM: University of New Mexico Press.

Wong, K. K. (1992). The politics of urban education as a field of study: An interpretive analysis. In J. Cibulka, R. Reed, & K. Wong (Eds.), *The politics of urban education in the United States* (pp. 3–26). London: Falmer.

Wong, K. K. (1994). "Governance structure, resource allocation, and equity policy" (Chapter 6, pp. 257–289), *Review of Research in Education*, 20, 1994.

Wong, K. K. (Ed.). (1996). *Advances in educational policy, vol. 2: Rethinking school reform in Chicago*. Greenwich, CT: JAI.

Wong, K. K., & Anagnostopoulos, A. (1998). Can integrated governance reconstruct teaching?: Lessons learned from two low-performing Chicago high schools. *Educational Policy*, 12(1&2), 31–47.

Wong, K. K., Dreeben, R., Lynn, L. E., Jr., & Sunderman, G. L. (1997). *Integrated governance as a reform strategy in the Chicago public schools*. Chicago, IL: University of Chicago, Department of Education & Irving B. Harris Graduate School of Public Policy Studies.

Wong, K. K., & Moulton, M. (1996). Developing institutional performance indicators for Chicago schools: Conceptual and methodological issues considered. In K. Wong (Ed.), *Advanced in educational policy, Vol. 2: Rethinking school reform in Chicago* (pp. 57–89). Greenwich, CT: JAI.

Wong, K. K., Sunderman, G., & Lee, J. Y. (1997). Redesigning the federal compensatory education program: Lessons from the implementation of Title I schoolwide projects. In M. Wang & K. Wong (Eds.), *Implementing school reform*. Philadelphia, PA: Temple University Center for Research in Human Development and Education.

Wright, D. (1982). *Understanding intergovernmental relations* (2nd ed.). Monterey, CA: Brooks/Cole.

CHAPTER

13

Success for All: Policy Consequences of Replicable Schoolwide Reform[1]

ROBERT E. SLAVIN

*Center for Research on the Education of Students Placed at Risk,
Johns Hopkins University*

American education has been in an uninterrupted state of reform for more than 15 years, at least since the publication of A *Nation at Risk* (National Commission on Excellence in Education) in 1983. Throughout that time, the main focus of reform has been on school governance and accountability. By the 1990s, almost all states had adopted standards, tests, and systems of accountability designed to recognize schools whose students are doing well and to punish those whose students are doing poorly. Discussions of school choice, vouchers, and privatization still dominate policy debates, as they have since the Reagan administration.

Yet throughout this time of national debate, student achievement has barely changed. Ironically, widespread improvements in scores on new state assessments have not led to improvements in performances on the National Assessment of Educational Progress (NAEP), which have generally stayed the same or slightly declined since the early 1980s. This discrepancy has led critics to suspect that increases in state test scores reflect nothing more than a one-time boost due to teachers' learning how to teach to new assessments,

[1]The research summarized in this paper was funded primarily by the Office of Educational Research and Improvement, U.S. Department of Education (Grant No. OERI-R-117-D40005). However, any opinions expressed are the author's and do not represent OERI positions or policies.

not to increases in actual learning. The problem, as studies are increasingly showing (e.g., Goertz, Floden, & O'Day, 1996), is that all of the hotly debated systemic reforms are having remarkably little impact on the day-to-day teaching of America's teachers.

Clearly, it is unlikely that student achievement will increase on a large scale unless teaching methods and materials improve broadly and significantly. This is a daunting task. In the United States there are 2.6 million elementary and secondary teachers in more than 100,000 schools. Helping even a small proportion of them to use markedly better instructional strategies would require a massive investment in professional development, even if there were complete agreement about what effective practices were.

Of course, professional development has always taken place in American schools, but its quality and effectiveness are highly variable. In particular, there is little evidence to support most instructional innovations, and even when such evidence exists, there is little capacity to provide the extensive training, follow-up, and assessment necessary to significantly improve teachers' practices. Islands of excellence appear, and are often documented, but there have been few mechanisms available capable of replicating effective practices.

MODELS OF REFORM

In recent years, this situation has begun to change. Beginning in the mid-1980s, in parallel to the development of systemic reform policies, a set of programs has formed that is designed to create substantial reforms throughout elementary and secondary schools. Most important, these programs are designed from the outset to be *replicable*. This is not to say that every school is expected to implement them in precisely the same way, but the schools implementing a given program do share at least a common set of principles and strategies, and national organizations supporting the programs provide extensive professional development, networking opportunities, and written guides to practice. Early examples include Comer's (1988) School Development Program, Levin's (1987; Hopfenberg & Levin, 1993) Accelerated Schools, and Sizer's (1984) Coalition of Essential Schools. Each of these national networks is currently engaged in hundreds of schools in all parts of the United States. Each nurtures national networks of reforming schools, including regionally based professional development groups. These programs do not, however, focus on instruction and curriculum but rather on school organization, community outreach, and internal innovation. Teachers are expected to create their own innovative approaches to curriculum and instruction according to very general guidelines, and as a result, schools involved in these networks vary enormously in the degree and nature of implementation. They can be characterized as *organizational development* approaches (see Slavin, 1998), because their intention is to build the school's own organizational capacity for reform rather than to implement specific instructional or curriculum practices. Perhaps for this reason, research on student achievement has not been a primary emphasis of these models. The major exception is the Comer project, which has carried out research on achievement, but a review of this research by Becker and Hedges (1992) concluded that the program's effects on nonacademic outcomes were much better documented than those on academic outcomes.

A second type of reform is seen in the work of the New American Schools Development Corporation (now simply New American Schools [NAS]). Starting in 1991, NAS funded the development of eight school reform designs specifically built for replication (see Stringfield, Ross, & Smith, 1996). Most resemble the earlier organizational development programs, and in fact, one, called ATLAS, grew out of a collaboration between Sizer and Comer and two other organizations. The development and dissemination of the NAS programs has given substantial impetus to the broader movement toward school reform based on replicable designs. For example, NAS as an organization was highly instrumental in the passage of the Obey-Porter Comprehensive School Reform amendment, described in a following section. Most of the NAS designs are currently working in no more than 50 schools. The two exceptions are built on the foundations of earlier large-scale programs: the National Alliance for Restructuring Education (Rothman, 1996), based on the New Standards Project, and Roots and Wings (Slavin, Madden, & Wasik, 1996), based on Success for All.[2]

A third type of reform has also evolved alongside the sytemic reform movement and the development of replicable organizational development approaches. This approach provides far more specific guidance to teachers, including teacher's manuals and student materials, and provides substantially more in-service for each teacher than do organizational development models. These might be called *faithful replication* models. Although it is not a whole-school strategy, Reading Recovery (Lyons, Pinnell, & DeFord, 1993) is the outstanding example of this approach. Starting in New Zealand in the early 1980s, this tutoring program for at-risk first graders is currently being used in more than 8000 U.S. schools with an elaborate network of university-based training programs and school-based teacher leaders operating nationally.

Unlike the organizational development programs, Reading Recovery expects schools to implement its procedures with fidelity and close adherence to the model. The national program, headquartered at Ohio State University, monitors the use of the program and will take legal action if its name is used without the program being implemented as intended. Also unlike the organizational development models, Reading Recovery carried out high-quality

---

[2]Roots and Wings and Success for All are registered trademarks of the Success for All Foundation.

research, with random assignment of students to tutoring and nontutoring conditions, from its earliest days (Pinnell, DeFord, & Lyons, 1988; Pinnell, Lyons, DeFord, Bryk, & Seltzer, 1994). This research has documented powerful impacts of the program for first-grade reading, although later research has questioned both the long-term impact and the cost-effectiveness of the model (Hiebert, 1994).

Although Reading Recovery has perhaps been the most successful of the faithful replication models, there are many others. Direct Instruction (Adams & Engelmann, 1996), dating back to the early 1970s, is reappearing in large numbers of schools. The National Diffusion Network, a U.S. Department of Education program that recognized and helped disseminate programs with some evidence of effectiveness, listed more than 500 programs before it was discontinued in 1996. Many of these remain in widespread use.

Whatever their particular merits and research bases, both the organizational development approaches and the faithful replication approaches have demonstrated unequivocally that educational programs can be broadly replicated far from their original sites. The concern expressed in the influential Rand Change Agent Study of the 1970s (McLaughlin, 1990) that externally developed programs cannot be replicated has been shown over and over again to be flatly wrong. Today, tens of thousands of schools are implementing one or another instructional design developed elsewhere.

Success for All

The first program to apply the faithful replication approach to reform of entire schools is the Success for All program (Slavin, Madden, Dolan, & Wasik, 1996). Success for All began in one Baltimore elementary school in 1987–1988, and since then has expanded each year to additional schools. As of fall 1998, it is in about 1130 schools in 300 districts in 44 states throughout the United States. The districts range from some of the largest in the country, such as Houston, Memphis, Philadelphia, Cincinnati, Chicago, New York, San Antonio, and Miami, to such middle-sized districts as Galveston, Texas, Rockford, Illinois, and Modesto and Riverside, California, to tiny rural districts, including two on the Navajo reservation in Arizona. Success for All reading curricula in Spanish have been developed and researched and are used in bilingual programs in many states. Almost all Success for All schools are high-poverty Title I schools, and the great majority are schoolwide projects. Otherwise, the schools vary widely. Under funding from NAS, a math program (MathWings) and a social studies/science program (WorldLab) were added to Success for All. Together, these elements constitute a program called Roots and Wings (Slavin, Madden, & Wasik, 1996).

Success for All and Roots and Wings have somewhat different components at different sites, depending on the school's needs and resources available to implement the program (adapted from Slavin, Madden, Dolan, &

Wasik, 1996). However, there is a common set of elements characteristic of all Success for All and Roots and Wings schools. These are described next.

Reading Program

Success for All and Roots and Wings use a reading curriculum based on research and effective practices in beginning reading (e.g., Adams, 1990) and on effective use of cooperative learning (Slavin, 1995; Stevens, Madden, Slavin, & Farnish, 1987).

Reading teachers at every grade level begin the reading time by reading children's literature to students and engaging them in a discussion of the story to enhance their understanding of the story, listening and speaking vocabulary, and knowledge of story structure. In kindergarten and first grade, the program emphasizes the development of oral language and pre-reading skills through the use of thematically based units, which incorporate areas such as language, art, and writing under a science or social studies topic. A component called Story Telling and Retelling (STaR) involves the students in listening to, retelling, and dramatizing children's literature. Big books as well as oral and written composing activities allow students to develop concepts of print as they also develop knowledge of story structure. There is also a strong emphasis on phonetic awareness activities, which help develop auditory discrimination and support the development of reading readiness strategies.

Reading Roots is typically introduced in the second semester of kindergarten or in first grade. This K-1 beginning reading program uses as its base a series of phonetically regular but meaningful and interesting minibooks and emphasizes repeated oral reading to partners as well as to the teacher. The minibooks begin with a set of shared stories, in which part of a story is written in small type (read by the teacher) and part is written in large type (read by the students). The student portion uses a phonetically controlled vocabulary. Taken together, the teacher and student portions create interesting, worthwhile stories. Over time, the teacher portion diminishes and the student portion lengthens, until students are reading the entire book. This scaffolding allows students to read interesting literature when they only have a few letter sounds.

Letters and letter sounds are introduced in an active, engaging set of activities that begins with oral language and moves into written symbols. Individual sounds are integrated into a context of words, sentences, and stories. Instruction is provided in story structure, specific comprehension skills, metacognitive strategies for self-assessment and self-correction, and integration of reading and writing.

Spanish bilingual programs use an adaptation of *Reading Roots* called *Lee Conmigo* ("Read with Me"). *Lee Conmigo* uses the same instructional strategies as *Reading Roots*, but is built around its own Spanish books and lessons.

Adaptations for second-language learners being taught in English are also widely used.

When students reach the primer reading level, they use a program called *Reading Wings*, an adaptation of Cooperative Integrated Reading and Composition (CIRC) (Stevens et al., 1987). *Reading Wings* uses cooperative learning activities built around story structure, prediction, summarization, vocabulary building, decoding practice, and story-related writing. Students engage in partner reading and structured discussion of stories or novels, and work toward mastery of the vocabulary and content of the story in teams. Story-related writing is also shared within teams. Cooperative learning both increases students' motivation and engages students in cognitive activities known to contribute to reading comprehension, such as elaboration, summarization, and rephrasing (see Slavin, 1995). Research on CIRC has found it to significantly increase students' reading comprehension and language skills (Stevens et al., 1987).

In addition to these story-related activities, teachers provide direct instruction in reading comprehension skills, and students practice these skills in their teams. Classroom libraries of trade books at students' reading levels are provided for each teacher, and students read books of their choice for homework for 20 minutes each night. Home readings are shared via presentations, summaries, puppet shows, and other formats twice a week during book club sessions.

Materials to support *Reading Wings* through the sixth grade (or beyond) exist in English and Spanish (called *Alas para Leer*). The English materials are built around children's literature and around the most widely used basal series and anthologies. Supportive materials have been developed for more than 100 children's novels and for most current basal series. *Alas para Leer* materials are similarly built around Spanish-language novels and the basals.

Beginning in the second semester of program implementation, Success for All and Roots and Wings schools usually implement a writing/language arts program based primarily on cooperative learning principles (see Slavin, Madden, & Stevens, 1989/1990).

Students in Grades 1 to 5 or 6 are regrouped for reading. The students are assigned to heterogeneous, age-grouped classes most of the day, but during a regular 90-minute reading period they are regrouped by reading performance levels into reading classes of students all at the same level. For example, a 2-1 reading class might contain first, second, and third grade students all reading at the same level. The reading classes are smaller than homerooms because tutors and other certified staff (such as librarians or art teachers) teach reading during this common reading period. Regrouping allows teachers to teach the whole reading class without having to break the class into reading groups. This greatly reduces the time spent in seatwork and increases direct instruction time, eliminating workbooks, dittos, or other follow-up activities which are needed in classes that have multiple reading groups. The regrouping is a form of the Joplin Plan, which has been found to increase reading achievement in the elementary grades (Slavin, 1987).

Eight-Week Reading Assessments

At 8-week intervals, reading teachers assess student progress through the reading program. The results of the assessments are used to determine who is to receive tutoring, to change students' reading groups, to suggest other adaptations in students' programs, and to identify students who need other types of assistance, such as family interventions or screening for vision and hearing problems. The assessments are curriculum-based measures that include teacher observations and judgments as well as more formal measures of reading comprehension.

Reading Tutors

One of the most important elements of Success for All and Roots and Wings is the use of tutors to promote students' success in reading. One-to-one tutoring is the most effective form of instruction known (see Wasik & Slavin, 1993). The tutors are certified teachers with experience teaching Title I, special education, or primary reading. Often, well-qualified paraprofessionals also tutor children with less severe reading problems. In this case, a certified tutor monitors their work and assists with the diagnostic assessment and intervention strategies. Tutors work one-on-one with students who are having difficulties keeping up with their reading groups. The tutoring occurs in 20-minute sessions during times other than reading or math periods.

In general, tutors support students' success in the regular reading curriculum, rather than teaching different objectives. For example, the tutor works with a student on the same story and concepts being read and taught in the regular reading class. However, tutors seek to identify learning problems and use different strategies to teach the same skills. They also teach metacognitive skills beyond those taught in the classroom program (Wasik & Madden, 1995). Schools may have as many as six or more teachers serving as tutors depending on school size, need for tutoring, and other factors.

During daily 90-minute reading periods, certified tutors serve as additional reading teachers to reduce class size for reading. Reading teachers and tutors use brief forms to communicate about students' specific problems and needs and meet at regular times to coordinate their approaches with individual children.

Initial decisions about reading group placement and the need for tutoring are based on informal reading inventories that the tutors give to each child. Subsequent reading group placements and tutoring assignments are made using the curriculum-based assessments described. First graders receive priority for tutoring, on the assumption that the primary function of the tutors is to help all students be successful in reading the first time, before they fail and become remedial readers.

Preschool and Kindergarten

Most Success for All and Roots and Wings schools provide a half-day preschool or a full-day kindergarten for eligible students. The preschool and kindergarten programs focus on providing a balanced and developmentally appropriate learning experience for young children. The curriculum emphasizes the development and use of language. It provides a balance of academic readiness and nonacademic music, art, and movement activities in a series of thematic units. Readiness activities include use of the Peabody Language Development Kits and Story Telling and Retelling (STaR) in which students retell stories read by the teachers. Pre-reading activities begin during the second semester of kindergarten.

Family Support Team

Parents are an essential part of the formula for success in Success for All and Roots and Wings. A family support team works in each school, serving to make families feel comfortable in the school and become active supporters of their child's education as well as providing specific services. The family support team consists of the Title I parent liaison, assistant principal (if any), counselor (if any), facilitator, and any other appropriate staff already present in the school or added to the school staff.

The family support team first works toward good relations with parents and to increase involvement in the schools. Family support team members may complete "welcome" visits for new families. They organize many attractive programs in the school, such as parenting skills workshops. Most schools use a program called Raising Readers, in which parents are given strategies to use in reading with their own children. Family support teams also help teachers implement a social skills curriculum, Getting along Together, which emphasizes peaceful solutions to interpersonal problems.

The family support team also intervenes to solve problems. For example, team members may contact parents whose children are frequently absent to see what resources can be provided to assist the family in getting the child to school. Family support staff, teachers, and parents work together to solve school behavior problems. Also, family support staff are called on to provide assistance when students seem to be working at less than their full potential because of problems at home. Families of students who are not receiving adequate sleep or nutrition, need glasses, are not attending school regularly, or are exhibiting serious behavior problems may receive family support assistance.

The family support team is strongly integrated into the academic program of the school. It receives referrals from teachers and tutors regarding children who are not making adequate academic progress and thereby constitutes an additional stage of intervention for students in need above and beyond that provided by the classroom teacher or tutor. The family support team also encourages and trains the parents to fulfill numerous volunteer roles within the school, ranging from providing a listening ear to emerging readers to helping in the school cafeteria.

Program Facilitator

A program facilitator works at each school to oversee (with the principal) the operation of the Success for All and Roots and Wings models. The facilitator helps plan the program, helps the principal with scheduling, and visits classes and tutoring sessions frequently to help teachers and tutors with individual problems. He or she works directly with the teachers on implementation of the curriculum, classroom management, and other issues, helps teachers and tutors deal with any behavior problems or other special problems, and coordinates the activities of the family support team with those of the instructional staff.

Teachers and Teacher Training

The teachers and tutors are regular certified teachers. They receive detailed teacher's manuals supplemented by 3 days of in-service at the beginning of the school year. In Roots and Wings schools, this level of in-service continues over a 3-year period as the main program elements are phased in.

Throughout the year, additional in-service presentations are made by the facilitators and other project staff on such topics as classroom management, instructional pace, and cooperative learning. Facilitators also organize many informal sessions to allow teachers to share problems and problem solutions, suggest changes, and discuss individual children. The staff development model used in Success for All and Roots and Wings emphasizes relatively brief initial training with extensive classroom follow-up, coaching, and group discussion.

Advisory Committee

An advisory committee composed of the building principal, program facilitator, teacher representatives, parent representatives, and family support staff meets regularly to review the progress of the program and to identify and solve any problems that arise. In most schools existing site-based management teams are adapted to fulfill this function. In addition, grade-level teams and the family support team meet regularly to discuss common problems and solutions and to make decisions in their areas of responsibility.

Special Education

Every effort is made to deal with students' learning problems within the context of the regular classroom, as supplemented by tutors. Tutors evaluate students' strengths and weaknesses and develop strategies to teach in the most effective way. In some schools, special education teachers work as tutors and reading teachers with students identified as learning disabled as well as other students experiencing learning problems who are at risk for special education placement. One major goal of Success for All and Roots and Wings is to keep students with learning problems out of special education if at all possible and to serve any students who do qualify for special education in a way that does not disrupt their regular classroom experience (see Slavin, 1996a).

Roots and Wings

Roots and Wings (Slavin, Madden, Dolan, & Wasik, 1994; Slavin, Madden, & Wasik, 1996), as noted earlier, is a comprehensive reform design for elementary schools that adds to Success for All innovative programs in mathematics, social studies, and science. Development of Roots and Wings was funded by NAS, a foundation mostly supported by large corporations.

Roots and Wings schools begin by implementing all components of Success for All, described earlier. In the second year of implementation, these schools typically begin to incorporate the additional major components. MathWings is the name of the mathematics program used in Grades 1 through 5. It is a constructivist approach to mathematics based on National Council of Teachers of Mathematics standards but designed to be practical and effective in schools serving many students placed at risk. MathWings makes extensive use of cooperative learning, games, discovery, creative problem solving, manipulatives, and calculators.

WorldLab is an integrated approach to social studies and science that engages students in simulations and group investigations. Students take on roles as various people in history, in different parts of the world, or in various occupations. For example, they work as engineers to design and test efficient vehicles, they form a state legislature to enact environmental legislation, they repeat Benjamin Franklin's experiments, and they solve problems of agriculture in Africa. In each activity students work in cooperative groups, do extensive writing, and use reading, mathematics, and fine arts skills learned in other parts of the program.

As of fall 1997, approximately 80 schools are adding either MathWings or WorldLab to their implementations of Success for All, making themselves into Roots and Wings schools.

RESEARCH ON SUCCESS FOR ALL
AND ROOTS AND WINGS

From the very beginning, there has been a strong focus in Success for All on research and evaluation. Longitudinal evaluations of the program were begun in its earliest sites, six schools in Baltimore and Philadelphia and one in Charleston, South Carolina. Later, third-party evaluators at the University of Memphis added evaluations in Memphis, Tennessee, Montgomery, Alabama, Fort Wayne, Indiana, and Caldwell, Idaho. Most recently, studies focusing on English language learners in California have been conducted in Modesto and Riverside by WestEd. Each of these evaluations has compared Success for All schools to matched comparison schools on measures of reading performance, starting with cohorts in kindergarten or in first grade and following the performance of these students as long as possible (details of the evaluation design appear next). Vaguaries of funding and other local problems have ended some evaluations prematurely, but most have been able to follow Success for All schools for many years. As of this writing, there are multiple years of continuous data, a total of 23 schools in nine districts (and their matched control schools) (summarized in Slavin et al., 1996). Information on these schools and districts is shown in Table 1.

Evaluation Design

A common evaluation design, with variations due to local circumstances, has been used in all Success for All evaluations. Every Success for All school involved in a formal evaluation is matched with a control school that is similar in poverty level (percent of students qualifying for free lunch), historical achievement level, ethnicity, and other factors. Schools are also matched on district-administered standardized test scores given in kindergarten or (starting in 1991 in six districts) on Peabody Picture Vocabulary Test (PPVT) scores given by the project in the fall of kindergarten or first grade.

The measures used in the evaluations were as follows:

1. *Woodcock Reading Mastery Test.* Three Woodcock scales—Word Identification, Word Attack, and Passage Comprehension—were individually administered to students by trained testers. Word Identification assesses recognition of common sight words, Word Attack assesses phonetic synthesis skills, and Passage Comprehension assesses comprehension in context. Students in Spanish bilingual programs were given the Spanish versions of these scales.
2. *Durrell Analysis of Reading Difficulty.* The Durrell Oral Reading scale was also individually administered to students in Grades 1 through 3. It presents a series of graded reading passages, which students read aloud, followed by comprehension questions.

TABLE 1
Characteristics of Success for All Schools in the Longitudinal Study

District/School	Enrollment	% Free lunch	Ethnicity	Date began SFA	Data collected	Preschool ?	Full-day kindergarten ?	Comments
Baltimore								
B1	500	83	B:96% W:4%	1987	88–94	Yes	Yes	First SFA school;
B2	500	96	B:100%	1988	89–94	Some	Yes	had additional funds first 2 years;
B3	400	96	B:100%	1988	89–94	Some	Yes	had additional funds first 4 years
B4	500	85	B:100%	1988	89–94	Some	Yes	
B5	650	96	B:100%	1988	89–94	Some	Yes	
Philadelphia								
P1	620	96	A:60% W:20% B:20%	1988	89–94	No	Yes	Large ESL program for Cambodian children
P2	600	97	B:100%	1991	92–93	Some	Yes	
P3	570	96	B:100%	1991	92–93	No	yes	
P4	840	98	B:100%	1991	93	No	Yes	Study only involves students in Spanish bilingual program
P5	700	98	L:100%	1992	93–94	No	Yes	
Charleston, SC								
CS1	500	40	B:60% W:40%	1990	91–92	No	No	
Memphis, TN								
MT1	350	90	B:95% W:5%	1990	91–94	Yes	No	Program implemented only in grades K–2
MT2	530	90	B:100%	1993	94	Yes	Yes	
MT3	290	86	B:100%	1993	94	Yes	Yes	
MT4	370	90	B:100%	1993	94	Yes	Yes	

Fort Wayne, IN								
F1	330	65	B:56% W:44%	1991	92–94	No	Yes	SFA schools (and controls) are part of desegregation plan
F2	250	55	B:55% W:45%	1991	92–94	No	Yes	SFA schools (and controls) are part of desegregation plan
Montgomery, AL								
MA1	450	95	B:100%	1991	93–94	No	Yes	
MA2	460	97	B:100%	1991	93–94	No	Yes	
Caldwell, ID								
CI1	400	20	W:80% L:20%	1991	93–94	No	No	Study compares two SFA schools to Reading Recovery school
Modesto, CA								
MC1	640	70	W:54% L:25% A:17% B:4%	1992	94	Yes	No	Large ESL program for students speaking 17 languages
MC2	560	98	L:66% W:24% A:10%	1992	94	Yes	No	Large Spanish bilingual program
Riverside, CA								
R1	930	73	L:54% W:33% B:10% A:3%	1992	94	Yes	No	Large Spanish bilingual and ESL programs; year-round school

Key: B: African American, L: Latino, A: Asian American, W: White

Reprinted with permission from Slavin et al., 1996.

3. *Gray Oral Reading Test.* Comprehension and passage scores from the Gray Oral Reading Test were obtained from students in Grades 4 and 5.

Analyses of covariance with pretests as covariates were used to compare raw scores in all evaluations, and separate analyses were conducted for students in general and for students in the lowest 25% of their grades.

The figures presented in this chapter summarize student performance in grade equivalents (adjusted for covariates) and effect size (proportion of a standard deviation separating the experimental and control groups), averaging across individual measures. Neither grade equivalents nor averaged scores were used in the analyses, but they are presented here as a useful summary.

Each of the evaluations summarized in this section follows children who began in Success for All or Roots and Wings in first grade or earlier, in comparison to children who had attended the control school over the same period. Students who started in a program after first grade are not considered to have received the full treatment (although they are of course served within the schools).

Results for all experimental-control comparisons in all evaluation years are averaged and summarized in Figure 1 using a method called multisite

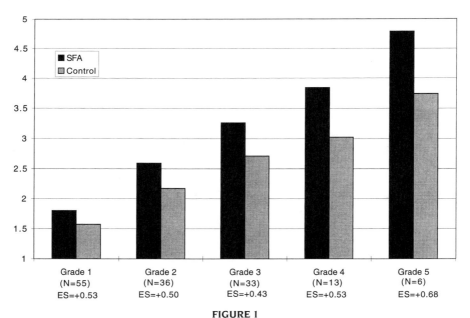

FIGURE 1

Comparison of Success for All (SFA) and control schools in mean reading grade equivalents and effect sizes (ES), 1988–1994. Reprinted with permission from Slavin et al., 1996.

replicated experiment (Slavin, Madden, Dolan, Wasik, 1996; Slavin, Madden, Dolan, Wasik, Ross, et al., 1996; Slavin & Madden, 1993). For more details on methods and findings, see Slavin, Madden, Dolan, and Wasik (1996) and Slavin, Madden, Dolan, Wasik, Ross, et al. (1996) and the full site reports.

Reading Outcomes

The results of the multisite replicated experiment evaluating Success for All are summarized in Figure 1 for each grade level, 1 through 5. The analyses compare cohort means for experimental and control schools; for example, the Grade 1 graph compares 55 experimental to 55 control cohorts, with cohort (50 to 150 students) as the unit of analysis. In other words, each bar is a mean of scores from more than 5000 students. Grade equivalents are based on the means and are only presented for their informational value. No analyses were done using grade equivalents.

Statistically significantly (p≤.05) positive effects of Success for All (compared to controls) were found on every measure at every grade level, 1 through 5. For students in general, effect sizes (ES) averaged around a half standard deviation at all grade levels. Effects were somewhat higher than this for the Woodcock Word Attack scale in first and second grades, but in Grades 3 through 5 effect sizes were more or less equivalent on all aspects of reading. Consistently, effect sizes for students in the lowest 25% of their grades were particularly positive, ranging from ES = +1.03 in first grade to ES = +1.68 in fourth grade. Again, cohort-level analyses found statistically significant differences favoring low achievers in Success for All on every measure at every grade level.

Roots and Wings

A study of Roots and Wings (Slavin, Madden, & Wasik, 1996) was carried out in four pilot schools in rural southern Maryland. The Roots and Wings schools serve populations that are significantly more disadvantaged than state averages. They average 48% free and reduced-price lunch eligibility, compared to 30% for the state; 21% of Roots and Wings students are Title I eligible, in comparison to 7% for the state. The assessment tracked growth over time on the Maryland School Performance Assessment Program (MSPAP), compared to growth in the state as a whole. The MSPAP is a performance measure on which students are asked to solve complex problems, set up experiments, write in various genres, and read extended text. It uses matrix sampling, which means that different students take different forms of the test.

In both third and fifth grade assessments in all subjects tested (reading, language, writing, math, science, and social studies), Roots and Wings students showed substantial growth. As shown in Figures 2 and 3, the State of Maryland gained in average performance on the MSPAP over the same time

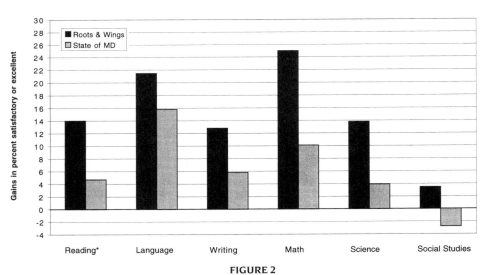

FIGURE 2
Relative gains on Maryland School Performance Assessment Program,
St. Mary's County Roots and Wings pilot schools, and state of
Maryland (MD) (percent satisfactory or excellent), Grade 3, 1993–1996.
*1993 reading scores were declared invalid. Gains are for 1994–1996.

period, but the number of Roots and Wings students achieving at satisfactory
or excellent levels increased by more than twice the state's rate on every
measure at both grade levels.

POLICY IMPLICATIONS OF SUCCESS FOR ALL

This is a time of both great opportunity and great danger in the educational
reform movement. On one hand, the public's concern about education is
high, the commitment to reform is broad, and recent policy changes (such
as the reauthorization of Title I) have removed significant obstacles to
change. Adoption in many states of tough, performance-based accountability systems has increased many educators' motivation to search for more
effective methods. However, although these systemic reforms at the policy
level may set the stage for improved teaching and learning, they have not yet
had a measurable impact. Since the publication of A Nation at Risk (National
Commission on Excellence in Education, 1983), the national conversation
about school reform has been continual, but actual student achievement has
stagnated. One of the most promising trends, the narrowing achievement
gap between majority and minority students, reversed itself in 1994 for the
first time since 1971 (National Center for Education Statistics, 1994).

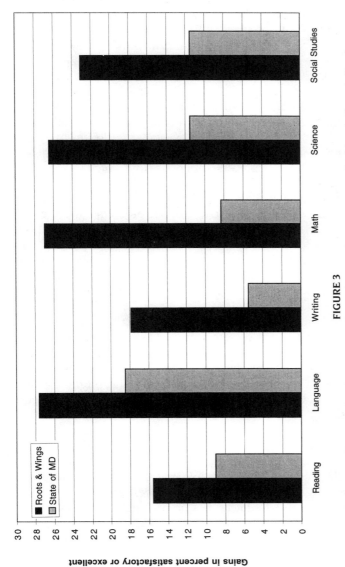

FIGURE 3

Relative gains on Maryland School Performance Assessment Program, St. Mary's County Roots and Wings pilot schools, and state of Maryland (MD) (percent satisfactory or excellent), Grade 5, 1993–1996.

It is possible, of course, that the systemic reforms being undertaken in many states and at the national level will ultimately be reflected in higher academic performance, and it seems certain that improving standards, assessments, and other governance reforms are a necessary part of an overall reform strategy. However, it is equally certain that these reforms are not enough. Student achievement cannot change unless teachers are using markedly better instructional methods and materials every day. Systemic reforms can provide incentives for schools and districts to upgrade teaching methods and materials, but otherwise they are too far from the classroom to make a substantial impact (see Goertz et al., 1996).

The research on Success for All and the demonstration that this program and many others can be replicated with integrity on a broad scale have profound implications for educational policies at all levels. They bring us closer to a day when educators will have available a range of well-developed, rigorously evaluated, and replicable programs from which to choose, rather than having to reinvent the wheel in every school. Educators will always have to adapt externally developed programs to meet local needs, but this is much easier than expecting every school to develop its own strategies from scratch. They dispel the myth that school-by-school change is too difficult, too uncertain, and too particular to local conditions to be broadly replicable. They show the effectiveness of national reform networks in building large-scale training capacity, maintaining their own high standards of practice and outcomes, and operating outside of particular school systems but within the public sector.

This is not to imply that the main policy implication of research on Success for All is to support the dissemination of this program. First, there are several programs with excellent evidence of effectiveness and of replicability (for reviews, see Fashola & Slavin, 1997; Slavin & Fashola, 1998; Slavin, Karweit, & Wasik, 1994). Second, there are many additional promising programs that are in need of assistance to complete their development, rigorous evaluation, and scaling up (see Slavin, 1997a). The currently available set of replicable programs known to have a substantial impact on student achievement when well implemented is too small. Much more research and development remains to be done to enlarge it. However, this current set, including Success for All, does provide visions of what could be accomplished in a policy environment committed to putting the best methods and materials possible into the hands of educators, who are enabled to make informed, thoughtful choices among them (see Slavin, 1996a).

The following sections discuss the implications of this perspective for several key areas of educational policy.

Reading by Age 9

During the last presidential campaign, President Clinton announced a bold objective: elimination of reading failure for all children by age 9. In an initiative called *America Reads*, he proposed spending $2.75 billion to provide stipends to volunteers and volunteer coordinators for elementary schools. There is research to support the effectiveness of volunteer tutoring of this kind, and volunteer tutors could play an important role in a comprehensive plan (Wasik, 1997). However, the administration acknowledges that this should not be the only strategy. It makes little sense to leave ineffective teaching practices in place in schools and then try to compensate for them using only volunteer tutors. *America Reads* is currently in legislative limbo; Congressman Bill Goodling, chair of the House Committee on Education and the Workforce, has proposed a compromise bill that would focus more on professional development in proven early literacy strategies.

The research on Success for All, Reading Recovery, and other early reading approaches demonstrates that high-poverty schools can routinely ensure the reading success of most at-risk children. If funds are to be made available to schools to combat reading failure, it would be important to allow schools to decide whether to use them on volunteer tutors, on proven programs in regular classrooms, on certified teacher tutors (as in Reading Recovery), or on other strategies with strong evidence of effectiveness. New literacy funds could be used to leverage Title I funds toward proven programs and away from the remedial pullouts and paraprofessionals that have been found to be ineffective in Title I/Chapter 1 programs (see the following section). The amount of money President Clinton proposed would be enough to give $40,000 to every elementary school in the United States, or $55,000 to each of 50,000 Title I schools. This is more than the total cost of materials and training for a Success for All school of 500 students. Even a small fraction of $2.75 billion could double or triple the entire national investment in educational research and development, currently less than $100 million per year. If we know that a rational process of development, evaluation, and dissemination can have a significant impact on children in thousands of schools within a reasonable time period, and if we already have on hand effective strategies capable of affecting the core of educational practice and of being replicated on a large scale, then this knowledge should be central to reform policies (see Slavin, 1997b).

Title I

Title I (of the Improving America's Schools Act, or IASA) is the largest single federal investment in elementary and secondary education. Currently funded at more than $8 billion, Title I and its predecessor, Chapter 1, primarily provide resources to high-poverty schools. Traditionally, Title I/Chapter 1 funds have overwhelmingly been used to pay for teachers to provide remedial instruction in small group pullout programs or to pay for instructional aides. These uses of Title I/Chapter 1 funds have been found in national studies to make little or no difference in the achievement of children who receive them (Puma et al., 1997). The 1993 reauthorization of Title I gave schools in which more than 50% of the students lived in poverty far greater flexibility to use their funds to benefit all students in the school, not just those who had already fallen behind. Still today the great majority of Title I schools continue to use their funds for pullout teachers and aides and on other investments with little evidence of effectiveness. Title I expenditures for proven programs are increasing; for example, Title I provides the overwhelming majority of funding for implementations of Success for All; the School Development Program, Reading Recovery; and other effective innovations. Yet although these innovations collectively serve thousands of schools, tens of thousands of Title I schools continue to invest in services that have been shown repeatedly to have little impact (see Slavin et al., 1994).

Title I needs to move to a new paradigm, in which Title I schools are made aware of a range of proven, effective models, incorporating professional development materials, staffing configurations, and so on. School staffs would have the opportunity to carefully consider the available alternatives, visit schools using them, view videotapes on them, and so on. Schools would not be required to adopt any particular program and could use programs not on the list or decide to create their own model. However, as the number of rigorously evaluated programs grows, schools might increasingly be required to justify using something else and to have their districts or other agencies carry out evaluations of their alternatives. Since its inception, the path of least resistance in Title I/Chapter 1 has been to pay for pullout teachers and aides; adopting proven programs has been difficult, whereas continuing discredited practices has been easy. This must change if Title I is to accomplish its goal of accelerating the achievement of poor children.

Obey–Porter Comprehensive School Reform Program

In November 1997, Congress passed a provision as part of the education appropriations bill that has profound implications for the perspective advocated here. This provision, proposed by Representatives David Obey of Wisconsin and John Porter of Illinois (Obey–Porter), provides $150 million, primarily for schools to use to help pay for the start-up costs of proven, comprehensive school reform designs. Schools will be able to apply for grants of at least $50,000 for up to three years to help them adopt programs with evidence of effectiveness and replicability. The bill named 17 examples of such programs, including both Success for All and Roots and Wings. However, schools are encouraged to select programs not on the list or to create their own if they can show convincing evidence of effectiveness.

Obey–Porter is a small program compared, for example, to Title I. Yet it could have a profound impact. For the first time, it puts serious funding and serious attention behind the adoption of proven programs. Of course, Obey–Porter will give thousands of schools an opportunity to adopt more effective whole-school strategies. Beyond this, however, it will give the entire education research and development enterprise a salience it has lacked. Perhaps most important, it will begin to tie Title I reform to programs with evidence of effectiveness, giving this crucial source of funding for high-poverty schools a much needed boost in popularity among educators and policy makers.

Although the potential of Obey–Porter is great, it is essential that this initiative be effective, and be *perceived* to be effective. An immediate problem the program has encountered is the limited capacity of existing reform organizations. Obey–Porter could fund as many as 2800 schools in 1998–1999. Yet the total national capacity of the 17 programs named in the legislation is on the order of 1000 to 1200, of which Success for All/Roots and Wings, the largest, would account for about 400. Even among the 17 programs, the degree of evidence of effectiveness is highly variable, and capacity to add schools is very low; only six of the programs are currently in more than 50 schools and some are in as few as 5.

The problem is that although Obey–Porter will greatly increase the *demand* for proven programs, there is no provision for increasing the *supply*. Funds are needed to help existing proven programs scale themselves up, to evaluate promising programs that would be good candidates for national scale-up, and to develop and evaluate promising new starts.

The passage of Obey–Porter has already created an enormous amount of interest and excitement about adoption of proven, comprehensive programs. At the policy level, the next essential step is to make certain that we have the programs and the evidence that schools across the country will be seeking.

Special Education

Research on Success for All, Reading Recovery, and other early intervention programs has profound implications for special education, especially for students with reading disabilities. This research shows that a substantial proportion of reading disabilities can be prevented with effective preschool, kindergarten, and first-grade programs, supplemented with one-to-one tutoring from well-trained, certified teachers for first graders who are struggling with reading. As noted earlier, studies of Success for All have shown that education placements for reading disabilities can be cut by 50% to 75%, not because students with reading disabilities are mainstreamed but because at-risk students never need special services (see Slavin, 1996b; Smith, Ross, & Casey, 1994). Further, students who are already in special education perform far better in Success for All than in control schools (Ross, Smith, Casey, & Slavin, 1995). Reading Recovery also has evidence that one-to-one tutoring for at-risk first graders can keep them out of special education (Lyons et al., 1993), and other evidence supports the same conclusion.

If we know that reading disabilities can be prevented, then it is foolish to continue current policies, which tend to assign large numbers of students with reading disabilities to long-term, expensive, relatively ineffective resource programs or (less often) self-contained special education. The recent reauthorization of IDEA could have provided an opportunity to replace remediation with effective early intervention, but this did not occur. Yet reform in this area is essential. For example, the law could be revised to require up to one year of one-to-one tutoring (paid for from special education funds) before a child could be assigned to special education for a reading disability. Only after tutoring has been tried and has failed could long-term special education become an option.

In addition, the law must be changed to remove the perverse incentive schools face to maintain or increase their special education caseloads. As things stand now, schools that invest in prevention and early intervention can be penalized (by loss of special education funds and personnel) if these interventions result in a smaller number of children going into special education. This must change. Schools should receive special education funds for high-incidence, low impact disabilities (such as learning disabilities and speech) based on demographic factors, not numbers of students placed. They must follow the law and provide services to children who do have serious learning disabilities, but if they can prevent children from falling behind they should not be penalized. For students who do end up in special education for learning disabilities, schools should be encouraged to select from among effective, rigorously evaluated models of service, as described earlier for Title I.

Systemic Reform

As noted earlier, American education policy has had a strong focus on *systemic reform*, a term that is used to describe coordinated, fundamental changes in federal, state, and local policies designed to set higher and more appropriate standards for student academic performance. In particular, the systemic reform movement has focused on establishing state and national standards, incorporating state-of-the-art performance assessments and accountability systems with real consequences for schools increasing or (especially) decreasing on these assessments. Another frequent element of systemic reform is the establishment of state curricular frameworks, which are then used to guide policies from textbook adoption to professional development. Systemic reforms also include changes in school governance, such as site-based management, choice, vouchers, charter schools, privatization, and regulatory reform.

Proponents of systemic reform (e.g., Smith & O'Day, 1991) generally recognize the limitations of this approach in affecting the day-to-day instruction of classroom teachers, but they argue that while school-by-school reforms may be desirable, there are few if any examples of effective school-by-school reforms working on a very large scale.

The research and dissemination of Success for All, the School Development Program, Reading Recovery, and other models have significantly shifted this discussion. These programs, largely operating independently of federal or state policies, have shown conclusively that large-scale school-by-school reform is possible. At the same time, studies of the outcomes of systemic reform are showing relatively little impact on classroom practice and student performance (Goertz et al., 1996). Systemic reforms can sometimes alter what teachers teach, but they rarely affect how well they teach it. The innovations most likely to be implemented and to be effective are those that provide specific materials, professional development, and other supports, in contrast to those that provide new standards and assessments but then leave educators to figure out how to accomplish these standards (Bodilly, 1996). Systemic reforms are still necessary to provide educators with appropriate standards and measures of success, to motivate educators to search for effective alternatives, and to make regulations and other policies consistent with a focus on schoolwide change. Yet neither school-by-school reform nor systemic reform can succeed without the other.

CONCLUSION

Research on Success for All and the widespread dissemination of this program and many others support a vision of school reform as a process capable of simultaneously setting higher standards for schools and assisting them with thoughtful selection and faithful, high-quality implementation of proven programs to meet those standards. The existence of reliable methods which, if properly implemented, can ensure that virtually all children can read in the elementary grades, has enormous implications for federal Title I and special education policies, as well as for President Clinton's commitment to ensure reading success for all children by third grade. If we know how to improve significantly the school success of all students, it is foolish to continue policies that fail to take this knowledge into account. Even as we expand our knowledge base, we need to use what we know. America's children deserve the best schooling we know how to provide them.

References

Adams, M. J. (1990). Beginning to read: Thinking and learning about print. Cambridge, MA: MIT Press.

Adams, G. L., & Engelmann, S. (1996). Research on Direct Instruction: 25 years beyond DISTAR. Seattle, WA: Educational Achievement Systems.

Becker, B. J., & Hedges, L. V. (1992). A review of the literature on the effectiveness of Comer's School Development Program. East Lansing, MI: Michigan State University.

Bodilly, S. J. (1996). Lessons from the New American Schools Development Corporation's development phase. Washington, DC: RAND Corporation.

Comer, J. (1988). Educating poor minority children. Scientific American, 259, 42–48.

Fashola, O. S., & Slavin, R. E. (1997). Promising programs for elementary and middle schools: Evidence of effectiveness and replicability. *Journal of Education for Students Placed at Risk*, 2(3), 251–307.

Goertz, M. E., Floden, R. E., & O'Day, J. (1996). *Systemic reform*. Washington, DC: U.S. Department of Education, Office of Educational Research and Improvement.

Hiebert, E. H. (1994). Reading Recovery in the United States: What difference does it make to an age cohort? *Educational Researcher*, 23(9), 15–25.

Hopfenberg, W. S., & Levin, H. M. (1993). *The Accelerated Schools resource guide*. San Francisco: Jossey-Bass.

Levin, H. M. (1987). Accelerated Schools for disadvantaged students. *Educational Leadership*, 44(6), 19–21.

Lyons, C. A., Pinnell, G. S., & DeFord, D. E. (1993). *Partners in learning: Teachers and children in Reading Recovery*. New York: Teachers College Press.

McLaughlin, M. W. (1990). The Rand change agent study revisited: Macro perspectives and micro realities. *Educational Researcher*, 19(9), 11–16.

National Center for Education Statistics. (1994). *The condition of education, 1994*. Washington, DC: U.S. Department of Education, NCES.

National Commission on Excellence in Education. (1983). *A Nation at Risk*. Washington, DC: U.S. Department of Education.

Pinnell, G. S., DeFord, D. E., & Lyons, C. A. (1988). *Reading Recovery: Early intervention for at-risk first graders*. Arlington, VA: Educational Research Service.

Pinnell, G. S., Lyons, C. A., DeFord, D. E., Bryk, A. S., & Seltzer, M. (1994). Comparing instructional models for the literacy education of high-risk first graders. *Reading Research Quarterly*, 29, 9–40.

Puma, M. J., Karweit, N., Price, C., Ricciuti, A., Thompson, W., & Vaden-Kiernan, M. (1997). *Prospects: Final report on student outcomes*. Cambridge, MA: Abt Associates.

Ross, S. M., Smith, L. J., Casey, J., & Slavin, R. E. (1995). Increasing the success of disadvantaged children: An examination of alternative early intervention programs. *American Educational Research Journal*, 32, 773–800.

Rothman, R. (1996). Reform at all levels: National Alliance for Restructuring Education. In S. Stringfield, S. Ross, & L. Smith (Eds.), *Bold plans for school restructuring: The New American Schools Development Corporation designs*. Mahwah, NJ: Erlbaum.

Sizer, T. (1984). *Horace's compromise: The dilemma of the American high school*. Boston: Houghton Mifflin.

Slavin, R. E. (1987). Ability grouping and student achievement in elementary schools: A best-evidence synthesis. *Review of Educational Research*, 57, 347–350.

Slavin, R. E. (1995). *Cooperative learning: Theory, research, and practice* (2nd ed.). Boston: Allyn & Bacon.

Slavin, R. E. (1996a). Neverstreaming: Preventing learning disabilities. *Educational Leadership*, 53(5), 4–7.

Slavin, R. E. (1996b). Reforming state and federal policies to support adoption of proven practices. *Educational Researcher*, 25(9), 4–5.

Slavin, R. E. (1997b). *Reading by nine: A comprehensive strategy*. Baltimore, MD: Johns Hopkins University, Center for Research on the Education of Students Placed at Risk.

Slavin, R. E. (1997a). Design competitions: A proposal for a new federal role in educational research and development. *Educational Researcher*, 26(1), 22–28.

Slavin, R. E. (1998). Sand, bricks, and seeds: School change strategies and readiness for reform. In A. Hargreaves, A. Liberman, M. Fullan, & D. Hopkins (Eds.), *International Handbook of Educational Change*. Dardrecht, The Netherlands: Kluwer.

Slavin, R. E., & Fashola, O. S. (1998). *Show me the evidence: Proven and promising programs for America's schools*. Thousand Oaks, CA: Corwin.

Slavin, R. E., Karweit, N. L., & Wasik, B. A. (1994). *Preventing early school failure: Research on effective strategies*. Boston: Allyn & Bacon.

Slavin, R. E., & Madden, N. A. (1993, April). *Multi-site replicated experiments: An application to Success for All*. Paper presented at the annual meeting of the American Educational Research Association, Atlanta.

Slavin, R. E., Madden, N. A., Dolan, L. J., & Wasik, B. A. (1994). Roots and Wings: Inspiring academic excellence. *Educational Leadership, 52*(3), 10–13.

Slavin, R. E., Madden, N. A., Dolan, L. J., & Wasik, B. A. (1996). *Every child, every school: Success for All*. Newbury Park, CA: Corwin.

Slavin, R. E., Madden, N. A., Dolan, L. J., Wasik, B. A., Ross, S., Smith, L., & Dianda, M. (1996). Success for All: A summary of research. *Journal of Education for Students Placed at Risk, 1*, 41–76.

Slavin, R. E., Madden, N. A., & Stevens, R. J. (1989/1990). Cooperative learning models for the 3 Rs. *Educational Leadership, 47*(4), 22–28.

Slavin, R. E., Madden, N. A., & Wasik, B. A. (1996). Roots and Wings. In S. Stringfield, S. Ross, & L. Smith (Eds.), *Bold plans for educational restructuring: The New American Schools*. Hillsdale, NJ: Erlbaum.

Smith, M., & O'Day, J. (1991). Systemic school reform. In S. Fuhrman & B. Malen (Eds.), *The politics of curriculum and testing* (pp. 233–267). Bristol, PA: Falmer.

Smith, L. J., Ross, S. M., & Casey, J. P. (1994). *Special education analyses for Success for All in four cities*. Memphis: University of Memphis, Center for Research in Educational Policy.

Stevens, R. J., Madden, N. A., Slavin, R. E., & Farnish, A. M. (1987). Cooperative Integrated Reading and Composition: Two field experiments. *Reading Research Quarterly, 22*, 433–454.

Stringfield, S., Ross, S., & Smith, L. (Eds.). (1996). *Bold plans for school restructuring: The New American Schools*. Hillsdale, NJ: Erlbaum.

Wasik, B. A. (1997). Volunteer tutoring programs: Do we know what works? *Phi Delta Kappan, 79*(4), 282–287.

Wasik, B. A., & Madden, N. A. (1995). *Success for All tutoring manual*. Baltimore, MD: Johns Hopkins University, Center for Research on the Education of Students Placed at Risk.

Wasik, B. A., & Slavin, R. E. (1993). Preventing early reading failure with one-to-one tutoring: A review of five programs. *Reading Research Quarterly, 28*, 178–200.

chapter 14

The Impact of the Teachers' Unions on Educational Policy and Outcomes

LEO TROY
Rutgers University

WHY TEACHER UNIONISM IS UNIQUE

Teachers' unions are probably the most powerful labor organizations in the American labor movement. They have a decisive impact on the size and allocation of resources in their industry, public education, unmatched by either any other public- or private-sector unions. Not only are the teachers' unions able to accomplish the usual union objectives—to increase compensation and negotiate changes in the workplace—but in contrast to almost all unions in the private and public sectors of the labor market, they are able to intensify the demand for their services—that is, to increase employment. When private-sector unions negotiate higher compensation, typically, these eventually reduce employment and membership. The membership of public-sector unions, except teachers, have recently experienced similar losses, as figures published by the U.S. Department of Labor over the past 3 years demonstrate. The teachers' unions are able to counter the normal union experience because their enormous political power, exercised through well-funded political action committees, has succeeded in increasing spending at all levels of government—federal, state, and local—for public education. State and local expenditures on public elementary and secondary education totaled almost $244 billion in 1994–1995. Of this amount, 62% went to instruction and another 34% to instructional support services (U.S. Department of Education, 1997). To this sum must be added more than $50 billion in federal budget support (U.S. Department of Education, 1997). Because education is a labor-intensive industry, these expenditures have translated into more jobs for teachers, even as the quality of education has declined.

This chapter examines and analyzes how the teacher unions evolved from organizations on the periphery of the American labor movement and labor markets to their present and future status of dominance and their anticipated leadership of the American labor movement. These developments have major consequences for the contemporary and future quality of public education in this country. Soon after the onset of the new millennium the anticipated merger of the two leading unions, the National Education Association and the American Federation of Teachers, will result in the largest union ever in the annals of labor organization in this and, for that matter, any other country. From this platform, the new union will be in a strategic position to gain even greater influence on the expenditures, quality, and direction of public education.

This chapter begins with a look at the historical origins of the teacher unions, their transition from self-proclaimed professionalism to unionism and bargaining, and then analyzes their effect on resource allocation and alternatives. The chapter continues with an examination of the unions' political power, their future as a merged organization, and the philosophy of this new powerhouse of labor.

THE TEACHER UNIONS: HISTORICAL ORIGINS

In contrast to the private labor market, unionism and bargaining in public education are relatively recent developments in the history of the United States. Collective bargaining did not begin in earnest in elementary and secondary public school education until the 1960s when the contemporary public-sector union movement, or what I call the *New Unionism*, originated (Troy, 1994). The private union movement began with the formation of the American Federation of Labor (AFL) in 1886; it was updated by the formation of the Congress of Industrial Organizations (CIO) in 1937. The lag in the development of public-sector unionism, of which the teachers unions are the most important component, can be attributed to the long-standing popular belief that government employees ought not and—from the perspective of public policy—should not be allowed to organize and bargain.

Public policy toward collective bargaining in the public economy changed, initiated by President Kennedy's Executive Order 10988 in January 1962. The order set off a boom in unionization and bargaining in the government labor market. The executive order itself applied to federal employees of all executive departments and agencies, with few exceptions. Only a tiny number of teachers were affected by the order because only a small number were employees of federal agencies as, for example, the teaching staff at American military installations abroad. Nearly all teachers and support staff in public education were employees of local and, to some extent, state governments. Constitutionally, these fell outside the jurisdiction of the executive order. The order fulfilled Kennedy's campaign pledge to the AFL-CIO to foster labor organization and bargaining (then referred to as collective negotiations) among federal employees. Anticipating that Congress would not enact legislation fostering unionism and bargaining for federal employees, Kennedy used the executive order to accomplish those goals.

The City of New York adopted policies encouraging bargaining by its employees in 1957, as did the state of Wisconsin. However, the model of government employee unionism and bargaining did not become nationalized until President Kennedy's order. His order was also imitated in Canada. In fact, it ignited a wave of public-sector unionism in Canada of greater scope and vigor than in any jurisdiction in the United States. Within 20 years, by about 1980, public-sector unionism became the dominant part of the Canadian union movement.

Soon after unionization at the federal level, unionization and bargaining was initiated among public school educators, as well as among other employees of state and local governments. Abetted by the willingness of officials in such key cities as New York to adopt bargaining legislation and to recognize and negotiate contracts with the representatives of the teachers' organized groups, the two principal teacher groups, the National Education Association (NEA)—an independent organization—and the American Federation of Teachers (AFT)—an affiliate of the AFL-CIO—quickly transformed themselves into unions. Both the NEA and the AFT dropped their historic, self-imposed prohibitions on strikes and bargaining and undertook both with zeal.

In reality, both organizations made the transformation from self-described professional organizations to organizations that supported unionism and bargaining prior to formally removing their self-imposed bans on bargaining and strikes. The new opportunities afforded by accommodating public employers—that is, the political leaders who saw the creation of new, powerful, and rich allies in future elections—initiated a period of active unionization of teachers and speeded up the transformation of public-sector organizations, especially teachers' organizations, into unions. Public policy and public management created what economists call a *bilateral monopoly*—that is, monopolistic conditions for both the unions and the public institutions in education with whom the teacher unions negotiated.

The new opportunities initiated a bitter rivalry between the two teacher unions to organize the country's large number of instructional and support staff. By and large, teachers in the big cities (New York, Chicago, and Los Angeles, for example) chose the AFT over the NEA to represent them. Recently, teachers in Dallas, Texas, voted to join the AFT. However, because the two unions are likely to merge in the next century, their organizational rivalry should end (Greenhouse, 1998). In anticipation of the merger, this chapter will refer to the anticipated union as the NEA-AFT. It also is likely that the new organization will be affiliated with the AFL-CIO, a step of historic significance for the NEA, which had always balked at association with the AFL-CIO or its predecessors. In the past, the NEA's affiliation would have been tantamount to an admission that the organization had abandoned its claim of professionalism and accepted its transformation into a union. In fact, that was an important block to the recent plan to merge.

THE TEACHERS' UNIONS:
THEIR EDUCATION IN COLLECTIVE BARGAINING

Although relatively new as full-fledged unions when compared to those in the private sector, the teachers' unions have had a long history of *proto-unionism* and extensive experience in *proto-bargaining* (Troy, 1994, p. 44). Consequently, they did not have to learn the basic practices of unionism and bargaining overnight.

The National Education Association

The NEA was established in 1857 as the National Teachers' Association, 29 years before the founding of the AFL, whose formation signaled the birth of the modern American union movement. The NEA changed its name to the National Educational Association in 1870, and finally settled on its present name by 1907. The NEA, which for years after its founding included principals and various supervisory personnel in its membership, therefore concerned itself in part with the administration of public education. Indeed, many of the teaching personnel within the NEA believed that their interests were often subordinated to those of the supervisory personnel. Eventually, principals and some supervisory personnel were excluded from the NEA. Shedding these groups shaped the organization's membership more like a traditional union well before it made the transition to full-fledged unionism.

The basic structural features of the NEA are the national and state association; local affiliates play a much more subordinate role than they do among standard trade unions. This structure has served the NEA's goals well, as public education is overwhelmingly a state and local function (which the expenditure figures presented earlier demonstrate). In fact, state government revenues and expenditures are currently more than double those of local governments (U.S. Department of Education, 1997), reinforcing the rationale for the state-based structure of the NEA. The NEA is composed of approximately 50 state-level teacher organizations, which operate in a semi-autonomous manner. The national level of the NEA provides both negotiating and political support while collecting a substantial portion of the state-level organization's dues. Neither the NEA nor the AFT and their affiliates, as public-sector unions, are subject to the National Labor Relations Act (NLRA). This means that public policy toward the teachers' unions is made at the state and local levels of government and therefore that government encouragement of unionism and collective bargaining varies from solidly prounion, to neutrality, and to opposition. It also enables the state affiliates of the NEA to wield extraordinary political power.

The American Federation of Teachers

AFT was organized and chartered by the American Federation of Labor in 1916 and has had a history of associating with unionist principles, even though for a long time it was not a practitioner itself. In contrast to the NEA, the AFT has relied more on the local organization as its basic structural unit, emulating most private-sector unions. The AFT also organized state groups, such as the NEA. The AFT's structure facilitated its transition to full unionism, but it more readily identified the organization with the union movement during a period of its history when it sought to represent itself as a professional rather than trade union organization. Of the two, the NEA became by far the largest organization—it was more than twice the size of the AFT on the eve of their failed merger in 1998.

New as Unions, Experienced as Negotiators

Although they lagged private unions in formal bargaining experience, both organizations had taken part in collective bargaining for years. Although they abjured formal bargaining and strikes, and even forbidden strikes in their constitutions, both dealt with salaries and working conditions through informal negotiations, lobbying, and political activities. In line with their claims of being professional organizations, the two proto-unions often veiled their bread-and-butter concerns under the rubric of educational policy. But as Wildman (1971) stated, "it is exceedingly difficult to distinguish between educational policy and salaries and working conditions" (p. 154), whether under full-fledged collective bargaining or the earlier methods of lobbying and sidebar negotiations that the two organizations employed.

The experience that the teachers' organizations acquired prior to becoming unions prepared them for de facto collective bargaining. To the informal discussions and lobbying the teachers' organizations practiced in the past, the teachers' unions added full-scale collective bargaining. Strikes (regarded by supporters of full-fledged teacher unionism as a sign of maturity) became commonplace, despite state and local laws that forbade them.

Teacher Bargaining Is New and Unique

But not only has teacher unionism come of age in straightforward collective bargaining, including reliance on the strike, teacher unionism today also wields its enormous political power to create a new and unique form of collective bargaining. This unique form of bargaining achieves results that cannot be matched in the private labor market. One of its most remarkable results is the ability of teachers' unions to increase the employment of teachers, an achievement private-sector unions are incapable of accomplishing. Typically, when private unions gain wage increases, they also reduce employment. In contrast, the teacher unions, through their political-action committees (often funded through compulsory dues payments) and their control of many parent-teacher associations, have gained increases in spending for education (and thereby for the teaching staff) from all levels of government—federal, state, and local. It is an example of eating your cake and having it too.

Another consequence of the new form of bargaining used by teachers' unions is its impact on managerial authority. Whereas bargaining in the private labor market encroaches on managerial authority, in the public labor market the teacher unions' encroachment on management goes much further—it curtails governmental sovereignty. The impact is qualitatively different and therefore, like the new style bargaining, unique. The difference is not a semantical distinction as adherents of public-sector bargaining portray; that is, that the impact of teacher unionism (and, for that matter, all public-sector unionism) on public management is no different from that in the private economy. There is a superficial similarity, but the managerial authority in the two labor markets differs significantly.

Public management's authority is derived from the electorate in an open society, whereas managerial rights in the private economy are derived from stockholders and private ownership; the curtailment of the rights of the electorate and of private employers is hardly equivalent. Encroachment on public management's authority shifts policy making from elected officials to collective bargaining. It infringes on the rights of the electorate, ostensibly the ultimate authority on educational policy. The curtailment of sovereignty is expanded further by arbitration procedures. The procedure adds another unelected person or tribunal to the bargaining process, one whose decisions compel a governmental response—financial and managerial—again divorced from the electorate. This impact is rarely recognized by the electorate because it is exercised at the local level, an arena infrequently in the headlines or on television. Most industrial relations specialists turn aside this transference of public authority as merely an extension of the curtailment of managerial authority in the public domain. They refer to it simply as "power sharing." However, it is not the sharing of power between constitutional bodies based on constitutional authority (as, for example, between the federal and state governments) but the sharing of power between sovereign elected authorities and unelected groups, unions, and arbitrators.

In public education the shrinking of the electorate's responsibilities is compounded by the impact of the new form of bargaining (collective bargaining cum political action) on the role of parents, the derivative consumer in the educational process. Not only does the new mode of bargaining intrude on parental interests in the education of their children, but the teachers' unions have often co-opted parent-teacher groups: Lieberman (1997) stated, "A profound but widely overlooked outcome of teacher unionization is that the National Congress of Teachers and Parents, widely known as the PTA, has become a tool of the NEA" (p. 225). Ultimately, the new form of teacher unionism' bargaining obfuscates, not to say thwarts, accountability for the poor record of public education among so many schools. Remedial actions are difficult to implement if responsibility for what goes on in the educational process is obfuscated.

The Road ahead for the Projected NEA-AFT

The new form of bargaining power—or, to adopt its supporters' terminology, "power sharing"—is likely to be greatly enhanced in the future, once the anticipated merger is consummated and the new leader of the American labor movement, the NEA-AFT, ascends to power within the AFL-CIO. As the future NEA-AFT matures in its new role within the American labor movement, the new union will doubtless obtain what might be considered its doctorate (Ed.D.) in collective bargaining. Its impact on resource allocation—and, indeed, its impact on the economy—will probably exceed that of the old unionism, if it has not already done so. Teacher unionism's combined political and economic power already gives it a comparative advantage over unions in the private sector.

Indications of its potential and its comparative advantage over the old unionism are the trends in the membership of the two teachers' unions, and a far higher proportion (80%) of the labor market teachers have organized (Stern, 1997) compared to any occupational group in the private labor market, particularly among professionals. Moreover, teacher unionism's comparative advantage in bargaining will grow as state and local governments extend their encouragement of unionization and bargaining for teachers or if a national law is passed covering unionism for teachers or for all state and local government employees. The potential for further unionization of teachers is considerable, despite the current high levels of penetration, because most local and a few state governments do not at this time have policies encouraging unionization and collective bargaining. Given the new colossus that the NEA-AFT would become, and the political knowledge and number of political operatives the predecessor unions currently field (Lieberman, 1997), enactment of governmental policies fostering teacher unionism and

bargaining will be a major goal of the NEA-AFT—and all of proponents of
the new unionism.

This trend can be called *convergence* with the private sector. By convergence,
I mean the demand of teachers' (and all public-sector) unions for labor law
equivalent to the National Labor Relations Act (NLRA), the federal law that
governs private-sector labor relations. Ideally, the teachers' (and all public-
sector) unions seek to nationalize labor law for all government employees,
including federal workers, and would support laws that legalize strikes across
a large swath of public employment, including teachers. The NEA-AFT would
prefer a national Teachers Labor Relations Act, designed only for their own
interests. Since 1985 it has been possible for Congress to adopt such legislation (*Garcia v. the San Antonio Metropolitan Transit Authority*, 1985). Unlike the
NLRA, a national Teacher Labor Relations Act would not be vulnerable to
the market forces that have weakened both the NLRA and the old (private-
sector) unionism. Because of the virtual immunity of public-sector teachers
to competitive forces, such a law would propel teacher unionism to new
heights and greatly enlarge the scope and impact of the subjects of collective
bargaining, a major goal of convergence by the teachers as well as all public
employee unions.

Although such developments are unlikely in the foreseeable future, the
consequences of such a law merit consideration because they are far-reaching
and because the Clinton administration has already moved in that direction
for federal employees and clearly intends to facilitate the application of that
model to all state and local public employees (of whom, of course, the teachers are the most important). Pursuant to Vice President Gore's National Performance Review of 1995, the administration established what it called
"partnership councils" (a euphemism for works councils) between agency
managements and their unions. Councils are expected to consult employees
on their ideas about the functioning of the governmental agency.

More important, under Clinton's E.O. 12871, the administration gave federal unions the right to negotiate matters hitherto only permissive by or at
the option of management. This sweeping change now mandates that federal
agencies' bargain with unions on such matters as "the numbers, types, and
grades of employees or positions assigned to any organizational subdivision,
work project, or tour of duty" and the "technology, methods, and means of
performing work" (Bureau of National Affairs, 1993). These inroads to managerial prerogatives exceed comparable inroads in private industry. What remains of the Civil Service system is more vestigial than real. Previously, the
administration and a Democratic Congress had relaxed the Hatch act's restrictions on federal employees' and their unions' political activities, further
ensuring the bilaterally monopolistic relations between union officials and
federal government officials.

With this model in hand, early in 1996 the Clinton administration established The Secretary of Labor's Task Force on Excellence in State and Govern-

ment Through Labor-Management Cooperation (hereafter, referred to as task force) to promote new structures of relations between state and local government employers and unions. The task force's most important recommendation was, not surprisingly, partnership councils at the state and local levels of government in imitation of those already set up at the federal level. If such councils were established at the state and local levels, teachers' unions, the most powerful group of public employees within state and local government, would benefit most. Thus, the teachers' unions urged the task force to recommend the expansion of the right to organize and bargain, because the absence of this right impedes what the unions referred to as mutual problem solving and the establishment of this right is essential to improving education through cooperation: "common goals [they said] cannot mean a union-free environment" and "excellence in education means management and the union set common goals" (Bureau of National Affairs, 1995). In addition, union leaders urged the task force to further reduce managerial rights now set by law and contracts.

In summary, the teachers' union and other union leaders seek a revolution in state and local government labor relations, a revolution that would dilute managerial authority and further erode state sovereignty. In its place they would substitute a new regime of works councils limited to unions and management, with authority for decision making transferred to these groups, and an even higher level of bilateral monopolistic practice. Although genuine cooperation between unions and management can contribute to efficiency, the typical result of such cooperation in the public sector often adds to the work rules' inefficiency, not efficiency, as is typical of bilateral monopoly. However, to date the task force has had little, if any, impact on public policies at the state and local levels.

Teachers' Unions and Resource Usage

From the perspective of economic analysis, teachers are an essential input in the production of educational output. Teachers' unions believe, or at least contend, that the unionization of teachers and collective bargaining contribute to an efficient use of scarce resources and to quality education. They rationalize unionization as a complement to the efficient use of instruction in the educational output and therefore share the goals of students, parents, and taxpayers for a quality system of education. However, there is general belief that the American system of public education has fallen short of the efficient use of its resources, as judged by results.

Therefore, the teachers' unions must be examined as one of the key factors responsible for the failure of the system. When organized into unions, the role that teachers play becomes transformed by the objectives of the union, objectives that may be responsible for an educational result that is short of objectively determined satisfactory measures. What, then, do teachers' unions want that all too frequently put their goals at odds with the achievement of quality education?

Teachers' unions share a goal basic to all unions: higher wages, shorter hours, and some control over working conditions. To achieve these goals, teachers' unions, like all unions, seek to establish as much control as possible over the educational production process. Because a monopoly, whether of businesses or labor, inevitably pursues goals in the interest of the monopoly, not the consumer of its product or service, the teachers' unions act in the same manner. Consequently, their goals are unlikely to coincide with those of the consumers—the students, parents, and the wider community.

In attempting to fulfill the historic trade union goals on wages, hours, and working conditions, teachers' unions are typically in conflict with the adoption and implementation of quality educational goals demanded by the community. As noted earlier, Wildman (1971) states "it is exceedingly difficult to distinguish between 'educational policy' and 'salaries and working conditions.'" Put another way, Hoxby (1996) stated, "[a] rent-seeking teachers' union can militate for school inputs [money] that maximize the objectives of teachers, rather than those of parents or administrators" (p. 712). As a consequence, Hoxby found that "teachers' unions may be a primary means whereby lack of competition among public schools translates into more generous school inputs and worse student performance" (p. 712). Not surprisingly, Hoxby (1997) concluded that more school choice for students in public schools "raises productivity, both by creating savings for taxpayers and by improving the achievement of students. And if given more choice among public schools, apparently parents are less likely to choose private schools" (p. 1). In view of these findings, President Clinton's proposed 1998–1999 budget increases for education should be considered more as additional financial rewards for the teachers' unions than as funding for educational improvement—a political move, not an educational one, and following a well-trodden path.

Educational Inputs and Outputs

Between 1965 and 1990, average spending per pupil nationally jumped in constant dollars from $2402 to $5582, average per pupil-teacher ratio declined from 24.1 to 17.3, the proportion of teachers with master's degrees more than doubled, and the median years of experience went up from 8 to 15. Meanwhile, between 1979 and 1989, average salaries of teachers increased 20% in real terms. These gains indicate that collective bargaining has produced impressive results for the teachers' unions (Stern, 1997, p. 37).

But, although educational inputs rose as a result of collective bargaining, the same cannot be said for the quality of the educational output. As Stern (1997) found, "During the same period, average SAT scores for public school students declined by 10 percent, dropout rates in urban school systems increased, and American students scored at or near the bottom of industrialized nations" (p. 37). Like Hoxby, who found that "teachers' unions increase school inputs but reduce productivity sufficiently to have a negative effect on student performance" (abstract, p. 671), another study also concluded that "[t]here appears to be no strong or systematic relationship between school expenditures and student performance" (quoted in Stern, 1997, p. 37). A study of expenditures and performance in New Jersey echoes those national conclusions. Using data on public high schools for 1988–1989, 1992–1993, and 1994–1995 supplied by the New Jersey Department of Education, this study found "no evidence that an increase in expenditures in poor urban districts in excess of the levels in most other districts will improve academic achievements" (Coate & VanderHoff, 1996, abstract, p. 1).

Educational Alternatives and the Teachers' Unions' Political Power

In the face of objective assessments of the damaging effects of teacher unionism on the value of increased public expenditures on education, why are alternatives so difficult to initiate? The answer is that public education dominates the elementary and secondary school market, and unions dominate the instructional labor market—a classic case of bilateral monopoly at work. Recall that the NEA's control extends to domination of the policies and programs of the national parent-teachers organization, which enhances its monopoly power. Only the introduction of competition will improve education in the public school system. And that competition need not be viewed as an all-or-nothing alternative, as the model of public and private higher education, discussed next, demonstrates.

Educational Alternatives

Although the introduction of competition is essential, what forms can it take and can competitive alternatives be introduced? One proposal has been to spur the formation and spread of unaffiliated local unions to compete with the NEA-AFT. Realistically, however, this response has virtually no chance of making any serious inroads against the hegemony of the existing and anticipated colossus of organized labor and poses no threat to the monopolistic position of the union and its partners in the educational process as now constituted. Moreover, why should unions, albeit localized, not share the monopoly educational policy goals of large-scale teacher unionism? Obviously they would, even though their impact on the quality of education could not be as severe.

Although competition in some form is an essential ingredient for the improvement of education, whatever the form, its implementation will be difficult to initiate, despite the record of improvements that competition has repeatedly demonstrated in the private economy. Perhaps the most attractive avenue for opening competition in education is to provide families with vouchers that will enable their children to attend either private schools (including parochial schools) or public schools of their choice (Flake, 1998, p. 27). Within the inner cities, vouchers are seen "as a continuation of blacks' struggle for civil rights" (Shlaes, 1998, p. A 22). Only a system of choice can undermine monopoly and return education to its original objective: investment in the human capital of the nation's oncoming generations. Adam Smith, in his classic *Wealth of Nations*, probably had this in mind when he endorsed public education, but he could not foresee how unionism would preempt that goal.

Unionization in Higher Education

A model for a competitive arrangement between public and private educational institutions has existed for more than a century in this country. It is higher education. Huge public investments have been made in colleges and universities throughout the country, subsidizing the cost for parents and students. However, the earliest institutions were private, and over the course of time an elite few retained their premier rank. Together with elite public universities, these private universities have set the standards within which faculty, students, and administrators in public (and other private) institutions have been forced to compete across the country. At the same time, the extent of unionization is nil at the premier private institutions and not extensive among the leading public universities. Indeed, where it has taken root, unionism often resulted from top administrative officers' desire to keep their institutions in tune with the times, as the states in which these universities were located adopted laws encouraging unionism and bargaining at public colleges and universities. Significantly, the extent of union organization is most widespread among community colleges, former teachers' colleges, and institutions most like public high schools. Typically either the NEA or the AFT represent the faculty and staff at these colleges. In a few instances, the American Association of University Professors (AAUP) may be the organized representative, whereas others have no union representation. Where teacher unionism does exist at colleges and universities, it plays the same role with the same objectives as teacher unionism in Grades K through 12. The impact is reduced at this level, however, because of the extent of competition that exists in higher education, a competition that extends to interpublic institutions. Overall, in higher education teacher unionism is not in a position to obstruct competitive forces.

Political Connections and Political Power

Such is not the case in public education from the kindergarten to 12th-grade levels. Political power complements the monopolistic position of teacher unionism and reinforces the power of the existing bilateral monopoly. At the federal level, the Clinton administration has acknowledged the political support it has received over the years by establishing programs that require large outlays and that at times are administered by former union officials now employed in the Department of Education. For example, the assistant secretary for research and educational improvement in the Department of Education, Sharon Robinson, was the former director of Issues at the NEA. Such political connections enable the NEA to shape and influence educational policies from within the administration and from outside. The effectiveness of this influence was illustrated when President Clinton vetoed legislation to provide scholarships that would have enabled poor students in the District of Columbia to attend private schools, a bill he initially indicated he would approve. The NEA opposed the vouchers, so President Clinton obliged his political ally by reversing field and vetoing the proposal.

The extent of the Clinton administration's connection to the teachers' unions is demonstrated by the following facts. At the 1996 Democratic convention, during which Clinton and Gore were nominated, the teachers' unions comprised 11% of all delegates, a larger proportion than that of the state of California. The NEA alone sent 405 members as delegates, compared to 34 who were sent as delegates to the Republican convention (Marx, 1997). During the campaign, the NEA contributed more than $9 million to Clinton-Gore and other Democratic candidates through political action committees (PACs). The NEA and AFT have numerous PACs, and claims of nonpartisanship ring hollow when faced with data showing the shares of spending. More important, union members volunteer time to Democratic candidates. Both organizations are also conspicuous in that they are not accountable to members in terms of their political commitments and finances (Stern, 1997).

As for their political action, the teachers' unions spent heavily to advertise in the media and donated in-kind contributions, which probably dwarfed their cash expenditures: Thousands of full-time campaign workers, phone banks, direct-mail advertisements, and, of course, the unions' own publications endorsed and supported Clinton-Gore and Democrats generally.

Although the unions are virtually committed to the Democrats, the Democratic party does not reflect the political makeup of their membership. Less than half (42%) of the members are Democrats and 30% are Republican; the political persuasion of the remaining members is unknown, undeclared, or independent (Marx, 1997). It has been estimated that the teachers' unions spent a total of $50 million on the 1996 national elections, compared to the AFL-CIO's reported outlay of $35 million. That they have the financial wherewithal, there can be no doubt. Combined, the teacher unions' receive an estimated $1.3 billion a year nationally and from all subordinate bodies. Together they employ approximately 6000 full-time staff members. On a full-time equivalent basis, the NEA-AFT employs more political operatives than the Republican and Democratic parties combined. About 3000 teacher union operatives receive more than $100,000 each per year in salaries and benefits.

The revenues of the teacher unions' subsidiary organizations, such as PACs and foundations, amount to more than $100 million annually (Lieberman, 1997). The high salaries and political expenditures are replicated by NEA state groups. In Michigan, the state affiliate of the NEA paid three retirees and 75 of its top employees (from a total of 298) more than $100,000 in salary and expenses in 1996, amounts greater than the governor of Michigan received (Hornbeck, 1997).

Union Goals

What are the goals of the teacher unions? Are they primarily interested in improving education or, instead, are they interested in fortifying and enlarging their political power in the country? A long-time and well-qualified student of the teachers' unions, Myron Lieberman, believes that the teachers' unions sabotage educational reform and hold students, parents, teachers, and taxpayers hostage (Lieberman, 1997). In light of the unions' political investment to maintain their monopolistic grip on education, is it any wonder that they forcefully oppose legislation, state and federal, which would introduce competitive alternatives? Or is it surprising that the teachers' unions fight curbs on their unrestrained political expenditures, so crucial to maintaining and expanding their monopolistic control?

THE PROJECTED NEA-AFT AND THE FUTURE OF LABOR ORGANIZATION

Because of its size, a merged NEA and the AFT would be of enormous significance to the future of the American labor movement and to American public education. If the two merge early in the new millennium, soon thereafter the new NEA-AFT will provide the leadership of the AFL-CIO. From that platform it will shape the philosophy, strategy, and political orientation of the American labor movement. It will be able to do so because the character of the union movement has steadily changed since the advent of the teacher unions (and other components of the new unionism) in the 1960s. Coupled with its steady growth in membership until 1994, and the decline of the membership of the old (private-sector) unionism from its peak in 1970, the balance of power between the two wings of organized labor will shift in favor of the new unionism early in the next millennium. The symbol of the organized employee will no longer be the muscular worker attired in traditional work clothing, but an employee dressed for the classroom or office. The transition to the new symbolism of unionism has already begun. The election of John J. Sweeney of the Service Employees International Union (SEIU) to the presidency of the AFL-CIO in 1995 marks the first shift in that direction.

The SEIU's membership is made up predominantly of public-sector employees, so Sweeney's elevation reflects the shift toward the coming dominance of the new unionism. When this development unfolds, as more organized workers in the American labor movement will be government employees, the American labor movement will have caught up with the transformation that has already occurred in all or most of the Group of 7 (G-7) countries. However, the American transformation will be unique when compared to other G-7 countries, because organized teachers, the new NEA-AFT, will be in the vanguard of the New American Labor Movement. Unlike some of the other unions in the public labor market, it appears that the NEA-AFT escaped the topping out, or losses of membership, that other public-sector unions have experienced over the past 3 years. Thus, in contrast to the old unionism (in which membership has hemorrhaged and is down more than 7.5 million members since 1970), market share (down from 36% in 1953 to under 10% in 1997), and other unions in the public sector, the NEA-AFT has been able to hold onto, if not actually gain, some membership since 1994. A continuation of this trend will strengthen the likelihood of the NEA-AFT's future as the coming leader of the American Labor Movement of the 21st century.

THE PHILOSOPHY OF THE PROJECTED NEA-AFT

What unions are and what they do are shaped by their philosophy. There is, of course, no official union philosophy. However, unions have developed principles—de facto philosophies—which guide their actions. Typically, these principles are derived empirically rather than theoretically. Laski (1949) found they are "generally more likely to develop after the trade union has twisted and turned to adapt itself to a developing situation than while the situation, in all its rich variety, is trying to find some stable basis of equilibrium in society" (p. 28). The process of twisting and turning to adapt to a developing situation describes how the NEA-AFT has been determining its philosophy, as have other unions, public as well as private. Although unions derive their philosophical outlook from experience, this is not to say that they have always drawn either the correct inferences or that their responses have been timely. However, history has demonstrated that the unions' empirically based philosophies are durable and continue to evolve. As Kovacs (1971) wrote nearly 3 decades ago:

> The philosophy of the labour movement cannot be examined in isolation without reference to its historical evolution, for the labour movement is a dynamic institution which passes through various stages of development. Thus in order to discover the philosophy behind the movement it is necessary to look at its pattern of growth. . . . [W]hile the development of the trade union movement is effected [sic] by the social and political structure in which it is allowed to grow, as a social force it, too, is influential in shaping the environment, directly or indirectly, through its collective activities and policies. (pp. 25–26)

Thus, the New American labor movement will reflect far more than a shift in the composition of union membership. The new unionism, and especially the new NEA-AFT, is characterized by a major difference in philosophy with the old unionism: The new unionism, particularly the NEA-AFT, demands a greater redistribution of the U.S. national income from the private to the public economy. The old unionism seeks a greater redistribution from private employers to private-sector union members. However, as taxpayers, many members of the old unionism oppose the redistributive goals of the new unionism.

For teacher unionism, the redistributive goal means continued expansion of expenditures for public education. Because the merged NEA-AFT would be largest affiliate of the AFL-CIO, and will almost certainly provide the leadership of that federation early in the next century, its political power to achieve this goal will be greatly magnified. Also, although private members may oppose the private-to-public economy redistribution, the leadership of private unions in the federation will promote solidarity with the public-sector group.

The evidence for the split attitudes is indicated by the voting profile of union members in presidential elections. Thus, in 1996, about one-third or more of all union members voted Republican, the party identified as favoring lower taxes. Because the voting profile of public-sector union members is about 90% Democratic, and because private-sector unionists comprise about 58% of all members, it is likely that the proportion of private unionists who voted Republican probably equaled or approached 45%. In the 1994 congressional elections, when Republicans won 40% of all union votes, it is almost certain that Republicans received more than half of private-sector union members' votes. In Ronald Reagan's election victories in 1980 and especially in 1984, private-sector union members were clearly a major segment of those workers who came to be known as Reagan Democrats.

These revolutionary changes in the union movement and its implications were neither addressed nor foreseen by professionals in industrial relations as recently as a half-dozen years ago. In the Industrial Relations Research Association' publication on The State of the Unions in 1991, of the two essays in the section titled "The Future" only one dealt at all with any aspects of public-sector unionism, and that in a minor way. The future, as these contributors envisioned it, continued to be focused on how the labor movement of the past, private-sector unionism, could be revived (Kochan & Wever, 1991; Piori, 1991).

CONCLUSIONS

The most important outcomes of teacher unionization and collective bargaining on education are their effects on public policy, especially on public spending. Through its unique combination of political power and influence, teacher unionism has shaped and often controlled public policies on education, policies that have perpetuated the poor performance of American public education and pushed costs higher. In fact, the unions' power to raise the cost of education (even as its quality declined) has contributed to municipal bankruptcy, de facto and de jure, as exemplified in the city of New York and the school district of San Jose, California. Both bankruptcies occurred more than 2 decades ago, but are reminders of what can happen.

The city of New York's de facto bankruptcy case exemplifies avoidance of federal judicial intervention under the bankruptcy code, whereas the San Jose (California) School District brought on that intervention. The city of New York went bankrupt de facto in 1975 when it was unable to market its debt. It was decided that legal bankruptcy had to be avoided, because under Chapter 9 a proposed plan of adjustment must show that 51% of the creditors accepted the reorganization plan. At the time, it was estimated that 160,000 individuals or families held nearly $5 billion of the city's debt, about two-thirds of the amount in outstanding bonds, and that, in addition, many registered bonds were held in nominee names. Because it would be manifestly difficult, if not impossible, to gain the approval of so many bondholders for a reorganization plan as required by the bankruptcy law, the city sought and found an alternative to the bankruptcy court—the state of New York (Spiotto, 1991a). Besides the administrative problems, the avoidance of bankruptcy was also a high political priority as the political costs would have been even greater.

Among the major contributors to the city's fiscal debacle were its unions, one of the most important of which was the United Federation of Teachers, the local affiliate of the AFT. Nevertheless, two analysts of the city's financial debacle, one now the secretary of Health and Human Services, refused to identify the role of the municipal unions. Instead, Shalala and Bellamy (1976) euphemistically identified only "groups" to whom "New York's elected officials . . . found it difficult to say no [to]" and from whom they could not obtain a quid pro quo (p. 1122). The word *union* never appeared in their analysis of New York City's fiscal crisis.

To avoid a de jure bankruptcy and federal court oversight, the state of New York was brought in as a surrogate for a bankruptcy court to resolve the financial debacle of the city. In the case of New York City, this step illustrated how the United Federation of Teachers and other municipal unions contributed to changing sovereignty by their contribution to local government bankruptcy: Instead of a bankruptcy court (itself an abridgement of sovereignty), the state of New York oversaw the adjustment and resolution of the city's debt. The state's first step as surrogate for a court was to create a new body with the authority to commandeer fiscal and governing powers normally vested by the electorate in city officials. Even Shalala and Bellamy described this as a "program of governance," which "eliminated the last vestiges of fiscal home rule of the City" (p. 1128). Governance of the city of New York's finances shifted from the elected officials of the city, except the mayor, to state officials (not elected for that purpose) and to state appointee experts (not elected at all). The new authority was titled the Emergency Financial Control Board. The mayor's authority was more nominal than actual. Decisions on the finances of New York City, a political entity with one the largest budgets of any political jurisdiction in the United States after the federal government, would now be decided mainly by individuals never elected by the people of the city! Although legal, the procedure should not obscure the real transfer of political power from the people to an administrative panel. These developments are surely serious reductions in the sovereign powers of the people and a change in representative democracy. The United Federation of Teachers and the other municipal unions were major factors in these reductions—first, in clipping sovereign power by its contribution to the bankruptcy and, second, in shifting elective authority to a de facto nonelective panel. Incidentally, the teachers' and other municipal unions took great pride in announcing the large amounts of investments they made in the bonds floated to refinance the city's debt (Troy, 1994).

Although New York City is the outstanding example of bankruptcy avoidance through the use of an alternative (the state of New York), the San Jose School District became the most significant example of bankruptcy among local government agencies in the recent past (Spiotto, 1991b). In 1983 the school district was unable to meet its debt to telephone and water utilities for unpaid services and unpaid wage increases to its employees. Most of its creditors were teachers, a situation that arose due to promised salary increases that the district could not meet, especially after the state of California adopted Proposition 13. The school district did not challenge its obligation to pay bondholders to avoid the stigma of repudiation and to undermine its future ability to borrow. Under the 1937 bankruptcy code, the school district could have gone into bankruptcy and the bondholders would have had to line up like all other creditors to receive any payment. In 1988 the bankruptcy code was amended to adopt the practice that the San Jose (and other bankrupt jurisdictions) had followed to protect bondholders. Under these rules, the credit worthiness of the jurisdiction was maintained. Moreover, unlike corporate bankruptcy, creditors cannot put the municipality into bankruptcy, irrespective of the mismanagement of its financial affairs. Municipal bankruptcy is voluntary and in fact could not proceed without the authorization of the state government.

In the San Jose case, the bankruptcy plan was agreed to under the terms of the Federal Bankruptcy Code and by a federal court. It secured the claims of the bondholders, but the school district challenged its obligations to pay its nonbonded debts, in particular the claims of the school district's teachers. In the plan adjusting the nonbonded debt, the court ruled that the school district could reject the contracts it had previously signed with its employees and roll back wages. However, the school district eventually resolved its dispute with the teachers and other employees by an agreement to fund about 60% of the promised increases.

The San Jose case paralleled a Supreme Court ruling upholding contract rejection in the private sector (*National Labor Relations Board v. Bildisco and Bildisco*, 1984). As a result, "given the fact that labor obligations are among the most burdensome problems faced by municipalities, as evidenced by the San Jose School District bankruptcy," the bankruptcy court's power to void collective bargaining agreements became very attractive to local governments (Spiotto, 1991b). However, the option of voiding agreements in the public sector are probably also more difficult now than at the time of the San Jose case.

In response to criticism of its obstructionist role in improving American education, but with no reference to the financial costs that can be imposed, the leaders of the NEA and the AFT have called for a new unionism (their term, which postdates the author's use of the phrase). A report commissioned by the NEA recommended that it take the lead in discussions of reform because the public has come to view the unions as heavy-handed special-interest groups. The report urged the NEA to change its message to focus on better teachers, better students, and better schools (Chaddock, 1997).

The report produced by the Kamber group, a prounion public relations organization in Washington, DC, is reminiscent of the study done by the Lou Harris Associates for the AFL-CIO in 1984. Like the Kamber report, it made recommendations to the federation that were intended to stop the decline of unionism in the private economy. However, since 1984, the old unionism has continued on its downward course toward the inevitable twilight zone (Troy, 1997). That zone is not oblivion, but a greatly reduced position of the old unionism in the private labor market. Just as the Harris report brought no relief to the old unionism, the Kamber report is unlikely to result in any substantive changes in the behavior of the teacher unions: As the French expression states, "the more things change, the more they stay the same." Across the Atlantic, the Labour government in the United Kingdom has adopted a policy of bypassing the country's powerful teachers' unions and their leaders by setting up machinery to consult directly with teachers about reforming education. Although indicative of the seriousness of the situation there (as here), it is unlikely to make any real headway because trade union members will be "exiled to Coventry," ostracized for participating in such endeavors (Carvel, 1997).

Were the issues not so serious, the Kamber recommendations could easily be dismissed. To expect a monopoly to surrender its power and its rich market is highly unlikely. To expect that the teaching unions would change, it is instructive to consider the recent actions of the NEA affiliate in California (the California Teachers Association, or CTA). The CTA wished to discourage business leaders from supporting a voter initiative to enact legislation that would require annual written approval from union members (private and public sector) to authorize their employers to deduct union dues earmarked for political purposes. The initiative was known as Proposition 226. The CTA warned business leaders that if they supported the measure, the union would sponsor legislation to raise business taxes by $10 billion annually (Skelton, 1997). Although businesspeople have few contacts with public-sector unions, many have contracts with unions in the private labor market. Although these unions also opposed the initiative, the CTA's retaliation to support taxes on business could only make private business more expensive in California, leading to unemployment from downsizing or out migration, affecting unionized and nonunion firms alike. This is another example of conflict between the objectives of the new and the old unionism in executing their philosophies. The initiative eventually lost. However, a similar initiative in the state of Washington led to legislation that resulted in the number of NEA members contributing $1 a month to the union's political fund to shrink from 48,000 to 8000.

Despite union opposition, a national poll found that 82% of respondents supported a federal version of the California initiative, known as the Payroll Protection Act. However, President Clinton denied choice by unionized workers to have that portion of their dues that unions spend for political purposes refunded to them. One of his first acts in 1993 was to void President Bush's executive order requiring government contractors to notify unionized workers of their legal right to a refund of the political portion of their dues. Surveys indicate that 78% of workers do not know that a legal right to a refund exists (Will, 1998).

The future does not yet promise any major changes to improve public education, even though competitive alternatives are present. Because the generally poor performance of public education can be seen as essentially a political matter, involving an entrenched bilateral monopoly, only a political corrective is possible. Because such an antidote is slow in developing, the monopoly will continue to successfully resist change for the better. In the private economy market forces, competition—the New Age of Adam Smith—acts as a corrective. President Clinton has embraced both sides of the argument: He has supported widening of the New Age of Adam Smith in the private economy and earned the rebuke of organized labor (seeking to prevent challenges to its monopolistic practices in the production of goods and services in the private economy) for so doing, but he remains steadfast in his opposition to exposing the bilateral monopoly in public education to the same forces that benefit consumers in the private economy.

To restore the promise that investment in human capital means to the students, parents, and the public, a protracted struggle lies ahead. Until the electorate sees the symmetry in the wisdom of competition in the private market and its application in public education, little can be accomplished.

Left unchecked by the electorate, the bilateral monopoly will expand its demands for more funds to finance continuing failure.

References

Bureau of National Affairs. (1993). *Government employees relations report*, 31, No. 1545, p. 1659. (From Lexis).

Bureau of National Affairs. (1995). *Government employees relations report*, 33, No. 1598, p. 72. (From Lexis).

Carvel, J. (1997, May 9). Blunkett by-passes teaching unions. *The Guardian*, p. A 5.

Chaddock, G. R. (1997, October 14). Teachers unions jump on bandwagon of school reform. The NEA and AFT embrace changes aimed at improving teacher and student performance. *Christian Science Monitor*, p. A 10.

Coate, D., & VanderHoff, J. (1996). The Abbott decision and the effects of increased state funding on educational attainment in poor urban school districts in New Jersey. Unpublished manuscript.

Flake, F. (1998, February 6). Vouchers: A hope for our kids. *The New York Post*, p. 27.

Garcia v. San Antonio Metropolitan Authority, et al. 105. S. Ct. (1985).

Greenhouse, S. G. (1998, January 27). Teacher groups to merge, creating largest U.S. union. *The New York Times*, p. A 12.

Hornbeck, M. (September 9, 1997). Teachers union pays execs $100,000: Some MBA brass make more than Engler, *Detroit News*, Sec. A, p. 1.

Hoxby, C. M. (1996). How teachers' unions affect education production. *Quarterly Journal of Economics*, 111, 671–718.

Hoxby, C. M. (1997). Does competition among public school districts benefit students and taxpayers? Evidence from natural variation in school redistricting. Unpublished manuscript.

Kochan, T. A., & Wever, K. R. (1991). American unions and the future of worker representation. In G. Strauss, D. G. Gallagher, & J. Fiorito (Eds.), *The state of the unions*, pp. 363–386. Madison, WI: Industrial Relations Research Association.

Kovacs, A. E. (1971). The philosophy of the Canadian union movement. In R. Miller & I. Fraser (Eds.), *Canadian labour in transition* (pp. 119–144). Scarborough, Ontario: Prentice-Hall.

Laski, H. (1949). *Trade unions in the new society*. New York: Viking.

Lieberman, M. (1997). *The Teacher Unions*. New York: The Free Press.

Marx, C. R. (1997, November 26). Teachers unions flex muscles. *Investors Business Daily*, p. A.1.

National Labor Relations Board v. Bildisco and Bildisco, 465 US 513 (1984).

Piore, M. J. (1991). The future of unions. In G. Strauss, D. G. Gallagher, & J. Fiorito (Eds.), *The state of the unions* (pp. 387–410). Madison, WI: Industrial Relations Research Association.

Shalala, D. E., & Bellamy, C. (1976). A state saves a city: The New York case. *Duke Law Journal*, pp. 1119–1132.

Shlaes, A. (1998, February 23). A chance to equip my child. *The Wall Street Journal*, p. A 22.

Skelton, G. (1997, October 6). In this fight, it doesn't matter who started it. *Los Angeles Times*, p. A 3.

Spiotto, J. E. (1991a). Municipal insolvency; bankruptcy, receivership, workouts and alternative remedies. Unpublished manuscript.

Spiotto, J. E. (1991b). *Strategies for communities in crisis: Is there life after a budget deficit?* Paper presented at the Government Finance Officers Association meeting.

Stern, S. (1997, Spring). How teachers' unions handcuff schools. *City Journal*, pp. 35–47.

Troy, L. (1994). *The new unionism in the new society: Public sector unions in the redistributive state*. Fairfax, VA: George Mason University Press.

Troy, L. (1997). The twilight of old unionism. In D. Lewin, D. J. B. Mitchell, & M. A. Zaidi (Eds.), *The human resource management handbook*, pp. 137–156.

U.S. Department of Education. (1997). National Center for Education Statistics. *Digest of Education Statistics.* NCES 98-015.

Wildman, W. A. (1971). Teachers and collective negotiation. In A. Blum (Ed.), *White collar workers.* (pp. 126–165). New York: Random House.

Will, G. (1998, February). The most important vote of the year. *The New York Post,* p. 47.

CHAPTER

15

The Pendulum Revisited: Faddism in Education and Its Alternatives[1]

ROBERT E. SLAVIN

Center for Research on the Education of Students Placed at Risk,
Johns Hopkins University

In 1989, I wrote an article in the *Phi Delta Kappan* called "PET and the Pendulum: Faddism in Education and How to Stop It" (Slavin, 1989). This article bemoaned the process by which educational innovations are so often adopted on a vast scale in the total or near-total absence of meaningful evidence of effectiveness. It used as a then-current example Madeline Hunter's Mastery Teaching or Instructional Theory in Practice (ITIP) model, focusing in particular on an adaptation called the Program for Effective Teaching (PET) disseminated throughout the state of South Carolina. The article tried to explain how the famous pendulum of educational innovation operates, and how it resembles changes in fashions rather than the progress over time typical of science-based professions such as medicine, engineering, or agriculture.

Now, 10 years later, it is interesting to reflect on the pendulum's progress. Madeline Hunter passed away a few years ago, and her programs, once everywhere, are now hardly remembered, much less used. More than a quarter-century after it was introduced, little evidence ever supported it; two studies

[1]Portions of this chapter are adapted from Slavin, 1989. This chapter was written under funding from the Office of Educational Research and Improvement, U.S. Department of Education (No. OERI-R-117D-40005). However, any opinions expressed are the author's and do not represent OERI positions or policy.

(Donovan, Sousa, & Walberg, 1987; Mandeville, 1988) found no effects of the program, and one (Stallings & Krasavage, 1986) found small positive effects that disappeared by the fourth implementation year.

Madeline Hunter's program may be gone, but faddism is still with us. In fact, the faddism following Madeline Hunter may be far worse than that which supported her methods; as she pointed out many times (e.g., Hunter, 1986), even if ITIP had not been evaluated, the principles on which it was based are very well established in research. In fact, the whole idea of ITIP was to make solid and extensively researched practices, such as the use of advance organizers, rapid pace, checking for understanding, rule-example-rule patterns in teaching concepts, and so on, practical and accessible to teachers on a mass scale. Later fads have often not even had this much research basis.

This chapter updates my 1989 paper, uses the model it proposed to discuss more recent fads in educational innovation, and describes new developments in policy, research, and practice that may someday get us off the pendulum of faddism in education.

Educational innovation is famous for its cycle of enthusiasm, widespread dissemination, disappointment, and eventual decline, the classic "pendulum." Of course, a similar pattern can be seen in most applied fields, but in many, there is steady generational progress, which is far more important than the latest fad. For example, there are fads in medicine, agriculture, and engineering, but these occur against a backdrop of steady, widely acknowledged, and irreversible progress. Generational progress does occur in education, but it is usually a product of changes in society rather than changes in educational techniques themselves. For example, the clearly beneficial trend toward desegregation and more equal treatment of minorities, and the resulting reduction of minority-white achievement gaps through the 1970s and 1980s, is true generational progress, but it arose from social, political, and legal changes, not from educational innovation per se. More often, educational change resembles change in such fields as fashion and design, which reflect changes in taste and social climate rather than true forward progress.

One major factor inhibiting systematic progress in education is a lack of respect for research and development in the change process. When Beltsville releases a higher-yielding seed, when the Food and Drug Administration approves a drug, farmers and physicians (respectively) confidently adopt the new product. In education, there is no Beltsville, no FDA, not even much agreement about what constitutes adequate evidence to support action. Educational indicators, such as standardized test scores and dropout rates, can take time to influence on a large scale and can be hard to ascribe to any one policy or practice.

If education is ever to go beyond the pendulum to make important progress in increasing student achievement, it must first change the ground rules under which innovations are selected, implemented, evaluated, and institutionalized. This chapter discusses the dynamics of the educational pendulum in light of several fads of recent years. Next, a series of steps is proposed that could provide an infrastructure capable of promoting lasting, clearly beneficial change in educational practice.

THE PENDULUM IN PRACTICE

One of the most important reasons for the existence of the educational pendulum is that in education, we rarely wait for or demand hard evidence before we adopt new practices on a wide scale. Of course, every innovator claims research support for his or her methods; at a minimum, there is usually some sort of a "gee whiz" story about a school or district that was "turned around" by the innovation. Alternatively, a developer may claim that although the program itself has not been formally evaluated, the principles on which it is based are supported by research. As noted earlier, this was the case with Madeline Hunter's program.

The recent quintessential boom-to-bust example of the pendulum of educational innovation is whole language, a philosophy of reading instruction that emphasizes reading of real literature, especially predictable texts in the early elementary grades, and de-emphasizes systematic instruction in phonics or word attack skills. Although based on the equally faddish and equally unevaluated language experience methods of the late 1960s and early 1970s, whole language burst on the scene in the early 1980s, largely as a reaction to frustration with what was perceived to be an overemphasis on isolated skills embodied by the widespread use in the late 1970s and early 1980s of such methods as mastery learning (Block & Burns, 1976) and, ironically, ITIP.

The research base for whole language was substantially weaker than that for ITIP, as there was very little research to support the principles on which whole language was based, much less the practices. Ken Goodman (1994) did cite some small-scale research to support the idea that children can learn from whole-word methods and rely heavily on context in their reading, but such findings do not point to any particular teaching strategy. In fact, influential advocates of whole language have often rejected the entire concept of quantitative research (e.g., Smith, 1988), arguing that outcome research only trivializes the reading process and advocating qualitative research that documents children's behaviors and social interactions but does not test them on formal assessments of any kind or compare them to control groups.

When reviews of a very limited body of research on whole language began to appear, they reported few benefits. Stahl and Miller (1989) found some gains among kindergarten children in whole-language classes, but children in the primary grades performed better in traditional programs. Adams (1990) did not focus on whole language per se, but did find evidence supporting a far greater focus on systematic teaching of phonics than was characteristic of whole language. A recent widely reported study by Foorman, Francis, Fletcher, Schatschneider, and Mehta (1998) found greater reading gains for children in phonetic programs than for those in whole-language-influenced basal programs. However, it was not so much these findings as the extremely poor performance of California fourth graders on the 1994 National Assessment of Educational Progress (NAEP) that probably ended the dominance of whole language. California, one of the states to adopt whole language first and most widely, tied with Louisiana for lowest reading scores in the nation (Campbell, Donahue, Reese, & Phillips, 1996). Initial protests that this was due to immigration turned out to be false; white students in California also tied with those in Louisiana for dead last. Of course, these low scores could be due to other factors, such as California's famously low per-pupil expenditures and large class sizes, but they certainly supported a national movement to seriously reexamine early reading practices. Today, state legislatures, school boards, and educators at all levels are precipitously backing away from whole language, or at least supporting a balance between systematic phonics and use of real books in early reading.

Another example of faddism at work is the Coalition of Essential Schools (Sizer, 1984). Unlike whole language but more like ITIP, the coalition is closely associated with the ideas of one person, in this case Theodore Sizer of Brown University. The coalition works primarily in secondary schools to help them engage in a process of reform built around nine essential principles. By design, coalition schools are not intended to all be the same; school staffs are expected to use the nine principles as a very general guide but to work out their own ways of putting these principles in practice.

Like advocates of whole language, Sizer explicitly rejected the idea that student achievement outcomes could or should be assessed in coalition schools and compared to outcomes in control schools. He argued that standardized tests could not capture the kind of higher-order learning supposed to be characteristic of coalition schools. However, neither Sizer nor anyone else has ever compared coalition students to control students on measures that might plausibly be seen as desired outcomes in coalition schools, such as creative writing samples, complex problem solving in mathematics, setting up science experiments, or analyzing historical documents, all of which are readily measurable.

Sizer has expressed his vision in a series of books (Sizer, 1984, 1992, 1996) that describe *hypothetical* experiences of a made-up teacher in a made-up school. To the extent that the program has given compelling examples of real schools, the main showcase has been Central Park East in New York City, a school that routinely produces outstanding performances in a student body that is primarily African American and Latino (see, for example, Meier, 1995). Rarely reported, however, is the fact that Central Park East is a magnet school, drawing from among New York City's one million students a small group of students (and teachers) who are highly motivated to attend the school and subscribe to its rigorous curriculum.

Evaluations of more typical coalition schools have focused on degree of implementation, not outcomes, yet even here the observations are not promising. A number of studies (e.g., Muncey & McQuillan, 1996; Stringfield, Millsap, & Herman, 1997) have found minimal implementation of the principles in schools *nominated as exemplars* by the national project. One study did examine standardized test outcomes in coalition schools and found that they declined over a 3-year period (Stringfield et al., 1997).

The coalition claims that more than 1000 schools are participating in the project but that only about 200 of these are really implementing the model. Some of the principles and practices typical of coalition schools, such as block scheduling, have spread far more widely than the program itself.

The disappointing results of evaluations of ITIP, of whole language, and of the Coalition of Essential Schools offer little hope that districts adopting these approaches on a broad scale will see any improvement in student achievement. Of course, this is important in its own right, but what is more important are the questions it raises: Why does it take so long for adequate evaluations of such widely used programs to be done? Why does American education jump so enthusiastically on such bandwagons in the total absence of any evaluation data to support them? Most important, how can we avoid having this sort of thing happen over and over in educational innovation?

ANATOMY OF THE PENDULUM

The cases of whole language, the Coalition of Essential Schools, and the Madeline Hunter movement provide vivid examples of the educational pendulum in action. Each is characterized by extraordinary breadth of adoption and near-total lack of positive evaluative evidence.

If change in education is ever to represent progress rather than just the swing of the pendulum, then we need to understand *why* and *how* the pendulum operates. Figure 1 illustrates a sequence of events that appears to characterize innovation in education. The major elements that make up the anatomy of the pendulum are described next.

The Upswing

1. *Program first proposed.* The first step in the pendulum process is usually publication of the idea in a popular educational periodical, such as *Instructor*, *Educational Leadership*, or *Learning Magazine*, or publication of a popular book. In the case of Madeline Hunter, publication of a series of small books in 1967–1969 and articles in *Instructor* were important points of departure. Sizer's (1984) popular book *Horace's Compromise* effectively launched the coalition.

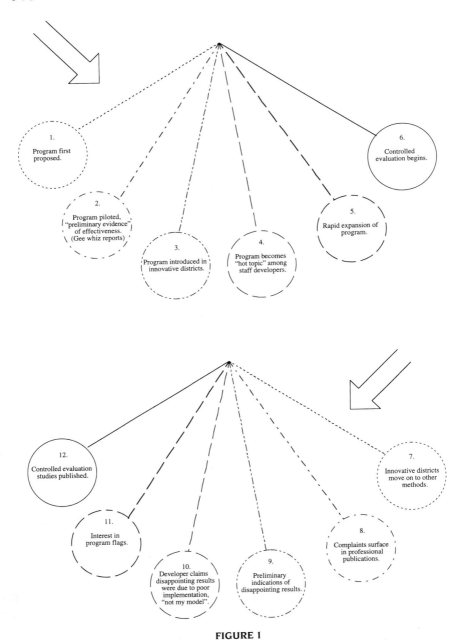

FIGURE 1

Anatomy of the pendulum: Phases 1–6, the upswing; Phases 7–12,
the downswing.

Whole language ideas appeared in a variety of practitioner-oriented reading journals, such as *Reading Teacher* and *Learning*.

2. *Program piloted: "Preliminary evidence" of effectiveness (gee whiz reports).* Early in the dissemination process, promising results are often reported from one or more school districts. These results are almost always highly flawed; at best, the data represent improvements over the previous year's scores, and at worst they may be completely anecdotal. In the case of ITIP, an unpublished, unavailable early evaluation in Long Beach, California, served the "gee whiz" function. Reports from Central Park East played this role for the coalition.

3. *Program introduced in innovative districts.* Certain school districts have a reputation for always being up on the latest innovations. There is an often-heard joke about such districts: "If the state superintendent said 'go to hell,' (District X) would make sure they got there first."

4. *Program becomes "hot topic" among staff developers.* One of the prime movers behind the educational pendulum is the fact that there is a substantial corps of staff developers, curriculum supervisors, and others whose job is to introduce the latest innovations to their school districts. These professionals are usually expected to be up on the latest developments; they are less often rewarded for sticking with a particular innovation for many years until it is well established and well evaluated within the district. What this means is that this year's hot instructional methods eventually become next year's old news. When a method becomes the talk of the Association for Supervision and Curriculum Development or American Association of School Administrators conventions, or of one of the curriculum conventions (e.g., International Reading Association, National Council of Teachers of Mathematics), then it has arrived at this critical stage.

5. *Rapid expansion of program.* As soon as a program becomes "this year's thing," training in it rapidly expands. Most of this training consists of one-day (or shorter) in-services given to large audiences of teachers, either by the developers or by staff development specialists who were just as enthusiastic about something completely different the year before. Rarely is classroom follow-up of any kind provided to ensure classroom implementation, at least at this stage in the pendulum swing. The coalition primarily provides summer institutes to selected teachers from many schools, not on-site training or followup. Whole language methods were often introduced in one-day workshops by staff developers, reading supervisors, or trainers working for textbook companies.

6. *Controlled evaluations begin.* Not until rapid expansion of a program is under way does serious controlled evaluation of the program usually begin. This occurs for many reasons. First, it is hard to evaluate a program until a lot of teachers are using it. Second, there is a lag between an awareness that a program is becoming widely used and an opportunity to study it; for example, grants may have to be sought to evaluate a program. As one example

of this, a decision by the federal Follow Through program to implement and evaluate promising programs directed at increasing time on task and implementing teacher effectiveness findings was made in 1980. This was the program that funded the influential Napa study of ITIP, which did not publish its final report until 1987, a lag of 7 years. The first outcome evaluation of the coalition appeared 13 years after *Horace's Compromise* (Sizer, 1984).

Ironically, controlled evaluations often begin at a program's peak of popularity, the very top of the pendulum's upswing, so the results of these evaluations often appear when the innovation is on the wane for other reasons.

The Downswing

7. *Innovative districts move on to other methods.* The downswing of the pendulum begins when the innovative districts who first give the method a try move on to something new. For example, many of the early Madeline Hunter enthusiasts moved on to training in such innovations as thinking skills education and cooperative learning or later to multiple intelligences or total quality management. Moving on to new methods is not, of course, just an indication of faddism; it may result from a saturation of the method within a district or a recognition of real or perceived problems with the method.

8. *Complaints surface in professional publications.* Every innovation, no matter how effective or popular, has its detractors. Until a program becomes widely known and used, however, articles written by detractors are of little interest and might not be published even if they were written; who cares if someone dislikes a method that few are using or discussing? However, once a method enters widespread use, its detractors are given a voice.

9. *Preliminary indications of disappointing results.* At about this point in the pendulum's downswing, early evaluation results begin to appear in the literature or to become known in some other way. These results are often disappointing. However, they may be flawed and therefore capable of being dismissed. This was the case with Madeline Hunter's program; the disappointing findings of the Napa study could indeed be criticized on the basis that the study was small, the control group was not initially equivalent to the experimental group, and so on. The *Elementary School Journal* devoted most of a special issue to the Stallings and Krasavage (1986) report of the Napa ITIP study and to responses to it, yet all the back-and-forth discussion missed the most important question: Why was this small and flawed study the first and only published evaluation of a program used in thousands of schools? Similarly, the Stahl and Miller review critical of whole language was often criticized, but it was limited by the small number and low quality of the research they had to review.

10. *Developer claims disappointing results due to poor implementation: "Not my model."* When results fail to support a developer's model, the developer is sure to claim that the model was not adequately implemented. Of course this may be true, but it is difficult to establish either way. When a developer

can point to well-designed studies in which the method *was* adequately implemented and *did* produce positive effects, this makes the "poor implementation" claim for a later study more supportable. In the case of the coalition, the frequent finding that little implementation took place calls into question the idea that the program *can* be successfully implemented on a broad scale.

11. *Interest in program flags.* At this stage, large numbers of districts move on to other programs, though not usually because of the disappointing evaluations. This is not to say that the program disappears everywhere or all at once, but just that districts dropping or no longer emphasizing the program begin to outnumber those that are beginning it.

12. *Controlled evaluation studies published.* At long last, controlled evaluation studies, reviews of research, and other articles begin to appear in top-quality research journals. However, the news, usually bad, arrives too late to make much difference as schools are already moving on.

STOP THE PENDULUM, I WANT TO GET OFF

The picture painted by Figure 1 is a dismal one. Obviously, the progression of events varies for each innovation, as does the length of time the process takes and the degree to which the innovation ever took hold. However, the history of dozens of once-popular innovations follows a pattern similar to that described here. In each case, the program entered widespread use and was then already on the wane before controlled evaluations with disappointing findings were published or generally recognized.

The pendulum process outlined here does assume that when finally evaluated, the program's effects turn out to be disappointing. Why is this so often true? One reason is that few educational innovations are *designed* to ensure positive effects in a fair evaluation. To be sure that a program would be effective in a fair control-group comparison, a developer would conduct many such evaluations him- or herself before going public. This rarely happens. However, it is unclear how much it would matter to the pendulum's progression if the program evaluations were positive. Direct Instruction, clearly the most effective early elementary reading program in the widely publicized Follow Through evaluation of the 1970s (Rhine, 1981), substantially waned in use outside of special education in the 1980s, as it conflicted with the zeitgeist of that time.

As each innovation moves through the pendulum process we do learn something that may be of use now or in the future. But if we are going to make generational, beneficial change in education, we are going to have to proceed in a different way.

Two majors changes will have to take place if we are to reduce faddism and increase responsible and lasting change in education. First, educators will have to demand high-quality evaluations of programs before they adopt them. Federal, state, and local governments can assist with this process in many ways. Second, school districts will have to shift staff development efforts from one-shot workshops on many topics toward extended training and follow-up for a smaller number of programs or practices of proven effectiveness, preferably carried out by well-trained, highly skilled trainers associated with the project rather than by local staff development experts who are expected to know how to train dozens of programs or practices. Emphasis in staff development must shift from scattershot presentations on what's *new* to systematic implementation of what *works*.

DEMANDING TOP-QUALITY EVALUATIONS

Educational administrators often complain that they lack the technical sophistication to evaluate the quality of program evaluations. Actually, evaluating evaluations is not so difficult or arcane. In selecting programs for dissemination, school administrators should look for the following characteristics

Has the Program Been Compared to a Comparable Control Group?

One hallmark of a top-quality program evaluation is that it compared schools or classes using the program to very similar schools or classes using traditional methods. Ideally, schools or classes were assigned at random to experimental or control conditions; more typically, it is possible to compare experimental schools to matched control schools. In either case, but especially the latter, it is essential to have evidence that experimental and control schools or classes were basically identical at pretest on as many factors as possible.

Many educational evaluations have used gains in percentile ranks or normal curve equivalents (NCEs) as criteria for program effectiveness, rather than using control groups. The theory is that if a school was performing at the 30th percentile last year and is now at the 45th percentile, it has improved compared to the norming sample. However, percentile or NCE gains have been found to inflate estimates of program effectiveness to an unknown but often substantial degree, so evaluations of this type should be approached with considerable skepticism (see Slavin & Madden, 1991; Slavin, Karweit, & Madden, 1988).

Did the Posttest Measure Assess Objectives Being Pursued Equally by Experimental and Control Classes?

Sometimes program evaluations look very positive because the program pursues nontraditional objectives and then assesses achievement on those objectives. For example, evaluations of IBM's Writing to Read program typically assessed the reading and writing skills of kindergartners and first graders (see Slavin, 1990). The writing assessments were obviously biased in favor of the program because writing was not traditionally taught at these grade levels. The reading measures at the kindergarten level were often biased because many traditional kindergarten programs that were used as control groups for Writing to Read were nonacademic in emphasis.

Was the Program Evaluated under Realistic Conditions over Realistic Time Periods?

Often programs are evaluated under highly artificial conditions or for brief time periods. Before adopting a program, administrations should be sure that a program has been evaluated in real schools somewhat like their own for at least a full school year. If the developer's positive evaluations were replicated by others, this increases confidence in the program's effectiveness.

EVALUATING NEW PROGRAMS

School districts that intend to adopt new programs on a substantial scale should first conduct evaluations of those programs on a smaller scale. These evaluations should compare experimental and control schools of classes on fair measures over extended time periods.

GOVERNMENTAL SUPPORT FOR PROGRAMS EVALUATION AND DISSEMINATION OF FINDINGS

If faddism is ever to end in education, decisions about adopting or maintaining programs must be made based on reliable, widely respected data. Federal or state governments can help bring this about in several ways.

1. *Provide a clearinghouse for program evaluations.* At a minimum, the federal government could maintain a central clearinghouse for evaluations of educational programs, particularly those conducted by school districts. A process of this type is currently being piloted by the U.S. Department of Education (see Klein, 1997). Districts could be encouraged to submit evaluations to this clearinghouse, and the evaluations that met a certain standard of methodological quality could be summarized from time to time. It is probable that among the 16,000 U.S. school districts, there are dozens of top-quality evaluations of many educational programs whose existence is known only to a few within the district. Unsuccessful evaluations are particularly unlikely to be disseminated beyond district boundaries. At minimal cost and effort,

the U.S. Department of Education could encourage districts to simply mail copies of such evaluations to a central location; for programs evaluated under federal monies, they could require a certain quality of evaluation and demand a copy of the results.

A somewhat similar function to this "clearinghouse" role was played by the U.S. Department of Education's Joint Dissemination Review Panel (JDRP) or Program Effectiveness Panel (PEP). Programs that JDRP/PEP reviewed were eligible for dissemination through the National Diffusion Network (NDN). However, the JDRP/PEP process was flawed in two major ways. First, the only source of evaluations was the developers themselves, who obviously had a stake in presenting the data in a positive light. Second, most JDRP/PEP-approved programs failed to use experimental-control comparisons; most used NCE or percentile gains which, as noted earlier, tend to overstate program effects.

2. Either as part of their funding of educational innovation or in a separate grants program, federal or state governments could contract with school districts to conduct top-quality evaluations of promising practices and disseminate their findings.

3. The best of all approaches would be to have federal or state governments fund one or more independent evaluation laboratories to conduct evaluations of promising programs and disseminate their findings. This could provide widely respected and believable results that districts could hardly ignore in making program adoption decisions (see Slavin, 1997).

CONCENTRATING RESOURCES
ON EFFECTIVE PROGRAMS

If we had a set of proven effective programs with effects that were beyond dispute, then attention would turn toward effective *implementation* of these programs. Serious educational change takes time and money; to move beyond faddism we need to invest in a small number of proven programs and make sure that they are properly implemented and are making the difference they should make. This implies that instead of running one-shot workshops, school districts would provide extensive training, classroom follow-up, peer coaching, circuit-rider assistance, or in-school program facilitators to help make the transition from traditional methods to more effective programs. If we know that a program is effective if properly implemented, then it is worthwhile to stick with the program for as long as it takes to *make* it effective.

An exciting recent development may actually put significant federal resources into programs with evidence of effectiveness. In 1997 Congressmen David Obey and John Porter introduced legislation that is providing a total of $150 million to schools to help them adopt comprehensive, schoolwide programs with evidence of effectiveness. Schools can apply for at least $50,000 per year for up to 3 years to defray the start-up costs of adopting (mostly) externally developed models that cover all major aspects of school organization and instruction. At present, the requirements for "rigorously evaluated" models are expected to be low; for example, the Coalition of Essential Schools itself is listed in the legislation as an example of a comprehensive program. States will each make their own determinations of which models meet the evaluation standards. Still, the linking of resources to evidence of effectiveness has revolutionary possibilities. Over time, states might increase their standards for evidence as programs with good evidence build up their capacity to serve large numbers of schools and as new evidence appears to support particular models. If the Obey-Porter initiative is perceived to be successful, it is likely that the far larger Title I program, at approximately $8 billion per year, will begin to encourage adoption of effective programs when it is reauthorized in 1999. If the more than 50,000 Title I schools were even encouraged, much less required, to use programs supported by rigorous research, faddism could finally be confronted in American education.

SWITCHING TO A FAD-FREE DIET

Faddism is so well entrenched in American education that uprooting it will take time and concerted effort, probably with significant government involvement. However, if education is ever to make serious generational progress, we must somehow stop the pendulum by focusing educational change efforts on programs that are *effective* rather than on those that are merely new and sound good. Otherwise, we will endlessly repeat the process that led us in and out of the open classroom, in and out of Madeline Hunter's ITIP, in and out of whole language, and in and out of the Coalition of Essential Schools. Our children deserve better.

References

Adams, M. J. (1990). *Beginning to read: Thinking and learning about print*. Cambridge, MA: MIT Press.
Block, J. H., & Burns, R. B. (1976). Mastery learning. In L. S. Shulman (Ed.), *Review of Research in Education* (Vol. 4, pp. 3–49). Itasca, IL: F. E. Peacock, Inc.
Campbell, J. R., Donahue, P. L., Reese, C. M., & Phillips, G. W. (1996). NAEP *reading report card for the nation and the states*. Washington, DC: U.S. Department of Education.
Donovan, J. F., Sousa, D. A., & Walberg, H. J. (1987). The impact of staff development on implementation and student achievement. *Journal of Educational Research*, 80, 348–351.
Foorman, B. R., Francis, D. J., Fletcher, J. M., Schatschneider, C., & Mehta, P. (1998). The role of instruction in learning to read: Preventing reading failure in at-risk children. *Journal of Educational Psychology*, 90(1), 37–55.

Goodman, K. (1994). Deconstructing the rhetoric of Moorman, Blanton, and McLaughlin: A response. *Reading Research Quarterly*, 29(4), 340–346.

Hunter, M. (1986). Comments on the Napa County, California Follow-Through project. *Elementary School Journal*, 87, 173–179.

Klein, S. S. (1997). A system of expert panels and design competitions: Complementary federal approaches to find, develop, and share promising and exemplary products and programs. *Educational Researcher*, 26(6), 12–20.

Mandeville, G. (1988, April). *An evaluation of PET using extant achievement test data*. Paper presented at the annual convention of the American Educational Research Association, New Orleans, LA.

Meier, D. (1995). How our schools could be. *Phi Delta Kappan*, 76(5), 369–373.

Muncey, D., & McQuillan, P. (1996). *Reform and resistance in schools and classrooms: An ethnographic view of the Coalition of Essential Schools*. New Haven, CT: Yale University Press.

Rhine, W. R. (1981). *Making schools more effective: New directions from Follow Through*. New York: Academic Press.

Sizer, T. (1984). *Horace's compromise: The dilemma of the American high school*. Boston: Houghton Mifflin.

Sizer, T. (1992). *Horace's school*. New York: Houghton Mifflin.

Sizer, T. (1996). *Horace's hope*. New York: Houghton Mifflin.

Slavin, R. E. (1989). PET and the pendulum: Faddism in education and how to stop it. *Phi Delta Kappan*, 70, 752–758.

Slavin, R. E. (1990). IBM's "Writing to Read" program: Is it right for reading? *Phi Delta Kappan*, 72, 214–216.

Slavin, R. E. (1997). Design competitions: A proposal for a new federal role in educational research and development. *Educational Researcher*, 26(1), 22–28.

Slavin, R. E., Karweit, N. L., & Madden, N. A. (Eds.). (1988). *Effective programs for students at risk*. Neeham Heights, MA: Allyn & Bacon.

Slavin, R. E., & Madden, N. A. (1991). Modifying Chapter 1 program improvement guidelines to reward appropriate practices. *Educational Evaluation and Policy Analysis*, 4, 369–379.

Smith, F. (1988). *Understanding reading* (4th ed.). Hillsdale, NJ: Erlbaum.

Stahl, S. A., & Miller, P. D. (1989). Whole language and language experience approaches for beginning reading: A quantitative research synthesis. *Review of Educational Research*, 59, 87–116.

Stallings, J., & Krasavage, E. M. (1986). Program implementation and student achievement in a four-year Madeline Hunter Follow-Through project. *Elementary School Journal*, 87, 117–138.

Stringfield, S., Millsap, M., & Herman, R. (1997). *Special strategies for educating disadvantaged children: Results and policy implications*. Washington, DC: U.S. Department of Education.

CHAPTER 16

The Role of Technology in Education: Reality, Pitfalls, and Potential

J. KEVIN MANEY
Miami University

INTRODUCTION

Education technology initiatives across the United States reveal a movement nationwide to develop a network infrastructure in K–12 classrooms and to infuse computer-based technologies into curriculum and instruction. For example, in 1996, 98% of all schools in the United States owned computers and the student-to-computer ratio was 10 to 1, an all-time low. Eighty-five percent of schools had multimedia computers but the ratio of students to these computers was a staggering 24 to 1. In the area of network access, 38% of schools reported using local area networks for student instruction, whereas 64% of schools had Internet access. However, only 14% of the *classrooms* in this country had Internet access (Coley, Cradler, & Engel, 1997). In the state of Ohio, three current state technology initiatives, SchoolNet, SchoolNet Plus, and Telecommunity have been funded. Combined, the three projects have dramatic implications for each other. The goal of SchoolNet is to provide network capacity for every K–12 classroom. The goal of SchoolNet Plus is to provide one computer workstation for every five students in Grades K–4, whereas the goal of Ohio's Telecommunity initiative is to increase collaboration among schools and service providers to enrich the public school curriculum. Combined, the three programs represent a $700 million

Handbook of Educational Policy

commitment by the state and service providers to infuse technology into K–12 education and set the stage for cultural transformation of teaching and learning in Ohio.

As computers and networks become more common in our schools, it becomes imperative for districts to develop policies that will train teachers to effectively use these resources as powerful learning tools as well as for their own professional development. However, unlike some advocates of expanding technology to make bold—and often unfounded—claims about the educational benefits of using technology in K–12 classrooms (often implying that technology is the answer to all educational woes), a more modest approach will be presented here.

This chapter explains why teachers are the key to the successful adoption and use of educational technology, briefly discusses the research findings about technology's effectiveness, examines some of the uses of education technology, identifies key issues involved with its adoption and use, and discusses some of the critical policy issues associated with adopting and using technology. The chapter concludes with some general recommendations to policy makers in the area of educational technology adoption and use.

TEACHERS, TECHNOLOGY, AND LEARNING

Technology, as defined in this chapter, refers to computer-based hardware and software. Despite some of the fantastic claims made by computer enthusiasts, it is not at all clear if technology can be effectively used in the classroom. There is, however, some research that indicates technology can have a positive impact on students' learning. If teachers are going to be asked to use technology, it is reasonable to ask if there is any empirical evidence that might provide compelling reasons for them to do so.

The following is a brief review and summary of research on the effectiveness of technology in the classroom, based on the work of Sivin-Kachala and Bialo (1993). Their synthesis was based on 86 research reviews and reports on original research projects from both published and unpublished sources. Of these 86 studies, 34 were published in professional journals and 15 were doctoral dissertations. Their synthesis concluded that technology is making a significant and positive impact in education. Important findings from the studies reviewed include the following:

1. Educational technology has demonstrated a significant positive effect on achievement. Positive effects have been found for all major subject areas, in preschool through higher education and for both regular education and special needs students.
2. Educational technology has been found to have positive effects on student attitudes toward learning and on student self-concept. Students

felt more successful in school, were more motivated to learn, and had increased self-confidence and self-esteem when using computer-based instruction. This was particularly true when the technology allowed learners to control their own learning.

3. The level of effectiveness of educational technology is influenced by characteristics of the student population, the software design, the teacher's role, how the students are grouped, and the level of student access to the technology.

4. Specific characteristics of the learning environment help to maximize the benefits of educational technology: (a) teachers are more effective after receiving extensive training in the integration of technology with the curriculum; (b) teachers should carefully plan, and actively participate in, learning activities that incorporate tool software; (c) teachers should offer students self-directed learning experiences and activities that encourage self-expression; and (d) students benefit from personal interaction among class members.

5. Introducing technology into the learning environment has been shown to make learning more student-centered, to encourage cooperative learning, and to stimulate increased student–teacher interaction.

6. Positive changes in the learning environment brought about by technology are more evolutionary than revolutionary (i.e., technology does not produce change overnight and its true effectiveness cannot be measured in the short term). These changes occur over a period of years as teachers become more experienced with technology.

7. Courses for which computer-based networks were used increased student-to-student and student-to-teacher interaction with lower-performing students and did not decrease the use of traditional forms of communication.

8. Greater student cooperation and sharing and helping behaviors occurred when students used computer-based learning that allowed them to compete against the computer rather than against each other.

As can be seen from these research findings, it would seem that technology has positive effects on student cognition and affect as well as promoting cooperative learning—all desirable outcomes. The other key finding is that *it is not the technology that makes the difference but rather how teachers adapt and apply technology that makes the difference.*

Research results yielded by from the Apple Classroom of Tomorrow (ACOT) Project (Sandholtz, Ringstaff, & Dwyer, 1997) also confirmed many of these findings. The ACOT project was a 10-year study of the effects of a technology-rich environment on students' learning and is one of the few examples of actual research done in technology-rich classrooms. ACOT began its work in seven classrooms that represented a cross section of elementary and secondary schools and in the United States eventually expanded its research to more than 100 elementary and secondary classrooms throughout the country. Currently, there are three ACOT sites in the United States: (1) Portal Elementary School, Cupertino Union School District, Cupertino, California; (2) Dodson Elementary School, Nashville Metropolitan School District, Nashville, Tennessee; and (3) West High School, Columbus Unified School District, Columbus, Ohio.

In the ACOT project, students and teachers were given two sets of computer workstations and peripherals, one for home and one for school, and independent researchers examined "how the routine use of technology by teachers and students would affect teaching and learning" (Sandholtz et al., 1997, p. 3). Researchers found that (1) teachers' beliefs about instructional practices have to change before their practices will change; (2) technology changes the interaction between students and teachers; and (3) change in teaching and learning brought about by technology is evolutionary, not revolutionary. In sum, there is evidence that technology, if properly used, can have a positive impact on the way students think and learn.

Effective Use of Technology: A Definition

Effective use of technology is defined here as using technology to help students achieve desired learning outcomes and to enhance students' learning experiences by providing them with resources, opportunities, and tools that would otherwise be unavailable to them. The implications of this definition are straightforward. Technology is not the most important variable in the learning process; instead, it is how teachers use the technology that is critical. Clearly the nature of learning and its required tasks must drive the use of technology and not *vice versa*. Teachers should always have compelling instructional reasons for using technology and if none can be found, then technology should not be applied to a given learning situation. As such, technology becomes one of many tools that teachers use to help their students learn instead of the only tool. For example, students studying World War II might use Internet e-mail or newsgroups to contact veterans groups from around the world and solicit their perspectives about the war. In this case, students are using network technology to help them do the things historians do (collecting primary data). Moreover, technology is being used appropriately to connect students to resources that otherwise would not have been readily available to them.

On the other hand, a questionable use of technology might be to use a software program in an elementary math lesson as electronic flash cards. Although drill and repetition foster encoding (the process of storing information into long-term memory) and are therefore necessary instructional strategies, the technology in this example is merely duplicating what could have been done more cost-effectively with traditional flash cards. Although drill and practice via computer may be—at least initially—motivating for some students, there is the concern that when using technology in this manner, students lose the human interaction with the teacher or other students. Similarly, if the learning objective is to develop children's handwriting skills, then having students use a word processor to write is highly inappropriate because it does nothing to help them develop this skill. However, if the learning objective is to develop a student's writing skills—that is, the objective focuses on the writing *process*—then having students use a word processor becomes highly appropriate because of its powerful editing tools, which makes revision of writing and reorganization of ideas much easier.

Effective uses of technology also demand excellent teaching skills and an understanding of how humans think and learn. Effective uses of technology require careful teacher planning and an understanding of how to use technology to help students achieve identified learning outcomes. Viewed this way, effective usage of technology and networks becomes primarily an issue of teaching and learning and *not* an issue of technical competence. In other words, teachers become the focus of attention rather than the technology, because effective use depends on how *teachers* use technology and not the technology itself. Although student outcomes are the end result, it is the teacher who arranges the learning experiences and decides how technology will be used to enhance the learning experiences of students.

Effective Uses and Engaged Learning

Approaches to learning also determine whether technology and networks are being used effectively. ACOT research (Sandholtz et al., 1997) suggests that technology is most successfully used in *engaged learning* contexts. The following are characteristics of engaged learning models:

- Students explore, assume the role of teacher when appropriate, produce their own knowledge, and manage their own learning
- Teachers act as facilitators and learning guides and design the curriculum to be used
- Learning tasks are authentic, the kinds of tasks that professionals deal with or that are real world, challenging, and multidisciplinary
- Assessment is authentic, performance based, ongoing, and often leads to new learning (Tinzmann et al., 1997).

In engaged learning models, teachers arrange learning experiences for their students and then have them use networks and technology to find appropriate information needed to complete their learning tasks. In other words, unlike direct instructional models where the teacher acts primarily as an information giver, the technology can serve as a primary source of information. The teacher's role becomes infinitely more complex in this model because instead of simply giving students the answer, teachers must now help them find the answers and make meaning from available data. Teachers use their expertise to model ways of thinking, data collection techniques, and problem-solving approaches for their students because in an Information Age, knowing how to find the answers becomes nearly as important as knowing the answers. This is not to suggest that teachers never serve as information givers. On the contrary, teachers must be prepared to provide structure and guidance for their students to help direct their learning activities.

At this point, a puzzle analogy may be useful in explaining the process of engaged learning. Engaged learning is like putting together a complex puzzle that might look differently each time it is constructed but the pieces still fit together. Students are given a challenging problem to solve or project to complete and the teacher helps the students find the pieces of the puzzle and put them together to form a finished product. Notice that the teacher does not put the puzzle together for the students; instead, the teacher helps the students fit the pieces together to form a whole. To ensure that this is done correctly, it is essential for the teacher to identify the necessary prerequisite knowledge and skills that students must have to piece the puzzle together successfully. The process of identifying prerequisite knowledge and skills when planning a lesson or unit demands that the teacher know the subject(s) very well and possess the ability to teach students different ways to fit the pieces together—that is, to problem-solve. If the teacher does not possess these skills, he or she runs the risk of not being able to provide adequate learning guidance for students, which would result in the students' inability to solve the assigned problem or complete the assigned project. This process is obviously time consuming and demands careful planning by the teacher. Teachers must also be aware of the characteristics of their students and adjust their structure and guidance appropriately. For example, younger learners and poorer learners generally need more structure and guidance, especially when they are learning new knowledge and skills. This would apply to both content domains and needed technical skills, such as Web browsing or using software programs. On the other hand, older learners and better learners typically need less structure and guidance. The primary role of structure and guidance for these students should be to help them develop and enhance the knowledge and skills they already possess.

Teachers are apt to find this new role simultaneously exhilarating and extremely frustrating. Helping students find the answers on their own and watching the lightbulb go on over their heads is infinitely rewarding. Getting to that point is a different matter, however. What the literature about engaged learning generally fails to point out are the difficulties associated with resocializing students to work in this new approach to learning. For example, when confronted with challenging problems or projects without being told specifically what to do, syllabus-bound students (i.e., students who feel the need to closely follow a prescribed course of study) feel very threatened and usually get defensive. Common complaints usually center around lack of perceived structure in lessons, which frequently means that they want to be given the right answer so they know exactly what to recite back to the teacher on a test. Even students who are not especially syllabus bound find engaged learning to be somewhat threatening, at least initially. After all, many students have spent most of their educational lives being socialized to view the teacher as the primary information giver who is able to answer all questions. These students tend to see their role as being recipients of information rather than constructors of knowledge; for them, the important thing is to memorize as much as possible so that they will be able to give the right answer to the teacher on tests and other forms of evaluation. Teachers who begin to use engaged learning approaches should therefore not be surprised to find initial student resistance to this model of teaching and learning (and sometimes the resistance gets personal). After all, it is somewhat unrealistic for teachers to expect to resocialize students to a different way of learning in a single school year or semester.

The good news is that once students begin to accept this model of learning, they frequently embrace it and generally benefit from it. Among other things, research indicates that students develop a more positive attitude about learning, spend more time on task, and take more initiative in their learning (Sandholtz et al., 1997). Teachers who find an engaged learning approach threatening should remember that they are as important as ever in the learning process; their roles have simply changed from information giver to learning guide. Teachers must still build or adapt a curriculum, provide meaningful learning experiences for their students, and help them achieve identified learning outcomes.

Moreover, teachers should not view direct instruction and engaged learning models as incompatible. Given the time constraints of daily schedules, the structure of most schools, the needs of students, and the demands of the content, teachers must often serve as information givers to help students when they run into the "brick wall" as they attempt to solve problems or complete projects. Using minilectures and other direct instructional approaches within the broader context of engaged learning is very much acceptable and often very useful to help meet the needs that these demands create.

At this point, not much has been said about the role of technology in engaged learning models. That is because technology becomes one tool of many that the teacher identifies to help students accomplish learning objectives. Although specific suggestions will be offered later, suffice it to say here that students use technology to acquire resources and information that might otherwise be unavailable to them. The teacher helps students use networks and technology to acquire the information, evaluate its usefulness and validity, and apply it to help solve problems or complete projects. It is obvious then that the teacher is the critical variable in determining whether technology is being used effectively because it is the teacher who arranges the learning experiences for the students and how they use technology to support those learning experiences. Teachers who worry that they will be replaced by technology would do well to remember B. F. Skinner's observation that any teacher who can be replaced by a computer should be.

Direct Instruction and Engaged Learning: A Comparison

The following example is intended to help clarify how technology might be used in an engaged learning approach to teaching and learning. Although the example pertains to teaching high school history, the principles remain constant through grade levels and subject matter.

In 1995 the world observed the 50th anniversary of the bombings of Hiroshima and Nagasaki—events that led to Japan's surrender and the end of World War II. During that year, the Smithsonian Institution unveiled a display that raised a firestorm of protest across the United States. Some veterans groups were outraged at the display, charging that it was biased against the United States and that revisionists were trying to rewrite history to fit their points of view. Others claimed that the Smithsonian's display represented a correct representation of the bombings and urged that the decision that led to the bombings be revisited. This controversy became a hot news topic and would therefore serve as an excellent authentic problem for students to work on.

In a direct instructional approach, the teacher might prepare a lecture outlining events that led to the decision to drop the bombs and present the pros and cons of doing so. The teacher might then test students' knowledge of these events by giving them an objective test or having them write an essay. The teacher might even ask the students to evaluate the decision to bomb the Japanese and students would dutifully write their essays, all the while hoping that their responses will be evaluated positively by the teacher. The reader will note that in this scenario, the teacher is the primary information giver and evaluator, while the students are essentially passive recipients of that knowledge (i.e., they were given the pros and cons of the argument and asked to decide which position was more valid). Video technology might be used in this lesson to show students the actual bombing of Nagasaki or the aftermath of the bombs. However, students would likely concentrate more on the teacher's presentation than the video because it is unlikely that they would be held accountable for the video during any formal evaluation of the lesson.

By contrast, a teacher using an engaged learning approach might pose this question to the students: Was the United States justified in dropping the bombs on the Japanese in 1945? This would represent an authentic problem because there is no one correct answer, multiple perspectives must be examined and accounted for, and it is a question that actual historians would discuss and write about. The teacher, through questions and minilectures, would help students identify the issues and contexts they would have to consider to construct a solution to the problem posed. The teacher might then divide students into small groups with the instruction that each group become an expert on various identified aspects of the issue. Students would be encouraged to identify and interview primary sources (firsthand accounts) who might provide added insights to the problem being studied. Students would be asked not only to conduct face-to-face interviews, but also to use e-mail or newsgroups to locate and interview people in this country and Japan. By entering into conversations with people and groups from both countries, students would gain insight into the multiple perspectives of the two former combatants.

The teacher would also help students identify other resources they could use to help them answer the problem posed. These resources might include film, video, text, graphics, pictures, and audio and the teacher would encourage student teams to share these resources and knowledge gained from them with other students and teams. As students collected information and began to form opinions and draw conclusions, the teacher would promote students' acquisition of a balanced view of the issue by posing thoughtful questions or suggesting other resources to review.

As students became more knowledgeable in their respective assigned aspects of the issue, the teacher would invite them to teach others. Students would be encouraged to use a word processor to reflect on their discoveries and the teacher might have them use a multimedia authoring tool to create a presentation that answered the question posed. Notice that the same organizational skills needed to write a cogent essay are also needed to develop a multimedia presentation of this nature. Students would have to decide what to include (and what to exclude), how to organize their material, how to present it in a meaningful way, and how to develop a persuasive argument through their presentations. By using multimedia, students could provide the audience with a more powerful, vicarious experience through the use of video, audio, pictures, and text. Perspectives gained from interviews of the various primary sources would also be showcased in these presentations and students would construct meaning of the issues from careful analysis of them. Because publishing on the Internet is relatively easy, the teacher might encourage students to do just that. Students would then have to consider publishing for a larger audience and adjust their presentations accordingly. The teacher might also have students invite local veterans groups to attend their presentations and encourage thoughtful conversations should disagreements arise.

The reader will note the fundamental differences in this approach to teaching and learning. In the engaged learning approach, the teacher acts as a learning guide, helping students locate resources that will help answer questions or solve problems that arise. The teacher models the behavior of experts by making suggestions to students regarding *how to study an issue* rather than giving students the right answer. To do this, the teacher must thoroughly plan this unit of study, identify necessary prerequisite knowledge and skills (i.e., the necessary pieces of the puzzle that students need to answer the question) and ensure that they research the issue in a balanced and thorough manner. Students systematically gather data and then draw conclusions based on evidence and not simply opinion. Rather than relying on the teacher to provide the answers, students are guided by the teacher to construct their own answers, which allows them greater control over their learning. Technology is used to enhance the students' learning by giving them both communication and authoring tools, which allow them to tap resources that would otherwise be unavailable. Network technology also allows students to publish their work in alternative media to reach broader audiences.

The reader will also notice that the necessary technological skills to be learned in this example (using search engines to locate Internet resources, e-mail, software authoring, multimedia production, and Internet publishing) are determined by the learning activities. As such, technology is used to support students' learning and not for its own sake. Furthermore, this approach to studying history allows for an interdisciplinary approach to learning. Concepts of physics, biology, environment, and statistics could easily be incorporated into this problem. Given the right scheduling structure, science, math, and history teachers could work collaboratively to teach students how to solve this problem.

Learning to Incorporate Technology

Teachers and administrators who are interested in using technology as a vehicle to advance engaged learning models must also realize that the process is evolutionary and not revolutionary. Indeed, there is evidence to support the notion that technology can be used as a catalyst for instructional change. Before that can happen, however, teachers must first change their beliefs about teaching and learning (Sandholtz et al., 1997). Apple Classrooms of Tomorrow (ACOT) researchers have identified a model of instructional evolution through which teachers progress as they begin to adopt and use technology. The five stages of development as identified by ACOT researchers (Sandholtz et al., 1997) are as follows:

- *Entry.* Teachers focus on technical issues, learn how to use the technology, become greatly concerned about time, and face typical first-year teacher problems (e.g., discipline, resource management, and personal frustration). As they become more certain about technical matters, there is less concern about time and teachers once again focus on instructional issues. This signals entry into the adoption stage.
- *Adoption.* Teachers show more concern about how technology is going to be integrated into daily instruction. During this phase, teachers incorpo-

rate computer-based activities designed primarily to teach their students *how* to use technology. Generally teachers attempt to integrate technology into direct instruction to support traditional modes of teaching and learning.

- *Adaptation.* Technology becomes thoroughly integrated into traditional classroom practice and student productivity emerges as a major theme. Teachers also note a change in the quality of student engagement in classroom tasks. In general, students spend more time on task and become more deeply engaged in their learning.
- *Appropriation.* This is less a phase of instructional evolution and more a personal milestone that is characterized by a change in the teacher's personal attitude toward technology. It is the point in which the individual comes to understand technology and uses it effortlessly to accomplish real work (invisible technology). It is a turning point for teachers and signals the end of efforts to simply computerize traditional instructional practices.
- *Invention.* Teachers experiment with new instructional practices and explore new ways to interact with their students and other teachers. Interdisciplinary project-based instruction, team teaching, and individually paced instruction become common. Teachers also begin to question old practices and speculate about the causes for change in their students' work. Invention represents the climax in the evolution of teachers' instructional strategies and beliefs.

As has been shown, technology is used effectively when it can enhance students' learning experiences and help support learning objectives. Furthermore, technology is used most effectively within engaged learning models but can also be used to support direct instruction, provided the teacher chooses to do so wisely. Direct instruction is usually efficient and teachers can relay great amounts of information to students in short periods of time through lecture. Consequently, it is relatively easy to cover formal courses of study and teachers do not feel the time constraints that are inherent with engaged learning. However, the learners tend to be passive recipients of information and there is not much emphasis placed on developing critical thinking skills. In this model, technology is typically used for drill and practice or secondary sources of information to supplement what the teacher gives. Teachers who want to remain the primary information giver will feel most comfortable in this model.

On the other hand, engaged learning models tend to change the roles of teacher, students, and technology. Students take an active part in their learning, collaborate in learning projects, and use networks and technology as one of several sources of information. Students also use technology and networks to publish their work in a variety of media and to broader audiences. The teacher is no longer the center of attention and the teacher's role shifts to that of learning guide. There is an emphasis on developing critical thinking skills, which has caused concern about how this approach affects student performance on standard testing, especially in states that mandate minimum competency tests for students. Research from the ACOT project (Sandholtz et al., 1997) suggests that their students' standardized test taking performance did not suffer as a result of being in engaged learning environments. Teachers who choose to use technology within an engaged learning approach would be wise to build courses of study that support identified learning outcomes on state proficiency tests and use network connectivity to help them find that information quickly and easily. Engaged learning also tends to be time consuming and teachers who use this approach will likely have to either rewrite their courses of study to reflect this reality or abandon the approach. Moreover, teachers who feel uncomfortable in allowing their students to actively collaborate to construct knowledge or who do not want to give up the role as primary information giver will likely not want to adopt engaged learning methods. In sum, both approaches to learning offer specific advantages and must be carefully chosen to best fit the learning situation as well as the needs of the learners.

EDUCATIONAL USES OF SOFTWARE AND NETWORKS

As stated previously, technology and networks, if they are to be used effectively, must support identified learner outcomes and provide students with access to resources and opportunities that otherwise would be unavailable. Approaches to learning that best utilize technology were also discussed. This section looks at possible uses of the Internet and software (word processors, databases, spreadsheets, etc.) that can be used across the curriculum to help students accomplish stated learning objectives and to enhance their learning experiences. Teacher use of these technologies as productivity tools will also be discussed.

Productivity Enhancement

Teachers can use technology as productivity tools and, as ACOT research (Sandholtz et al., 1997) has shown, most teachers start using these software packages to help them become more productive and to support traditional instructional patterns. For example, teachers might use a word processor to write lesson plans and produce attractive instructional handouts for their students. The powerful features of word processors make adding graphics and revising work easy so that teachers, once they have learned how to take advantage of these features, can efficiently produce lesson plans and attractive documents for their students.

Teachers can use databases to store data about their students to help reduce paperwork. For example, teachers can keep textbook inventories on databases and create mailing labels to be used when communicating with parents. Teachers can merge database fields with a word processing document to easily create customized form letters. These letters, incorporating, for example, information from an electronic gradebook, can be used to help keep parents better informed about their student's academic progress and enhance teacher-parent communications.

Fostering Communications

Likewise, schools can use telecommunications software or the World Wide Web to stimulate communications between teachers, administrators, and parents. As schools gain network capacity, teachers can use telecommunications software and e-mail to more conveniently communicate with one another. Although it would be inappropriate to use electronic communications to replace face-to-face conversations when the latter is just as convenient, teachers can use the power of network connectivity to help break down the isolation of the self-contained classroom. Teachers in large school buildings will find this tool especially helpful in communicating with other teachers whom they would not normally see during the course of a school day. For example, teachers might use e-mail to share information about a student they both have and about whom they are concerned. Teachers can browse the Web to find resources to help them create more effective lesson plans or to locate competency test outcomes or standards relevant to their class or grade level so that they can incorporate these outcomes in their lesson plans. Schools could host electronic bulletin boards where parents could locate courses of study and find tips on helping their children develop better study habits. Districts could also develop a Web site where teachers from several districts (or even states) could construct, edit, and share lesson plans with each other. In all these cases, teachers and schools are using technology to increase their productivity and communications with other important constituents. Moreover, if schools expect teachers to eventually adopt and use technology, the latter will have to be convinced that there is a relative advantage in doing so. Showing teachers ways to use technology to reduce paperwork and increase productivity is a good place to start in this process. Finally, benefits accrue for school districts as a whole. For example, in an age where many schools are having trouble securing adequate local funding, it seems imperative that they use the connectivity power of networks to project a positive presence into their respective local communities.

Learning Tools

Teachers can also use forms of technology as powerful learning tools. Word processors have been demonstrated to have a positive effect on the writing process (Sandholtz et al., 1997). Students who use word processors to write have been shown to be more fluent in developing their thoughts and editing their work because the powerful editing tools of word processors make revising papers much easier. Databases can store data on various subjects and teachers can have students use a database's sort-and-search tools to find meaningful patterns within the data and draw conclusions. Spreadsheets are used primarily to manipulate quantitative information and can be used to complete complex calculations for students within the broader contexts of problem solving. Authoring tools allow students to organize data and incorporate various media—video, sound, text, and pictures, etc.—to create powerful multimedia presentations. Digital cameras, flatbed scanners, video authoring tools, and a host of resources on the Web make it easy to include multimedia resources in student presentations and are quite cost efficient. However, as alluded to previously, using multimedia for its own sake is not good a reason to use it. Instead, there should always be some compelling instructional rationale behind its use. Moreover, there is some research to suggest that multimedia can be used as an effective learning tool (Moore, Myers, & Burton, 1994).

The World Wide Web can be used to publish students' projects and connect them with other people and resources around the world. As a general rule, teachers and students should use technology to do the time-consuming, repetitive, and labor-intensive tasks (i.e., the "dirty work"), which in turn allows them to pursue the thinking, learning, and creative activities that humans do best. The following hypothetical examples illustrate some possible effective uses of computers. These examples are not comprehensive or exhaustive; rather, they are intended to stimulate thinking about how technology could be effectively used in engaged learning contexts.

Social Studies

Social studies students could use databases to analyze and correlate different variables. For example, students could use databases to search for and compile information about the gross domestic product, demographics, and birth and death rates to help them compare developed and underdeveloped countries. Students could use databases and spreadsheets to examine variables to discover whether there are significant relationships between them. Teachers and students could use the Internet to locate other classrooms across the country and then discuss national and regional issues with their on-line counterparts. Students could access databases on the Web and use the latest information to help them analyze current events in politics or economics. Simulations could be used to help students explore difficulties in developing the national budget or in conducting foreign policy.

Health and Physical Education

In health and physical education classes, computer and network technologies could be used to show the heart beating and allow students to introduce variables that would have positive or negative impacts on the human heart (smoking, exercise, cholesterol, etc.). Computer simulations could also be used to teach CPR or allow students to construct healthy diets and then analyze the effects of their proposed diets on their health. By combining text, graphics, and video, the computer allows students to become active problem-solvers of important health issues rather than simply memorizing verbal information about health or physical education.

Science

In science, teachers could use computer-based technologies to conduct experiments in class that would otherwise be too dangerous or costly. For example, students could use the computer and interactive videodisc to conduct experiments that test the chemical reaction of Group 1 elements that would normally produce an explosion if actually mixed. Moreover, since computers are able to infinitely replicate experiments and introduce new variables, students who are absent during labs would have the opportunity to conduct experiments that they would have otherwise missed. Computers could also be used as "smart tools" that actually collect data. For example, a thermometer could be attached to a computer and the computer programmed to record and graph temperatures every second. By doing so, students could analyze the effectiveness of different insulations or track the effect of temperature on other variables such as metals or chemicals. Finally, students could use simulations to perform realistic dissections of animals and humans, thus giving them greater insights into anatomy and physiology and providing them with resources that might otherwise be unavailable to them.

Mathematics

Computers would allow math students to develop high-level problem-solving skills because they free students from doing often lengthy and difficult computations. For example, students could use database, spreadsheet, and statistical programs to raise and answer such questions as "Does life expectancy rise with income rather than with physicians per thousand?" or "What significant trends are developing in manufacturing or business?" The reader will also note the interdisciplinary nature of these questions.

Foreign Languages

Foreign language teachers could use video conferencing and chat rooms on the Web to locate classes of students in other countries and communicate with them on a regular basis. For example, a German class in the United States might connect with an English class in Germany to practice their respective language skills with each other and to share cultural practices or discuss current international problems. If time differences prevented real-time conversations, students could use e-mail or Web communication tools to communicate with each other.

Cross-Disciplinary Uses

All teachers could use word processing programs to facilitate students' writing and thinking processes. Because computers significantly ease the editing process, students would be encouraged to write several drafts, thus developing and refining their ideas and critical-thinking skills. Results from the ACOT project have demonstrated that this indeed happens when students have regular access to word processing programs (Sandholtz et al., 1997). Teachers could also have their students use the Web to locate current resources and people relevant to their courses of study and to publish their work for broader audiences.

By now, it should be readily apparent to the reader that computer-based technologies allow a more seamless integration of different subject areas. Because the real world is rarely as compartmentalized as schools, especially secondary schools, an integrated approach to curriculum and instruction can be viewed as an extra benefit of using computer-based technologies. Although this chapter has ignored using computers for such things as drill-and-practice in favor of using them to develop critical-thinking and cognitive skills, this should not be interpreted to mean that drill-and-practice activities are inappropriate instructional devices. Rather, it must be recognized that computers are generally not the most cost-effective way to administer drill-and-practice activities.

As a final note, it must be reemphasized that these scenarios will not become realities unless teachers are adequately trained to use computer-based technologies in ways that facilitate critical-thinking skills. Moreover, teachers are unlikely to even consider using computers as tools of instruction until they become comfortable with them as productivity tools for their own personal use. Without a comprehensive faculty development program and adequate funding to implement it, purchasing computer-based hardware is an exercise in futility and a waste of scarce resources, something that school districts can ill afford. Consequently, the issues of technology adoption are examined next.

ADOPTION ISSUES

If schools are to ultimately use technology in effective ways, it is critical that they carefully consider the issues involved in its adoption and use by teachers and students so that policies can be developed that will produce desired results. Schools must base their policies on the best contemporary research and practices so that adequate professional development opportunities can be offered to ensure that teachers know how to use technology effectively. Perhaps most important, school leaders and parents must realize that technology adoption is a slow process and not given to immediate results. Table 1 shows nine principles, distilled from relevant research, that should provide guidance to those formulating policies related to the adoption and integration of technology into curriculum and instruction in elementary and secondary schools.

These principles, consistent with the ACOT model of instructional evolution previously discussed, suggest that professional development is the critical element so that teachers view technology as *one* tool for learning and not the solution to every educational problem. Moreover, if schools are to

TABLE 1
Nine Principles of Technology Adoption

Principle	Description
Principle 1	Technology adoption is not about technology at all; rather, it is about using technology to improve teaching and learning. In other words, it is really about reforming and restructuring curriculum and instruction.
Principle 2	Technology can have a significant impact on teaching and learning, depending on how it is used by teachers (Sandholtz et al., 1997).
Principle 3	Change is a process, not an event. The process of adopting significant innovations (like technology) will take 3 to 5 years (or longer) to complete (Hall & Hord, 1987; U.S. Congress, Office of Technology Assessment, 1995; RAND Corporation, 1975–1978).
Principle 4	Understanding the point of view of the participants in the change process is critical (Hall & Hord, 1987). In the context of schools, this initially refers to teachers and principals.
Principle 5	Teacher change is not unidirectional. Instead teachers progress through stages of concern in an idiosyncratic manner (Dwyer, Ringstaff, & Sandholtz, 1990).
Principle 6	These stages of concern can be systematically and empirically measured using the Stages of Concern Questionnaire (SoCQ) developed by Hall, George, and Rutherford (1979). The results of the SoCQ can be used to guide further faculty development as well as evaluate past efforts.
Principle 7	Teachers' beliefs about instruction and schools is an important factor that underlies schools' resistance to change. This fact must inform and guide planning and implementation of significant change efforts. This does not mean abandoning beliefs, but gradually replacing them with more relevant beliefs shaped by experiences in an altered context (Dwyer et al., 1990).
Principle 8	Transformation of teachers' instructional processes follows a predictable pathway that can be expedited through staff development programs (Sandholtz et al., 1997).
Principle 9	Without long-range professional development programs, teachers will use technology to support traditional instructional patterns and accomplish some productivity gains, but little else follows (Sandholtz et al., 1997).

successfully adopt and use technology, a K–16 approach must be used in which preservice teachers are trained to use technology as tools for learning. This is essential because most school districts do not have the adequate financial resources to provide thorough professional development for entry-level teachers. The following section provides one possible model that has been successfully used to train both pre- and in-service teachers and is part of Project TEAM (Technology in Education Adoption Model) developed by Maney, Brooks, and Perry (1997).

THE TECHNOLOGY IN EDUCATION ADOPTION MODEL FOR PROFESSIONAL DEVELOPMENT

The goal of TEAM is to systematically provide multiple opportunities for undergraduates to use and integrate technology into curriculum and instruction so they will be more likely to adopt and use education technology as teachers. TEAM recognizes the importance of learning technology within the context of authentic educational experiences and attempts, through a series of courses, to provide students with multiple opportunities to teach with technology instead of simply teaching them how to use technology. TEAM has been implemented in the School of Education and Allied Professions at Miami University, Oxford, Ohio, and is based on the following precepts. To help teachers learn to adopt and use technology, it is critical that they learn needed skills within the context of their jobs. There is a critical difference between knowing how to use technology and knowing how to *teach with* technology. Consequently, teachers must be given multiple opportunities to teach with technology and to watch others model it. Networks can be especially valuable for this purpose because they can be used to connect pre-service and in-service teachers with others who are using technology in educational contexts. Although there must be some direct instruction involved in learning to use the technology, the key task is to get teachers to use the technology within the contexts of their jobs. It is not sufficient to have teachers describe how they would use technology to teach; they must actually teach with technology and peer teaching is an excellent way to accomplish this. Doing so sets the framework for needed skills and teachers learn that they do not have to know everything about a software application. In other words, they learn technology on a need-to-know basis and the learning outcomes drive the uses of technology, not vice versa. Peer teaching also allows skill development to be embedded within the context of teaching the lesson because other teachers serve as students and use technology to accomplish assigned tasks and projects.

For example, databases could be learned in the contexts of productivity tasks or engaged learning discussed previously. Accordingly, teachers might learn to use a word processor to write objectives, develop a problem or project to teach, plan lessons that use a database to help solve the problem or complete the project, and then actually teach a lesson or lessons to their peers using a database and any handouts produced on the word processor. Teachers could then have their students (i.e., other teachers) present their solutions to the given problem or completed projects using desktop publishing capabilities of software suites. This, in turn, provides further skill development and repetition and reinforces the idea that learning activities dictate the needed technology skills and not vice versa.

For some teachers, a more effective strategy might be to show them how to use technology to help them ease the drudgery of daily paperwork and other record-keeping tasks. Once teachers see the relative personal advantages of using technology, they tend to be more open to suggestions about using it as a learning tool. This process can to be problematic unless new users clearly see personal advantages of using technology as they struggle to learn to use it.

BARRIERS TO ADOPTION

Network connectivity, *provided teachers are trained to effectively use it*, seems to offer great hope in leveling the playing field in terms of equity and access to adequate educational resources. However, several significant barriers stand in the way. First, if students and teachers are going to effectively use networks to support learning outcomes, they must have access from their classrooms. Because only 14% of the nation's classrooms have Internet access (Coley et al., 1997), this becomes a major stumbling block because of the high cost of retrofitting and hardwiring school buildings. Moreover, even if the problem of access is overcome, teachers must still be trained to help their students effectively use Internet resources for learning purposes. For example, teachers will have to know where and how to look for resources so that they can be effective learning guides for their students. Evaluating Web-based resources is also an essential skill because the Internet, besides hosting a wealth of valuable educational resources, is also the single largest source of *mis*information in our society. Curiously, however, many teachers seem to faithfully accept the legitimacy of most Internet resources and fail to apply critical tools of scholarship to them. This is a very dangerous practice and teachers and their students must learn to treat Internet-based resources the same way they do other resources.

Also, if teachers are not professionally developed to use technology effectively, computer-based technology will likely go the way of countless other failed educational innovations, despite the computer's ubiquitous presence in society. Furthermore, there are other major barriers that may prevent its adoption and use. The following are the most common barriers to technology adoption: (1) time, (2) access, (3) teacher attitudes toward technology, and (4) technical support.

Time

Teachers must be given adequate time to learn new technologies. Finding time to learn new skills is becoming increasingly difficult as teachers are asked to do much more than just teach. Moreover, if engaged learning models are to be adopted and used, schools will have to consider alternatives to the traditional 40- or 50-minute class periods.

Access

This includes access to the technology both at school and at home and the latter is closely related to the barrier of time. If teachers do not have access to technology and networks *in their classrooms*, they will be unlikely to use it. No matter how well-intentioned a media center person or computer lab teacher might be, it is just not convenient for most teachers to take their classes to another room (if that room is even available) on a regular basis. The key is to get computers and network access into classrooms and teachers' homes so that they have time to develop their skills in using and teaching with these resources.

Teacher Attitudes toward Technology

Simply put, if teachers are not convinced that they or their students will benefit from using technology or engaged learning approaches, they will adopt neither. This becomes especially problematic because teachers are often frustrated by technology as they initially begin to use it. For example, it is hard to tell new users that e-mail will increase their ability to communicate with others when it has taken them hours to figure out how to send a message! For the most part, these issues can be dealt with by providing adequate and timely technical support.

Many teachers also fear technology for a number of reasons. Teachers do not want to look like fools in front of their students, parents, or colleagues, and many teachers doubt their own ability to use the technology. Some teachers also believe that their own students must see them as the expert in everything. Yet many feel that their students know more about technology than they do and, as a result, feel threatened by the technology. Consequently, these teachers are reluctant to adopt and use technology and will not likely do so until their beliefs about teaching and learning change.

Technical Support

If teachers are going to adopt and use technology, there must be a support infrastructure available to help them troubleshoot and solve technology-related problems. Hopefully, as teachers' skills grow, their support network will grow as well and take advantage of network connectivity to administer troubleshooting. Schools would also be wise to enlist the help of capable students in this task.

One example of such an approach was implemented in the Talawanda City Schools in Oxford, Ohio. A student "tech squad" was formed when the district made the decision to adopt technology and is one of the key reasons why technology has been successfully adopted there. The tech squad is a group of high school students who use their technological skills and knowledge to help teachers solve network and computer-related problems as they occur. As part of its support system, the tech squad uses a network bulletin board where users can ask questions and e-mail for help.

Although these are not the only potential barriers that prevent schools from adopting and using technology, they are the most commonly reported ones in the research and schools must develop effective policies to deal with them.

SAFE USE OF NETWORKS

As previously discussed, students and teachers can use the Internet to acquire additional resources to support and enhance teaching and learning. The Web can also be used as an additional medium for publishing, capable of reaching literally a worldwide audience of potential readers. However, because the world of cyberspace mirrors the human world (and all that is good and bad about it), it is imperative that parents, teachers, and school and community leaders formulate policies that provide reasonably safe environments in which students can work and publish. This section identifies essential issues that policy makers need to consider.

Fair Use

Students and teachers who use resources from the Web in their work or projects must reference any materials that are not theirs, just as they would in more traditional forms of publishing. Currently the issue of copyright has not been settled for Web-based resources. However, teachers would be wise to have their students seek permission from the publisher if they are going to rely heavily on resources from a particular Web site. At minimum, students should *always* site the URL (Web address) from which they acquired their information or resources in their work. Generally speaking, it is acceptable to use Web-based resources for educational publishing.

Academic Freedom versus School Liability

The issue of academic freedom versus school liability tends to be exacerbated in cyberspace because of the Internet's ability to quickly access resources and reach large audiences. Although there are no hard and fast rules, it is advisable for districts to formulate Internet policy that mirrors their policy on these issues concerning more traditional means of publishing. This will tend to be a community or local issue and will be guided by the values of a local constituency. Whatever the policy, students should be given reasonable freedom to express their ideas and teachers must help students publish ideas in ways that are not patently offensive or grossly distorted. In terms of Web publishing, schools must also establish reasonable guidelines to protect their students, and teachers must regularly remind students of these guidelines. For example, students should never publish their home addresses or include their phone numbers or any other sensitive material in their published material. It is an unfortunate reality that students must be protected from dangers on the Web, but schools must also move to protect their students from similar dangers in the world of humans.

Obscene Material

Similarly, this is an area of growing concern, primarily because of the explosion of pornographic Web sites. Unfortunately, however, there are no quick fixes or easy solutions to this problem. Schools and Internet service providers can construct firewalls to block access to certain Web sites and domains. However, this is not always effective because of the fluent nature of the Web; sites can appear, disappear, and reappear overnight and use a different URL or domain that can sometimes defeat the firewalls. Internet service providers can limit access to certain newsgroups and block spam (unsolicited e-mail that is usually an advertisement for a product or service), but here again, only with limited success for the same reasons. If students are going to use e-mail, then teachers must regularly monitor their mail and limit times they use it. The most effective strategies are close supervision of student activity while they are using the Internet and limiting their access to e-mail. This will require careful planning and classroom management on the part of teachers and these skills must be developed in any professional development they receive. Teachers would also be wise to make their students aware of the problem but not to blow it out of proportion. Doing so will likely arouse students' prurient interests and may even aggravate the problem.

Combined with blocking mechanisms that can be established by the district's network administrators and the Internet service provider, schools can be reasonably certain that students will be shielded from obscene materials. However, none of these methods are foolproof and policy makers would be well advised to include parents in formulating acceptable use policies and procedures for students to use the Internet. Once formulated, schools should post the policies on their Web sites (if available) and require parents to read and sign it. Parents who refuse to sign the policy form or who do not want their sons or daughters using the Internet should have their wishes honored and those students should be allowed to acquire resources from alternative and more traditional sources (e.g., libraries or media centers) without penalty.

Viruses

There is some disagreement among experts as to whether viruses actually pose a problem. On one hand, whenever two or more computers are networked, it is always possible to transmit a virus from machine to machine. However, most reputable Web sites regularly monitor resources for viruses and generally do not allow infected files to be transferred. To be safe, school districts might consider purchasing antivirus software and installing it on each machine. When considering antivirus software, schools should find out how frequently the manufacturer updates its virus definitions because new viruses seem to appear on a regular basis and therefore the antivirus software needs the updated virus definitions to detect and destroy any new viruses. Teachers could then regularly configure the software to automatically scan for viruses during the evening and encourage their students to do the same with any resources they might download at home or school. Moreover, students and teachers should always know the source of any materials used, text or otherwise, and should be reluctant to download anything that cannot be confirmed to be virus-free.

RECOMMENDATIONS

School leaders, district administrators, and legislators each play a role in formulating sound policies for purchasing technology, developing professional development opportunities for teachers, and planning instructional approaches that will prepare American students for the future. Effective policies should be informed by knowledge of emerging notions of engaged learning; the possibilities for using technology to aid teaching, learning, communication, and school-related record-keeping tasks; stages of implementation; and the barriers to successful adoption of education technology. This chapter has addressed these issues, grounded in what can be learned about these topics in the relatively new and underdeveloped research literature.

Based on the issues and challenges described previously, the following recommendations are offered to promote the opportunity for schools to successfully adopt and effectively use technology. Where possible, relevant research is cited to support the specific recommendation.

Recommendations for District and Central Office Leaders

1. At the district level, the commitment for technology adoption and support must come from the superintendent and board of education. This commitment is manifested primarily in the development of a permanent line item in the school district's budget for technology, of which, at least 15% should be earmarked specifically for faculty development. This commitment also includes supporting a culture of responsible risk taking by principals, teachers, and students.

2. School districts need to keep parents and the community well informed about the progress of technology adoption/restructuring. District leaders and teachers must work to create realistic expectations about technology adoption and results. They need to help the community understand that technology adoption is a change process and that it will take time to evaluate its success or failure. Consequently, school leaders and teachers should speak to the community in terms of years instead of months or days. In addition, generating and maintaining community support by building partnerships and collaborative relationships with parents and other key community leaders is critical. This can be done by inviting parents and key community leaders to help plan for technology use and adoption.

3. To foster communication with parents and the community, school districts might purchase a telecommunications server/electronic bulletin board system and allow parents and the community to use it free of charge, if possible. This will help generate public support and keep the community informed about school and technology-related issues.

4. As part of a broader academic community, schools can seek to form partnerships with nearby colleges or universities. These institutions can help in developing an action research program to track the progress and results of the change efforts of the district. In turn, schools can work with a college or university to provide student teachers with the opportunities to watch mentor teachers teach with technology and use it in their own teaching.

Recommendations for Principals

1. Building principals should be encouraged to take the lead in technology adoption. Teachers and principals are the key to technology adoption. Principals are responsible for developing a building culture that sets high

but achievable instructional expectations and encourages responsible risk taking using technology.

2. Principals should also model technology and articulate an instructional vision for its use for both faculty and students. To do this, principals must first learn about the issues of teaching with technology. Moreover, for schools to successfully adopt technology, a well-defined instructional vision must precede a technological one. If the building principal and faculty do not have ideas as to how technology should be used, none should be purchased until they do.

3. Likewise, principals need to keep current with developments in cognitive science and encourage faculty to do the same. Some research data suggest that teachers are more willing to use technology when they understand that it will support their theoretical orientation to teaching and learning.

4. Accordingly, districts and individual buildings should develop a technology plan. Faculty should be given a substantial role in generating building plans because they must also develop an instructional vision for technology. Principals must also include teachers in hardware and software decision making. Excluding faculty from basic technology decision making essentially takes away their ownership of it.

5. Building principals must understand that traditional standardized tests may not be particularly good measures of the kinds of learning fostered by innovative uses of some technologies. Consequently, they should work with faculty to develop new assessment tools. Principals must also keep this in mind when evaluating teachers who use technology as instructional tools. In other words, to make accurate evaluations of teachers teaching with technology, principals must be aware of the capabilities of technology and its impact on learning.

6. School districts should consider incorporating incentives into teacher evaluation instruments and the collective bargaining that reward good teaching with technology. This has the effect of institutionalizing instructional uses for technology and will be manifested primarily at the building level. It is also directly related to fostering the appropriate building culture that encourages technology use and responsible risk taking. However, districts and principals should not force technology on faculty. Principals must accept that some faculty members do not want to use technology and commit appropriate resources to those who do.

7. Building principals and faculty should consider alternative configurations for class schedules and teaching approaches that will allow teachers and students to collaborate in ways that fully utilize technology. Similarly, principals should help to ensure that technology is placed in their buildings where it is convenient for students and teachers to use it. In most instances, this means the classroom, as opposed to computer labs. Although this strategy reduces opportunities for public relation "sound bytes," involving the

display of sparkling computer labs during an open house, it is critical for the adoption of technology.

Recommendations for the Development of Professional Development Policies

1. It is imperative that school leaders and policy makers realize that professional development is *essential* for successful technology adoption. Moreover, it is essential for school leaders to realize that teachers are key to technology adoption and take a slow approach with them. Without a systematic, sustained professional development program, it is a waste of resources to purchase hardware and software. For example, the U.S. Office of Technology Assessment (1995) recommends that at least 30% of the technology budget should be earmarked for professional development.

2. Consequently, it is critical for building and district administrators to develop sustained, systematic professional development programs that adequately train faculty to use technology. One shot in-services are simply inadequate for professional development in the areas of technology, teaching, and learning. However, one of the barriers to increasing technology training for teachers is the competing priorities for limited professional development time (U.S. Office of Technology Assessment, 1995). Principals and superintendents will have to balance these needs as they allocate scarce resources for professional development. One strategy that district and building leaders might pursue is to first show teachers how technology can help make their professional lives easier, such as cutting down paperwork and facilitating communications between colleagues and parents. Teachers will not use technology if they do not see any relative advantage in doing so. Logically, districts might develop policies that allow teachers to initially use technology for instructional management and to support their current teaching practices until they become comfortable using the technology.

3. A district's professional development plan must also recognize that if the instructional potential of technology is ever to be realized, curriculum integration must be the focal point of professional development. A goal of district's professional development plan should be to ensure that mastering technology is not viewed as a stand-along competency—that is, technology must be integrated into curriculum and instruction and not viewed as something distinct from curriculum and instruction. However, curriculum integration is a difficult, time-consuming, and resource-intensive endeavor that district and building leaders must account for in their planning.

4. Based on the Office of Technology Assessment (OTA) findings (1995), a school district's professional development program should also make teachers aware of the resources technology can offer them as professionals

in carrying out many aspects of their jobs. OTA found that very little time is currently invested in training or helping teachers to use technologies. Consequently, to achieve sustained use of technology, school leaders must provide teachers with hands-on learning, time to experiment, easy access to equipment, and ready access to support personnel. Furthermore, a number of different approaches have been successful for training teachers to use technology. These include (1) technology-rich model schools, (2) the train the trainer model, (3) providing expert resource people, (4) giving every teacher a computer, (5) training administrators alongside teachers, and (6) establishing teacher resource centers. Based on these findings, districts are advised to use multiple training and support strategies (U.S. Office of Technology Assessment, 1995).

5. School and building leaders must also recognize that most successful strategies to enhance technology implementation make significant investments in three elements of teacher support: (1) appropriate and timely training, (2) expertise to support and help teachers, (3) time for teachers to learn and reflect, and (4) opportunities to work with colleagues in the same building (U.S. Office of Technology Assessment, 1995). Moreover, when planning professional development programs, school leaders and policy makers are advised to consider these commonly expressed teacher wants/concerns when developing professional development programs: (1) assistance in how to use various technologies, in part to avoid being embarrassed in front of their students; (2) opportunities to understand what technologies can do, in part to visualize applications in their own classrooms; (3) more knowledge about how to organize and effectively manage their students in technology-based environments; and (4) more knowledge about how to teach with technology or how to organize learning activities to make optimal use of technologies. The U.S. Office of Technology Assessment (1995) has found that although teachers want opportunities to educate themselves about technology, they often do not have the time during the school day to do so. Therefore, a key to successful professional development is to find (or make) time for teachers to learn to use and teach with technology. In fact, lack of time may be the single most important barrier to the adoption of technology (Maney, 1994; Sheingold & Hadley, 1990; U.S. Office of Technology Assessment, 1995).

6. Similarly, it is difficult to structure training for teachers with widely varying experience and knowledge about technology. Consequently, to provide timely and appropriate training for faculty regardless of their experience or knowledge, professional development planners should consider administering the Stages of Concern Questionnaire (SoCQ) (Hall et al., 1979) at regular intervals to measure teachers' changing concerns about technology. School leaders and planners can construct faculty Concerns Profiles from the SoCQ, which can help them address the divergent needs and concerns of faculty as well as measure the success of prior training. Although this strategy

is more time consuming, ultimately it will prove to be more successful because the diverse concerns of faculty are being simultaneously addressed and relevant training applied that matches those concerns.

7. ACOT literature (Sandholtz et al., 1997) suggests that professional development is most effective when it is conducted on-site and is embedded within the appropriate contexts of faculty receiving the training. Therefore, whenever possible, district and building leaders should conduct professional development on-site and have teachers use only the equipment that will be available to them (and their students) on a regular basis. Moreover, the training provided should be as closely associated with the teachers' curricular goals as possible.

8. Last, school and building leaders must realize that it is critical for professional development to move beyond the basics of learning technology and concentrate on how to teach with technology. Ideally, this would also extend to a local college or university's teacher training program (if available) and be coordinated with programs designed to train preservice teachers to teach with technology. Regardless of local higher education resources and programs, at minimum, school districts must establish professional development programs for new teachers to ensure that their teaching-with-technology skills develop concurrently with other needed professional skills. Possible indictors of successful professional development programs would be the steady integration of technology into curriculum and instruction, as well as a trend toward interdisciplinary and collaborative teaching and learning. Accordingly, evaluation procedures must reflect these new practices.

This chapter examined the issues involved with successfully adopting and using technology in K–12 schools. It showed that technology can be used effectively in schools and argued that effective use of technology consists of using it to support desired learning outcomes and within engaged learning contexts. Policy development and reform initiatives must recognize that teachers are the key to the successful use of technology and that effective professional development is the key to teacher use of technology. Moreover, policy makers must recognize that technology adoption is a gradual process and consequently seek to measure the effectiveness of technology in education longitudinally.

References

Coley, R. J., Cradler, J., & Engel, P. K. (1997). *Computers and classrooms: The status of technology in* U.S. *schools*. Princeton, NJ: Educational Testing Service Policy Information Center.

Dwyer, D. C., Ringstaff, C., & Sandholtz, J. H. (1990). *The evolution of teachers' instructional beliefs and practices in high-access-to-technology classrooms: First-fourth year findings*. Teachers' Beliefs and Practices Research Summary No. 8. Cupertino, CA: Apple Computer, Inc.

Hall, G. E., George, A., & Rutherford, W. L. (1979). *Measuring stages of concern about the innovation*: A *manual for use of the* SoC *questionnaire*. Washington DC: U.S. Government Printing Office. (ERIC Document Reproduction Service No. ED 147 342).

Hall, G. E., & Hord, S. M. (1987). *Change in schools: Facilitating the process.* Albany: State University of New York Press.

Maney, J. K. (1994). *The adoption of multimedia technology in selected public high schools (9–12) in northwest Ohio.* Unpublished doctoral dissertation, The University of Toledo.

Maney, J. K., Brooks, D. M., & Perry, B. E. (1997). *The technology in education adoption model* (TEAM). http://www2.eap.muohio.edu/TEAM/

Moore, D. M., Myers, R. J., & Burton, J. K. (1994). What multimedia might do . . . and what we know about what it does. In A. W. Ward (Ed.), *Multimedia and learning: A school leader's guide.* Alexandria, VA: Institute for the Transfer of Technology to Education of the National School Boards Association.

RAND Corporation. (1975–1978). *Federal programs supporting educational change* (Vols. 1–8). Santa Monica, CA: Author.

Sandholtz, J. H., Ringstaff, C., & Dwyer, D. C. (1997). *Teaching with technology: Creating student-centered classrooms.* New York: Teachers College Press.

Sheingold, K., & Hadley, M. (1990). *Accomplished teachers: Integrating computers into classroom practice.* Washington DC: U.S. Government Printing Office. (ERIC Document Reproduction Service No. ED 322 900).

Sivin-Kachala, J., & Bialo, E. R. (1993). *The Report on the Effectiveness of Technology in Schools 1990–1992.* Washington DC: Software Publishers Association.

Tinzmann, M. B., Rasmussen, C., Foertsch, M., McNabb, M., Valdez, G., & Holum, A. (1997). *Learning with technology.* Oak Brook, IL: North Central Regional Educational Laboratory.

U.S. Congress, Office of Technology Assessment. (1995). *Teachers and technology: Making the connection.* Washington DC: U.S. Government Printing Office.

Methodological Advances for Educational Policy Analysis

CHAPTER

17

Meta-Analytic Effects for Policy[1]

HERBERT J. WALBERG and JIN-SHEI LAI

University of Illinois at Chicago

Rational policy analysts, evaluators, and practitioners choose policies, programs, practices, and instructional methods that suit such criteria as costs, ease of implementation, and appropriateness for their philosophies, conditions, and student characteristics. Until recently, they could not consider perhaps the most important criterion—the impact of alternatives on learning and other educational outcomes. Meta-analysis now provides *effect size* estimates of alternative policies, techniques, and methods as an additional basis for policy planning and evaluation.

EFFECT SIZES

Simply described, an effect size is the difference between the means of a group using a new method and a control group (divided by the control group or pooled group standard deviation to provide a uniform scale). Effect sizes allow comparison of effects from different studies even though they have employed tests of varying numbers of items and difficulties. Much like a calibrated meter stick in measuring distance, they allow comparison of learning effects across studies and methods of teaching. Other things being equal, programs or methods with bigger effect sizes are preferable: We should choose Method A over Method B if Method A has the larger effect size. However, effect sizes cannot serve as the sole criterion of choice.

[1]The Non-Directed Research Fund of the Korean Research Foundation supported the preparation of this chapter.

Effect sizes may best be evaluated by comparing them with one another. What does it take to be rich or tall? Given the relevant numbers, we can readily agree that one person is richer or taller than another, but cutting points are debatable and subjective. Rather than setting arbitrary cutting points for effect sizes, we will generally report the numbers for the reader's own weighing.

Estimates of learning effects are fallible, as are other considerations. Administrators, for example, may find costs much larger than expected and programs more difficult to implement than program manuals suggest. Similarly, the learning effects of a program may be smaller than average because of variations in, say, the staff training or program fidelity. Still, policy decisions must be made, and information about estimated effects should undoubtedly be weighed as one factor in decision making, program design, evaluation, and policy analysis.

Effect sizes can be useful for a variety of policy decisions. Teachers may want to choose among instructional methods. State or central-office administrators may want to plan staff development offerings. Program planners may want to consider the likely effects of practices they might incorporate in programs they develop or revise. Those who choose programs may weigh the effects of programs or program components.

OVERVIEW

This chapter provides the most recent and largest collection of educational effects known to us. From two compilations of meta-analyses of learning studies, we grouped 275 mean effect estimates (based on 8707 effect sizes) into 16 categories of educational practices and conditions. This wide variety—including behavioral treatments of special-needs children, patient education, and staff development—will help to show the dependency of effects on underlying principles of learning and instructional purposes and circumstances. Each is briefly characterized for the sake of comparison and contrast. They are not described in operational detail because many are familiar to educational policy analysts and because interested readers should read the original studies and meta-analyses, which may be found by consulting references to previous compilations of meta-analyses.

For several reasons, reading original meta-analyses, studies, and other cited references in the studies is recommended before making important decisions about educational policy or next research steps. These documents describe the methods in detail, their variations in practice, and how they are implemented. They may provide information on training required, costs, difficulty of implementation, recommended grade levels and conditions of use, and other information for decision making.

Though reasonable care was taken in compiling the estimates, it seems certain that some numerical errors have affected them. Not only are the original studies subject to errors of execution and reporting, but meta-analysts have employed different samplings of studies, formulas, and adjustments to calculate effect sizes. Most of the replicated estimates reported here yield fairly close correspondence, but they may have been subject to the same systematic errors.

Thus, the estimates in this review should be considered approximations. Replicating all meta-analyses using current recommended methods (Glass, McGaw, & Smith, 1981; Hunter, Schmidt, & Jackson, 1983; Hedges, 1984) would be highly desirable but labor intensive and unlikely. A more practical alternative would be collections of effect sizes of studies carried out since the latest meta-analyses. Until this is done, the present collection may provide initial estimates for comparisons, contrasts, and decisions.

BASIS OF THE ESTIMATES

The two largest collections of estimates of educational effects served as the basis of the present compilation. In the *American Psychologist* (flagship journal of the American Psychological Association), Lipsey and Wilson (1993) compiled effect sizes from 302 meta-analyses of psychological experiments and quasi-experiments intended to induce change in attitudes, behaviors, cognitions, and emotions. They showed "a strong, dramatic pattern of positive overall effects that cannot readily be explained as artifacts of meta-analytic technique or generalized placebo effects" (p. 1181). They concluded that meta-analytic "results are more creditable than conventional reviews" and that "well-developed psychological, educational, and behavioral treatment is [sic] generally efficacious" (p. 1181).

Lipsey and Wilson's purpose was to estimate the general efficacy of psychological (including educational) treatments. They showed few trivial effects: 90% of them were .10 or larger, 85% were .20 or larger, and the mean was .50. Lipsey and Wilson also showed that the effects were not artifacts of faulty research methods; rather findings were robust across studies of varying quality. True experiments (with random assignment of subjects to groups), for example, showed effects only .05 greater than quasi-experiments (that employed statistical equating). Published studies showed an effect .14 greater than unpublished ones, which reveals a journal bias to publish studies showing larger effects. Still, the difference is small relative to the mean effect of .50.

Lipsey and Wilson's calculations showed that methodologically strong studies resulted in average effects only .03 greater than methodologically weak ones. This suggests inclusive selection criteria because "weaker" studies such as quasi-experiments are often less contrived than stronger ones such as true experiments; if the results are consistent across both sets, the evidence is more creditable.

Lipsey and Wilson's smaller studies showed an effect .23 lower than larger ones. Studies with placebo control groups showed a placebo effect (a psychological benefit of thinking one is being efficaciously treated) of .19. When estimated effects with these biases were adjusted for their particular biases, the overall mean effect was .47, only 6% smaller than the unadjusted mean effect of .50. The mean psychological treatment effect compared favorably with effects of surgery and medical treatments compiled in the Lipsey and Wilson article.

Since it was not their purpose, Lipsey and Wilson made no attempt to compare effects of various treatments (aside from their methodological characteristics). As pointed out previously, however, alternate treatments or practices are of keen practical interest in professional fields including education. For this reason, this review combines Lipsey and Wilson's more recent educational effect estimates with the previous and partly overlapping compilation of Walberg (1991) to provide a comprehensive synthesis.

For several reasons, the combined set of educational effect estimates is considerably larger than that in either source. The Lipsey and Wilson collection contains effect estimates for peripheral treatments on the border between educational and psychological practice such as special education placement of learning-disabled and other children that escaped previous education compilations. These were included in the present review as were peripheral methods included by Walberg, such as educational staff development and physician and patient education.

The Lipsey and Wilson (1993) compilation is more recent and larger in the number of meta-analyses included. On the other hand, it intentionally omitted meta-analyses of "separable elements of intervention that do not, by themselves, constitute freestanding treatment (e.g., "use of advance organizers in a teacher's lesson plan," p. 1182). Such specifics of instruction are of interest in educational design and were included in Walberg's (1991) synthesis. In addition, Lipsey and Wilson took the most aggregated effects from each meta-analysis whereas educational meta-analyses often report separate estimates for student groups and planned treatment variations. Because these were included by Walberg and are of interest in educational practice, they are retained in the present synthesis.

EDUCATIONAL EFFECT ESTIMATES

This section is divided into several parts. Preliminary analyses show the overall statistical pattern of the educational effect sizes. The next section groups the effects into 15 categories. Subsequent sections discuss specific findings within each of these categories. The last section identifies several rudimentary principles that suggest the beginnings of an empirically based theory of classroom instruction.

Overall Educational Effects

As shown in the stem leaf in Figure 1, the 275 educational practices range in effect size from -.03 to 1.43 (the highest leaf of the 1.4 stem is .03 indicating an effect of 1.43). The mean is .373 (SD = .306) and the mode is .170—their relation indicating moderate positive skew; that is, most effects are moderate, say, .15 to .75, but a few stand out as particularly efficacious for various reasons subsequently discussed. The six high outliers above 1.0 (which are subsequently discussed) further illustrate this skew. The stem leaf also shows 25 negative effects (9% of the total) in which control groups learned more than experimental groups.

Other things being equal, policy makers and educators should choose methods and techniques that yield the greatest learning effects. Other things are rarely equal, of course, and they need to consider such things as costs, training requirements, ease of implementation, and their own, their institutions', and their students character and educational philosophy. Thus, the

```
Stem Leaf
                                                              Box plot
14  23
                                            2                  0
13
12  055
                                            3                  0
11  7
                                            1                  0
10  145
                                            3                  I
 9  00445689
                                            8                  I
 8  13488
                                            5                  I
 7  0111122334555688
                                           16                  I
 6  0011112355666788
                                           16                  I
 5  0000000112333444555566777789
                                           29              +-----+
 4  0000011111122223355555577777888888999
                                           38              I     I
 3  00122222233333344455555556777778888999
                                           38              *--+--*
 2  00000111222223344555556688888889999
                                           33              I     I
 1  00001223344455566666667777777778889999
                                           37              +-----+
 0  001112225566666778889
                                           21                  I
-0  988777743321
                                           12                  I
-1  643333322
                                            9                  I
-2  630
                                            3                  I
-3  0
                                            1                  I
    ----+----+----+----+----+----+----+---
```

FIGURE 1
Stem and leaf for all techniques.

effect sizes should be considered important but not sole selection criteria for designing and evaluating educational programs.

Effect Categories

Preliminary review of the findings showed that the practices could be roughly grouped into 15 categories shown in Table 1 in order of average effect. In a few cases, the practices within categories were somewhat dissimilar, but the logical grouping seemed for more useful than other orderings such as alphabetical or chronological. The effect sizes within categories are discussed in subsequent sections.

Differences among the Categories

An F-test for the differences among these categories was significant (F = 6.49 p < .0001). As illustrated in the 15 following sections, however, there are huge differences in the effects within categories. A post-hoc Tukey test showed that behavioral elements of teaching stand out in comparison to the other categories. The research demonstrating these behavioral effects has been unusually rigorous and well controlled. As pointed out in subsequent section, however, such research has been carried out in somewhat contrived settings often with a focus on short-term outcomes.

As illustrated in subsequent sections, categories and techniques with clear objectives, teacher- or media-centered control, and less learner autonomy tended to have larger effects on outcomes. This tendency does not suggest the unqualified superiority of behavioral training but a trade off between instructional- and student-centered approaches, either of which may be more appropriate depending on educational goals and instructional conditions as illustrated in the rest of this review.

Behavioral Elements of Instruction

Following E. L. Thorndike and B. F. Skinner, Dollard and Miller (1950) emphasized three components of teaching—cues, engagement, and reinforcement—similar to input, process, and output in physiology and systems theory. Their influential conception stimulated early observational research on what teachers do rather than on their age, experience, certification, college degrees, and other characteristics less connected with what their students learn.

Shown in Table 2, the behavioral elements of teaching show the largest average of effect among the 15 categories. Because the mean of all effects is .31, the effects of psychological elements of teaching are huge except for the 1950s technique of behavioral objectives instruction, which was far less efficacious. Table 2 and subsequent tables generally rank the various methods from largest to smallest within categories.

TABLE 1
Categories of Effects

Category	Numbers of effects	Means of effects	SD	Graphic representation
Behavioral elements of instruction	209	.872	.448	XXXXXXXXXXXXXXXXXXXXXXXXXXXXXXX
Reading methods (and prose devices)	262	.663	.418	XXXXXXXXXXXXXXXXXXXXXX
Teaching patterns	33	.630	.113	XXXXXXXXXXXXXXXXXXXXX
Staff development	291	.584	.281	XXXXXXXXXXXXXXXXXXXX
Special programs	1122	.555	.301	XXXXXXXXXXXXXXXXXXX
Computer-assisted instruction	777	.463	.172	XXXXXXXXXXXXXXX
Student grouping	1065	.409	.338	XXXXXXXXXXXXXX
Instructional systems	1528	.389	.240	XXXXXXXXXXXXX
Mathematics methods	366	.382	.377	XXXXXXXXXXXXX
Teaching method	1585	.363	.232	XXXXXXXXXXXX
Science effects	1447	.292	.235	XXXXXXXXXX
Learner autonomy in science	171	.290	.262	XXXXXXXXXX
Writing methods	99	.234	.269	XXXXXXXX
Open education	821	.199	.255	XXXXXXX
Social environment	1424	.084	.231	XXX

Note: Each "X" represents 0.03.

TABLE 2
Effects of Behavioral Elements of Instruction

Technique	Number of effects	Effect size	Graphic representation
Cues	17	1.25	.XXXXXXXXXXXXX
Reinforcement	39	1.17	.XXXXXXXXXXXX
Corrective feedback	20	0.94	.XXXXXXXXXX
Engagement	22	0.88	.XXXXXXXXX
Behavioral objectives instruction: elementary through adults	111	0.12	.X

Note: Each "X" represents 0.1.

Cues, as operationalized, show what is to be learned and explain how to learn it. Their quality can be seen in the clarity, salience, and meaningfulness of explanations and directions provided by teachers, instructional materials, or both. Ideally, as the learners gain confidence, the salience and numbers of cues can be reduced.

Engagement is the extent to which learners actively and persistently participate until appropriate responses are firmly entrenched in their repertoires. Such participation can be indexed by the extent to which the teacher engages students in overt activity—indicated by absence of irrelevant behavior, concentration on tasks, enthusiastic contributions to group discussion, and lengthy study.

Corrective feedback remedies errors in oral or written responses. Ideally, students waste little time on incorrect responses, and teachers rapidly detect and remedy difficulties by reteaching or using alternate methods. When necessary, teachers also provide additional time for practice.

Reinforcement, both immediate and direct, is reflected in the efforts elicited by athletics, games, and other cooperative and competitive activities. Some activities are intrinsically rewarding. As emphasized by some theorists, classroom reinforcement may gain efficacy mainly by providing knowledge of results.

For several apparent reasons, the general category of behavioral elements of teaching had by far the largest effects. In the Thorndike-Skinner tradition, behaviorists employed rigorous experimental methods in classroom research. Often working with single subjects or small groups, they were able to manipulate stimuli with precision and employ powerful reinforcers for which students work either for their extrinsic merit or for their information, symbolic, or competitive value. Experimenters, for example, established a baseline in physical activity or the mastery of spelling or vocabulary words (calculating a mean and standard deviation across a time series), then applied a reinforcement schedule and saw sharp changes in performance. In special education settings and in the control of misbehavior, such programs had impressive results that hardly required statistical inference to detect.

Employing behavioral methods in more realistic classroom settings, however, yielded far less impressive results as indicated by the poor record of behavioral objectives that enjoyed a heyday in the 1950s. Since behavioral techniques can only be fully employed in special circumstances, there is a question of whether they should be included in this review. In the end, it was decided to keep them in for the sake of completeness and to indicate the sizes of effects that can be attained when educators gain more complete control of learning environments than they ordinarily have.

Reading Methods

Ten reading methods and pictorial devices in prose generally showed large effects. Divided into three subcategories, the results are shown on Table 3.

TABLE 3
Effects of Reading Methods and Pictorial Devices in Prose

Technique	Number of effects	Effect size	Graphic representation
Reading Methods			
Adaptive speed training	28	0.95	.XXXXXXXXXX
Reading improvement study skills programs: college	28	0.94	.XXXXXXXXX
Reading methods	9	0.61	.XXXXXX
Reading instruction strategies: elementary	31	0.60	.XXXXXX
Pictorial devices in prose			
Transformative	18	1.42	.XXXXXXXXXXXXXX
Interpretive	24	0.75	.XXXXXXXX
Organizational	21	0.72	.XXXXXXX
Representative	79	0.54	.XXXXX
Adjunct pictures	16	0.22	.XX
Decorative	8	−0.12	X.

Note: Each "X" represents 0.1.

Adaptive speed training involves principles similar to those of comprehension teaching (discussed later) in that learners are taught to monitor and control their reading progress. It shows learners how to vary their pace and depth of reflection according to the difficulty of material and their purposes in reading and the difficulty of the text. It yields big effects on the capacity to shift gears in reading.

Reading methods vary widely, but their largest effects seem to occur when teachers are systematically trained almost irrespective of particularities of methods. Phonics or *word-attack* approaches, however, have moderate advantage over whole-word approaches in the teaching of beginning reading—perhaps because early misconceptions are avoided. Phonics may also reduce the need for excessive reteaching and correctives.

Pictures in the text can be highly helpful, although they increase the cost of books and occupy space that could otherwise be used for prose. Several types of pictures can be distinguished; in order of their effects they are as follows:

- *Transformative* pritures encode information into concrete memorable form, relate information in a well-organized context, and provide links for systematic retrieval.
- *Interpretive* pictures, like advance organizers, make text comprehensible by relating abstract to concrete terms and the unfamiliar and difficult to previous knowledge.

Herbert J. Walberg and Jin-Shei Lai

- *Organizational* pictures, including maps and diagrams, show the coherence of objects or events in space and time.
- *Representational* pictures are photos or other concrete representations of what the prose relates.
- *Decorative* pictures present information incidental to (and possibly irrelevant to or conflicting with) intended learning (researchers might concede that decoration may add interest if not information). Decorative pictures and other adjunct texttual devices with small effect sizes add little value and might justifialy be omitted.

As the research demonstrates, pictures can provide vivid imagery and metaphors that facilitate memorization, show what is important to learn, and intensify the effects of reading and listening. Pictures may allow students to bypass the text; but memorable, well-written prose may obviate pictures.

Teaching Patterns

Patterns of teaching integrate elements and methods of teaching. These more inclusive formulations (shown in Table 4) follow the evolution of psychological research on education. Behavioral research moved in the 1950s from psychological laboratories to classrooms, where short-term, controlled experiments were conducted on one element at a time. In the 1970s, educational researchers tried to find patterns of effective practices from observations of ordinary teaching.

Thus, early behaviorists traded educational realism for theoretical parsimony and scientific rigor; later researchers strove for broader classroom application. Fortunately, the results from both approaches appear to converge. It seems possible, moreover, to incorporate the work of cognitive psychologists that took place during the 1980s into an enlarged understanding of teaching.

Explicit teaching also known as *direct instruction* (shown in Table 4) can be viewed as traditional or conventional whole-group teaching done well. Because most teaching methods have changed little in the last three-quarters of

TABLE 4
Effects of Teaching Patterns

Technique	Number of effects	Effect size	Graphic representation
Comprehension teaching	20	0.71	.XXXXXXX
Explicit or direct teaching	13	0.55	.XXXXXX

Note: Each "X" represents 0.1.

a century (Hoetker & Ahlbrand, 1969) and may not change substantially in the near future, it is worthwhile knowing how the usual practice can excel. Because it has evolved from ordinary practice, explicit teaching is relatively easy to carry out, does not disrupt conventional expectations, and can incorporate teaching practices such as advance organizers (discussed subsequently).

Early reviews of correlation studies (see Rosenshine and Stevens, 1986, for many references) discussed the traits of effective teachers, which include clarity, task orientation, enthusiasm, and flexibility, as well as their tendencies to structure their presentations and occasionally use student ideas. From later observational and control-group research, Rosenshine and Stevens identified six phased functions of explicit teaching: (1) daily review, homework check, and, if necessary, reteaching; (2) rapid presentation of new content and skills in small steps; (3) guided student practice with close monitoring by teachers; (4) corrective feedback and instructional reinforcement; (5) independent practice in seatwork and homework with high, more than 90 percent, success rate; and (6) weekly and monthly review.

Comprehension Teaching

The descendants of Aristotle in the Anglo American tradition of Bacon, Locke, Thorndike, and Skinner objected to philosophical "armchair" opinion. Midcentury behaviorists, particularly John Watson, insisted on hard empirical facts about learning. But they also saw the child's mind as a blank tablet and seemed to encourage active teaching and passive acquisition of isolated facts. Around 1980, cognitive psychologists reacted to such atomism and William James's "bucket of knowledge" metaphor by reviving research on student-centered learning and "higher mental processes," in the learner-centered tradition of Plato, Socrates, Kant, Rousseau, Dewey, Freud, and Piaget.

The Russian psychologist Lev Vygotsky (1978) developed an influential psychological compromise between learner- and teacher-centered views. Emphasizing the two-way nature of teaching, he identified a *zone of proximal development* extending from what learners can do independently to the maximum they can do with the teacher's help. Accordingly, teachers should set up *scaffolding* for building knowledge but remove it when it becomes unnecessary. In mathematics, for example, the teacher can give hints and examples, foster semi-independent practice, then remove support—not unlike the common sense prompting and fading of behavioral cues. Vygotsky's insight helped open research on transferring a degree of autonomy and monitoring to students.

In the 1980s, cognitive research on teaching sought ways to encourage self-monitoring, self-teaching, and meta-cognition to foster independence. Skills were important, but the learner's monitoring and management of them had primacy, as the explicit teaching functions of planning, allocating time, and review (discussed in the previous section) are partly transferred to learners.

Pearson (1985), for example, outlined three phases of metacognitive teaching: (1) modeling, where the teacher exhibits the desired behavior; (2) guided practice, where the students perform with help from the teachers; and (3) application, where the student performs independently of the teacher—much like explicit teaching functions. Pallincsar and Brown (1984), moreover, described *reciprocal teaching*, in which students take turns leading dialogues on pertinent features of a text. By assuming the planning and executive control ordinarily exercised by teachers, students learn planning, structuring, and self-management—which is perhaps why tutors learn from teaching and why we say that if you want to learn something well, teach it. Comprehension teaching encourages students to measure their progress toward explicit goals. If necessary, they can reallocate time for different activities. In this way, self-awareness, personal control, and positive self-evaluation can be enlarged.

Staff Development

Programs to help teachers in their work have had good effects. The nine techniques in Table 5 are all larger than .35 except whole-language teacher training on students' reading achievement.

TABLE 5
Effects of Staff Development

Technique	Number of effects	Effect size	Graphic representation
Staff development training: changing teacher's attitudes	112	1.01	.XXXXXXXXXX
In-service teacher education on teacher achievement	•	0.90	.XXXXXXXXX
Feedback to teachers: individual academic performance, K–12	21	0.70	.XXXXXXX
Teacher consultation for modifying teacher behavior and attitudes	40	0.66	.XXXXXXX
In-service teacher education on teacher classroom behavior	•	0.60	.XXXXXX
Microteaching	47	0.55	.XXXXXX
Feedback of student rating to college instructors	17	0.38	.XXXX
In-service teacher education on teacher achievement	•	0.37	.XXXX
Whole-language training on reading	54	0.09	.X

Note: Each "X" represents 0.1.
• Indicates the reviews examined did not include information on the number of studies involved in these comparisons.

Microteaching, developed at Stanford University in the 1960s, is a behavioral approach for preservice and in-service training that has substantial effects. It employs explanation and modeling of selected teaching techniques; televised practice with small groups of students; discussion, corrective, and reinforcement while watching a playback; and recycling through subsequent practice and playback sessions with new groups of students.

In-service teacher education also proves to have good effects. Somewhat like the case of physician training, the biggest effects are on teacher knowledge; but effects on classroom behavior and student achievement are also large. The meta-analysis suggests that authoritative planning and execution seem to work best; informal coaching by itself seems ineffective. Instructor responsibility for designing and teaching the sessions works better than teacher presentations and group discussions. The best techniques are observation of classroom practices, audiovisual feedback, and practice. The best combination of techniques is lecture, modeling, practice, and coaching. The size of the training group, which can range from one (in a tutoring situation) to greater than 60, makes no detectable difference.

Some apparent effects may be attributable to participant selectivity rather than to superior efficacy. Federal-, state-, and university-sponsored programs, for example, appear more effective than locally initiated programs. Competitive selection of participants and college credit apparently work better as incentives than extra pay, certificate renewal, and no incentives. Independent study seems to have larger effects than workshops, courses, minicourses, and institutes.

Whole-language training of teachers had little effect on students' reading achievement. It is possible that this method has subtle undetectable effects, but the factual burden of proof still lies with its advocates.

Special Programs

Table 6 shows 21 strategies in this category. All programs have the effects larger than .2 except the perceptual-motor training for disabled students. Several of these are more curricular than instructional: nutrition education, vocabulary instruction, primary prevention, career education, and moral judgement programs. They illustrate what might be called, perhaps tautologically, the "iron law of curriculum": Students tend to learn what they are taught.

Early intervention programs include educational, psychological, and therapeutic components for disabled, at-risk, and disadvantaged children from one month to 66 months of age. The immediate and large outcome advantages, however, faded rapidly and disappeared after 3 years.

Preschool programs also showed initial learning effects that were unsustained. It appears that young children can learn more than is normally assumed; but like other learners, they can also forget. The key to sustained

TABLE 6
Special Program

Technique	Number of effects	Effect size	Graphic representation
Nutrition education programs: high school	6	1.25	.XXXXXXXXXXXXX
Guidance and consulting program: regular high school curriculum	6	1.20	.XXXXXXXXXXXX
Vocabulary instruction: elementary to college	52	0.90	.XXXXXXXXX
Superior patient education	70	0.84	.XXXXXXXX
In-service training of MDs on physician knowledge	41	0.81	.XXXXXXXX
Superior patient education: physician performance	41	0.74	.XXXXXXX
Primary prevention ed programs in schools	41	0.55	.XXXXXX
Preschool early intervention	326	0.50	.XXXXX
Career education program: K–12	18	0.50	.XXXXX
Full versus half-day kindergarten	11	0.48	.XXXXX
Handicapped students as tutors	19	0.48	.XXXXX
Career counseling interventions	58	0.48	.XXXXX
Pullout programs: gifted	9	0.47	.XXXXX
Vocabulary instruction: poor readers: 3–12 grades	15	0.47	.XXXXX
Handicapped students: psycholinguistic training	34	0.39	.XXXX
Counseling and guidance: high school	77	0.38	.XXXX
Superior patient education: patient outcomes	41	0.34	.XXX
Handicapped students: mainstreaming	11	0.33	.XXX
Moral judgement: junior high to adults	55	0.25	.XXX
Preschool early intervention: preschool programs	11	0.22	.XX
Handicapped students: perceptual motor training	180	0.08	.X

Note: Each "X" represents 0.1.

gains may be sustained programs and effective families—not one-shot approaches.

  Handicapped students classified as mentally retarded, emotionally disturbed, and learning disabled have been subjects in research that has several important implications. The perceptual motor-training program emphasizes skills training as preparation for cognitive learning. Though some researchers argue that such training can improve integrative abilities, it seems less effective than other special programs.

Mainstreaming studies show that mildly to moderately handicapped students can prosper in regular classes. They may avoid the stereotyped, invidious labeling often associated with misclassifications and pullout programs. Or they may benefit from higher academic expectations.

Psycholinguistic training of special-needs students yields positive effects; it consists of testing and remedying specific deficits in language skills.

Patient education can affect mortality, morbidity, and lengths of illness and hospitalization. In studies of patients' learning about drug use for hypertension, diabetes, and other chronic conditions, one-to-one and group counseling (with or without instructional materials) produced the greatest effects—in contrast to leaving instruction to bottle labels or patient-package inserts. Labels, special containers, memory aids, and behavior modification, nonetheless, were successful in minimizing later errors in drug use. The most efficacious educational principles were specification of intentions; relevance to learner needs; personal answers to questions; reinforcement and feedback on progress; facilitation, such as unit-dose containers; and instructional and treatment regimens suited to personal convenience, such as prescribing drugs for mealtime administration.

In-service physician training shows large effects on knowledge and on laboratory performance; but only moderate effects of training can be found for patient outcomes. Knowledge and performance, even in practical training, may help but hardly guarantees successful application in practice.

Under the category of special programs, it may be useful to mention research on *brain-centered learning* even though the effects of such techniques remain to be meta-analyzed. At the request of the U.S. Army, the National Academy of Sciences evaluated exotic techniques and shortcuts for learning and performance enhancement described in popular psychology and presumably being exploited in California and U.S.S.R. (Druckman & Swets, 1988). Little or no evidence, however, was found for the efficacy of learning during sleep, mental practice of motor skills, integration of left- and right-brain hemispheres, parapsychological techniques, biofeedback, extrasensory perception, mental telepathy, mind-over-matter exercise, and neurolinguistic programming (in which instructors identify students' mode of learning and mimic the students' behavior as they teach).

Computer-Assisted Instruction

Ours may be the age of computers, and they have already been shown to have substantial effects on learning. With the hardware costs declining and software increasing in sophistication, computers are more prevalent in classroom activities. Good software can convey complicated ideas as concrete, vivid images.

As Table 7 shows, computers appear to have special advantages for younger and handicapped students (one of the few indications of aptitude-treatment

TABLE 7
Computer-Assisted Instruction

Student group or technique	Number of effects	Effect size	Graphic representation
Early elementary	13	1.05	.XXXXXXXXXXX
Handicapped	26	0.66	.XXXXXXX
Exceptional elementary and high school	18	0.66	.XXXXXXX
Learning disabled and mentally retarded	15	0.57	.XXXXXX
Computer versus conventional: elementary students	25	0.48	.XXXXX
Computer versus conventional: elementary students	28	0.47	.XXXXX
Computer versus conventional: elementary students	28	0.45	.XXXXX
Japanese elementary and secondary	4	0.45	.XXXXX
Adult	24	0.42	.XXXX
Secondary: college	11	0.42	.XXXX
Elementary: secondary	33	0.42	.XXXX
Secondary: elementary and secondary	42	0.42	.XXXX
Computer programming instruction: cognitive outcome	65	0.41	.XXXX
Secondary: mathematics	46	0.39	.XXXX
Computer programming: elementary and secondary	72	0.38	.XXXX
Simulation and games	93	0.35	.XXXX
Math: elementary and secondary	40	0.35	.XXXX
Secondary	42	0.32	.XXX
Computer versus conventional: secondary classroom	51	0.32	.XXX
College	101	0.26	.XXX

Note: Each "X" represents 0.1.

interaction among the meta-analyses). Computers may be more patient, discreet, nonjudgmental, even encouraging about students' progress. Another explanation, however, is plausible. Elementary schools provide less tracking and differentiated courses for homogeneous groups. Computers may adapt to larger within-class differences among elementary students and special-needs children allowing them to proceed at their own pace and avoiding invidious comparisons between students.

Stimulation and games, with or without computer implementation, require active, specific learner responses and may strike a balance between book learning and the dynamic, complicated, and competitive real world. Their interactiveness, speed, intensity, movement, color, and sound add interest and information to academic learning. If games are not geared to a curricular objective, however, they can also waste time—as in arcade games.

Student Grouping

Teaching students what they already know and what they are yet incapable of learning are equally wasteful. For this reason, traditional whole-class teaching of heterogeneous groups can present serious difficulties and inefficiency. Ability grouping shows a range of positive effects, and acceleration of talented elementary students seems particularly efficacious (see Table 8).

Acceleration programs identify talented youth (often in mathematics and science) and group them together or with older students. Such programs provide counseling, encouragement, contact with accomplished adults, grade skipping, summer school, and the compression of the standard curriculum into fewer years. The effects are huge in elementary schools, substantial in junior high schools, and moderate in senior high schools. The smaller effects at advanced levels may be attributable to the smaller advantage of acceleration over tracking and differentiated course placement practiced in most high schools.

The effects of acceleration on educational attitudes, vocational plans, participation in school activities, popularity, psychological adjustment, and character ratings were mixed and often insignificant. These outcomes may not be systematically affected in either direction.

Ability grouping is based on achievement, intelligence tests, personal insights, and the subjective opinions. In high school, ability grouping leaves deficient and average students unaffected but yields benefits for talented students and on improving students' attitudes toward the subject matter. In elementary schools, the grouping of students with similar reading achievement but from different grades yields substantial effects. Within-class grouping in mathematics yields worthwhile effects, but generalized grouping does not. Five meta-analyses, moreover, showed small effects. Ability grouping effects appear contingent, which may be a reason for the controversies about it.

Tutoring, because it gears instruction to individual or small-group needs, yields big effects on both tutees and tutors. It yields particularly large effects in mathematics—perhaps because of the subject's well-defined scope and organization.

In whole-group instruction, teachers may ordinarily focus on average or deficient students to ensure that they master the lessons. But when talented students are freed from repetition and slow progression, they can proceed quickly. Grouping may work best when students are accurately grouped according to their specific subject matter needs rather than IQ, demeanor, or other irrelevant characteristics. To distinguish such needs, however, may not be easy.

Instructional Systems

Instructional systems require special arrangements and planning, and they often combine several components of instruction. Moreover, they tend to

TABLE 8
Effects of Student Grouping

Technique	Number of effects	Effect size	Graphic representation
Acceleration of talented students: elementary	3	1.43	.XXXXXXXXXXXXXX
Tutoring: training the conservation concept, preoperational students	302	0.98	.XXXXXXXXXX
Acceleration of gifted students	13	0.88	.XXXXXXXXX
Acceleration of talented students: junior high school	9	0.76	.XXXXXXXX
Tutoring of special educational students by other special educational students	19	0.65	.XXXXXXX
Psychological and affective interventions: underprepared learners	14	0.63	.XXXXXX
Tutoring in mathematics	153	0.61	.XXXXXX
Tutoring of special educational students by other special educational students	19	0.59	.XXXXXX
Enrichment programs, gifted students	20	0.55	.XXXXXX
Ability grouping in elementary school: cross-grade reading groups	14	0.45	.XXXXX
Tutoring in all courses	65	0.41	.XXXX
Student tutoring of elementary and secondary students	52	0.40	.XXXX
Ability grouping on subject matter attitudes	8	0.37	.XXXX
Ability grouping in high school talented students	14	0.33	.XXX
Student tutoring of elementary and secondary: effects on tutors	38	0.33	.XXX
Ability grouping in elementary within-class mathematics	5	0.32	.XXX
Between class ability groupings: gifted students	23	0.32	.XXX
Acceleration of talented students: senior high school	7	0.28	.XXX
Between and within class ability: elementary	39	0.22	.XX
Ability grouping in senior high school	18	0.20	.XX
Between class ability: elementary	31	0.19	.XX
Between and within class ability: secondary	52	0.10	.X
Ability grouping in junior high school	33	0.05	.
Ability grouping in average and deficient students	27	0.02	.
Between class ability: K–12	50	0.01	.
Ability grouping in elementary self-contained classes	14	0.00	.
Between and within class ability: secondary	29	−0.03	.

Note: Each "X" represents 0.1.

emphasize adaption to student needs rather than relying on a fixed pattern of teaching for all such direct whole-group instruction. To reflect the evolution of research, the discussion begins with the earlier and less efficacious systems near the bottom of Table 9.

TABLE 9
Effects of Instructional System

Technique	Number of effects	Effect size	Graphic representation
Mastery learning: require mastery before next unit	3	0.99	.XXXXXXXXXX
Mastery learning: unit mastery level, 91–100	17	0.73	.XXXXXXX
Creative drama: elementary, effect on achievement	16	0.67	.XXXXXXX
Mastery learning: duration of program up to 1 month	12	0.65	.XXXXXXX
Mastery learning: Grades 1–12 and college	43	0.61	.XXXXXX
Mastery learning: college	27	0.58	.XXXXXX
Creativity training techniques: creative performance	106	0.57	.XXXXXX
Mastery learning: Keller versus Bloom: college	103	0.52	.XXXXX
Mastery learning: 81–90	15	0.51	.XXXXX
Keller's personalized system of instruction	72	0.49	.XXXXX
Mastery learning: precollege	22	0.49	.XXXXX
Creative thinking training programs: Torrance Test of Creative Thinking	46	0.47	.XXXXX
Adaptive instruction	37	0.45	.XXXXX
Mastery learning: 70–80	17	0.38	.XXXX
Individualization: science	131	0.35	.XXXX
Mastery learning: 17 or more weeks	6	0.30	.XXX
Individualization: mathematics	153	0.29	.XXX
Programmed instruction: college	56	0.28	.XXX
Mastery learning: primary and secondary	17	0.25	.XXX
Programmed instruction: science branched	5	0.21	.XX
Programmed instruction: linear	47	0.17	.XX
Individualization: science	131	0.17	.XX
Individualization: mathematics	153	0.16	.XX
Programmed instruction: mathematics	153	0.10	.X
Individualization: high schools	51	0.10	.X
Programmed instruction: secondary	48	0.08	.X
Individualization: mathematics, self-paced modularization	41	−0.07	X.

Note: Each "X" represents 0.1.

Programmed instruction, popular in the 1950s, mechanically presents a series of *frames,* each of which conveys an item of information and requires a student response. *Linear programs* present a graduated series of frames with knowledge increments so small that learning steps may be nearly errorless and continuously reinforced by progression to the next frame; such programs are adaptive in that able students proceed quickly.

Branched programs direct students back when necessary for reteaching; to the side for correctives; and ahead when they already know parts of the materials. The ideas of continuous progress and branching influenced later developers who tried to optimize learning by individualization, mastery learning, and computer-assisted instruction. Despite such sophisticated theorizing, programmed instruction—perhaps because it was overly atomistic—had small effects and has been eclipsed by computer-assisted instruction.

Individualization adapts instruction to individual needs by varying speed or branching and by using booklets, worksheets, coaching, and the like. Perhaps because they have been vaguely defined and operationalized, individualized programs have had small effects. Other systems such as mastery learning appear more effective for adapting instruction to the needs of individual learners.

Mastery learning combines the behavioral elements of teaching (see previous sections) with suitable amounts of time. Formative tests are employed to allocate time and guide reinforcement and correct feedback. Kulik and Kulik (1986) reported substantial effects for mastery learning. Mastery programs that yielded larger effects established a criterion of 95 to 100 percent mastery and required repeated testing to ensure mastery before allowing students to proceed to additional units (which yielded a gigantic effect of one standard deviation). Mastery learning yielded larger effects on less able students, and reduced the disparities in performance to 82% that of control groups.

Mastery, as Bloom (1976) pointed out, takes additional time; the Kuliks found that it required a median of 16% (and up to 97%) more time than did conventional instruction. Given the huge effects of behavioral elements of instruction, the large effects of mastery learning are not surprising.

Mastery learning studies lasting less than a month yielded larger effects than those lasting more than four months. Retention probably declines sharply no matter what the educational method, but the decline can be more confidently noted about mastery, because it has been more extensively investigated.

Bloom (1976) and his students have reported larger effects than has Slavin (1987), who reviewed their work. Guskey and Gates (1986), for example, reported an effect of .78, estimated from 38 studies of elementary and secondary students. Anderson and Burns (1987), in response to Slavin, pointed out two reasons for larger effects in some studies, especially those under

Bloom's supervision: Bloom was more interested in what is possible than in what is likely; he has sought to find the limits of learning. His students, moreover, have conducted tightly controlled experiments over times shorter than a semester or a year.

Adaptive instruction combines mastery, cooperative, open, tutoring, computer, and comprehension approaches into a complex system to tailor instruction to individual and small-group needs. It includes managerial steps executed by a master teacher, including planning, time allocation, task delegation to aides and students, and quality control. It is a comprehensive program for the whole school day rather than a single method that requires simple integration into one subject or into a single teacher's repertoire. Its achievement effects are substantial but its broader effects are probably underestimated, because adaptive instruction aims at diverse ends including student autonomy, intrinsic motivation, and teacher and student choice, which are poorly indicated by the usual outcome measures.

Mathematics Methods

Studies of mathematics instruction yielded a large effect for manipulatives and a range of other effects. They are shown in Table 10.

Manipulative materials, such as Cuisinnaire rods, balance beams, counting sticks, and measuring scales, allow students to engage directly in learning rather than to passively follow abstract teacher presentations. The students taught through the manipulative materials receive feedback immediately by handling the materials; their advantages apparently lie in seeing abstract ideas in concrete embodiments and quick checking of hypothesized answers.

Problem solving in mathematics yields positive effects. It requires comprehension of terms and their application to varied examples. It may motivate students by showing them the application of mathematical ideas to real-world

TABLE 10
Effects of Mathematics Methods

Technique	Number of effects	Effect size	Graphic representation
Manipulative materials	64	1.04	.XXXXXXXXXX
Problem solving	33	0.35	.XXXX
New mathematics	134	0.24	.XX
Math instructional method: K–12	102	0.15	.XX
Systematic methods of math problem solving: elementary and secondary	33	0.13	.X

Note: Each "X" represents 0.1.

questions. The two effect estimates, however, are discrepant; one meta-analysis puts the effect size near average of all effects compiled in this review, the other as closer to the mode. Many other replicated estimates in other tables are close to one another, but this discrepancy, which may be attributable to meta-analytic methods, samplings of studies, or numerical errors, should be a warning about the fallibility of the estimates, the need for further replications, and the value of checking against original source studies.

The new mathematics produced beneficial results, although not as big as the new science curricula. Both reforms may have their learning advantages partly by testing what they taught.

Teaching Methods

Table 11 shows the componential features of teaching repertoires. The effect estimates suggest that when the affective or informational content of cues, engagement, reinforcement, and feedback is improved, learning improves—although not as much as observed in short-term, highly controlled studies of pure behavioral elements of teaching.

Advance organizers are brief overviews of subject matter that abstractly relate new concepts or terms to previous learning. They are effective if they bridge new to old learning. Those spoken by the teacher or graphically illustrated in texts work best.

Adjunct questions alert students about key questions to answer—particularly in texts. They work best on questions repeated on posttests, and moderately well on questions related to the adjuncts. As we might expect, however, adjunct questions distract attention away from incidental material that might otherwise be learned.

Goal setting sets forth objectives, guidelines, methods, or standards for learning. Like adjunct questions, goal setting sacrifices incidental-intended learning.

Learning hierarchies assume that instruction can be made efficient if facts, skills, or ideas that logically or psychologically precede others are presented first. Teaching and instructional media sequenced in this way appear slightly more effective. Learners, however, may adapt themselves to apparently ill sequenced materials and presentations. It may be advantageous to learn to do so, since human life may depart from logical progression.

Pretests are benchmarks for determining how much students learn under various methods of teaching. Educational psychologists have found, however, that pretests themselves can have positive cuing effects if they show students what will be emphasized by instruction and on posttests.

Two techniques show negative effects: Adjunct questions and goal setting on intended outcomes distract students' attention away from the incidental material.

High expectations transmit teachers' standards of learning and performance. These may function as both cues and incentives for students to engage actively with extended effort and perseverance.

Frequent tests increase learning by requiring sustained effort and providing feedback. Their effects are larger, however, on performance on quizzes than on final examinations.

Questioning also appears to work by increasing students' engagement and may encourage deeper thinking, as in Plato's accounts of Socrates. Questioning has bigger estimated effects in science than in other subjects.

Corrective feedback, as a component of ordinary instruction, remedies errors by reteaching, using the same or a different method. It has moderate effects that are somewhat higher in science than in other subjects—perhaps because science often requires conceptual thinking.

Homework by itself constructively extends engagement or learning time. Corrective feedback and reinforcement in the form of grades and comments on homework raise its effects dramatically.

Praise has a small, positive effect. For young or disturbed children, praise may lack the power of tangible and token reinforcers used in psychological experiments. For students able to see ahead, grades and personal standards may be more powerful reinforcers than momentary encouragement. As cognitive psychologists point out, moreover, the main classroom value of reinforcement may lie in its information for the student about his or her progress rather than in its power to reward.

Science Effects

Many science curricular and instructional effects are shown in Table 12. Twenty-three effects are larger than the grand mean, .37, of all methods.

Inquiry teaching requires students to formulate hypotheses, reason about their creditability, and design experiments to test their validity. Inquiry teaching yields substantial effects—particularly on the understanding of scientific processes.

Audio tutorials are taped-recorded instructions for using media such as laboratory equipment, manipulative, and readings for topical lessons or whole courses. This simple approach yields somewhat better results than conventional instruction, allows independent learning, and has the further advantage of individual pacing—allowing students to pursue special topics or take courses on their own.

Original source papers derive from the "Great Books" approach of University of Chicago President Robert Maynard Hutchins and his colleague Mortimore Adler, who saw more value in reading Plato or Newton than predigested textbook accounts. Those who trade depth for breadth believe it is better to know few transcending ideas than many unconnected bits of soon forgotten information. They have shown that such knowledge can be acquired by

TABLE 11
Effects of Teaching Method

Technique	Number of effects	Effect size	Graphic representation
Adjunct questions: repeated	61	0.96	.XXXXXXXXXX
Homework with teacher comment	2	0.83	.XXXXXXXX
Homework with graded	5	0.78	.XXXXXXXX
Advance organizers: bridging, previous knowledge	•	0.75	.XXXXXXXX
Advance organizers: bridging, previous material	•	0.71	.XXXXXXX
Advance organizers: presentation mode, spoken	•	0.68	.XXXXXXX
Visual media: nursing education	12	0.68	.XXXXXXX
Questioning in science	11	0.56	.XXXXXX
Remediation-feedback: in science	28	0.54	.XXXXX
Instruction in problem solving: science and math	68	0.54	.XXXXX
Wait time in science	2	0.53	.XXXXX
Adjunct questions: related	61	0.50	.XXXXX
Frequent testing: attitudes	5	0.50	.XXXXX
Interactive video instruction	63	0.50	.XXXXX
Interactive video instruction: industrial training and higher education	28	0.50	.XXXXX
Frequent testing: quizzes	4	0.49	.XXXXX
Focusing in science	25	0.48	.XXXXX
Pretests: outcome cognitive	•	0.48	.XXXXX
Advance organizers: overall effect	29	0.45	.XXXXX
Feedback	15	0.45	.XXXXX
Technology based instruction: Japanese and Americans	116	0.41	.XXXX
Advance organizers: presentation mode, written and illustrated	•	0.40	.XXXX
Goal setting, on intended outcomes	21	0.40	.XXXX
Increased testing in science	33	0.37	.XXXX
Advance organizers: presentation mode, written only	•	0.34	.XXX
Instructional stimulation games versus conventional instruction	33	0.33	.XXX
Coaching programs, aptitude tests: elementary to college	35	0.33	.XXX
Training in test taking skills: elementary and secondary	24	0.33	.XXX
High expectations	77	0.32	.XXX

continues

TABLE 11 (*Continued*)

Technique	Number of effects	Effect size	Graphic representation
Practice test taking: elementary to college	40	0.32	.XXX
Pretests: outcome attitude	•	0.29	.XXX
Homework with assigned	47	0.28	.XXX
Stimulation games	93	0.28	.XXX
Questioning	14	0.26	.XXX
Pretest-posttest: same	•	0.25	.XXX
Coaching programs: achievement test performance	30	0.25	.XXX
Advance organizers: in science	16	0.24	.XX
Training in test taking skills: standardized achievement, elementary	24	0.21	.XX
Postiethwait's audio-tutorial method: college	47	0.20	.XX
Frequent testing: final examinations	30	0.19	.XX
Coaching programs: SAT aptitude tests, college	22	0.19	.XX
Learning hierarchies	15	0.18	.XX
Praise	14	0.16	.XX
Visual-based instruction: college	65	0.15	.XX
Coaching programs: SAT	12	0.15	.XX
Modality based instruction	39	0.14	.X
Technology, nontechnology and combination: math advantage	127	0.14	.X
Behavioral objectives	111	0.12	.X
Pretest-posttest: different	•	0.11	.X
Advance organizers: bridging, unspecified bridging	•	−0.02	.
Adjunct questions: unrelated	61	−0.13	X.
Adjunct questions: unrelated goals setting	20	−0.20	XX.

Note: Each "X" represents 0.1.
• Reviews without information on numbers of effect sizes are indicated with a period.

studying and discussing science papers of historical or scientific significance. Such an approach can be considered a variant of inquiry teaching.

The effects of team teaching, departmentalized elementary programs, and media-based instruction are near zero. They apparently do not produce superior effects; on the other hand, they are no worse than conventional methods. The null results for media-based instruction, however, suggest choices that may be convenient or cost saving. Because live television and canned

TABLE 12
Science Effects

Technique	Number of effects	Effect size	Graphic representation
Teaching students to control variables in science education: Grades 1–12; college	62	0.73	.XXXXXXX
New curricula on creativity	5	0.71	.XXXXXXX
New curricula on problem solving	4	0.71	.XXXXXXX
New curricula on scientific understanding	28	0.61	.XXXXXX
New curricula on spatial relations	2	0.57	.XXXXXX
Innovative science teaching techniques: Grades 6–12	51	0.55	.XXXXXX
Diag testing and feedback versus none: middle school, college	21	0.53	.XXXXX
New curricula on subject attitude	6	0.51	.XXXXX
New curricula on science attitude	25	0.50	.XXXXX
Innovative science versus tradition: Grades 6–12	33	0.47	.XXXXX
New curricula on general science achievement	111	0.43	.XXXX
Inquiry teaching	68	0.43	.XXXX
Tests of neutral content	11	0.41	.XXXX
Science method attitude	10	0.41	.XXXX
Mathematics achievement	18	0.40	.XXXX
Communication skills	5	0.40	.XXXX
Tests of new content	9	0.39	.XXXX
General outcomes	105	0.37	.XXXX
Primary and secondary	105	0.37	.XXXX
Innovative science teaching techniques: Grades 6–college	160	0.35	.XXXX
Three major activity-based elementary science program	57	0.34	.XXX
New curricula on social studies achievement	2	0.25	.XXX
Innovative approaches to teaching college economics	48	0.20	.XX
New curricula on critical thinking	31	0.19	.XX
New curricula on scientific skills	28	0.17	.XX
Audio tutorial	7	0.17	.XX
New curricula on logical thinking	14	0.16	.XX
Teaching biology as inquiry: high school and college	59	0.16	.XX
Original source papers	13	0.14	.X
New curricula on reading achievement	23	0.10	.X
Instructional systems in science education: K–12	130	0.07	.X
Team teaching	41	0.06	.X

continues

TABLE 12 (*Continued*)

Technique	Number of effects	Effect size	Graphic representation
Media-based instruction: television	40	0.06	.X
Inductive versus deductive approaches: Grades 4–12	24	0.06	.X
New curricula on synthesis and analysis	11	0.05	.X
New curricula on fact recall	8	0.02	.
Media-based instruction: film	58	−0.07	X.
New curricula on self-concept	10	−0.08	X.
Departmentalized elementary program	3	−0.09	X.
New curricula on tests of old content	1	−0.13	X.

Note: Each "X" represents 0.1.

film can be broadcast, they can provide equally effective education over wide areas (even the world by satellite). Students today, moreover, can interact on-line with distant teachers and fellow students.

Learner Autonomy in Science

The National Science Foundation sponsored many studies of student inquiry and autonomy, which showed that giving students opportunities to manipulate science materials, to contract with teachers about what to learn, to inquire on their own, and to engage in activity-based curricula all have substantial effects, as shown on Table 13. Self-direction, however, had smaller positive effects; and pass-fail grading and self-grading had small negative effects.

TABLE 13
Learner Autonomy in Science

Technique	Number of effects	Effect size	Graphic representation
Student manipulatives	24	0.56	.XXXXXX
Contracts for learning	12	0.47	.XXXXX
Inquiry/discovery	38	0.41	.XXXX
Activity-based curricula	57	0.35	.XXXX
Self-directed study	27	0.08	.X
Pass-fail or self-grading	13	−0.13	X.

Note: Each "X" indicates 0.1.

Writing Methods

Seven aspects of teaching writing have been meta-analyzed. As shown in Table 14, they show a wide range of effects, including negative effects of emphasizing grammar and mechanics.

Inquiry requires students to find and state specific details that convey personal experience vividly, to examine sets of data to develop and support explanatory generalization, or to analyze situations that present ethical problems and arguments.

Scales are criteria or specific questions students apply to their own and others' writing to identify points for improvement.

Sentence combining shows students how to build complex sentences from simpler ones.

Models are presentations of good pieces of writing for students to follow.

Free writing allows students to write about whatever occurs to them.

Grammar and mechanics include sentence parsing and analysis of the parts of speech.

Open Education

In the late 1960s, open educators increased autonomy in primary grades by enabling students to join teachers in planning educational purposes, means, and evaluations. In contrast to teacher- and textbook-centered education, students were given a voice in choosing what to learn. Open educators tried to foster cooperation, critical thinking, constructive attitudes, and self-directed lifelong learning. Table 15 shows that open education may be effective in promoting several of these ideals.

TABLE 14
Effects of Writing Methods

Technique	Number of studies	Effect size	Graphic representation
Inquiry	6	0.57	.XXXXXX
Scales	6	0.36	.XXXX
Sentence combining	5	0.35	.XXXX
Instruction programs: composition, elementary to college	60	0.28	.XXX
Models	7	0.22	.XX
Free writing	10	0.16	.XX
Grammar-mechanics	5	−0.30	XXX.

Note: Each "X" indicates 0.1.

TABLE 15
Effects of Open Education

Technique	Number of studies	Effect size	Graphic representation
Cooperativeness: handicapped-nonhandicapped and ethnically group	98	0.75	.XXXXXXXX
Cooperativeness: effect on achievement and productivity	122	0.72	.XXXXXXX
Cooperativeness: versus competitive and individualistic, adult	133	0.62	.XXXXXX
Cooperativeness: students with mild disabilities	11	0.31	.XXX
Cooperativeness: K–12	37	0.30	.XXX
Creativity	22	0.29	.XXX
Independence	22	0.28	.XXX
Cooperativeness	8	0.23	.XX
Attitude toward teachers	17	0.20	.XX
Mental ability	16	0.18	.XX
Adjustment	9	0.17	.XX
Attitude toward school	50	0.17	.XX
Curiosity	7	0.17	.XX
Cooperativeness: handicapped K–12 in mainstream classrooms	13	0.16	.XX
Self-concept	60	0.07	.X
Locus of control	16	0.01	.
Anxiety	19	−0.01	.
Mathematics achievement	57	−0.04	.
Language achievement	33	−0.07	X.
Leading achievement	63	−0.08	X.
Achievement motivation	8	−0.26	XXX.

Note: Each "X" indicates 0.1.

According to Giaconia and Hedges's (1982) synthesis, open education has worthwhile effects on creativity, independence, cooperation, attitudes toward teachers and schools, mental ability, psychological adjustment, and curiosity. As shown on Table 15, the results were generally modest, although the effects on cooperativeness, creativity, and independence were substantial. The achievement effects were small and negative. Giaconia and Hedges concluded that open programs most effective in producing the nonachievement outcomes sacrificed some academic achievement on standardized measures. These programs emphasized the role of the child in learning, use of diagnostic rather than norm-referenced evaluation, individualized instruction, and manipulative materials; but such programs neglected to emphasize three other components thought by some to be essential to open programs: multiage grouping, open space, and team teaching.

Giaconia and Hedges (1982) speculated that children in the most extreme open programs may do somewhat less well on conventional achievement tests because they have little experience with them. At any rate, it appears that unless they are radically extreme, open classes enhance several nonstandard outcomes without detracting much from academic achievement.

Social Environment

Table 16 shows the effects of various types of social environments. As in the other categories, the effects show considerable variability.

Cooperative learning programs delegate some control of the pacing and methods of learning to groups of two to six students who work together (and

TABLE 16
Effects of Social Environment

Technique	Number of effects	Effect size	Graphic representation
Cooperative learning	182	0.78	.XXXXXXXX
Small versus large class size	59	0.53	.XXXXX
Classroom morale, cohesiveness	50	0.23	.XX
Classroom morale, satisfaction	54	0.22	.XX
Small versus large class size	77	0.21	.XX
Small versus large class size	77	0.20	.XX
Classroom morale, material environment	49	0.18	.XX
Classroom morale, goal direction	51	0.17	.XX
Classroom morale, democracy	50	0.17	.XX
Classroom morale, task difficulty	50	0.13	.X
Classroom morale, formality	57	0.06	.X
Classroom morale, competition	35	0.06	.X
Classroom morale, diversity	47	0.02	.
Classroom morale, speed	48	−0.02	.
Classroom morale, cliqueness	46	−0.12	X.
Classroom morale, disorganization	50	−0.13	X.
Classroom morale, apathy	48	−0.14	X.
Classroom morale, favoritism	46	−0.16	XX.
Classroom morale, friction	53	−0.23	XX.

Note: Each "X" indicates 0.1.

sometimes compete with other groups within classes). Their success may be attributable to (1) relief from the exclusively teacher-to-student interaction of whole-group teaching, (2) the time freed for students' interaction with one another on substantive matters, and (3) frequent opportunities for targeted cues, engagement, correctives, and reinforcement by fellow students. As in comprehension teaching, moreover, the acts of mutual tutoring and teaching may encourage students to think about subject matter organization and productive time allocation.

Class size appears to have moderate effects on learning, although somewhat larger effects on attitudes. The size of the effect, however, is ill represented by single numbers. The effect of class-size decrements appears quite small in the range of 12 to 30 students, but it is larger below these levels especially among class sizes of 2 to 5. Still, few classes and studies are in this range, partially because of the obvious expense. Because fewer studies have concerned this range, the effects may be somewhat uncertain. In any case, many changes in teaching practices are larger in effect and nearly costless.

Classroom morale is associated with achievement gains, greater subject matter interest, and the worthy end of voluntary participation in nonrequired subject-related activities. Morale is assessed by asking students to agree or disagree with such statements as "Most of the students know each other well" and "The class members know the purpose of the lessons." The better the students' perception of classroom morale (i.e., friendly, satisfying, goal directed, and challenging), the more they learn. Students who perceive student cliques, disorganization, apathy, favoritism, and friction learn less. (Unlike the previous research described, this research is based on correlational methods, and the effects listed are average correlations of morale indicators with learning gains.)

Time Influences on Learning

The previous sections of this review address the quality of education, more particularly the effectiveness of practices and conditions. For comparison, Table 17 shows the estimated influence of the quantity of education obtained from Frederick's (1993) review. Approximately 375 estimates were available, 88% of which showed a positive relation of time and learning. Many of the correlational studies were statistically controlled for student ability or pretests, but these might best be ignored in favor of the effect size estimates in the last column, which are comparable to the estimates reported in previous sections. Averaging across all of them yields an effect of .47—moderately higher than the average, .37—of the quality estimates.

This comparison, however, is somewhat arbitrary. With a few exceptions (social environments and class size in Table 16), the other practices and conditions are categorical and usually dichotomous; students were either exposed or unexposed to them. Time, however, is continuous like human

TABLE 17
Time Influences on Learning in Various Types of Research Studies

Area researched	Number of estimates	Percent positive	Correlation mean (N)	Effect mean (N)
Studies in which instructional time was extended	162	83%	.27 (34)	.40 (57)
Earlier start in school or extra preschool	49	73	.08 (1)	.27 (32)
Lenghtening the school day or week	26	88	.40 (7)	.96 (7)
Lenghtening the school year	11	91	.22 (5)	— (0)
Learning extended by homework/study	43	88	.23 (19)	.41 (18)
Extracurricular participation	33	85	.46 (2)	— (0)
Studies of how school time was used	103	96	.43 (50)	.49 (18)
Program length or long-term study	42	93	.57 (21)	.69 (5)
Attendance rate	6	100	.48 (4)	.32 (1)
Efficient time use	55	93	.31 (25)	.42 (12)
Theoretically-driven studies	111	90	.35 (53)	1.10 (6)
Less time needed to learn a topic	18	89	.70 (6)	— (0)
Studies of time on task	79	89	.26 (37)	1.10 (3)
Matching time spent to time needed	14	100	.47 (10)	1.10 (3)
All above studies	376	88	.37 (137)	.47 (81)

height: The average point advantage of height in basketball depends on the height difference between taller and shorter players arbitrarily divided for study. Similarly, the time effect estimates depend on the mix of time differences sampled. (It might be argued that the analogy in quality of instruction estimates is the degree of valid implementation of the practice, which may vary considerably.) Regression of achievement effects on time differences would allow a less arbitrary estimate such that an achievement effect might be calculated for each additional hour or other time unit of study.

In any case, the time associations with learning are highly consistent. The correlational studies carried out in natural settings have more generalizability or external validity. The experimental and quasi-experimental studies have more causal or internal validity. Both show consistent effects. To improve learning substantially, both quality and quantity are probably necessary rather than either-or.

CONCLUSION

Hundreds of educational practices compete for the attention, time, and energies of busy policy makers and educators intent on improving student learning—a widely shared goal in the United States and elsewhere. The last half century yielded many studies of these practices, which may be found among thousands of journal articles and other reports; it seems certain that no scholar has read them all—even within a single subject matter. Because such research is relatively inaccessible, such organizations as the American Educational Research Association and the National Association for Research in Science Teaching have published at least seven handbooks running up to 900 pages by generalists and subject matter specialists narratively summarizing the findings. Sponsored by the 29 scholarly and practitioner organizations, editors have further condensed these authoritative handbooks to about 200 printed pages (Cawelti, 1995).

To complement such huge narrative review and condensation, the present review draws together the largest collections of quantitative estimates of the effects of educational practices, classifies them, and compares the averages of their effects. For reasons mentioned in the introduction, the estimates may be considered approximations that deserve replication and continued updating. Along with such considerations as cost, feasibility, philosophy, and subjective preferences, they might be recommended as one criterion for selecting and evaluating policies and practices—under the assumption that decision makers consult the meta-analyses that provide the estimates, related narrative reviews, and a sampling of recent studies.

No united theory is offered here to tie the results together, but a few general principles can be suggested. Based on the huge amounts of research summarized here, they constitute a few rudiments of an empirically based general theory of instruction. If nothing else, they illustrate that older and perhaps commonsense research findings as well as newer findings have important practical implications, including the following:

When they can be applied, behavioral principles get results. Though perhaps unfashionable in today's academic settings, training works (that is, education with clear measurable goals, control of stimulus conditions and reinforcement, and objective criteria of success). It is employed widely and successfully not only with special-needs students but also in patient education and in the military, industry, and business firms (Morrison, 1991). Conventional classrooms, however, may rarely approximate the conditions required to fully employ behavioral principles.

Conventional, whole-group direct teaching works fairly well. However, its efficiency is impaired by individual differences among students. It is obviously wasteful to teach some students what they already know and others what they are yet incapable of learning. Grouping students, mastery learning, and attainment of national goals by given grade levels may help to place students on a more even footing allowing direct teaching to be targeted and accelerated.

Meta-cognitive strategies work well and yield extra benefits. Teaching students to teach themselves enables them to monitor and regulate their learning. They learn not only knowledge and skills but how to allocate their chief resource—time for study—and become more independent learners.

Tutoring and cooperative learning also yield double benefits. Students tutoring others learn how to organize facts and ideas for presentation. They and those working with a few others in cooperative groups can also learn social skills.

Time counts. No matter how measured, time is consistently associated with learning gains. This association is perhaps the most consistent finding in educational research.

Curriculum exposure makes a big difference. Though almost tautological, students tend to learn what they are taught. Therefore, careful selection of content is crucial, particularly if the curriculum is to be well articulated among units and grade levels.

Sharing some discretion with students over what and how to study can promote their attitudes toward school. This practice also improves students' capacities to work well with one another and to carry out independent study.

References

Anderson, L. W., & Burns, R. B. (1987). Values, evidence, and mastery learning. *Educational Research*, 57, 215–223.

Bloom, B. S. (1976). *Human characteristics and school learning*. New York: McGraw-Hill.

Cawelti, G. (1995). *The handbook of research on improving student achievement*. Alexandria, VA: Educational Research Service.

Dollard, J., & Miller, N. (1950). *Personality and psychotherapy*. New York: McGraw-Hill.

Druckman, D., & Swets, J. A. (1988). *Enhancing human performance*. Washington, DC: National Academy Press.

Frederick, W. C. (1993). Extending and intensifying learning time. Washington, DC: Report for the Under Secretary of Education, U.S. Department of Education.

Giaconia, R. M., & Hedges, L. V. (1982). Identifying features of effective open education. *Review of Educational Research*, 52, 579–602.

Glass, G. V, McGaw, B., & Smith, M. L. (1981). *Meta-analysis in social research*. Beverly Hills, CA: Sage.

Guskey, T. R., & Gates, S. L. (1986). Synthesis of research on the effects of mastery learning in elementary and secondary classroom. *Educational Leadership*, 43, 73–80.

Hedges, L. V. (1984). Advances in statistical methods of meta-analysis. In W. H. Yeaton & P. M. Wortman (Eds.), *Issues in data synthesis: New directions for program evaluation* (pp. 25–42). San Francisco: Jossey-Bass.

Hoetker, J., & Ahlbrand, W. P. (1969). The persistence of the recitation. *American Educational Research Journal*, 6, 145–167.

Hunter, J. E., Schmidt, F. L., & Jackson, G. B. (1983). *Meta-analysis: Cumulating research findings*. Beverly Hills, CA: Sage.

Kulik, J. A., & Kulik, C. (1986). Mastery testing and student learning. *Journal of Educational Technology Systems*, 15, 325–345.

Lipsey, M. W., & Wilson, D. B. (1993). The efficacy of psychological, educational, and behavioral treatment. *American Psychologist*, 48, 1181–1209.

Morrison, J. E. (1991). *Training for performance: Principles of applied human learning*. New York: John Wiley & Sons.

Pallincsar, A. M., & Brown, A. (1984). Reciprocal teaching of comprehension fostering and comprehension monitoring activities. *Cognition and Instruction*, 1, 117–176.

Pearson, D. (1985). Reading comprehension instruction: Six necessary steps. *Reading Teacher, 38*, 724–738.

Rosenshine, B., & Stevens, R. (1986). Teaching functions. In M. C. Wittrock (Ed.), *The handbook of research on teaching* (pp. 328–375). New York: Macmillan.

Slavin, R. E. (1987). Mastery learning reconsidered. *Review of Educational Research, 57*, 175–213.

Vygotsky, L. (1978). *Mind in society*. Cambridge, MA: Harvard University Press.

Walberg, H. J. (1991). Productive teaching and instruction: Assessing the knowledge base. In H. C. Waxman (Ed.), *Effective teaching* (pp. 33–62). Berkeley, CA: McCutchan.

CHAPTER

18

Mixed-Method Research:
Introduction and Application

JOHN W. CRESWELL
University of Nebraska, Lincoln

Research information used by policy analysts helps policy makers change ways of thinking about an issue, evaluate the merits of alternative proposals for action, mobilize support for a position or point of view, improve existing programs, and raise issues for the attention of decision makers (Hutchinson, 1995). Policy research needs to be of high technical quality, comprehensive, and jargon-free (Hutchinson, 1995). Mixed-method research has the potential to address these needs because it incorporates everyday, qualitative language as well as quantitative, technical data.

A mixed-method study is one in which the researcher incorporates both qualitative and quantitative methods of data collection and analysis in a single study. This type of a study enables a policy researcher to understand complex phenomena qualitatively as well as to explain the phenomena through numbers, charts, and basic statistical analyses. A multimethod approach to policy research holds potential, according to Rossman and Wilson (1991), for understanding the complex phenomena of our social world, seeing this world through multiple lenses, and using eclectic methodologies that better respond to the multiple stakeholders of policy issues than a single method or approach to research.

INTRODUCTION

In the broad area of social science research, mixed-method studies have caught the attention of writers who call it a "third paradigm" in evaluation research (Datta, 1994, p. 68) and a "research style in its own right, one as distinctive in its way as the more conventional styles" (Brewer & Hunter, 1989, p. 28). In 1989, Greene, Caracelli, and Graham reported 57 mixed-method evaluation studies; Datta (1994) found 18 evaluation studies from 1959 to 1992; and Creswell, Goodchild, and Turner (1996) discussed 19 mixed-method studies about postsecondary educational institutions. In policy research, however, only a few published studies exist (Rossman & Wilson, 1991), such as the recent, combined quantitative and qualitative approaches applied to distance education (Atman et al., 1991), to a community-based needs assessment model (Loos, 1995), to barriers to student success (Kinnick & Ricks, 1993), and to the nature of instruction in high school transition courses (White et al., 1996). Such examples illustrate the applicability of mixed-method approaches to policy research, but they provide little insight into how a policy researcher might conduct this form of inquiry or assess the contribution of a study.

This chapter attempts to clarify the terms used in mixed-method research in the social science literature, construct a brief historical overview of mixed-method studies, and advance eight steps useful in conducting and evaluating a mixed-method project. The chapter ends with an illustration of each step as applied to a specific study in the field of education.

THE LANGUAGE AND RHETORIC
OF MIXED-METHOD RESEARCH

The language and rhetoric of educational research have long provided a framework for understanding procedures and design (Firestone, 1987). Policy researchers also need a common language to understand a mixed-method design. Unfortunately, what is involved in this form of study and what it is to be called remains cloudy, even confusing.

The reader in this area is met with a plethora of terms. Writers have referred to it as multitrait/multimethod research (Campbell & Fiske, 1959), integrating qualitative and quantitative approaches (Glik, Parker, Muligande, & Hategikamana, 1986/1987; Steckler, McLeroy, Goodman, Bird, & McCormick, 1992), interrelating qualitative and quantitative (Fielding & Fielding, 1986), methodological triangulation (Morse, 1991), multimethodological research (Hugentobler, Israel, & Schurman, 1992), multimethod designs and linking qualitative and quantitative data (Miles & Huberman, 1994), combining qualitative and quantitative (Bryman, 1988; Creswell, 1994; Swanson-Kauffman, 1986), mixed-model studies (Datta, 1994), and mixed-method research (Greene et al., 1989; Caracelli & Greene, 1993; Rossman & Wilson, 1991).

Central to all of these terms is the idea of combining or integrating different methods. The term, *mixed method*, seems appropriate, although this author has used others (Creswell, 1994; Creswell et al., 1996; Creswell & Miller, 1997). *Mixing* provides an umbrella term to cover the multifaceted procedures (to be discussed shortly) of combining, integrating, linking, and employing multimethods.

Next, a definition of a mixed-method study can help policy makers start on common ground to understand the design of this form of research. A *mixed-method study* is one in which the research uses at least one quantitative method and one qualitative method to collect, analyze, and report findings in a single study (Fielding & Fielding, 1986; Greene et al., 1989). Two issues are embedded in this definition. First, what are the methods associated with quantitative and qualitative research? At the simplest level, quantitative research involves gathering numeric information through instruments. Typically, in a quantitative study, a researcher gathers information from a mailed survey instrument, from an instrument administered to individuals as an intervention in an experiment, or from current or historical policy documents. Qualitative research involves collecting text (e.g., interview data, fieldnotes of the researcher) or visual information (e.g., pictures, videotapes, photographs) from participants at a site or setting. (See Creswell, 1998 for an extended list of qualitative data collection procedures.) In qualitative research, the policy researcher becomes the instrument for data collection rather than relying on a predetermined instrument (Bogdan & Biklen, 1992).

The second issue is whether a mixed-method study is a single study or multiple studies in an extended program of research, such as described by Brewer and Hunter (1989). In this chapter, the discussion refers to a *single* study because it is the form typically reported in mixed-method policy studies, and it becomes the type of information policy researchers use to make decisions.

How would this single study employing both quantitative and qualitative methods be organized? To mix quantitative and qualitative methods, an investigator might administer an instrument to a sample of a population (quantitative data collection). Then the investigator analyzes the data, selects outlier cases, and conducts intensive interviews with a few individuals in the sample (qualitative data collection). Alternatively, a researcher might observe individuals in a setting (qualitative) and survey a large sample from which these individuals are taken (quantitative) to combine the findings and to determine whether the in-depth picture from observations converges or matches the more general survey findings. These are two popular models discussed in the literature about mixed-method designs.

A BRIEF HISTORY OF MIXED-METHOD RESEARCH

Before a more extensive discussion of these design issues, it might be helpful to briefly examine the etiology of this form of research. Mixed-method research emerged in the early 20th century as writers discussed multiple forms of social science fieldwork (e.g., Chapin, 1920; Young, 1939). However, it was not until 1959, and the multitrait, multimethod approach advanced by Campbell and Fiske, that a mixed-method approach came into sharp focus. Campbell and Fiske discussed using multiple quantitative methods in psychological experiments of personality traits to determine that it was the trait and not the method that caused differences in the outcomes of a study. They used more than one quantitative measure and assessed and compared numeric scores.

Several years later, the discussion continued in the form of combining *fieldwork*, a term used to denote in-depth case studies (qualitative research) at the site or location of the study, coupled with surveys (quantitative research). Sieber (1973) discussed this "new style of research" and advocated the "integration of research techniques" within a single study, suggesting that such a combination opened up "enormous opportunities for mutual advantages in each of three major phases—design, data collection, and analysis" (p. 1337).

What were these opportunities? Several writers following Sieber began to explore the purposes or reasons for mixing methods. Jick (1979) drew on a navigation term from military science—*triangulation*—in which individuals used multiple reference points to locate an object's exact position to advance one reason for conducting a mixed-method study. By triangulation he meant that different methods, each administered independently, could "uncover some unique variance which otherwise may have been neglected by a single method" (p. 603; also see Mathison, 1988). In his study of the effects of a merger on employees, Jick illustrated triangulation by collecting data through surveys, semistructured interviews, unobtrusive and nonparticipant observations, and archival materials. His approach was to corroborate or converge the results from these alternative qualitative and quantitative approaches and systematically attempt to reduce potential bias inherent in any one method of data collection.

Other writers soon pointed out that triangulation, or converging findings from several methods, was only one reason for a mixed-method study. As for convergence of findings, Rossman and Wilson in 1985 discussed the reasons for elaborating on findings from one method to another and for initiating findings from one method to new interpretations, new areas for exploration, or new research questions. More recently, Rossman and Wilson have advocated for three purposes: corroboration (as with triangulation, the search for consistencies in findings), elaboration (enhancing the results from one method to the other), and development (efforts to inform one method from the other method) (Rossman & Wilson, 1991).

The discussion about purposes or reasons raised important issues in the design of a mixed-method study, a conversation that continues today. In this discussion, two trends are noteworthy. First, authors linked methods to the process of research. For example, two sociologists, Brewer and Hunter (1989) discussed the multimethod research of surveys, experiments, fieldwork, and nonreactive measures in formulating research problems, collecting data, sampling, measurement, and establishing causal explanations of social phenomena. In a study of 57 mixed-method evaluation studies, Greene et al. (1989) not only specified five purposes for mixed-method studies, they also explored design considerations, such as the use of similar or dissimilar methods, the equal or unequal status of the methods, and the implementation of the methods (interactively or independently, sequentially or simultaneously). Later, Caracelli and Greene (1993) extended their discussion to the important question of how to analyze and interpret data from a mixed-method study—discussing data transformation, typology development, extreme case analysis, and data merging.

A second trend was to draw visual models of mixed-method designs. For example, three visual models capture the procedures of conducting mixed-method studies (Creswell, 1994; Creswell et al., 1996). These models are represented in visual images, including and going beyond those presented by Steckler et al. (1992) and Miles and Huberman (1994). For example, in 1994, Creswell reported on a two-phase model, in which the qualitative part followed the quantitative part; a dominant-less-dominant model, in which qualitative or quantitative constituted the more substantial part of a project; and a mixed-methodology model, in which qualitative and quantitative approaches were combined in all phases of the process of research.

Creswell's work also addressed a range of research issues, from specifying a worldview and epistemology to interpreting the results. His mixed-methodology model raised a question in the mixed-method literature: the relationship between paradigm (or worldview) and method, a topic hotly debated (see, e.g., Reichardt & Rallis, 1994). By arguing for the primacy of the research problem rather than epistemological compatibility in a mixed-method study, a more productive line of thinking emerges to advanced knowledge about mixed-method designs. Regardless of this larger philosophical debate, the visual models help portray the process of research, raise questions about the implementation and sequence of the quantitative and qualitative methods in a study, and emphasize the relative weight given to these both quantitative and qualitative methods in a single study (Morse, 1991).

BASIC PROCEDURES IN DESIGNING AND COMPOSING A MIXED-METHOD STUDY

Many factors play a central role in designing and composing a mixed method study for policy research. What follows are eight basic procedures in designing a mixed-method study, drawing on a multidisciplinary literature and organized into a series of steps that should be used by policy analysts seeking to conduct and evaluate a mixed-method study.

1. *Determine if a mixed-method study is needed to study the problem.* After the initial identification of a problem (and an accompanying literature review to determine that the topic needs to be addressed, has been understudied, or has been overlooked), consider whether a mixed-method study is needed to examine the problem. This topic has occupied the attention of several mixed-method writers: deciding on the purpose of a study. Unfortunately, of the many purposes or reasons presented for this design (e.g., see Rossman and Wilson, 1985; Greene et al., 1989; Steckler et al., 1992; Miles & Huberman, 1994), authors unnecessarily complicate the situation. They label these purposes with names that do not adequately present a reason for conducting a mixed-method study. Three major reasons exist for conducting a mixed-method study:

- More information or better information can be learned from converging or triangulating the results from qualitative and quantitative methods than from one method alone. One rationale, then, is to converge information from the findings from qualitative and quantitative methods administered independently from each other.
- Results from one method can be extended by using another method. The nature of quantitative methods is to focus inquiry on a discrete set of variables to test specific hypotheses or research questions. Alternatively, the nature of qualitative inquiry is to open the study through presenting the large, interconnected complexities of a situation. Thus, each type of method has advantages and can extend, in certain ways, understanding a researchable problem. This occurs when the researcher sequences the two types of methods, either qualitative first as exploratory, followed by quantitative as explanatory, or vice versa. Further, many researchers begin with the qualitative phase first if the problem has not been explored much in the literature.
- Quantitative measures and instruments grounded in the views of subjects or participants in the study can be developed. In this case, the researcher develops quantitative measures from a qualitative exploration because measures are not currently available, extant measures do not represent the population being studied, or the topic has not been explored much by other investigators.

2. *Consider if a mixed-method study is feasible.* There are general requirements about the feasibility of a study, such as studying a realistic problem, being able to adequately gather the information, undertaking a study of interest to others, and relating the project to career goals (Creswell, 1994). But beyond these requirements, mixed-method researchers have an additional challenge of collecting extensive information. Thus, the design of a mixed-method study requires that the researcher provide evidence of skills, resources, time, and costs of conducting the study. Mixed-method designs require expertise

in both qualitative and quantitative research. The need for skills and funds is compounded by extensive data collection involving both time and cost (Bryman, 1988). The costs may not be borne equally by the researcher and participants or subjects in a study (Brewer & Hunter, 1989). If the researcher's burden is substantial, the resources needed may place a mixed-method design outside the reach of policy researchers. Obtaining resources may be difficult given the need for policy centers and funding agencies to seek numbers and fund few qualitative projects. Finally, the audience for a mixed-method study may be limited at present to journals, book-length works, receptive faculty graduate committees, and policy decision makers.

3. *Write research questions that can be examined both qualitatively and quantitatively.* The next step is to write research questions (or hypotheses) testable through both qualitative and quantitative methods. Quantitative questions specify the relationship among independent and dependent variables, and they may be written in the null form but are typically written to convey a direction (e.g., the more resources, the more centralized the decision making). Qualitative questions are open ended and nondirectional in nature, and they seek a description of the phenomenon being addressed. Moreover, they can be encoded with terms to denote the type of qualitative tradition being used. For example, in grounded theory, the researcher develops or generates a theory; in an ethnography, the investigator describes and interprets a culture-sharing group; in a case study, the researcher presents an in-depth description and analysis of a bounded system such as an event, program, or activity (Creswell, 1998).

4. *Review and decide on both quantitative and qualitative types of data collection.* Incorporated in a mixed-method design is the need to determine the types of methods typically associated with qualitative and quantitative inquiry. A mixed-method study would consist of at least one quantitative method and one qualitative method of data collection in a single study.

Simply stated, quantitative methods reflect closed-ended information measured on an instrument or gathered through a structured form of interviewing and observing. The type of information is numeric, and it can be reduced to aggregated information (Bryman, 1988). The researcher asks participants in a study to respond, rate, rank, or check information on an instrument that can be evaluated for validity and reliability. Alternatively, the researcher may check the appropriate place on the scale of a structured observational protocol or interview protocol. The central point is that the data can be recorded or represented by a number that is available for statistical analysis.

For qualitative methods, four primary forms of open-ended qualitative data exist: observations, interviews, documents, and audio-visual material (Creswell, 1994). Within each of these types variations exist, such as different roles of an observer (from participant to outside observer) or the multiple forms of documents (from private to public archives). An elucidation of the many forms can be found in a recent book on *Qualitatitive Inquiry and Research Design* (Creswell, 1998).

5. *Assess the relative weight and the implementation strategy for each method.* What relative weights should be given to the qualitative and quantitative components of a study? Morse (1991) and Greene et al. (1989) introduced the concept of weight in mixed-method studies. Morse (1991) suggested that studies might be either theoretically driven by the qualitative method or theoretically driven by the quantitative method, and she used capital letters to signify the method given the greatest weight by the investigator. To a certain extent, this approach is useful, but it tends to encourage, once again, thinking about distinct attributes of the qualitative and quantitative paradigms and raises questions about how one defines the theory in both the qualitative and quantitative approaches. Greene et al. (1989), on the other hand, used the term, *status*, to refer to either equal or unequal weight of the qualitative and quantitative methods. They suggested that a study's qualitative and quantitative methods,

> have equally important or central roles vis-à-vis the study's overall objectives. . . . the status design characteristic should directly reflect the relative weight and the influence of the qualitative and quantitative methods with respect to their frequency and their centrality to study objectives. (p. 264)

Thus, it is useful to consider the weight of each method as a reflection of the amount of discussion given to each method and its centrality to the study objectives rather than its importance as a theoretical orientation for a study.

A further point is how the quantitative and qualitative methods are implemented. Policy researchers might implement the methods either sequentially or concurrently. If the purpose of the study is to build from one method to another or to develop an instrument from qualitative data, the sequential approach is used. If the intent of the study is to converge or triangulate the findings, then the methods may be administered at the same time. Additionally, the methods can be implemented independently as in a sequential approach, or dependently, an approach where the methods are administered to the same population or group of people.

6. *Help the reader visualize the design by presenting a visual model.* The simultaneous and sequential approaches can be visually portrayed for the reader. Some form of visual mapping of procedures has a long tradition in experimental research, such as the classic notations provided by Campbell and Stanley (1966), in which the X's represent an exposure of a group to an experimental variable or event and the O's portray an observation or measurement. A visual mapping has utility as well in mixed-method studies. Three important elements should go into this visual model: the sequence of the qualitative and quantitative phases of the study (recognizing that both parts might be implemented simultaneously if the intent is to triangulate or

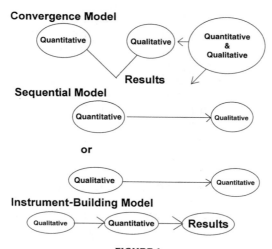

FIGURE I
Three models of mixed-method designs.

converge findings), the independence or dependence of each method, and the relative weight given to each method.

Those designing mixed-method research might draw circles to indicate methods and arrows to indicate sequence, dependence, and weight (with capital letters) (Morse, 1991). Thus, for the three reasons for conducting a study mentioned earlier, these visuals might be represented by the three models shown in Figure 1. In the *convergence model*, the researcher collects both qualitative and quantitative data and then examines both data to determine the findings of a study. In the *sequential model*, two phases are used with the second phase building on or extending the first phase of research. In the *instrument-building model*, the investigator's intent is to develop an instrument that appropriately reflects (and is generated from) views from people who will use or who will be administered the instrument. Thus, the researcher begins with an exploratory qualitative method of data collection, analyzes the information, and then uses it to form questions and scales on an instrument.

7. *Determine how the data will be analyzed.* Which one of these visual models the policy researcher chooses to use affects the form of data analysis and interpretation of the results (Caracelli & Greene, 1993). In this discussion, data analysis will be treated separately from data collection, a position not always supported in the qualitative research literature, but one that adds to the heuristic value of this discussion.

For the convergence model, the intent of the study is to converge the findings, to assemble results that are more powerful (and potentially less biased) than if only one method were used. Accordingly, the data analysis for quantitative methods proceeds independently from the data analysis for the qualitative methods. As suggested by Caracelli and Greene (1993), an integration of data at the analysis stage does not take place; instead, the integration occurs at the interpretation stage of a study. The researcher examines whether the results from the quantitative and qualitative methods confirm each other or contradict each other. If they contradict each other, then several steps can be taken: one can explain the contradictions, gather more information to resolve the contradiction, or state that such contradiction is a limitation or weakness in the study.

In the sequential model, the data analysis proceeds sequentially with the data from the first method analyzed, and then this analysis is used to shape the direction of the second method. For example, the qualitative observations can be transformed (Caracelli & Greene, 1993) into quantitative categories or variables to be tested empirically by the quantitative phase. The analysis becomes one of identifying themes in the qualitative data and then measuring and employing statistical analysis to test hypotheses or research questions. This quantitative phase may also be to examine outlier or extreme cases in more depth (Caracelli & Greene, 1993). Alternatively, if a researcher begins with a quantitative approach and gathers survey data on an instrument, a factor analysis might be used to identify factor loadings and establish constructs or a chi-square analysis to make comparisons. These constructs or comparisons can then be used in methods of observing or interviewing qualitatively to provide more detail about the constructs or comparisons.

In the instrument-building model, the analysis proceeds from reducing the qualitative observations, interviews, and documents (as well as other forms) into variables and specific questions for instrument development. In qualitative data analysis, the process involves reading through the text, reducing it to a sizable set of themes, condensing these themes to a small number, and finding evidence for each theme (see Creswell, 1994; Tesch, 1990). Each of these themes might be variables for the quantitative instrument, and the evidence used to compose specific questions on the instrument.

8. *Assess how the quality of the study will be determined.*

Although standards exist for evaluating quantitative studies (Miller, 1991) and qualitative studies (Creswell, 1994, 1998; Maxwell, 1995), no specific guidelines have been articulated for a mixed-method study. However, from the preceding discussion, a reasonable set of guidelines for policy analysts and researchers to use in evaluating a mixed-method study would include the following:

- Does the study employ at least one method associated with quantitative approaches and one method associated with qualitative approaches in a single study?

- Has the author presented reasons for why a mixed-method study is needed?
- Is the study feasible, given the amount of data to be collected, the monies, time, and expertise required?
- Have research questions been written for both the quantitative and the qualitative methods in the study?
- Have the quantitative and qualitative methods been clearly identified?
- Has the implementation of the methods been specified, especially in terms of sequence (simultaneous versus sequential), dependence (independent versus dependent), and relative weight?
- Has the author presented a visual model of the procedures?
- Have the procedure for data analysis and interpretation been specified so that the reader can determine how the data will be converged, extended, or developed?

9. *Develop a plan for a mixed-method study.* The design of a mixed-method study can be improved if researchers have some guidance as to a general outline for their plan. Although guidelines exist for quantitative and qualitative designs (Creswell, 1994; Marshall & Rossman, 1995; Miller, 1991), comparable guidelines for the overall format of a mixed-method study are apparently still being developed. Accordingly, a plan should incorporate the procedures identified and consider such issues as timing, sequence, and quality considerations.

One potential set of design guidelines is shown in Figure 2. These guidelines incorporate the traditional elements of design, such as the problem, the purpose statement, and the literature review. When considering the issues of design, the reader is reminded of Brewer and Hunter's (1989) point that one cannot separate the methods of research from the larger process of design in which it is embedded.

The plan shown in Figure 2 highlights the need for the author to present a clear rationale for why a mixed-method study is being undertaken, to pose both qualitative (i.e., open-ended) and quantitative (i.e., close-ended) questions, to include a visual model of the actual design, and to discuss both qualitative and quantitative data collection and analysis procedures.

APPLYING THE STEPS OF A
MIXED-METHOD STUDY

It is not enough to plan a study or to identify procedures; a concrete example should aid policy researchers who conduct or evaluate mixed-method studies. The following sections illustrate such a study by Russek and Weinberg (1993) on the implementation of technology-based computer and calculator materials in elementary classrooms in a suburban school district. This study

I.   Introduction to the Study

        Problem

        Past research about the problem

        How present study will address deficiencies in past
            research

        What audience(s) will profit from problem being
            addressed

II.   Purpose of the Study

        Rationale for a mixed-method study

        Identification of the qualitative and quantitative
            questions

III. Related Research Literature (optional)

IV.   Procedures

        Relationship of Methods to Paradigms

        Visual Model of Mixed-Method Approach

        Type of Research Design within Each Method

        Researcher's Resources and Skills

        Data collection within the type

            Sampling strategy and researcher's role

            Types of data to be collected

            Sequencing of data collection

            Relative emphasis on qualitative/quantitative

        Data analysis within the type

        Approach to validity and verification

        Overall organization of the integrated findings and

            anticipated results

V.   References

VI.   Appendices: Instruments, Interview/Observational Protocol,
        etc.

FIGURE 2

A format for designing a plan to conduct a mixed-method study.

illustrates the convergence model of a mixed-method study as shown in Figure 1.

Description of the Study

Russek and Weinberg (1993) sought to explore the impact of computers and calculators in a suburban school district with 7000 students. As part of a large National Science Foundation 4-year project to develop and field test technology-based elementary mathematics curriculum materials, the researchers studied 16 teachers in six elementary schools to examine their implementation of computers and calculators. The stated purpose of the study was as follows:

> to determine during the first year of field testing, the extent to which two sets of supplementary mathematics lessons, one utilizing the calculator and one utilizing the computer, were implemented by elementary school teachers, and the factors that governed such implementation. (p. 132)

The article refers to a mixed-method study, and the researchers included at least one form of qualitative and quantitative data in a single study. In terms of a specific mixed-method model, this study represents convergence through the triangulation of data, drawing on both qualitative and quantitative information.

Need for a Mixed-Method Study

Early in the process the authors argued that their study employed a mixed-method approach because each method provided "distinct strengths" to broaden the study and afforded "deeper insights" (Russek & Weinberg, 1993, p. 131) into the nature and extent of technology implementation. The authors mentioned the advantage of triangulation "to achieve a more complete picture of empirical reality" (p. 131). Even though they begin with qualitative data collection followed by quantitative collection, their analysis suggested some attempt to blend or converge the results from the methods.

Feasibility of the Study

This issue is not addressed explicitly, although the authors devote several pages to elucidating the key characteristics of qualitative research and ethnographic research. With federal funding, they embarked on elaborate qualitative and quantitative methods of data collection. Thus, lack of skills, money, time, and effort did not seem to be a problem.

Research Questions

Although they did not specify detailed research questions, they posed one open-ended qualitative question, "What is going on here?" and one quantitative question, "What are the explanations for what we see happening?" (Russek & Weinberg, 1993, p. 131) in the introduction to the study. The quantitative question clearly sought to specify the variables that explain the implementation of technology.

Types of Data Collection

In a section on data collection, the authors mentioned that they gathered both qualitative and quantitative data, which can be enumerated as follows:

1. Qualitative data
   - informal in-depth interviews of teachers and administrators
   - informal classroom observations
   - school documents
   - teacher-written responses to open-ended questions or questionnaires

2. Quantitative data
   - classroom observation checklists
   - lesson evaluation forms
   - workshop evaluation forms
   - a self-evaluation questionnaire
   - stages of concern questionnaire

Relative Weight and Implementation Strategy

Although many pages in this study present the qualitative and ethnographic approach to research, in the analysis and interpretation phase of this study, the authors provide equal weight to qualitative and quantitative methods. They suggest that they began with the qualitative phase of data collection by interviewing and observing and then followed this segment by administering the instruments. Because the quantitative phase was decided before the study began, their study might be characterized as a sequential one in which the qualitative results led to quantitative measures and instruments. Alternatively, one might view the study as two methods implemented concurrently, an approach consistent with the convergence model of mixed-method design.

Visual of the Design

This project might have been enhanced if the authors had presented a visual model of their procedure. Such a model was not available to the reader, but the authors might have presented one model that they began with and a second that they ended with. A speculation about how such a visual might have looked is shown in Figure 3. The first would be a sequential qualitative followed by quantitative approach; whereas, the second would be the

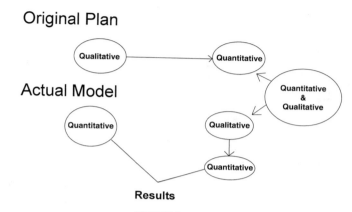

FIGURE 3

Possible diagram of mixed-method model for Russek and Weinberg (1993) study.

actual model, in which the researchers took quantitative data in the form of an index of implementation and compared it with qualitative data that was quantified into categories (high and low) on three factors found qualitatively to impact implementation (teachers expressions, volunteer attitude, and skills/knowledge). In the end, they compared the two numeric sets of data.

Analysis of the Data

The specific form of data analysis used by Russek and Weinberg (1993) would, according to Caracelli and Greene (1993), be called *data transformation*. For example, in a single table Russek and Weinberg (1993) compared the degree of implementation of teacher verbal reports (qualitative), classroom observations (qualitative), and lesson evaluation forms (quantitative) (Table 2, p. 139). To do this, they transformed the verbal reports and classroom observations into categories rated *low*, *moderate*, and *high*. For each teacher, then, the reader could visually inspect ratings on the three methods of data collection. From this they concluded that "there appears to be good agreement among indicators; triangulation has resulted in convergence" (p. 139).

As a second example, they created an index score for each teacher on calculator implementation. This score represented the proportion of lessons completed and a quality weighting factor describing the effectiveness of the teacher in fulfilling the objectives of the lessons completed. Thus, a quantitative score was available. They then transformed qualitative expressions about implementation on three factors, teacher commitment, preactivity attitudes, calculator skill, and knowledge into *low, moderate* and *high* ratings. In a Venn diagram, they plotted the quantitative index score and the transformed qualitative views in a figure to show that those individuals with a high quantitative implementation score also had a high score when measuring commitment, preactivity attitudes, and skills.

Quality Criteria

In terms of the criteria for assessing the quality of a mixed-method study mentioned earlier, the Russek and Weinberg (1993) study adequately addressed most of the criteria. Its strength was in the use of multiple forms of quantitative and qualitative data; it presented a distinct model of convergence and discussed the issue of triangulating data, and it was labeled a mixed-method study. The authors might have enhanced their discussion by presenting a visual model and by discussing the type of mixed-method approach they employed and how it shifted during their study.

CONCLUSION

This chapter suggests that mixed-method designs are beginning to emerge in policy research. As policy researchers conduct or evaluate mixed-method studies, they need to recognize that this form of design goes by different names and has a history of an increased clarification of design topics in recent years. Accordingly, this chapter advances eight steps to consider when planning or evaluating a mixed-method study.

Policy researchers should assess the need for such a study, followed by exploring its feasibility in terms of time, cost, and expertise. Then the analyst needs to write research questions that relate to qualitative and quantitative methods of data collection and identify the specific forms of data to be collected. The analyst can then consider the relative weight, the sequence, and a visual diagram for the study. Also, the specific procedures for data analysis must relate closely to the model or purpose for the study identified at the outset of the project. In the end, a policy study can combine the best of both quantitative and qualitative methods and provide useful narrative as well as quantitative data for decision making.

References

Atman, K. S., Donaldson, J. F., Gunawardena, C. N., Egan, M. W., Sebastian, J., Welch, M., Page, B., Miller, G. E., Bajtelsmit, J. W., Leiter, R. B., & Moore, M. G. (1991). *Distance education symposium, selected papers, part 3*. Papers presented at the American Symposium on Research in Distance Education, ACSDE Research Monograph Number 9. University Park, PA: Pennsylvania State University.

Bogdan, R. C., & Biklen, S. K. (1992). *Qualitative research for education: An introduction to theory and methods* (2nd ed.). Boston: Allyn & Bacon.

Brewer, J., & Hunter, A. (1989). *Multimethod research: A synthesis of styles.* Newbury Park, CA: Sage.

Bryman, A. (1988). *Quantity and quality in social science research.* London and New York: Routledge.

Campbell, D., & Fiske, D. (1959). Convergent and discriminant validation by the multitrait–multimethod matrix. *Psychological Bulletin, 56,* 81–105.

Campbell, D. T., & Stanley, J. C. (1966). Experimental and quasi-experimental designs for research. In N. L. Gage (Ed.), *Handbook of research on teaching* (pp. 1–76). Chicago: Rand McNally.

Caracelli, V. J., & Greene, J. C. (1993). Data analysis Strategies for mixed-method evaluation designs. *Educational Evaluation and Policy Analysis,* 15(2), 195–207.

Chapin, F. S. (1920). *Field work and social research.* New York: Century.

Creswell, J. W. (1994). *Research design: Qualitative and quantitative approaches.* Thousand Oaks, CA: Sage.

Creswell, J. W. (1998). *Qualitative inquiry and research design: Choosing among five traditions.* Thousand Oaks, CA: Sage.

Creswell, J. W., Goodchild, L., & Turner, P. (1996). Integrated qualitative and quantitative research: Epistemology, history, and designs. In J. Smart (Ed.), *Higher education: Handbook of theory and research* (Vol. XI). New York: Agathon Press.

Creswell, J. W., & Miller, G. A. (1997). Research methodologies and the doctoral process. In L. F. Goodchild, K. E. Green, E. L. Katz, & R. C. Kluever (Eds.), *Rethinking the dissertation process: Tackling personal and institutional obstacles* (pp. 33–46). New Directions for Higher Education, No. 99. San Francisco: Jossey-Bass.

Datta, L. (1994). Paradigm wars: A basis for peaceful coexistence and beyond. In C. S. Reichardt and S. F. Rallis (Eds.), *The qualitative–quantitative debate: New perspectives* (pp. 53–70). New Directions for Program Evaluation, No. 61. San Francisco: Jossey-Bass.

Fielding, N. G., & Fielding, J. L. (1986). *Linking data.* Beverly Hills, CA: Sage.

Firestone, W. A. (1987). Meaning in method: The rhetoric of quantitative and qualitative research. *Educational Researcher,* 16(7), 16–21.

Glik, D. C., Parker, K., Muligande, G., & Hategikamana, D. (1986/1987). Integrating qualitative and quantitative survey techniques. *International Quarterly of Community Health Education,* 7(3), 181–200.

Greene, J. C., Caracelli, V. J., & Graham, W. F. (1989). Toward a conceptual framework for mixed-method evaluation designs. *Educational Evaluation and Policy Analysis,* 11(3), 255–274.

Hugentobler, M. K., Israel, B. A., & Schurman, S. J. (1992). An action research approach to workplace health: Integrating methods. *Health Education Quarterly,* 19(1), 55–76.

Hutchinson, J. R. (1995). A multimethod analysis of knowledge use in social policy. *Science Communication,* 17(1), 90–106.

Jick, T. D. (1979). Mixing qualitative and quantitative methods: Triangulation in action. *Administrative Science Quarterly,* 24, 602–611.

Kinnick, M. K., & Ricks, M. F. (1993). Student retention: Moving from numbers to action. *Research in Higher Education,* 34(1), 55–69.

Loss, G. P. (1995). A blended qualitative–quantitative assessment model for identifying and rank-ordering service needs of indigenous peoples. *Evaluation and Program Planning,* 18(3), 237–244.

Mathison, S. (1988). Why triangulate? *Educational Researcher,* 17(2), 13–17.

Marshall, C., & Rossman, G. B. (1995). *Designing qualitative research* (2nd ed.). Newbury Park, CA: Sage.

Maxwell, J. A. (1995). *Qualitative research design: An interactive approach.* Thousand Oaks, CA: Sage.

Miles, M. B., & Huberman, A. M. (1994). *Qualitative data analysis* (2nd ed.). Thousand Oaks, CA: Sage.

Miller, D. C. (1991). *Handbook of research design and social measurement* (5th ed.). Newbury Park, CA: Sage.

Morse, J. M. (1991). Approaches to qualitative–quantitative methodological triangulation. *Nursing Research,* 40(1), 120–123.

Reichardt, C. S., & Rallis, S. E. (1994). The relationship between the qualitative and quantitative research traditions. In C. S. Reichardt and S. F. Rallis (Eds.), *The qualitative–quantitative debate: New perspectives* (pp. 5–11). New Directions for Program Evaluation, No. 61. San Francisco: Jossey-Bass.

Rossman, G. B., & Wilson, B. L. (1985). Number and words: Combining quantitative and qualitative methods in a single large-scale evaluation study. *Evaluation Review*, 9(5), 627–643.

Rossman, G. B., & Wilson, B. L. (1991). *Numbers and words revisited: Being "shamelessly eclectic."* Washington, DC: Office of Educational Research and Improvement. (ERIC Document Reproduction Service No. 337 235).

Russek, B. E., & Weinberg, S. L. (1993). Mixed methods in a study of implementation of technology-based materials in the elementary classroom. *Evaluation and Program Planning*, 16, 131–142.

Sieber, S. D. (1973). The integration of field work and survey methods. *American Journal of Sociology*, 78, 1335–1359.

Steckler, A., McLeroy, K. R., Goodman, R. M., Bird, S. T., & McCormick, L. (1992). Toward integrating qualitative and quantitative methods: An introduction. *Health Education Quarterly*, 19(1), 1–8.

Swanson-Kauffman, K. M. (1986). A combined qualitative methodology for nursing research. *Advances in Nursing Science* 8(3), 58–69.

Tesch, R. (1990). *Qualitative research: Analysis types and software tools.* Bristol, PA: Falmer.

White, P. A., Porter, A. C., Gamoran, A., & Smithson, J. (1996). *Upgrading high school math: A look at three transition courses.* Washington, DC: Office of Educational Research and Improvement.

Young, P. V. (1939). *Scientific social surveys and research* (1st ed.). New York: Prentice-Hall.

chapter 19

Basic Concepts in Hierarchical Linear Modeling with Applications for Policy Analysis*

J. DOUGLAS WILLMS
Atlantic Centre for Policy Research
University of New Brunswick

INTRODUCTION

Can Monitoring Efforts Meet the Needs of Policy Makers and Teachers?

State and provincial departments of education expend considerable resources collecting and analysing data that describe the performance of their educational systems. Many school districts also conduct their own performance evaluations. Policy makers want to know whether the achievement of learning outcomes in their jurisdiction is changing over time, as they develop and implement educational reforms. They want to know whether there are

*This chapter is a revised version of a manuscript prepared for the Joint Conference of the International Association of Survey Statisticians and the International Association for Official Statistics, organized in conjunction with the National Institute of Statistics, Geography and Informatics of Mexico, held in Aguascalientes, Mexico, 1–4 September 1998. The author is grateful for support received from the New Brunswick Department of Education, the Canadian Social Sciences and Humanities Research Council (Grant No. 410-92-1569), and the Spencer Foundation. The Atlantic Centre for Policy Research is supported by the Canadian Institute for Advanced Research and the University of New Brunswick. Opinions reflect those of the author and do not necessarily reflect those of the funding agencies. The author also appreciates the assistance of George Frempong and Donnalouise Watts in preparing the manuscript.

inequalities in achievement among students with differing socioeconomic backgrounds, among ethnic groups, and between males and females. They are particularly interested in how well their students fare compared with those in other jurisdictions. Their belief is that monitoring school performance is necessary for making day-to-day decisions concerning the allocation of resources, the efficacy of certain programs, and the strengths and weaknesses of their schools and schooling systems. They hope that routine monitoring encourages a process of self-examination and motivates educators to provide a better education.

But many principals and teachers oppose performance monitoring. The move toward high-stakes testing, whereby policy makers use monitoring data to make decisions about school closures or to reward or sanction some teachers, has created mistrust and skepticism among many educators. They are justifiably critical because in many jurisdictions schools and districts have been compared in their achievement scores without considering the characteristics and background of the students enrolled in them or the wider economic and social context in which each school operates. Educators also maintain that monitoring promotes "teaching to the test," thereby limiting both the formal and informal curricula and deterring educators, parents, and children from critically examining the wider purposes of schooling. Many teachers feel that school assessment places unrealistic demands on their time and resources and that ultimately it reduces their authority in deciding what is taught and how it is taught.

An important question therefore is whether performance monitoring can serve the needs of policy makers charged with ensuring that all students receive a quality education while at the same time supporting the day-to-day work of principals and classroom teachers. If it is to do the latter, the information furnished by monitoring must contribute to principals' and teachers' working knowledge. It must yield information that describes which aspects of the curriculum have been mastered by the majority of students and which aspects require further attention. It should identify the school and classroom *processes* that affect student learning, such as the disciplinary climate of the school, student-staff relations, and parental involvement. It must kindle a process of *critical inquiry* (Sirotnik, 1987)—a dialectic around questions and activities pertaining to school improvement.

Hierarchical Linear Modeling as an Analytical Tool

Hierarchical linear modeling (HLM) is a particular regression technique that is designed to take into account the hierarchical structure of educational data (Raudenbush & Bryk, 1986). Generally, regression analysis is often used in monitoring to examine the relationships among a dependent variable, such as academic achievement, and one or more independent variables, such as students' prior academic experience and their family socioeconomic status. One of the assumptions underlying traditional regression approaches is that the observations are independent; that is, the observations of any one individual are not in any way systematically related to the observations of any other individual. This assumption is violated, for example, if some of the observed students are from the same family or, as is nearly always the case with monitoring data, students are from the same classroom or school. Consequently, the use of traditional regression approaches with most monitoring data yields biased estimates of the relationships among variables.

Moreover, policy makers are often interested in the relationships among variables describing features of different levels of an hierarchical structure, such as students, classrooms, schools, and school districts. For example, a common question is whether a reduction in class size is likely to lead to an improvement in students' test scores. However, traditional regression techniques assume that all data are collected at the same level. Twenty years ago, educational researchers debated whether the student, the classroom, or the school was the appropriate level for analysis. However, this was the wrong question, and researchers called for techniques that explicitly modeled the multilevel structure of the data. Advances in statistical theory and computing enabled researchers to solve this level-of-analysis problem (Bryk & Raudenbush, 1992; Goldstein, 1995), and now computer programs that can be used to analyse multilevel monitoring data are widely accessible (see Resources, this volume). These methods allow one to systematically ask new questions about how policies and practices affect students' outcomes. The advantage of HLM is that it allows the analyst to explicitly examine the effects on student outcomes of policy-relevant variables, such as class size or the implementation of a particular reform.

HLM can be understood by thinking of the analysis as being conducted in two steps. In the first step, analyses are conducted separately for every school (or some other unit) in the system, using student-level data. For example, students' test scores in mathematics (the outcome measure of interest) could be regressed on a set of student-level predictor variables, such as the students' socioeconomic status, and a dichotomous variable indicating whether the student was male or female. In this case, the regression model for each school would be expressed as follows:

$$(Mathematics)_{ij} = \beta_{0j} + \beta_{1j}(SES)_{ij} + \beta_{2j}(Female)_{ij} + \epsilon_{ij}$$

where $(Mathematics)_{ij}$, $(SES)_{ij}$, and $(Female)_{ij}$ are the scores on these variables for the ith student in the jth school. The analysis yields j separate sets of the regression parameters, β_0, β_1, and β_2, one set for each school. The model can be constructed such that β_0 indicates the level of performance for each school, after adjustment for SES and sex, and β_1 and β_2 indicate the extent of inequalities between students with differing SES and sex.

In the second step, the regression parameters from the first step of the analyses (i.e., levels of performance and extent of inequalities) become the outcome variables of interest. These are regressed on school-level data describing schooling processes. For example, one could specify a regression of the adjusted levels of performance on the average class size for the school, and a measure of the school's disciplinary climate:

$$\beta_{0j} = \gamma_{00} + \gamma_{01}(ClassSize)_j + \gamma_{02}(Discipline)_j + U_{01}$$

The analyses at this level yield estimates of the magnitude of the impact of the policy variable. In this example, the estimate of the parameter γ_{01} indicates the expected gain (or loss) in mathematics scores for an average reduction in class size of one student. The estimate for γ_{02} indicates the average effect of the intervention across the schools in which it had been implemented. The statistical and computing techniques on which HLM is based incorporate into a single model the regression analyses specified in both steps. It estimates the parameters of this model using iterative procedures (Goldstein, 1995; Raudenbush & Bryk, 1986).

Thus, the basic idea underlying HLM is that there are separate analyses for each unit in an hierarchical structure. The simple two-level model described here can be applied to address a range of questions that policy makers might pose. There are more complex hierarchical linear models; indeed, the statistical analyses specified at each level are not limited to linear regressions, and the models can include three- or even four-level models. The remainder of this chapter is divided into four sections. The first of these sets out some criteria for successful monitoring, and poses four questions that provide a useful framework for analysing monitoring data. The next three sections provide examples of hierarchical linear models based on data collected at national, provincial, and district levels. Each of these sections describes a simple example in some detail and then discusses some of the more complex models that can be used for specific purposes. The concluding section returns to the question, "Can monitoring efforts meet the needs of policy makers and teachers?" It argues that we require better data and more exacting analyses of monitoring data.

CRITERIA FOR SUCCESSFUL MONITORING

The indicators normally used in school monitoring, such as test scores or dropout rates, derive their meaning in one of three ways: through comparisons among jurisdictions, such as schools or districts; by comparison to some fixed standard; or from their trend over time. The problem with the first of these—making comparisons among schools or districts—is that there are always winners and losers. It is impossible, for example, for all schools to score above the state or provincial average. Rather than foster self-examination, such comparisons tend to pit schools against each other within local communities and encourage them to compete for certain teachers and students. Three important criteria for comparisons derived for monitoring purposes, if they are to be useful to teachers and be accepted by them, is that (1) they take into account the background characteristics of students attending the schools, (2) they are based on fixed standards, and (3) they emphasize *changes* in the school's or district's performance over time (Willms, 1992).

Most of the research on school and teacher effectiveness, and efforts to monitor school performance, have aimed to address four principal questions:

- To what extent do schools or districts vary in their outcomes?
- To what extent do outcomes vary for students of differing status?
- What policies and practices improve levels of schooling outcomes?
- What policies and practices reduce inequalities in outcomes among students of differing status? (Willms, 1992)

These questions constitute a useful framework for the study of HLM, because they have the same structure as the basic two-level hierarchical linear model.

The first question concerns the *level* of schooling outcomes attained by students in a schooling system. In its simplest form, it entails straightforward comparisons among schools and districts based on indicators such as average test scores or the percentage of students dropping out of school before graduation. The question can be extended to ask, "To what extent do schools or districts vary in their outcomes after account is taken of students' background characteristics?" This question pertains to the added value of schools or districts and is fundamental to gauging the effects of particular schooling processes or interventions or to determining where efforts at improving schools or districts might best be placed.

The second question is about equality of outcomes in a schooling system. The term, *gradients*, is being used by analysts to refer to the relationship between schooling outcomes and, for example, socioeconomic status (SES). If the gradient is steep for a schooling system, it means there are large disparities between students from advantaged and disadvantaged backgrounds. If it is shallow, it means there is greater equality of student outcomes. In monitoring school performance, a useful starting point is to determine how steep the SES gradient is for the entire system and whether gradients are particularly steep or shallow in particular schools or districts. The same idea applies to questions concerning differences among ethnic groups or between the sexes. For example, an analyst approaching monitoring from a multilevel perspective would determine the magnitude of achievement differences between males and females for the entire system and ask whether the gap varied among districts or schools.

The third and fourth questions ask *why* some schools have better or worse outcomes than others and *why* some schools are more or less successful in reducing inequalities among students of differing status. These questions are more difficult to answer because they require an understanding of the culture and internal workings of school life: the formal and informal rules governing the operation of a school; how students are organized for instruction; the nature of interactions between students, parents, and teachers; and their attitudes, values, and expectations. Because schooling is a such a complex phenomenon, monitoring can never be an exact science. However, the research on school effectiveness over the past 30 years has yielded some consistent findings, which are useful starting points for monitoring school performance.

NATIONAL LEVEL ANALYSES OF INTERPROVINCIAL DIFFERENCES

The primary purposes of assessment at national or international levels are to provide a basis for a continuing record of progress, to make comparisons among various jurisdictions (e.g., states and provinces, school districts), and to evaluate the effectiveness of particular kinds of educational programs (Willms & Kerckhoff, 1995). This section describes analyses based on Canadian data from the Third International Mathematics and Science Study (TIMSS), a study conducted in 41 countries in 1994 (Beaton et al., 1996).

In Canada, the federal government provides transfer payments to the ten provinces and two territories that have constitutional jurisdiction over education. Thus, it is common for provinces to enroll separately as member countries in international studies of education. In the case of the TIMSS, Canada participated as a member country, and five provinces—British Columbia, Alberta, Ontario, New Brunswick, and Newfoundland—participated separately. The analyses presented in this section describe the middle-school results for these provinces and for students from the other five provinces who elected to take the tests in French. The majority of these students were from Quebec.

The hierarchical analysis of these data examines the relationship between mathematics test scores and three predictor variables: socioeconomic status, sex, and immigrant status. The test scores were converted to a grade-equivalent metric, such that differences among provinces and the effects of the predictor variables can be gauged in terms of years of schooling. The SES variable is a statistical composite of variables describing the mothers' and fathers' levels of education and the number of educationally related possessions available in the home. Sex was coded such that the coefficients indicate the difference between females and males (positive coefficients indicate higher scores for females). Immigrant status was coded such that the coefficients indicate the difference between immigrants and nonimmigrants (positive coefficients indicate higher scores for immigrants). The hierarchical linear model has two levels: students and provinces. It provides national estimates of levels and gradients and separate estimates for each province.

National Results

Table 1 displays the overall regression results for Canada. They can be thought of as the average within-province regression results. The intercept, 7.43, is the (weighted) mean of the provincial means. At the student level, the mean score is 7.5, because the data were standardized such that the average Grade 7 students had a mean of 7.0 and the average Grade 8 students had a mean of 8.0. (Although it may not be intuitively obvious, the mean of the provincial means can be larger or smaller than the overall student mean. In this case it is smaller because there are more provinces with mean scores below 7.5.)

The average coefficient for SES is 0.71. It indicates that for each one-unit increase in SES, the typical student's score increased by about 7 months of schooling. (The school year in Canada is approximately 10 months in every province.) The negative coefficient for female indicates that, on average, females scored slightly lower than males; however, the size of the difference represents only about 1 month of schooling and is not statistically significant. The negative coefficient for immigrants indicates that, on average, immigrants scored 6 months of schooling lower than nonimmigrants.

TABLE I
Variation among Provinces in Levels of Mathematics Scores, Sex Differences, Socioeconomic Gradients, and Differences between Immigrants and Nonimmigrants Third International Mathematics and Science Study, 1994[a]

	Adjusted mean	Sex difference	SES gradient	Immigration effect
National results	7.43*	−.12	.71**	−.58
Provincial results				
Newfoundland	7.31	−.21	.83	−.67
New Brunswick	7.09	−.15	.79	−.48
Other (French)	8.77	.22	.51	−1.81
Ontario	6.97	−.28	.78	−.30
Alberta	7.67	−.18	.71	−.33
British Columbia	7.26	−.27	.70	.46

*$p < .05$
**$p < .01$
[a]Beaton et al., 1996.

Provincial Levels and Gradients

Hierarchical linear modeling also yields estimates of the levels and gradients for each province. Provincial estimates can vary not only because of "true" differences among them, but also because of sampling error (some provinces have relatively small samples) and measurement error (the tests themselves are not perfectly reliable). The estimates furnished by HLM are adjusted according to how reliably they have been estimated. HLM does this by borrowing strength from the data for the full national sample and shrinking each estimate toward the national average according to how accurately the level and gradient were estimated. Thus the estimates for provinces with small samples, such as Newfoundland in this example, are shrunk more toward the national mean than provinces with larger samples, such as Ontario. This shrinkage does not figure heavily in this example, however, because the sampling strategy entailed an oversampling of students in smaller provinces. Shrinkage is more important in cases where the second- and third-level units are schools and districts.

The bottom part of Table 1 displays for each province the HLM estimates of adjusted levels of mathematics achievement, the SES gradients, and the differences in performance between males and females and between non-immigrants and immigrants. Figure 1 displays the adjusted levels and SES gradients. The background-adjusted estimates of mathematics results (column 1) can differ substantially from the unadjusted results, because the provinces differ considerably in their demographic characteristics, particularly with respect to socioeconomic status and the percentage of minority students.

The finding of most immediate concern to Canadian educators is that students in the "Other (French)" category performed over a full grade level better than their counterparts elsewhere in Canada, whereas students in Ontario, the most affluent province, had the worst results. The superior performance of Quebec students in mathematics has been evident from other national and international studies for more than a decade, yet there has been little effort to systematically examine why these differences persist. These interprovincial differences are not apparent in the literacy skills of children when they enter school at age 5. They appear as early as Grade 2, increase gradually during the elementary and middle school years, and are evident in general literacy skills of youth aged 16 to 25 (Willms, 1996, 1997). We are using the TIMSS and other data to determine the most important schooling processes that lead to these differences.[1]

---

[1]Frempong and Willms (in progress) are examining the effects of curriculum coverage on levels and gradients, and they are comparing them to the effects associated with various aspects of school climate. The hypothesis is that, compared with other provinces, Quebec has a tighter fit between the *intended* curriculum of the provincial government and the *enacted* curriculum of the classroom. The research is being supported by Manulife Financial, Statistics Canada, and Human Resources Development Canada.

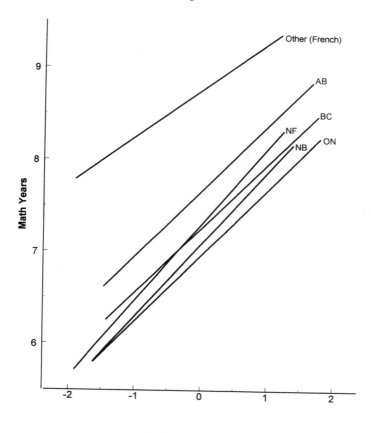

Socioeconomic Status

FIGURE 1

Relationship between mathematics scores and socioeconomic status
for Grades 7 and 8 students (adjusted for sex and immigration status).
AB, Alberta; NF, Newfoundland; BC, British Columbia; NB, New Brunswick;
ON, Ontario. From Third International Mathematics and Science Study,
1994 (Beaton et al., 1996).

Modeling Several Outcomes

The hierarchical linear models presented earlier can be extended to a multivariate, multilevel model, in which several outcome measures are modeled
simultaneously (Goldstein, 1995; Thum, 1997). The multivariate HLM has an
intra-individual level as its first level, which simply summarizes the set of
scores for each individual. For a three-level multivariate HLM, the second and
third levels of the model are similar to the two-level model presented above,
except that there is a separate set of equations for each outcome measure.

Analysts can perform separate two-level HLM analyses for each outcome measure, but they may wish to know also whether provinces (or districts or schools) that are effective in reading were also effective in mathematics, or whether schools that had high test scores also had low dropout rates. The multivariate HLM provides a means for directly assessing these issues.

Frempong and Willms (1998) have fit a multivariate HLM to the data for the separate subtests (i.e., fractions, geometry, algebra, statistics, measurement, and proportionality) of the mathematics test used in TIMMS. Given the large interprovincial differences in mathematics scores reported earlier, we wondered whether certain domains of achievement were particularly difficult for particular groups, such as children with low SES, or males or females. Also, domain-specific analyses have implications concerning the emphasis of curriculum in each province, and the methods of instruction (Kupermintz, Ennis, Hamilton, Talbert, & Snow, 1995; Muthen, Huang, & Booil, 1995). We found that provinces varied most in their results on the fractions subtest. Also, the SES gradients were steepest for fractions, proportionality, and statistics, and sex differences were greatest for proportionality and measurement. Figures 2 and 3 provide a summary of the findings.

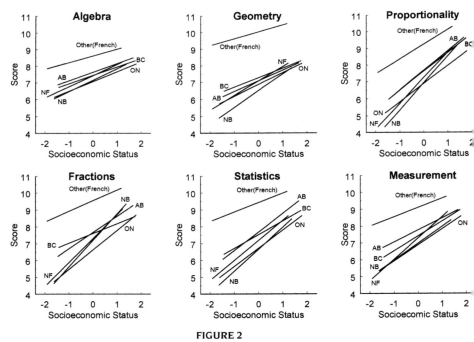

FIGURE 2

Relationship between mathematics scores and socioeconomic status, by achievement domain. From Third International Mathematics and Science Study, 1994 (Beaton et al., 1996).

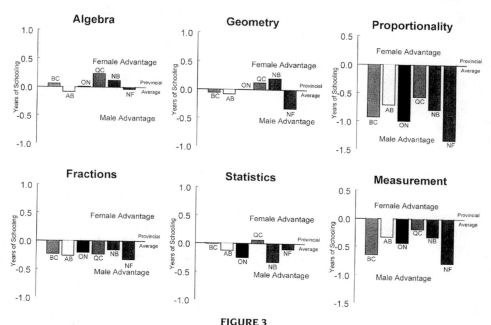

FIGURE 3

Relationship between mathematics scores and sex, by achievement domain. From Third International Mathematics and Science Study, 1994 (Beaton et al., 1996).

Multivariate multilevel models can also be used to examine the degree of consistency among people assessing the same phenomena. For example, a monitoring system might include assessments from students, teachers, and parents of the quality and quantity of homework assignments. The modeling would reveal whether these three groups were consistent in their judgments, and if not, whether the inconsistencies were related to the type of school or program. A similar model could be used to assess the extent of consistencies among test raters and to discern whether consistencies were related to either the type of student or the type of school.

PROVINCIAL AND DISTRICT-LEVEL ANALYSES TO ESTIMATE ADJUSTED LEVELS AND GRADIENTS

Hierarchical analyses of monitoring data at the provincial or district levels can be used to examine variation among schools in their adjusted levels of achievement and in their gradients. The example used in this section is based on the 1996 data of the New Brunswick Elementary School Climate Study. The study is based on data derived from questionnaires administered to the full population of Grades 6 and 8 students and to all elementary and middle-school teachers. These data are merged with students' test scores in mathematics, reading, science, and writing. The student questionnaire included measures of four affective schooling outcomes: self-esteem, general well-being, sense of belonging, and general health. It also asked questions pertaining to educational possessions in the home, the family's participation in cultural activities, and family size and structure. The latter variables were used to construct a composite measure of SES.

Unadjusted Results

The hierarchical analysis presented in this section has three levels: students, schools, and districts. The first set of analyses are null models for each of the four achievement measures and the four affective measures. These analyses provide information on the extent to which schools and districts vary in their schooling outcomes, before account is taken of students' background characteristics. Table 2 shows the proportions of variance at each of these levels. The analyses indicate that most of the variation is within schools, rather than between schools or between districts. Interdistrict variation is relatively small, representing less than 2% of a standard deviation for each measure.

Proportions of variation can be misleading, however, because many of the schools or districts can have scores that are very close to the provincial mean, yet there can be outliers that deserve attention. Figure 4 displays the unadjusted results for mathematics. On tests at this grade level, an effect size of 1.0 is roughly equivalent to 1 year of schooling. The figure indicates that schools do differ substantially in their test scores and that the variation is significant in both substantive and statistical terms. Displays of unad-

TABLE 2
Variation among Schools and School Districts for Eight Schooling Outcomes New Brunswick Elementary School Climate Study, 1996[a]

	Percentage of variation		
	Within schools	Between schools	Between districts
Mathematics	89.1	9.1	1.8
Reading	94.5	5.1	0.4
Science	90.2	9.0	0.8
Writing	90.9	8.0	1.1
Self-esteem	93.7	6.2	0.0
General well-being	92.0	7.8	0.2
Sense of belonging	96.7	3.0	0.2
General health	97.8	1.4	0.8

[a]Willms, 1994.

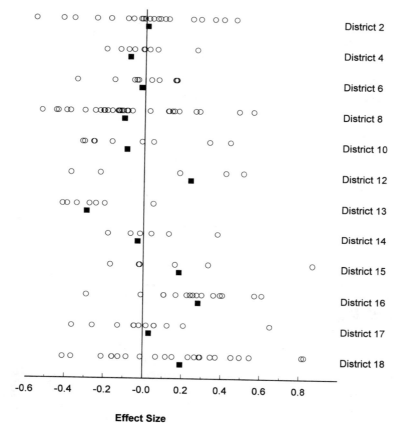

FIGURE 4
Estimates of average Grade 6 mathematics scores (unadjusted) for schools
and districts in New Brunswick. (○) School means, (■) district means.
From New Brunswick Elementary School Climate Study, 1996 (Willms, 1994).

justed results are useful in that they indicate actual levels of performance.
However, they can result in misleading conclusions if the analyses are not
taken further to include adjustments for the family backgrounds of students.

Results Adjusted for Student Background

Table 3 describes the results of analyses examining the relationships of each
outcome measure with SES and sex. Figure 5 displays the SES-adjusted results for mathematics. For this set of outcome measures, self-esteem has the
strongest relationship with SES; general health has the weakest relationship.

TABLE 3
HLM Estimates of Sex Differences and SES Gradients
New Brunswick Elementary School Climate Study, 1996[a]

	Sex difference (Female–Male)	SES gradient
Mathematics	−.069**	.147**
Reading	.172**	.183**
Science	−.148**	.150**
Writing	.437**	.163**
Self-esteem	−.052	.292**
General well-being	.215**	.161**
Sense of belonging	.338**	.122**
General health	−.131**	.085**

**p<.01
[a]Willms, 1994.

After controlling for sex and SES, there is less variation among schools and districts in their outcomes. The extent of the decrease is evident by comparing the variation among schools in mathematics scores within each district, before and after adjusting for students' background (i.e., comparing Fig. 4 with Fig. 5).

Although these analyses provide estimates of SES-adjusted levels of achievement, which provide a fairer means of comparing schools, they should not be misconstrued as estimates of school effects—that is, the added value attributable to what happens at school. Estimates of school effects require longitudinal data, such that gains in achievement can be assessed for each school (see Raudenbush & Willms, 1995; Willms & Kerckhoff, 1995).

Models for Dichotomous Variables

Often the dependent variable of interest is some event, such as whether a student attains mastery of a particular set of skills, drops out of school, begins using illegal drugs, or pursues a university-bound curriculum. In these cases we are interested in the *likelihood* or *probability* of the event occurring for children with certain characteristics. The logistic HLM provides a means for modeling dichotomous variables. The analysis furnishes estimates of the overall *likelihood* of an event occurring and the *odds ratio* for each variable. These are analogous to levels and gradients discussed earlier. It also provides shrunken estimates of likelihoods and odds ratios for each school or district.

Rumberger's (1995) study of dropping out of middle school employs a logistic HLM. His model specifies the probability of a child dropping out of school as a function of family background variables and several risk factors,

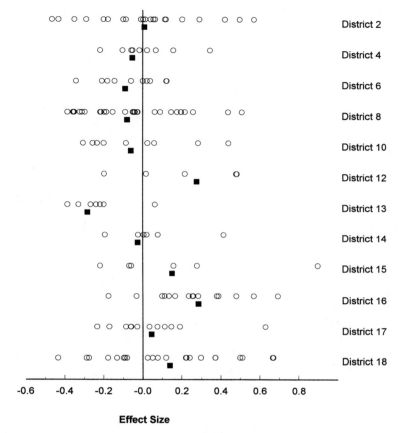

Effect Size

FIGURE 5

Estimates of average Grade 6 mathematics scores adjusted for
socioeconomic status in schools and districts in New Brunswick.
(O) School means, (■) district means. From New Brunswick Elementary
School Climate Study, 1996 (Willms, 1994).

such as having moved during the schooling year or having previously repeated a grade. His analysis indicated that on average, the likelihood of a
child dropping out of middle school was about 6%. However, children who
had repeated a grade were more than four times as likely to drop out, even
after controlling for their achievement scores in Grade 8 and a wide range of
variables describing their family SES and attitudes toward school.

When the dependent variable is a dichotomous variable, measured on
three or more occasions, a set of statistical techniques called survival analysis is appropriate for addressing certain questions. In survival analysis, the

interest is in the proportion of children that continue to display a particular trait over time, such as the proportion of children that remain in school from year to year during the secondary school period or the proportion of children that have never taken drugs. Survival analysis uses logistic regression techniques to examine the effects of independent variables on the likelihood that a child will change status (e.g., drop out of school or take drugs) at a particular time. The independent variables can be either time invariant, such as the child's sex, or time variant, such as the child's attitude toward school. Thus, one can ask questions such as "What is the likelihood that a boy will drop out of school at each grade level, compared with the likelihood of a girl dropping out?" It may be that the critical age for dropping out differs for boys and girls. It could also be that early school failure is an important determinant of dropping out for boys, whereas some other factor, such as low self-esteem, is a more important determinant of dropping out for girls.

The HLM survival analysis enables the researcher to ask such questions in a multilevel framework. In essence, it not only asks *why*, but also *when* particular events are likely to occur. Ma and Willms (1998) used an HLM survival analysis to examine the factors affecting students' persistence in taking advanced mathematics courses. The analysis found that there were two critical transitions when students were most vulnerable to dropping out of advanced mathematics: the transition from Grade 8 to Grade 9 and from Grade 11 to Grade 12. The rates of dropping out at these transition points varied among schools and were related to the SES composition of the school. We also found that children's early experience in mathematics had a strong influence at the first critical transition, but attitudes played a more dominant role at the second transition.

The analysis also uncovered an important finding pertaining to gender differences. Many accounts of gender differences in mathematics suggest that females "leak out" of mathematics, implying that it is a gradual process during the high school career. Our analysis found that this is not the case. In fact, the achievement scores and participation rates in advanced mathematics for females were comparable to those of males through to the end of Grade 11, but during the final year of high school a disproportionate number of females dropped out of advanced mathematics. This was the case even after taking into account students' prior test scores in mathematics.

PROVINCIAL AND DISTRICT-LEVEL ANALYSES THAT
EXAMINE SCHOOLING PROCESSES

After estimating adjusted levels of performance and social-class gradients, as described in the previous section, attention naturally turns to the two questions about why schools differ in their outcomes: "What policies and practices improve levels of schooling outcomes?" and "What policies and practices reduce inequalities in outcomes among students of differing status?" The goal is to identify and measure those schooling processes that might explain variation among schools in their outcomes and then to use the techniques of multilevel modeling to discern which factors are most important. However, identifying and monitoring schooling processes is even less of an exact science than estimating levels and gradients. The term *schooling processes* refers to a wide array of factors that describe the context and setting of a school (e.g., enrollment, average class size, teachers' experience, urban or rural), as well as evaluative factors that portray the internal workings of school life (e.g., how pupils are organized for instruction, the nature of interactions between students and teachers, and the formal and informal rules governing the operation of the school). Willms (1992) provided a schema for collecting data on schooling processes. It was derived from a review of the literature on school climate, and emphasized indicators that (1) provided a balanced picture of the schooling system across levels, (2) facilitated self-examination, (3) were viewed by teachers and principals as factors that could be changed through policy and practice, and (4) were relatively easy and inexpensive to measure.

Three of the processes that meet these criteria, and are important determinants of levels of academic achievement, are the disciplinary climate of the classroom and school, parental involvement in the child's learning both at school and at home, and *academic press*, which refers to the extent to which school staff value academic achievement and hold high expectations for all students. Valid and reliable indicators of these constructs can be obtained with student and teacher questionnaires. The questionnaires for the New Brunswick Elementary School Climate Study have about 20 items for each of these constructs.

These constructs have been found to be strongly related to academic achievement in national studies of school effectiveness (e.g., Ho & Willms, 1996; Ma & Willms, 1996; Pallas, 1988). Our experience with process measures suggests that classroom discipline is particularly important, as gauged through student reports of the extent to which classes are disrupted by a few troublesome students and the amount of time teachers spend dealing with disciplinary matters (Ma & Willms, 1996). With respect to academic press, peers also play an important a role in establishing high expectations and norms for success. Parental involvement at home has a strong effect on a child's learning and, at least at the upper elementary level, has a stronger effect than volunteering or participation in school governance.

Although national and provincial studies have helped to identify the most important processes, there is usually not enough statistical power to detect the effects of process variables in district-level analyses. Thus, the technology is not sophisticated enough to discern precisely why a particular school is performing poorly or well. Therefore, for the Elementary School Climate

Study, we simply prepare a two-page profile for each school on an annual basis. The profile is a graph that displays the school's levels of performance on each of the schooling outcomes listed in Table 2. The profile also provides the school's scores on several dimensions of disciplinary climate, academic press, and parental involvement. Teachers and administrators have used these profiles to inform their discussions concerning the school's mission and their plans for school improvement. This work is in its early stages. We intend to extend the school profile to cover other schooling processes, including teacher morale and commitment, the instructional approach used by the teacher, and student–teacher relations.

An important aspect of school climate, which is especially relevant to questions concerning inequalities of outcomes, concerns the manner in which students are allocated to schools, classrooms, and instructional groups. Some schooling systems are highly differentiated because of residential segregation. Children are usually assigned to particular schools according to school *catchment areas*, and the geographical boundaries of these areas are seldom drawn with the aim of achieving a heterogeneous mix of students with respect to SES or ethnicity. But in addition to residential segregation, other district and school policies can further increase differentiation. For example, magnet schools, charter schools, and special schools for gifted students can result in greater between-school differentiation. Similarly, tracking and specialized programming at the secondary level tends to increase differentiation.

The extent to which students are differentiated is important because their reference group can have a substantial effect on schooling outcomes, over and above the effects associated with students' own ability and social class (Dreeben & Gamoran, 1986; McPherson & Willms, 1986; Willms, 1986). When disadvantaged students are concentrated in particular schools or classrooms, they tend to have poorer schooling outcomes than if they were in less differentiated settings. Students from advantaged backgrounds tend to do well in most settings, especially when teachers adopt techniques appropriate for heterogeneous groups (Cohen & Lotan, 1995). This contextual effect is attributable not only to peer effects but also to other factors associated with school climate. For example, teachers in classrooms with a disproportionately high percentage of students who have learning or behavior problems are likely to find it difficult to maintain a positive disciplinary climate or to achieve a high level of parental support. Consequently, gradients are more likely to be steeper in highly differentiated systems.

Multilevel modeling can be used to examine the extent of differentiation for a schooling system, either along social class lines or between minority and majority groups (Willms & Paterson, 1995). It can also help administrators discern whether observed differentiation is occurring predominantly between schools within communities or between classrooms and programs

within schools. In the same way that multilevel models can be used to estimate the effects of various aspects of school climate on levels of performance, they can be extended to examine the effects of differentiation on
gradients.

POLICY IMPLICATIONS

HLM is a powerful analytical tool that can be used to achieve more exacting
analyses of monitoring data. Like any analytical tool, it cannot compensate
for deficiencies in the quality of data collected. However, the framework on
which HLM is based, and the wide range of problems to which it can be
applied, compels one to consider collecting data that can be useful for
addressing policy-relevant questions. Many monitoring systems have emphasized simple comparisons among schools in their average levels of performance, without paying attention to the social context of the schools or to
the factors that lead to improved performance. When analysts appreciate
the possibilities afforded by HLM, they tend to shift their focus away from
this good-schools/bad-schools paradigm and design better monitoring programs. With better data, their analyses can emphasize changes in school and
district performance over time, examine inequalities in outcomes among
advantaged and disadvantaged groups, and ask questions about the effects
of policies and practices aimed at improving schooling outcomes.

A simple example illustrates this point. One of the most controversial
issues in educational practice, not only among policy makers but also among
teachers and parents, is whether children ultimately benefit by repeating a
grade when they have not adequately learned the subject matter for a particular grade. The research on this issue is unequivocal: it indicates that children make the best progress if they are promoted with their peers (Shepard &
Smith, 1989). Studies that have compared retained and promoted students
with equivalent academic ability have found that retained students tend to
fall further behind academically and are more prone to dropping out of
school during the middle and secondary school years (Rumberger, 1995). In
Canada and the United States, despite these findings, policies on grade
retention vary considerably among school districts. In many cases, the decision to retain a child is a school matter and is often at the discretion of a
classroom teacher. Given this widespread variation in retention policies and
practices, a basic element of monitoring systems should be the tracking of
all students' progress from grade to grade during their schooling career.
However, it seems that few monitoring systems have sufficient data to address even basic questions like, "What proportion of students are retained at
each grade level?" or "Is there a long-term trend toward less retention?" If
the requisite data were available, the analyst could use HLM to address

questions such as "What types of students are most likely to repeat a grade?"; "Do schools vary in their retention rates?"; and "What school-level factors are related to retention rates?"

Can monitoring efforts meet the needs of policy makers and teachers? If monitoring systems are to furnish information that can inform policy decisions and lead to better classroom practice, two requirements must be met. First, policy makers must reconsider the kind of data that are being collected. Assessment procedures need to be extended beyond testing in reading and mathematics to cover a broad range of outcomes, including noncognitive outcomes such as self-esteem and physical health. The monitoring must also garner information about aspects of schooling processes, such as the disciplinary climate of the school, student-staff relations, homework practices, and parental involvement. The measures must be sensitive to changes in school policy and practice and responsive to the efforts of school staff. Second, we require analyses that extend beyond simple comparisons of schools or districts in their average test scores. If monitoring is to be used for purposes of accountability, comparisons should emphasize changes in school performance relative to a fixed standard and take into account the socioeconomic characteristics of the school. They also must also portray the extent of inequalities along social-class lines and between the sexes. Analyses are more useful to administrators and teachers if they address some of the *when* and *why* questions: When do the critical transitions occur for students as they progress through the schooling system? Why do some schools have better academic results than others? How are students allocated to different types of programs? What is the nature of the school and classroom learning climate in these programs? Hierarchical linear modeling provides an analytic framework and is the appropriate tool for analysing multilevel data.

References

Beaton, A. E., Mullis, I. V. S., Martin, M. O., Gonzalez, E. J., Kelly, D. L., & Smith, T. A. (1996). *Mathematics achievement in the middle school years*: IEA's Third International Mathematics and Science Study (TIMSS). Chestnut Hill, MA: Boston College.
Bryk, A. S., & Raudenbush, S. W. (1992). *Hierarchical linear models for social and behavioral research: Applications and data analysis methods.* Newbury Park, CA: Sage.
Cohen, E. G., & Lotan, R. A. (1995). Producing equal-status interaction in the heterogeneous classroom. *American Educational Research Journal, 32*(1); 99–121.
Dreeben, R., & Gamoran, A. (1986). Race, instruction, and learning. *American Sociological Review, 51,* 660–669.
Frempong, G., & Willms, J. D. (1998, April). *Social class gradients in middle school students' mathematics achievement: A multivariate multilevel analysis of the TIMSS data.* Paper presented at the annual meeting of the American Educational Research Association, San Diego.
Goldstein, H. (1995). *Multilevel statistical models* (2nd ed.). London: Arnold.
Ho, S.-C., & Willms, J. D. (1996). The effects of parental involvement on eighth grade achievement. *Sociology of Education, 69,* 126–141.

Kuppermintz, H., Ennis, M. M., & Hamilton, L. S. (1995). Enhancing the validity and usefulness of large-scale educational assessments: INELS 88 mathematics achievement. *American Educational Research Journal, 32*(3), 523–554.

Ma, X., & Willms, J. D. (1995, April). *The effects of school disciplinary climate on eighth grade achievement.* Paper presented at the annual meeting of the American Educational Research Association, San Francisco.

Ma, X., & Willms, J. D. (1998). *Dropping out of advanced mathematics: How much do students and schools contribute to the problem?* Manuscript presented for publication.

McPherson, A. F., & Willms, J. D. (1986). The socio-historical construction of school contexts and their effects on contemporary pupil attainment in Scotland. In A. C. Kerckhoff (Ed.), *Research in sociology of education and socialization* (pp. 227–301). Greenwich, CT: JAI.

Muthen, B., Huang, L., & Booil, J. (1995). Opportunity to learn effects on achievement: Analytical aspects. *Educational Evaluation and Policy Analysis, 17*(3), 371–403.

Pallas, A. M. (1988). School climate in American high schools. *Teachers College Record, 89*(4), 541–553.

Raudenbush, S. W., & Bryk, A. S. (1986). A hierarchical model for studying school effects. *Sociology of Education, 59*, 1–17.

Raudenbush, S. W., & Willms, J. D. (1995). The estimation of school effects. *Journal of Educational and Behavioural Statistics, 20*, 307–335.

Rumberger, R. W. (1995). Dropping out of middle school: A multilevel analysis of students and schools. *American Educational Research Journal, 32*(3), 583–625.

Shepard, L. A., & Smith, M. L. (1989). Flunking grades: A recapitulation. In L. A. Shepard, & M. L. Smith (Eds.), *Flunking grades: Research and policies on retention* (pp. 214–235). London: Falmer.

Sirotnik, K. A. (1987). Evaluation in the ecology of schooling: The process of school renewal. In J. I. Goodlad (Ed.), *The ecology of school renewal: Eighty-sixth yearbook of the National Society of Education* (pp. 41–61). Chicago: University of Chicago Press.

Thum, Y. M. (1997). Hierarchical linear models for multivariate outcomes. *Journal of education and behavioral statistics, 22*(1), 77–108.

Willms, J. D. (1986). Social class segregation and its relationship to pupils' examination results in Scotland. *American Sociological Review 51*(2), 224–241.

Willms, J. D. (1992). *Monitoring school performance: A guide for educators.* Lewes: Falmer.

Willms, J. D. (1994). The Elementary School Climate Study. Proposal submitted to the Social Science and Humanities Research Council.

Willms, J. D. (1996). Indicators of mathematics achievement in Canadian elementary schools. In HRDC (Ed.), *Growing up in Canada: National longitudinal study of children and youth* (pp. 69–82). Ottawa, Ontario: Human Resources Development Canada and Statistics Canada.

Willms, J. D. (1997). Literacy skills and social class. *Policy Options, 18*(6), 22–26.

Willms, J. D., & Kerckhoff, A. C. (1995). The challenge of developing new social indicators. *Educational Evaluation and Policy Analysis, 17*(1), 113–131.

Willms, J. D., & Paterson, L. (1995). A multilevel model for community segregation. *Journal of Mathematical Sociology, 20*(1), 23–40.

PART

V

American Educational Policy Making: Past and Future

American Educational Policy: Constructing Crises and Crafting Solutions

GREGORY J. CIZEK and VIDYA RAMASWAMY
University of Toledo

Policy making is frequently the business of responding or reacting. When a problem, issue, or situation arises that is not adequately addressed by existing mechanisms (legal, procedural, regulatory, etc.), then policies are often developed or revised so that they better respond to the diversity of contexts to which they are applied. The more serious the problem, issue, or situation is, the more far-reaching the policy development is likely to be. A problem that reaches crisis proportions cries out for remedy by legislators and educational policy makers.

One starting point of this chapter is the observation that educational policy making in the United States appears, largely, to be crisis driven. That is, policy development in education is prompted by the presence of a crisis. Unfortunately, it also appears that American education, from the perspective of those who comment from within the field, is in a pervasive, continual state of crisis—or, at least, in a continual state of crisis *claims*. If crises are related to policy development in American education, then claims of crisis themselves warrant scrutiny.

The following sections of this chapter examine the phenomenon of crisis in American education. First, the chapter investigates the meaning of the word *crisis*. Second, the chapter reports on a literature review that describes the extent of crises in U.S. education since the 1960s. Third, the chapter

Handbook of Educational Policy

497

attempts to distill factors that prompt education professionals to conclude that a crisis exists, common aspects of proposed solutions, the effectiveness of the remedies, and ownership of educational crises. The chapter concludes with recommendations of several alternatives to the current crisis orientation of educational policy making.

WHAT IS A CRISIS?

On October 22, 1962, President John Kennedy revealed that an offensive military buildup was occurring in Cuba. His subsequent deployment of an air and naval blockade of Cuba created a tension between the United States and the Soviet Union such that the two countries began preparations for nuclear warfare. Six days later, Kennedy and Soviet premier Khrushchev negotiated a diplomatic solution that eventually ended the crisis. This situation, the so-called Cuban Missile Crisis, looms in American history as a clear illustration of a true crisis: an event or set of circumstances which, if unabated, threatens significant, irreversible harm.

A crisis need not portend only substantial harm, however. According to *Webster's Ninth New Collegiate Dictionary*, a crisis can be "the turning point for better or worse in an acute fever or disease," or simply "a decisive moment." The connotation of harm is also presented though, with an alternative meaning of crisis being "an unstable or crucial time or state of affairs in which a decisive change is impending; *esp.*, one with the distinct possibility of a highly undesirable outcome" (*Webster's*, 1985, p. 307).

The milder connotation of the term crisis signifies simply a decision point. According to this definition, most of human existence could be said to be spent in crisis, in that humans make decisions—from pedestrian to profound—thousands of times each day. However, the stronger connotation suggests that whatever action (or inaction) occurs at that point influences whether the resolution of the problem or issue is likely to be highly favorable or unfavorable. A crisis presents a decisive moment in which whatever decision is made results in decisive change. It is this stronger sense of the word that is probably most frequently encountered in common usage. The following section examines claims about decisive moments—crises—in education and whether decisive changes have resulted.

EDUCATION IN CRISIS

Research in any disciplinary area can be seen as problem driven. All researchers address problems—sometimes theoretical, sometimes applied in nature. Problems are sometimes solved, although the process of research frequently does not end with a solution; rather, it culminates in refining the questions asked, delimiting the universe of possible solutions, or generating new problems. Speaking specifically about the field of education, and about the mechanism by which educational research affects educational policy, Glass (1987) stated the matter succinctly: "Researchers do not solve problems, they set them" (p. 9). If that is the case, educational researchers are prolific indeed.

The Extent of Crises in Education

As one strategy for examining the hypothesized presence of a crisis orientation in educational research and policy making, a review of research was conducted. The purpose of the review was not to identify all relevant materials, nor to estimate some proportion of the universe of educational research focussing on crises. The review process was, admittedly, not as rigorous or exhaustive as that which might be prepared for a dissertation chapter on a specific topic. Instead, the purpose of the review was only to gauge, roughly, the extent to which educational problems are cast as crises.

Two sources were used for the review. First, the ERIC database, a collection of research reports, evaluations, conference papers and presentations, and journal articles pertaining to the field of education, was searched. The ERIC search was limited to more recent entries—those from 1966 to the present. It is recognized that this source would not contain all relevant work because the ERIC system is somewhat selective in soliciting and accepting submissions for entry into the database. The ERIC search also does not catalog theses or dissertations. We judged, however, that uncataloged conference papers, project reports, program evaluations, and products of graduate student research would probably have less influence on educational policy making than more accessible, cataloged, published works.

A second source was the library collection of our own university—a medium-sized public institution in the midwestern United States. This source was used for the purpose of including books and other nonprint holdings on the topic of crisis and to sample materials published prior to 1966. Admittedly the holdings of a single university library do not capture the universe of published works on the topic. However, if a bias exists, it would favor inclusion of more popular, influential works over less influential ones. As a check on the comprehensiveness of the local holdings, a search was conducted via a database of all holdings of all public universities and all participating private universities in the state. This search identified only a few items not previously identified. It is likely that a search of the Library of Congress holdings would have revealed additional items.

Search Results

Using the key word search method for terms used in the titles or abstracts of ERIC entries, a total of 6024 entries were identified containing the keyword *crisis*. Using the same key word, 3314 library holdings were identified. A preliminary review of these results indicated that the search returned many entries for crises related to a variety of topics not directly bearing on education, such as energy, health care, ecology, violence, child care, insurance, midlife crises, and so on. Additional key words were subsequently added to the search in an attempt to further limit the results to materials more directly related to education. For both the ERIC and library searches, the following key word combinations were used: crisis and classroom, crisis and education, crisis and school(s). Table 1 shows the results of these combinations.

The design of the search procedure may have failed to identify additional works that might have been included. Because the search used ERIC and library sources in which the term crisis was used in the abstract, summary, or title of the work, books or articles that clearly focused on specific educational crises in American elementary and secondary education but did not actually use the term in their abstract or title may have been overlooked. It is difficult to evaluate the nature or extent of this potential bias.

All items identified in the search were further reviewed for possible inclusion in a final set of materials. In the set of materials identified in the ERIC database, the set was further reduced to include only the following: materials written in the English language; materials dealing with American education; and materials cataloged as journal articles (denoted with the prefix EJ), as opposed to materials entered as other education-related documents (denoted ED). This procedure also probably created a bias in favor of more accessible, influential materials, and reduced the set of ERIC materials to 356 items. All abstracts for this set of materials were read to determine whether the article should be retained for further analysis. A subjective process was used in this final step to eliminate a few materials that appeared as journal articles and met key word search criteria but did not seem to directly focus on an educational crisis. For example, an article by Bledsoe (1978) was

TABLE 1
Literature Review Search Results

Key word(s)/descriptor(s)	ERIC search results	Library search results
Crisis	6024	3314
Crisis and education	2275	179
Crisis and classroom	306	9
Crisis and school(s)	1446	72

identified in the ERIC search because of an abstract which read, in part, "More teachers should learn to accommodate needs of children experiencing a values crisis associated with divorce. First step is for school system, schools, and teachers to become better prepared to teach human values." This article was not retained for further analysis.

In the set of materials identified in the library holdings search, a similar process was used. Abstracts of all materials were read to determine whether the material was available in the English language, dealt with American education, and focused on a primarily education-related issue. Items that did not meet these criteria were not retained for further review.

Varieties of Crisis

Even limiting the search as described, hundreds of books and journal articles describing crises in American education remained. An attempt was made to organize these materials into logical sets. For example, some items had an international focus, comparing educational problems in the United States with those in other countries or regions, including Africa, Austria, Australia, Canada, Europe, Germany, Great Britain, Japan, Poland, South Africa, and the Soviet Union. We concluded that the American educational system is not the only one in crisis.

A second group of materials dealt with educational crises in the United States, but at a broad level. At the most global level, some writers situated problems in American education as part of a larger context. For example, a book by Bereday (1969) reported on the proceedings of the International Conference on the World Crisis in Education (see also Coombs, 1985). Griffin and Falk (1993) contextualized the issue as part of "a planet in crisis." A book of proceedings from a conference at the University of Minnesota described the urgent educational tasks precipitated by the "crisis of mankind" (University of Minnesota, 1947). Several authors situated educational crises as part of a larger societal crisis (e.g., Keach, Fulton, & Gardner, 1967), a cultural crisis (e.g., Agger & Goldstein, 1971; Griffen & Marciano, 1972; Johnson, 1951), or as one element in an "age of crisis" (Broekman, 1997).

Focusing at a somewhat narrower level, though still perceiving general educational crises, a third group of materials addressed the crises of western education (Dawson, 1961), liberal education (McKenzie, 1995), and Catholic education (Koob, 1994). More than 20 books and journal articles described a general crisis in American elementary and secondary education (e.g., Fine, 1947; Scott, Hill, & Burns, 1959; Stanley, 1980). More than 50 books and articles addressed crises in American higher education (e.g., Froomkin, 1983; Sommer, 1995). Numerous books and articles targeted a crisis in urban education (e.g., Kantor & Brenzel, 1992; Kerber & Bommarito, 1965); one author addressed the crisis of suburban youth (Larkin, 1979). Some writers identified educational crises according to specified subgroups of students, including adolescents (Lerner, 1994), African American males (O'Brien, 1989), Chicanos/Latinos (Rodriguez, 1994), and homeless children (Gore, 1990). Several authors narrowed the issue to that of crisis in American secondary education (e.g., Brown, 1984; Eulie, 1985; Wittes, 1970). The narrowest of the general crisis works focused specifically on a crisis in curriculum reform (Guyton, 1984).

Three other groupings of research and writings about educational crises in the United States could be discerned. One group of materials targeted highly specific crises related to discrete aspects of education. A sampling of these writings identified numerous crises in such diverse areas as character and citizenship (Longstreet, 1989; Starratt, 1994); school food service (Pannell, 1990); liability insurance (Munson, 1986); home-school relationships (Wise & Thornburg, 1978); school boards (Pois, 1964); testing (Glass, 1979); scheduling (Distenfeld & Richardson, 1983); school building heating, ventilation, and energy usage (Wiles, 1979); learning styles (Gibbons & Phillips, 1978); and crises precipitated by site-based management (Lausberg, 1990) and the need for an additional fourth grade classroom (Tyson, 1993).

A second set of materials described what authors called *identity crises* related to some profession or area in the field of education. The literature review revealed that all of the following experienced (or are still experiencing) identity crises: art education; physical education, early childhood special education, elementary and middle school social sciences, inorganic chemistry, school psychology, the social sciences, higher education generally, and community college instructors specifically.

The final set of writings addressed subject-specific crises; 108 titles were identified as focusing on subjects taught in American elementary and secondary school classrooms. This set was of particular interest because it revealed that the sense of crisis in American education extends across nearly all subject areas in elementary and secondary education. (Although not the focus of this research, the sense of crisis apparently extends into many disciplines of postsecondary education as well.)

Table 2 illustrates a sample of the writings produced by the ERIC and library searches related to subject-specific crises. At least one caveat is warranted regarding the list provided in Table 2. The list shows only one sample reference for each variety of crisis. Frequently—for example in math and science—numerous works have been written on a topic. However, in an attempt to balance the goals of informing the reader and maintaining a manageable reference list for this chapter, only one illustrative reference is cited for each subject area.

Because the ERIC search was limited to more recent holdings (i.e., 1966-present), it was expected to reveal a substantial representation of writings related to crises in science and mathematics that dominated the educational policy debates of the 1960s and 1970s. As expected, crises in math and science were most frequently cited; crises in literacy and special education

TABLE 2
Sample References for Subject-Area-Specific Crises

Subject area	Sample reference
Agricultural education	Swanson, 1991
Art education	Topping, 1990
Biology education	Yager, 1982
Business education	Bronner, 1991
Calculus education	Kast, 1993
Computer-assisted design (CAD) training	Yuen, 1990
Computer literacy	Molnar, 1978
Drama/theater education	Rough, 1994
English	Eagleton, 1991
Gifted education	Renzulli & Reis, 1991
Health education	Greensher, 1978
History	Fitch, 1988
Journalism	Rische, 1977
Legal education	Martini, 1996
Literacy	Ruiz, 1993/1994
Literary education	Squire, 1985
Literature	Farrell, 1981
Mathematics education	Stanic, 1986
Music education	Prescott, 1981
Physical education	Stroot, 1994
Physics education	Layman, 1983
Poetry	Wade & Sidaway, 1990
Reading	Chall, Jacobs, & Baldwin, 1990
Science education	Cadoree, 1990
Special education	Miller, 1981
Vocational education	Jacobs, 1993
Writing	Brereton, 1978

were also mentioned repeatedly. Perhaps the most striking aspect revealed in Table 2 is related to the pervasiveness of a sense of crisis, with crises being asserted as affecting nearly every aspect of the elementary and secondary curriculum—if not from A to Z, at least from A to V—ranging from agricultural to vocational education.

We conclude that crisis is a pervasive and enduring feature of American schooling, if only as reflected in professional commentary and scholarship within the field of education. The next section of this chapter, examines the sufficiency of evidence marshaled to support the many and varied claims of educational crises.

Evidence of Crises in Education

An abundance of evidence often accompanies the pronouncement of a crisis. For example, in the so-called Cuban Missile Crisis mentioned previously, American intelligence reports from within Cuba, U.S. military surveillance photographs, diplomatic contacts, and other sources of information provided an accumulation of data to support the dire declaration.

A second purpose of the review of research reported in this chapter was to examine the extent to which evidence accompanies declarations of crisis in American education. Four evidentiary possibilities were considered: (1) quantitative or statistical evidence, (2) qualitative or anecdotal evidence, (3) a combination of quantitative and qualitative evidence, and (4) no evidence provided. To address this second purpose, a subset of the published works focusing on subject-area specific crises was selected. Publications were selected from the areas listed in Table 2, with an attempt to represent each area with at least one published work. In some subject areas, only a single published piece was identified (i.e., literature). In other areas for which multiple publications existed, the subset was formed by including only those references that would likely be retrievable by others interested in this topic (e.g., an article comparing the crises in special education in the United States and Canada that appeared in the *British Columbia Journal of Special Education* was not included in the subset.)

A total of 35 published works were retained in the final subset. Each publication was read and coded to indicate the presence or absence of evidence supporting the claim of a crisis, the type of evidence, the presence or absence of suggested solutions, and types of solutions. Before proceeding, it should be noted that the coding initially involved only recording a characteristic, without a corresponding judgment about the quality of the evidence or logical connection of the evidence to the claim of crisis. For this step, *any* presentation of material purporting to support the claim that a crisis existed was recorded as evidence without judging the merits of that evidence in support of the claim.

Of the 35 publications involving subject-area specific crises, a majority ($n = 30$, 85.7%) included some evidence in support of the claim that a crisis existed. Five publications (14.3%) gave no evidence in support of the claim of a subject-area crisis. Of the works providing any type of evidence, the most frequently occurring evidentiary type was quantitative (37.1%), followed by qualitative (31.4%), and a combination of evidentiary types (17.1%).

An example of the typical presentation of quantitative evidence provided can be seen in an article by Molnar (1978) who predicted a coming crisis in computer literacy attributable to a proliferation of publications related to science and technology. Molnar reported that nearly 100,000 scientific and technological journals are produced in the world and that 80,000 technical reports are produced in the United States, with that number increasing at a rate of 14% per year.

An example of typical presentation of qualitative information as support for the presence of a crisis is found in an article by Gundlach who chronicled complaints from college professors about the "new illiteracy" among high school students (1981, p. 14). Interestingly, one writer's (Miller, 1981) argument regarding a crisis in special education was buttressed using a *lack* of data on the topic as supporting evidence.

Finally, some authors chose to present both quantitative and qualitative data. For example, in the course of addressing the crisis in literature, Farrell (1981) both described the agonizing experience of listening to censors at textbook adoption hearings and offered statistical information about American reading habits (e.g., 68% of Americans had not read a book in the past five or more years). Another example comes from the work of Renzulli and Reis (1991) in their discussion of gifted education. The authors summarized large-scale data collections, which show average Japanese students achieving higher than the top 5% of American students in college preparatory mathematics; the authors also presented an anecdote related to the inability of a small group of children to solve problems from a fifth grade mathematics textbook.

Quality of the Evidence

Overall, quantitative evidence was cited most frequently, and changes in counts were often cited as quantitative evidence. As noted earlier, the appropriateness of this kind of evidence was not evaluated in the process of recording whether evidentiary support of a crisis claim existed. However, the quality of any empirical data or logical rationales must be taken into account when evaluating the evidence in support of a crisis. In many of the published works examined as part of this research, though, authors did not engage in internal evaluation of the evidence, and the evidence presented did not provide *prima facie* support for the claim that a crisis exists.

One aspect of this problem is illustrated in the article by Molnar (1978), cited earlier, which focused on an impending crisis in computer literacy. Molnar's quantitative rationale included reference to the burgeoning number of periodicals in science and technology. In this case, the tacit assumption seems to be that an increasing number of periodicals produces a negative consequence—a crisis—although that case is not made. It seems equally plausible that a *decrease* in the number of scientific and technological journals would also be cause for concern, as would stagnation in the number of journals under given conditions. Also, it is not at all clear that an increase in publications necessitates additional computer literacy; it is conceivable that the publications referred to target audiences who already possess the type of literacy advocated.

A related problem common to many publications that provide quantitative evidence in support of a claim that an educational crisis exists is related to reliance on discrepancy data. For example, crises in teacher education have been announced based on quantitative evidence of disparities between proportions of teachers and students of various ethnic groups (e.g., King, 1993; Rong & Preissle, 1997), although Cizek (1995) has shown that numerical discrepancies alone do not provide a sound basis for concluding that a crisis exists.[1] Of itself, data that show differences, discrepancies of proportion, or deviation from prior trends do not signal that a decision point is at hand that portends great benefit or harm.

Proposed Solutions for Educational Crises

In 31 of the 35 publications reviewed, authors offered some advice about how to address the crisis that had been identified. In five of the publications, authors identified crises but failed to propose strategies to address them. Advice within the individual sources varied from a single recommendation to a constellation of remedies. Overall, a total of 61 recommendations were made. An analysis and distillation of the content of the recommendations yielded four general categories of solutions: teachers, curriculum, enrollment, and other.

Authors tended to perceive teachers as the policy route most likely to promote a satisfactory resolution to a crisis. Twenty-nine suggestions were made regarding teachers' attitudes, training, pedagogy, and teaching conditions; 15 recommendations concerned curriculum innovation and evaluation; three suggestions centered on student enrollment changes (these were contained in articles that identified an enrollment decrease as the cause of a crisis); and 14 proposals recommended assistance from other sources such as administrators, parents, industry, and so on.

Recommendations related to teachers are exemplified in the works such as Sobel (1983) who suggested ways of improving conditions for math teachers in the form of higher salaries for practicing teachers and more favorable

---

[1]Claims of an impending educational crisis due to a shortage of elementary and secondary school teachers has been a stable feature of the educational literature for some time. Recently, the claim has again received attention in the press and was elevated in its credibility by inclusion in the 1998 presidential state of the union address. However, the claim has been examined by Feistritzer (1998) who calls to mind an interesting observation about the use of data in support of crisis claims. Feistritzer used data from the National Center for Education Statistics (NCES) and the U.S. Bureau of Labor Statistics (BLS) to allay fears of impending teacher shortages. She quotes a BLS official familiar with the data on teacher supply and demand, who concluded that "We don't see anything that would indicate there will be general teacher shortages" (p. 8). Apparently, sometimes even the presence of data to the contrary is insufficient to head off claims of crisis.

loans for teachers in training. Teachers were implored to teach more passionately (Farrell, 1981), to be more responsive to high ability students (Renzulli and Reis, 1991), and to more completely integrate computers into the educational process (Kelly, 1981).

Recommendations centering on curriculum reform are illustrated in the work of Renzulli and Reis (1991) who advocated redressing the problem of "dumbing down" of the curriculum in gifted education programs. Curriculum-related recommendations included those at a general level, such as the suggestion that American students should have a common literary experience (Ostler & Dahlin, 1995). Other authors mentioned specific changes to the curriculum in a field, with suggestions ranging from moving toward a multidisciplinary approach in special education (Skrtic, 1986) or a more quantitative approach in history (Fitch, 1988).

The third category of suggestions had to do with increasing student enrollment. Low enrollments were frequently mentioned vis-à-vis post-Sputnik efforts to promote achievement in mathematics and science (Kelly, 1981; Layman, 1983; Yager, 1982).

Support from other sources was also sought to rectify a crisis situation. Public support was identified as a means of helping art education to overcome a crisis (Hoffa, 1979). Bass (1982) described the role parents can play in solving the problem of declining music education programs. Vogel (1991) recommended a cooperative effort by physical educational specialists, classroom teachers, administrators, parents, and health industry experts to solve the crisis in youth physical fitness and wellness.

Analysis of the proposed solutions to educational crises reveals that when solutions are proposed they share what might be called a top-down perspective, as represented by solutions geared toward improving teaching, curriculum, and enrollment, or garnering outside assistance. Interestingly, no author mentioned factors related to students, families, or sociocultural factors—arguably three of the most powerful variables in the mix.

For example, recent research has revealed the importance of student volition (see Corno, 1993) and that in the United States effort receives less emphasis than ability, compared to Japan where families encourage beliefs in effort within a climate of interpersonal cooperation (Holloway, 1988). If it is desired that students spend more time in tasks related to educational achievement, it may be necessary for schools to concentrate more on developing students' interest in education and sense of confidence in their own capabilities as effective solutions to general educational crises (Deci, Vallerand, Pelletier, & Ryan, 1991).

Other scholars have argued that any general educational crisis in the United States is more social than academic. A study of Indochinese refugee families in the United States found that families, including siblings, played a significant role in inculcating a sense of personal efficacy and love of learning in children (Caplan, Choy, & Whitmore, 1992). Other studies have demonstrated that time spent on homework in combination with help received from families for doing homework may be a more powerful predictor of mathematics achievement in the elementary grades than the curriculum used in schools (Stigler, Lee, Lucker, & Stevenson, 1982). Increasingly, research is demonstrating that a successful educational system needs to take into account the ways in which student motivation to succeed can be strengthened with the help of teachers and families. Schools cannot function merely as academic systems but are part of a larger social context, which must be addressed as part of crafting solutions to educational crises.

CRISIS OWNERSHIP AND THE POLITICS
OF EDUCATIONAL POLICY MAKING

The ubiquity of crisis claims in education has reached, some might say, crisis proportions. The review of literature conducted for this chapter unearthed thousands of documents about crises in education. With only one notable exception, described later in this section, the review of literature revealed no counterclaims or rebuttals of crisis claims.

The publications reviewed described crises covering virtually every aspect of schooling as a system: enrollment, personnel, curriculum, funding, organization, and functioning. The history of crisis claims is not only wide but enduring. The literature search revealed influential educators describing educational crises spanning the past 70 years, and much more. Filler (1965) compiled the writings of *Horace Mann on the Crisis in Education* during the 1800s in a book of the same title. Rury and Cassell (1993) chronicled the crisis of public schooling in a single urban city since 1920. Kilpatrick (1932) addressed *Education and the Social Crisis* in a book with that title. Books have described the entire American school system—from elementary schools to universities—as being in crisis in the 1940s (Fine, 1947), the 1950s (Scott, Hill, & Burns, 1959), the 1960s (Miller & Gilmore, 1965), the 1970s (Corwin, 1974), and the 1980s (Sommer, 1984). Given this long history of crisis, a more recent book with the title *To Save Our Schools, To Save Our Children: The Approaching Crisis in America's Public Schools* (Frady, 1985) seems a little tardy in predicting what has been documented for over half a century. A quotation reproduced in Silberman's book, *Crisis in the Classroom* (1970) illustrates the longevity of the sense of crisis:

> For more than a hundred years much complaint has been made of the unmethodical way in which schools are conducted, but it is only within the last thirty that any serious attempt has been made to find a remedy for the state of things. And with what result? Schools remain exactly as they were. (p. 158)

The longevity of the sense of crisis is highlighted not simply in the fact that the source of the quotation perceived a problem that was extant for more than 100 years, but also in the fact that the remarks were penned by John Comenius, an educator writing in 1632. Finally, although it focuses on a single subject area, the title of a more recent article seems to capture most accurately the lingering crisis state of affairs in American education: "Art Education in (Perpetual) Crisis" (Hoffa, 1979).

A Dissenting Opinion

Given the intensity of debates on nearly every aspect of educational policy, it is difficult to imagine that debates have not arisen regarding the crisis state of American education. Occasionally, an author has expressed refinement or mild dissent. For example, Ayers (1994) described a selective crisis in American education; Kagan and Tippins (1993/1994) explored some of the benefits of schools in crisis; Fantini (1982) urged an end to the crisis-oriented approach to problems in urban schools. Houston and Schneider (1994) did not directly refute the popular notion of trouble in the American educational system but objected to the process used for constructing the U.S. Department of Education's state-by-state ranking of academic performance.

One source, however, flatly disputed the notion of crisis in the American school system. In their book of the same title, two commentators, educational researchers David Berliner and Bruce Biddle, asserted that troubles in American education are a "manufactured crisis" (1995). Berliner and Biddle did not focus on a specific crisis, such as the subject-specific crises represented in Table 2. Instead, their work is a reaction to the sense of a general crisis in American education.

Berliner and Biddle's (1995) work is unique on several counts. First, their book presents the case that nearly all aspects of American schooling labeled "in crisis" by other authors—including student performance, international comparisons, educational spending, shortages of scientists and engineers, the quality of teaching and textbooks, decline in civic and moral virtue, and public discontent with American education—are not nearly so troubled. Also, in contrast to many of the writings on educational crises reviewed for this chapter, their work also relies more on data and logical analysis than it does on rhetoric or undersubstantiated claims.

Their assertions about American education are also outliers in the universe of crisis literature. For example, although many recent American educational reformers and policy makers have discovered much to emulate in the educational practices of other countries, Berliner and Biddle began their book by condemning Japanese schools "for brutality and for promoting over-achievement" (1995, p. 2). Berliner and Biddle also rejected many of the recommendations frequently mentioned as remedies for educational crises, such as curriculum reform or additional time spent by students on school subjects. Among other things, they suggested more research and more compassion as efficacious routes to school improvement.

```

Perhaps Berliner and Biddle's (1995) most curious thesis is that perceptions of crisis in American education are not merely unfounded, but are the product of "organized malevolence" on the part of neoconservative federal policymakers who were "throttling research and misusing evidence about education" (p. xiii). They identified the first publicly malevolent act as being the U.S. Department of Education's release of the influential document, A Nation at Risk (National Commission on Excellence in Education, 1983). Berliner and Biddle contended that a loose conspiracy of media elites, unelected bureaucrats, industrialists, and other right-wing malcontents—for example, newspaper columnist George Will, former assistant secretary of education Chester Finn, University of Chicago sociology professor Alan Bloom, religious leader Pat Robertson, and the philanthropic foundation of beer maker Adolph Coors—were responsible for creating, disseminating, and perpetuating the diverse and sundry myths about a purported American educational crisis.

According to Berliner and Biddle, the conspirators were abetted by a mass media that was willing and able to confuse the American populace. They argued that perceptions of crisis in American education and potential strategies derived from comparative studies are mere illusions:

> [F]or more than a dozen years, this groundless and damaging message has been proclaimed by major leaders of our government and industry and has been repeated endlessly by a compliant press. Good-hearted Americans have come to believe that the public schools of their nation are in a crisis state because they have so often been given this false message by supposedly credible sources. (1995, p. 3)

In deference to Berliner and Biddle's (1995) work, it is entirely plausible that the public sense of general crisis in American education may have been aroused in the 1980s following the release of A Nation at Risk. The authors have also demonstrated that some of the folklore of American educational problems certainly makes for sensational headlines and a heightened sense of crisis. For example, they referenced the dubious origins of surveys that supposedly compared "the public's lists of top school problems" from the 1940s and 1980s (p. 171). The root of the comparison is shown to lie more in urban legend than in historical fact.

However, their analysis is demonstrably incorrect on other counts. First, as the review of research on educational crises demonstrates, the sense of crisis in American education clearly predates the release of A Nation at Risk by several decades. The scientific requirement of "temporal precedence" (Cook & Campbell, 1979, p. 10) dictates that neither the education report, nor the contemporaneous conspirators mentioned by Berliner and Biddle, could possibly be identified as the cause for a phenomenon that began earlier in time. The literature of crisis in education demonstrates an abiding penchant for claims of general crisis in American education. Any search for causation must begin with the hundreds of books and articles bemoaning then-current states of affairs, cutting across political ideologies, authored
```

primarily by those within the profession, and beginning long before many of those identified as coconspirators by Berliner and Biddle were born.

Second, although a willing press and an ignorant public have been blamed for convoluted conspiracies ranging from the assassination of President Kennedy to alien landings at Roswell, New Mexico, these agents offer little power for explaining the pervasive sense of crisis about American education. An alternative hypothesis seems more likely: Public perceptions about the state of American education have been formed much more ably by the claims of crises and testimony of educational researchers—in research, books, journal articles, and commentaries, spanning almost a full century in time and nearly every aspect of the American schooling system in breadth.

CONCLUSIONS AND CONJECTURES
ABOUT CRISES IN EDUCATION

As Berliner and Biddle (1995) suggested, the message of educational crisis has been drummed into the heads of Americans for several decades. However, if Berliner and Biddle (1995) have seen the enemy, it is probably us. Educational crises are owned by their creators—educational analysts and researchers enmeshed in a culture of crisis. If educational policymaking is the business of responding to crises, there has been no lack of stimulus. A crisis orientation is weaved throughout decades, maybe centuries, of the literature on American education, produced from within the system. Educational crises appear to proliferate at an alarming rate, with crisis density increasing in the 1980s and 1990s. It is not known how this proliferation compares with other disciplines, only that education is sorely afflicted. Claims of crises infuse published writings in education research journals, books, and magazines. These sources reveal crises to be omnipresent, undifferentiated, and intractable.

The literature reviewed for this chapter reveals that crises are rarely foreseen, never reported as being prevented, and, despite an apparent multitude of opportunities, are almost never solved. (One notable exception is contained in a 1988 article by Reid titled, "School Lunch: A Crisis Overcome.") Despite an abundance of literature on crisis prevention and crisis management, educational crises do not appear to be tackled as these literatures would recommend. It is typical for a crisis to be merely claimed, accompanied most often by evidence of questionable quality and recommendations of unknown efficacy.

Further, education writers fail to make distinctions between varieties of crisis; the need for an extra fourth-grade class in the 1990s and the need to address explosive racial hostility in the schools of the 1960s are expressed on a par with each other. Even schoolchildren are enculturated into the ethos of crisis: One social studies journal article provided a simulation game for elementary school students called "The Chocolate Milk Crisis" to help children understand how to deal with the shortage of chocolate milk in their cafeteria (Derrico & Karsotis, 1981).

Educational researchers have not failed to suggest strategies for attenuating crises. For example, one book's subtitle offered a straightforward (and notably confident) precis of its contents: "A *Blueprint for Fixing What Is Wrong and Restoring America's Confidence in the Public Schools*" (Hagerty, 1995). However, even the works of educators who claim to have discovered and are willing to reveal the solutions for a debilitating crisis are apparently ignored, judged impractical, or simply passed by as attention is turned to yet another crisis. The literature on educational crises contains little in the way of follow-up reports that assess or document the efficacy of proposed courses of action and little solid guidance to inform policy makers.

With such a state of affairs, it can be tempting to view educational crises as mere fodder for political cannons or as the canons of educational policy making. Chicken Little said, "The sky is falling!" and returned to reiterate, "The sky is falling!" Education writers cry, "A crisis of this sort!" and later, "A crisis of another sort!" Both seem genuinely distressed when no one believes; both are easily ignored. If Chicken Little has the quality of consistency, writers in the field of education can boast of variety. Perhaps both protesteth too much.

Real challenges do exist in the arena of American education. They range from the mundane matters of configuring fourth-grade classrooms to the societal conundrum of race relations in a multicultural republic. Each pole presents decision points, and policy makers can craft strategies to respond to both. However, only some situations are truly crises. The following recommendations might further the goal of responding to all crises, great and small.

More Accurate Classification

A first and facile recommendation is that education writers refrain from invoking the term *crisis* in most situations. Vexing situations exist along a continuum, with crisis anchoring only one end. Temporary uncertainty about the place of inorganic chemistry in the science curriculum is an *issue*; bureaucratic regulations are a *nuisance*; the rising cost of liability insurance is a financial *problem*; lunchroom scheduling may range from *inconvenience* to *difficulty*; reductions in the rigor of school textbooks is a *concern*; absences of civic and moral virtue in students and vision on the part of educational leaders are a *shame*. In the United States, there may be crises, but they are qualitatively different than these dilemmas. The level of deprivation presented by the absence of chocolate milk from an elementary school cafeteria stands in marked contrast to the austerity described in a 1989 United Nations report on education in Tanzania that reported:

It is not uncommon to find a teacher standing in front of 80–100 pupils who are sitting on a dirt floor in a room without a roof, trying to convey orally the limited knowledge he has, and the pupils take notes on a piece of wrinkled paper using as a writing board the back of the pupil in front of him. There is no teacher guide for the teacher and no textbooks for the children. (cited in Samoff, 1994, p. 5)

More accurate categorization and less frequent invocation of crisis may have the desirable side effect of increasing the status of educational research. Educational researchers have openly repined their inability to compel educational policymakers or to translate research findings into effective legislation and classroom practice. The impotence of educational research was highlighted by Kaestle (1993, p. 23) who bemoaned "The Awful Reputation of Education Research" in the title of an article on that topic. Kennedy (1997) developed four hypotheses to account for the lack of influence of educational research on classroom practice. Kleine and Greene suggested other "factors contributing to the irrelevancy of educational research" (1992, p. 187). In a follow-up to Kaestle's article, Sroufe (1997) offered his suggestions for improving the awful reputation of educational research.

Ultimately, some of the hypotheses may be proved, and some suggestions for improving the reputation of educational research may be helpful. Regardless of progress on these fronts, we believe that a terrible trifecta involving crises in education may also help explain the comparatively poor reputation of educational research: Excessive claims of crisis; frequently inadequate evidence, and insufficiently demonstrated and practicable solutions may represent additional reasons why policy makers are not as moved by the claims of educational researchers as many would hope.

Apply the "So What?" Test

A second recommendation is that authors of publications illuminating educational problems should be more critical of the evidence when claiming a crisis. Consumers of such publications must also read with the same critical eye, constantly asking the rather frank question, "So what?" Application of the "So what?" test can be illustrated using one of the articles uncovered in the literature search, titled "The Crisis in Biology Education" (Yager, 1982), in which dramatic changes were proposed for secondary school science programs, materials, goals, and instruction. The author listed a wealth of evidence to support the claim of crisis. Among the evidence:

- No growth in students' interest in science across the high school years
- A greater interest in technology than in science
- Fewer than 10% of students are reported to be "attentive" in their high school science classes
- Only a modest percentage of high school graduates seem interested in pursuing science as a career

Reasonable application of the "So what?" test might disqualify all of the preceding evidence as bearing at all on the possibility of there being a crisis in high school biology. For example: (1) no rationale was provided for the expectation that there *ought* to be increasing interest in science across the 4 years of high school, and no evidence was given to suggest that interest in other subject areas was increasing at the expense of science; (2) there is no reason to believe students' greater interest in technology is inappropriate (it may indeed even be a positive factor in influencing students' interest in science); (3) no "index of mean attentiveness" was provided (the rate for science classes could be considerably *higher* than for, say, American government) tempting readers who had not been in close contact with large groups of adolescents lately to infer that 10% is a low value; and (4) only modest percentages of high school graduates pursue any given career, there being no ideal criterion by which to assess whether the "right" percentage are pursuing science. It may be that industry forecasts of shortages exist, specifying the need for a certain number of scientists compared to projected numbers of graduates. Even with such predictions in hand, a crisis may never materialize if the need for scientists falls short of projections, if the number of high school graduates increases, if graduates with backgrounds other than science are found to be qualified for the jobs, or if all of these occur.

Demonstrate the Effectiveness of Solutions

A third recommendation is that education professionals offer policy makers a firmer foundation for action. The review of literature conducted for this chapter shows that evidence to support proposed plans for addressing crises is often absent, skimpy, or equivocal. Policy makers should demand that specific, well-reasoned, and realizable remedies accompany well-justified claims of educational problems. It is too easy to suggest that increased funding is necessary or to chant the mantra that "more research" is needed. It is chimeric to proffer solutions touting improbable results, such as universal literacy, 100% graduate rates, and the like. It is insufficient to shout "We must get serious!" about this or that problem.

Proposals for change should also be accompanied by statements regarding reasonably anticipatable results. For example, in the case of the high school biology crisis, what results might likely be expected if the curriculum, pedagogy, and resources were changed as suggested by the author? Might we expect interest in science to exceed interest in technology or literature? Would attentiveness in biology classes reach 20%?

Additionally, the research conducted for this chapter revealed a marked tendency for proposed solutions to be predominately of the top-down variety. To name just a few, proposals for a more integrated curriculum, increased pay for teachers, a longer school year, or more developmentally appropriate pedagogy might individually make small contributions to an improved educational *system*. However, policy makers might do well to first ask what effect these changes would have on student *learning* and to recognize that improvements in one do not necessarily result in improvements in the other. For example, Berliner and Biddle (1995) reviewed the evidence for a longer school year and found that such a change might result in no student gains without dramatic changes in students' textbooks, which appear to constrain what students are exposed to in any academic year.

Top-down solutions also fail to take into account what is known about the most powerful influences on student learning. Even if *all* of the solutions mentioned earlier (integrated curriculum, increased pay, and so on) were carried out, there would likely be little impact if students were disinterested, resistant, or absent. It is important, therefore, that policymakers seek solutions that take into account the complexities of the educational process, such as student motivation, parental involvement, and community and cultural support for education. Thus, if more scientists are needed, it may not be enough to change the curriculum or change the teaching method. It may be necessary to find out why students are inattentive, attracted to other fields, or not profoundly affected by their science programs so that any potential solution is more meaningful and has greater potential for success. Policy makers cannot afford to be isolated from those for whose betterment the policy is being created.

A New Paradigm for Educational Policy Making

Our most fundamental, and admittedly most ethereal, recommendation is that educational policy making be radically reconceptualized. The paradigm that appears to characterize current policy development—constructing crises and crafting solutions—is a long-lived (if not particularly corrective) lens through which improvements in American education are pursued. The starting point for reconceptualization is also a stopping point: eschewing a crisis orientation.

Beyond avoiding casting each decision point as a crisis, a new approach to policy development would not involve responding or reacting to events, but innovation and anticipation of what challenges the future holds. Policies might always be needed to respond to problems in the current function of schools. But effective policy development should not simply be targeted at rectifying past or present ills but at identifying and refining the roles schools can perform well, who they serve, and which roles and services they are suited to contribute in the years ahead. Advances in educational policy development will also accrue from refining systems that are apparently already functioning smoothly today.

References

Agger, R. E., & Goldstein, M. N. (1971). *Who will rule the schools: A cultural class crisis.* Belmont, CA: Wadsworth.

Ayers, W. (1994). Can city schools be saved? *Educational Leadership, 51*(8), 60–63.

516   Gregory J. Cizek and Vidya Ramaswamy

Bass, L. P. (1982). The crisis in music education. *Music Educators Journal*, 68(7), 30–31.

Berliner, D. C., & Biddle, B. J. (1995). *The manufactured crisis: Myths, fraud, and the attack on America's public schools*. Reading, MA: Addison-Wesley.

Bereday, G. Z. F. (Ed.). (1969). *Essays on world education: The crisis of supply and demand*. New York: Oxford University Press.

Bledsoe, E. (1978). Divorce and values teaching. *Journal of Divorce*, 1(4), 371–379.

Brereton, J. (1978). Learning from the writing crisis. *Teachers College Record*, 80(2), 356–364.

Broekman, H. (1997). Education in an age of crisis. *Momentum*, 28(1), 52–55.

Bronner, M. (1991). Workforce 2001—Can we cope? The coming crisis in business education. *BEA Journal of Metropolitan New York*, 5, 7–12.

Brown, B. F. (1984). *Crisis in secondary education: Rebuilding America's high schools*. Englewood Cliffs, NJ: Prentice-Hall.

Cadoree, M. (1990). *The crisis in science education*. Washington, DC: Library of Congress, Science Reference Section, Science and Technology Division.

Caplan, N., Choy, M. H., & Whitmore, J. K. (1992). Indochinese refugee families and academic achievement. *Scientific American*, 266, 36–42.

Chall, J. S., Jacobs, C. A., & Baldwin, L. E. (1990). *The reading crisis: Why poor children fall behind*. Cambridge, MA: Harvard University Press.

Cizek, G. J. (1995). On the limited presence of African American teachers. *Review of Educational Research*, 65(1), 78–92.

Cook, T. D., & Campbell, D. T. (1979). *Quasi-experimentation: Design & analysis issues for field settings*. Boston: Houghton Mifflin.

Coombs, P. H. (1985). *The world crisis in education: The view from the eighties*. New York: Oxford University Press.

Corno, L. (1993). The best laid plans: Modern conceptions of volition and educational research. *Educational Researcher*, 22(2), 14–22.

Corwin, R. G. (1974). *Education in crisis: A sociological analysis of schools and universities in transition*. New York: Wiley.

Dawson, C. (1961). *The crisis of Western education*. New York: Sheed and Ward.

Deci, E. L., Vallerand, R. J., Pelletier, L. G., & Ryan, R. M. (1991). Motivation and education: The self-determination perspective. *Educational Psychologist*, 26, 325–346.

Derrico, P., & Karsotis, A. T. (1981). The chocolate milk crisis: A consumer economics simulation unit for grades 1–6. *Social Studies Journal*, 10(1), 18–21.

Distenfeld, J., & Richardson, D. (1983). Innovative ways of using staff members: The role of the school psychologist. *NASSP Bulletin*, 67(463), 105–109.

Eagleton, T. (1991). The enemy within. *English in Education*, 25(3), 3–9.

Eulie, J. (1985). The crisis in American secondary education: A failure of state leadership. *Clearing House*, 59(3), 137–142.

Fantini, M. D. (1982). Toward a national public policy for urban education. *Phi Delta Kappan*, 63(8), 544–546.

Farrell, E. J. (1981). Literature in crisis. *English Journal*, 70(1), 13–18.

Feistritzer, C. E. (1998, January 28). The truth about the "teacher shortage." *Wall Street Journal*, p. 8.

Filler, L. (1965). *Horace Mann on the crisis in education*. Yellow Springs, OH: Antioch.

Fine, B. (1947). *Our children are cheated: The crisis in American education*. New York: Holt.

Fitch, N. (1988). The crisis in history: Its pedagogical implications. *Historical Methods*, 21(3), 104–111.

Frady, M. (1985). *To save our schools, to save our children: The approaching crisis in America's public schools*. Far Hills, NJ: New Horizon Press.

Froomkin, J. (Ed.). (1983). *The crisis in higher education*. New York: Academy of Political Science.

Gibbons, M., & Phillips, G. (1978). Helping students through the self-education crisis. *Phi Delta Kappan*, 60(4), 296–300.

Glass, G. V (1979). Looking at minimal competence testing: Educator versus senator. *Education and Urban Society*, 12(1), 47–55.

Glass, G. V (1987). What works: Politics and research. *Educational Researcher*, 16(3), 5–11.

Gore, Jr., A. (1990). Public policy and the homeless. *American Psychologist*, 45(8), 960–962.

Greensher, J. (1978). Crisis in school health education. *Journal of the New York State School Board Association*, 13, 19–24.

Griffen, W. L., & Marciano, J. D. (Eds.). (1972). *Education for a culture in crisis*. New York: MSS Information Corp.

Griffin, D. R., & Falk, R. (Eds.). (1993). *Postmodern politics for a planet in crisis: Policy, process, and presidential vision*. Albany, NY: State University of New York Press.

Gundlach, R. A. (1981). Is there a writing crisis in the high school? *Momentum*, 12(4), 14–16.

Guyton, E. (1984). Curriculum reform: The crisis in teacher education. *Action in Teacher Education*, 6(3), 7–15.

Hagerty, R. (1995). *The crisis of confidence in American education: A blueprint for fixing what is wrong and restoring America's confidence in the public schools*. Springfield, IL: Charles C. Thomas.

Hoffa, H. (1979). Art education in (perpetual) crisis. *Art Education*, 32(1), 7–12.

Holloway, S. D. (1988). Concepts of ability and effort in Japan and the United States. *Review of Educational Research*, 58, 327–354.

Houston, P. D., & Schneider, J. (1994). Drive-by critics and silver bullets. *Phi Delta Kappan*, 75(10), 779–782.

Jacobs, J. (1993). Vocational education and general education: New relationship or shotgun marriage? *New Directions for Community Colleges*, 21(1), 75–84.

Johnson, C. S. (1951). *Education and the cultural crisis*. New York: Macmillan.

Kaestle, C. F. (1993). The awful reputation of educational research. *Educational Researcher*, 22(1), 23–31.

Kagan, D. M., & Tippins, D. J. (1993/1994). Benefits of crisis: The genesis or a school–university partnership. *Action in Teacher Education*, 15(4), 68–73.

Kantor, H., & Brenzel, B. (1992). Urban education and the "truly disadvantaged:" The historical roots of the contemporary crisis. *Teachers College Record*, 94(2), 278–314.

Kast, D. (1993). Collaborative calculus. *Primus*, 3(1), 53–61.

Keach, E. T., Fulton, R., & Gardner, W. E. (Eds.). (1967). *Education and social crisis*. New York: Wiley.

Kelly, W. H. (1981). Physicist: An endangered species? *Physics Teacher*, 19(2), 87, 144.

Kennedy, M. M. (1997). The connection between research and practice. *Educational Researcher*, 26(7), 4–12.

Kerber, A., & Bommarito, B. (Eds.). (1965). *The schools and the urban crisis*. New York: Holt, Rinehart, & Winston.

Kilpatrick, W. H. (1932). *Education and the social crisis*. New York: Liveright.

King, S. H. (1993). The limited presence of African American teachers. *Review of Educational Research*, 63(2), 115–149.

Kleine, P. F., & Greene, B. A. (1992). Story telling: A rich history and a sordid past. *Educational Psychologist*, 28(2), 185–190.

Koob, C. A. (1994). National Catholic Educational Association: 90 years meeting crisis with confidence. *Momentum*, 25(1), 34–37.

Larkin, R. W. (1979). *Suburban youth in cultural crisis*. New York: Oxford University Press.

Lausberg, C. H. (1990). Site-based management: Crisis or opportunity? *School Business Affairs*, 56(4), 10–14.

Layman, J. W. (1983). The crisis in high school physics education: Overview of the problem. *Physics Today*, 36(9), 26–30.

Lerner, R. M. (1994). The crisis among contemporary American adolescents. *Journal of Research on Adolescence*, 4(1), 1–4.

Longstreet, W. S. (1989). Education for citizenship: New Dimensions. *Social Education*, 53(1), 41–45.

Martini, M. R. (1996). *Marx not Madison: The crisis of American legal education*. Lanham, MD: University Press of America.

McKenzie, P. (1995). Education and training: Still distinguishable? *Vocational Aspects of Education*, 47(1), 35–49.

Miller, S. R. (1981). A crisis in appropriate education: The dearth of data on programs for secondary handicapped adolescents. *Journal of Special Education*, 15(3), 351–360.

Miller, M. V., & Gilmore, S. (Eds.). (1965). *Revolution at Berkeley: The crisis in American education*. New York: Dell.

Molnar, A. R. (1978). The next great crisis in American education: Computer literacy. *AEDS Journal*, 12(1), 11–20.

Munson, M. L. (1986). Self-insurance: A haven for school districts facing hostile carriers. *School Business Affairs*, 52(6), 20–21.

National Commission on Excellence in Education. (1983). *A nation at risk: The imperatives for educational reform*. Washington, DC: U.S. Department of Education.

O'Brien, E. M. (1989). 1988 ACE annual report sounds the alarm: Higher education community must act on the crisis of the black male. *Black Issues in Higher Education*, 5(21), 3, 17.

Ostler, L. J., & Dahlin, T. C. (1995). Library education: Setting or rising sun. *American Libraries*, 26(7), 683–684.

Pannell, D. V. (1990). Has a financial crisis hit school food services? *School Business Affairs*, 56(4), 10–14.

Pois, J. (1964). *The school board crisis: A Chicago case study*. Chicago, IL: Educational Methods.

Prescott, M. P. (1981). An overview: The crisis in music education. *Music Educators Journal*, 68(3), 35–38.

Reid, J. E. (1988). School lunch: A crisis overcome. *School Business Affairs*, 54(11), 24–29.

Renzulli, J. S., & Reis, S. M. (1991). The reform movement and the quiet crisis in gifted education. *Gifted Child Quarterly* 35(1), 26–35.

Rische, T. (1977). California crisis: Journalism as English. *Communication: Journalism Education Today*, 11(4), 10–20.

Rodriguez, R. (1994). Higher education crisis looms for Chicanos/Latinos. *Black Issues in Higher Education*, 11(3), 20–23.

Rong, X. L., & Preissle, J. (1997). The continuing decline in Asian American teachers. *American Educational Research Journal*, 34(2), 267–293.

Rough, W. (1994). Crisis? What crisis? High school theater education in a diverse America. *Drama/Theater Teacher*, 6(3), 42–44.

Ruiz, R. (1993/1994). Language policy and planning in the U. S. *Annual Review of Applied Linguistics*, 14, 111–125.

Rury, J. L., & Cassell, F. A. (1993). *Seeds of crisis: Public schooling in Milwaukee since 1920*. Madison, WI: University of Wisconsin Press.

Samoff, J. (1994). Crisis and adjustment: Understanding national responses. In J. Samoff, (Ed.), *Coping with crisis: Austerity, adjustment, and human resources* (pp. 5–27). New York: Cassell.

Scott, C. W., Hill, C. M., & Burns, H. W. (Eds.). (1959). *The great debate: Our schools in crisis*. Englewood Cliffs, NJ: Prentice-Hall.

Silberman, C. E. (1970). *Crisis in the classroom*. New York: Random House.

Skrtic, T. M. (1986). The crisis in special education knowledge: A perspective on perspective. *Focus on Exceptional Children*, 18(7), 1–16.

Sobel, M. A. (1983). The crisis in mathematics education. *Educational Horizons*, 61(2), 55–56.

Sommer, C. (1984). *Schools in crisis: Training for success or failure?* Houston, TX: Cahill.

Sommer, J. W. (Ed.). (1995). *The academy in crisis*. New Brunswick, NJ: Transaction.

Squire, J. R. (1985). The current crisis in literary education. *English Journal*, 74(8), 18–21.

Sroufe, G. E. (1997). Improving the 'awful reputation' of education research. *Educational Researcher*, 26(7), 26–28.

Stanic, G. M. (1986). The growing crisis in mathematics education in the early twentieth century. *Journal for Research in Mathematics Education*, 17(3), 190–205.

Stanley, M. (1980). Social science and legitimate policy discourse: American public education as a case instance. *Teachers College Record*, 81(3), 270–292.

Starratt, R. J. (1994). *Building an ethical school: A practical response to the moral crisis*. New York: Falmer.

Stigler, J. W., Lee, S.-Y., Lucker, G. W., & Stevenson, H. W. (1982). Curriculum and achievement in mathematics: A study of elementary school children in Japan, Taiwan, and the United States. *Journal of Educational Psychology*, 74, 315–322.

Stroot, S. A. (1994). Contemporary crisis or emerging reform?: A review of secondary school physical education. *Journal of Teaching in Physical Education*, 13(4), 333–341.

Swanson, G. I. (1991). The future of agricultural education: A view from the bleachers. *Journal of Agricultural Education*, 32(3), 10–17.

Topping, R. J. (1990). Art education: A crisis in priorities. *Art Education*, 43(1), 20–24.

Tyson, G. D. (1993). Creating a classroom on the run. *Principal*, 73(1), 44–45.

University of Minnesota. (1947). *The crisis of mankind: The urgent educational tasks of the university in our time*. Minneapolis, MN: University of Minnesota Press.

Vogel, P. R. (1991). Crisis in youth fitness and wellness. *Phi Delta Kappan*, 73(2), 154–156.

Wade, B., & Sidaway, S. (1990). Poetry in the curriculum: A crisis of confidence. *Educational Studies*, 16(1), 75–83.

Webster's ninth new collegiate dictionary. (1985). Springfield, MA: Miriam-Webster.

Wiles, D. K. (1979). *Energy, winter, and schools: Crisis and decision theory*. Lexington, MA: Lexington Books.

Wise, G., & Thornburg, K. (1978). Home–school relationships: An educational crisis. *Education*, 99(2), 180–187.

Wittes, S. (1970). *People and power: A study of crisis in secondary schools*. Ann Arbor, MI: University of Michigan Center for Research on Utilization of Scientific Knowledge.

Yager, R. E. (1982). The crisis in biology education. *The American Biology Teacher*, 44, 328–336.

Yuen, S. C. (1990). Incorporating CAD instruction into the drafting curriculum. *Technology Teacher*, 50(3), 30–32.

chapter 21

Educational Policy Analysis: The Treads behind, the Trends ahead

ANNE C. LEWIS
Education Policy Writer

In the mid-1980s—before national standards or international tests that people paid attention to, before the tight labor market, and before a tremendous turnover in the teacher force—some policy makers wondered how the relatively benign National Assessment of Educational Progress (NAEP) could become more of a report card for the country. They asked a politician—former Tennessee governor Lamar Alexander—to head up a study whose outcome was predetermined because the agenda was all about accountability.

One aspect of the study queried national education leaders, primarily association heads, about an expanded NAEP, especially state-by-state comparisons. Their response was about as ho-hum as one could get. NAEP was a very minor occurrence for students. Few at the local level paid any attention to the results, and as long as Greg Anrig, president of the Educational Testing Service, was in charge of NAEP, no one was particularly concerned about any great surprises coming from an expanded NAEP. People trusted him to be fair and open. Little thought was given to a potentially profound change in accountability.

Had they known the rollercoaster ride they were destined for, these leaders and the ones who have followed them might have asked more questions and tried harder to shape the educational policies that were to rule their professional lives. It was not the phenomenon of NAEP per se, but the

Handbook of Educational Policy
521

study's melding of political agendas with educational policy making that was significant, a departure that has consumed American education for more than a decade. If there is any general theme running through the contributions to this volume, it is this interplay between political aims—let's be frank, political ideologies—and educational policy. True, local education systems have always reflected local politics, and national policy making that began in the mid-1960s was more intrusive than any before it, but it primarily concerned education at the fringes—of poor children, those with disabilities, or those with home languages other than English. It also tended to be nonpartisan.

The positive aspect of the crescendo of policy making that has taken place in recent years is that research and experience have tempered the political agendas. On the negative side, however, is the reality that not enough of the expertise gets into policy making. This is not endemic to education. Decision-making based on myths or, at best, half-truths dominates all aspects of society today. Politics is about competing policies, but also about character and purposes and ends, as Michael J. Sandel (1997) wrote in *The Kettering Review* the "anxieties of the times" and erosion of self-government and sense of community, he says, have all but erased public discourse around civic aspirations and moral actions (though morality plays are on the increase). Politics is sort of left hanging out there without what Sandel terms the communal storytelling that could help it bring society together.

This dominance of a different kind of politics certainly seems reflected in the national debate over the privatization and support of separateness in education. Another example is the contrast between policy making for the Chicago school district and for the Boston school district. Both are now under control of mayors' offices, but a 3-year limit on the new arrangement imposed by the Illinois legislature forced Chicago officials to make very expedient, political decisions about changes in the system. Schools are being held accountable on the basis of scores on a nationally standardized test, wholly inappropriate for such accountability and divorced from the standards adopted for the Chicago schools. Student retention is being used as a major tool to force improved achievement levels. These are silver-bullet, almost symbolic efforts, more akin to politics than the more deliberate, policy making efforts underway in Boston. There, the superintendent, not under such a tight political timeline to produce success, has focused on adopting standards, creating a new performance-based assessment system, and preparing teachers for standards-based classrooms.

The propensity for politics to undermine well-intended policy making is quite evident in the partial unraveling of the 1994 Clinton administration agenda for education. It was a marvel of interlocking policies—Goals 2000 providing seed money to support the move toward higher standards for all students in the reauthorization of the Elementary and Secondary Education Act, particularly Title I, and the extension of standards to a new system for school-to-work transitions. The problem is that the politics on Capitol Hill changed with the 1994 elections, and the administration's high goals gave way to strategies aimed at just saving the structure of the various initiatives. States have been allowed to do almost anything they wanted with the funds, aimed at mollifying those who sought to eliminate a federal presence in educational policymaking altogether. Requirements that states show "adequate, reasonable progress" among Title I students, for example, were so watered down as to be meaningless in terms of narrowing the academic gap between poor and more affluent children. This meant that states did not have to address problems with opportunity to learn standards. The administration turned more to middle-class concerns and away from an emphasis on the most disadvantaged in its original policy package.

With education quality now the most important issue for the public, political agendas will hold sway well into the next century. The late American Federation of Teachers president Albert Shanker once said that education would not become important as a political issue until the public makes a connection between it and the country's economic security. After years of hearing that economic argument for reform from business leaders, the public has become convinced and, consequently, so have those who run for top state and national offices.

So, can educational policymaking be anything more than an appendage to political decisions? Can it finesse more rational approaches to changing the education system? Can it provide the character and purpose that Sandel said are missing from the political process? Despite some of the disillusioning examples cited, educational policy making is in a better position to answer those questions in the affirmative than it has ever been. There has been substantial capacity building among a cadre of researchers and analysts who can provide advice on policy making. Most governors and legislators and some members of Congress acknowledge that educational policy making needs to be systemic, not piecemeal. Furthermore, there is some evidence that these decision makers realize their political symbolism needs to be tempered with informed educational policies lest they wind up at the far end of a limb.

Much successful policy making has taken place, many issues remain mired in what appear to be battles between politics and educational policy making, and some very important areas are ripe for intensive policy analysis. Let's discuss examples of each.

POLICY MAKING THAT MADE A DIFFERENCE

The most comprehensive, state-level policy making that affects education rarely gets into the literature for educators because it is not specific to schooling. However, the Oregon benchmarks initiative was the first major effort to look at *results*. It was and remains an innovative policy thrust that has survived changes in governance at the state level and integrated specific goals for education with overall goals for the quality of life in the state.

In the mid 1980s, Oregon leadership in government and business realized the state was losing its traditional economic base—lumbering—and needed to find replacements. Instead of focusing only on economic development, however, the Progress Board and other groups organized a grassroots effort to develop benchmarks in many areas, including water quality, worker skills, health and education. The process used data to establish baseline information on more than 200 indicators. In education, these included enrollment in early childhood programs; readiness for learning to read; student achievement; sufficient supports for students; involvement by students in community service; preparation for work; and, because it is a Pacific Rim state, an indicator on the proficiency (not just course taking) of young people in a foreign language.

Before the benchmarks were developed, Oregon already had adopted changes in high school graduation requirements that established a Certificate of Initial Mastery and a Certificate of Advanced Mastery. The former is needed to graduate from high school. This is a performance-based system; for the certificates, students take state tests and complete performance assessment tasks, and samples of their work are scored by teachers using scoring guides. This new graduation system was blended into the benchmark plan, which sets interim goals and final goals for the year 2002. The most interesting policy implication is how the high school plan is influencing college admission expectations. They, too, have become standards based and performance based. Beginning in 2001, students from Oregon public high schools will be expected to demonstrate proficiency in English and math to be admitted to an Oregon public campus, based on activities and tests. The goal, according to higher education officials, is to ensure that students admitted to college can do college-level work. (Similar plans are underway in Washington State, Colorado, and Wisconsin.)

The Oregon benchmark process, initially independent of official government action, became a formal activity through the establishment of an ongoing process by the legislature. Budgets of various state agencies, for example, are drawn up with the indicators in mind. The developers went back to the grassroots, asking town meetings to decide on core benchmarks, about 20, such as having every child fully immunized, reducing teenage pregnancy, and updating worker skills. Two characteristics make this an interesting initiative for policymakers. First, it reflects an environment in government in Oregon that welcomes policy innovation and has attracted experienced, forward-thinking policy analysts into government and civic leadership. Secondly, it acknowledges the interdependence of all the factors influencing better results in education: health, social supports, cultural strengths, environmental quality, and job preparation and creation. Much has been written and accomplished about collaborative services around children and families with the reasoning that children and young people cannot learn well unless they are healthy, have positive community influences, and there are suffi- cient supports around their families. These efforts often have been legis- lated. Oregon's accomplishment is that it created collaboration through a democratic process.

A second example of successful policy making in education is the work of the National Commission on Teaching and America's Future. Responding to the belated realization in many policy circles that teacher quality is the back- bone of school reform, this high-powered commission representing teachers, administrators, researchers, and governors studied the issues for 2 years and issued an important report, *What Matters Most: Teaching and America's Future*, in September 1996. The politics within the commission considerably taxed the diplomatic skills of its director, Linda Darling Hammond of Teachers College/Columbia University, but she was able to move the commission toward significant recommendations. One fact in its success often is not available to other efforts at reform—consistency of leadership. Cochair of the commission, for example, is Governor James Hunt of North Carolina, who led the National Board for Professional Teaching Standards through its formative years. Similarly, the emphasis in the commission report on stan- dards for students and teachers can be attributed to Al Shanker, who led the American Federation of Teachers (AFT) campaign for higher student stan- dards; and the commission's call for accreditation of all teacher education programs can be attributed to another member, Arthur Wise, who has been reforming the quality of teacher preparation as head of the National Council for the Accreditation of Teacher Education.

What is significant about the commission's report and work is that it focuses specifically on building a systemic policy framework for improving the quality of teaching. Its recommendations follow a teacher's career—from selection into a program, through quality, performance-based preparation, preferably with a fifth year as an internship—into a licensing and certifica- tion system based on performance standards. This is followed by an induc- tion period during which a teacher receives support and peer evaluation; quality professional development; changes in school environments that al- low high-quality teaching to occur; and, finally, incentives and rewards for continual growth and improvement, such as support and rewards for obtain- ing National Board certification.

Many of the pieces in the commission's plan already existed. Its report refers to a three-legged stool for improving the profession: accreditation of preparation programs by NCATE, use of the standards in licensing and cer- tification developed by an interstate consortium, and incentives/rewards for professional growth through National Board certification. Twelve states immediately signed on to participate in developing the systemic policies, and others are engaging in conversations and in some of the commission's activities. The commission also developed a special project to improve the quality of teaching through comprehensive policies in urban school districts. Some of the recommendations are controversial, such as the elimination of substandard preparation programs and procedures to ensure a qualified, competent, and caring teacher in every classroom (meaning that ineffective teachers must leave the classroom). The commission's scope inevitably put it in political hot water. For example, the Council of Chief State School Officers would not support requiring NCATE approval of teacher preparation programs, even though it is the only national accrediting group approved by the U.S. Department of Education. States do not want to be dictated to, the chiefs said, but it remains to be seen whether their governors agree with this position.

A third example comes from a 1994 survey of elementary teachers in California by David Cohen and Heather Hill, working with a research group at Michigan State University under the auspices of the Consortium for Policy Research in Education. They explored the effect of state policy changes on classroom practice and student performance, finding that systemic policy initiatives did affect classroom practice and did result in higher student achievement.

In 1985 California swirled with activity to improve curriculum and raise standards for students. It adopted a new mathematics framework and new textbooks. Displeased with the limited improvements made in the texts, state officials stimulated the development of other materials, especially teaching modules known as replacement units. About three weeks' worth of classroom work, these units more closely followed the changes in math instruction embedded in the new frameworks. California officials encouraged changes in teacher education to match the frameworks, using the replacement units, and it used its new student assessment plan, the California Learning Assessment System, as another way of pushing changes in content and instruction.

Some of the professional development organized to respond to the math framework was grounded in the improved student curriculum state policymakers wanted, according to the researchers. Most was not. Only about 15% of the teachers surveyed participated in professional development that was focused on the curriculum, supported by peers, extended over time, and provided opportunities for reflection and feedback. Those who had this kind of professional development were more likely to change their classroom practice than teachers who attended short-term workshops or those focused on noncurriculum strategies, such as cooperative learning. The students of teachers who had quality professional development also scored higher on CLAS.

Cohen and Hill concluded that "educational policy is an instrument for improving teaching and learning." State agencies were not the only ones responsible for changing teacher practice and improving student achievement. Related agencies, such as higher education, and professional organizations also played a part. Working together, the researchers noted, "this diverse set of agents was able to create somewhat more coherent relationships among teachers' learning opportunities, their practice, school curriculum and assessments, and student achievement, than are typical in the United States."

This success is overshadowed, of course, by the political controversies over CLAS and the math curriculum. CLAS was criticized by conservatives for too much attention to critical thinking and not enough on the "basics" and for test items that one researcher noted had not passed through the political screen. It was vetoed by the governor, and a new math curriculum emphasizing the basics was adopted by the state board.

The last example perhaps illustrates issues in which political agendas and educational policy making are locked in combat. However, it belongs more to the successful category because for the few years where state-level policies linked with classroom practice and content, the policies did bring about change.

All of these examples—the Oregon benchmarks, the National Commission on Teaching and America's Future, and the efforts in California to integrate curriculum reform, teacher development, and new assessment—characterize *systemic* policy making, especially at the state level. It is a shift from programmatic, categorical or short-term policy making that characterized much of efforts at school reform during the 1980s. Research and analysis by the Consortium for Policy Research in Education certainly helped policy makers make the shift. Similarly, the National Governors' Association, prodded into action by the National Education Summit in 1989, has followed systemic reform among the states. It noted in a 1993 report that "creating the policy environment that underlies systemic reform is proving more difficult than anticipated. It is easier to add new policies than subtract old ones. It is easier to mandate than enable. It is easier to monitor than assist." However, it added, the conflicts "signal that deep changes are underway." Policy making in education has produced its share of conflicts.

POLICY MAKING TIPPED OVER INTO POLITICS

Unfortunately, the "math wars" that produced a turnaround in state board policies *are* an example of politics subsuming educational policy making. It is ironic that millions of students in California are returning to traditional back-to-basics kind of content knowledge at the same time the Third International Mathematics and Science Study reveals that this kind of instruction leaves American students way behind students in other countries where learning concepts through problem solving is emphasized. But we never said politics was rational!

As the century closes, perhaps the most dramatic intermingling of political agendas and policy making is the reliance of states on academic bankruptcy policies to force accountability. Each January state-of-the-union addresses by governors add more states to the list of those threatening to take over consistently failing school districts as evidence that political leadership was willing to get tough. Almost half of the states had such laws by 1997. Where the takeovers have occurred, the targeted school districts, almost always in urban areas, usually needed some kind of intervention. The consistent failure of the schools—as shown in high dropout rates, low student achievement, mismanagement, and poor school board-union relationships—also left the public school systems vulnerable to more radical political solutions, such as vouchers that parents could use in public or private alternatives. Voucher plans existed in Milwaukee and Cleveland, where the courts ordered the state superintendent to take over in 1995. Members of Congress fought perennially over a voucher plan for the District of Columbia, even though Congress established emergency powers for the District that took away authority from the local school board.

Despite the bravado of politicians in threatening to save urban districts, the states actually painted themselves into a corner on this issue and by 1998 were seeking policies that would give them a way out. Takeovers for academic bankruptcy began in New Jersey in the early 1990s but 8 years later had not produced higher student achievement in any of the districts subjected to state control. Conditions in the schools improved, but not the central reason for takeovers—student performance. When the state of Maryland realized that its accountability plan, which called for reconstituting schools where students consistently failed the state's assessments, was going to result in the reconstitution of as many as one-third of the schools in Baltimore, it turned to more creative policy making. The legislature approved a new governance system for Baltimore, taking absolute control away from the mayor and establishing greater teacher and school accountability. It also gave the schools an infusion of additional funds in return for diminished local control.

At conferences of states with takeover laws in 1997, the Education Commission of the States pushed for new rounds of policy making rather than politics on the issue of interventions with failing districts. The policy makers who attended the meetings agreed that the best solutions were local. "State intervention may be accepted locally in order to correct mismanagement, but state initiatives that threaten local values and interests in an arbitrary manner, though more likely to be efficient and time-saving, may be viewed as an invading army," an ECS report said. A better policy thrust, the state policymakers said, would be for states to concentrate on encouraging coherence and communication across sectors, such as mobilizing state and local efforts at economic development on behalf of school reform. States also could bring best-practices knowledge to local districts and help them create stability in leadership and practices. Even so, Ohio approved an academic bankruptcy plan in 1997, and the governor of Wisconsin gave Milwaukee 2 years to make significant improvements on several indicators or else face a state takeover.

POLICY MAKING TO WATCH

At the end of the 1990s, almost all policy making in education centered on accountability—whether by individual teachers, schools, or districts. Undoubtedly, technology had made incredible amounts of data available to policymakers to track accountability. In Kentucky, accumulated data from the state's assessment system embroiled policy making in minute details over administering schools as the state's "distinguished educators" moved into schools in decline or in crisis and recommended (for the former) and required (for the latter) changes in classroom practice. Tennessee's value-added initiative, involving millions of data items that pinpointed the effectiveness of teachers (as determined by student test scores) had the potential to move accountability policies from the school level, as in most states, to the classroom level.

Most states and districts had not yet worked out the tension between the decentralization of authority through site-based decision making and the centralization of accountability measures, primarily through new state assessment systems based on state standards. For example, districts such as Louisville and Long Beach, which were committed to standards-based reforms, had to figure out how to persuade schools to design professional development that supported the district's goals. Incidentally, one of the fastest disappearing claims for an innovation that would produce revolutionary changes in schools is that of local school autonomy. This was the policy panacea of the early 1990s. By the end of the decade, it had been transformed into the concept of schools as "learning communities," still having the autonomy to make decisions to create such environments but not dependent on autonomy alone to create needed changes.

The role of assessment as a tool for accountability will continue to be debated well into the next century. Certainly, California's experience with CLAS and the modifications forced on the Kentucky assessment system by the legislature after its problems with reliability and unanticipated consequences confirm that testing is a technical issue taken over by politicians. The use of a norm-referenced standardized test in Chicago to evaluate schools—a decision made by a political appointee head of the schools who was not an educator—was unwise by all measures but considered necessary for public accountability.

The most significant challenge to policy making, however, came from Congress. Even though the 1994 reauthorization of the Elementary and Secondary

Education Act required Title I programs to emphasize high standards and quality efforts, such as qualified teachers and schoolwide professional development, it was generally acknowledged that schools did not comply and that states were not monitoring the implementation of reforms in Title I programs. So Congress approved a new pilot project, infusing more than $140 million into primarily Title I schools willing to adopt certain models of whole-school change or other models that met certain criteria. Ever since the 1970s the idea of going to scale on school reforms through models had been discounted as either impossible or undesirable.

The Comprehensive School Reform program, adopted through the appropriation process and thus without much public discussion, was considered a forerunner for the redesign of the $8 billion Title I program. If that happened, schools would become consumers of verified models of school improvement, such as Success for All, Accelerated Schools, or High Schools That Work (Congress listed 17 possible models). This would be a massive change in policy, affecting everything from teacher training to what entity should be responsible for accountability (e.g., the state, the federal government, or the program developers).

Even before the program began, its implications were being debated. For example, a RAND study of the eight models participating in the New American Schools initiative points out that an important factor in the successful adoption of the models was density—having a number of schools using the same model in the same geographic area. This is a factor not taken into consideration at all in the criteria outlined by the Comprehensive School reform program. There also was the immediate problem of capacity. The most widely used model among all those listed was Success for All, which had been implemented in about 750 schools by 1997. For the models to be able to stretch themselves over the thousands of schools receiving Title I funds in a short time would tax their resources and expertise.

In all of these policy making efforts, there is a steady undercurrent flowing across them, one that acknowledges the ultimate policy makers are not in central offices and capitol buildings but in families and communities expressing what they believe children should know and be able to do and how to determine those things. Yet the fractured and sound-bite-driven lives of most families, not just the poor, have muted consistent involvement in decisions about children's schooling. Often, the public voice is heard only when policies are onerous. Just as often, uninformed public voices are the only ones heard because the policies are so poorly articulated.

The issues that families, schools and policy makers struggle with as they shape adequate educations for children will not get any less complex in the future. One needs to hope that politics and educational policy making can learn enough from each other in the years ahead to make each enterprise successful—the former in expressing public will and the latter in informing the public's decisions.

References

Education Commission of the States. (1997, March). ECS conference highlights state takeovers of failing urban schools. *Perspectives* Denver, CO: Education Commission of the States.

National Commission on Teaching & America's Future. (1996, September). *What Matters Most: Teaching and America's Future*, New York, NY: Teachers College, Columbia University.

National Governor's Association. *Transforming education: Overcoming barriers.* (1993). Washington, DC: National Governors' Association.

Sandel, M. J. (1997, summer). In search of a public philosophy. *The Kettering Review*, pp. 51–59.

State policy and classroom performance: Mathematics reform in California. (1998, January). CPRE *Policy Briefs*. University of Pennsylvania, Philadelphia, PA.

Resources

The following resources were compiled by the chapter authors and the editor for readers who wish to gain additional information about a topic related to educational policy. Resources are listed by chapter and consist of both traditional forms (i.e., books or journal articles not listed in the reference section of a chapter) and electronic versions (e.g., e-mail addresses and Internet Web sites for organizations involved in educational policy). Note: For a few chapters, additional resources have not been listed here; for information on those topics, readers are referred to the appropriate references listed at the end of the chapter.

Chapter 1 (Pullin)

Center for Law and Education
Jeff Horner, President
1875 Connecticut Ave., Suite 510
Washington, DC 20009

Telephone: 1-202-462-7688

Education Law Association
818 Miriam Hall
300 College Park
University of Dayton
Dayton, OH 45469-2280

Telephone: 1-937-229-3589
E-mail: ela@udayton.edu
Internet: www.educationlaw.org

Education Law Reporter
West Publishing Company
610 Opperman Dr.
St. Paul, MN 55123

Telephone: 1-800-937-8529
Internet: www.westlaw.com

Kirp, D. L., & Jensen, D. N. (1986). *School days, rule days: The legalization and regulation of education.* Philadelphia, PA: Falmer.

Yudof, M. G., Kirp, D. L., & Levin, B. (1992). *Education policy and the law* (3rd ed). St. Paul, MN: West.

Chapter 2 (Goertz)

Consortium of Policy Research in Education (CPRE)
Robb Sewell
University of Pennsylvania
3440 Market St., Suite 560
Philadelphia, PA 19104-3325

Telephone: 1-215-573-0700
E-mail: cpre@gse.upenn.edu
Internet: www.upenn.edu/gse/cpre

Wisconsin Center for Education Research (CPRE affiliate)
Allan Odden
University of Wisconsin
1025 Johnson St., Suite 653
Madison, WI 53706-1796

Telephone: 1-608-263-4260
E-mail: odden@macc.wisc.edu
Internet: www.wcer.wisc.edu/cpre/

New America Schools
1000 Wilson Blvd., Suite 2710
Arlington, VA 22209

Telephone: 1-703-908-9500
E-mail: csef@air-ca.org
Internet: www.air.org/csef_hom/

Education Finance Statistical Center
William J. Fowler, Jr.
National Center for Education Statistics/OERI
555 New Jersey Ave., N.W.
Washington, DC 20208

Telephone: 1-202-219-1921
E-mail: william_fowler@ed.gov
Internet: www.nces.ed.gov/edfin

American Education Finance Association
George Babigian, Executive Director
5249 Cape Leyte Dr.
Sarasota, FL 34242

Telephone: 1-914-349-7580
E-mail: aefa+@pitt.edu or gbabigian@aol.com
Internet: info.pitt.edu/~aefa

Chapter 3 (Kennedy)

American Educational Research Association
Denise McKeon
1230 17th St., N.W.
Washington, DC 20036-3078

Telephone: 1-202-223-9485
Internet: www.area.net

National Education Association
Sylvia Seidel
1201 16th St., N.W.
Washington, DC 20036

Telephone: 1-202-833-4300
Internet: www.nea.org

Education Week
6935 Arlington Rd., Suite 100
Bethesda, MD 20814-5233

Telephone: 1-301-280-3100
E-mail: webster@epe.org
Internet: www.edweek.org/

Chapter 4 (Lumpe)

Educational Theory
Education Building
University of Illinois
1310 S. Sixth St.
Champaign, IL 61820

Telephone: 1-217-333-3003
E-mail: EdTheory@uiuc.edu
Internet: www.ed.uiuc.edu/coe/eps/educational-theory/

The Advancement of Sound Science Coalition
Steven Milloy, Executive Director
1155 Connecticut Ave., N.W., Suite 300
Washington, DC 20036

Telephone: 1-202-467-8586
E-mail: milloy@cais.com
Internet: www.junkscience.com/

Chapter 5 (Michaels/Ferrara)

Northwest Regional Education Laboratory
Dr. Robert Blum, Director
School Improvement Program
101 S. W. Main St., Suite 500
Portland, OR 97024-3297

Telephone: 1-503-275-9615
E-mail: blumb@nwrel.org
Internet: www.nwrel.org/scpd/

Mid-continent Regional Education Laboratory
2550 S. Parker Rd., Suite 500
Aurora, CO 80014

Telephone: 1-303-337-0990
E-mail: info@mcrel.org
Internet: www.mcrel.org/resources/links/index.asp

Maryland State Department of Education
200 W. Baltimore St.
Baltimore, MD 21202

Telephone: 1-800-246-0016
Internet: www.msde.state.md.us

Chapter 6 (Engler/Whitney)

Office of the Governor
Romney Building
111 S. Capitol St.
Lansing, MI 48933

Telephone: 1-517-373-3400
Internet: www.migov.state.mi.us/

Teach Michigan
Paul DeWeese, President
321 N. Pine
Lansing, MI 48933

Telephone: 1-800-Teach Mi
E-mail: research@teach-mi.org
Internet: teach-mi.org

Mackinac Center or Public Policy
Lawrence Reed, President
140 West Main Street
P.O. Box 568
Midland, MI 48640

Telephone: 1-517-631-0900
E-mail: mcpp@mackinac.org
Internet: www.mackinac.org

Michigan Association of Public School Academies
Daniel Quisenberry, President
124 West Allegan St., Suite 750
Lansing, MI 48933

Telephone: 1-517-374-9167
E-mail: mapsa@charterschools.org
Internet: www.charterschools.org/core.html

Chapter 7 (Roeber)

Foreign Language Standards

American Council on the Teaching of Foreign Languages. (1995). *Standards for foreign language learning: Preparing for the 21st century.* Yonkers, NY: Author.

American Council on the Teaching of Foreign Languages
6 Executive Plaza
Yonkers, NY 10701-6801

Telephone: 1-914-963-8830
E-mail: actflhq@aol.com
Internet: www.actfl.org

Arts Education Standards

Consortium of National Arts Education Associations. (1994). *National standards for arts education: What every young American should know and be able to do.* Reston, VA: Music Educators National Conference.

Music Educators National Conference
1806 Robert Fulton Drive
Reston, VA 22091

Telephone: 1-703-860-4000
E-mail: mbmenc@vais.net
Internet: www.menc.org

Civic Education Standards

Center for Civic Education. (1994). *National standards for civics and government.* Calabasas, CA: Author.

Center for Civic Education
5146 Douglas Fir Rd.
Calabasas, CA 91302-1467

Telephone: 1-818-591-9321
E-mail: center4civ@aol.com
Internet: www.civiced.org/

Economic Education Standards

Saunders, P., & Gilliard, J. (Eds.). (1995). *A framework for teaching basic economic concepts with scope and sequence guidelines.* New York: National Council on Economic Education.

National Council on Economic Education
1140 Avenue of the Americas
New York, NY 10036

Telephone: 1-800-338-1192
E-mail: ncee@eaglobal.org
Internet: www.nationalcouncil.org/

English Language Arts Standards

National Council of Teachers of English and International Reading Association. (1996). *Standards for the English language arts.* Urbana, IL: National Council of Teachers of English.

National Council of Teachers of English
1111 West Kenyon Road
Urbana, IL 61801

Telephone: 1-800-369-6283
E-mail: www.ncte.org/contact/
Internet: www.ncte.org

Geography Standards

Geography Education Standards Project. (1994). *Geography for life: National geography standards.* Washington, DC: National Geographic Research and Exploration.

National Council for Geographic Education
16A Leonard Hall
Indiana University of Pennsylvania
Indiana, PA 15705-1087

Telephone: 1-412-357-6290
Internet: www.nationalgeographic.com/resources/ngo/education/
                standards.html

Health Education Standards

Joint Committee on Health Education Standards. (1995). *National health education standards: Achieving health literacy.* Reston, VA: Association for the Advancement of Health Education.

Association for the Advancement of Health Education
1900 Association Drive
Reston, VA 20191-1599

Telephone: 1-800-213-7193
E-mail: aahe@aahperd.org
Internet: www.aahperd.org

Mathematics Standards

National Council of Teachers of Mathematics. (1989). *Curriculum and evaluation standards for school mathematics.* Reston, VA: Author.

National Council of Teachers of Mathematics
1906 Association Dr.
Reston, VA 20191-1593

Telephone: 1-703-620-9840
E-mail: infocentral@nctm.org
Internet: www.nctm.org

Science Education Standards

National Committee on Science Education Standards and Assessment. (1995). *National science education standards*. Washington, DC: National Academy Press.

National Research Council
National Academy of Sciences
2101 Constitution Ave., N.W.
Washington, DC 20418

Telephone: 1-202-334-2000
Internet: www.nap.edu/readingroom/books/nses/

Social Studies Standards

National Council for the Social Studies. (1994). *Expectations of excellence: Curriculum standards for social studies*. Washington, DC: Author.

National Council for the Social Studies
3501 Newark St., N.W.
Washington, DC 20016

Telephone: 1-202-966-7840
E-mail: information@ncss.org
Internet: www.ncss.org/standards/

Physical Education Standards

National Association for Sport and Physical Education. (1995). *Moving into the future, national standards for physical education: A guide to content and assessment*. St. Louis, MO: Mosby.

National Association for Sport and Physical Education
1900 Association Drive
Reston, VA 20191

Telephone: 1-800-213-7193
E-mail: naspe@aahperd.org
Internet: www.aahperd.org/naspe/naspe.html

United States and World History Standards

National Association for History in the Schools. (1995). *National standards for United States history: Exploring the American experience*. Los Angeles, CA: Author.

National Association for History in the Schools. (1995). *National standards for world history: Exploring paths to the present.* Los Angeles, CA: Author.

National Association for History in the Schools
Department of History
University of California, Los Angeles
405 Hilgard Ave.
Los Angeles, CA 90095-1473

Telephone: 1-310-825-8388
E-mail: gnash@ucla.edu
Internet: www.sscnet.ucla.edu/nchs/

Workplace Readiness Standards

Secretary's Commission on Achieving Necessary Skills. (1991). *What work requires of schools: A SCANS report for America* 2000. Washington, DC: U.S. Department of Labor.

SCANS/2000 Program
Johns Hopkins University Institute for Policy Studies
Wyman Park Building, 5th Floor
3400 N. Charles St.
Baltimore, MD 21218

E-mail;   scottab@jhuvms.hcf.jhu.edu
Internet: infinia.wpmc.jhu.edu

Chapter 9 (Bourque)

National Assessment Governing Board
National Assessment of Educational Progress
800 North Capitol St., N.W., Suite 825
Washington, DC 20002-4233

Telephone: 1-202-357-6938
E-mail: jewel_bell@ed.gov
Internet: www.nagb.org

National Assessment Governing Board
Voluntary National Tests
800 North Capitol St., N.W., Suite 601
Washington, DC 20002-4233

Telephone: 1-202-357-7500
Internet: www.nagb.org

National Center for Education Statistics
Steve Gorman
555 New Jersey Ave., N.W., Room 404G
Washington, DC 20208

Telephone: 1-202-219-1937
E-mail: steve_gorman@ed.gov
Internet: nces.ed.gov/naep/

Chapter 10 (Stevenson/Hofer)

National Center for Education Statistics
Office of Educational Research and Improvement
United States Department of Education
555 New Jersey Ave., N.W.
Washington, DC 20208-5574

Internet: nces.ed.gov/timss/

Educational Testing Service
Policy Information Center
Paul Barton
Rosedale Rd., MS 04-R
Princeton, NJ 08541-0001

Telephone: 1-609-734-5694
E-mail: pic@ets.org
Internet: www.ets.org/sppolicy.html

Chapter 11 (Dunn)

Social Policy Report
Nancy G. Thomas, Editor
Society for Research in Child Development
505 East Huron St., Suite 301
Ann Arbor, MI 48104-1522

Telephone: 1-970-925-5516
E-mail: ngthomas@umich.edu

Phi Delta Kappan
Pauline B. Gough, Editor
P.O. Box 789
Bloomington, IN 47402

Telephone: 1-800-766-1156
E-mail: kappan@pdkintl.org
Internet: www.pdkintl.org/Kappan/Kappan.htm

Chapter 12 (Wong)

Center of Research in Human Development and Education
Temple University
1301 Cecil B. Moore Dr.
Philadelphia, PA 19122-6091

Telephone: 1-800-892-5550
E-mail: lss@vm.temple.edu
Internet: www.temple.edu/LSS

Chapter 13 (Slavin)

Success for All
3505 N. Charles St.
Johns Hopkins University
Baltimore, MD 21218

Telephone: 1-800-548-4998
E-mail: sfa@successforall.net
Internet: www.successforall.net

Steve Ross, Lana Snith
CREP, 115 Brister Library
University of Memphis
Memphis, TN 38152

Telephone: 1-901-678-3413 or -2396
E-mail: smith.lana@coe.memphis.edu
               ross.steve@coe.memphis.edu

Education Partners
2601 Mariposa Dr., Suite 100
San Francisco, CA 94110

Telephone: 1-415-985-9148

Chapter 14 (Troy)

Education Policy Institute
4401-A Connecticut Ave.
Box 294
Washington, DC 20008

Telephone: 1-202-244-7535
E-mail: info@educationpolicy.org
Internet: www.educationpolicy.org/

Martin P. Catherwood Library
Cornell School of Industrial and Labor Relations
Cornell University
Ithaca, NY 14853-3901

Telephone: 1-607-255-2184
Internet: www.ilr.cornell.edu/library.html

American Federation of Teachers
555 New Jersey Ave., N.W.
Washington, DC 20001

E-mail: askaft@aol.com
Internet: www.aft.org

National Education Association
1201 16th St., N.W.
Washington, DC 20036

Telephone: 1-202-833-4000
Internet: www.nea.org

Chapter 16 (Maney)

Technology in Education Adoption Model (TEAM)
Attn: Kevin Maney
Miami University
Department of Teacher Education
Oxford, OH 45056

Telephone: 1-513-529-6443
E-mail: maneyjk@muohio.edu
Internet: www2.eap.muohio.edu/team/

Apple Classroom of Tomorrow (ACOT)
E-mail: acot@research.apple.com
Internet: www.apple.com/education/K12/leadership/acot/library.html

Apple Learning Interchange
E-mail: jlengel@ultranet.com
Internet: ali.apple.com

Chapter 17 (Walberg/Lai)

Cooper, H. (1988). *Synthesizing research*. Thousand Oaks, CA: Sage.

Cooper, H., & Hedges, L. V. (Eds.). (1994). *The handbook of research synthesis*. New York: Russel Sage Foundation.

Reynolds, A. J., & Walberg, H. J. (Eds.) (1998). *Evaluation research for educational productivity*. Greenwich, CT: JAI Press.

Chapter 19 (Willms)

HLM
Scientific Software
1525 East 53rd St., Suite 530
Chicago, IL 60615-4530

Telephone: 1-800-247-6113
Fax: 1-312-684-4979

MLN
The Multilevel Models Project
Department of Mathematical Sciences
Institute of Education
London, England

Telephone: 44-171-612-6682

Chapter 20 (Cizek/Ramaswamy)

National Library of Education
80 F Street, N.W.
Washington, DC 20202

Telephone: 1-800-424-1616
E-mail: library@inet.ed.gov
Internet: www.ed.gov/NLE/
        or   www.accesseric.org:81/

Chapter 21 (Lewis)

Consortium for Policy Research in Education (CPRE)
Susan Fuhrman
Graduate School of Education
University of Pennsylvania
3440 Market St., Suite 560
Philadelphia, PA 19104-3325

Telephone: 1-215-898-6993
E-mail: cpre@gse.upenn.edu
Internet: www.upenn.edu/gse/cpre/

National Center on Education and the Economy (NCEE)
Attn: Marc Tucker
700 11th St., N.W., Suite 750
Washington, DC 20002

Telephone: 1-202-783-3668
E-mail: info@ncee.org
Internet: www.ncee.org/

Education Commission of the States (ECS)
Attn: Christine Johnson
707 17th St., Suite 2700
Denver, CO 80202-3427

Telephone: 1-303-299-3600
E-mail: ecs@ecs.org
Internet: www.ecs.org/

Biographical Statements

MARY LYN BOURQUE

Mary Lyn Bourque (Ed.D., University of Massachusetts, 1979) is chief psychometrician for the National Assessment Governing Board, where she is responsible for policy-related technical issues, particularly standard setting, on the National Assessment. A former secondary school science teacher, she has also served as director of testing for a large urban district and has directed the scoring and evaluation unit of a state regional service center. As president of New England Evaluation Designs, she provided consulting services to local and state departments and foreign ministries of education and provided professional development services for teachers and administrators in applied measurement topics. Dr. Bourque is a member of the National Council for Measurement in Education and the American Educational Research Association, and she has authored numerous technical reports and articles on applied measurement issues. She has published in *Reading Research Quarterly*, *Educational Measurement: Issues and Practices*, *Education*, and was a contributor to *Monitoring the Standards of Education*, an international publication sponsored by the International Academy of Education. Her research interests focus on large-scale assessment, standard setting, and applied measurement issues.

JAMES G. CIBULKA

James G. Cibulka is professor and chair of the Department of Education Policy, Planning, and Administration at the University of Maryland, College Park. He received his A.B. from Harvard College magna cum laude, majoring in government, and his Ph.D. from the University of Chicago, majoring in educational administration and educational policy and politics. Before joining the faculty of the University of Wisconsin–Milwaukee, where he was affiliated for 23 years, he worked in the public schools of Chicago, Illinois, and

Duluth, Minnesota. Dr. Cibulka has served as a consultant to many school systems and a number of state departments of education on education policy issues. He has been an expert witness on urban education reform, state education reforms, and metropolitan equity issues. Cibulka also served as a senior research scholar at the U.S. Department of Education. He has written widely on education policy issues and is the author, coauthor, or coeditor of six books, many journal articles, and policy reports. Currently he is conducting research on redesign and deregulation of categorical programs, reconstitution of failing schools, and development of schools as learning communities.

GREGORY J. CIZEK

Gregory J. Cizek is currently associate professor of Educational Research and Measurement at the University of Toledo, where he teaches courses in assessment, statistics, and research design. His specializations and research interests include assessment policy, classroom assessment, and standard setting. He is the author of more than 100 journal articles, book chapters, books, conference papers, and other publications. His work has been published in *Educational Policy, Educational Researcher, Review of Educational Research, Journal of Educational Measurement, Phi Delta Kappan*, and elsewhere. He was a contributor to the previous volume in this series by Academic Press titled *Handbook of Classroom Assessment*.

Dr. Cizek received his Ph.D. in measurement, evaluation, and research design from Michigan State University. He worked for 5 years at American College Testing (ACT) in Iowa City, Iowa, managing national licensure and certification testing programs. He has also worked as a policy analyst for the Michigan Senate, as a test development specialist for the Michigan Educational Assessment Program (MEAP), and as an elementary school teacher. In 1997 he was elected and named vice president of an Ohio school district board of education.

JOHN W. CRESWELL

John W. Creswell earned his Ph.D. in higher education from the University of Iowa in 1974. His major interests are qualitative and quantitative research methods in education and issues related to the American professorate. He teaches qualitative research methods, survey methods, and qualitative and quantitative research designs. His research interests are mixed method designs, qualitative methods, faculty research productivity, and departmental leadership. Creswell has authored seven books and currently writes about research design in education and the social sciences.

THOMAS G. DUNN

Thomas G. Dunn is professor of educational psychology at The University of Toledo. He teaches courses in instructional and cognitive psychology as well as behavior management. His research interests include expertise in various professions, how to influence the development of higher levels of competence in various professions, the nature of the knowledge that experienced professionals (e.g., teachers and doctors) use during professional activities, and cognitive influences in self-management. His work has appeared in journals of educational psychology, teacher education, medical education, educational technology, and law.

JOHN ENGLER

John Engler was elected Michigan's 46th governor in 1990. First elected to public office in 1970 at the age of 22, Engler began a series of nine straight election victories, including state representative, state senator, and Michigan Senate majority leader. Engler holds degrees from Michigan State University and Thomas M. Cooley Law School.

Engler was recently named to the National Assessment Governing Board for the National Assessment of Educational Progress (NEAP). In 1996 he was selected as chairman of the Republican Governors' Association.

Engler's policy initiatives in education have influenced national debates on education reform. U.S. Secretary of Education Richard Riley called Engler "a leader in education and testing initiatives [who] has fought for higher standards, better assessments, local control, interdistrict school choice, and a charter schools law." In 1994, he was awarded the Thomas Jefferson Freedom award by the American Legislative Exchange Council Board of Directors, who noted that "No one in America in the late 20th century has done more to reinvent government."

STEVEN FERRARA

Steven Ferrara is director of research and psychometrics for the American Institutes for Research (AIR) contract to develop new voluntary testing national tests in Grade 4 reading and Grade 8 mathematics. Prior to joining AIR in September 1997, he was state director of student assessment (1991–1997) and Chief of Measurement, Statistics, and Evaluation for the Maryland State Department of Education (1985–1991). Steve earned a Ph.D. in educational psychology in 1989 and an Ed.S. in program evaluation (1984) from Stanford University, an M.Ed. in special education (1978) from Boston State College, and a B.A. in English from the University of Massachusetts at Amherst (1973). Ferrara was a high school special education teacher in Massachusetts for 5 years. He began his teaching career as a Head Start teacher. He has also taught GED preparation courses for adults and graduate-level courses in educational measurement and evaluation at Stanford University, the Johns Hopkins University, University of Maryland College Park, and Western Maryland College.

Ferrara is on the board of directors of the National Council on Measurement in Education (NCME) and has been an editorial board member for *Applied Measurement in Education* and *Educational Measurement: Issues and Practice*. He has published in professional journals and delivered presentations on test design and development, computer-adaptive testing, local item dependence, scaling and equating, test score generalizability and validation, effects of assessment policy on educational reform, performance assessment, and classroom assessment. He has been a consultant to various state assessment programs, testing and accrediting companies and organizations, local school systems, and U.S. foreign universities.

MARGARET E. GOERTZ

Margaret E. Goertz is a professor in the graduate school of education at the University of Pennsylvania and a codirector of the Consortium for Policy Research in Education. Previously, she was executive director of the Education Policy Research Division of Educational Testing Service. A past president of the American Education Finance Association, Goertz's research focuses on issues of education finance, state education reform policies, and state and federal programs for special needs students. Her current research activities include studies of standards-based reform in education and the allocation of school-level resources. She recently coauthored the book, *From Cashbox to Classroom: the Struggle for Fiscal Reform and Educational Change in New Jersey* (Teachers College Press, 1997). Goertz received a Ph.D. in social science from the Maxwell School of Syracuse University in 1971.

BARBARA K. HOFER

Barbara K. Hofer is a research associate at the Center for Human Growth and Development at the University of Michigan. She received an Ed.M. in human development from the Harvard Graduate School of Education and a Ph.D. in education and psychology from the University of Michigan. Her research interests are the interrelation of culture and cognition, motivation and schooling, adolescent and early adult development, and personal epistemology. She is currently working on a longitudinal study on the transition to adulthood in Japan, Taiwan, and the United States.

MARY KENNEDY

Mary Kennedy is a professor at Michigan State University. Her scholarship focuses on the relationship between knowledge and teaching practice, on the nature of knowledge used in teaching practice, and on how research knowledge contributes to practice. She has published two books addressing the relationship between knowledge and teaching and has won four awards for her work. Prior to joining Michigan State University in 1986, her work mainly focused on policy issues and on the role of research in improving policy. She has authored numerous journal articles and book chapters in these areas and has authored reports specifically for policy audiences, including the United States Congress.

JIN-SHEI LAI

Jin-Shei Lai is a research assistant professor in the Department of Occupational Therapy at University of Illinois at Chicago. She received a B.S. in occupational therapy from the National Taiwan University. She completed her graduate work at the University of Illinois at Chicago. She received a Ph.D. in educational psychology and a master's degree in occupational therapy specializing in pediatrics.

Her recent interests have focused on outcomes research (mathematic learning and health services). In addition, she has been investigating gender differences in mathematical achievement. Currently, she is collaborating with international researchers from Sweden, Finland, Scotland, and Netherlands in various health care projects.

ANNE C. LEWIS

Anne C. Lewis is an education policy writer specializing in national issues and trends. She has been national columnist for Phi Delta Kappan for more than 15 years and the narrative documenter of urban school reform funded by the Edna McConnell Clark Foundation for seven years. She authored *Restructuring America's Schools* for the American Association of School Administrators as well as numerous reports for such agencies/groups as the Education Commission of the States, the U.S. Department of Education, the National Education Goals Panel, the National Center on Education and the Economy, and several other foundations. A former award-winning newspaper reporter, she edited *Education* USA for 10 years and is a past president of the Education Writers Association.

ANDREW T. LUMPE

Andrew T. Lumpe is an associate professor in the Department of Curriculum and Instruction at Southern Illinois University-Carbondale. Dr. Lumpe is a former public school science teacher and currently serves as the president of the Giant City School Board in Carbondale, Illinois. His research interests include science teaching, learning, curriculum, and teacher professional development. He has published articles in the *Journal for Research in Science Teaching*, *American Biology Teacher*, *Journal of Science Teacher Education*, and *School Science and Mathematics*. He has served as a principal or coprincipal investigator for numerous externally funded grant projects.

J. KEVIN MANEY

J. Kevin Maney, Ph.D., is an assistant professor of education technology for the Department of Teacher Education at Miami University, Oxford, Ohio, where he works with preservice teachers to help them learn how to integrate technology into curriculum and instruction. Since coming to Miami, Maney has introduced many innovative teaching practices and developed a significant Web presence to support his teaching agenda. He also works closely with area schools and teachers to advance the adoption of education technology, the primary focus of his research and scholarship. Prior to coming to Miami, Maney taught senior high social studies for 18 years and then served as technology director for a county educational service center.

HILLARY R. MICHAELS

Hillary R. Michaels is a senior research scientist at CTB McGraw-Hill in Monterey, California, where she manages research on large-scale assessment and studies measuring growth in student achievement. Previously, Michaels was a senior research associate at the Mid-continent Regional Educational Laboratory in Denver, Colorado, and an assessment specialist at the Maryland Department of Education. Dr. Michaels' research interests include score interpretation and factors that affect score validity such as assessment format, scoring, and student motivation. She has worked with a number of school districts to facilitate appropriate assessment use and in the creation of comprehensive assessment systems.

DIANA PULLIN

Diana Pullin holds both a law degree and a doctoral degree from the University of Iowa. As a practicing attorney, she has represented school districts, teachers unions, parents, student, and educators in a broad range of matters concerning education law, civil rights, and employment. She is most known for her representation of a statewide class of students in Florida who successfully challenged the state's requirement that students pass a minimum competency test in order to receive a high school diploma (*Debra P. v. Turlington*).

As an academic, she has served as a member of the tenured faculties of the School of Education at Boston College and the College of Education at Michigan State University. From 1987–1994, she served as dean of education at Boston College. She has taught courses in education law, higher education law, special education law, law and testing, public policy, and law and society. She is the author of many articles, book chapters, and one book in these areas and in the area of education reform.

Dr. Pullin has served as president of the board of directors of the Center for Law and Education. She has also served as member at large of the Joint Committee on Education Evaluation and as a member of the Joint Committee on Psychological Testing and Assessment of the American Psychological Association, the American Educational Research Association, and the National Council on Educational Measurement. She has served as a consultant to many organizations including the Council of Chief State School Officers, the National Research Council, and the National Center for Education Statistics.

VIDYA RAMASWAMY

Vidya Ramaswamy is a doctoral candidate in the department of Educational Psychology, Research, and Social Foundations at the University of Toledo. She earned a bachelor's degree in Psychology and a master's degree in education and counseling psychology from the University of Bombay, India. Her doctoral work focuses on fostering prosocial behavior in preschool children in classroom settings.

Previously, Ramaswamy has collaborated on research projects involving daycare and the process of collaborative consultation to improve education in preschool settings. She has been involved in research investigating parenting and drug addiction in mothers of preschool-aged children.

EDWARD D. ROEBER

Edward Roeber is currently vice president of external relations at Advanced Systems in Measurement and Evaluation. In this position, he works with state policy leaders to foster long-term improvements in student achievement and school reform. His current work involves development of alternate assessments for students with severe disabilities. From 1991 to 1998, Roeber was the director of Student Assessment Programs for the Council of Chief State School Officers (CCSSO). In this position, he was responsible for assisting states in the development of their statewide student assessment programs.

Prior to joining CCSSO, Roeber was director of the Michigan Educational Assessment Program, Michigan Department of Education in Lansing, Michigan from 1972 to 1991 and a consultant with the Education Commission of the States, working on the National Assessment of Educational Progress in the areas of music and visual arts. Roeber received his Ph.D. in measurement and evaluation from the University of Michigan in 1970.

He has consulted with a number of states as well as national organizations on the design and development of large-scale assessment programs. He has authored numerous articles, reports, and other publications, particularly on the development of innovative assessment programs, as well as the use and reporting of student achievement information. In addition, he has made numerous presentations to various groups around the country.

ROBERT E. SLAVIN

Robert Slavin is currently codirector of the Center for Research on the Education of Students Placed at Risk at Johns Hopkins University. He received his B.A. in psychology from Reed College in 1972 and his Ph.D. in social relations in 1975 from Johns Hopkins University. Dr. Slavin has authored or coauthored more than 180 articles and 15 books, including *Educational Psychology: Theory into Practice*, *School and Classroom Organization*, *Effective Programs for Students at Risk*, *Cooperative Learning: Theory, Research, and Practice*, *Preventing Early School Failure*, *Every Child, Every School: Success for All*, and *Show Me the Evidence: Proven and Promising Programs for America's Schools* (in press). He received the American Educational Research Association's Raymond B. Cattell Early Career Award for Programmatic Research in 1986, the Palmer O. Johnson award for the best article in an AERA journal in 1988, and the Charles A. Dana award in 1994.

HAROLD W. STEVENSON

Harold W. Stevenson is a professor of psychology at the University of Michigan. He received his undergraduate training at the University of Colorado and received his Ph.D. from Stanford University. He has studied issues of learning and motivation in both experimental and applied settings since his days as a graduate student. He has served as president of the Society for

Research on Child Development, the International Society for the Study of Behavioral Development, and the American Psychological Association Division of Developmental Psychology. He has received numerous awards, including, most recently, the APA award for the application of psychology to applied problems.

LEO TROY

Leo Troy is distinguished professor of economics at Rutgers University-Newark. His research and publications have focused on unions over nearly the last half-century. He has been published in leading journals in the United States and the United Kingdom; among them are *The Harvard Journal of Law and Public Policy*, *The University of Chicago Law Review*, *The British Journal of Industrial Relations*, *Industrial Relations*, *Industrial and Labor Relations Review*, and the *Journal of Labor Research*.

His work on unions is widely recognized outside academia. Since February 1996, his work has been cited in more than 120 newspaper, magazine, and wire accounts regarding labor organization and unions' financial operations. These include the *New York Times*, the *Los Angeles Times*, the *Wall Street Journal*, the *Washington Post*, *USA Today*, and numerous wire services. He has been interviewed frequently on radio, including NPR, the BBC World Service, and French National Radio.

Professor Troy earned his Ph.D. at Columbia University and is a member of Phi Beta Kappa. He has been the recipient of numerous research awards including two from the National Science Foundation. He has twice been a Visting Fulbright Professor in England and prior to his appointment at Rutgers he worked at the National Bureau of Economic Research. Professor Troy is a veteran of World War II and the grandfather of three grandchildren.

HERBERT J. WALBERG

Herbert Walberg is research professor of education and psychology at the University of Illinois at Chicago. He served on the National Assessment Governing Board, referred to in the United States as the national school board given its mission to set education standards for U.S. students. The National Assessment provides information on changes in educational achievement in the United States as well as comparisons of individual states.

Holding a Ph.D. from the University of Chicago and formerly assistant professor at Harvard University, he has edited more than 55 books and written about 350 articles on such topics as educational productivity and exceptional human accomplishments. A fellow of four academic organizations including the American Psychological Association and the Royal Statistical

Society, Walberg is a founding member of the International Academy of Education, headquartered in Brussels.

In his research, Walberg employs experiments and analyses of large national and international data sets to discover the factors in homes, schools, and communities that promote learning and other human accomplishments. He also employs meta-analyses to summarize effects of various educational conditions and methods on learning and other outcomes, the results of which have important bearings on policies formulated by legislatures and courts. He carried out comparative research on Japanese and American schools for the U.S. Department of Education. He organized a radio series and book about American education distributed in 74 countries for the U.S. Department of State and the White House. He currently serves on a committee that selects students with near perfect SAT scores for merit scholarships at top universities.

Walberg served as the chair of the scientific advisory group for the Paris-based Organization for Economic Cooperation and Development project on international educational indicators. He also advised UNESCO and the governments of Israel, Japan, Sweden, and the United Kingdom on education, research, and policy. He currently chairs the board of the Heartland Institute—a think tank that provides policy analysis for the U.S. Congress, state legislators, and news reporters. He is listed in Who's Who in America and Who's Who in the World.

GLEAVES WHITNEY

Gleaves Whitney is senior speech writer for Michigan Governor John Engler, a position he has held since 1992. He is also Senior Fellow of the Russell Kirk Center for Cultural Renewal. Since 1995, he has served on the colloquium faculty of the Intercollegiate Studies Institute.

Whitney has authored one book, *Colorado Front Range* (1983) and has contributed to several others, including *American Middle East Policy: Is Free Speech Threatened* (1988), *American Perestroika: The Demise of the Welfare State* (1995), and *Encyclopedia of the American Right* (1998). His work has also appeared in national publications, including *The Wall Street Journal*, *New York Times*, *National Review*, *Christian Science Monitor*, and *Policy Review*.

Prior to his work in the governor's office, Mr. Whitney taught history at the Droste-Hulshof Gymnasium (Germany), Colorado State University, and the University of Michigan.

J. DOUGLAS WILLMS

J. Douglas Willms is a professor in the faculty of Education at the University of New Brunswick. He is a member of the Human Development Program and a research fellow with the Canadian Institute for Advanced Research. Previously, he has worked as an elementary and secondary schoolteacher in Maple Ridge, British Columbia; as an engineering officer in the Canadian Armed Forces; as a teacher educator at the University of Lethbridge; and as a faculty member at the University of British Columbia.

Willms holds a bachelor's degree in engineering physics from the Royal Military College, a diploma in education and an M.A. in educational psychology from the University of British Columbia, an M.S. in statistics and a Ph.D. in education (diploma in educational evaluation) from Stanford University.

Willms teaches courses in research methods, policy studies in education, and school effectiveness. He is the author of *Monitoring School Performance: A Guide for Educators* (Falmer Press), coeditor with Stephen Raudenbush of *Schools, Classrooms, and Pupils: International Studies of Schooling from the Multilevel Perspective* (Academic Press), and more than 50 research articles pertaining to the accountability of schooling systems and the assessment of school effects and educational reforms. His studies of school performance have included research projects in Canada, the United States, England, Scotland, Thailand, India, and Jordan. He is the founder of the Atlantic Centre for Policy Research in Education at the University of New Brunswick.

KENNETH K. WONG

Kenneth K. Wong is associate professor in Department of Education and the College at the University of Chicago. A political scientist by training, he has conducted research in urban school reform, school politics, intergovernmental relations, and federal educational policies. He authors or edits several books and serves as a member of the editorial board in several professional journals. He was awarded the Spencer Fellowship from the National Academy of Education for 1989–1990. In recent years, his research has been supported by the Spencer Foundation, the Social Science Research Council, the Joyce Foundation, the National Science Foundation, and the U.S. Department of Education. Currently, he is principal investigator of a study on school governance reform in Chicago and Birmingham (England). He is also a senior research associate in the federally funded Laboratory for Student Success at Temple University.

Index